Drama, Poetry and Music
Late-Renaissance Italy

Drama, Poetry and Music in Late-Renaissance Italy

The life and works of Leonora Bernardi

Virginia Cox and Lisa Sampson

with a translation by Anna Wainwright and contributions by Eric Nicholson, Eugenio Refini and Davide Daolmi

First published in 2023 by
UCL Press
University College London
Gower Street
London WC1E 6BT

Available to download free: www.uclpress.co.uk

A CIP catalogue record for this book is available from The British Library.

ISBN: 978-1-80008-432-2 (Hbk.)
ISBN: 978-1-80008-431-5 (Pbk.)
ISBN: 978-1-80008-430-8 (PDF)
ISBN: 978-1-80008-433-9 (epub)
DOI: https://doi.org/10.14324/111.9781800084308

Contents

List of figures and tables

Figures

Table

List of contributors

Virginia Cox is Senior Research Fellow at Trinity College, Cambridge, and Honorary Professor of Early Modern Italian Literature and Culture at the University of Cambridge. Her publications include *Women's Writing in Italy, 1400–1600*, *The Prodigious Muse: Women's Writing in Counter-Reformation Italy* and *Lyric Poetry by Women of the Italian Renaissance* (all Johns Hopkins University Press, 2008, 2011 and 2013).

Davide Daolmi is Associate Professor of Music History at the University of Milan and a specialist in early music; his publications include *Storia della musica: Dalle origini al Seicento* (Mondadori, 2019) and critical editions of Gioachino Rossini's *Petite messe sollennelle* (Fondazione Rossini, 2013) and Francesco Cavalli's *Orione* (Bärenreiter, 2015).

Eric Nicholson is a tenured faculty member at New York University Florence, an actor and director of classic theatre (plays by Aristophanes, Shakespeare, Molière and others), and the author of publications on early modern drama, including the co-translated and co-edited *Lovers' Debates for the Stage*, by Isabella Andreini (University of Chicago Press, 2022).

Eugenio Refini is Associate Professor of Italian Studies at New York University. He works on the reception and interplay of literary culture and music; his publications include *The Vernacular Aristotle: Translation as Reception in Medieval Italy* (Cambridge, 2020) and *Staging the Soul: Allegorical Drama as Spiritual Practice in Baroque Italy* (Legenda, 2023).

Lisa Sampson is Reader in Early Modern Italian Studies and Co-director of the Centre for Early Modern Exchanges at University College London. She has published on Italian theatre, women's writing, courts and academies, including *Pastoral Drama in Early Modern Italy*, and the co-edited *The Italian Academies, 1525–1700: Networks of Culture, Innovation and Dissent* (both Legenda, 2006 and 2016).

Anna Wainwright is Assistant Professor of Italian Studies and Core Faculty in Women's and Gender Studies at University of New Hampshire. She is co-editor of *Innovation in the Italian Counter-Reformation* (University of Delaware Press, 2020) and the author of publications on women, race and emotion in early modern Italy.

Abbreviations

Libraries and archives

ASF   Archivio di Stato, Florence
ASM   Archivio di Stato, Modena
BCIS   Biblioteca Comunale degli Intronati, Siena
BEM   Biblioteca Estense, Modena
BMV   Biblioteca Marciana, Venice
BNCF   Biblioteca Centrale Nazionale, Florence
BSL   Biblioteca Statale, Lucca

Primary works

All Italian works listed below are cited in the editions available on http://
www.letteraturaitaliana.net/, with the exception of BC, Gr*L*, *L III*, *M*, and
M*Op*. For all other sources full citations are given in the bibliography.
For classical works this volume references book and line number(s) (e.g.
Met IV.639–61 for Ovid's *Metamorphoses*, Book IV, lines 639–61). For
vernacular epic poems the references are first to canto, then stanza and
line where relevant (e.g. *OF* V.46.1 for *Orlando furioso*, Canto V, stanza
46, line 1). References to Petrarch's *Canzoniere* give poem number (in
small roman numerals) and lines where required (e.g. *C* cv, line 2 for
Canzoniere, 105, line 2); the same format applies to Tasso's *Rime* (*R*).
For plays, references give in order the act and scene numbers, with lines
where relevant (e.g. *Am* I.2.365 for Tasso's *Aminta*, Act I, scene 2, line
365).

Aen   Virgil, *Aeneid*
Am   Tasso, *Aminta*
BC   Bulgarini and Chiariti, letters (BCIS, C. II. 25)
C   Petrarch, *Canzoniere (Rerum vulgarium fragmenta)*
Ecl   Virgil, *Eclogues*
GL   Tasso, *Gerusalemme liberata*
Gr*L*   Grillo, *Lettere*
Inf   Dante, *Inferno*

L III	Marino, *La Lira, Parte 3*
M	[Bernardi], *Tragicomedia Pastorale* [*Clorilli*], and *diverse rime* (BMV, MS It. IX, 239)
Met	Ovid, *Metamorphoses*
MOp	Matraini, *Le opere in prosa*
OF	Ariosto, *Orlando furioso*
Par	Dante, *Paradiso*
R	Tasso, *Rime*
TC	Petrarch, *Triumphus cupidinis (Trionfi)*
TF	Petrarch, *Triumphus fame (Trionfi)*
TP	Petrarch, *Triumphus pudicitie (Trionfi)*

Secondary works

Full citations are given in the bibliography.

ABC*i*	Adorni Braccesi, *Una città infetta*
B*No*	Berengo, *Nobili e mercanti nella Lucca del Cinquecento*
B*Tr*	Bertelli, *Trittico: Lucca, Ragusa, Boston*
C*Ly*	Cox, *Lyric Poetry by Women of the Italian Renaissance*
C*Pr*	Cox, *The Prodigious Muse*
C*Wo*	Cox, *Women's Writing in Italy, 1400–1650*
DBI	*Dizionario biografico degli italiani*
DM*Gr*	Durante and Martellotti, *Don Angelo Grillo*
L*St*	Lucchesini, *Della storia letteraria del Ducato Lucchese*
P*Sc*	Pieri, *La scena boschereccia*
S*Fr*	Sforza, *F. M. Fiorentini ed i suoi contemporanei lucchesi*
S*Pa*	Sampson, *Pastoral Drama in Early Modern Italy*

Acknowledgements

This volume is the product of at least a decade of research, planning and writing, by a team of collaborators that has expanded with the years. The names of the authors of each section on the table of contents gives a headline notion of who is responsible for which parts, but it does not do full justice to the extent of the 'team' or the collaboration involved. Thus, Virginia Cox is credited with Section 1's reconstruction of Leonora Bernardi's biography and with the edition of Bernardi's verse in Section 3.1. These two sections, however, depend vitally on research carried out within the archives and libraries of Modena, Lucca, Siena and Florence by Anna Wainwright and Lisa Sampson at a relatively early stage in the project (2015–17). This established key details of Bernardi's life, such as her husband's murder in Florence in 1585, and uncovered a substantial proportion of her lyric output. Section 1 also profited immensely from Ida Caiazza's generous and engaged help with research in Lucca in 2021–2, which clarified Bernardi's family relationships and unravelled the dramatic story of her entanglement with her nemesis, Girolamo Sbarra. Bruce Edelstein then kindly helped continue this work by transcribing the letter from the Florentine Archivio di Stato presented in the Appendix to Section 1. Eric Nicholson and Eugenio Refini, meanwhile, provided vital input to Section 3.1.4, presenting Ottavio Rinuccini's verse for Bernardi, through their work on the manuscripts containing these poems in Florence and Rome.

As Section 2.4 relates, an important – and immensely enjoyable – stage in the development of the project was the production of Bernardi's pastoral, *Clorilli*, staged in the gardens of Villa La Pietra in Florence in May 2018. Acknowledgements of the many collaborators on this production, from the set designer, actors and technicians to the funding bodies, are contained in the Appendix to Section 2.4, where the original programme for the play is reproduced. Here, it is necessary only to acknowledge Eric Nicholson's vast input to the project, as director, actor and coordinator, and as abridger and adaptor for the stage of Anna Wainwright's translation. All of us involved in the project were struck by the extent to which the process of bringing this lost play together as a living production and considering the ways in which it might speak to audiences today fed vitally into the edition, translation and study of the work contained in this volume.

The transcription and exploration of the complex manuscript of *Clorilli* in Section 2 have also benefited from expert advice on linguistic and poetic matters from Virginia Cox, Eugenio Refini, Brian Richardson and Rodney Sampson. Elisabetta Lugano, Elisabetta Sciarra and other staff at the Marciana Library of Venice have provided invaluable clarifications regarding the manuscript's physical make-up. Ongoing dialogue with Anna Wainwright as she was preparing her translation, and in order to write the joint notes, has also provided important checks and balances for the Italian text. The Note on the Translation in Section 2.3 provides further details on the collaborations underpinning Anna Wainwright's work, including for a second theatrical production of *Clorilli* at the University of New Hampshire in spring 2019.

We would also like to offer thanks to Margaret King for her support at an early stage in the project; Chiara Ferrari for preparing a preliminary transcription at the start of the project (in 2014); Monica Milianti for research help in Lucca; Francesca Masiero and Jack Hayes for research help in Venice and London; Paul Greene for helping bring clarity to the geographical and genealogical complexities of Part I through his artwork (Figs 1–3); the British Academy for the award of a Mid-Career Fellowship (in 2016) to Lisa Sampson, which enabled some key research in Italy; Chris Penfold and the editorial board of UCL Press for important suggestions for how to expand the scope of the project; and the reader for the Press and Tim Carter for extremely useful late close readings and corrections. Our thanks go also to Alice Greaves and her team for her invaluable, precise guidance through the copy-editing and production process. Last, but not least, many thanks go to our families. Without their essential 'backstage' support and encouragement, this volume would not have been the same.

VC and LS, 20 March 2023

1
Context, life, legacy
Virginia Cox

The story of the poet, dramatist and singer Leonora Bernardi Belatti (1559–1616) offers a telling object lesson in the sketchiness of cultural memory. More particularly, it illustrates the depth of oblivion into which the literary culture of later sixteenth-century Italy has fallen. Talented, well-connected and lionized during her lifetime, Bernardi lapsed after her death into such invisibility that, by the eighteenth century, even the most diligent local historians in her hometown of Lucca could assemble few facts about her life and writings. She passed through the nineteenth and twentieth centuries with virtually no attention from scholars. Only since 2008, when the pastoral drama edited in this volume resurfaced, has Bernardi begun to come newly into focus. She emerges now as a distinctive and intriguing figure, flourishing at a moment when creative women enjoyed an exceptional level of cultural visibility in Italy. Her biography, reconstructed here in detail for the first time, has much to tell us about women's engagement with literature and music in the late Cinquecento and about the complex and imbricated cultural geographies of central and northern Italy at this time. Bernardi's story is also of great interest for the history of early modern women's literary sociability, in that it offers an exceptionally well-documented case of a female-hosted private literary 'academy', of a type that is increasingly recognized as anticipating the salons of seventeenth-century France. Finally, Bernardi's dramatic life offers a rare and thought-provoking case of an early modern woman who survived scandal and public shaming in part through her own cultural agency: a striking contribution to our evolving under-standing of gender attitudes and mores at this time.

1.1 Context

1.1.1 A troubled city: Lucca in the Cinquecento

Lucca is located in north-western Tuscany, on the Serchio river, not far from its mouth on the Tyrrhenian seacoast: a walled city on a plain that stretches away eastwards towards the towns of Pescia and Pistoia. To the north lies the mountainous region of the Garfagnana, with the Emilian cities of Modena and Reggio beyond, while on the coast north from Lucca stand the towns of Massa and Carrara, the latter home to the great marble quarries from which Michelangelo sourced his stone.

At the time of Bernardi's birth, Lucca was a distinctive place geopolitically: a small, ancient city-republic squeezed between two powerful and restless dukedoms (see Fig. 1). To the south and east lay Florence, capital of the rapidly expanding duchy of Florence, ruled by Cosimo I de' Medici (1519–74). Two years before Bernardi was born, in 1557 Cosimo had formally annexed Florence's once-powerful rival Siena, after a protracted and crippling war. To the north, the Garfagnana region was partly in the possession of the Este dukes of Modena and Ferrara. Besides these two looming powers, Lucca had a less threatening border to the north-west, with the small marquisate (from 1568, principality) of Massa and Carrara, governed by the family of Cybo-Malaspina, under its long-ruling lord, Alberico I (1534–1623).

Although it could hardly compete with Florence or Ferrara, culturally or politically, Renaissance Lucca was far from a backwater. While the population of the city itself was not large (*c.* 20,000 in 1500, around the same size as Siena), that of the state, including the surrounding agricultural *contado*, was around 100,000.[1] Lucca was a wealthy and cosmopolitan place, home to a flourishing mercantile tradition, particularly strong in the silk trade and the manufacture of luxury goods. Many Lucchese patricians had ties with northern Europe through their mercantile activities, especially with Antwerp, Lyons, Bruges and London. Politically, with the exception of the short-lived *signoria* of Paolo Guinigi (1400–30), Lucca was governed as a republic; indeed, it proved one of the longest-standing of the medieval Italian city-republics, surviving down to the Napoleonic period with its ancient civic institutions intact. The city was ruled by a legislative Great Council, with elected members drawn from the three main districts (*terzieri*) of the city; together with an executive council consisting of nine Anziani (lit. 'Elders') and a Gonfaloniere ('Standard-Bearer') – the head of state – both elected for two-month periods. A third council, known as the Trentasei ('Thirty-Six') acted as electoral college for the Anziani, as well

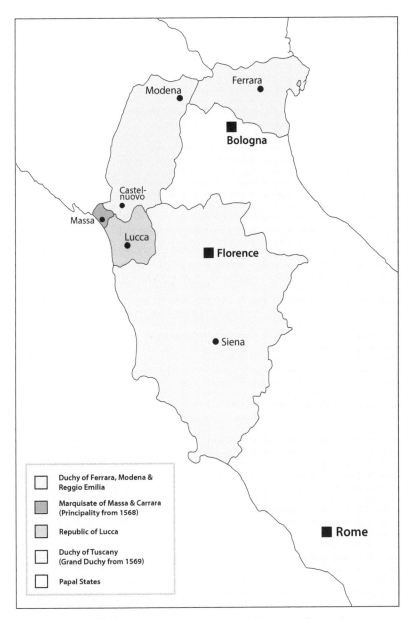

Figure 1 Simplified political map of central Italy between Florence's annexation of Siena (1557) and the devolution of Ferrara to the papacy (1598). Artwork by Paul Greene.

as having consultative functions. Informal consultative councils, known as *colloqui*, and ad hoc committees to deal with particular issues, made up the chief remaining political organs of the state.[2]

Informally, from the fifteenth century, election to high office was dominated by men from wealthy families, predominantly silk merchants. Although around 150 families were formally qualified for office, families who regularly supplied Anziani and Gonfalonieri were limited to a couple of dozen.[3] This oligarchical regime was challenged in the early 1530s, in the uprising of the Straccioni, or 'Ragged Ones', when the artisan stratum of Lucchese society, in league with some intellectuals, such as notaries and priests, attempted to break the wealthy merchants' monopoly on power. This rebellion, quickly put down, had the indirect effect of tightening the patriciate's grip on power, as in the better-known case of the ill-fated rebellion of the Ciompi (woolworkers) in Florence in the 1370s.[4] New constitutional laws drawn up in 1556 (named the 'Riforma Martiniana', after their author, Martino Bernardini) formally limited involvement in the Lucchese government to established city families, confirming the oligarchic nature of the republic and the primacy of the city of Lucca over its surrounding *contado*.

The period from the Straccioni revolt to the time of Bernardi's birth was a troubled one for Lucca, in political and religious terms. The failure of the Straccioni rebellion and the repression that followed had helped swell the numbers of Lucca's political exiles. After several minor plots against the regime in the 1530s, two more ambitious conspiracies followed in 1542 and 1546. The first was orchestrated by Pietro Fatinelli (1512–43), a Lucchese who had spent most of his adult life outside the city. The second, more shocking, was that of Francesco Burlamacchi (1498–1547), a man from one of the most powerful Lucchese merchant families and Gonfaloniere at the time of his planned coup. Burlamacchi's intent was to 'liberate' Pisa from Florentine dominion and to overthrow the Medici regime, replacing it with a free league of Tuscan cities. The plot, and its long judicial aftermath, exacerbated existing tensions between Lucca and Florence.[5]

In the same decade – and not unconnectedly – Lucca became an increasing concern to the Catholic Church, as it sought to secure religious orthodoxy in the face of the spreading influence of Reformist thinking in Italy, the so-called evangelical or spiritual movement. Lucca was a noted centre of this movement in the early sixteenth century, home briefly in the early 1540s to leading Reform intellectuals such as Pietro Martire Vermigli (1499–1562) and Celio Secundo Curione (1503–69).[6] The city's commercial ties to northern Europe facilitated the spread of Reformist ideas among its elites, as did its connections with Modena and Ferrara, also home to Reform-leaning groups. Under increasing pressure from the Inquisition to control the spread of 'heresy', the Lucchese government formed its own committee for religious affairs in 1545, charged with policing the city's orthodoxy. Scrutiny was lax in practice, however, given the widespread sympathy with Reformist thinking among the governing elites, as witnessed by the appointment of the Erasmian Aonio Paleario (c. 1500–70) as superintendent of the city's schools in 1546. In 1553, the Inquisition was reported to regard Lucca as the worst-infested nest of heresy in Italy.[7]

The later 1550s marked a turning point in Lucca's religious history, as the city's combative bishop, Alessandro Guidiccioni (1524–1605), embarked on an energetic campaign to reimpose Catholic orthodoxy. In 1556, tensions between Guidiccioni and the Lucchese government reached a point of crisis, with both parties appealing to Rome. The religious divide had become strongly politicized since the conspiracies of the 1540s. Burlamacchi was a Reformist, and the combination of religious and political radicalism in his thought hardened surrounding rulers' perception of Lucca's religious toleration as politically dangerous.[8] Fatinelli had defended his coup attempt against Lucca as an attempt to overthrow a heretical regime. By the late 1550s, the ambitious Carafa family, headed by Pope Paul IV, approached Cosimo de' Medici to propose a joint campaign against Lucca, under the pretext of extirpating heresy.[9]

Following this exceptionally turbulent period in the city's history, the last four decades of the sixteenth century saw a relative return to order in both the political and religious realms. From the mid-century, many Lucchese Reform sympathizers fled Italy for northern Europe, settling first mainly in Geneva, where 50 households of Lucchese origin are registered in 1560, and afterwards in Lyons, when that city formally adopted the Calvinist faith in 1562.[10] In 1562, Lucca officially prohibited its religious exiles from living in Italy, France, Flanders or Spain, lest they contaminate orthodox co-nationals doing business in those realms. Although pockets of religious dissidence remained (an apostolic visit in 1575 by the bishop of Rimini, Giovanni Battista Castelli, flushed out a handful of Protestant sympathizers, who fled to Lyons to escape arrest), Lucca had been largely recaptured by this point for Catholic orthodoxy.[11] Bishop Guidiccioni threw himself into the task of reforming Church affairs within the city and the broader *contado*, holding a series of synods from 1564 to regulate all aspects of ecclesiastical practice, with special emphasis on the conduct of priests and on the religious education of lay adults and children.[12]

Politically, after the fall of Siena left the remainder of Tuscany in the hands of the duchy of Florence, the energies of the Lucchese government were largely concentrated on ensuring the city's continuing independence and republican status. Key to this was the protection of the Spanish and Austrian Habsburgs. Lucca had a tradition of imperial patronage since the later Middle Ages, reaffirmed by Charles V in the 1520s and renewed by successive emperors, in return for a generous subsidy.[13] The city also gained the patronage of the Spanish crown, with Charles's son, Philip II; indeed, later sixteenth-century Lucca has been described as 'first a Spanish, then an imperial city'.[14] Despite this high-profile support, Lucca remained keenly alert to its precarious status. One of the great civic enterprises in the later sixteenth and early seventeenth centuries in the city was the raising of the powerful circle of walls that remain today the most striking visual feature of the city. The city's calm continued to be troubled by conspiracies and treacheries, real or suspected. A sharp-eyed Venetian ambassador to Florence, Andrea Gussoni (1546–1615), described the relation of Lucca to Florence in the 1570s as like that of a quail to a sparrowhawk, which it constantly watches in terror over its shoulder.[15]

The most threatening conspiracy in later sixteenth-century Lucca was that orchestrated in the 1590s by the Lucchese patrician Bernardino Antelminelli. Stripped of his patrician honours by the Lucchese government, for reasons that remain obscure, Antelminelli became an agent for Grand Duke Ferdinando de' Medici, receiving a pension from him in return for laying the ground for a pro-Florentine coup that was intended to take place following the death of Philip II. Antelminelli was arrested in Genoa in 1596, while attempting to sound out potential Genoese collaborators, and he was executed in Lucca the following year, along with two of his sons. The episode vividly illustrates the febrile atmosphere of the period, as does the fact that the Lucchese government continued to pursue Antelminelli's surviving son, Alessandro (1572–1657), for decades after the conspiracy, as he moved around Europe under an assumed name.[16]

It was not from Florence alone that Lucca felt itself and its territories under threat in this period. Ferrara and Modena, to the north, were also a source of unease. The Garfagnana, where Lucchese towns and fortresses stood alongside others under the jurisdiction of the Este, was an obvious flashpoint. A war in all but name took place in the region in 1583, when Alfonso II d'Este sent troops with the intention of extending his territories there and seizing the strategically crucial pass near San Pellegrino (Passo delle Radici). Further, more 'official' wars between Lucca and the

Este dukedom of Modena took place in 1602–3 and in 1613. Girolamo Tommasi and Carlo Minutoli's patriotic 1847 *Sommario della storia di Lucca* – still useful as a source for this under-investigated period of Lucchese history – represents this whole period as one of permanent threat for Lucca, depicting the city as a David between two Goliaths.[17] It was in this complex and uncertain civic climate that Leonora Bernardi's life in Lucca was lived out.

1.1.2 Poetry, music and spectacle in Lucca

In respect of cultural history, Lucca cannot be said to have excelled, by the high standards of Renaissance Italian cities. The energies of its patrician elite were more occupied by commerce, government service and religious speculation than by the study of classical literature or vernacular poetry.[18] While the young nobles of nearby Siena were building a national reputation in the 1530s for their poetic and theatrical experimentation, their Lucchese peers were often abroad, honing their business skills in Lyons or Antwerp. Even those Lucchese who made significant contributions to literary culture in this period, such as the Dante commentators Alessandro Vellutello (1473–1550) and Bernardino Daniello (d. 1565), or the dramatist Agostino Ricchi (1512–64), spent the greater part of their careers outside the city. The same is true of the poet and papal administrator Giovanni Guidiccioni (1480–1541), the most celebrated Lucchese *letterato* of the sixteenth century.

In keeping with the practical orientation of Lucchese cultural life, the city's first sixteenth-century *ridotti* – informal gatherings of learned men –seem to have been scientific and philosophical, as much as literary, in their orientation. A first such gathering was hosted by Silvestro Gigli, deacon of the church of San Michele; a second by Cristofano Guidiccioni (1536–82), a Greek scholar and translator of Sophocles and Euripides; a third by Giuseppe Bernardini (1524–*c.* 1580), who had studied with the celebrated literary theorist Francesco Robortello (1516–67), during the latter's employment as lecturer in the humanities at Lucca between 1539 and 1543. Bernardini's *ridotto* was sufficiently ambitious to employ a tutor, Ascanio Santini, to lecture on astronomy and on Aristotle's moral philosophy.[19] Finally, in 1584, a more formal, literary academy was constituted, the Accademia degli Oscuri, with the full apparatus of regulations, emblems and academic names that characterized such institutions in the Italian sixteenth century.[20]

The extent to which, by the 1580s, the Lucchese patriciate had evolved culturally towards a more courtly, less strictly mercantile model is well illustrated by the profile of the founder of the Oscuri, Gianlorenzo Malpigli. Malpigli spent part of his youth in Ferrara, where his father, Vincenzo Malpigli, resided, and he was a close acquaintance of Torquato Tasso, who featured him as the title character in two of his dialogues of the mid-1580s. In the first of these, *Il Malpiglio primo, overo de la corte*, Tasso represents Gianlorenzo as strongly attracted to a career as a courtier, while his father is hopeful that he will take up his place as a citizen and statesman of the Lucchese republic.[21] The activities of the Accademia degli Oscuri reflect both these cultural models, the courtly and the republican. On the 'courtly' side, the academy staged theatrical performances, some quite lavish, with musical *intermezzi* and architectural stage settings.[22] On the 'republican' side, a distinctive activity of the Oscuri was that of feigned embassies (*finte ambascerie*): a ludic exercise in diplomatic oratory that helped young patricians to train for their political careers.[23]

Music had a strong tradition in Lucca, perhaps stronger than that of 'letters', especially after the foundation of the state-funded palace consort (Cappella Palatina) in 1543, which was charged with providing the music for ceremonial occasions.[24] With the posts of organist to the cathedral of San Martino and head of the Cappella Palatina in its gift, Lucca had the capacity to retain at least some talented musicians and composers within its walls, even if others, such as Niccolò Malvezzi (d. 1574) and his more famous son Cristofano (1547–99) were drawn away to more lucrative musical centres such as Florence. The composers Jacopo Corfini (*c.* 1540–*c.* 1591) and Gioseffo Guami (1542–*c.* 1611) were successively employed as organists of San Martino, while the trombonist and composer Niccolò Dorati (1513–93) was a member of the Cappella Palatina for a half-century from its foundation. The consort attained a fame that extended well beyond the boundaries of the city. Its musicians were frequently requested by neighbouring rulers, and occasionally they were engaged for high-profile international events, such as the 1585 wedding of Carlo Emanuele I of Savoy to Catalina Michaela, daughter of the king of Spain.[25] The state and cathedral musical establishments collaborated each year on the festivities to honour the Feast of the Exaltation of the Cross in September – an event that attracted musicians from all over central and northern Italy and showcased the musical excellence of Lucca.

1.1.3 Women's participation in Lucchese cultural life

The extent to which women participated in elite culture in Lucca is not easy to establish (although, as we will see, documents associated with Leonora Bernardi provide valuable information on this score). Certainly, in Italy as a whole in the later sixteenth century, traditional conceptions of women's role as limited to child-rearing and the efficient running of the household were no longer wholly dominant. A broader vision of women's cultural role, originating in the princely courts, had by this time permeated through to the provincial elites of Italy, and it was not unusual for women to attain local fame for their attainments in music and poetry, or for the elegance of their manners and conversation.[26] This was strikingly the case in some contexts, such as Siena, where the literary talents of the city's women became a source of civic pride in the 1530s and 1540s, and where mixed social gatherings (*veglie*) offered women a chance to shine for their intelligence and wit, as much as their beauty and grace.[27]

We have much less evidence for this type of mixed social gathering in Lucca, whose social norms seem to have been closer to Florence's more conservative, sex-segregated model.[28] More generally, women of the Lucchese elite seem to have been relatively disadvantaged with regard to their peers elsewhere. The importance Lucchese elite families accorded to the *domus* or *casato* over the *stirps* – the individual's blood line – meant that male offspring were privileged over female to an extent unusual even within the generally patriarchal world of Renaissance Italy. In the words of the historian Marino Berengo, 'women in Lucchese families of the Cinquecento appear even more silent and outside history ... than is the case in Venice or Florence, and their ability to wield influence, even indirect, on civic life, was practically non-existent'.[29] It is notable that evidence of Lucchese women's cultural engagement during the first half of the sixteenth century is largely limited to convents, notably the new foundation of San Domenico and the relaunched San Giorgio, both influenced by the radical Dominican Reformist thought of Girolamo Savonarola (1452–98). Both convents were important centres for manuscript production, with San Domenico boasting among its founders the scribe and illuminator Eufrasia Burlamacchi (1478–1548), a substantial portion of whose production survives.[30] San Giorgio had among its earliest prioresses the learned Beatrice Palmieri (*c.* 1462–1532), granddaughter of the humanist Giovanni Aurispa (*c.* 1376–1459) and the author of a life of St Dominic, as well as of many 'laude, sonnets, prayers and sacred plays'.[31]

Although the evidence for mixed lay cultural sociability in Lucca is thin, we do have one literary document of a *veglia*-type gathering there: a dialogue by the Erasmian thinker Ortensio Lando (1510–*c.* 1558). Lando spent a month in Lucca in 1532 as the guest of the wealthy, powerful, Reform-sympathizing Buonvisi family, and he preserved a record of the visit in his *Forcianae quaestiones* (1535), named for the Buonvisi villa at Forci, north of the city. The dialogue depicts a lively mixed conversation, in which – most unusually for this period – a woman, Camilla Guinigi Bernardi, takes the role as leading speaker during a discussion of women's status and role.[32] Lando's dialogue suggests that Reform circles in Lucca may have fostered the same distinctive type of mixed-sex elite sociability that we see so strikingly in other settings, such as in the circles of Juan de Valdés in Naples and of Reginald Pole in Viterbo.[33] Further evidence of this is offered in the records of a heresy trial of the mid-1550s against a palace guard, Rinaldo da Verona, which describes regular religious discussion groups hosted by two Lucchese patricians in the later 1540s, among the attendees of which two women are named.[34] This is of relevance to our study of Leonora Bernardi, in that the families of her parents, and particularly that of her mother, Lucrezia Trenta, were profoundly involved with the Reform movement in Lucca. Lucrezia's father, Silvestro Trenta, was among those attending the group denounced by Rinaldo da Verona, as was Matteo Gigli, the father-in-law of Leonora's aunt, Elisabetta Bernardi (see Figs 2–3).[35] Another relative of Lucrezia Trenta is found among the speakers of Lando's dialogue: Caterina Calandrini Sbarra, daughter of Lucrezia's great-uncle, the prominent statesman and diplomat, and notable Reform sympathizer, Filippo Calandrini (d. 1554).[36]

Beyond the city itself, we should also recall that the Lucchese hinterland contained some of Italy's most famous spas (*terme*) in this period, at Corsena and Villa (now Bagni di Lucca), and that the culture of these places was notably courtly and cosmopolitan, bringing together men and women of the elites from the whole of Europe.[37] Lucchese patricians, male and female, frequently socialized at the *terme*, and some families, such as the Buonvisi, owned houses there, so we can reasonably consider these locations as an extension of Lucca's elite literary scene. Several figures we will encounter as literary contacts of Leonora Bernardi's were keen visitors to the Lucchese *terme*, including Angelo Grillo (*c.* 1557–1629) and Scipione Bargagli (1540–1612).[38] Earlier in the century, the leading female Petrarchist poet and prominent Reform sympathizer Vittoria Colonna (1490–1547) spent the spring and summer of 1538 at the *terme* and presumably socialized with

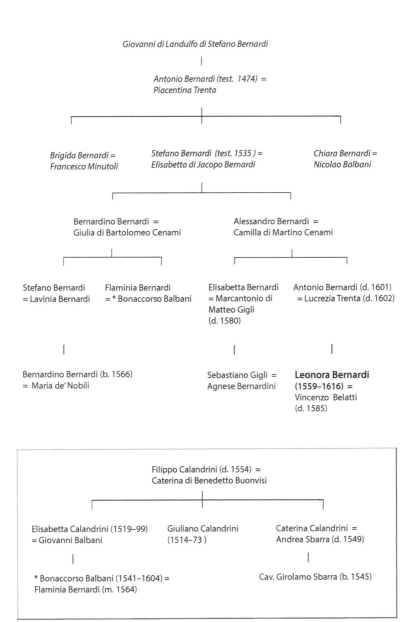

Giovanni di Landulfo di Stefano Bernardi
│
Antonio Bernardi (test. 1474) =
Piacentina Trenta

Brigida Bernardi =
Francesco Minutoli

Stefano Bernardi (test. 1535) =
Elisabetta di Jacopo Bernardi

Chiara Bernardi =
Nicolao Balbani

Bernardino Bernardi =
Giulia di Bartolomeo Cenami

Alessandro Bernardi =
Camilla di Martino Cenami

Stefano Bernardi
= Lavinia Bernardi

Flaminia Bernardi
= * Bonaccorso Balbani

Elisabetta Bernardi
= Marcantonio di
Matteo Gigli
(d. 1580)

Antonio Bernardi (d. 1601)
= Lucrezia Trenta (d. 1602)

Bernardino Bernardi (b. 1566)
= Maria de' Nobili

Sebastiano Gigli =
Agnese Bernardini

**Leonora Bernardi
(1559–1616) =**
Vincenzo Belatti
(d. 1585)

Filippo Calandrini (d. 1554) =
Caterina di Benedetto Buonvisi

Elisabetta Calandrini (1519–99)
= Giovanni Balbani

Giuliano Calandrini
(1514–73)

Caterina Calandrini =
Andrea Sbarra (d. 1549)

* Bonaccorso Balbani (1541–1604) =
Flaminia Bernardi (m. 1564)

Cav. Girolamo Sbarra (b. 1545)

Figure 2 Simplified genealogical table of the Bernardi family, showing figures discussed in Section 1 in roman type and others in italic. Artwork by Paul Greene.

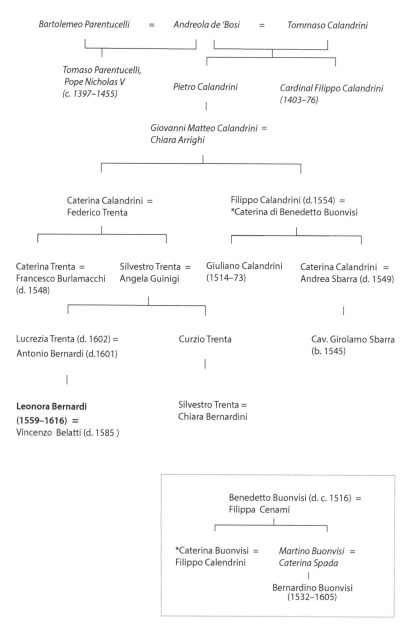

Figure 3 Simplified genealogical table of the Trenta family, showing figures discussed in Section 1 in roman type and others in italic. Artwork by Paul Greene.

local Reform-minded patricians; she also attended the electrifying sermons given in the cathedral of Lucca by the radical Capuchin preacher Bernardino Ochino (1487–1564).[39]

Colonna's Lucchese sojourn of 1538 is likely to have given her poetry special currency within the city, as it began to circulate in print from that same year. Traces of her legacy in Lucca have been detected in musical settings of her poems by Lucchese composers such as Corfini and Dorati.[40] Her influence may also be seen in the writings of Lucca's first significant female literary figure, Chiara Matraini (1515–1604), author of an important volume of Petrarchist *rime* published by the local printing house of Vincenzo Busdraghi in 1555. Matraini was one of a handful of female poets who had substantial collections published in the 1540s and 1550s, together with Tullia d'Aragona (from 1547), Laura Terracina (from 1548) and Gaspara Stampa (1554), based, respectively, in Florence, Naples and Venice.[41] Four years after the publication of Matraini's *Rime*, in 1559, Busdraghi brought out the first anthology of poetry by women, containing verse by more than 50 named authors, ranging from luminaries such as Colonna and her fellow aristocrat Veronica Gambara (1485–1550) to provincial Tuscan women unattested as authors elsewhere.[42]

Despite these two publications, we should be wary of assuming that Lucca had established itself by this point as a propitious environment for women's writing. The 1559 anthology, although published in Lucca, was edited by a native of Piacenza; the well-known writer, translator and editor Lodovico Domenichi (1505–64), a contact of Matraini's. No woman identified as Lucchese finds a place in its pages, not even Matraini herself. Scrutiny of Matraini's writings from the 1550s suggests that she was a somewhat isolated figure in her home city, in a way that in part reflects her non-patrician background, still unusual in this period for a woman writer. The famous cluster of Sienese female poets and 'learned women' of the 1530s and 1540s, who might have served as her closest role models – Virginia Salvi (*c.* 1510–post 1571), Laodamia Forteguerri (1515–post 1572), Aurelia Petrucci (1511–42) – all came from the patrician elite of their city, while Matraini was the daughter of a family of upwardly mobile dyers and weavers who played a prominent role in the Straccioni uprising and paid a heavy price when the rebellion was put down.[43]

It is not until Bernardi's own generation that we see something more like a tradition of women's writing emerging in Lucca, with Laura Guidiccioni Lucchesini (1550–*c.* 1597), Silvia Bendinelli Baldini (fl. 1588–95) and Bernardi herself.[44] The names of three further

Lucchese literary women of this era are known to us, all, like Bernardi and Guidiccioni (though not Bendinelli, the daughter of a schoolmaster), from leading patrician families. These were Angela Cenami Spada (fl. 1566), the wife of Gherardo Spada, dedicatee of Domenichi's anthology of female-authored verse; Eufrasia Tegrimi (c. 1514–77), a nun at San Giorgio; and Chiara Bernardini (fl. 1598), perhaps a relative of Bernardi's by marriage.[45] The elderly Matraini, a contemporary of Tegrimi's, reprised publication in the final decades of the sixteenth century, bringing out four works of religious prose and two revised editions of her verse and letters between 1581 and 1602. Lucca's adjacent states also offered notable examples of female literary and intellectual talent. Florence could boast the much-admired Laura Battiferri (1523–89), author of two acclaimed collections of verse (1560 and 1564), as well as Maddalena Salvetti (c. 1557–1610), a contemporary of Bernardi and Guidiccioni.[46] In Modena, meanwhile, Tarquinia Molza (1542–1617), granddaughter of the acclaimed poet Francesco Maria Molza, attained fame from the 1560s as a poet and erudite and as an outstanding musician and singer.[47] The striking figure of Molza was doubtless important in diffusing the cultural type of the 'respectable' female singer-poet (as opposed to courtesans, or figures close to the courtesan type). In Lucca, both Bernardi and Laura Guidiccioni correspond to this model.

Guidiccioni offers in many ways the closest parallel to Bernardi in her background, life and writings (although very little of her work survives). Nine years older than Bernardi, she was the daughter of a Lucchese patrician family of intellectual distinction. The poet Giovanni Guidiccioni was a cousin of her father's, and her brother was the Greek scholar Cristofano Guidiccioni, whom we encountered earlier as founder of an academy. Laura's husband, Orazio Lucchesini, also had literary interests, and he is recorded among those attending the *ridotto* of Giuseppe Bernardini. According to a nineteenth-century source citing family manuscripts, Laura Guidiccioni herself hosted cultural gatherings for the 'most famous intellects' (*più chiari spiriti*) of the city, presumably in the 1570s or 1580s, until one of her circle, Ippolito Santini, a canon at the cathedral, persuaded her that her talents were wasted in her home city, and that she deserved to experience the greater 'glory and splendour' that might be hers at the court of Florence.[48] The letters of her mother, Caterina de' Benedetti, who accompanied her to the Medici court in 1588, bear out Santini's analysis; Caterina sounds star-struck by the reception of her brilliant daughter and the sophistication of the musical establishment at court.

1.2 Life

1.2.1 1559–79: Girlhood and marriage (Lucca, Castelnuovo)

Leonora Bernardi was born in 1559 into a silver-spoon background in Lucca, the daughter of Antonio d'Alessandro Bernardi (1535–1601) and Lucrezia di Silvestro Trenta (d. 1602) (see Figs 2–3).[49] Both were members of prominent patrician families, among the few dozen Sergio Bertelli has defined the 'inner group' of the early modern Lucchese oligarchy.[50] Bernardi's paternal great-grandfather, Stefano d'Antonio Bernardi, was elected to the Anziani 14 times between 1496 and 1535, and he was four times Gonfaloniere, the highest office of the republic. Her father, Antonio Bernardi, was elected as Anziano five times between 1563 and 1583, and he was three times Gonfaloniere, in 1570, 1580 and 1586.[51] On her mother's side, Leonora was related to the most famous – or infamous – Gonfaloniere of Lucchese history, the conspirator Francesco Burlamacchi, whose wife, Caterina Trenta, was Lucrezia Trenta's aunt.[52] Lucrezia's paternal grandmother, Caterina Calandrini, was the sister of the Reformist statesman Filippo Calandrini, and aunt of the religious exile Giuliano Calandrini (1514–73), who left Lucca for Geneva in 1566, seven years after Leonora Bernardi's birth.[53]

Curiously, Leonora Bernardi began her rise to fame – and her connection with the Medici family – while still in the womb. As the chronicle of Giuseppe Sanminiati records, while pregnant with Leonora, Lucrezia Trenta attracted the admiration of the seventeen-year-old Francesco de' Medici, future grand duke of Florence, when he visited Lucca in the Carnival season. Francesco was so taken with the beautiful young woman – probably still in her teens – that he offered to act as godfather to her child, who was named for his mother, Eleonora of Toledo.[54] It is intriguing to speculate about the political meaning of the episode, especially when we consider that the powerful cleric and Medici client Ugolino Grifoni (1504–76), who held the rich benefice of Altopascio, near Lucca, stood proxy for Francesco at Leonora's baptism.[55] That Medici cultivation of patronage relationships with Lucchese patrician families could have a strategic dimension at this time is well illustrated by the story of the Antelminelli conspiracy of the 1590s.

An oblique glimpse of the culture – and perhaps also the religious sympathies – of the Bernardi–Trenta household is offered by a literary work printed in Lucca in 1566, *Il vero soggetto d'amore*: a short treatise on love by Antonio Renieri, or Rinieri, published by the author's son Claudio. The dedicatory letter to the work, addressed to Lucrezia Trenta, makes it clear that the young Claudio, in his early twenties, was at this time based in Lucca, in exile from his hometown, Colle di Val d'Elsa, near Siena.[56] The letter expresses gratitude to Lucrezia for her support in the 'calamity' of his banishment and flatteringly proposes Lucrezia and her husband as living examples of the noble, virtuous, good-looking, married lovers the work defines as 'the true subjects of love'.[57] Although Claudio Renieri is an obscure figure, we know something of his father, Antonio (1515–94), the author of *Il vero soggetto*: he was a schoolteacher, a poet in Latin and Italian, a member of the Sienese Accademia degli Intronati and a correspondent, among others, of the religious dissenter Aonio Paleario.[58] Given Paleario's presence in Lucca in the 1540s and the strong Reformist connections of Lucrezia Trenta's family, it is suggestive that Antonio Renieri's son should have sought her protection during his exile in Lucca. Although Claudio says little specific about Lucrezia, only praising her generic 'rare qualities' and 'merits', his dedication of this work to her suggests that she was known as a woman of literary interests.

Leonora Bernardi probably grew up in the palace of the Bernardi family near the church of San Salvatore in Mustolio.[59] We know little of her childhood or adolescence, although she was clearly educated to a high standard, especially in music and literature. It is even possible that Claudio Renieri was engaged as tutor to her, given his references to his 'service' or clientelage (*servitù*) to the Trenta–Bernardi household, and the strong educational bent of his family (his three younger brothers, as well as his father, all had teaching careers).[60] The two earliest records we have of Leonora, in works of the mid- to late 1570s, when she was in her late teens, both mention her artistic talents, as well as praising her beauty and charm. The first is a letter by an obscure *letterato*, Cesare Argiliani (sometimes also referred to as Angiloni), published with accompanying poems in 1575. The second is a dialogue by a better-documented figure, Niccolò, or Nicolao, Granucci (*c.* 1530–1603), published in appendix to a translation of Boccaccio's *Teseida* in 1579. Granucci's dialogue speaks rather vaguely of Leonora 'performing so elegantly and gracefully in every sort of artistic activity that she deserves the highest appreciation and praise'.[61] More precisely, Argiliani's letter expresses the hope that the composer and organist of Lucca cathedral, Jacopo Corfini, might set some of his verse to music, for her to sing, accompanying herself on the spinet.[62]

By the time these works were published, Leonora Bernardi was married, even though Granucci's dialogue, datable to 1577, describes her only as 'the most noble young lady Madonna Leonora, daughter of the Honourable Messer Antonio Bernardi, and goddaughter of the Grand Duke'.[63] Argiliani's text attests to a three-week stay on the part of Leonora in Castelnuovo di Garfagnana, one of the principal towns of that mountainous region, and the poems that accompany it speak of the desolation of the inhabitants on seeing her depart.[64] The occasion for this visit was her wedding to a gentleman of Castelnuovo, Vincenzo di Pietro Belatti. Bernardi was 16 at the time of her marriage: young for a bride, but not unusually so by the standards of the day. The couple had at least two children. Francesco, perhaps named for Leonora's godfather, Francesco de' Medici, appears as first-born in Vincenzo's will of October 1580, but he presumably died young, since we find no further mention of him.[65] A second son, Pierpaolo, survived into adulthood.

Intriguing information concerning Bernardi's marriage is offered by a published *consilium* (legal opinion) by a celebrated Ferrarese jurist Ippolito Riminaldi (1529–89), datable to the years following Vincenzo Belatti's death in 1585. The context is a dispute between the Bernardi family and the guardians of Leonora's underage son, Pierpaolo Belatti, who contested the return of her dowry from Vincenzo's estate, as the law required. The guardians challenged the validity of a 1574 dowry acknowledgement (*confessio dotis*) recording Vincenzo's receipt of 2,000 scudi from Antonio Bernardi, on the grounds that no other documentation existed for this payment.[66] They also questioned the legality of a document drawn up in 1575, at the time of the couple's wedding, whereby Vincenzo gave his wife a gift (*donatio*) of exactly that same sum. Reading between the lines of the *consilium,* this arrangement seems to have functioned as a workaround, to save Leonora's family from having to find the sum in one payment, with the 2,000 scudi instead being paid in instalments by her paternal grandmother, Camilla di Martino Cenami, over a period of eight years.[67]

Interestingly, there is some suggestion in the *consilium* that this unusual system of payment may reflect Vincenzo's lesser social status in relation to his wife. The amount of Leonora's dowry was respectable but not exceptional for a patrician bride of the 1570s, when dowries of over 3,000 scudi were not unknown.[68] A generation earlier, in 1551, Leonora's great-uncle Bernardino di Stefano Bernardi had left a bequest for the dowry of his daughter Flaminia of 1,500 ducats, extendable to 2,500.[69] It is also true that her marriage to Vincenzo Belatti is a rare case of a marital allegiance within Leonora's extended family in Lucca that was not straightforwardly endogamic, in the sense of being limited to families who were core members of the Lucchese political elite. His main attraction as a match was presumably his wealth, welcome at a time when Leonora's family may have suffered financial losses following the collapse of a number of leading Lucchese mercantile enterprises in the summer of 1574.[70] A late sixteenth-century Modenese writer describes Belatti as 'one of the wealthiest men in the Garfagnana'.[71] We also find mention of his 'notable riches' (*considerevole ricchezza*) in a letter of 1581, discussed in Section 1.2.2.

1.2.2 1579–84: Married life (Lucca, Florence, Ferrara)

As a native of Castelnuovo, Leonora's husband, Vincenzo Belatti, was a subject of Alfonso II d'Este (1533–97), duke of Ferrara and Modena, and he naturally sought advancement through service to the Este dynasty. Our first evidence of this is a letter of 1581 from Duke Alfonso's cousin Marfisa d'Este (*c.* 1554–1608) recommending Belatti to Cardinal Luigi d'Este (1538–87), the family's representative in Rome. The previous year, Marfisa had married Alderano Cybo-Malaspina (1552–1606), heir to the lordship of Massa and Carrara, close to Belatti's hometown of Castelnuovo. Marfisa's letter suggests that Belatti was seeking a position in Cardinal Luigi's household, although the cardinal refused on the grounds that he was already 'too encumbered with courtiers'.[72]

We have little documentation of Leonora Bernardi's movements during the early years of their marriage, with the exception of two letters in the Gonzaga Archives in Mantua, which place her in Lucca in late 1584. The letters give an intriguing glimpse of the contacts she had made by this point in the world of the courts. Both letters are dated 21 December. The first is from Giulio Cesare Gonzaga of Gazzuolo (1552–1609), younger brother of Tasso's great friend Scipione Gonzaga, and it is addressed to the heir to the duchy of Mantua, Vincenzo Gonzaga (1562–1612). The letter notifies Vincenzo that Giulio Cesare, who was bound for the Lucchese *terme*, has received the madrigals Vincenzo has sent him, and that he will convey them to the 'Signora Leonora Bellata' in Lucca that same day. The second letter, from Leonora herself, is addressed to Vincenzo's wife, Eleonora de' Medici (1567–1611) and proffers thanks to Vincenzo for the gift.[73]

The letters are intriguing as documentation of an acquaintance between Bernardi and the Medici–Gonzaga couple, who would vie in the 1580s with Alfonso d'Este and his duchess, Margherita Gonzaga (1564–1618), Vincenzo's sister, as courtly patrons of literature and music. The most likely occasion for their meeting is the celebration of the couple's marriage in Florence in April 1584, which was conducted in typically lavish style by the bride's father, Grand Duke Francesco. A description of the wedding festivities, by the duke of Urbino's envoy Simone Fortuna, notes that there were few ambassadors present, other than a 'gentleman of the republic of Lucca, with a most honourable entourage'.[74] It may well be that Leonora Bernardi was part of this entourage, as would be fitting for a goddaughter of the grand duke. A letter of December 1585 addressed to Francesco de' Medici confirms that she visited Florence some time before that date ('Your Highness has met her in Florence; she sang and played and she was most charming').[75] The Medici–Gonzaga wedding is one possible occasion for this visit, while another is Francesco's own marriage to Bianca Cappello in October 1579, when Bernardi would have been around 20 years old. The Lucchese ambassador who attended the latter event was a relative of Bernardi's, Marcantonio Gigli (d. 1580), the husband of her aunt, Elisabetta d'Alessandro Bernardi, and son of the Reformer Matteo Gigli.[76]

At some time in the mid-1580s, Vincenzo Belatti entered the service of Duke Alfonso d'Este. He is registered in December 1585 as among the 'gentilhuomini' of the duke.[77] A volume of music by the Ferrarese composer Andrea Nigrisoli, published in February of that year, is dedicated to 'Sig. Cavalier Vincenzo Bellati'. The first *canzonetta* praises Vincenzo and Leonora together, hailing them as the 'prize of our age'.[78] That Leonora spent time with her husband in Ferrara is also suggested by a publication of 1607, which contains the posthumous second edition of a literary work by the courtier and poet Annibale Pocaterra (1559–93), along with a biography of Pocaterra and other material relating to Ferrarese literary life. Bernardi is named in this edition as one of 16 poets in Ferrara between the time of Tasso's confinement in the hospital of Sant'Anna in 1579 and Giambattista Guarini's departure from Ferrara in 1588 who excelled in composing madrigals. She is also praised as a singer, whose voice added 'new sweetness' to her verse. The text further mentions, intriguingly, that Bernardi had ventured beyond lyric to pen a pastoral play.[79]

Another source for Bernardi's presence in Ferrara is a passage in a collection of lives of illustrious citizens of Modena composed by Francesco Forciroli (c. 1560–?1624) around the end of the sixteenth century. Writing of Tarquinia Molza, who had moved to Ferrara in 1583 to take up a position at court, Forciroli states that she was forced out in 1592 as a result of competition from Bernardi, whom he represents as newly arrived in Ferrara. The anecdote is confused in historical terms. Although Bernardi did move to Ferrara in 1592 (see Section 1.2.5 below), this was not her first sojourn there, and by then Molza had already left the city (in 1589). Despite its factual inaccuracy, however, Forciroli's description of Leonora offers interesting evidence of her reputation in her husband's home territory and the early circulation of her verse. Forciroli describes her as 'not only most beautiful and most charming, but also skilled in letters, and more than commonly accomplished in vernacular poetry, as may be seen from the poems of hers that are going around'.[80]

The opportunity to experience the culture of one of the most remarkable courts in Italy doubtless marked a watershed for Bernardi. Although this was Ferrara's last season as a quasi-independent princely court – the city and its territories devolved to its overlord, the pope, after Duke Alfonso died without issue in 1597 – it remained a place of extraordinary cultural vitality. In literary terms, the Ferrarese court in this period was synonymous with the names of Tasso and Guarini. Ferrara saw the composition of Tasso's great epic, the *Gerusalemme liberata* (completed in draft, 1575–6, and published in full in 1581), and of his archetypal pastoral play, *Aminta* (likely written and produced 1573; published 1580). Where music was concerned, the greatest innovation of the time was the creation in 1580 of a female vocal consort, the *concerto delle dame*, which performed for exclusive audiences, under the patronage of the duke.[81] This featured some of the most famous virtuoso singers of the time, including Tarquinia Molza and Laura Peverara (c. 1550–1601). A similarly groundbreaking female dance group was also formed, known as the *balletto delle donne*, or *balletto della duchessa*, made up of ladies of the court.[82]

A final possible testimonial to Bernardi's first Ferrarese sojourn is Tasso's sonnet 'Mentre ancor non m'abbaglia il dolce lume' ('While the sweet light does not yet dazzle me'), first published in 1586 (*R* mccxv).[83] The poem is unusual for an encomiastic sonnet, as the poet seems to have been asked to write in praise of a lady whose identity was masked. As Tasso noted in the *argomento* of the annotated 1593 edition of his verse:

> [The poet] says he is imagining the beauty of a gentlewoman he has never seen or heard and whom he does not know by name, even though she was famed for the excellence of her musicianship, and for other fine aspects of her body and mind.[84]

A note in the same edition glosses the poem's mention of the river Serchio, often used to identify Lucca by antonomasia, by saying that 'the lady's homeland had been communicated to the Poet, even though her name was not revealed'.[85] Ingeniously, Tasso makes poetic capital from the very vagueness of this strange commission, thematizing the fact that he must praise the lady without knowing her, as a poetic fancy or a 'lovely veil' (*bel velo*).

Starting with Angelo Solerti in the 1880s, several scholars have hypothesized that the mysterious subject of Tasso's sonnet was Laura Guidiccioni.[86] Bernardi seems a stronger candidate, however, given her connections with Ferrara at this time. Various mutual acquaintances might have commissioned the sonnet, including two already mentioned, Gianlorenzo Malpigli and Giulio Cesare Gonzaga.[87] Perhaps the most likely candidate, however, is the Genoese Benedictine poet Angelo Grillo, later well documented as a friend and admirer of Bernardi's. Although we have no firm evidence of when Bernardi and Grillo first met, it is not unlikely that they coincided in Ferrara in 1585. Grillo visited the city at least once in the autumn of that year, in connection with his friendship with Tasso. In the 1593 edition of Tasso's *Rime*, one of the few to be produced under the poet's own supervision, 'Mentre ancor non m'abbaglia il dolce lume' is followed by a canzone addressed to Grillo's sister, Girolama Grillo Spinola. Grillo's letters document this as written in October 1585, at the time of Grillo's visit to the city.[88]

If Tasso's sonnet to the Lucchese gentlewoman was written at Grillo's request, that would help explain the commission's most unusual feature, the suppression of the addressee's name. An element of semi-playful discretion and shielding was part of Grillo's persona at this time, as a monk unusually attracted to secular culture; he famously wrote love poetry in the 1580s under the allusive pseudonym 'Livio Celiano', the surname suggesting both hiding (*celare*) and jest (*celia*). It may also be true that Bernardi, like other gentlewoman-poets, tended towards discretion in the display of her talents; certainly, she seems to have made no attempt to publish her pastoral, and the sole surviving copy of her play acknowledges her authorship only in a cryptic fashion, using a phrase reminiscent of Tasso's framing of his sonnet, 'Gentildonna lucchese'.[89] A further hint that would point to Grillo as commissioner of the sonnet is the similarity between the phrasing in Tasso's 1593 *argomento* and a caption relating to Bernardi found in Grillo's *Prima parte delle rime* of 1589, which describes her as 'a lady of that city [Lucca], of rare and singular beauty of body and mind, and supremely talented at singing, playing, and writing verse' ('rara e singolare di *bellezza di corpo e d'animo*, & *eccellentissima* nel cantare, nel sonare, e nel poetare'; compare Tasso's 'famosa per l'*Eccellenza* de la Musica, e per *altre belle parti del corpo, e de l'animo*').[90] This suggests that it was only on reading this edition of Grillo's verse – in which he himself features very prominently as correspondent and object of praise – that Tasso became aware of the identity of the mysterious *gentildonna* that his friend had commissioned him to praise.

1.2.3 1585–88: Widowhood, scandal, banishment (Ferrara, Lucca, Florence)

Tragically, it was not only to her artistic talents that Bernardi owed her fame in these years. As the Ferrarese chronicles of Marcantonio Guarini and Giovanni Maria di Massa inform us, on Christmas Eve of 1585, 'as the Ave Maria was sounding', Vincenzo Belatti was shot dead in the courtyard of the ducal palace in Ferrara. The following day, Christmas Day, Belatti's body was buried 'with funeral pomp' in the Chiesa dello Spirito Santo, and the day after that, the hired assassin, from Pistoia, was gruesomely executed, being quartered alive.[91] A letter from Camillo Albizzi, the Florentine ambassador, to Francesco de' Medici confirms the details of the shooting with a few insignificant discrepancies. Startlingly, Albizzi's letter reports a rumour that Belatti's wife or her relatives were behind the killing:

> They have chosen not to divulge who ordered it [the murder], but it is said that it came from his wife or her relatives, who are certain gentlemen of the Bernardi family.[92]

Another, better-informed letter from Albizzi, of 13 January 1586, identifies the *mandante* (instigator of the crime) as 'Cavalier Sbarra' of Lucca, a knight of Malta. The two chronicles report the same news.[93] We learn from the chronicle of Massa – and from a letter of Belatti's – that this was Sbarra's second attempt at the killing; four months earlier, in August, he had already sent an assassin to Ferrara.[94] The man had been apprehended and imprisoned, only to be executed on 4 January – again, by the exceptionally brutal means of quartering – in the wake of the second, successful murder attempt. A third hired assassin may have escaped, given that a later, eighteenth-century Lucchese source records that in 1588, three years after the event, 'a certain Captain Luca da Menabbio', guilty of various other killings, was captured and imprisoned, and that 'it was said that he had been guilty of Signor Belatti's murder'.[95]

It cannot be excluded that Bernardi and her family were involved in her husband's murder, as Albizzi's initial report suggested. Although our Florentine and Ferrarese sources for the murder investigation may not have been aware of this connection, the 'Cavalier Sbarra' identified by the second assassin as having ordered the killing was a cousin of Leonora's mother, Lucrezia Trenta. Girolamo, or Geronimo, Sbarra (b. 1545) was the son of Caterina di Filippo Calandrini, daughter of Lucrezia's great-uncle, and of Andrea Sbarra (d. 1549), a merchant operating between

Lucca and Naples and a follower of the Reformer Juan de Valdés (see Fig. 3).[96] A further connection was forged between the two families when Caterina's nephew, Bonaccorso Balbani (1541–1604), married Antonio Bernardi's cousin Flaminia Bernardi in 1564 (see Fig. 2, inset). Girolamo Sbarra joined the Order of the Knights of Malta in 1566, and an emblem book of 1583 (Vincenzo Ruscelli's expanded edition of Girolamo Ruscelli's *Le imprese illustri*) speaks of him fighting in the Lepanto campaign in the early 1570s and subsequently enjoying a successful military and administrative career in the service of Venice.[97] Further documentation of his career is offered by a letter he addressed to the soldier and military engineer Sforza Pallavicino (1520–85) in June 1572, containing a detailed eyewitness report on the failed expedition to recapture the fortress of Castelnuovo (modern-day Hercegnovi, in Montenegro).[98] A notarial document signed in Venice in 1573 shows that Sbarra was acquainted with the 'Luca da Menabbio' identified in 1588 as Belatti's assassin – a certain Luca Pulcinelli, from Menabbio (now Benabbio), near Bagni di Lucca.[99]

We have little evidence for Bernardi's life in the years immediately following her husband's murder. A scene (II.5) in her play, however, seems to place her in Florence, in circles close to the court, in the summer of 1587. The scene narrates an episode involving an *à clef* character, Cellia, seemingly modelled on Marfisa d'Este, who is said to have 'left the proud, royal banks of the Po to bring happiness to lovely Etruria' (i.e. to have visited Tuscany from Ferrara). The passage almost certainly refers to a visit that Marfisa and her husband, Alderano Cybo, paid to Francesco de' Medici and his duchess, Bianca Cappello, in August 1587, a few months before the ducal couple's sudden deaths in October of that year. Marfisa and Alderano first stayed briefly with the ducal couple at their villa in Pratolino, around eight miles north of Florence, before travelling on with them to Florence itself. A letter from Alderano suggests that they were much feted in both places, 'receiving every honour possible', while a chronicle speaks of them entering Florence 'met by all the nobility of the city'.[100]

Bernardi's account in the play contributes to our knowledge of this visit by suggesting that a cortege of Tuscan noblewomen also played a part in the Florentine ceremonies of greeting. The speakers in II.5, Clorilli and Licasta, describe how 'all the nymphs of the surrounding countryside' rushed to pay tribute to Cellia-Marfisa. More specifically, Clorilli recalls a meeting on the river Mugnone, which runs between Pratolino and Florence, as Cellia made her journey 'to the Arno'. It seems likely that Bernardi herself was present at this event; certainly, she would have been a natural choice for the welcome party, as Francesco's goddaughter and presumably an acquaintance of Marfisa d'Este from her Ferrara days. It is possible, indeed, that Licasta is a proxy for the author, given the similarity of their names (seven letters: 'L . . . a') and the fact that Licasta stands outside the action of the play, figuring only in this single, highly distinctive *à clef* scene (which is discussed further in Section 2.1.3 below).[101] Subsequently to the Mugnone encounter, Licasta is also represented as having paid a visit to Cellia in her 'happy abode' by the sea near Massa, where Cellia delivered a memorable invective on the treacherousness of men. The scene as a whole seems intended to memorialize Bernardi's early widowhood as a gilded time of courtly sociability – and, perhaps, to draw on a metaphor strikingly developed by Cellia in her speech, as a moment of calm between storms.

The next tempest was not slow in coming. As the Lucchese chronicler Lorenzo Trenta recounts, on 10 July 1588, Cavalier Girolamo Sbarra accosted Leonora Bernardi in Piazza di San Michele in Lucca and began to harangue her (*cominciò a ragionare e vituperare*), saying that, if he were allowed a safe conduct to do so, he would denounce to the Lucchese government a murder plan dating to a few years before (see Section 1.5.1 for a transcription). After an attempt to get his case heard, Sbarra returned to the piazza, loudly repeating his denunciation and stating that Antonio Bernardi had promised Leonora to him in marriage but had since reneged on the promise. He further claimed that he and Leonora had had an affair, and that a daughter had been born from the liaison. He 'had many letters from her in which she called him her husband, and he was, in effect'.[102]

In the wake of these scandalous tirades, Sbarra was arrested and imprisoned, while Leonora Bernardi and her parents were summoned to appear before the *podestà* (chief magistrate) within a week, on pain of death and the confiscation of their possessions. Instead, they escaped to Florence, to find refuge with 'that grand duke', as the chronicler puts it: the new grand duke of Tuscany, Cardinal Ferdinando de' Medici (1549–1609), who had succeeded Francesco the previous year. Ferdinando appears to have welcomed Bernardi and her parents, giving them a house and a stipend of some kind. In September 1588, after two months of imprisonment, Girolamo Sbarra was banished not only from Lucca but 'beyond the confines of Italy' (*fuori de' confini di Italia*).[103] If he breached these terms, he would be considered a political rebel. Sbarra's sentence of exile refers to the safe conduct he was granted, which presumably assured him that he could depose his evidence without risking a capital sentence. The Council describes his sentence as respecting the terms of this assurance, but also as taking into account the severity of his offences, including the 'temerity and ill-doing' of his public denunciations, which risked disturbing the peace of the city.[104]

A document in the Archivio di Stato of Florence, transcribed in Section 1.5.3, offers further evidence of Sbarra's accusations against Leonora and her parents, as well as offering intriguing insights into his motives and character. The document – a kind of open letter, addressed by Sbarra to the citizens of Lucca – is located in a miscellany containing disputes between gentlemen submitted for adjudication to successive Medici rulers of Florence, suggesting that Antonio Bernardi may have approached Ferdinando I with a request for mediation. Sbarra's letter is a remarkable, rancorous diatribe, which paints him as a victim and Leonora Bernardi as a 'false siren' who has led him to his doom. In Sbarra's account, apparently 'published' on 6 July, a few days prior to his assault on Bernardi in Piazza San Michele, Bernardi seduced him into a prolonged sexual affair, which resulted in a child (Sbarra uses the masculine *figliolo*, by contrast with Lorenzo Trenta, who spoke of a daughter). She also apparently persuaded him to abandon his long-term service to the Republic of Venice and his membership of the Order of Knights of Malta, promising to marry him if he could secure a papal dispensation from the vows of his celibate order. Once he had attained this, she reneged on her promise, perhaps lured by the prospect of a more lucrative match.

The opening lines of Sbarra's letter make it clear that it was written in response to an alternative narrative being circulated by Antonio Bernardi, that he, Sbarra, was 'an insolent and temerarious man' attempting to claim his daughter's hand 'by force'. The letter's peroration, begging the 'honourable gentlemen' of Lucca to 'set aside passion' and give ear to his story, suggests that Antonio's version had already gained traction within the city. To counter this narrative, Sbarra offers up evidence in the form of a series of letters, supposedly from Leonora, attesting to their affair. Copies of these seem to have circulated with his own 6 July letter, while the originals are said to be deposited with a supporter, Lorenzo di Giovanni Buonvisi (1539–1621), who is willing to display them on request. While this may appear powerful evidence, there are elements in Sbarra's account that might lead us to suspect that this epistolary documentation was forged, not an unusual practice in this period.[105] Sbarra confesses that the letters displayed are a few survivors out of 'infinite' numbers received, that they are undated and that they do not make up a 'continuato filo', an uninterrupted narrative. Moreover, several details in the love narrative that Sbarra's letter reconstructs (the birth of a child, the lady's betrayal of the lover during his absence, his threat to expose her story) resemble the plot of a contemporary letter-collection, Alvise Pasqualigo's *Lettere amorose*, first published in 1563.[106] It is possible that Sbarra elaborated the story of his affair with Leonora by drawing on this curious autobiographical epistolary romance, containing purported real-life letter exchanges between Pasqualigo and 'Vittoria', a Venetian married woman. Sbarra may even have been personally acquainted with Pasqualigo, a Venetian patrician and a soldier by profession, who, like Sbarra, spent time in the garrisons of Venetian-ruled Dalmatia in the 1570s.[107]

Two things that come over with great clarity in Sbarra's letter are the strength of his erotic fascination with Leonora Bernardi and his determination to ruin her chances of marriage if he cannot have her himself. Tellingly, Sbarra states that, before going public with his tale, he approached the Bernardi family with an offer to preserve his silence if Leonora were to enter a convent, suggesting that his anger might have been assuaged if he knew she was unable to marry. Earlier evidence of Sbarra's feelings for Bernardi is offered by Vincenzo Ruscelli's 1583 commentary on his emblem, which consisted of an image of the fixed star Regulus with a lion. Among the interpretations Ruscelli offers is that the emblem may be an allusion to Sbarra's 'honest' – presumably Platonic – love for a lady to whom he felt himself astrologically predestined, noting that the *leone* included in the emblem was intended to recall her name.[108] Ruscelli speaks of Sbarra having first met this lady at a time when her 'rare qualities and virtues' (or 'talents', *virtù*) had attracted 'universal acclaim' (*universal grido*). Together with Sbarra's own description of Bernardi in his 1588 letter as a 'celebrity' (*persona celebre*), this suggests that her fame may have been an element in his attraction to her, as well as her beauty and high birth. While it must be emphasized that we do not have sufficient information properly to assess the veracity of Sbarra's claims regarding his relations with Bernardi, there seems much in his behaviour that maps onto modern analyses of the psychology of stalking, in a manner sinisterly adumbrated by his Virgilian motto, *Qua ducitis adsum* ('Wherever you lead, I am there').[109]

Whatever the truth of the story, Sbarra's assault on Bernardi's reputation did not prevent her and her family from being welcomed in Florence. We have confirmation of this in a letter from the Ferrarese ambassador to the Tuscan court, Ercole Cortile, dating to 13 August 1588, only a month after their exile from Lucca.[110] Discussing the musical resources available to the new grand duke, Cortile lists six 'ladies who sing very well' (*donne che cantano assai bene*). Five are well known to musical historians: Vittoria Archilei and Laura Bovio, already recorded as singing at the Florentine court in 1584, at the wedding of Vincenzo Gonzaga and Eleonora de' Medici; Lucia di Filippo Gagnolanti, first wife of the composer Giulio Caccini; Bernardi's Lucchese compatriot Laura Guidiccioni; and a very young Ippolita Recupito, described as 'a girl whom His Highness [Ferdinando] has brought from Rome'.[111] The sixth, only recently identified as Leonora, is 'the daughter of Antonio Bernardi, who was the wife of Signor Bellati'.[112] Given the scandal of the previous month, it is intriguing to see Cortile mentioning Leonora so neutrally, especially when writing to the Duke of Ferrara, who had witnessed Vincenzo Belatti's murder. This may suggest that Sbarra's accusations had not followed her to Florence or that they were not given credence there.

A detail in Cortile's report deserving of further consideration is that Ferdinando's musical establishment in August 1588 included two Lucchese gentlewomen from prominent political families, Leonora Bernardi and Laura Guidiccioni. Both had arrived in the same year, the first of Ferdinando's rule, and both were accompanied by well-connected male relatives, Antonio Bernardi and Guidiccioni's husband, Orazio Lucchesini, respectively. The latter, at least, had a clear role in Ferdinando's Lucchese policy, which sought to destabilize and ultimately to overthrow the government. Working in conjunction with Laura Guidiccioni's artistic collaborator, Emilio de' Cavalieri, Lucchesini coordinated the Florentine network of informers within the city and facilitated the planning of the Antelminelli conspiracy. He was formally banished from Lucca on two occasions: once in 1593, and then definitively in 1597.[113]

We have less information on the Bernardi family's activities, but it seems probable that the welcome that Ferdinando offered them in their exile had political motivations, as well as doubtless reflecting interest in Leonora's musical talents and family loyalty to her as his brother's goddaughter. Antonio Bernardi was a prominent man, with a distinguished background in politics and diplomacy. Lucrezia Trenta, too, brought significant family connections, not least through her nephew Settimio d'Andrea Bernardi, already launched on a successful political career.[114] While there is no evidence that the Bernardi family were regarded as traitors to the republic – indeed, as we will see, they were permitted to return to Lucca in the 1590s – it seems more than likely that their political connections in a 'target city' were part of their perceived capital as exiles.

1.2.4 1588: Poetic rehabilitation (Florence)

Four months before the Sbarra scandal broke, driving the Bernardi family from Lucca, the city experienced an epoch-defining religious event. On 30 March 1588, in a loggia near one of the city gates, a young soldier, Jacopo di Piero di San Romano, lost heavily while gambling. Disgusted at his losses, he threw a set of dice at a painted image of the Virgin, only for his arm strangely and spontaneously to break. Following due investigation by the bishop, Alessandro Guidiccioni, the episode was confirmed as a miracle, and a great civic procession escorted the now detached painting into the church of San Pietro Maggiore, where it became the object of a significant cult, drawing pilgrims from the *contado* and further afield.[115] The event was celebrated in verse by the Latin poets Filippo Sergiusti, Scipione Bendinelli and Belisario Morganti and by the vernacular poets Cesare and Michele Garzoni and Gaspare Casentini, while Laura Guidiccioni's acquaintance Ippolito Santini was appointed by Bishop Guidiccioni to narrate the miracle and its aftermath in prose.[116] The miracle also appears to have inspired more personal Marian poetry, such as Silvia Bendinelli's sonnet 'Lofty Queen, to you with humble heart' ('Alta Regina, a te con humil core') and the poems contained in Chiara Matraini's 1590 *Breve discorso sopra la vita e laude della beatissima Vergine e madre di Dio*.[117]

The exiled Leonora Bernardi, too, seems to have added her voice to this Lucchese Marian outpouring, with what would prove her most celebrated poem, the canzone 'Se pur fin su ne gli stellanti chiostri' ('If even on high, within the starry cloisters'). Although there is nothing within the text that explicitly relates to the 1588 miracle, a printed edition of 1591 annotates the poem as 'On the Virgin who appeared in Lucca', while a manuscript copy in Siena dates the poem to 1588 (see Section 3.1.1).[118] More specifically, it seems near certain that we can date the poem to the early months of Bernardi's exile in Florence. Following an initial section of praise of the Virgin, the canzone turns to the travails of the suffering poet, who prays that, with Mary's aid, she can defy 'the thoughts of the vulgar throng' and see its 'vain efforts' shattered like glass (see Section 3.1.2 for the text). In a still more explicit allusion to the author's predicament, the initial, praise section of the canzone introduces, as 'types' of the Virgin, not merely the Old Testament heroines Judith and Esther, who were often invoked in this role, but also a less expected figure, the Roman Vestal Virgin Tuccia, who was accused of incest, a capital offence for a Vestal. Tuccia purged herself of the charge by a miracle: that of carrying water intact in a sieve.

The ostensible argument of the *exemplum*, spelled out in the poem, is that the Virgin redeems her sex by purging the sin of Eve. An implicit comparison is also suggested, however, between the poet and Tuccia – both women falsely accused of unchastity, who defend themselves by fearlessly speaking out. The comparison becomes still closer if we look at the version of the anecdote in Valerius Maximus's *Memorable Deeds and Sayings*, where Tuccia's story is grouped with a series of anecdotes illustrating acquittals in criminal cases faced by those 'beset by *invidia*' (malevolence or envy). Valerius's Tuccia, confident of her innocence, 'boldly' prays to the goddess Vesta to allow her to prove her chastity and is rewarded by the miracle of the sieve. Bernardi's votive canzone to her own virgin 'goddess', Mary, manifests the same assurance that justice will triumph in her case.[119]

In addition to this defiant assertion of her innocence, Bernardi's canzone contains a discreet allusion to the complexity of her situation, as a widow who – unlike the *ur*-widow-poet of sixteenth-century Italy, Vittoria Colonna – cannot in sincerity embody the widow's role of adoring, Artemisia-like devotion to her deceased husband that her culture admired. Buried in the autobiographical stanzas of the poem is an allusion to the timeline of the poet's anguished suffering ('black horror and death'): not, as we might expect, three years, taking us back from 1588 to the murder of her husband, but rather 13 years, taking us back to the year of their marriage. To readers aware of Bernardi's situation, the canzone thus serves as the allusive confession of a *malmaritata* – an ill-married wife – whose decade of marital unhappiness has been followed by the further anguish of a violent widowing, then by public humiliation and shame. Bernardi's allusion to the misery of her marriage also helps us to understand why, in the aftermath of Belatti's killing, on the evidence of the Florentine ambassador's initial letter, Ferrarese court gossip pointed to his wife's relatives as the prime suspects in the case.

Most unusually for a poem that is not a correspondence sonnet, we have two direct 'replies' to Bernardi's canzone, which offer indications of its early reception. Bernardi's acquaintance from her Ferrara days, Angelo Grillo, wrote a sonnet in praise of the canzone, acclaiming Bernardi as a Marian poet of rare genius and having the Virgin herself, in a passage of prosopopeia, acclaim 'Leonora' as her chosen Muse. Read in the light of Bernardi's predicament at the time, the Virgin's emphasis on the poet's chastity is noteworthy; she is 'purer than any other [woman]' and thus permitted to speak of Mary, who shuns praise 'from any impure tongue' (see Section 3.1.3). Grillo was a close friend of the Lucchese patrician Nicolao Tucci (1541–1615), and both were stationed in Genoa in 1588,

Tucci in the service of Cardinal Antonmaria Sauli, Grillo as a monk in the monastery of Santa Caterina.[120] It is possible that Tucci was the conduit through which Bernardi's poem reached Grillo, as Tucci was acquainted with Antonio Bernardi, who had accompanied him as Lucchese envoy on a diplomatic mission to the imperial court at Vienna in 1576.[121] Grillo's published *Prima parte delle rime* of 1589, where his sonnet on Bernardi's canzone appears, also contains a rather obscure sonnet exchange with a Lucchese cleric, Monsignor Guido Tegrimi, archdeacon of the cathedral, in which both poets allude flatteringly to a musical 'phoenix' of Lucca, identified in the annotations as Bernardi. Tegrimi's sonnet speaks of this phoenix as having supplied Grillo with 'delicious, sweet sustenance' (*cibo . . . soave, e dolce*), presumably her canzone, while Grillo's alludes to a 'base, rustic song' (*carme rustico vil*) that is circulating in Lucca, presumably his sonnet.[122] If this interpretation is correct, we are perhaps catching an echo of the reception of Bernardi's and Grillo's Marian poetic exchange within Lucca, and a glimpse of her support network there. Interestingly, Tegrimi's poem speaks of the soothing and consolatory effects Grillo's poetry is having 'here' (i.e. in Lucca) as it circulates, 'blessing all those wretched and unhappy'.[123]

A second response to Bernardi's canzone is an *ottava rima* poem by the poet and librettist Ottavio Rinuccini (1563–1621), found in two manuscripts in Florence. In one of these sources, prepared under Rinuccini's supervision, the poem is accompanied by a madrigal and by a note stating that it was written 'about a canzone by the Sig[no]ra L.B.' (see Section 3.1.4 for the text). The poem replies to the canzone, reassuring Leonora that her prayers will be listened to in Heaven, and that she will soon find the serenity she seeks. Cast partly in the language of love lyric, the poem says little that relates specifically to Bernardi's predicament, but to early readers who were aware of it, phrases like 'innocent beauty' (l. 18) and 'the decent and holy thoughts of your chaste heart' (l. 21) are likely to have had particular meaning, as is a passage that insists on the choral nature of sympathy for Bernardi ('everyone weeps for your ill fortune, every breast is pierced by your pain'; ll. 27–8). The poem also alludes to Grillo's support, when it talks of a 'divine Angel' watching over Bernardi (l. 30).

Rinuccini's poem is of special interest given his closeness to the Florentine court and especially its performance culture. Around 25 years old in 1588, he was already well-integrated in Florentine intellectual and literary society, and he was soon to make his debut as a poet for Medici spectacles.[124] We can probably take him to be voicing a collective court position towards Bernardi in the poem, rather than simply a personal view. It is possible, too, that Grillo's warm support of Bernardi owed something to Medicean sympathies. A madrigal sequence published in his 1589 *Prima parte delle rime*, sent to Grand Duke Ferdinando, 'during the time when he was also a cardinal' (i.e. between October 1587 and November 1588), attests to his contacts with the Florentine court, as do the numerous poems in that collection celebrating Ferdinando's marriage to the French princess Christine of Lorraine (1565–1637).[125]

Nonetheless, whatever other factors may have moved him, it is difficult to imagine a well-respected cleric such as Grillo risking his reputation through a public friendship with a woman accused of sexual irregularity and conniving in murder if he did not believe in her innocence. Many of his later letters to Tucci speak of Bernardi not simply with affection but with admiration, both for her literary talents and her moral and spiritual qualities (see Section 1.2.7 below). Of special interest in this context is a passage in a letter of 1610, written when Leonora was in her early 50s, which praises her for the 'virile constancy' with which she met misfortune, as well as for the 'spiritual blessings of a soul truly united with God'.[126] More specifically, Grillo speaks of Bernardi as 'that noble lady who never bent her fine soul to persuasions or to the consensus of popular opinion'.[127] Especially in a letter addressed to Tucci, his likely conduit for news of the Sbarra scandal of 1588, it seems quite probable that the phrase may allude to that episode, with 'persuasions' referring to Sbarra's aggressive erotic pursuit and 'popular opinion' to what Bernardi refers to in her canzone as 'the thoughts of the vulgar throng'.

1.2.5 1589–98: Exile (Florence, Ferrara)

We have little information on the next few years of Bernardi's life, after the dramas of 1588, although she appears to have continued within the sphere of Medici court patronage. The prologue to the surviving version of her pastoral suggests that it was conceived for performance in the presence of Ferdinando and Christine ('Dinando' and 'Cristilla'), probably around 1590 or 1592 (see Section 2.1.4). Around this same time, Bernardi's *canzone* to the Virgin appeared for the first time in print, in a poetic anthology published in Genoa (see Section 3.1.1). Bernardi's shorter lyrics also began to appear in print in the early 1590s, set to music, although without attribution (see Section 3.2.1 below).

A further possible trace of Bernardi's experiences in these years is found in the Licasta scene of *Clorilli*, discussed in Section 1.2.3 above. In the episode recounting Licasta's visit to Cellia-Marfisa d'Este at Massa, she is said to have encountered a gallant male figure, Ormindo, who speaks warmly against misogyny and in praise of women. This may be a tribute to the Bolognese poet Giulio Cesare Croce (1550–1609), who had dedicated a work on these same themes to Marfisa in 1590: the *ottava rima* poem *La gloria delle donne*, one of the relatively rare 'elite' products of an author mainly known for his comic and popular street verse.[128] Intriguingly, Croce states in the poem that Marfisa's 'court' contains women quite capable of answering back themselves to misogyny through their own 'valour, wit, prudence, vivacity, and spirit' – perhaps a challenge to which Bernardi self-consciously responded in the play.[129] Whether the allusion in *Clorilli* records an actual meeting with Croce, or, as seems more likely, a virtual, textual encounter, it serves to associate Bernardi with Croce as fellow celebrants of Marfisa d'Este and co-participants in the *querelle des femmes*. Croce's text is likely to have elicited a degree of interest in Bernardi's circles in Florence, since, among the creative women he celebrates in the poem were two figures well known at the Medici court, Laura Guidiccioni and Laura Bovio, both members, together with Bernardi, of the vocal consort mentioned in Ercole Cortile's letter of 1588.[130]

The next archival evidence we have concerning Bernardi's life is a letter of 11 July 1592 from the soon-to-be cardinal Cinzio Aldobrandini (1551–1610), nephew of the recently elected Pope Clement VIII, to Alfonso d'Este, duke of Ferrara. The letter recommends Bernardi to Alfonso's protection, requesting his clemency (*clemenza*) for her and asking that he accord her his 'special and preferential favour' while she is *costì* (i.e. in Ferrara).[131] The letter refers to Bernardi by her married name ('la S[igno]ra Leonora Bellati') and describes her as 'not unworthy, on account of her *virtù*' (*non indigna per la sua virtù*), with the latter term meaning either moral virtue or artistic talent. How Bernardi obtained Aldobrandini's support in this plea is not clear, though one likely conduit was the Lucchese cardinal Giovanni Battista Castrucci (1541–95), who had benefited from the patronage of Nicolao Tucci in his early career.[132] Also unsure is the reason for Bernardi's return to Ferrara, although the relationship with Marfisa d'Este attested in her play offers one possibility. Another may have been considerations of safety. If the Bernardi family was concerned about potential further harassment from Girolamo Sbarra, Ferrara and the Este court may have seemed their safest residence option. Lucca's banishment of Sbarra beyond 'the confines of Italy' was unlikely to have reassured them, given the political divisions of Italy and the lack of reliable extradition norms. After Lucca itself, Ferrara was plausibly the most dangerous city in Italy for Sbarra to set foot in, having ordered the murder of a subject and courtier of Duke Alfonso before the duke's own eyes a few years before.

The duration of Bernardi's second sojourn in Ferrara is unknown. A letter of Grillo's locates her in the city in the summer of 1598. We do not know whether she remained there throughout the intervening years, though the fact that a letter from Antonio Bernardi of 1595 locates him in Ferrara may suggest that the family moved there for the whole period.[133] Grillo's 1598 letter, written from Venice, replies to a request from Leonora that Grillo exert his influence within the Cassinese Congregation on behalf of 'Padre Don Gervasio', probably the Neapolitan monk of that name recorded elsewhere as a literary acquaintance of Tasso and of Berardino Rota.[134] Grillo concludes his letter to Bernardi by stating that he hopes to see her in Ferrara before she leaves for her 'homeland' (*patria*). Another letter of Grillo's, to their mutual Lucchese acquaintance Nicolao Tucci, probably dating to 1599, speaks of Bernardi having been 'about to set off for Lucca' when he saw her in Ferrara the previous year.[135] This suggests that, by 1598, the Bernardi family did not see their decade-old sentence of banishment as a bar to a return to their home city, even though, as we will see, the sentence was not formally revoked until the summer of the following year.

The timing of the Bernardi family's departure from Ferrara is significant. Alfonso II d'Este, the last Este duke of Ferrara, had died without issue in October 1597, and, by the time of Leonora's letter to Grillo, the city had already passed into the hands of its overlord, the papacy. In May 1598, Clement VIII entered the city, with a vast entourage from the papal court in train. That Bernardi and her family planned to leave shortly afterwards suggests that their sojourn in Ferrara may have been connected with the court and, more precisely, the old establishment of Alfonso, his consort Margherita Gonzaga (1564–1618), and his sister, Lucrezia d'Este (1535–98), who continued Este traditions of poetic and musical patronage throughout the dying years of the dynasty's reign in Ferrara.[136] If we accept the recent, intriguing hypothesis put forward by Aoife Brady that Lavinia Fontana's (1552–1614) *The Visit of the Queen of Sheba to King Solomon* in the National Gallery of Dublin is a record of the court of Ferrara in the 1590s, with Margherita and Alfonso in the role of protagonists, then it is even possible that Bernardi features within the striking group portrait of the Queen of Sheba's female entourage.[137] In any case, the painting offers us a vivid evocation of the material and cultural richness of the court of Ferrara during the period of Bernardi's second sojourn in the city. It also opens up the intriguing possibility that Leonora may have become acquainted in this period with Fontana, the greatest female artist of the period, celebrated hyperbolically by Croce in *La gloria delle donne* as the equal of Michelangelo and Raphael.[138]

A letter of January 1598 from Leonora's son, Pierpaolo, to his guardians in the Garfagnana gives a sense of the status that the Bernardi family enjoyed within the city. The letter proudly announces that the writer, probably in his late teens, has been selected as one of a select group of young men ('the foremost' of the city) who are to accompany the baldaquin of the cardinal legate Pietro Aldobrandini (1571–1621) as he arrives in Ferrara as governor of the city.[139] Pierpaolo urgently requests funding from his guardians to cover the costs of the extravagant livery he must wear for the occasion. The young men selected for this escort were knighted by Aldobrandini a few days after the ceremony and given gifts, including gold and silver commemorative medals. Thirty-eight ladies (*gentildonne*) were also present at this ceremony and received medals, of whom Bernardi could well have been one.[140]

Perhaps unsurprisingly, given his troubled childhood, Pierpaolo Belatti appears to have been a wayward adolescent, to judge from a letter addressed to Antonio Bernardi by an unidentified correspondent in September 1598. Vincenzo Belatti's will had stipulated that, in the event of his early death, his son's estate was to be managed by guardians until he reached the age of 25.[141] The 1598 letter makes it clear that this constraint was chafing on the young man, who was keen to throw himself into expensive aristocratic pursuits such as hunting.[142] The author speaks in highly-coloured terms of Pierpaolo being immersed in 'his usual dissipations' (*le solite dissolutezze*) and having 'lost all fear' of reproach. The letter concludes on a note of weary fatalism: only divine intervention can bring the youth to hand.

1.2.6 1599–1603: The *ridotto* years (Lucca)

After her return from Ferrara, Leonora Bernardi seems to have remained in Lucca more or less stably until her death in 1616. The first years of this period, to 1604, are incomparably the best-documented portion of her life. We owe this documentation principally to the rich correspondence between her Lucchese admirer Domenico Chiariti and the prominent Sienese *letterato* and academician Belisario Bulgarini (1539–1619). This *carteggio* survives in manuscript in the Sienese Biblioteca degli Intronati, within Bulgarini's very copious archive.[143]

Chiariti is now remembered by literary historians, if at all, for a letter addressed to Camillo Pellegrino in 1598, relating to the Ariosto–Tasso dispute.[144] He appears to have been well-connected, however, with a significant network of literary acquaintances. In addition to Bulgarini, he corresponded with the Lombard poet Giuliano Goselini (1525–87), the Piedmontese writer Annibale Guasco (1540–1619) and the Sienese linguist and university professor Diomede Borghesi (1540–98).[145] Latin verse to him is found in a collection by Bernardino Baldini (1515–1600) and his emblem is discussed in Camillo Camilli's *Imprese* (1586).[146] Within Lucca, we find Chiariti the title speaker of a 1599 dialogue by the otherwise unknown Count Silvio Feronio, which portrays him as an expert on literary and linguistic matters. A few details of Chiariti's life transpire from his letters to Bulgarini. He studied at Padua University – presumably in the 1570s, since he notes that he was a contemporary there of Alessandro Guidiccioni Jr (1557–1633), bishop of Lucca from 1600 – and he spent two years in France in 1595–7.[147] We also know from letters that he and the Benedictine poet Benedetto Guidi exchanged with Goselini that Chiariti was in Venice in 1580, where he helped see an edition of Goselini's *Rime* through the press.[148] A published work by Bulgarini speaks of him being 'in Heaven' in 1608, supplying a *terminus ante quem* for his death.[149]

Besides Bernardi, Chiariti was in contact with other female intellectuals. A reply sonnet from Chiariti to Chiara Matraini is published among the prefatory verse to her last published work, the *Dialoghi spirituali* (1602), and a sonnet exchange with the Venetian writer Moderata Fonte appears in an anthology of 1589.[150] A sonnet addressed to Chiariti by an otherwise unknown Milanese poet, Maria de' Ferrari, is found in an anthology of 1591, in which Chiariti is described in the index as a *musico famoso* (famous musician).[151] Chiariti also seems to have known Tarquinia Molza, as we find him soliciting a sonnet from Goselini on the subject of her widowhood in early 1580.[152] Finally, as the Bulgarini letters attest, he was a close acquaintance of a Florentine lady living in Paris, Cornelia Doni Gorini, a lady-in-waiting of Maria de' Medici, also a contact of Ottavio Rinuccini's. Bulgarini describes Doni Gorini in a printed work as *virtuosa* and *scienziata* (talented – or virtuous – and learned), and she seems to have shared Chiariti's and Bulgarini's linguistic and literary-theoretical interests.[153]

Bernardi first appears in Chiariti's letters to Bulgarini in a letter dated 15 September 1599, where he introduces her in rapturous terms:

A gentlewoman of this city is here at the moment, Leonora Bernardi Belatta. She is young, beautiful and marvellously talented. She is a Sun in her beauty, a Minerva in her wisdom, and a Thalia in her grace. And, although she is most honoured, I would not name her to you were she not also exemplarily respectable.[154]

From this point, Chiariti serves as a self-appointed publicist for Bernardi, sending letters and poems in praise of her not only to Bulgarini, but to other correspondents such as Grillo.[155] Shortly after the letter cited above, he writes to Bulgarini to solicit an encomium of Bernardi for him to show around in Lucca – not, he quickly notes, because the lady herself is concerned with such matters, but to satisfy some of her relatives and friends, who are hungry to hear her praised.[156]

Chiariti's flamboyant announcement of Leonora's presence in the city probably indicates the time of her return to Lucca. Archival documents in the city show that Antonio, Leonora and Lucrezia Bernardi successfully requested 'liberation' from their sentence of exile in August 1599 – the month before Chiariti's letter – even though their sentences were not formally struck from the records until June 1601.[157] It is intriguing to speculate what kind of negotiations went on behind the scenes to clear their path to rehabilitation, and we should perhaps not rule out that they garnered favour through information-gathering during their time in Ferrara, given Lucca's keen political interest in its borders with Modena. Leonora's acquaintance Nicolao Tucci reported to the Lucchese government in 1588 a warning he had received from the Spanish ambassador in Genoa that it should not rely on information from official ambassadors or envoys in dealing with wily princes like those of Ferrara and Florence; rather, it needed to 'keep its eyes open in many parts and employ more secret means'.[158] Exiles such as the Bernardi could be of use to foreign princes, but they could also potentially serve as *mezzi segreti* for their home governments, if they hoped to return to the fold.

We learn a few details from Chiariti of Bernardi's domestic situation after her return to Lucca. During her first few years back, her parents were still alive, and Leonora lived with them, in their house in town and a country villa to which she often retreated. We also hear mentions of visits to unnamed female relatives, and there are several references to a cousin, Bastiano, or Sebastiano, Gigli, who visited Bulgarini in Siena in 1600 as her 'ambassador' (*ambasciatore*), bearing a letter of greeting from her, along with a copy of 'li scherzi del Chiabrera' (Chiabrera's *Scherzi e canzonette morali*, published in Genoa in 1599).[159] Sebastiano was a member of the Accademia degli Oscuri, and he is recorded as taking part in a joust organized by the academy in 1592 and as acting in a comedy in 1593.[160] Like his father, Marcantonio – and many others of his family – he also served the Republic as a diplomat, most notably as ambassador to Spain in 1607–10.[161]

Notable as an absence in Chiariti's letters is Bernardi's son, Pierpaolo, who appears from other documentation to have resided in his father's hometown of Castelnuovo di Garfagnana.[162] In October 1602, Leonora Bernardi wrote to Virginia de' Medici, duchess of Modena, on his behalf, requesting help with a lawsuit Pierpaolo was pursuing against his guardians, presumably for mismanagement of his funds (see Fig. 4, in Section 2.2.2).[163] Earlier that same year, on 13 May, in the Church of Santi Giovanni e Reparata in Lucca, Pierpaolo had married Caterina d'Ippolito Guidiccioni, in a match very likely arranged by his mother.[164] The detail is intriguing, given that Caterina was a niece of the now-deceased Laura Guidiccioni, providing suggestive evidence of Bernardi's relationship with the family of her closest cultural counterpart in Lucca. The marriage was doubtless also intended to solder the young Pierpaolo's connections within the Lucchese patriciate, and perhaps to prevent him from gravitating back entirely into his dead father's Garfagnana sphere.

The most historically important aspect of Chiariti's reporting on Bernardi is the very full account he gives of her literary sociability, and specifically the *ridotto* or 'academy' she hosted in her home (Bulgarini uses both terms).[165] We know of other such female-run household academies in this period, including a famous one hosted by Margherita Sarrocchi in Rome.[166] In no other case, however, do we possess such a detailed account of the cultural interests of such a *ridotto* and the role played by its 'Diotima' or 'Aspasia', as Bulgarini terms Bernardi in one letter.[167]

The activities of Bernardi's *ridotto* are comparable with those of male literary academies, often centring on the discussion of recently composed works. In February 1600, for example, Chiariti speaks of reading two literary works *chez* Leonora in the presence of 'several gentlemen with expertise in these matters': Piero Segni's funeral oration for the literary theorist Giacomo Mazzoni, which includes attacks on those – such as Bulgarini – who had argued against Mazzoni's defences of Dante; and a counter-attack by Bulgarini.[168] Segni's oration was in print, while Bulgarini's was in manuscript (it was not published until 1608).[169] This episode provides fresh documentation of women's engagement with literary-theoretical debates in this period, alongside Eleonora di Garzia de Toledo's 1575 request to the Accademia degli Alterati in Florence for an opinion on Alessandro Piccolomini's annotations on Aristotle's *Poetics*.[170] A published work by Bulgarini records that Cornelia Doni Gorini intervened in these same, long-running debates on

Dante, defending Bulgarini's position against the Florentine bishop of Carpentras, Orazio Capponi (1552–1622).[171]

Another, related topic we see featuring in some sittings of the *ridotto* is language and the correct form of the literary vernacular. In February 1603, for example, Chiariti reports a meeting at Leonora's house to discuss the 'orations of Sig[nor] Celso': three recently published speeches on linguistic topics by the poet and linguist Celso Cittadini (1553–1627), employed at the university-level Studio of Siena as a lecturer in that field.[172] Other sessions of the *ridotto* were devoted to reading poetry: Bulgarini's poems on the marriage of Maria de' Medici and Henry IV in October 1600, for example, and the *rime* of the Sienese *letterato* Scipione Bargagli in February 1602.[173] Bargagli's *rime* are said to include poems in praise of various ladies of Lucca, seemingly written some years previously, since some are now dead or 'in the shadows of their years' (*nelle tenebre degli anni*). Those still living include Bernardi herself and another poet, Chiara Bernardini, said to have written a madrigal on the death of Diomede Borghesi in 1598. This may be Leonora's relative of that name, the wife of her cousin Silvestro di Curzio Trenta (see Fig. 3). The same letter that reports on the reading of Bulgarini's poems for Maria de' Medici also details a discussion of women's emblems and mottos (*le imprese delle donne*). Chiariti mentions, in particular, a critique of Tarquinia Molza's device of a vine encircling an elm tree, with the motto *Non sufficit alter*, referring to Molza's decision not to contemplate a second marriage.[174] The meeting debated whether *Nec alter* would have been a more elegant motto, and referred the matter to Bulgarini, who responded with a detailed discussion of the point.

In addition to these secular pastimes, we catch glimpses of a religious inflection to Bernardi's *ridotto*. Sundays seem to be marked by a regular gathering of clerics (*ecclesiastici*) and laymen. Presumably discussion on these days was generally religious in character, although the only Sunday gathering on which Chiariti reports in details sees the clerics detained by their duties – it is Palm Sunday 1603 – leaving Chiariti to entertain the lay audience with a letter from Bulgarini on linguistic issues.[175] Earlier that same year (1 January, the Octave of the Nativity), Chiariti truncates a letter to Bulgarini in his eagerness to reach Bernardi's house, where Padre Vincenzo Domenici, 'a most excellent theologian', is expected to deliver what Chiariti calls a *sermone*, a religious disquisition of some kind.[176] The detail is interesting, as it offers our first indication of Leonora's involvement with the Congregation of the Chierici Regolari della Madre di Dio (Clerics Regular of the Mother of God), with which Domenici was closely associated. The Congregation was first instituted in 1574 in Lucca as an informal grouping of young priests under the leadership of Giovanni Leonardi (1541–1609). It was formalized by Bishop Guidiccioni in 1583, and it received confirmation from Pope Gregory XIII the following year. Domenici is recorded in Rome in the late 1580s, studying theology, alongside two of the earliest members of the Congregation, Cesare and Giulio Franciotti, and he is recorded as one of the instructors in a Congregation-run seminary opened in Lucca in 1592.[177]

It is frustratingly rare that, as in the case of Domenici, Chiariti names men associated with Leonora's *cenacolo*. In general, we hear solely of 'fine wits' (*belli spiriti*) or 'most noble intellects' (*nobilissimi intelletti*). Chiariti's Palm Sunday report mentions an Ascanio Cenami among the attendees, and a few more names are supplied by a curious episode in August 1602, when Chiariti and Bulgarini asked Bernardi to host a meeting to discuss a recent work by Bulgarini, without Chiariti being present. Bernardi's role seems to have been that of literary spy, taxed to report on her attendees' judgement of the works – the thought presumably being that they would speak more candidly in Chiariti's absence, since his friendship with Bulgarini was well known.[178] Those named as having received Bulgarini's work in this instance are Ludovico Arnolfini, a member of the Moricone family (probably Moricone Moriconi) and a member of the Altogradi family (probably one of the brothers Alessandro and Niccolò Altogradi).[179] All these figures were from patrician families with traditions of political service, Cenami and Arnolfini from the inner elite, and Moriconi the son of a famous lawyer. Arnolfini was among the founding members of the Accademia degli Oscuri, and Moriconi was also a member (respectively, 'il Contrario' and 'l'Aggiustato').[180] Both Arnolfini and Moriconi were doctors of law, and the Altogradi, too, were a family with strong legal connections.[181] Moriconi's cultural interests are attested by the dedication to him of a translation of George Buchanan's spiritual tragedy *Jephthes* by Scipione Bargagli, published in Lucca in 1587.[182]

Chiariti's letters also occasionally afford glimpses of Bernardi's interactions with women. A letter of 20 September 1603 records a gathering attended by a Genoese gentlewoman, Ersilia Doria Lomellini. A letter of 25 June of the same year mentions that Leonora has been detained in her villa, hosting 'the wife of Signor Orazio Lucchesini', who is visiting from Pescia. The reference must be to a second wife of Lucchesini, as Laura Guidiccioni had died several years earlier. Chiariti refers quite casually to the fact that Lucchesini is 'banished' (*sbandito*) from Lucca (as we saw earlier, he had been implicated in the Antelminelli conspiracy a few years earlier).[183] Bernardi's willingness to receive the wife of a traitor to the republic is a matter of note, especially given her own family's past as exiles and the fact that her home city was at war at this time. Although Este Modena was the official enemy in the 1603 Garfagnana war, suspicions also attached to Florence and to Ferdinando I, whose own territorial interests in the Garfagnana would be well served by a Lucchese defeat.[184]

One potential female acquaintance of Bernardi's is not mentioned in Chiariti's letters: the elderly but still active Chiara Matraini. Connections were not lacking between these two Lucchese women of letters: Chiariti exchanged sonnets with Matraini, and Matraini's *Dialoghi spirituali* were dedicated to Bernardi's acquaintance Marfisa d'Este. Praising Lucca in a letter of 24 October 1599 as a home to 'most noble intellects' and 'superhuman ladies', Bulgarini cites Matraini as an example of the latter, 'the most illustrious Signora Chiara Matraini, now living, and gloriously destined to immortality'.[185] It is possible that Bernardi, and others of her caste, kept their distance from Matraini because of her family's involvement in the revolt of the Straccioni (on which see Section 1.1.1). Nicolao Tucci's unsympathetic treatment of the Straccioni rebels in his unpublished history of Lucca, written in 1598–9, is likely to be representative of patrician attitudes to this still well-remembered episode of Lucchese history.[186]

Angelo Grillo's letters to Tucci help us round out our knowledge of Bernardi's cultural life in Lucca. A letter dating to 1602–4 sketches out a circle of Lucchese friends with whom Grillo expects Tucci to share verses he has sent him: 'Sig[nora] Leonora' and 'Sig[nori] Tegrini [*sic*] & Fortini', jointly described as 'the Muses and Apollos themselves'.[187] The second male figure named is Tucci's protégé, Antonio Fortini (d. 1657), a young priest who enjoyed a reputation as a poet.[188] The first-named is probably Francesco Tegrimi, whom Grillo also mentions, along with Fortini, in a letter datable to 1604–7.[189] A further indication that Bernardi was part of the audience with whom Grillo shared verse pre-publication is found in a letter to Tucci datable to 1600, in which Grillo discusses two Latin poems on Mary Magdalene that Tucci has sent him, one by Tucci himself and the other by Cardinal Silvio Antoniano (1540–1603). Grillo reciprocates by sending a series of madrigals he has composed, inspired by a *Magdalene* by Titian, asking for Tucci's critical opinion and also the 'judgement (*giudicio*) of Signora Leonora, by which I mean that with which she polishes her own creations and renders them so beautiful'.[190]

An earlier letter from Grillo to Tucci, datable to 1599–1602, contains an encomium to Bernardi that is interesting for what it reveals of contemporary attitudes to 'exceptional' women. After praising some poems of Tucci's, Grillo remembers himself to Bernardi, commenting that her 'magnanimity' is now so well proven that 'we need have no fear of those dangers into which other women so easily fall, especially exceptional ones (*le singolari*), as Your Lordship has said'.[191] That the 'dangers' are vanity and pride is clear from what follows. Leonora is so well shielded by her greatness of soul that 'she cannot change, if not for the better, and what is given to her as a prize she accepts instead as a spur'.[192] 'These clouds of human praise', Grillo continues, 'cannot rise so high that they can disturb the serenity of a noble soul, which, united with its origin [God], can barely see them from on high, except as tiny, dark, and fleeting shadows'.[193]

To the extent that we can infer Tucci's remarks from Grillo's reply, it seems likely that Tucci expressed concern that Bernardi risked having her head turned by the adulation she received from men in her circle. Whether Grillo shared Tucci's view that 'singular' women were prone to such vanity is not clear, even though he politely concurs with the view. Grillo's letters and verse show him to have been exceptionally supportive of women of talent.[194] Shortly after this letter was written, as abbot of San Paolo Fuori le Mura in Rome, he commissioned an altarpiece from Lavinia Fontana – a rare case of a major ecclesiastical commission being given to a female artist.[195] It is not unlikely, however, that Tucci's anxiety was shared by others of his Lucchese compatriots. As a culturally active woman in a town with relatively little experience of the type of mixed-sex social gatherings familiar in court settings, Bernardi was treading a delicate path, and this doubtless conditioned her behaviour to some extent. A slightly earlier letter from Grillo, this time to Chiariti, describes Leonora as possessed of 'brilliant, God-given gifts' which she nonetheless keeps 'shrouded in such a cloud of modesty that, where she could turn night into a bright day for her name and that of others', she is instead 'so reserved and restrained by her own rigour that she leaves us in a state of desire'.[196]

1.2.7 1603–16: Religious retreat (Lucca)

Two of the most fascinating passages in Chiariti's letters on Bernardi are those that describe elaborate dinners she hosted to commemorate the Feast of the Innocents (28 December). The guest list for these dinners appears to be all-male (at least, no woman other than Leonora is mentioned). In 1602, the guests are said to be 12 in number. They are invited to stay for dinner quasi-spontaneously; then Leonora leaves the room to oversee preparations, while her guests are left to be entertained by the young medic Bernardino Vecoli (b. 1576), who speaks at length (perhaps, Chiariti says, a little too lengthily), on nutrition 'according to the doctrine of Galen', and on preventative medicine (*de sanitate tuenda*).[197] The dinner goes on for five or six hours, in a salon marvellously illuminated with lights hung from the ceiling with trompe-l'oeil marble fixtures. A portative organ provides music. Chiariti says little of the menu, other than mentioning a concoction of distilled apple with which the banquet ends, but he describes the setting in detail. Perfume burns continually, deliciously scenting the room, and the guests are delighted to have orange-flower water brought for them to wash their hands 'without leaving the table'.[198] Even the toothpicks are magnificent, 'wondrously worked from juniper wood'.[199] Sumptuous as the 1602 dinner was, it was outdone, in Chiariti's judgement, by the following year's 'stupendous feast'.[200]

Despite the appearance of effortless luxury afforded by these banquets, Bernardi's days of good living were numbered. Her father, Antonio Bernardi, had died on 1 October 1601.[201] Her mother, Lucrezia Trenta, died suddenly the following April, leaving her daughter 'desperate' (*disperata*) with grief.[202] Antonio's death had financial implications for his daughter, as his estate was bound by a *fideicommissum* dating to the 1535 will of his grandfather, Stefano d'Antonio Bernardi. This mandated that his property, in the absence of a direct male heir, should pass to the closest male in the *stirps*, and, failing that, to more distant Bernardi male relatives.[203] In Chiariti's words, with Antonio's death, Leonora 'lost the enjoyment of notable wealth'.[204] The lavish banquet of the Innocents in 1602 was paid for, Chiariti tells us, surprisingly, by an admirer, the wealthy silk merchant Bernardino Buonvisi (1532–1605), a man in his 80s, who is 'decently in love with her, and, with an unconfessed ambition' – presumably to marry her – 'offers her any service he can'.[205] The two had a family connection, in that Bernardino's aunt, Caterina Buonvisi Calandrini, was also Lucrezia Trenta's great-aunt by marriage (see Fig. 3, inset).

Leonora Bernardi's dramatic life had a dramatic last act. In a letter of 1604, probably December, a letter from Bulgarini, in reply to a lost letter from Chiariti, informs us that Leonora had decided to withdraw from the world – not to a convent, but rather in a private, secular religious retreat, within her own home.[206] Bulgarini expresses conventional moral admiration for this choice, but he concludes on a note of bafflement, remarking on the displeasure her retirement must cause to 'these most noble spirits, her academicians (for they will, in a sense, have lost their Diotima, who could have served God without entirely forsaking this highly virtuous conversation)'.[207] Although any explanation must be conjectural, the reason for Bernardi's retirement from the world may have been in part financial. Her veteran admirer Buonvisi died in January 1605, and he may have been in his final illness at the time of her decision. It is possible that, having long enjoyed her role as glittering hostess, Bernardi preferred a sudden withdrawal from view on her own terms to the humiliation of living on in public with reduced means.

Whatever her motives, Bernardi seems to have embraced her religious retirement with conviction. In February 1605, she invited Chiariti to her house to take back some books he had lent her, and they spoke briefly in the presence of her confessor about the motives for her retreat. Bernardi's explanation, as reported by Chiariti, is that 'finding herself in the winter of her years and the shadows of the senses, it was expedient for her, to warm herself and light her path, to turn to her spiritual Sun'.[208] Although we cannot know whether this is a paraphrase, rather than a verbatim record, it is tempting to think that the Colonnaesque metaphorical language that Chiariti cites may reflect Bernardi's own words. Consistently with his own monastic vocation, Angelo Grillo responded with enthusiasm to the news of Bernardi's retreat from the world, exclaiming in a letter to Tucci:

> What fine things can we expect from Signora Leonora, now that she has chosen the better part? How I praise her, and how I envy her those devout tears, and those fiery sighs, and those moments of tenderness, filled with virile constancy. What have women not done on the path of the spirit? There is no reading matter that moves me more than that of holy women, who have left the way behind them for us to follow.[209]

At some point before 1610, Leonora lost her sight, and the dedicatory letter of a spiritual work of 1615 speaks of her as bedridden and having lost the use of her hands, presumably through arthritis.[210] The author, Cesare Franciotti (1557–1627), congratulates her on this shutting down of the senses as a gift from God, enabling her to concentrate her entire energy on Him. Fortunately, Bernardi was not without companionship in these difficult last years. Franciotti speaks of her being accompanied by a person who cares for her with the love of an only daughter (*unigenita figlia*). The phrase is probably intended to emphasize the devotion of Leonora's carer, rather than literally to designate their relationship. We have no other record of Leonora having a daughter, if we exclude

Lorenzo Trenta's allusion to her alleged illegitimate child with Girolamo Sbarra (see Section 1.5.1.).

The 1615 dedication is interesting, in that it confirms Bernardi's involvement with the Clerics Regular of the Mother of God, discussed earlier in connection with Vincenzo Domenici. Cesare Franciotti, from a prominent Lucchese patrician family, was one of the core members of the Congregation from its earliest days, and he became famous as a preacher, performing with great success in Rome (1589), Naples (1600) and Siena (1605).[211] The Congregation attained a strong following among Lucchesi of all social strata, but it encountered resistance initially from the ruling elite of the city, which viewed it with suspicion as a 'Trojan horse' for papal interference in the political and religious life of the city and as too closely associated with the Jesuits.[212] Chiariti may well have been a victim of these tensions if, as seems likely, he is the Domenico di Bartolomeo Chiariti who was tortured and briefly imprisoned in December 1588 under suspicion of having leaked details of Lucchese Council deliberations concerning a proposed abolition of the Clerics Regular to a representative of the Lucchese clergy in Rome.[213] The Congregation appears to have reciprocated the Lucchese government's suspicions. Bernardi's acquaintance Domenici was removed from his teaching post at their seminary in 1597–8, during a visit to Lucca by the Congregation's founder, Giovanni Leonardi, on the grounds that he was too 'close to the Republic' (*da la parte de la Repubblica*).[214]

A last literary work of Bernardi's deserves mention, one dating to the time of her retreat and known through the letters of Grillo: a narrative poem on Saint Eustace, the early Christian martyr, who converted while hunting, on seeing a crucifix appear between a stag's horns. Bernardi's choice of genre is interesting. Vernacular sacred epic (and epyllion) was reaching the height of its vogue at this time, and was practised equally by religious and by lay authors.[215] At least one other poet in Bernardi's circle in Lucca, Francesco Tegrimi, composed a religious epic, on the first Christian emperor, Constantine, while in Florence an unfinished Old Testament epic by Maddalena Salvetti was published posthumously in 1611.[216] Grillo's enthusiasm for this genre is manifested in an interesting letter to Tucci, datable to around 1605, in which he discusses Francesco Bracciolini's recently published *La croce racquistata*, some cantos of which Grillo had read in draft. Grillo mentions Tegrimi's epic-in-progress in the letter, and he also alludes more obliquely to a similar project involving Tucci's protégé Antonio Fortini.[217] A surviving trace of this Lucchese interest in *ottava rima* religious poetry is Tucci's meditative *poemetto* on the Virgin of Loreto, published several times from 1590, including, most intriguingly, in Tasso's *Rime spirituali* of 1597.[218]

Our first mention of the *Eustachio* occurs in a letter from Grillo to Tucci datable to June 1606, in which, after further discussion of Bracciolini's epic (which Tucci has now read and admired), Grillo speaks of his pleasure in hearing that Bernardi's poem is progressing.[219] Another letter of Grillo's, dating to 1607 at the latest, suggests that the poem is now near to completion. This last-cited letter of Grillo's states that he heard a passage of the text (*particella*) read aloud to him by Leonora herself during a visit to Lucca.[220] While Grillo politely declines to act as 'reviewer' (*censore*), on the grounds that the burdens of his day job as abbot of San Paolo Fuori le Mura leave him no time for literary pursuits, he happily accepts the role of 'reader' and 'admirer', and he speaks with enthusiasm of the 'lights and splendours' (*lumi e splendori*) of this 'noble poem', concluding that he 'would be pleased to see her give it the finishing touch, so others may give it the first palm in this genre'.[221]

Grillo's mention of having heard Leonora read from her poem during a visit to Lucca suggests that her retreat from the world may have been less absolute than Chiariti's or Franciotti's testimony would suggest. Some evidence indicates that she may have attended gatherings at which Fortini and Tegrimi were present, at the house of Tucci's nephew by marriage, Mario Fiorentini, as late as 1615, following Tucci's death.[222] Also of interest in this regard is a letter from Grillo to Tucci of 1610, in which he mentions Bernardi and Tucci as co-participants in what he calls 'spiritual feasts' or symposia (*spirituali conviti*), probably alluding to the same *ridotto*, later 'inherited' by Fiorentini. Intriguingly, the two works Grillo mentions in connection with these gatherings are both secular: Tucci's own unpublished commentary on Tacitus, whose progress Grillo was watching with interest, and a copy of a work by the young poet Girolamo Preti (1582–1626), probably his idyll, *La Salmace*, which Grillo suggests as potential light relief.[223]

Bernardi's final appearance in Grillo's letters, dating to 1616, is found in a reply to her son Pierpaolo, who has written to notify him of her death. Grillo describes her loss as 'a great misfortune not merely for Lucca . . . but for the whole of Italy and for our age, of which she was such a rare ornament'.[224] His eulogy emphasizes her exceptionality and her 'valour and virile virtue', which made her a 'woman who not only exceeds woman, but also exceeds man'.[225] Grillo concludes by speaking admiringly of Bernardi's decade-long period of religious seclusion, imagining her now enjoying 'that heaven, which she sowed for herself on earth with such a long preparation for this last and perilous pass'.[226]

1.3 Legacy

Bernardi's most immediate and intriguing legacy may be seen in the figure of Isabetta Coreglia (fl. 1628–50), last in the micro-tradition of early modern Lucchese women writers that started with Chiara Matraini.[227] Connected to Bernardi through their mutual acquaintance Antonio Fortini, Coreglia has much in common with Bernardi both in terms of her life and her literary choices, although she differed considerably in her openness to print publication. Like Bernardi, she was known as a musical *virtuosa* as well as a poet and dramatist. Like Bernardi, without entering a convent, she embraced a religious identity, in Coreglia's case that of a Carmelite tertiary. Her surviving works include a volume of *Rime spirituali e morali* (1628) and two pastoral dramas, *Dori* (1634) and *Erindo il fido* (1650). She is also known to have composed a narrative poem or tragedy on an Old Testament theme, *Absalon*.[228] It is likely that Coreglia was acquainted with Bernardi's works, since she was related to the Bendinelli family, who appear to have inherited Bernardi's manuscripts.[229] It is possible that the opening scene of *Erindo il fido*, which features two older shepherds in conversation, is a conscious echo of the opening scene of *Clorilli*.[230]

Coreglia aside, Leonora Bernardi appears to have disappeared from memory not long after her death in 1616. Only her rare appearances in print during her lifetime, and a few posthumous printings of her religious verse in editions of Cesare Franciotti's writings (see Section 3.1.1) kept her memory alive.[231] The oblivion into which she fell is reflected in the thinness of the biographical information given for her in Luisa Bergalli's *Componimenti poetici delle più illustri rimatrici d'ogni secolo* (1726) and Francesco Saverio Quadrio's *Storia e ragion d'ogni poesia* (1739–52), where she first resurfaces to notice. Bergalli shows awareness of Bernardi's appearance in Grillo's *Rime*, while Quadrio mentions her appearances in Pocaterra and in the 1591 anthology.[232] Both authors give her name as 'Leonora Bellati Bernardi' and Quadrio makes explicit the assumption that Bernardi was her married surname. This detail was corrected in 1750 by Domenico Vandelli, whose biography of Tarquinia Molza accurately records that Leonora was a Bernardi by birth and the wife of Vincenzo Bellati [*sic*], although Giovanni Maria Mazzucchelli, in his entry on 'Lionora [*sic*] Bellati' in *Gli scrittori d'Italia* (1753–63), retains the erroneous earlier position.[233]

It was among historians working in Modena and Lucca in the second half of the eighteenth century, and especially through the efforts of Girolamo Tiraboschi (1731–94), that the first steps were made towards serious research on Bernardi's life. Tiraboschi's first mentions of Bernardi, in 1781, do little more than repeat the information in Vandelli.[234] Later, however, by 1786, he had new details, deriving from the Lucchese erudite Tommaso Francesco Bernardi (1719–94): the names of Leonora's father and son, and the correct spelling of her marital surname, Belatti.[235] Tiraboschi also seems to have commissioned a collaborator, Giovanni Battista Moreali (1699–1786), to conduct further, literary research on Bernardi, which survives in manuscript. Moreali gathered information about Bernardi found in the printed record, including rare texts such as Argiliani, Granucci and Nigrisoli. He also speculated that she might be the 'Gentildonna lucchese' to whom two poems are attributed in Agostino Ferentilli's 1579 anthology *Della scielta di stanze di diversi autori toscani*, although current scholarship attributes these to Chiara Matraini.[236] Further biographical details regarding Bernardi are found in an unpublished volume of notes on the literary history of Lucca compiled by Tommaso Trenta (1745–1836), who was also in touch with Tiraboschi. In compiling his notes, Trenta reviews literary sources already tapped, such as the works of Argiliani and Grillo, but he also adds important biographical details, such as Leonora's date of birth, her mother's name and the fact of Vincenzo Belatti's murder in Ferrara.[237]

This Settecento research also shed light on the fate of Bernardi's writings. Moreali states that Bernardi's poetry passed into the Bendinelli family and, after this, into the collections of the Lucchesini. A manuscript catalogued in the library of Scipione Lucchesini, but which Moreali could not locate, is listed as 'Clorillo, a pastoral drama by Signora Leonora Bernardi de' Belatti, dedicated to the Most Serene Grand Duchess of Tuscany'.[238] Further mention of a lost pastoral by Bernardi, again in the Lucchesini family library, is found in Cesare Lucchesini's *Storia letteraria del Ducato Lucchese* (1825–31). Lucchesini reports the title of the play as *Clorindo*, on the evidence of the Lucchese literary historian Bernardino Baroni (1694–1781). While it is possible that Bernardi composed two plays of similar title, it is more likely that Moreali and Baroni were describing the same manuscript. The similarity of Moreali's title, *Clorillo*, to the name of the principal character in the play edited in this volume makes it plausible that the lost manuscript of the Lucchesini library was a copy of this same work.

No further advances in scholarship on Bernardi were made in the nineteenth or twentieth centuries. Even passing mentions of Bernardi are rare after Lucchesini's *Storia letteraria*, although her canzone was republished in 1853 in an anthology of Marian verse (see Section 3.1.1), and Giovanni Sforza's 1879 monograph on Francesco Maria Fiorentini contains a brief discussion of Bernardi that incorporates new material from Grillo's letters.[239] A few brief mentions of Bernardi are found in later studies, but it was not until the re-emergence of a manuscript of her pastoral in Venice in 2008 that she became the focus of the closer biographical and literary study attested in this volume.[240]

1.4 Conclusion

Knowledge of Leonora Bernardi's life and works contributes to studies of late-Renaissance Italy in several ways. Most obviously, it enriches our understanding of women's place in elite literary and musical culture in a period that remains significantly under-researched. It helps reinforce the recent scholarly trend towards recognizing the era of the Counter-Reformation as one in which literature, both religious and secular, flourished and evolved, and in which male attitudes to female cultural activity were often open and supportive, in a way that defies previous stereotypes of the era.[241]

In terms of the cultural geography of the period, Bernardi's writings and life story help illuminate the intense traffic between Ferrara and Florence in the 1580s and 1590s, and the ways in which important Ferrarese innovations such as pastoral drama and female vocal consorts made their way to the Medici court. Bernardi's biography also helps shed light on Lucchese culture in this little-studied period and on the city's transregional relationships, both with feared and admired 'great powers' such as the Este and Medici dukedoms, and with smaller centres such as Siena. Of special interest for Lucchese history is the rich documentation concerning Bernardi's *ridotto*, with its distinctive mixture of secular and religious activities. An articulated study of literary and religious sociability in Lucca at the turn of the Seicento, encompassing formal institutions such as the Accademia degli Oscuri and the Chierici Regolari della Madre di Dio, and more informal gatherings such as Bernardi's *ridotto* and Tucci's *veglie*, would be valuable as a granular case study in the dynamics of Italian Counter-Reformation culture, helping illuminate the context in which distinctive early modern Lucchese practices developed, such as the tradition of political-religious Senate sermons to which Renzo Sabbatini has recently called attention.[242]

Through these considerations, the example of Bernardi helps productively complicate our understanding of women's position and role within a republic such as Lucca, which seems in most regards to have marginalized women. As we have seen (in Section 1.1.3), Lucchese women have been characterized as 'silent' and 'outside history', deprived of any 'ability to wield influence, even indirect, on civic life'. A recent edition of Chiara Matraini's late works presents Lucca as an environment in which intellectually aspiring women were disadvantaged by 'insufficient education . . . restriction to a purely domestic vocation, and the suspicion with which female intellectuals were regarded'.[243] This unmitigatedly negative view needs to be revised in Bernardi's case, despite the many disadvantages she struggled with, some directly connected with her sex. Bernardi was certainly not silent, even if she chose not to publish her writings (a choice that may reflect practice in her Lucchese circles as much as gender convention, given that neither Tucci nor Fortini published their writings).[244] Nor is it necessarily true that she stood outside history and lacked all influence on civic life. Not only did her *ridotto* serve as an important meeting place for the Lucchese secular and clerical elites, but her achievements and connections also made her a soft-power asset to the republic, at a time when 'singular women' were an increasingly recognized source of cultural capital in Italy.[245] In some respects, such as in her closeness to the Clerics Regular of the Mother of God, she may be seen as at the forefront of religious and cultural change in Counter-Reformation Lucca. By the early 1620s, not long after her death, the long-enduring tensions between this order and the governing elite of Lucca had finally given way to a new collaboration, and vocal supporters of the Clerics Regular from patrician families such as the Trenta, Sbarra and Arnolfini – the first two, of course, with connections to Bernardi – began to be elected to the Anziani and the Gonfalonierato.[246] By the middle of the decade, all laws passed to limit the power of the order within Lucca had been rescinded.

Finally, thinking about the rich case study offered by Bernardi's life in Lucca might help ease our way towards more nuanced ways of understanding the transition from Reformation to Counter-Reformation in Italy. Bernardi was born into a city famous – or infamous – for its infiltration by the 'heresies' affecting northern Europe. Her mother's family was one of the dynasties, or networks of dynasties, most closely associated with this trend. Bernardi's own life, as a friend of a poet as quintessentially 'Counter-Reformation' as Angelo Grillo, and a sympathizer with an order as quintessentially 'Counter-Reformation' as the Clerics Regular of the Mother of God, might seem to represent almost the antithesis of the lives of her theologically questing ancestors among the Calandrini, Trenta and Burlamacchi clans. If we look beyond theological speculation to cultural patterns, however, things become more complex. It is not difficult, for example, to note continuities between the type of mixed religious *cenacolo* we recognize as characteristic of the evangelical movement in Italy and Bernardi's much later *ridotto*, similarly bringing together devout laymen and women to talk of divine things on the margins of the institutional Church. Similarly, it is striking that Bernardi sought religious respite towards the end of her life not in a situation of formal claustration, as a boarder in a convent, but rather in a self-chosen and self-enforced lay seclusion, where she presumably set her own spiritual routine. Traditional distinctions between Protestantism as a religion that privileged a direct, personal communion with God on the part of the worshipper, contrasted with Catholicism's insistence on institutional mediation, would struggle to make sense of this highly distinctive and original early modern female life.

1.5 Appendix: Documents of the scandal of 1588

1.5.1 Lorenzo Trenta's chronicle

This account is found, in a near-identical form, in Baroni, 'Notizie', ms. 1105 (Bernardi), pp. 135–6 (72r–v) and Baroni 'Notizie', ms. 1132 (Sbarra), pp. 95–6 (49r–v). The transcription is mainly taken from the latter source (vol. 1132), with two phrases, given in italics, from the former. The attribution to a volume of memoirs by the historian Lorenzo Trenta is found only in vol. 1105.[247] The dates and details given in Trenta's chronicle tally with those in archival sources, such as ASL Sentenze e bandi, 480 (Bernardi) and 676 (Sbarra), except that the latter gives the date of Sbarra's exile as 12 September 1588, rather than 11 September.

This document, like those in Sections 1.5.2 and 1.5.3, has been transcribed with the original punctuation and spelling.

In questo anno 1588 Girolamo d'Andrea Sbarra a 10 luglio in Piazza di S. Michele cominciò a ragionare, e vituperare M.ᵃ Leonora Ved.ᵃ rel. del Sig.ʳ Vincenzo Belatta da Castelnuovo, asserendo che se lui poteva aver salvo condotto dalli Sig.ⁱ Anziani voleva scoprire un trattato di un'omicidio commesso pochi anni sono, e se ne andò a Palazzo adomandando a i segretari e *all'Ill.mi Sign.ri questo ma che se l'averà o no non lo so.*[248]

Ma ritornato in Piazza, per ogni luogo che si fermava ragionava dicendo: Antonio Bernardi l'aveva promesso dare la sua figlia per moglie, ma che non l'aveva voluto mantenere la parola, che aveva molte lettere di mano di lei che lo chiamava suo marito, e che cosi era, e per tale l'aveva avuto in suo dominio, e piu volte narrato il che e il come, e che ne aveva avuta una figlia.

Lo Ecc.o Consiglio avutone cognizione volle che il Cav. Sbarra costituisse Prigione, e ne fu delegata la causa al Potestà, e a i sig. Giuseppe Altogradi M. Agostino Sinibaldi, e a Niccolo Narducci, e che Antonio Bernardi, la moglie, e la figlia fossero citati dandogli tempo a comparire fra otto giorni e difendersi dall'imputazioni dategli dal Cav. Sbarra e non comparendo dentro il tempo cadessero in pena di testa e confiscazione de' beni.

A dì 11 luglio 1588 furono citati per tutti i canti della Piazza e nessuno di loro comparì mai, ma s'erano di già per avanti avventati dalla Città, e andati a Firenze, dove raccolti da quel Granduca, datoli casa e possessioni, e anco provigione da potere vivere.

Il Cav. di poi a' 11 di s[ettem]bre 1588 fu mandato in bando dalla terra e confinato fuori d'Italia. *Cosi scrive Lorenzo Trenta nelle sue memorie appo lo signor Biagio Torre.*

On 10 July of the present year, 1588, in Piazza S. Michele, Sig. Girolamo d'Andrea Sbarra began to harangue Signora Leonora, the widow of Signor Vincenzo Belatta of Castelnuovo, asserting that, if he could have a safe conduct from the Signori Anziani, he would reveal the plan for a murder committed a few years before. He went to the Palace [of Justice] and asked this of the secretaries and the Most Illustrious Lords [the Anziani], but whether he will be allowed [the safe conduct], I do not know.

But, returning to the Piazza, wherever he paused, he continued his speeches, saying that Antonio Bernardi had promised to give him his daughter as a wife, but that he had chosen not to keep his word. He said that he had many letters written by her in which she spoke of him as her husband, and that he was indeed her husband, and in that role had held her at his disposal; and he repeated several times exactly the what and the how, and he said he had had a daughter with her.

The Most Excellent Council, having been apprised of this, called for Cavalier Sbarra to be taken into custody, and the case was delegated to the Podestà, and to the lawyers Giuseppe Altogradi, Agostino Sinibaldi and Niccolò Narducci. Antonio Bernardi, his wife, and his daughter were cited and given eight days to appear and defend themselves against Cavalier Sbarra's accusations. If they did not appear within this time, they would be liable to the punishment of death and confiscation of their goods.

On 11 July, they were summonsed on every side of the Piazza, but none of them ever appeared. They had already dashed off from the city and gone to Florence, where they were received by that Grand Duke, and given a house and possessions, and the means by which to live. The Cavaliere was then on 11 September exiled from Lucca, with orders to remain outside Italian territory.

Thus writes Lorenzo Trenta in his memoirs, which are in the possession of Signor Biagio Torre.

1.5.2 Girolamo Sbarra's sentence of banishment

Sbarra's sentence, dating to September 1588, two months after his public denunciation of Leonora Bernardi, is found in ASL Sentenze e bandi, 676, among the records of criminal sentences and banishments issued by the Lucchese Consiglio Generale. The record is signed by Tolomeo dal Portico, Chancellor of the Republic from 1588 to 1599.[249]

Nello Cl[arissi]mo Consiglio generale celebrato alli xii di sett[em]re 1588 fu proposto il fatto di Geronimo Sbarra carcerato a instanza dello Cl[arissi] mo Consiglio et fu decreto:

Che detto Gironimo Sbarra[,] attese le condittioni del salvacondutto concessoli, et attesa la temerità e mal proceder suo in havere publicato lettere et manifesti con pericolo di turbare la quiete publica[,] s'intenda et sia relegato a stare perpetuamente fuori de' confini di Italia, et non servando d[etta] relegatione s'intenda *ipso facto et ipso iure* senz'altra dechiaratione incorso in pena di rebellione, et militino contra di lui tutti i decreti et statuti nostri che parlano contra i ribelli, et nella osservanza di d[etta] relegatione debba d[etto] Gironimo incaminarsi et andare retta via subito che sarà escarcerato, et per ciò si debba escarcerare ?pertanto il presente giorno.

The meeting of the Worshipful General Council that took place on 12 September 1588 considered the case of Geronimo Sbarra, held in prison on the orders of the Worshipful Council, and it was decreed: That the said Geronimo Sbarra, taking into account the safe conduct granted to him, and considering his temerity and ill-doing in publishing letters and declarations, at the risk of disturbing public order, be banished and remain permanently beyond the confines of Italy. Should he fail to observe this banishment, he will be understood ipso facto et ipso iure *(by that act and by law), without need for further decree, to have incurred the penalty for rebellion, so that all our laws and statutes relating to rebels will apply in his case. In obedience to this sentence of banishment, the said Geronimo must set off and leave directly as soon as he is released from prison, and he should hence be released this same day.*

1.5.3 Girolamo Sbarra's open letter

The document is found in a miscellany in the Archivio di Stato in Florence containing material relating to issues of honour referred to successive Medici rulers of Florence for mediation or adjudication (Miscellanea Medicea 129, 'Scritture di duelli e paci dal 1543 al 1613').[250] *The opening words of the text state that it was 'published' by Girolamo Sbarra on 6 July 1588 (meaning, presumably, circulated in manuscript copies). The location of the surviving document suggests that Antonio Bernardi or, less probably, Sbarra himself referred the dispute to Ferdinando I de' Medici in the hope of a resolution.*

Misc. Med. 129, cc. 296r–297v

[c. 296r] La presente scrittura fu publicata in Lucca dal Cav.re Sbarra il giorno delli 6 di lug[lio] 1588 nel q[u]al tempo le lettere che sono nominate in essa originali si mostrorono a chi hebbe desiderio di vederle, et per fino alli XI del d[etto] mese, che esso Cavaliere si constituì prigione, et che furono retirate dal principe tali lettere[,] lui passeggiò sempre per la città et comparse alla piazza secondo il suo solito con due soli ?ser[vitori], né da alcuna persona fu mai parlato alla presenza sua, contro la detta scrittura et lettere publicate come si può giustificare per infiniti testimonij.

[296r] The present document was published in Lucca by Cavalier Sbarra on 6 July 1588. At the said time, the original letters that are mentioned in the document were shown to whoever desired to see them. Until the 11th of the said month, when the Cavaliere was imprisoned and the Prince had the letters confiscated,[251] *the Cavaliere constantly strolled around the city and appeared in the piazza in his customary way, accompanied only by two servants, and no one spoke out in his presence against the said document or the letters he had published, as infinite witnesses can attest.*

Geronimo Sbarra a chi legge

Geronimo Sbarra to the reader

Poiché Antonio Bernardi mi va lacerando in cospetto del mondo per homo insolente et temerario imputandomi che per forza pretendo per moglie M.a Lionora vedova relitta del Cav[aliere] Belatta sua figl[iola] sono astretto da questo modo di procedere contro mia voglia far palese quello che ragionevolmente doveva occultarsi, affine che venuto in ?luc[e] la verità si conosca da tutti chi è questa donna, che piena di superbia, hoggi mi vilipende tanto, la quale non si sdegnò di adoperare altre volte tutto il suo ingegno per alettarmi et ingannarmi, in maniera che, spinto da ardentissimo amore perso il lume delle ragioni [sic] per contentarla et aiutarla in esso travaglio mi sono rovinato a fatto, et abandonato la servitù di tanti anni, che tenevo con la ser[enissi]ma Re[pubbli]ca di Venetia, et a sua persuasione uscito delle Religione di Malta, nella quale da me era stato preso già ventidue anni sono la croce di Cavaliere. Reputando che gentildonna nobile di età di ventinove anni stimata virtuosa dovesse essere veridica et fedele et mi rendo sicuro, che sì come [c. 296v] confesso meritare grande biasimo, essendomi tant'oltre lassato trasportare l'amoroso affetto sarò anco conpassionato da quelli che vederano con quanto sotile artifitio mi fu posto questo veleno, et credo che pochi sarano coloro liquali non fussero stati allettati et ingannati dal canto di così falsa serena. Fra questa donna et me sono passate infinite lettere, che sì bene ne è in essere ogni minima parte, tutta via per gratia del sig[n]or ne restano tante che bastaranno per mia giustificatione, la copia delle quali cavata fedelmente si vede dopo questa più ordinatamente che sia possibile e se bene non ci sono li giorni del mese, et dell'anno, da molti particulari si cava il tempo in circa che furono scritte e si comprende che pure questa gran donna generò et parturì un figliolo di me che sono (chi la sente hora) la feccia di tutti li homini, poiché tanto me disprezza, et abhorrisce, vederassi poi chiaramente che non solo me desidera per Marito, ma come tali tratta et scrive con me et tale sempre mi nomina sottoscrivendosi Moglie et Lenora [sic] Sbarra sollecittandomi con tanto affetto e con tanta vehementia a procurare la mia Dispensa per publicare il matrimonio, che laserò a ogni uno giudicare se in persona di qualità tale et che parlava et scriveva nel modo che si vede dovevo o potevo temere che cadesse in eterno mutatione ne io mai gliene detti minima cagione né mi alterai o dolsi se non quando mezzo di tanto ardore viddi che indotta da Avaritia acconsentì di lasciarmi per darsi a persona che havesse della Robba, né io potendo tollerare un mancamento che così infame vedevo farmi, volendo fare noto al ?P[adr]e per mezo di dui suoi parenti la fede havuta da costei et ogn'altra cosa passata tra di noi da Madonna Lucretia Bernardi sua M[adr]e fui con molti prieghi astretto alla presenza di persona che per ?hora sì tace a procurare la dispensa promettendomi che la figliola saria mia moglie et giurandossi [c. 297r] esser vero, che per il passato haveva sempre dissuaso Leonora da maritarsi meco ma che ?hora me assicurava essersi mutata di opinione, però che senza discoprire a [sic] loro a Antonio per al hora io cercassi liberarmi, come ho dopoi fatto. Andando a Roma in persona da dove mentre vi dimorai, ?chiedè molte volte per fino all'ultimo che io ritornai a Lucca ?part[icola]re ragguaglio nello stato che si trovava il negotio della mia libertà, con mie lettere alla medesima Madonna Leonora, in essi sempre chiamandola Moglie et sottoscrivendosi marito, et sempre furono recevute et accettate da lei per mano dell'istessa persona, che si trovò presente al ragionamento et promessa fattami da madonna Lucretia, la quale persona che li sia parente ancora, quando sarà astretta con forte giuramento a dare conto del vero non doverà volere dannare l'anima sua per fomentare uno assassinamento come è questo, che me vien fatto, et hoggi chiaro conosco dal principio al fine essere stato tradito da tutti tre loro perché quanto a Antonio Bernardi poco avanti la partita mia per Roma scrisse una lettera all'illustrissimo signor Cardinale Castruccio pregandolo a favorirmi nel negozio della dispensa et se bene per l'accidente narrato delle preghiere che prima me haveva fatte la moglie di tacerli, il vero pare si dovesse credere che non havesse integra notitia di questi andamenti. Dal modo suo di procedere noto a tutta la città et dallo haversi gettato doppo li spalli l'honore ?disprechando il remedio che per ocultare questi inconvenienti et vituperij poteva prendere allo stato suo ha dato ?certo testimonio ch'ogni cosa sia stata ordita con suo volere et di comune consenso et si comprende che Leonora al presente partito, che le venne avanti di persona facultosa[,] avara come superba diede segno qual fusse la sua vera voluntà[,] se ben sciocco et ch'io non seppi in quel punto conoscere il mio errore et ho di poi tocco con mano che fu falsissimo, che il signor Martino Buonvisi havesse intention di pigliarla lui per Moglie, anzi perché ?ricercatone si ritiro da più corteggiarla come con speranza di goderla come amante da prima faceva [.] Lei di ciò sdegnata si mostrava a me nelle sue lettere di disprezzarlo et di non haverlo havuto per marito et io che li credevo adattavo [c. 297v] all'intelletto quelle cose che nutrivano il veleno quale mi ha ridotto in questo termine. Li originali adunque delle lettere che si leggeranno sono di proprio pugno della signora Lionora Bernardi, il cui carattere come di persona celebre [è] conosciuto da molti, et sono depositati in Lucca in mano del signore Lorenzo del signore Giovanni Buonvisi acciò che si possino vedere [cancelled: acciò che si possino] da chi lo desidera per testimonio vero et esemplare al mondo del premio che da questa ingrata ho havuto per ricompensa di quanto huomo puoi mai fare per amata Donna. Il che sia specchio alli altri poiché a me ne resta il solo pentimento. Di più che alla promessa, che mi fece madonna Lucretia Bernardi, come si è detto lei medesima cola figliola confermorno al signor Settimio Bernardi che si contentavono ottenendo la mia libertà che il matrimonio havesse effetto et per confermatione di ciò si mette inmediate dopo le lettere di lei la copia di una poliza scrittami il signore Settimio suddetto pochi giorni dopo che fu entrato in Palazzo come si vede dal tenore di essa che fu di luglio 1587 et io partì per Roma alli X del detto mese di luglio del detto anno per la quale dice, ch'aricorderia alle donne la perseveranza poiché si conosce per tal poliza che io havevo qualche timore di essere ingannato come è seguito. Si avverte li signori lettori che sì come qualche lettere sono rimaste in essere miracolosamente perché non doveva mai cadere in pensiero di doversi venire a questo così mancandocene infiniti non possono ?servare continuato filo, ma basta che si giustifica largamente quanto costei bramava essermi Moglie sì come in fede quanto a Dio et quanto a me mentì, come ho fatto mi dichiaravo libero tale la tenevo atteso con tal fede dal canto suo era senza conditione o minimo dubio che per qualsivoglia accidente potessi mutarsi, sicché trovandosi libera et persona del suo volere facciasi giudizio se merita scusa nissuna et se al mondo si può trovare donna più falsa et disleale et dallo scelerato procedere che ha fatto con il cavaliere Belatta primo marito et meco di più perfida et iniqua natura di costei [.] Si fa anche noto qualmente visto l'ostinatione del non volere effettuare il promesso matrimonio ho fatto ?offrirsi a tutti loro per mezzo del signor Lorenzo del signor Giovanni Buonvisi, che monachandosi Leonora io porrei silentio a tutto et mi ?quieterai se bene tacendo non giustificavo il mondo et anche questo partito è stato ributtato da loro onde spero che sarà conosciuto da tutti che non per malignità et iniqua natura mia sono venuto a questa publicatione ma per pura difesa, pregando ogni honorato gentilhuomo a spogliarsi di passione et considerare se io merito compassione et quanta sia la sfacciata arroganza et superbia di Antonio Bernardi della moglie et della figliola.

Since Antonio Bernardi is tearing into me in the presence of the whole world, accusing me of being an insolent and foolhardy man who is using force to press my claim to marry his daughter Madonna Leonora, widow of Cavalier Belatta, I have no choice, given his mode of proceeding, other than reluctantly to make public what should have remained hidden. The truth must be brought out into the light, so that all will know who this lady is: she who now, filled with pride, despises me so, yet who did not disdain in past times to use all the force of her intellect to seduce and deceive me, until, driven by the most ardent love, and having lost the light of reason, in order to please and abet her, I have ruined myself entirely. I have abandoned my years' long service to the Most Serene Republic of Venice, and I have left, at her persuasion, the Religion of Malta, within which I took up the cross of a knight twenty-two years ago. Since I judged that a noble gentlewoman, of the mature age of twenty-nine and of virtuous repute, would be honest and faithful, I am quite sure that [296v] – although I freely admit I deserve great blame, having allowed myself to be so carried away by amorous feeling – I will also win compassion from those who will see with what subtle artifice I was fed this poison. I believe there are few men who would not have been seduced and deceived by so false a siren.

This lady and I have exchanged infinite letters, of which only a very few survive. However, by God's grace, there are enough remaining to serve as my justification. Following this document, you will see copies of these letters, faithfully copied and ordered as accurately as possible. Even if there is no indication of the days of the month, or the years when they were written, many details allow you to reconstruct approximately the time when they were written. You will see from the letters that this great lady even conceived and bore a child of mine – I, who, to judge from her words now, am the dregs of humanity, so greatly does she despise and loathe me. You will also see clearly that not only does she desire me as her husband, but she treats me and writes to me as such and she always names me as such, signing her letters 'wife' or 'Lenora [sic] Sbarra'. And she urges me with great emotion and vehemence to obtain my dispensation, so we could make the marriage public.[252]

I will leave everyone to judge whether, in a person of such quality, who spoke and wrote to me in such a manner, I should or could have feared that her feelings would ever undergo a change. Certainly, I never gave her the least cause for it. I never changed towards her or complained of her, except when, in the midst of such ardour, I saw that, induced by avarice, she showed herself prepared to leave me in order to give herself to a man who possessed wealth. Unable to tolerate such an infamous betrayal, I resolved to inform her father, through two relatives of hers, just how she had broken faith with me and everything that had happened between us. But Madonna Lucretia Bernardi, her mother, convinced me with her pleas to seek a dispensation, in the presence of a person whose name I will not reveal for the moment, promising me that her daughter would be my wife. She swore to me [297r] that, though it was true that she had always dissuaded Leonora from marrying me, she had now changed her mind [and urged me] to secure my freedom and not to tell Antonio.

I did as she said. I went to Rome in person, and while I was there, right down to when I finally returned to Lucca, she constantly asked that I send detailed reports on how things stood with my negotiations for my freedom, enclosing letters to the said Madonna Leonora. In these letters, I always called her 'wife' and signed myself as her husband, and they were always received and accepted by her, [and delivered] by the hand of the same person who was present at my conversation with Madonna Lucretia, when she made me that promise. That person, who is also a relative of hers, if they are compelled to tell the truth by a strong oath,[253] will surely not want to commit their soul to damnation in order to abet a murder like this which I am having to suffer.

It is clear to me now that the whole thing was planned from the start by the three of them. Where Antonio Bernardi is concerned, he wrote a letter just before my departure to Rome to the Most Illustrious Lord Cardinal Castrucci,[254] requesting that he favour me in the business of the dispensation. So, despite what I have told you about his wife's pleas that I keep the story from him, it seems that the truth must be that he had full knowledge of all that was happening. By his mode of proceeding, which is known to the whole city, and having thrown away his honour by scorning the remedy that he could have taken to hide these improprieties and shameful acts, he gave clear evidence that everything was planned with his consent and of common accord. It is clear that Leonora, as avaricious as she is proud, when the present match was offered to her by a wealthy person gave a sign of what her true desire was, although I foolishly at that point still did not recognize my error. I have since been able to verify that it was entirely false that Signor Martino Buonvisi had the intention of taking her as his wife.[255] When he was asked about it, he withdrew from courting her, as he had been doing, wishing to make her his mistress. Angered by this, she initially feigned to despise him in her letters and [claimed that] she had not considered him as a husband, and I, who believed her, [297v] persuaded myself of those things that fed the poison which has reduced me to this state.

The originals of the letters that you will read after this are written in the handwriting of the Signora Lionora Bernardi, which writing is well know to many, since she is a famous person. They have been deposited in Lucca in the hands of Signor Lorenzo, the son of Signor Giovanni Buonvisi,[256] so that they may be viewed by anyone who wishes as a true and exemplary witness to the world of the recompense I received from this ingrate in return for all that a man can do for a beloved woman. May this serve as a mirror for others, as I have nothing left but repentance. As for the promise that Madonna Lucretia Bernardi made to me, as described above, she herself together with her daughter confirmed to Signor Settimio Bernardi that,[257] if I could obtain my liberty, they were happy for the marriage to go ahead. As confirmation of this, you can see immediately after her letters a copy of a pledge written for me by Signor Settimio Bernardi a few days before he entered the government, as you can see by the tenor of the document. That was in July 1587, and I left for Rome on the 10th of that month of July in the said year. The pledge stated that he would remind the two women to keep their word. You can tell from this pledge that I had some fears of being deceived, as turned out to be the case.

I would remind my gentle readers that, if a few letters have survived, it is by a miracle, because it never occurred to me that things would ever end in this way. Since infinite others are lost, the narrative does not maintain a continuous thread, but it should be enough that it proves how much this lady longed to be my wife, and also how much, in faith, she lied both to God and to me. Just as I declared myself to be free, so too I assumed that she was. I had not the least suspicion that she would change her mind. She was free and subject to her own will, so judge for yourself whether there is any excuse for her behaviour and whether any falser and more disloyal woman can be found on earth. To judge from her evil behaviour towards Cavalier Belatti and myself, there can be no more perfidious and iniquitous nature on earth than hers. It should also be noted that, given her obstinate refusal to agree to the promised marriage, I made an offer to her and her parents by means of Signor Lorenzo di Giovanni Buonvisi to the effect that, if she agreed to become a nun, I would preserve my silence and be satisfied, even if this meant I could not justify myself to the world. This too they refused. So, I hope it will be recognized by all that it is not my malignant and iniquitous nature that prompts me to publish my story in this way; rather, I do it entirely out of self-defence. I pray that every honourable gentleman will set aside all passion and consider whether I deserve his pity and how great is the shameless arrogance and pride of Antonio Bernardi, his wife and their daughter.

Notes

1 Grell, *Brethren*, 22.
2 On the Lucchese political system, see BNo, 19–31; BTr, 19–25. On the economy, see BNo, 64–82, 280–90.
3 Grell, *Brethren*, 22; BTr, 387–8; BNo, 25–30.
4 On the revolt of the Straccioni and its aftermath, see BNo, 117–46; Sabbatini, *La sollevazione*.
5 See Giuli, 'Dietro la quiete', 147–9; Hewlett, 'Fortune's Fool'; BNo, 147–9; Hewlett, 'Republic in Jeopardy'.
6 On the Reform movement in Lucca, see ABCi; also Caponetto, *Aonio Paleario*, 80–5; Grell, *Brethren*, 22–37; BTr, 273–80.
7 BTr, 278; BNo, 147–234.
8 See Hewlett, 'Fortune's Fool'; BTr, 275–6.
9 BNo, 231–2.
10 On the history of this exiled community, see Grell, *Brethren*. Two of the most prominent Lucchese families among the exiles were the Burlamacchi and Calandrini, both related to Leonora Bernardi's mother, Lucrezia Trenta (see Section 1.2.1).
11 On the embers of religious dissidence in Counter-Reformation Lucca, see Adorni Braccesi, 'Il dissenso'; Ragagli, 'La Repubblica'.

12 Adorni Braccesi and Ragagli, 'Guidiccioni'.
13 Mazzei, 'La Repubblica', esp. 299–301, 305–8; also B*No*, 11–19; Sabbatini, *Le mura*, 121–34.
14 Sabbatini, *Le mura*, 134.
15 'I Lucchesi . . . stanno appresso il granduca come la quaglia appresso lo sparviero'. Gussoni, 'Relazione', 390. The analogy seems to have become a commonplace; see Giuli, 'Dietro la quiete', 163.
16 See Bertoni, 'Antelminelli'; Miani, 'Antelminelli'; Giuli, 'Dietro la quiete', 164–5; Tommasi and Minutoli, *Sommario*, 472–4.
17 Tommasi and Minutoli, *Sommario*, 467–9 on the 1583 Garfagnana conflict, and 485–91 on the events of 1602–3. See also Mazzei, *La società*, 1–2; Giuli, 'Al servizio', 138–40. Verse seemingly relating to this troubled period of Lucchese history is found in the manuscript containing Bernardi's pastoral play (see Section 2.2).
18 See B*No*, 266–70.
19 On these gatherings, see Bertacchi, *Storia*, 5; L*St*, 50–1.
20 Bertacchi, *Storia*, 3–8; L*St*, 52–3. On Italian Academies generally, see Everson et al. (eds), *The Italian Academies*.
21 Cox, 'Il Malpiglio'.
22 Pellegrini, *Spettacoli*, viii.
23 Bertacchi, *Storia*, 14–5.
24 On music in Lucca, see Nerici, *Storia della musica*; Biagi-Ravenni, 'I Dorati'.
25 Biagi-Ravenni, 'I Dorati', 70–1.
26 C*Pr*, 1–19.
27 Eisenbichler, *The Sword and the Pen*; McClure, *Parlour Games*.
28 C*Wo*, 129 and 322 n. 37.
29 B*No*, 38. On the position of women in Lucca, see also B*Tr*, 221–57, *passim*; Vellutini, *Donne e società*; Sabbatini, 'Famiglie e potere', 239–46.
30 Tozzi, 'I codici miniati'; Vandi, 'Sister Eufrasia Burlamacchi'.
31 Coli, *La cronaca*, 440–1.
32 Cox, 'The Female Voice', 58; Cox, 'Note', 80.
33 C*W*, 72–4; Cox, 'The Female Voice', 62–4.
34 AB*Ci*, 269–70.
35 AB*Ci*, 269–70. See also AB*Ci*, 57 for gatherings hosted by the Erasmian humanist Gherardo Sergiusti (1492–1542), also attended by Gigli, to which women were sometimes admitted. Genealogical information in this section is drawn from BSL Baroni, 'Notizie', mss 1105 (Bernardi), 1113 (Gigli) and 1136 (Trenta).
36 AB*Ci*, 66–7.
37 For lists of distinguished visitors to the Lucchese baths in the Cinquecento, see Mazzei, 'Il viaggio', 662–6, 674–89.
38 DM*Gr*, 191 n. 93; Borsellino, 'Bargagli'.
39 For Colonna's stay in Lucca and its environs, see AB*Ci*, 94–5.
40 Piéjus, 'Musical Settings', 332–6.
41 CL*y*, 23–6. On Matraini, see also Rabitti, 'Matraini'; Marcheschi, *Chiara Matraini*. For editions of her works, see Matraini, *Lettere e rime*; *Rime e lettere*; *Selected Poetry and Prose*; M*Op*.
42 C*Wo*, 105–6.
43 Marcheschi, *Chiara Matraini*, 7–11.
44 On Bendinelli, who lived in Piacenza during her married life, see C*Wo*, 139, 141; C*Pr*, 255; Coller, *Women, Rhetoric*, 234–5. On Guidiccioni, see Megale, 'Guidiccioni'; Solerti, 'Laura Guidiccioni'; Magini, 'Cronache'; Kirkendale, *Emilio de' Cavalieri*, 186–212.
45 On Bernardini, see Section 1.2.6 below. On Cenami, dedicatee of the 1568 Lyons edition of Lodovico Paterno's *Le nuove fiamme*, where she is praised for her literary skills in vernacular prose and verse, see L*St*, 172; Stella, 'La parola d'autrice', 46–7. On Tegrimi, see Coli, *La cronaca*, 483–6.
46 On Battiferri, see Kirkham, *Laura Battiferra*; on Salvetti, Wainwright, 'The Fair Warrior'.
47 See Catelli, 'Molza'; Cox, 'The Female Voice', 73–4; Stras, 'Recording Tarquinia'.
48 L*St*, 168.
49 For Antonio's date of birth (3 June 1535), see Baroni, 'Notizie', ms. 1105, 36r. For the dates of his and Lucrezia's deaths, see Section 1.2.7.

50 B*Tr*, 387–8; also AB*Ci*, 9. On the Bernardi and Trenta families, see Mansi, *I patrizi*, 73–80; 463–68.

51 B*Tr*, 392–3. See Fig. 2, which draws on information in Baroni, 'Notizie', ms. 1105 (Bernardi), 51.

52 See Fig. 3, drawing materials from Baroni, 'Notizie', ms. 1136 (Trenta). The Burlamacchi connection is intriguing, not least because it connects Lucrezia with the distinguished convent artist Eufrasia Burlamacchi, on whom see Section 1.1.3. Eufrasia was Francesco Burlamacchi's second cousin.

53 See Grell, *Brethren*, 35.

54 Saltini, 'L'educazione', 158; see also Renieri, *Il vero soggetto*, dedicatory letter. I have estimated Lucrezia's age from a letter by the Lucchese *letterato* Domenico Chiariti which describes her as 'not yet sixty' at the time of her death in April 1602, suggesting that she was born at the earliest in 1542. For the context, see Section 1.2.6.

55 Saltini, 'L'educazione', 158. On Grifoni's relations with the Medici and within Lucca, see Giuli, 'Dietro la quiete', 163; Adorni Braccesi, 'Giuliano da Dezza', 110.

56 For Claudio's date of birth (1545), see Pidatella, 'Antonio Renieri', 450, n. 16.

57 Renieri, *Il vero soggetto*, dedicatory letter of 1 September 1566, unnumbered. For discussion of the dialogue, see Pidatella, 'Antonio Renieri', 459–62; also, for brief mention, Riccò, *Giuoco e teatro*, 15–16.

58 See Sacré, 'Quaestiunculae', 215–223.

59 See Nuttall, 'Filippino Lippi's Lucchese Patrons', 103 and n. 78, which notes that the palace was demolished to make way for the piazza before the church, leaving only a tower, the Torre della Veglia.

60 Renieri, *Il vero soggetto*, dedicatory letter; Pidatella, 'Antonio Renieri', 450; Machiavelli, *Tizia*, 21–22.

61 'ella riesce con tanto garbo, e con tanta gratia in ogni sorte d'operar virtuoso, che merita esser amata, e grandemente lodata'. Boccaccio, *La Theseide*, 144v.

62 'terrebbesi felice se quattro de' suoi versi fossero da Messer Jacopo Corfini musicati, e felicissimo poi se voi, Madonna Eleonora, coll'angelica vostra e soavissima voce gli cantaste gorgheggiando sulla spinetta'. Magini, 'Cronache', 43–4.

63 'la nobilissima Giovane M[adonna] LEONORA figliuola dello spet[tabile] Antonio Bernardi, figlioccia del Gran Duca'. Boccaccio, *La Theseide*, 144v.

64 Moreali, 'Memorie', 354v. I have not been able to locate an extant copy of Argiliani's text and rely on Moreali's summary.

65 Testament of Vincenzo Belatti, 17 October 1580, in ASM, Archivio Estense, Cancelleria, Carteggi e documenti di particolari, 107.

66 Riminaldi, *Consiliorum*, 7, 82–5 (*Consilium* DCCLV). Riminaldi makes it clear that he is drawing on a previous, fuller opinion by another lawyer, Giovanni della Torre. On Riminaldi, see D'Urso, '"Ed egli puote"'.

67 For discussion of similar instances, though involving notional loans, rather than gifts, see Meek, 'Il matrimonio', 366. Riminaldi refers to Bernardi's grandmother only as 'Camilla'. Her full name is found in Baroni, 'Notizie', ms. 1105 (Bernardi).

68 Sabbatini, 'Paolino Vellutelli', 594.

69 Coli, *La cronaca*, 149–50.

70 On this financial crisis, see de' Ricci, *Cronaca*, 127–8; Miani, 'Arnolfini'; Minutoli, *Memorie*, 74. De' Ricci names members of the Arnolfini, Pentesi, Guinigi and Bernardini families as protagonists of the crash, but Minutoli couples the Bernardi with the Bernardini as owners of one of the firms involved. Miani notes that many smaller investors in these enterprises were severely affected by the collapse.

71 'de'più facoltosi uomini della Garfagnana'. Forciroli, *Vite*, 223.

72 'troppo gravato di famiglia'. Masetti Zannini, *Marfisa d'Este*, 108–9.

73 Picinelli, *Le collezioni Gonzaga*, 3:74. On Giulio Cesare Gonzaga's presence at the Bagni di Lucca in early January 1585, see Mazzei, 'Il viaggio', 675 n. 91.

74 'un gentil uomo della repubblica di Lucca, molto onorevolmente accompagnato'. Fortuna, *Le nozze*, 16.

75 'è stata consciuta da V[ostra] A[ltezza] che cantava e sonava et era gentilissima'. Camillo Albizzi, letter to Francesco de' Medici of 30 December 1585, in ASF, Archivio Mediceo del Principato, filza 2902. The context of this important letter is discussed in Section 1.2.3.

76 Ceruti, *Appunti*, 79; Baroni, 'Notizie', ms. 1113 (Gigli).

77 Guarini, 'Diario', 1.161. See also Guerzoni, *Le corti estensi*, 259, which records a 'Magnifico Signor Vincenzo Bellan [*sic*]' among Alfonso's retinue of 'signori e gentilhuomini' in 1585.

78 'il valor dell'età nostra'. Nigrisoli, *Delle canzonette*, 1. Stras, *Women and Music*, 258, erroneously dates the marriage of Vincenzo and Leonora to Carnival 1585 in Ferrara.

79 Pocaterra, *Due dialoghi*, 16. See the discussion in Section 2.1.2.

80 'non solo bellissima et leggiadrissima, ma letterata insieme, et nella poetica volgare più che mezzanamente dotta, come si scorge dalle sue canzoni che vanno attorno'. Forciroli, *Vite*, 223.

81 On the *concerto delle dame*, discussed further in Section 2.1, see Durante and Martellotti, *Cronistoria*; Stras, *Women and Music*, 241–88.

82 Treadwell, '"Simil combattimento"'.

83 Tasso, *Delle rime et prose . . . parte quarta*, 126.

84 'Dice d'imaginarsi la bellezza d'una Gentildonna non veduta, non udita, non conosciuta per nome, quantunque fosse famosa, per l'Eccellenza de la Musica, e per altre belle parti del corpo, e de l'animo.' Tasso, *Delle rime*, 40.

85 'perche al Poeta era manifesta la patria, benche fusse occulto il nome'. Tasso, *Delle rime*, 41.

86 See Solerti, 'Laura Guidiccioni', 803–4, followed by Megale, 'Guidiccioni'; Guccini, 'Intorno alla prima'; Magini, 'Cronache', 41–44; Kirkendale, *Emilio de' Cavalieri*, 188.

87 On Tasso's acquaintance with Gonzaga, see McClure, 'Women', 777–81.

88 DM*Gr*, 129–30.

89 See Section 2.2.1.

90 Grillo, *Rime*, Tavola, unnumbered, under *incipit*, 'Chi può vincer Vincenzo, o pur chi perde[?]'. For discussion of the sonnet glossed, addressed to Monsignor Guido Tegrimi, see Section 1.2.4. The annotations to this volume are by Giulio Guastavini.

91 Guarini, 'Diario', 1: 160–1, 163; Massa, *Memorie*, 54 and 131. Massa reports Belatti's name as 'Vintenio Blata'.

92 'Non hanno volute divulgare a requisit[ion]e di chi fusse fatto, ma tuttavia s'è detto esca dalla moglie ò parenti di lei, che sono certi gentilhuomini de' Bernardi.' Albizzi, letter to Francesco de' Medici of 30 December 1585, in ASF, Archivio Mediceo del Principato, filza 2902.

93 Guarini, 'Diario', 1: 163; Massa, *Memorie*, 131.

94 For Belatti's own testimony, see his letter to Duke Alfonso II d'Este of 3 August 1585, in ASM, Archivio Estense, Cancelleria, Carteggi e documenti di particolari, 107, where he speaks of an 'assassinamento concertato contra di me' ('murder attempt orchestrated against me').

95 ASL, Inv. 26 ('Carte di Tommaso Trenta'), 1: 28.

96 The Sbarra family tree is found in Baroni, 'Notizie', ms. 1132. On Andrea Sbarra, see Mazzei, 'A proposito di modelli', 45–6.

97 Bonazzi, *Elenco*, 296; Ruscelli, *Imprese illustri*, 42–3.

98 BMV MS It. X. 40 (= 6415), 77r–81v. The letter is dated 29 June 1572, and it was sent from Zara in Venetian Dalmatia (now Zadar, in Croatia).

99 Antonio da Callegarini, document of 30 July 1573, in ASL Principale, Diplomatico, Sbarra 1551–1600. In the document, Sbarra appoints his brother, Ferdinando, then in Lucca, to recover a debt from Pulcinelli.

100 'mia moglie e io riceviamo tutti questi honori che siano possibili a credere'; 'incontrati da tutta la nobiltà della città'. Masetti Zannini, *Marfisa d'Este*, 142 n. 6 (see also 137); de' Ricci, *Cronaca*, 495. De' Ricci dates the couple's arrival in Pratolino to 19 August.

101 Note that, as detailed in the notes to II.5 of *Clorilli*, the name Licasta may derive from a figure in Bernardo Tasso's *Amadigi* (1560), like Leonora a young widow whose husband dies a violent death. Other *à clef* characters in II.5 include Licasta's companion 'wise Ilia', said to have accompanied her at the Mugnone event and the Massa visit, and a male feminist, Ormindo, on whom see Section 1.2.5.

102 The text of the relevant passage of the chronicle is found in the Appendix to this section.

103 ASL, Sentenze e bandi, 676 (12 September 1588); also Baroni 'Notizie', ms. 1132 (Sbarra), p. 96 (49v). See Sections 1.5.1–1.5.2. The Bernardi family's sentence is found in ASL, Sentenze e bandi, 480 (20 July 1588)).

104 'temerità e mal proceder suo'. ASL, Sentenze e bandi, 676; see Section 1.5.2.

105 On forgeries of letters in early modern English judicial contexts, see Gordon, 'Material fictions', esp. 90–1 on cases involving courtship and marriage.
106 On Pasqualigo and the *Lettere amorose*, see Caiazza, 'Pasqualigo, Alvise'; Caiazza, 'Alvise Pasqualigo'. I am grateful to Ida Caiazza for alerting me to the similarities between Pasqualigo's *Lettere* and Sbarra's narrative of his affair with Bernardi.
107 Ruscelli, *Imprese illustri*, 43, states that Sbarra was appointed governor of Traù (Trogir) in 1572–3. Further documentation of his time in Dalmatia is offered by his 1572 letter to Sforza Pallavicino, discussed above in the text. Pasqualigo's dedications of his comedy, *Il Fedele*, and his pastoral drama, *Gl'intricati*, place him in the garrison of Zara in 1575 (Caiazza, 'Pasqualigo').
108 Ruscelli, *Imprese illustri*, 44.
109 Ruscelli, *Imprese illustri*, 42. The phrase is found in *Aen.* II.701.
110 Newcomb, *The Madrigal*, 1: 272 (document 67).
111 'una fanciulla che ha pur anco condotta Sua Altezza da Roma'. For discussion of Cortile's letter, see Newcomb, *The Madrigal*, 1: 90–2; Fenlon, 'Preparations', 213. Bovio's and Archilei's performance at the 1584 wedding is recorded in Fortuna, *Le nozze*, 13.
112 'la fig[li]a d'Antonio Bernardi che fu moglie del Bellati'. Stras, *Women and Music*, 258.
113 On Lucchesini's political activities as a Medici agent, see Bongi, *Storia*, 65–71; Ragagli, 'La Repubblica', 264–9. On Cavalieri's involvement, see Magini, 'Cronache', 56; Kirkendale, *Emilio de' Cavalieri*, 80.
114 See Appendix, notes to 1.5.3.
115 Paoli, 'Nell'Italia', 539–41; M*Op*, 487–90; Ragagli, 'La Repubblica', 236–41.
116 For works published in Lucca, see M*Op*, 489 n. 8, to which should be added Morganti, *Deiparae Virginis . . . encomium*; also Sergiusti, *De Virginis imagine . . . carmen* (published in Siena), Garzoni, *Historia* (published in Florence) and Casentini, *Il vero suggetto* (published in Florence and reprinted in Lucca).
117 Bendinelli, *L'ode*, A4r; M*Op*, 543–602, *passim*. On Bendinelli, see C*Wo*, 139, 141; C*Pr*, 255; Coller, *Women, Rhetoric*, 234–5.
118 For a reading of the canzone in the context of the Lucca miracle of 1588, see Cox, '"L'umil prego ascolta"'.
119 The passage in Valerius Maximus (8.1) is discussed in Mueller, *Roman Religion*, 51–2. On *invidia*, see Mueller, *Roman Religion*, 154–6. The reception of Tuccia in Italian Renaissance art and culture is discussed in Miziolek, '"Exempla"', 81–82; Eycken, 'Tuccia', 64–80.
120 DM*Gr*, 182 n. 78. On Tucci, see Rizzolino, '*Angelus Domini*', 183–213; Rizzolino, 'Nicolao Tucci'; Sabbatini, 'Tra amministrazione'; Sabbatini, 'Tucci'; also, among older literature, L*St*, 198–200; S*Fr*, 483–6.
121 Sabbatini, 'Tucci'.
122 See Grillo, *Parte prima*, 67r, for Grillo's sonnet to Tegrimi (inc. 'Chi può vincer Vincenzo, o pur chi perde[?]'), and 113r for Tegrimi's to him (inc. 'Nuntio sacro del Ciel, in cui si perde'). The edition presents Grillo's poem as the *proposta* and Tegrimi's as the *risposta*, but this may be an error, in that Grillo's poem has the air of a response. For the identification of the 'phoenix' of the sonnets with Bernardi, see Giulio Guastavini's *argomento* in the *Tavola* to the volume (unnumbered but alphabetically ordered by *incipit*).
123 'Canta dunque di questa, e si raggiri / qui la tua Musa, ch'ogni affetto molce, / e bea qualunque misero, e infelice'. Grillo, *Parte prima*, 113r.
124 See Fantappiè, 'Rinuccini'.
125 For the madrigal sequence, see Grillo, *Parte prima*, 23r–25r, and *Tavola*, unnumbered, under 'Al gran Duce, al gran Padre, al Figlio grande'. For the poems to Christine of Lorraine and to Ferdinando, see 86r–93r.
126 'viril constanza . . . . beneditioni d'anima veramente unita con Dio'. Gr*L*, 483. The letter is datable to 1610, from its mention of a catastrophic flood of S. Benedetto Mantovano, where Grillo was abbot, as having taken place 'last year' (Gr*L*, 482). For the date of the flood (November 1609), see DM*Gr*, 240.
127 'questa nobil donna, che non piegò mai quel generoso animo a persuasioni, nè a consenso d'openion popolare'. Gr*L*, 2.483.
128 Croce, *La gloria delle donne*, 13. The comparison that Bernardi's Ormindo makes between the female sex and a 'fiammeggiante / piropo' (flaming pyrope [a type of garnet]; II. 5, lines 226–7) may intentionally echo Croce's use of the same simile to describe women, burnished

by Marfisa's example (*La gloria delle donne*, dedicatory letter, A3r). Bernardi adorns the image with an etymological adjective, 'fiammeggiante' (Greek 'pyropos' means 'flame-like'). For discussion of Croce's text, see Collina, 'La gloria delle donne'.

129 Croce, *La gloria delle donne*, 30.

130 Croce, *La gloria delle donne*, 13 and 19. Guidiccioni is referred to by her married name as 'Laura Luc[c]hesina'.

131 'particolare e favorita racc[ommandatio]ne'. Aldobrandini to Alfonso d'Este, letter of 11 July 1592, in ASM, Archivio Estense, Cancelleria, Carteggi e documenti di particolari, 18 (Aldobrandini).

132 See Foa, 'Castrucci'. See also Sbarra's letter of 1588 in the Appendix (1.5.3), where Antonio Bernardi is said to have written to Castrucci requesting a favour in 1587.

133 ASM Archivio Estense, Cancelleria, Carteggi e documenti di particolari, 107 (Bernardi).

134 GrL, 1: 158. On Don Gervasio, see Solerti, *Vita di Torquato Tasso*, 2: 271.

135 'in procinto per Lucca'. GrL, 1: 874. The letter to Tucci was written from Subiaco, where Grillo was abbot from May 1599.

136 Stras, *Women and Music*, 289–320; Durante and Martellotti, 'Carlo Gesualdo', esp. 199–200. Alfonso's heir, Cesare d'Este, and his consort, Virginia de' Medici, had already left Ferrara for Modena in January 1598, accompanied by many members of the court. Bernardi's acquaintance Marfisa d'Este was absent from Ferrara, in Massa with her husband, for much of the period between 1594 and 1598.

137 Brady, 'Lavinia Fontana', esp. 26–31.

138 Croce, *La gloria delle donne*, 19–20.

139 ('dei primi di qua'). Pierpaolo Belatti, letter of 9 January 1598, in ASM, Archivio Estense, Cancelleria, Carteggi e documenti di particolari, 107.

140 The detail is supplied by an anonymous festival pamphlet (*Narratione*, unnumbered). See also, on Cardinal Aldobrandini's entry, Mitchell, *1598*, 22–5.

141 Vincenzo Belatti, testament of 17 October 1580, in ASM Archivio Estense, Cancelleria, Carteggi e documenti di particolari, 107. This same folder contains numerous letters relating to Pierpaolo's affairs during this period of guardianship.

142 Anonymous to Antonio Bernardi, letter dated 25 September 1598, in ASM Archivio Estense, Cancelleria, Carteggi e documenti di particolari, 107.

143 Bulgarini's correspondence with Chiariti (henceforth cited as 'BC') is mainly contained in BCIS, C. II. 25. See the brief discussion in Danesi, *Cento anni*, 15.

144 Tasso, *Opere*, 10: 231–2.

145 Goselini, *Lettere*, 46v–49r, 109v–110r, 133v–142v; Guasco, *Lettere*, 36–9; Borghesi, *La prima*, 16r–17r, 24r–25r, 38v–39r. On Chiariti's literary relationships, see Durante and Martellotti, 'Amorosa fenice', esp. 176, 208–9, 224–6, 265–7.

146 Baldini, *Lusus*, 45, 108; Camilli, *Imprese*, 2: 39–41.

147 BC, 193 (1 November 1597) for the stay in France; 261r–v (25 July 1601) for his university studies.

148 See the summary in Durante and Martellotti, 'Amorosa fenice', 241–3.

149 Bulgarini, *Annotazioni*, 11. The dedicatory letter to the work is dated 15 November 1608.

150 For Matraini, see Matraini, *Lettere e rime*, 463–4 and MOp, 630, 662. For Fonte, see Caporali, *Le piacevoli rime*, 4v–5r, and Durante and Martellotti, 'Amorosa fenice', 266–7.

151 *Scelta di rime* (described in Section 3.1.1 (Sc)), index. Verse by Bernardi and the Genoese poet Livia Spinola also appears in this collection. Ferrari's sonnet is reproduced in Durante and Martellotti, 'Amorosa fenice', 266.

152 Goselini, *Lettere*, 109v–110r (letter of 8 February 1580). The sonnet is found in Goselini, *Rime*, 222.

153 Bulgarini, *Annotazioni*, 59. See also on Doni Gorini, Feronio, *Il Chiariti*, 62–3; Campbell, 'Marie de Beaulieu', 870 and n. 94.

154 'Ritrovosi ora in questa città una nostra gentildonna, Leonora Bernardi Belatta, la qual è giovane, bella, e virtuosa à maraviglia. È un Sol di bellezza, una Minerva di sapere, et una Talia di grazia. Et avvenga, ch'ella sia onoratissima; se essemplarm[en]te non fosse da bene, io à V. S. non la nominerei.' BC, 230.

155 See GrL I: 638–39 for a letter from Grillo to Chiariti, thanking him for a letter he has sent him, enclosing verse in praise of Bernardi. The letter dates to 1599–1602.

156 Letter of 22 September 1599 (BC, 224). Bulgarini's very fulsome display letter, dated 24 October 1599, is found at 225.

157 ASL Consiglio generale, Riformagioni pubbliche 82 (25 August 1599); cfr. ASL, Sentenze e bandi, 480, where the formal quashing of the sentence is recorded.

158 'conveniva star con gl'occhi aperti in più luoghi, et haver mezzi più segreti'. Sabbatini, 'Tra amministrazione', parag. 37.

159 BC, 238r (letter of 6 January 1600). Sebastiano was the son of Marcantonio Gigli and of Leonora's paternal aunt, Elisabetta d'Alessandro Bernardi. He married an Agnese di Damiano Bernardini. See Baroni, 'Notizie', ms. 1113 (Gigli); Coli, La cronaca, 607 n. 467.

160 Bertacchi, Storia, 27; Pellegrini, Spettacoli, viii.

161 Coli, La cronaca, 607 n. 467. On the prominence of the Gigli within early modern Lucchese diplomacy, see Giuli, 'Al servizio', 131–3.

162 Pierpaolo Belatti to Cesare d'Este, letter of 8 December 1603, in ASM, Archivio Estense, Cancelleria, Carteggi e documenti di particolari, 107. The letter requests compensation for livestock stolen during the 1602–3 Garfagnana war (on which see Tommasi and Minutoli, Sommario, 485–91).

163 Leonora Bernardi to Virginia de' Medici, letter of 8 October 1602, in ASM, Archivio Estense, Cancelleria, Carteggi e documenti di particolari, 107.

164 Baroni, 'Notizie', ms. 1104, 138 (also mentioned in Tiraboschi, Biblioteca Modenese, 6: 27). Caterina's will, of 24 October 1626, leaves her estate to a Guidiccioni nephew, suggesting that the marriage was without issue.

165 See BC, 282v for the term ridotto and 242v for the term accademia.

166 On such gatherings, see Cox, 'Members, Muses', 157–9. For a discussion of an earlier, ill-fated attempt by Chiara Matraini to host what a contemporary chronicler called an accademia in Lucca in the 1540s, see Cox, 'Members, Muses', 141 and MOp, 799.

167 BC, 282v.

168 BC, 241 (letter of 9 February 1600).

169 Segni, Orazione; Bulgarini, 'Brevissima Giustificazione . . . intorno a quanto fù segnato contro di lui nell'Orazione recitata per la morte di M. Jacopo Mazzoni, nell'Accademia della Crusca da Sig. Pier Segni', in Annotazioni, 223–6. On the debates on Dante, which started in the 1570s, see Katinis, Sperone Speroni, 106–36.

170 Cox, 'Members, Muses', 141.

171 Bulgarini, Annotazioni, 59, 62; also 11. A letter from Chiariti to Bulgarini of 1 April 1598 (BC, 198) states that Capponi refused Gorini's challenge to a debate, claiming that he had left secular studies behind him.

172 BC, 320r–v (letter of 12 February 1603); Cittadini, Tre orationi.

173 BC, 252r–v (letter of 11 October 1600); 254r–v (letter of 7 February 1602).

174 Camilli, Imprese illustri, 3: 48–51. Camilli notes that Molza's motto is an adaptation of Virgil's phrase 'non deficit alter' (Aen. VI.143).

175 BC, 325r–326r (letter of 26 March 1603, reporting on a meeting held on 23 March).

176 The detail is found in a letter of the following week, 8 January 1603 (BC, 327r–v).

177 Carbonaro, 'L'altro Cesare', 8; Ragagli, 'La Repubblica', 271.

178 See BC, 292r–295v. The work to be discussed was Bulgarini, Riprove, another skirmish in the Dante debates.

179 Arnolfini is named as a recipient of the Riprove in a letter of 7 August 1602 (BC, 293r–v), Moriconi and Altogradi in a letter of 14 August 1602 (292r–v). Chiariti refers to Altogradi and Moriconi purely by their surnames. For their identification, see Danesi, Cento anni, 30.

180 LSt, 52; Biralli [Bargagli], Delle imprese, 10, 14.

181 Biralli, Delle imprese, 10; Gamurrini, Istoria, 437–8; LSt, 6: 145–7, 153.

182 See Martini, 'Aggiornamento', 149–50, which also notes the dedication to Moriconi of a Latin ode by Filippo Albertini, written to welcome a returning Lucchese ambassador to Spain, and published in 1592.

183 Giuli, 'Dietro la quiete', 164; Magini, 'Cronache', 56, 60–1.

184 Tommasi and Minutoli, Sommario, 486–7, 490.

185 'nobiliss[imi] spiriti . . . soprumane donne, e sig[no]re'; 'fa pieniss[i]ma fede di ciò, tra l'altre innumerabili, la molto Ill[ust[re Sig[nor]ra Chiara Matraini, oggi vivente, per eternamente vivere gloriosa'. BC, 225r.

186 For Tucci's account, see Sabatini, 'Tra amministrazione', paragraphs 28–32. On the Matraini family's involvement in the Straccioni revolt, and its consequences for Chiara, see Marcheschi, Chiara Matraini, 7–11.

187 'le Muse & gli Apolli istessi'. GrL, 1: 930. The letter was sent from Rome, where Grillo was

stationed from 1602–7. It seems to date to a time prior to Bernardi's religious retreat in late 1604.

188　*SFr*, 350–2, 485.

189　*GrL*, 1: 409. On Tegrimi, see *SFr*, 356–7.

190　'Non escludo il giudicio della Signora Leonora. Quello dico co 'l quale pulisce e fa sì belli i suoi parti.' *GrL*, 1: 386. For the date of the letter, see DM*Gr*, 191. On Grillo's ekphrastic religious verse, see Ferretti, 'L'ecfrasi mistica', with mention of the Titian poems at 117 n. 14.

191　'Alla Signora Leonora di nuovo mi offero, della cui magnanimità siamo horamai tanto sicuri, che non habbiamo à temere, che non la guardi da quei pericoli, ne' quali sogliono incorrere assai spesso le altre donne, & massime le singolari, come Vostra Signoria dice.' *GrL*, 1: 880–1.

192　'ella non si può alterare, se non in meglio; & quel, che le concede per premio, accettare per istimolo'.

193　'Queste nubi di lodi humane . . . non arrivano tanto alto, che possano turbare la serenità d'un'anima gentile, ch'unita al suo principio à pena le scorge di là suso, quasi ombre picciole, fosche, e caduche.'

194　See C*Pr*, 23–5, 27–8, 31.

195　Cox, '"Consenti, o pia"'.

196　'quei chiari doni, che riceve dal cielo . . . involti sotto nube di tanta modestia, che dove potria ella far della notte un chiaro giorno al suo nome, & à gli altrui, si stà tanto raccolta, & ristretta nel proprio rigore, che ce li fa tal hora desiderar troppo'. *GrL*, 1: 639. The letter, which dates from Grillo's time in Subiaco (1599–1602), replies to a letter of self-introduction from Chiariti, accompanied by poems in praise of Bernardi.

197　BC, 326r. Vecoli was a relative and protégé of Bernardi's friend Nicolao Tucci, to whom the precocious Bernardino had dedicated a volume of philosophical disputations in 1595. See L*St*, 1, 122–4; *SFr*, esp. 178–9; Bongi, *Lucrezia Buonvisi*, 103 n. 1; also Guidotti, 'Vecoli' on the family.

198　'senza levarsi da tavola'. BC, 327r (letter of 8 January 1603).

199　'stecchi, per li denti, maestrevolmente lavorati di legno di ginepro'. BC, 327r (letter of 8 January 1603.)

200　'stupendo convitto più risplendente del fatto l'anno passato'. BC, 391r (letter of 31 December 1603).

201　Baroni, 'Notizie', ms. 1105, 138; also *GrL*, 1: 397 for a letter from Grillo to Tucci of spring 1602 mentioning the news.

202　BC, 285r–v. See also 180–2 for three sonnets by Chiariti on Lucrezia's death and Leonora's grief.

203　Palma, *Liber primus*, 134–5; B*No*, 33. In the event, Antonio's cousin Bernardino di Stefano Bernardi (b. 1566), the grandson of Antonio's uncle, another Bernardino di Stefano, inherited. On Stefano d'Antonio Bernardi's will, see B*No*, 33. On the patrilinear character of Lucchese inheritance practices and the frequent use of *fideicommissi*, see Sabbatini, 'Famiglie e potere', 238, 240.

204　'venne a perdere il godimento di notabile ricchezza'. BC, 327r (8 January 1603). Chiariti also mentions the *fideicommissum* in a letter of 23 February 1600.

205　'un nostro gentiluomo, che onestamente l'ama, e con tacita ambizione, à tratto, à tratto la serve'. BC, 327r (letter of 8 January 1603). On Buonvisi, see Luzzati, 'Buonvisi, Bernardino'.

206　This choice was unusual, but not unknown in the period; see C*Pr*, 227–8.

207　'cotesti Nobilissimi Spiriti Accademici (poi che haveranno, in un certo modo, perduta la loro Diotima, che poteva anco servir à Dio, senza lassar affatto la tanto virtuosa conversazione)'. BC, 378v.

208　'mi parlò in questa sentenza: cioè, ch'ella trovandosi nel verno della sua età, e nelle tenebre del senso, esserle stato spediente per iscaldarsi, e per illuminarsi, ricorrere al Sole spirituale'. BC, 378r (letter of 2 February 1605).

209　*GrL*, 2: 288. 'Ma che belle cose dee far la Signora Leonora, hora ch'ella s'è eletta la miglior parte? O quanto la lodo, o quanto le invidio quelle divote lagrime, & quei focosi sospiri, & quelle tenerezze, piene di viril costanza. Che non hanno fatto le donne per la via dello spirito? Io non leggo letione, che mi muova più che quella delle sante donne, che doppo di loro hanno lasciata la via del seguirle.'

210　Franciotti, *Pratiche spirituali*, 3–5. I consulted the 1622 edition. The first edition came out with Ottaviano Guidoboni in Lucca in 1615. A rough *ante quem* date of the onset of Leonora's blindness is supplied by a letter from Grillo to Tucci of 1610 (Gr*L*, 482–83). Grillo speaks of it as of sudden onset ('la precipitata cecità').

211 See Del Gallo, 'Franciotti'; Carbonaro, 'L'altro Cesare'.

212 See Ragagli, 'La Repubblica', 193–204, on the 1570s and 1580s (the description of the Clerics Regular as a 'Trojan horse' is at 194); 274–6, on the 1590s; and 362, on the early seventeenth century.

213 Ragagli, 'La Repubblica', 202. Anna Mario, in Matraini, *Le opera in prosa*, 630 n. 2, identifies Domenico Chiariti as the son of a Niccolò, but this appears to be a misreading of her source, Adorni Braccesi, 'Giuliano da Dezza', 128 and 130 n. 152. Camilli, *Imprese*, 2: 40, identifies Domenico's father as Bartolomeo, a jurisconsult.

214 Ragagli, 'La Repubblica', 273–4.

215 Cox, 'Re-thinking', 19–21, 23–34.

216 L*St*, 50; C*Pr*, 157–63.

217 Gr*L*, 1: 922. A further mention of these two works in progress is found at Gr*L*, 2: 288.

218 See Rizzolino, '*Angelus Domini*', 215–70 (including an edition of the poem); also Rizzolino, 'Nicolao Tucci'.

219 Gr*L*, 1: 926.

220 'n'intesi in Lucca dalla voce della medesima Signore una particella'. Gr*L*, 1: 409.

221 'Piacimi che gli dia l'ultima mano, perche altri gli dia la prima palma in questo genere.'

222 S*Fr*, 353. Sforza speaks of Bernardi, 'almost blind and ailing' ('quasi cieca e infermaticcia'), attending *veglie* in the Fiorentini household after Tucci's death in March 1615. His source is an autobiographical work by Mario Fiorentini's son, the physician and historian Francesco Maria Fiorentini (1603–73).

223 Gr*L*, 2. 483. Grillo speaks of Preti's work as having 'just come out' ('venuto pur hora in luce'), so he may be referring to the second, Venice, edition of 1609. For Tucci's work on Tacitus, see Sabbatini, 'Tucci', parag. 24. Further on this *ridotto* in Lucca and its literary interests, see Rizzolino, 'Nicolao Tucci', 50–53.

224 'gran iattura che fà non pur Lucca . . . ma l'Italia, e l'età nostra, della quale ella era sì raro ornamento'. Gr*L*, 3: 10.

225 'i vari pregi del valore, e della virtù virile . . . donna non solamente più che donna, ma più che huomo ancora'.

226 'gode . . . quel cielo, che si seminò in terra con sì lunga preparatione a questo estremo, e periglioso passo'.

227 See Capucci, 'Coreglia'; Coller, *Women, Rhetoric*, 172–245; C*Wo*, 209–10, 215–6. On the tradition of Lucchese women's writing from Matraini to Coreglia, via Bernardi and Silvia Bendinelli, see C*Pr*, 2, 68; Coller, *Women, Rhetoric*, 234–5.

228 Coller, *Women, Rhetoric*, 175–6.

229 Coreglia identifies Antonio Bendinelli, the dedicatee of her *Rime*, as her uncle. Moreali, 'Memorie' states that Scipione Bendinelli owned Bernardi's manuscripts before they passed into the hands of the Lucchesini family.

230 Coller, *Women, Rhetoric*, 222.

231 See, for example, Marracci, *Bibliotheca*, 37–8.

232 Quadrio, *Della storia*, 4/1: 288; also 5/2: 401 for a mention of Bernardi's pastoral. For Bergalli, see Section 3.1.1 of this volume.

233 Vandelli, 'Vita', 15–6; Mazzuchelli, *Gli scrittori d'Italia*, 2, ii: 663. Vandelli's source is Francesco Forciroli; see above, Section 1.2.2.

234 Tiraboschi, *Biblioteca modenese*, 1:190.

235 Tiraboschi, *Biblioteca modenese*, 6/1: 26–7.

236 Marcheschi, *Chiara Matraini*, 67–8.

237 Trenta, 'Carte'.

238 'Clorillo, favola pastorale della Sig[no]ra Leonora Bernardi de' Belatti alla Sereniss. Gran Duchessa di Toscana'. Moreali, 'Memorie'.

239 S*Fr*, 353–5.

240 For mentions prior to 2008, see, for example, Bandini Buti, *Poetesse e scrittrici*, I: 75; Durante and Martellotti, *Cronistoria*, 48 and 113 n. 69; S*Pa*, 103; C*Wo*, 141, 147, 322 n. 76. Subsequently, see C*Ly*, 244–8, 279–80, 392; C*Pr*, 67–8, 92–118, 255–6; Coller, *Women, Rhetoric*, esp. 235.

241 C*Pr*; McHugh and Wainwright, eds. *Innovation*.

242 Sabbatini, 'Immagini'.

243 'l'educazione insufficiente . . . il destino volto alla "casalinghitudine", il sospetto con cui una donna-intellettuale è considerata'. MOp, 25.

244 On Tucci's resistance to publishing his work, see GrL, 3: 8.

245 CWo, 102–8, 144–8.

246 Ragagli, 'La Repubblica', 362–5.

247 On Trenta, see LSt, 1.195; Bratchel, 'Chronicles', 7–8 n. 3.

248 Cfr. Baroni, 'Notizie', ms. 1132: 'all'Ill.mo Sign.re questo che lo averà o no non so'.

249 Bongi, Inventario, 138. See 400–402 of the same volume for a description of ASL Sentenze e bandi.

250 For discussion, see Paoli, 'I Medici arbitri d'onore'.

251 'The Prince' indicates the Gonfaloniere, Francesco di Tomaso Trenta, from a relatively distant branch of Leonora's mother's family. The introduction to Sbarra's letter represents Sbarra as having been at large in Lucca in the days between 6 and 11 July 1588, contradicting Lorenzo Trenta's chronicle, which suggests that he was in prison at that time.

252 This seems to suggest that, in Sbarra's reconstruction, the couple considered themselves to be married through mutual consent, despite not having undergone a public ceremony. This was a common and legal way to marry before the Council of Trent.

253 The gender of the 'persona' is not specified in the original.

254 Giovanni Battista Castrucci, made cardinal by Sixtus V in 1585. See Section 1.2.5.

255 This is likely to be Martino di Benedetto di Martino Buonvisi, who held office between 1580 and 1598 (BTr, 396). He was a nephew of Leonora's later admirer Bernardino Buonvisi, on whom see Section 1.2.7.

256 This is likely to be Lorenzo di Giovanni di Lorenzo Buonvisi (1539–1621), mentioned briefly in Luzzati, 'Buonvisi, Lorenzo'. He held office in government between 1567 and 1598 (BTr, 396).

257 Settimio d'Andrea Bernardi was Lucrezia Trenta's nephew, the son of her sister Cassandra di Silvestro Trenta. He was 'ordinario' in July–August 1587 (the moment referred to in the text), gonfaloniere in 1593 and 1599 and ambassador to Florence in 1600–3 (BTr, 393; Bongi,, Inventario,186. He first held office in 1578.

2
Clorilli and late-Renaissance theatre

2.1 Bernardi's *Clorilli* and pastoral drama between Ferrara and Florence

Lisa Sampson

Leonora Bernardi apparently composed her *Tragicomedia pastorale* (*Clorilli*) some time during the 1580s or early 1590s, when her reputation as a singer and writer of lyric verse had been firmly established beyond her native Lucca in the vibrant court of Ferrara.[1] The play seems to have been prepared for performance at the grand-ducal court of Florence in the early 1590s. Writing a full-length, original play represents an ambitious bid for cultural recognition on the part of Bernardi; it may also have served to shore up her personal reputation after she was dramatically widowed in 1585 and exiled in 1588 from Lucca under a cloud of scandal (see Section 1.2.3). In choosing to write a pastoral drama, Bernardi was engaging with a 'third genre' of erudite drama, alongside neo-classical comedy and tragedy, one which became consolidated around the mid-sixteenth century and rapidly became very popular on-stage and, increasingly, in print. Variously known as *favola*, *tragicomedia*, *commedia pastorale* or *boschereccia*, this dramatic form developed out of diverse types of multimedia performance and poetry. The genre was often associated, especially in its early phase, with Bernardi's adopted city, Ferrara, and the lively, intersecting circles of the court of the Este dukes, the university and local academies, but it was also widely adopted across the peninsula and beyond.

This chapter explores Bernardi's play by developing three main lines of enquiry. First, it considers her work against the contemporary tradition of pastoral drama. This was canonized especially by the leading poets in Ferrara, Torquato Tasso (*Aminta*, composed 1573?, printed 1580) and Battista Guarini (*Pastor fido*, 1589/90), but a handful of pioneering female dramatists also engaged with the genre around the same time. Evidence suggests that Bernardi had access to the kind of elite milieus in which pastoral drama and verse were cultivated, given her recognition as a *virtuosa* poet and singer. However, cultural participation as a woman involved complex poetic negotiations and strategic attention to the intended audience. A second aim of the chapter is therefore to analyze *Clorilli*, focusing on its structure, themes and style, and its perceived pro-feminist concerns, which attracted attention among Bernardi's contemporaries. Finally, this chapter aims to explore the striking performative aspects of *Clorilli*, especially in relation to the high-profile experimentation with hybrid pastoral forms at the Florentine court (including opera), as well as a largely 'invisible' tradition of female performances.

2.1.1 Pastoral drama: The Ferrarese tradition

Ferrara in Bernardi's day was a leading centre for the development and theorization of an erudite and courtly tradition of pastoral drama. This interest stemmed from pioneering experimentation since the mid-1540s by intellectuals with drama and poetry, especially following the rediscovery of Aristotle's *Poetics*.[2] In 1545 Giambattista Giraldi Cinthio prepared his *Egle* as a modern reworking of the little understood ancient satyr drama, though it also integrated aspects of dramatic courtly eclogues (based loosely on ancient verse eclogues) and pastoral spectacle. Agostino Beccari's *Il sacrificio* (*The Sacrifice*) (performed 1554) is commonly accepted as a starting point for the new genre of pastoral drama, though dramatists would thereafter experiment widely with different plot structures and pastoral topoi.[3] Following Beccari, many dramatists included: a cast of noble-hearted shepherd and nymph lovers in an Arcadian setting, with a disruptive satyr; a largely comedic structure, developed over multiple, interweaving plot strands; and various episodes, such as dreams, magical transformations and performative elements, including a pseudo-religious ritual and comic by-play. Pastorals were normally produced in verse over the sixteenth century, mixing lines of hendecasyllables and *settenari* (eleven and seven syllables, respectively). Their association with lyric poetry, together with their green setting, also allowed for a varied musical dimension.

Pastoral drama gained wider recognition and legitimization particularly as a result of Tasso's *Aminta* (first performed probably in

1573), which was much performed and extensively imitated. In 1598 the dramatist critic Angelo Ingegneri mentioned 'a good thousand' pastoral plays available in manuscript and print, stimulated by Tasso's example.[4] These included five-act pastorals by some of the first known Italian secular women dramatists: the aristocratic Barbara Torelli, who completed her manuscript *Partenia* by 1586; the noblewoman Maddalena Campiglia, whose *Flori* was printed in 1588; and Isabella Andreini, a famous diva actress, whose *Mirtilla* enjoyed great success in print from 1588.[5] Tasso's most influential imitator and competitor, the Ferrarese Battista Guarini, had his much disputed masterpiece, *Il Pastor fido*, printed for the first time in Venice (1589/90) after it had circulated for some years in manuscript form. Various failed attempts were made to stage it from 1584–5 in Ferrara, Turin and Mantua, until its first performances in Siena and possibly Rimini (*c*.1592–3) and elsewhere until the spectacular ones in Mantua 1598.[6]

Bernardi may well therefore have been at the vanguard of female-authored pastoral when she started her composition. Besides Tasso's and Guarini's authoritative models, she was perhaps aware of the examples of Torelli and especially Campiglia, which brought a more spiritual dimension to the genre, thereby 'converting' it according to new literary trends and shifting the subject matter 'onto more classically feminine terrain'.[7] However, by the turn of the 1590s (when internal evidence suggests her *Tragicomedia pastorale* was performed), the dramatic field had become more critically conflicted. Guarini's still unpublished *Pastor fido* had, since 1586, ignited vigorous critical debates, especially in academies across northern Italy, which continued well into the next century. Citing Cicero, Plato, Aristotle and Horace, among others, critics objected to *Pastor fido*'s lack of 'verisimilitude' and its 'monstrous' hybrid nature as a tragicomedy. According to the neo-Aristotelian Giason Denores, its combination of what were deemed the 'incompatible' genres of comedy and tragedy, each with its distinct end and affect, was a breach of the Aristotelian ideal of unity. In Denores's view, this confused the purpose of drama, which was to teach its audiences morality.[8] The varied characters, themes and plot of the pastoral tragicomedy were also considered to transgress conventions for the simple and humble pastoral eclogue. As a vehement response to these and other objections, two pseudonymous polemical treatises, probably by Guarini, were printed in 1588 and 1593. They defended the *Pastor fido*, hailing it as the first and only example of the new 'unified' genre of pastoral tragicomedy.[9] This work is argued to combine artfully only *tempered* aspects of comedy and tragedy which can appropriately co-exist (without excessive licence or gruesome deaths). The end of tragicomedy is solely comedic and hedonistic: to purge melancholy and delight its audiences through the imitation of comic and tragic actions without tragic catharsis. Importantly, this is considered the appropriate end for modern Christian audiences, who will receive instruction from the Gospel – not from drama.[10]

This background is of relevance when considering Bernardi's play, which, as the prologue self-consciously highlights, has a tragicomic structure with a happy ending (*lieto fin*, line 134). Miseries (*avversi casi*), grief and weeping are transformed into delightful 'sweet accents' (lines 139, 143) and a Golden Age is restored as a result of the Medici infant's presence (though by implication the prologue's speaker, the enchantress Linfadusa, is also responsible). The play thereby provides an apparently secular parallel to Bernardi's famous contemporary verse, which stages her appeal for her personal grief to be purged by the Virgin. However, the prologue's hint at Virgil's messianic fourth *Eclogue* potentially points to a spiritual message beyond courtly encomium to which the implied dedicatee, Christine of Lorraine, may have been particularly receptive.[11]

It is impossible to know whether Bernardi herself chose the more unusual designation *Tragicomedia pastorale*, which appears in the title of the Marciana manuscript.[12] If so, it would suggest her willingness to join the contemporary polemic focused on Guarini's *Pastor fido*, which continued to provoke criticism long after. Certainly, it seems safe to assume that, especially in Ferrara, a noblewoman of Bernardi's social and literary standing would have been apprised of critical questions as she began composing her own pastoral. This likelihood is strengthened by the fact that the first printed defence of Guarini's masterpiece (*Verrato*, 1588) was published in Bernardi's adopted city Ferrara, and that the second was printed in Florence, shortly after her own play was apparently meant to be performed there.[13] Her play, furthermore, reflects aspects of Guarini's model for tragicomic dramaturgy and lyric style, as discussed below. It should be noted, however, that while the *Pastor fido* debate was undoubtedly hostile in academic contexts, it ultimately probably piqued wider public interest in pastoral drama. Certainly, this genre was a very popular one for staging by the late 1590s and was suited for contemporary tastes. In Ingegneri's view, pastorals represented a seemly alternative to the increasingly stale and licentious comedy, and bloodthirsty and lugubrious tragedy. As such, they were appropriate for audiences and dramatists of both sexes. Among the handful of excellent examples that he singles out are the plays of both Torelli and Andreini.[14]

Pastoral drama could, for various reasons, offset suggestions of impropriety, licence and indecorous visibility typically associated with the stage, which particularly concerned 'decent' women. The pastoral's theoretically humble status (compared to epic or neo-classical tragedy) allowed the author to present modestly limited ambitions. It also represented apparently simple and 'natural' elements, though these coexisted artfully with fictional or literary ones. The secluded, green setting of pastoral opened up a space far from the troubling realities of courts or cities, in which personal and emotional expression conventionally perceived as feminine could appropriately resonate. Yet shepherds and nymphs still typically assimilated courtly values, and the setting allowed veiled compliments to courtly figures and contexts. Importantly, the genre's concern with love, expressed predominantly in lyric verse in the fashionable Petrarchan mode, 'allowed virgins and honest women onto the stage (which would not be permitted in comedy), giv[ing] rise to noble emotions befitting tragedy itself'.[15] Ingegneri's words here seem to silently allude to his staging of his own pastoral play (*Danza di Venere*, printed 1584) under the aegis of the Marquise Isabella Pallavicino Lupi of Soragna (near Parma); this featured her fourteen-year-old – and marriageable – daughter in the title role, accompanied by her ladies-in-waiting as nymphs, and involved choral (and possibly solo) singing and dancing. By the time Bernardi was composing her play, there was an emerging tradition of similar highly exclusive and reserved ('secret') female pastoral performances, including ballets, associated with female rulers and consorts (see Section 2.1.5).[16]

2.1.2 Court and academies in Ferrara

Unfortunately, scarcely any concrete evidence exists of the circumstances of Bernardi's composition of her pastoral drama or of her involvement in its subsequent transmission. However, we may surmise that her husband's connections with the Ferrarese court facilitated her undertaking by enabling her access to the restricted, elite cultural circles in which poetry and drama were discussed and practised, often alongside musical experimentation. These connections would explain the intriguing comments about Bernardi and her play in the anonymous preface added posthumously to *Dui dialoghi della vergogna* (*Two Dialogues on Shame*, 1607) by the Ferrarese intellectual Annibale Pocaterra (1559–93). This lists her among 16 prominent poets who in the 1580s and early 1590s excelled in writing madrigals, a short and flexible poetic form much in vogue at that time, including for musical settings. Bernardi is described in this context as singing her own verse, in which she displayed her wit (*ingegno*) and vocal skills – qualities suggested in surviving examples (see Sections 3.1.5 and 3.2.1). She is also said to have 'successfully dared to compose a pastoral play [*favola pastorale*] in which she avenges her sex against those poets who unjustly seek glory through criticism of the female sex'.[17] The author of this description remains anonymous, though internal evidence points to a connection with a Ferrarese academy. Elio Durante and Anna Martellotti consider the author to be Alessandro Guarini, son of the more famous poet Battista and brother of the virtuoso singer Anna. Alessandro appears as one of the interlocutors in Pocaterra's *Dialogues* but (out of modesty) is not cited among the poets in the preface. Pocaterra had himself been a member of the Accademia degli Umili and the prestigious Accademia Ferrarese, like Tasso and Guarini; some poets cited in the preface were also linked to the all-male Accademia di Lettere, Armi e Musica (Academy of Letters, Arms and Music) and the prestigious Intrepidi academy (founded 1601).[18]

Groupings of this sort offered a space to explore new philosophical ideas, and to discuss and experiment with poetry, drama and musical performance. They also enabled members, who were frequently associated with the local court and university, to widen their range of cultural and social connections. While Bernardi is not documented as a formal member of any academy, her mention in the Pocaterra preface alongside many known figures from these circles suggests she may have been somehow affiliated, particularly in view of her status as a *virtuosa* performer, since such skills were valued in this kind of elite gathering.[19] At a conservative estimate, some 25 academies were active in Ferrara in the sixteenth century, especially in the second half, including six that were devoted solely to music.[20] In this respect, Ferrara proportionately includes a higher concentration than significant cultural centres of the period such as Florence, Rome and Padua. University professors, court officials and intellectuals often belonged to several academies at a time in order to supplement their studies. The Ferrarese academies, following Vincenzo Maggi's appointment at the university in 1543, were also important contexts for the rigorous critical discussion of Aristotle's *Poetics*.[21] As such, these environments were crucial for the major literary debates at the time and the contemporaneous elaboration of 'modern' aesthetic responses to this problematic work. Debates concerned especially the genres of romance and epic, provoked by the Ferrarese masterpieces of Ariosto (*Orlando furioso*, final edition 1532) and Tasso (*Gerusalemme liberata*, printed 1581); and drama, including the tragedy *Canace* by Sperone Speroni (incomplete, 1542), as well as Guarini's tragicomedy *Pastor fido*. Academies seem to have been important spaces for reading aloud, discussing and composing plays, though fully staged performances were probably restricted given the relatively limited spaces of the private homes in which they often met.[22]

During the 1580s, when Bernardi appears to have been in Ferrara – and was presumably contemplating her own *Tragicomedia pastorale* – there was, as mentioned, strong interest in Tasso's *Aminta* and in Guarini's composition of *Pastor fido*.[23] Especially in academic contexts, which overlapped with the court, there was a prolific production of pastoral drama as well as of highly innovative madrigals, many on pastoral subjects. These latter were deemed by the Ferrarese musician Luzzasco Luzzaschi to be a perfect poetic form for his time, with their 'brevity, wit [*acutezza*], nobility and sweetness', which pushed musicians to 'discover new ways and new inventions', characterized by exquisite and pleasing artifice.[24] They foreshadowed the new style of musical composition known as *seconda prattica*, later associated especially with Claudio Monteverdi (1567–1643), in which text and music were interconnected at all levels.[25] Many of the academic pastoral plays were never printed and some are now believed lost, as Bernardi's own pastoral was until 2011, when the author's name was deciphered on the sole known manuscript copy.[26] Of the 16 madrigalists celebrated in Pocaterra's preface active in Ferrara from the 1580s and early 1590s, four produced pastoral plays, including Bernardi. The others were Cesare Cremonini (1550–1631), who wrote the pastoral *Le pompe funebri* (printed 1590), which was staged before Leonora d'Este;[27] Count Alfonso Fontanelli (1557–1622), author of a lost pastoral and with expertise in staging and music; and Count Guidobaldo Bonarelli (1563–1608).[28] Bonarelli, in particular, is of interest in Bernardi's case, since he composed one of the most important pastoral plays of the post-Guarinian period, *Filli di Sciro* (performed Mantua 1604?, printed 1607), which was meant to be staged in the new theatre built by the Intrepidi academy of Ferrara, of which he became a founder member.[29] Some common features in Bernardi and Bonarelli's pastoral plays might suggest shared influences.[30]

Intriguingly, the Pocaterra preface also lists three other women alongside Bernardi. Of these, Sidonia Zerbinati is still unknown; her production is exemplified solely by a spiritual madrigal. The other two are recognized for their prominent role in the cultural and musical milieus of Ferrara in the late-sixteenth century. The published poet Orsina Cavaletti (Caval(l)etta) (1531–92) famously appears alongside her husband, Ercole, and Forestiere Napolitano (a figure for Tasso) as an interlocutor in the latter's dialogue on Tuscan poetry (*La Cavaletta*, 1587).[31] Her verse, unusually all secular, includes 10 sonnets and 18 madrigals, and Cavaletti has been described as one of the 'earliest adopters' of the latter form as it evolved at the Ferrarese court in the late 1580s, where it was linked closely with female performance.[32] Cavaletti's madrigal cited in the Pocaterra volume celebrates the virtuoso singer Laura Peverara, and appeared in a collection dedicated to Duchess Margherita Gonzaga d'Este for the famed consort of singing ladies, the *concerto delle dame* (which included Battista Guarini's daughter Anna).[33] More significant still among the madrigalists celebrated in the Pocaterra preface was the exceptionally learned poet, philosopher and singer-musician Tarquinia Molza (1542–1617). She became a key figure at the Ferrarese court from 1583, when she was employed specifically to train the female singers who gave prized exclusive performances (*musica secreta*), until her departure for Modena in 1589 (see Sections 1.1.3 and 1.2.2).

Bernardi's inclusion among these women on Pocaterra's list, together with a sample of their poetry, strongly suggests her prominence within reserved circles active in madrigal production for musical fruition (*poesia per musica*) linked to the court. During the later 1580s and 1590s it is well known that court musicians were continually on the lookout for texts of this nature, given the duke's mania for exclusive virtuoso musical performances, including by the female singers in his *concerto delle dame*. Given the high frequency of performances before distinguished guests and musical connoisseurs at court, there was an urgent need for variety and novelty, especially in the commissioned repertoire for the *musica secreta*. Guarini had been unwilling to write *poesia per musica* on command, which he felt was beneath his dignity. In the end, though, he had to adapt to necessity, particularly given the high regard for musicians at court. By the time Guarini published his first authorized volume of *Rime* in 1598, about a fifth of the verse had appeared previously in unauthorized musical collections, often unattributed, incorrectly reproduced or otherwise altered.[34] Similarly, Guarini's *Pastor fido*, which was mostly written during the years of intensive madrigal production from 1580/81, included various madrigal texts, sometimes slightly adapted, which were in turn excerpted by others and set to music. This led to the accusation later by the poet Giambattista Marino (1569–1625) that this play was simply a hotchpotch (*pasticcio*) of madrigals.[35] Guarini's practice of madrigal composition for musical settings alongside pastoral drama presents a further context for understanding Bernardi's style of composition.

While there is no firm evidence that Bernardi or the other women listed in the Pocaterra volume were formal members of Ferrarese academies, they may well have had contacts at least with members, especially via overlapping courtly groupings. An interesting possible venue is the Accademia di Lettere, Armi e Musica, mentioned above, of which four of the male madrigalists listed in *Dui dialoghi* were at one time members (according to an undated handwritten list): Cesare Cremonini and Annibale Pocaterra, as 'censors of letters' (*censori delle lettere*); Alfonso Fontanella, as 'music adviser' (*consigliere della musica*); and Ercole Castelli.[36] As Virginia Cox has suggested, women enjoyed informal relationships beyond membership with their local academies in many parts of Italy, as patrons, muses, active participants and audiences of public events.[37] Around the late 1580s in Parma and Vicenza, respectively, the dramatists Barbara Torelli and Maddalena Campiglia apparently gained advice from members of their prestigious local academies on structural and other aspects of their pastoral plays. Yet in Ferrara it is less clear that formal academies provided an equally enabling culture for women, despite the mixed sociability at court and the presence of some important female cultural patrons, such as the Duchess Margherita Gonzaga d'Este (from 1579), and Marfisa d'Este (c.1554–1608), who had some connection with Bernardi. Tarquinia Molza, for instance, seems to have met freely with musicians and *letterati* in her court apartments while in Ferrara, but her only documented link with a more formal academy is with the Innominati of Parma (by 1581).[38] The lack of any known female academy members in Ferrara may be explained by the strong connections of these institutions with male-dominated university spheres and the court. The high concentration of cultural capital in male intellectuals may have limited the need to enhance local prestige by promoting a learned or *virtuosa* woman, as Cox has hypothesized was more common in academies in provincial centres.[39]

In sixteenth-century Ferrarese academies women seem to have played a limited role as audiences for more public events. Court members of both sexes are described as enjoying sessions hosted by the Accademia degli Umili – as a break from private lectures on Aristotle's *Ethics* – which 'question[ed] or discuss[ed] the subject of love in Tuscan, that is, in the presence of the princes, princesses, noblewomen and *cavalieri* who had been formally invited'.[40] In this context Annibale Pocaterra's eloquence was apparently so pleasing that even the women doubly preferred it to jousts and other delightful spectacles. Women similarly attended Torquato Tasso's virtuoso defence of 50 theses on love (*Conclusioni amorose*) organized by the Accademia Ferrarese over three days at Carnival time in 1568. During this event Orsina Cavaletti is said to have intervened as a very capable opponent of Tasso, with whom she remained a close friend also during his years of imprisonment in Sant'Anna. Though the account itself is likely spurious, it is perhaps significant that she is said to have objected specifically to the 21st *conclusione*: 'Man by his nature loves more intensely and stably than woman.'[41] As we will see, this contention seems to have inspired Bernardi too in *Clorilli*. Cavaletti apparently defended her position with great conviction, though the substance of her argument is not preserved. The tradition of Ferrarese debates on love performed before literati and ladies, informed by philosophical precepts, would continue also into the seventeenth century within the Accademia degli Intrepidi. Guidubaldo Bonarelli was called upon by the academy in 1606 to defend the 'double love' of his character Celia in *Filli di Sciro* in *Discorsi* – a defence that lasted over three days; and in 1609 Alessandro Guarini gave a lecture entitled 'L'Anticupido', dramatized as a trial of Cupid and Venus.[42]

Bernardi's formative years in Ferrara in the 1580s, and perhaps after, when she was close to the court and possibly to academy circles which privileged female *virtuose*, must therefore have provided her with first-hand experience of highly innovative experimentation with composition and performance of pastoral drama and verse, especially madrigals. In addition, she would have likely attended debates on love of both a serious and ludic nature appealing to a female audience – which form a core part of the subject matter of pastoral drama. As Molza's case demonstrates, these were, however, played out against the background of real restrictions and envious hostility to female protagonism in practice. This context will be important to bear in mind in evaluating Bernardi's pastoral play and its striking pro-feminist polemic, as highlighted in the preface to Pocaterra's *Dialogues*.

2.1.3 Bernardi's *Clorilli*: Structure and themes

Bernardi's pastoral play observes most of the conventions of the recently established genre noted above. However, the action takes place in a pastoral Etruria (a fictionalized Tuscany), which sets up an interesting parallel with its likely performance setting in the context of the Medicean court and alerts the audience to possible 'real-life', or biographical, references. The plot follows the interlinked love affairs of two sets of shepherds and nymphs, observing a double structure similar to that proposed by Guarini for tragicomedy, and also ending happily. Bernardi's setting is strictly private or domestic, though, without staged religious or political action. The 'serious' framing plot involves the couple Dalinda and Fillinio, on which depends a more comedic plot which follows the travails of the younger Clorilli and Filemone (developed mainly in Acts 1–3). In the first scene we learn that the two couples had been separated two years earlier as the result of a disastrous attempt by the elderly shepherd Alcone to arrange an unwanted marriage between his daughter (Dalinda) and a friend's son (Filemone), when both parties secretly loved another. Dalinda soon took matters into her own hands to avoid the wedding. The night before, she daringly set out to elope with her lover, Fillinio, in contravention of all moral and social codes.[43] This plan failed, though. It gradually emerges over the course of the play that Dalinda had fled from their appointed meeting place at the appearance of a savage bear and, on returning, found what appeared to be the mauled body of her lover. The desperate Dalinda was then restrained from suicide and sheltered in seclusion by a holy woman (Lidia, V.3), thus safeguarding her virtue and her life. Fillinio, similarly misled by indications that his beloved had been devoured by the same beast, had then fled Etruria. These lovers appear separately during the play – Fillinio in Acts 2–3 and Dalinda in Acts 4–5 – to return to their original meeting place by a fountain, each believing the other dead and wishing to die, but also filled with uncertain hope. These lovers, in fact, never meet on-stage in the play, though their final union is implied.

Compared to this near-tragic framing plot, with its echoes of Ovid's tale of Pyramus and Thisbe, and strong romance elements and lyric pathos, the plot-line featuring Clorilli and Filemone offers more opportunities for staged comedic dispute and action.[44] The action starts with Filemone attempting to woo back Clorilli, as he had tried to do since Dalinda's disappearance released him from their arranged marriage. Clorilli will have none of this; she declares herself disillusioned with her lover and with love. Following her lover's rejection, she had lost her wits and roamed the forests like Ariosto's paladin Orlando, until she joined a group of female companions and recovered her 'original liberty' ('libertà primiera').[45] She perceives as a betrayal her lover's passive acquiescence to his father's wishes and his thoughtless disregard for fidelity. Indeed, a clear contrast is set up in the play between Filemone's timid, submissive stance and the heroic constancy displayed by Fillinio and Dalinda, whose sworn promise (*fede*) and 'immense love' (IV.4.50–1) led her to defy her father.

Clorilli's feelings for her erstwhile suitor have therefore changed to scornful rejection (*sdegno*), a stance later upheld by her companion nymph Licasta. Yet her main female confidante, the older nymph Armilla, tries to soften these feelings by appealing to Clorilli on behalf of Filemone and arranging a meeting between them. Filemone's male adviser, Coribante, meanwhile counsels his young charge that: 'A virile man should not pass his time shedding vain tears' ('inutil pianto ad uom viril non lice / sempre versar'). The shepherd should 'become virile and strong as [he was] before' ('qual prima / torna virile e forte').[46] He needs to 'man up' and actively *persuade* Clorilli – physical force is not mentioned, though – or use *disprezzo* (scorn) to reclaim his freedom from love. However, the lovers' long-awaited meeting (III.6) is preceded by a series of destabilizing events: a satyr's attack on Clorilli; an ensuing fight scene in which Fillinio drives off the satyr; Fillinio's recognition by Clorilli as her long-lost brother, and their fraternal embrace. This last 'spectacle-in-a-spectacle' is observed by Filemone as he arrives for his meeting with Clorilli, and he misconstrues it as a secret tryst. This finally precipitates his jealous rage, which only heightens Clorilli's disdain; in despair, he beats a hasty exit from the stage to commit suicide. This reported act (IV.3) eventually moves her to pity her lover, and she attempts suicide herself on-stage before she too departs. However, at the start of Act V we learn from a second messenger that Filemone had in fact miraculously avoided death when jumping from a cliff. The lovers are reconciled off-stage after Clorilli revives Filemone with her tears and kisses, and their marriage is celebrated.[47] Both plots end well, then, as is customary in pastoral.

Anyone familiar with Tasso's *Aminta* will recognize that *Clorilli* draws self-consciously on this canonical work for many elements of the plot, quite apart from the lyric diction; at one point a character even includes a tongue-in-cheek, intradiegetic reference.[48] *Clorilli* contains the same motifs of the despairing shepherd and recalcitrant nymph, the suicide attempts and false accounts of death. However, Bernardi introduces the innovation of splitting Tasso's action between two pairs of lovers.[49] Her pastoral also more clearly distinguishes between the tragedic and comedic, especially through her two female characters, and integrates a new framing romance plot, though it lacks the more explicitly heroic-epic dimension that Guarini introduced to pastoral drama.[50] From the opening, *Clorilli* highlights the private tragedy caused by forced marriage, elopement and amorous exile – following an apparent brutal death. One might even speculate whether the plotline also contained biographical hints, referencing the murder of the husband of Bernardi, her possible entanglement with an unwanted lover, exile from Lucca and safe haven in Tuscany, as described in Section 1. Also, like *Pastor fido*, Bernardi's dramaturgy differs substantially from that of Tasso by giving much more emphasis to dynamic performative elements, notably by staging the satyr–nymph scene (III.2–3), as will be discussed below

(Section 2.1.5). However, compared to these male pastoral dramatists, her overall tone is marked by greater moral decorum, limiting the sensuality and erotic suggestions that were often part of the genre's broader appeal.

Bernardi's play presents some innovations from contemporary pastoral, therefore, in respect of its arguments and tone. Thematically, one of its noticeable departures from Tasso is the avoidance of the conventional dilemma of chastity as against love.[51] This is not a play charting the growing emotional and sensual awareness of naïve, virginal lovers, as in *Aminta*, aided and observed by experienced advisers, or presenting a sort of rite of passage. The backstory makes it clear that Bernardi's nymphs have both had experience of love at the time of the action (though probably not consummated).[52] Dalinda and Fillinio have even privately exchanged a ring. The drama is triggered, rather, by the imposition on Dalinda of a loveless (*infelice*) marriage, when she is already in love, as in the main plot of Guarini's *Pastor fido* and many other comedies and tragedies. Unlike in *Pastor fido*, though, Bernardi does not dramatize the conflict between family or divine duty and love. Instead, the arranged marriage to a wealthy suitor – whose desirability is insisted upon by Dalinda's father and Armilla – prompts an important polemic in *Clorilli* regarding the importance of respecting individual free will, fidelity and mutual respect between the sexes.[53] These ideas, which are also represented in Torelli's *Partenia*, are particularly centred around *Clorilli*'s two female protagonists, who together have an unusually important stage presence.

Clorilli appears in one third of the scenes – 10 of 30 – the second highest number of any character in the play (by contrast, *Aminta*'s female protagonist, Silvia, appears only in three scenes in Acts 1 and 4). Clorilli is also the only one of the four lovers to appear in both the 'comedic' (Acts 1–3) and the 'tragedic' parts (Act 4) of the play, and is the only one never to appear alone voicing a lament.[54] This character's role is therefore developed interactively and would have required a highly skilled and versatile actor. As noted, Clorilli appears at the start as part of a band of huntress nymphs devoted to Diana (Delia) and the single life. Her bitter experience of being jilted has armed her with a sense of the perfidy of men, so she spars with a ready tongue with Armilla and, later, her former lover. From her opening dialogue (I.2), she shows her wit and sprightly irony. To the older nymph's observation that she has 'lost the most beautiful, the wisest, the kindest shepherd Tuscany has ever seen', Clorilli adds: 'You'd have done well to add "the most faithful" to that description' (I.2.69–71). Further, she counters the accusation of ingratitude by saying: 'I was never ungrateful, adored Armilla, for I returned false (*finto*) love with the most perfect and true love' (I.2.122–4). She also reasons that 'men are never in a hurry to kill themselves' and that she would not be to blame if Filemone did so.[55]

Clorilli's words, therefore, show a control and balance of both emotions and language, normally hallmarks of 'masculine' identity.[56] Her combative stance and conceits draw on a more 'realist' sub-genre of love poetry characterized by scorn (*sdegno*) that became popular in Ferrara in the late 1580s, though the gender roles are here reversed: normally, an angry rejected male lover chastises his cruel (female) beloved.[57] Models for Clorilli's witty ripostes can be found in the quips of court lady Emilia Pia in Castiglione's *Il cortegiano* and in parlour games played in elite mixed-sex groupings, as in Siena. Yet Clorilli's forthright rhetorical defence of her rejection of Filemone in debate (*contrasto*) also points to the more confrontational poetic duelling found in the courtesan poet Veronica Franco's *capitoli*, albeit rigorously without erotic or sexual allusions. Professional actresses of the day, such as Isabella Andreini, known for her masculine roles, provided further eloquent and more ambivalent examples of women in bold debate with their supposed lovers, using witty put-downs and even open mockery, thereby 'transcend[ing] conventional, decorum-enforcing limits placed on their gender's voice'.[58] By contrast, Clorilli's lover Filemone mostly appears as a passive, 'feminized' figure. His brief show of *sdegno* prompted by jealousy when they meet on-stage (III.6) melts into a paean of praise; later he is reported as acknowledging his failings (IV.3). He therefore sharply contrasts with the shepherd protagonist in Francesco Bracciolini's popular contemporary pastoral play *L'amoroso sdegno* (*Lover's Scorn*), whose *sdegno* is linked with virile heroism and justifies his imagined eroticized violence against his resistant nymph (Clori), whom he finally 'tames'.[59] Ultimately, Bernardi undermines the ethics and effectiveness of *sdegno* in stimulating love: Clorilli is moved to near-tragic pity, regret and finally love by Filemone's reported suicide and repentance, not by his scorn

With the comedic couple out of the way by Act 4 scene 3, the stage is cleared for the long-awaited entry on-stage in the following scene of the second female protagonist, Dalinda. This character's appearance re-activates the framing romance plot and recalls the allusive predictions in her father's opening account of his dream (I.1). It also complements the return to Etruria of her grieving lover, Fillinio (II.1). In keeping with its more tragic quality, this plot strand provides less scope for dramatic action or interaction, relying, rather, on the narration of events off-stage by messengers. Since the 'tragic-romance' lovers never meet during the play's action, the drama lies in whether news of Fillinio's safety (which the audience knows to be true) can be brought to the desperate Dalinda before she takes flight, or worse ensues. Her solo lament (IV.5), which explores conflicting emotions, hopes and fears, forms the culmination of the most tragic act (see Section 2.1.5) before the happy conclusion. The two female protagonists in *Clorilli* thus adopt determining roles in terms of the play's generic mediation between comedy and tragedy, as in Torelli's *Partenia*.[60] However, in Bernardi's case they never appear together on-stage. A strong contrast is also set up in performance styles between the two female protagonists, as was characteristic in *commedia dell'arte* plays. These often featured rival performances between the two leading ladies, as showcased in the singing competition in Andreini's *Mirtilla* (III.5).[61]

While the two main plot-lines in Bernardi's tragicomedy remain generally distinct, the Aristotelian ideal of unity of plot is maintained by various structural and thematic means. The two plots intersect at the play's mid-point (at III.3, the 15th of the 30 scenes), via the character of Fillinio, who is both the lover of Dalinda and the brother of Clorilli. Fillinio first appears at the start of Act 2, after he has returned incognito from a period of voluntary exile to end his life by the fountain where his beloved Dalinda had apparently died. Fillinio's lyrical first words underscore the motif of return and recognition,[62] but his suicide attempt is thwarted bathetically by the approach of Filemone. Thereafter Fillinio goes to hide in a cave (*grotta*) to avoid revealing his return. In the absence of indications to the contrary, he seems to remain hidden until his re-entry to the stage on hearing Clorilli's cries when the satyr Ruscone attacks her (III.3). This moment is of structural importance, bringing brother and sister together, and sparking their mutual recognition and the *peripetia* (reversal) of the play. Bernardi does not offer a fully developed recognition sequence of the kind Aristotle admired in tragedy, and which Guarini developed in his own *Pastor fido*, modelled on Sophocles's *Oedipus Rex*.[63] Instead, she focuses on the tragicomical, theatrical potential of the reunion scene. The brother and sister's joyful embrace on-stage foreshadows, in a duly chaste manner, the later off-stage reunions between the separated lovers. Ruscone's recognition of Fillinio will later be relayed to Dalinda to encourage hope for her lover's safety (IV.4.137–9). Most importantly for the plot development, Filemone's witnessing of his beloved's embrace with a presumed love rival sparks the lover's jealous rage, breaking the stasis of his 'effeminizing' despair.

This device of a lover's mistaken identification of a beloved's presumed adultery is, of course, not new to Bernardi. It was used in various pastoral plays in the period, including Luigi Groto's popular *Pentimento amoroso* (1576) and Chiabrera's *Gelopea* (1604), besides being implied in Guarini's *Pastor fido*.[64] Most famously, it recalls the scene in Ariosto's *Orlando furioso* (V.46–54) where a maid named Dalinda impersonates her mistress Ginevra, a Scottish princess, and, before the eyes of Ginevra's horrified lover, embraces a rival suitor. This textual echo in Bernardi's dramatic scene – which interestingly connects her two female protagonists, Clorilli and Dalinda – must have been especially resonant to Ferrarese and Florentine elites in the early 1590s, following the recent high-profile debates there on Ariosto's *Furioso*, besides frequent performances of the work also in music and by women. This episode – stage-managed by a vindictive, rejected knight-suitor to impugn Ginevra's chastity and have her condemned to death according to a harsh law condemning female adultery – would have been of interest since it crystallizes Ariosto's engagement with the debate on women.[65] Bernardi may also have given it prominence for personal reasons, since it highlights the treachery of publicly accusing an innocent noblewomen of infamy, as she herself had apparently experienced at the hand of a declared 'lover', Cavalier Sbarra. Such a defensive allusion to a falsely accused woman would connect her play discreetly with her famous, and probably contemporaneous, Marian *canzone* (see Sections 1.2.3–4 and 3.1.2 (i)). Interestingly, in the play Clorilli never attempts to defend herself against the unjust accusations of infidelity; Filemone's mistaken conclusion is explained to him only off-stage after the lovers' reconciliation.[66] More broadly, then, this scenario pinpoints at the play's centre the proto-Baroque theme of misleading appearances, and the ambiguity of spectacle – *spettacolo*, a term self-consciously insisted upon to describe apparent deaths, suicide attempts and acts of violence.[67] This concept negates the Aristotelian principle of mimesis, and the stable norms of verisimilitude, decorum and observable truth on-stage, opening it up to what José Antonio Maravall has called 'lyrical engineering of the human world'.[68]

The theme of deception and doubts about false appearances recurs throughout the plot, linked predominantly with the question of love, which was so intrinsically associated with the pastoral. The issue of epistemological uncertainty is foregrounded in the opening scene, where Alcone (Dalinda's father) recounts a dream intrinsically ambiguous in its truth status which has left him poised between 'doubt and hope, . . . happiness and sadness'.[69] Over the course of the play there are repeated references to veiled speech and misleading sightings, including accounts of both the male lovers' deaths. Dalinda, for instance, recounts seeing Fillinio's defaced and barely identifiable corpse (a point which perhaps hints suggestively at Bernardi's own murdered husband).[70] Fillinio, however, is more sceptical about the signs of Dalinda's death caused by a wild beast (III.4.105–28), and alludes to the instructive case of Tasso's misled protagonist in *Aminta* (lines 141–9). Fillinio was not yet 17 at the time of falling in love with Dalinda (notably Bernardi herself was married at 16).[71] Yet, he showed greater awareness of potentially false appearances and inferences, and more scope for action than the other young female protagonists and Filemone. Clorilli describes her extreme youth when engaged to Filemone, which meant she could not ask him to disobey his father. This question of naivety and the social dangers that this poses, in contrast with the moral responsibilities and empowerment that come with experience, form an important thread in *Clorilli*.[72] It may be linked also with the polemic in the play relating to the relations between the sexes, which, as we have seen, drew comment from Bernardi's contemporaries.

Bernardi's tragicomedy explores various kinds of interpersonal relationships, from familial bonds between fathers and children and siblings, to friendship and erotic love. The focus remains firmly on earthly, human relationships, therefore, leaving aside explicit mention of spiritual or Neoplatonic love, unlike in Torelli's *Partenia* or Maddalena Campiglia's *Flori*. The play opens strikingly by considering the responsibilities and rights of fathers towards their children in the significant matter of deciding whether and who they should marry. The elderly Alfesibeo, the father of Fillinio and Clorilli, openly critiques his close friend, Alcone, for forcing his daughter into an arranged marriage, a bond that lasts until death (I.1.167–71), despite her express wish to observe celibacy. While the social norm of filial obedience per se is not in question, Alfesibeo believes that children of both sexes (*figli*) have been granted the freedom (*libertade*) by both Nature and God to choose their partner as they wish (I.1.172–5). His view upholds recently codified Tridentine principles, meant to avoid the abuse common among elites of arranging marriages for their offspring for financial and family reasons – a point insisted upon forcefully also in Torelli's *Partenia*.[73] Alfesibeo therefore considers Alcone's suffering due to Dalinda's failed marriage and disappearance to be a deserved punishment for 'transgress[ing] the laws of men and of Heaven'. Dalinda too is reported angrily critiquing her father's cruelty: '[M]ay your wish be fulfilled by my death, for I shall yield and obey you!'[74] As she later explains, her rebellious act in leaving home, with all its near-tragic consequences, was a response to being forced (*forzata*) (IV.4.56). Dalinda's actions are not uniformly excused in the play: Coribante describes her elopement as the counsel of Love 'gone mad' (*furioso*) (IV.4.61). However, the happy outcome of Dalinda's love 'implicitly condones her filial disobedience as justified by her fidelity to love'.[75]

The strongest critique in the play is reserved for deceptive male lovers. This polemic centres round Clorilli. It is played out through her interaction first with the older nymph, Armilla (who appears in seven scenes over Acts 1–4), and culminates in the single, crucial scene with Licasta, a companion huntress (II.5). This scene presents a tour de force denunciation of men's professed love and fidelity as an elaborate act to ensnare naïve nymphs. Conventional anti-feminist tropes are imaginatively turned on their head with witty gender reversal: men become the 'enemy sex' (*nemico sesso*) (II.5.77), avaricious, fickle and mendacious, using the typically feminine snares of beauty, jewellery and false virtue.[76] The scene's rhetorical excess with its elaborate extended metaphors mirrors that of the male lovers themselves. They are 'rare masters of lying words, and they know how to disguise Fraud so well, in matters of Love . . ., that you would say it was the very truth'.[77] These dissembling lovers with their pale faces, tears, sighs, and rich promises are in fact metaphorically linked to the elegantly adorned but horrid figure of Fraud, disconcertingly gendered as female according to allegorical conventions.[78] The common metaphor of the shifting sea (*instabil mar*) is used to describe men's changeable desires (*volubil voglie*) (lines 43, 160). It is tempting here to see a response by Bernardi to the above-mentioned thesis of Tasso's *Conclusioni* that Orsina Cavaletti had apparently debated ('Man by his nature loves more intensely and stably than woman') in Licasta's conclusion that: 'The most unfaithful and fickle nymph would seem like constancy itself compared to even the most steadfast of shepherds.'[79] A similar theme also informed Ottavio Rinuccini's *Mascherata di donne tradite* (*Masque of Deceived Women*) performed in Florence around the 1580s or 1590s.[80]

How are we to interpret this polemical scene: as aggressive denunciation or playful provocation and parody? The premise of male deception recalls a long tradition of anti-courtly satire, which represented the courtier as a self-serving, grasping, dissembling flatterer, effeminized by the court arts, which included love.[81] Male deceits practised against naïve women had already been critiqued in Castiglione's *Il cortegiano* and, more ambiguously, in Ariosto's *Orlando furioso*. Bernardi could also draw on a tradition of misandry in writings by women, including references in pastoral and convent drama.[82] Yet the ending of *Clorilli* brings a more conventional reconciliation between the sexes through marriage, rather than the more challenging choice of the single life or a companionate bond (as in Campiglia's *Flori*). The lively prose dialogue by the Venetian Moderata Fonte (d. 1592), *Il merito delle donne* (*The Worth of Women*), composed likely around the same time as *Clorilli*, perhaps suggests a counterpart to Bernardi's approach. Fonte presents an anti-men polemic as part of a ludic debate on the relations between the sexes, which touches upon real lived experience, but within a self-consciously fictionalized frame. Intriguingly, one of Fonte's main upholders of the anti-men thesis is a fiery young patrician widow named Leonora, who persistently denounces male injustices, though she ultimately stops short of decrying social conventions and marriage in practice. She is also the only one of Fonte's seven female speakers whose name lacks obvious literary or patriotic significance.[83] Given that Fonte was in touch with Ferrarese literary circles, one wonders whether there may have been any connection between her and Leonora Bernardi.[84] In any case, this dialogue exemplifies how such a polemic can be playfully advanced and explicitly retracted, though the suggestions remain hovering. Indeed, in Bernardi's case, the anti-male polemic would undoubtedly have gained even greater vividness by being staged, compared with the subdued, off-stage reconciliations between the lovers.

Even so, perhaps to offset potential criticism, Licasta's argument is undercut by various ambiguities, particularly through referencing off-stage authority figures. First, a long set-speech is attributed to 'Cellia', a name which connotes concealment and teasing (*celiare*). Bernardi's Cellia has been convincingly identified by Virginia Cox as an allusion to the flamboyant Ferrarese princess Marfisa d'Este (*c.* 1554–1608), who became Marquise of Massa and Carrara.[85] Besides patronizing spectacle, Marfisa performed in the all-female *balletto* of the Duchess of Ferrara, sometimes in male attire, including in a pastoral entertainment by Guarini staged in 1582 which similarly presented a gendered dispute highlighting the theme of male deceits.[86] In 1606 the character Celia in Bonarelli's *Filli di Sciro* also famously became the subject of a three-day academic debate in Ferrara for her scandalous and 'impossible' equal love for two shepherds.[87] Second, an aporia is created by Licasta's concluding reference to an unidentifiable *male* authority, Ormindo 'the strong' (*il forte*), who supports the nymphs' misandrist view: Clorilli describes him as the exception to the rule that men are faithless liars, while Licasta says all men are tarred with the same brush.[88] Overall, then, Licasta's argument to persuade Clorilli is teasingly provocative, like the paradoxical theses discussed in staged academic and courtly debates on love. The self-conscious artifice of this scene is further enhanced by Bernardi's allusion to Tasso's resonant 'anti-theses' against courtly love which run through *Aminta*. Most famous is his hedonistic Golden Age chorus to Act 1, which celebrates Love unfettered by the restraints of honour. It is characterized by the dictum: 'if it pleases it is allowed' ('s'ei piace ei lice', line 681). Bernardi's Licasta seems to target this with a critical twist: she states that Fraud's forehead bears the words 'to satisfy one's desires, all is permitted' ('per saziare le sue voglie il tutto lice', II.5.54).[89] She thereby explicitly draws attention to the implicitly fraudulent *male* perspective from which these desires are expressed, realized and enjoyed. However, Bernardi's anti-male-lovers thesis is undermined in the following scene (II.6), by eulogistic reference to 'real' courtly love in the form of the grand-ducal couple as perfect 'lovers and consorts' sanctioned by God.

Bernardi's happy ending ultimately appears to revert to conventional views on love, justifying Armilla's efforts to soften Clorilli, prove Filemone's fidelity and reunite the lovers. Indeed, Clorilli herself is criticized by Armilla for her ambiguous words (*finto parlar*), which initially misled him to accept the unwanted marriage,[90] and for her excessive cruelty – playing on the assonance of *fera* (beast) and *fiera* (fierce or proud) – recalling the accusations made against Tasso's Silvia. Coribante also presents love for Clorilli as enslaving and feminizing Filemone. Coribante urges his younger charge through his noble scorn (*sdegno*) to recover '[his] original liberty' ('la libertà primiera') by breaking 'those chains which have bound [him] as a slave to the tyrant Love' ('quelle catene onde t'avvinse / alla sua servitù tiran[n]o Amore' (I.5.83, 61–4). Yet blame is also attached to Filemone. His passive compliance with his father's authority has resulted in the melancholic wasting of his assets and youth, according to a topos regarding Petrarchan lovers. Filemone too accepts his own responsibility for distancing Clorilli: 'You were the cruel forger of your own misery' ('Tu crudel fab[b]ro fosti / delle miserie tue'), since his father's wishes would not have prevailed if Filemone had not surrendered to him his 'blind will' ('cieco volere').[91] Nonetheless, within the play his attitude is still preferable to the potentially destructive effects of trying to fulfil one's 'desires' at all costs, as witnessed by the actions of the predatory satyr.

The closest we get on-stage to an exemplary relationship between the sexes marked by companionship and protection is that between Clorilli and her brother Fillinio. Their fraternal love is compassionate (and appropriately chaste), and the siblings also show their mutual care for their aged father (Alfesibeo), just as he had initially spoken up for the rights of youths regarding marriage. By contrast, romantic love has no place on-stage. It is evoked between Fillinio and Dalinda solely through their individual recollections of the past, or through their tremulous hopes for future happiness. Clorilli and Filemone only chastise and lament on-stage when they meet. As in *Aminta*, mutual affection and reconciliation between the sexes are thus reserved for the audience's imagination via messengers' accounts. But the play ultimately also rejects the alternative 'freer' and virtuous all-female sociability that Clorilli enjoys at the start of the play, hunting and conversing with fellow nymphs following a pastoral topos, and critiquing men. This nymph's voluntarily chosen period of feminine seclusion or exile – like Dalinda's stay with the priestess Lidia – proves only a *temporary* space for self-evaluation, protection and deter-mination, for chaste pleasures and for healing from emotional scars and the violence of societal impositions. It allows for the recovery of the self in preparation for a return to the patriarchal social order of Etruria, rather than leading to the configuration of more challenging, alternative models of female autonomy, as proposed in Campiglia's *Flori*.[92]

In the end, earthly love according to the natural desires of the young couples themselves appears to triumph over societal and paternal impositions. Their fathers do not explicitly sanction these unions, since they left the stage in Act 2 scene 6, after encountering the priest at Jove's temple, hopeful of their offspring's return. However, the play ends somewhat ambiguously. The nuptial festivities are only reported from off-stage; the manuscript text lacks a full choral closure, though in practice this might have been supplied symbolically though song or dance.[93] The last words of the play are spoken by the explicitly 'pastoral' messenger figure, Aurindo, who contrasts with the authorita-tive shepherds at the close of Tasso's *Aminta* and Bonarelli's *Filli di Sciro* by pointing out his error in reporting Filemone's death (IV.3). His moral status is further undercut by his flippant rejection of the heroic love attained in the action after much suffering; he favours instead more easily gained love – a position that self-consciously recalls the provocative last chorus of *Aminta*.[94] The double agency proposed for the happy ending of *Clorilli* is also left unresolved. In the play's action, the elderly shepherds refer to omniscient Jove steering events with his 'immutable eternal knowledge' like a 'loving father' (II.6. 12, 14). Yet Dalinda attributes the happy outcome to Lidia, the wise (off-stage) 'priestess of the great goddess [Diana?]' ('de la gran Dea ministra', V.3.77), whose holy care kept the nymph alive despite her suicidal grief.[95] The prologue, on the other hand, as noted, presents the benign enchantress, Linfadusa, as the presiding authority, the *genius loci* of Etruria, who will restore the pastoral setting to its former Golden Age state of happiness through her power, as befitting the 'real' occasion of the dynastic birth. This ancient female guardian figure opposes the tyrannical male god Love, whom she declares brings only pain and death. Linfadusa thus suggests a timeless, benign and restorative maternal presence mediating events – alongside the classical gods worshipped within the play. Questions of gender and authority are thus set up from start to finish. These can be connected to its intended performance context at the Florentine court, to which we will now turn.

2.1.4 Bernardi's pastoral in Florence: Contexts of performance

As we have seen, Bernardi's dramaturgy was strategically positioned vis-à-vis Ferrarese models of pastoral drama (and romance), but it also conspicuously signals its Tuscan frame of reference and specific connection with the Medici grand dukes Ferdinando de' Medici (r. 1587–1609) and Christine of Lorraine (1565–1637). The prologue openly praises the couple, with their infant son Cosimo (lines 57–63), emphasized through capitalization in the manuscript (Fig. 6). In the action too they are evoked under the thinly veiled names of Cristilla and Dinando, and compared to Jove and Juno or Diana (II.6.61–8, 78–9). As in other courtly pastorals and staged eclogues, a number of *à clef* pastoral names are suggested in the play, especially in Act 2 scenes 5–6, presumably for the amusement and celebration of known figures at court.[96] These are now hard to identify with certainty, especially since Bernardi uses several standard pastoral names which also appear in other plays (specifically, Amarilli from Guarini's *Pastor fido*, and Silvia and Tirsi from Tasso's *Aminta*). The Marciana manuscript containing the play makes no mention of a performance, unlike some other printed pastoral plays. This is, of course, no grounds for assuming that one did not take place or was not envisaged. Indeed, the prologue strongly suggests its specific preparation to celebrate the birth of the much-feted Medici heir, and later grand duke, Cosimo II (b. 12 May 1590, r. 1609–21) – or, more likely, his christening on 26 April 1592, for which various occasional music and poetry was composed.[97] A (lost) manuscript of the play existing in the library of Scipione Lucchesini in the eighteenth century was evidently dedicated to Christine of Lorraine, perhaps by Bernardi herself, and so may have contained information on such a courtly event – probably a one-off.[98] The copyist of the Marciana manuscript containing the play may have felt it superfluous for readers to transcribe the play's original dedication, though the lack of mention of a performance may have been deliberate to preserve the author or copyist's privacy, or for political reasons (see Section 2.2.2).

The prologue to *Clorilli* positions the setting of the action in contemporary Etruria (Tuscany), which now appears as a restoration of a Golden Age Etruscan past ushered in by the 'new Cosimo'. The evocation of renewal of a glorious history predating Roman times had been key to Cosimo I de' Medici's cultural policies, formed especially in response to disputes over dynastic prestige with Ferrara in the 1540s to 1580s.[99] Like imperial rulers and earlier Medici, Cosimo I also adopted the classical motif of the returning Golden Age; he was, for example, depicted as Augustus in a statue for the Uffizi by Vincenzo Danti (*c.* 1568–72).[100] *Clorilli*'s action reinforces this idea of cyclical return, since it takes place exactly two years after the departure of the 'romance' lovers on the day of funeral games honouring the 'departed Cosmino' ('estinto Cosmino') – presumably a thinly veiled reference to Cosimo, whose death on 21 April 1574 was still commemorated in the 1590s.[101] The play's action seems to suggest a performance before a Medici villa, in the lush countryside near Fiesole, a few miles north of Florence. There are frequent references in the play (especially in the prologue) to Fiesole with the backdrop of 'high hills' ('alti colli') and the off-stage river Mugnone.[102] Villa La Petraia near Castello is a possible candidate, given the deictic reference to it standing just before them ('*qui* dirimpetto', emphasis mine; II.6.107), and the description of its splendid private gardens, various fountains and fishing lake. This villa was notably given to the Grand Duchess Christine of Lorraine in August 1589 by Ferdinando I de' Medici after their marriage, and she is envisaged there as a 'new Diana' with her nymphs.[103] Bernardi seems to allude specifically in the play to frescoes that were commissioned by leading artists to adorn the villa's courtyard on heroic dynastic themes from Medici and Lorraine ancestry, and to lifelike marble statues.[104] Villa Pratolino is another possible performance venue. It was created by Bernardo Buontalenti for Grand Duke Francesco de' Medici and used to welcome Marfisa d'Este (Cellia in the play) and her husband in 1587. This villa was famous throughout Europe. It had cascades, grottoes, ingenious water features, an elevated amphitheatre-style space behind the villa, hunting grounds and a statue of the river Mugnone (as alluded to in *Clorilli*), which was associated in Medici iconography with Fiesole (the daughter of Atlas) and depicted as a Diana figure to evoke the grand-ducal consort, Bianca Cappello.[105]

Central to the action is the fountain by the laurels ('fonte de gli Allori', I.2.18), which provides the backdrop for Fillinio and Dalinda's earlier apparent deaths (II.1), the satyr's attack (III, 2) and Clorilli's apparent betrayal of her lover (III.5), as well as the suicide attempts of Fillinio and Clorilli (II.1, IV.3). This fountain evokes Apollo's famous tragic love for the nymph Daphne, and the sublimation of his desire in the form of poetry after she was transformed into a laurel tree, as well as perhaps more playfully the famous Florentine court artist Alessandro Allori (1535–1607) and his son Cristofano (1577–1621). Alessandro, trained and adopted by Bronzino, was an important designer of Medici spectacles for Ferdinando I. He prepared, for instance, some of the ephemeral architecture for the entry of Christine to Florence in 1589 and costume designs for Laura Guidiccioni Lucchesini's pastoral ballet *La disperazione di Fileno* (*Fileno's Despair*) (1590).[106] The fountain – and the water imagery which is prevalent in the play (see Section 2.4.2) – may also symbolically refer to the baptism of the Medici couple's first son. Tuscan allusions are even wittily integrated at a rhetorical level. Clorilli, for instance, gives a playful twist to the typically pastoral figure of *adynaton* (*impossibilia*): 'you will sooner see waves of the Mugnone return to their source [i.e. Fiesole] ... than you will hear it said ... "Clorilli is Filemone's lover once more"'.[107] For encomiastic reasons, this kind of 'domesticating' approach was not unusual at the time in pastoral drama, although the genre was often located in a mythological Arcadia. In fact, four of the seven known early modern pastoral plays by women (including Bernardi's) follow this pattern. Alexandra Coller has linked this tendency with the potentially closer relationship of these plays with 'contemporary social, cultural, and political realities'.[108] In this respect, Tasso's *Aminta* again provided an important precedent, since it playfully equated the pastoral space mostly with the Ferrarese court to compliment and entertain audiences. However, it is also ostensibly an ambiguously transitional space ('luogo di passo', III.1.1212) and evokes off-stage wilder terrains not found in Ferrara (Acts 4–5).[109]

Bernardi's transposition of the 'Ferrarese' pastoral to Tuscany (Etruria) results in an almost perfectly self-contained Arcadian-type setting with the standard pastoral *loci* – which could be found also in Medici villas: woods and a fountain, a cave ('antro di Tesbina'), a backdrop of a temple, mountains, river and hunting grounds; more specifically, an underground fountain ('fonte sotterra') is also mentioned (as found at Pratolino), and the sea further off.[110] We hear virtually nothing of problematic other spaces or times beyond the present of the court reality which could hint polemically at alternative political or ethical orders, as explored in Guarini's *Pastor fido* or Bonarelli's *Filli di Sciro*. There are, however, some slight exceptions to this pattern. In Act 2 scene 7, the 'uncivilized' satyr, Ruscone, sets up a potentially ambiguous comparison of himself to Jove. Boasting ludicrously, he calls himself a god of the woods, which in his view justifies resorting to rape to satisfy his love for the nymph Clorilli – as Jove had done with his conquests male and female.[111] He asks rhetorically: 'Oh is it not fitting for a god to be rapacious (*rapace*)? / [. . .] And who will blame me, if I too follow the example of that most powerful god [Jove]?'[112] While ostensibly presenting a comic juxtaposition, this comparison more problematically recalls Alcone's praise of the grand duke as Jove-like in the previous scene; some audience members would perhaps also remember Ferdinando's propensity for earthly pleasures as a cardinal in Rome until 1587.[113] Significantly, Licasta's above-mentioned polemic about men also points to wider geographic vistas. This reports the words of Cellia (Marfisa d'Este), who had previously come from the banks of the Po (Ferrara) to Tuscan shores (II.5.93–7), and is described looking out at the sea. Cellia's long reported speech (lines 133–96) is striking for breaking the self-contained space of the play. However, like Tasso's controversial Mopso episode, it may have been added later, or could have been intended for a particular performance occasion or readers. The marginal marks in the manuscript at lines 71 and 264 may indicate that the lines between could be cut, which would make the scene a more typical length.[114]

Bernardi's presentation of the pastoral space and chronology, and her intertextual references, self-consciously suggest her literary negotiation of the Ferrarese *pastorale* for Florentine circles. The process suggests what Françoise Graziani calls *translatio arcadiae*, mirroring Guarini's operation of transposing Golden Age Arcadia to the Savoy court in his prologue to *Pastor fido*, which was planned for a performance in Turin in 1585.[115] When writing her pastoral play, Bernardi would have been aware of distinctively different literary and performance traditions of Ferrara and Florence, and the strong cultural rivalry between these centres. This continued after the Medici won the struggle for political precedence in 1569, when Cosimo I was made grand duke. It is most prominently exemplified by the academic debate surrounding Ariosto's *Orlando furioso* (from 1575) and especially relative to Tasso's *Gerusalemme liberata* (printed 1581), which intensified around 1582–6.[116]

Pastoral drama in these years, as we have seen, represented a similarly contested genre. This kind of drama appeared surprisingly late and in a 'proportionately more limited' way in Florence compared with other centres.[117] By contrast, the city was celebrated for its innovative stage technologies, from Brunelleschi in the fifteenth century through to Vasari and Buontalenti later in the next century, and for its longstanding pre-eminence in comedy, besides its early experimentation with vernacular tragedy.[118] Famously, Machiavelli had suggested that only a Tuscan can effectively deploy the necessary native wit (*motti*) and 'salty' language (*sali*) to prompt laughter in comedy, pointing to the inferiority of Ariosto's Ferrarese comedies in this respect.[119] By the mid-sixteenth century, when Tuscan (Florentine) was becoming accepted as the 'pure' vernacular tongue following intense linguistic debates under Cosimo I's cultural direction, Florence still continued to favour the production of comedy, as distinct from Ferrara's experimentation with other mixed genres. However, pastoral and rustic forms of spectacle continued to be performed in Florence over the sixteenth century as interludes within the acts of plays (*intermedi*), in civic and popular *feste* such as Carnival and May performances or for occasional purposes as eclogues, which were sometimes printed.[120] The most distinctive rustic drama produced in Tuscany was by the skilled Sienese artisan theatre practitioners known collectively as the Congrega de' Rozzi. Their famed productions from the early century continued to be popular in print, partly in censored form, well after Siena was eventually formally annexed by Florence in 1559.[121]

The competitive political and cultural relationship between Florence and Ferrara that persisted into the early 1580s can be traced in Florentine attitudes to pastoral and Ferrarese *literati*. In 1582, when relations were tense, Raffaello Gualterotti claimed in a preface to his comedy *La Virginia, rappresentazione amorosa* that he had updated the version that had been performed earlier by substituting the pastoral characters with comic-style Tuscan gentlemen and ladies to achieve greater contemporaneity and verisimilitude, reflecting conversations in local villas.[122] However, the marriage in early 1586 of Cesare d'Este and Virginia de' Medici, the daughter of Cosimo I and half-sister of Grand Dukes Francesco and Ferdinando, brought some rapprochement.[123] The Medici–Estense wedding festivities in Florence in February of that year featured a performance of Giovanni de' Bardi's (lost) comedy *L'amico fido*, perhaps echoing the title of Guarini's play, which inaugurated the Medici theatre in the Uffizi with an extravagant pastoral stage set designed by Buontalenti for the inter-act spectacles (*intermedi*).[124] Guarini also seems to have contributed three short choruses for these festivities in Florence.[125] Around the same time the dramatist seems to have become connected with the great Tuscan linguistic authority Lionardo Salviati, via Lorenzo Giacomini from the Florentine Accademia degli Alterati, which paved the way for Salviati's corrections to the still unpublished *Pastor fido* (July 1586).[126]

The earliest example of a full-length Florentine pastoral play stems from only shortly before the Medici–Estense wedding. The prolific comic dramatist Raffaello Borghini composed his *Diana pietosa, commedia pastorale* (*Merciful Diana, A Pastoral Comedy*) apparently after being inspired by a visit to Villa di Castelnuovo, near the Medici villa Castello, and close to Villa La Petraia, where Bernardi's *Clorilli* may have been performed a few years later.[127] The fact that Guarini's *Pastor fido* was closely studied, read aloud and discussed among leading intellectuals in the Florentine academies such as the Alterati from 1586, which intersected with villa groupings, may have further stimulated critical interest in this genre.[128] Salviati in his comments on the play to Guarini explicitly appreciated its 'excellent' and graceful lyric language and its effective structure, though he expressed some slight reservations, for example regarding the lack of verisimilitude and unity at times in favour of theatrical effect. As Silvio Pasquazi has argued, Salviati had no objection to most of the major complaints raised in the debate against the *Pastor fido* by the Paduan Denores and others. Even so, no explicit Florentine academic defence of the work was prepared, unlike for the Ariosto–Tasso debate. Perhaps this may be connected with Salviati's ambiguous comment that of the 'many learned and judicious gentlemen of the Accademia degli Alterati [who] heard [his reading of] the play', those he had spoken to 'were confused [*confusi*] by it, as well as admiring it'.[129] Despite the apparent coolness of academicians towards this pastoral drama, relations between Guarini and Salviati thereafter intensified through their mutual procurement of honours. The Florentine was invited to the Ferrarese court in 1587, and Guarini was invited to join the Accademia Fiorentina later that year, and the Accademia della Crusca in July 1588.[130]

By this time, Guarini may have been entertaining hopes of finding employment in Florence after having left the court of Ferrara in high dudgeon. Grand Duke Ferdinando de' Medici had become interested in staging the still unprinted and unperformed *Pastor fido*, under the direction of his close ally, the soon-to-be Cardinal Francesco Maria Del Monte (1549–1627). This play was even considered for the celebrated festivities marking the grand duke's marriage in 1589.[131] However, both projects came to nothing, doubtless partly because of the diplomatic risks involved in poaching the prized poet of the duke of Ferrara and his dramatic masterpiece. Guarini duly sought openings elsewhere therefore, and only after the Estense duke's death did Guarini return to Florence (1599–1600), invited to a court post by the Medici grand duke and honoured in the famous local academies.[132] Nonetheless, throughout this period, Ferdinando seems to have cultivated a recognized taste for pastoral drama, perhaps one developed in Rome. Pietro Lupi's pastoral play *I sospetti* (*The Suspicions*), printed in 1589 (in Florence and for Lucca) by fellow members of the Svegliati Academy of Pisa after it had been performed there, references the 'great Medici heroes' ('i gran Medici eroi') in the concluding chorus.[133] In 1589 the Ferrarese Bernardino Percivallo's *L'Orsilia boschereccia* was performed during the grand duke's wedding with Christine of Lorraine, and was dedicated to Cesare d'Este. The Venetian Francesco Contarini specifically dedicated his very popular *La fida ninfa* (1598) to Ferdinando I.[134]

Bernardi therefore seems to have been preparing her pastoral drama in Florence around the time when this genre was gaining great popularity both in court and academy circles. She seems to have skilfully positioned her *Clorilli* between the Ferrarese and Florentine cultural traditions. Not only does she strategically reference Ariosto's *Orlando furioso*, which was mostly defended against Tasso's *Gerusalemme liberata* in Florentine critical debates on romance epic, but also the Ferrarese pastoral 'classics', which had recently gained favour among Florentine elites. As a talented singer and poet herself, whose verse was popular with composers (see Section 3.2), Bernardi must also have had a keen awareness of experimentation from the 1590s by Florentine poets and musicians with hybrid forms of pastoral, involving the 'convergence of a number of overlapping developments in music, dance and theatre'.[135] This coincided with Grand Duke Ferdinando's decision to use the Pitti Palace for court performances and to restructure the Boboli Gardens as a *locus amoenus* as part of his political self-styling. Between 1590 and 1595 three pastoral ballets by the Lucchese Laura Guidiccioni, entirely set to music by Emilio de' Cavalieri, the superintendent of the arts at the Medici court, were staged in the 'Hall of Statues' of Palazzo Pitti, which overlooked the gardens; these included *Il giuoco della cieca* (*Game of blind-man's buff*, 1595), which reworked a danced scene from Guarini's *Il pastor fido* (III.2).[136] Within elite intellectual circles, the singer-composer Jacopo Peri (1561–1633) also began experiments, perhaps as early as 1594, to emulate the declamatory style of ancient Greek tragedy with pastoral subjects. *Dafne*, the first known *melodramma*, or opera – of which only the libretto by Ottavio Rinuccini (1563–1621) and portions of Peri and Jacopo Corsi's music survive – was performed three times from carnival 1598. This stimulated intense competitive activity, leading to the first surviving opera, *Euridice*, in 1600.[137]

2.1.5 Female pastoral at the Medici court: Drama, poetry and music

It is probably relevant for Bernardi that several female members of the Medici court, and younger Medici males, were avid patrons of pastoral performances and music, in which they sometimes also participated privately. Performances were associated especially with the youthful Grand Duchess Christine of Lorraine and the two younger Medici princesses and cousins, Maria de' Medici (1575–1642), the future queen consort of France (from 1600), and Leonora (Eleonora) Orsini (1571–1634). Maria and Leonora were very close in the 1580s, at least until the latter's marriage in 1592. Leonora Orsini was herself a skilled singer and also a composer, raised at the Medici court under the tutelage of her uncle Ferdinando after the scandalous murder of her mother Isabella de' Medici in 1576.[138] Although performances patronized or given by courtly women remain largely invisible in the historical record, evidence suggests their frequency and variety during the years of Ferdinando I's rule and around the time of *Clorilli*'s probable performance. In 1590, Ottavio Rinuccini's *Maschere di bergiere*, dedicated to Christine, was performed by the virtuoso singer Lucia Caccini in the role of a shepherdess fleeing civil war in France who 'sought the aid of Florence and of Mari[a]'s future husband Henri de Bourbon [Henry IV of France]'. Melinda Gough considers it likely that Maria attended this performance, which she possibly even danced in.[139] In the same year, a Carnival performance of Tasso's *Aminta* was given with inter-act madrigals by Guidiccioni and Cavalieri, commissioned by Maria de' Medici and probably Leonora Orsini.[140] Tasso is documented as being in Florence around then, as a guest of the music patron Jacopo Corsi (a close collaborator with Rinuccini), and later in April or early September, when he was hosted by Grand Duke Ferdinando.[141] It was for the same Carnival of 1590 that the first of the above-mentioned pastoral ballets (*Il Satiro*) by Laura Guidiccioni and Emilio de' Cavalieri was originally performed in Palazzo Pitti; their *Disperazione di Fileno* may have been staged there privately too or at a smaller villa such as Villa Careggi. Peri and Rinuccini's *Euridice* was also staged privately in Palazzo Pitti on the order of the then heavily pregnant Christine on 28 May 1600 – before its public staging in October.[142]

Bernardi, as a slightly younger compatriot of Laura Guidiccioni, may similarly have sought to capitalize on courtly interests in 'female pastoral', especially by Medici women, as patrons, audience and performers. She (like Guidiccioni) would have had access to the grand-ducal court as one of a select group of virtuoso singing ladies at least in August 1588 (see Section 1.2.3). This had been re-formed during the period of frantic preparations for the arrival of Christine of Lorraine (at the end of April 1589). A female *concerto* had operated since 1584 at the court of Francesco I de' Medici, the father of Maria, in part to rival the above-mentioned female consort of the Este dynasty. This was, however, dissolved in 1588 by Ferdinando I, after his brother's death (19 October 1587), mainly for political reasons, to purge his brother's 'luxuries' and cultural establishments; a smaller-scale *concerto de' castrati* (two *castrati* and an accompanist) was created instead. It is not clear how long Bernardi's association with the singing ladies lasted beyond the single record in 1588, but she may also have contributed – perhaps by supplying poetic texts as well – to the unofficial group formed soon after by Maria de' Medici and Leonora Orsini, perhaps linked with Roman circles.[143] The Estense ambassador reported that the two princesses began in 1588 to 'set up a *musica di donne* in their rooms'.[144] Bernardi's likely access to the princesses at court, and possible contacts by then also with Rinuccini (see Section 3.1.4) could well have prompted her to prepare her pastoral play for their entertainment, as the *Aminta* performance had been – and possibly even for their participation. It may be linked with what Giuseppe Gerbino has described as an emerging demand for a special type of female pastoral theatre in the 'marketplace of the court'.[145] The fact that no documentation has yet been found of a performance might even strengthen a hypothesis of a female patron since, as Suzanne Cusick argues, the patron's gender clearly affected choices of genres, performance spaces and historical visibility.[146]

Given Bernardi's likely familiarity with a wide array of pastoral performances in two of the most pioneering cultural centres of late-sixteenth-century Italy, involving also music and dance, one might expect her *tragicommedia pastorale* to show a high level of performability. To some extent this does indeed seem to be the case, but it is not immediately apparent from looking at the Marciana manuscript. As noted, the manuscript provides no paratextual information on the performance context, nor staging instructions, following the Aristotelian convention that the verbal text alone should allow the audience to visualize the action – there should be no need of 'inartistic' spectacle.[147] No chorus appears in the action, or between the acts, as sometimes found in pastoral plays, especially for large-scale performances. This, too, is not surprising, since classical-style choruses were difficult to write, especially given the conflicting theoretical understandings of these. They were also complex and expensive to perform and needed well-equipped theatre spaces.[148] For some occasions these were added later, such as for formal performances or for print publication (as for *Aminta*). Decorum was also an issue in this regard, especially for female dramatists. When Barbara Torelli considered adding choruses to her manuscript *Partenia* around 1591, her mentor and correspondent, Muzio Manfredi, considered these unsuitable since '[her] pastoral contained a private action'.[149] Probably for these various reasons (and especially if designed for a private setting), Bernardi's manuscript play contains no inter-act spectacles (*intermedi*) or special effects of the kind found in showy Medici-sponsored comedies to celebrate their patrons using sophisticated new technologies and stage sets.

However, *Clorilli* opens with a madrigal, performed and likely sung by Venus, who is searching for her son Cupid. As noted in the rubric, Venus here addresses 'the Author' ('Venere alla Autora'), a gentle lady (*gentil signora*) presumably present in the audience or on-stage, who is suspected of hiding Cupid in her breast; the goddess warns in the final line that this will lead to great suffering (*pena*). The madrigal thus wittily alerts women to love's power for concealment and torment, a main theme of the play. Interestingly, the idea of Cupid being hidden in a female lover's breast is found also in one of Bernardi's Ferrarese madrigals cited in the Pocaterra volume ('Tacete (oimè) tacete'), where it is given a new twist.[150] The madrigal opening the play – by Bernardi, or perhaps another author, such as Ottavio Rinuccini, addressing her in playful, erotic dialogue – appears to respond to Tasso's *Amor fuggitivo* (*Fugitive Love*). This monologue by Venus apparently formed a postlude to Tasso's *Aminta*, balancing the errant Cupid's appearance in the prologue. Tasso's Venus, unlike in *Clorilli*, considers it impossible that Cupid will be housed in the hard hearts of ladies, whereas men will be more hospitable.[151]

Other sung madrigals may well also have been added to *Clorilli* between the acts, as for the recent Florentine *Aminta* performance, perhaps performed off-stage as invisible *intermedi*, or choreographed 'mute' spectacle.[152] It is possible that some, or all, of a series of five undated madrigals by Rinuccini in a Florentine manuscript collection of his lyric and performance verse (*c.* late 1580s–90s) were used, especially since these directly precede his poetic response to Bernardi's famous Marian *canzone* (composed 1588) (designated enigmatically as the work of 'Sig[nor]a L. B.').[153] The fourth of these madrigals is specifically described as being 'created [performed?] at Fiesole' ('Madrigale fatto a Fiesole'), a locale that, as mentioned, figures as a setting for the play – especially in the prologue and close.[154] The five madrigals vary in length (from 6 to 14 lines), but are all voiced from the perspective of a male lover (*servo d'amore*, 36r) celebrating his beloved lady as a virtuosa singer. In the first, she is a 'little angel' (*angeletta*, 35r) – a term also used by Rinuccini in his response to Bernardi's *canzone* (see Section 3.1.4 (i), line 3). The second and third madrigals describe her singing accompanied by a golden lyre, where the instrument bow (*arco*) and her sweet notes and glances treacherously disguise Cupid's dangerous bow and darts.[155] By the fourth, the lover is dying of desire for her voice, which in the shorter fifth madrigal is presented as siren-like. If Bernardi herself played the prologue to her play (Linfadusa) – as was common for dramatists and creatively envisaged in the 2018 production – or appeared as a singer, or indeed as the anti-male character Licasta (as hypothesized in Section 1.2.3), a male perspective for the inter-act interludes would have set up an interesting contrast in these framing elements, like that between Cupid and Venus in *Aminta*. While there is no firm evidence to connect the madrigals to *Clorilli*, the series broadly matches the play's tonal arc. In particular, those representing the female 'archer' would follow Acts 2 and 3, featuring the sharp-witted huntress Clorilli; the fourth has a more tragic tonality, appropriate following Dalinda's lament (IV.5); the last in its closing couplet concludes with the sensually suggestive wish to 'hear / your sweet accents and then die'.[156]

These factors, and the fairly modest forces required in *Clorilli* (a cast of 13, of which some parts could potentially be doubled),[157] suggest that Bernardi may have meant her play for a reserved type of in-house staging. Christine's talented ladies (and possibly some male courtiers) could even have performed this in her private residence or a garden setting – as had become popular in northern Italian courts by the late-sixteenth century.[158] As Muzio Manfredi noted in relation to his plan to perform Torelli's *Partenia* in spring 1587, 'pastoral stage-sets can be prepared quickly and with little expense, and the effect is beautiful and honorable'.[159]

Clorilli, like many pastoral plays, generally seems static by modern standards, with its many long lyrical passages. The 'performative' features that stand out most distinctively for the modern reader (and audience) are associated especially with the active comedic roles of Clorilli and the satyr Ruscone. These roles suggest the fast-paced, interactive performance-style of *commedia dell'arte* players, who excelled both in verbal virtuosity and physical feats. Since the 1560s companies had prominently included actresses, who were instrumental to developing a wide range of tonalities also in pastoral and tragic roles.[160] These practices influenced the diva Isabella Andreini's own pastoral play *Mirtilla* (1588), which included at its centre a satyr's attack on the assertive nymph Filli, whom the actress was known for playing, involving an extended *lazzo*, or gag scene. Interestingly, the company of the great diva (the Gelosi) entertained the court in Florence in April 1592, as part of the baptism festivities around the time Bernardi's play may have been staged.[161] Andreini had memorably gained prominence in Florence in 1589 as a result of her star performance on the Uffizi stage for the Medici wedding in the comedy (*La pazzia*). She had charmed the grand duchess by improvising also in French, and thereafter sent Christine two elegantly produced celebratory manuscript poems.[162] It is tempting, then, to imagine the actress inspiring a performance of Bernardi's play, if not being actually involved in an aristocratic performance for reasons of decorum.

Clorilli's encounter with the satyr, which stretches over two central scenes in Act 3, implies an *arte*-style realization, with plenty of physical action to flesh out the unusually meagre text (29 lines in all).[163] In particular, a fight scene must have been required between Fillinio's threat to the satyr to stop attacking Clorilli, and Ruscone's grudging response in the next line: '[Fillinio] You won't let her go? We'll soon see about that! / [Satyr] Here, I'll let her be. Oh, deceitful Clorilli!'[164] The scenario of a satyr's attack on a nymph had by the early 1590s become a standard element (or 'theatergram' to use Louise Clubb's term) in pastoral drama. It was adopted and variously realized by dramatists of both sexes, including Andreini, Campiglia, Valeria Miani and Isabetta Coreglia (in both *Dori*, 1634 and *Erindo il fido*, 1650).[165] But whereas Andreini and Miani (and some male dramatists such as Beccari, Leone de' Sommi, Contarini and Guarini) envisaged an active nymph turning the tables on her assailant to taunt him in increasingly aggressive ways, Bernardi's scene apparently casts Clorilli in the more decorous position of a 'damsel-in-distress', like Campiglia's protagonist Flori. The sparse writing of the scene may, however, have left possibilities for more female agency in performance, as envisaged in the NYU Villa La Pietra performance directed by Eric Nicholson in 2018, where Clorilli steps in herself to trick and overcome the satyr after Fillinio's arrival onstage. Noticeably, though, Bernardi avoids the kind of eroticism typical of contemporary *arte* performances, or in plays such as Tasso's *Aminta* (III.1), where the off-stage nymph is represented as a passive, naked victim of assault. Bernardi therefore seems to tread a more decorous, tragicomic mid-path, consonant with her elevated social status.

It is difficult to know to what extent *Clorilli* may have featured music and dance internally to the play in performance, in addition to possible inter-act interludes, as noted above. It is tempting to imagine it did, especially given Bernardi's background, the strong associations of the pastoral mode with music, and the tastes at the Medici court. The quite substantial length and wordiness of her five-act play (3,039 lines), especially when compared to the slight pastoral libretti of Rinuccini (*Dafne* and *Euridice*, respectively 445 and 790 lines), would seem to rule out music featuring throughout. It is possible, though, that some passages were intoned (sung or chanted) at discrete lyric moments. No specific indications are given in the text of any dancing, though some may have been added, as for the 2018 performance (see Section 2.4.5 and fig. 16). This omission may have been intentional to distinguish Bernardi's work from the pastoral ballets of Guidiccioni, which were, as mentioned, also prepared in the early 1590s with Emilio de' Cavalieri for private court performances – though not, it seems, for the birth or baptism of Cosimo II.[166]

However, certain passages of *Clorilli* bear a strong imprint of Bernardi's familiarity with poetry for musical setting. The play may, like Guarini's *Pastor fido*, have recycled some of her own madrigal texts (see Section 2.1.2), just as she quoted liberally and deliberately from other pastoral plays, recalling to some extent the 'centonizing' or 'rhapsodic' practices of other poets and learned actors such as Isabella Andreini.[167] Bernardi engages at certain key moments in conspicuously complex word-play, anaphora, assonance and alliteration, aural effects which were much valued also in *poesia per musica* and especially in madrigals together with witty conceits. Filemone's speeches in particular, but also Fillinio's, often incorporate such effects, though one cannot say with any certainty whether (or how) these were meant to be intoned on-stage.[168] Filemone's opening lament, for example, includes a 15-line section using anaphora – *cantai* ('I sang') three times, *or* ('now') twice – and closes with three rhyming couplets (I.5.12–26). The effect of the alliterative *m* and repeated *or / o* also enhances his conceit of 'sweet death': 'Or s'è voler di lei, ch'io *mora amando / morrommi*, e fia il *m*orir soave, e dolce' ('Now if it is her will that I die from love, / I will die, and my death will be sweet and gentle') (I.5.95–6). Yet Bernardi conspicuously rejects the often-daring eroticism in Tasso and Guarini's pastoral verse, which in the latter's case was heavily criticized.[169]

Probably the most likely point for the play text to be intoned is Dalinda's elegiac lament on her lost love Fillinio (Act 4 scene 5), which forms an emotional high point in the play as a moment of intense soliloquy. By the time Bernardi was writing, laments had a long history as a sub-genre across literary, dramatic and musical media, typically representing a woman abandoned by her faithless lover. Recent high-profile vernacular literary models were found in the (epic-)romances of Ariosto and Tasso, as well as in tragedy, serious comedy (*commedia grave*) and pastoral drama; they were also popular in *commedia dell'arte* performances and would soon become the eagerly anticipated 'emotional core' of early opera.[170] Dalinda's monologue (72 lines) takes the form of six irregular and unrhymed stanzas, separated by a two-line refrain, which is slightly varied in the final two stanzas. It portrays the heroine's emotional journey through states of horror, self-blame, pleading for forgiveness, disbelief, anger, desperate grief and wonder that she is still alive. She ends resigned to waiting for news, but wishing to join her lover in death. Emily Wilbourne argues that long laments in declamatory style, punctuated by irregular refrains, became common in opera based on *commedia dell'arte* models, and recalled the 'half-song, half-speech of recitative's ideal'. Dalinda's lament, which is unique in using a refrain within *Clorilli*, may also have been fully sung, like the celebrated one of Arianna by Rinuccini and Monteverdi, the only surviving part of their opera *Arianna* (1608) today.[171] This would have given Dalinda's lament high seriousness, differentiating it from those recited by Filemone and Fillinio in the tragicomic first three acts. A sung lament would respond to the significant contemporary interest in expressive and more or less virtuosic solo singing in the courts and academies of Ferrara and Florence. In contrast, Dalinda's later hymn-like praise of this most happy day ('Felicissimo giorno') invoking Lidia, the holy nymph who saved her life, mostly in *settenari* and partly rhymed (V.3.17–75), would present an appropriate 'tragicomic' balance.

As Ellen Rosand has noted, the lament imposed a structure on the subject's 'uncontrolled passion' through the text's combinations of contrast and recurrence.[172] It also became a vehicle to express an individual performer's virtuosity with improvisatory aspects, and to articulate fractured 'feminine' subjectivity, sometimes in eroticized ways.[173] Bernardi must surely have had opportunities to observe at first hand the virtuoso solo performances of laments by male actors and singers, as well as by female ones. She may well have seen Isabella Andreini and the celebrated singer Vittoria Archilei, both of whom performed publicly during the 1589 Medici wedding festivities. Archilei, as noted, also performed privately alongside Bernardi in the Florentine *concerto* in 1588, as well as in Guidiccioni and Cavalieri's pastoral ballet *Disperazione di Fileno*, during the 1590 season.[174] One wonders whether such experiences of female *virtuose* influenced Bernardi's writing of Dalinda's lament. Tim Carter has suggested this was the case for Monteverdi, who wrote his Arianna lament for the actress Virginia Ramponi Andreini in the form of heightened musical declamation.[175]

It is certainly striking how Dalinda's lament is given particular relief within the tragic part of the play before the conclusion. Yet this character remains firmly decorous, and relatively moderate in her emotions, as befitting an elite tragicomedy – more in the style perhaps of a performance by Bernardi herself of her above-mentioned *canzone* for the Virgin, suggesting an autobiographical complaint.

In the absence of direct evidence of *Clorilli*'s performance, it is tantalizing to consider this possibility in the early 1590s, especially in relation to Christine of Lorraine, who is explicitly celebrated as a consort and mother in the prologue alongside Ferdinando, and who seems to have been the dedicatee of a lost manuscript of the play.[176] The play itself evokes a private, female-oriented setting, focused around Cristilla (Christine) in her idyllic personal domain of Villa La Petraia (II.6). In reality, too, the grand duchess delighted in these gardens and commissioned a meadow lawn in 1589 for festivities, which could include dances by peasant women ('contadine').[177] Grand Duke Ferdinando had assembled numerous talented and beautiful women to form an honourable retinue for Christine on her arrival in Florence from France as his bride, like that of her grandmother Catherine de' Medici.[178] Thereafter Christine is known for fostering a gynocentric culture, or 'women's court', particularly documented during her regency (1607–36).[179] Her principal 'nymphs', mentioned in *Clorilli* with *à clef* names as being united by blood with the great 'Dinando' (Ferdinando) (II.6.102), might be identified as his nieces, the Medici princesses Maria de' Medici (Amarilli) and Leonora Orsini (Onoria), who, as mentioned, evidently enjoyed pastoral performances. A further candidate for a nymph was Flavia Peretti Damasceni (1574–1606), the grand-niece of Pope Sixtus V and wife from 1589 of the music-loving Virginio Orsini – the brother of Leonora, famously evoked as Duke Orsino in Shakespeare's *Twelfth Night* (1601). She was close to Maria de' Medici, and herself an amateur performer and widely celebrated by writers, including Tasso and Maddalena Campiglia (in madrigals for *Flori*), as well as perhaps in a manuscript madrigal by Bernardi.[180] With her husband, Peretti played an active presence at the Florentine court from 1590. She was a keen patron of female musicians and dance, and in Rome with her husband was a co-patron of many significant *virtuosi* (including Luca Marenzio, Isabella Andreini and Vittoria Archilei), shared with the grand-ducal court of Florence.

The context of a 'women's court' could explain the emphasis on maternal figures at the frame-level of *Clorilli*: in the opening madrigal, Venus presents herself as a 'suffering mother' ('afflitta madre', line 2) seeking her son; Linfadusa in the prologue describes her care for her beloved charge Dardano, 'reborn' in the infant Cosimo. The theme of marriage is also emphasized with some criticism, as noted, exploring the theme of male abuses: it may be relevant in this respect that the hypothesized performance of Bernardi's play in 1592 for Cosimo II's baptism coincided with the year of Leonora Orsini's (unhappy) marriage. Yet in *Clorilli* the female protagonists, unusually, realize their choice of marriage partner, despite societal pressure. Ultimately, though, the play is decorously resolved by the combined powers of divine female and male presences (Linfadusa and Cupid or Jove), under the aegis of the grand-ducal couple.

In conclusion, *Clorilli* draws knowingly on consolidated contemporary conventions and models of pastoral drama, but adds some striking and contextually specific elements and witty adaptations of topoi, including pro-feminist twists as in the early female-authored pastorals by Torelli and Campiglia. It also provides an interesting example of the rich contamination of theatrical, poetical and musical forms of pastoral just shortly before *melodramma* was developed. Importantly, *Clorilli* illustrates aptly the competitive cultural exchanges between Ferrara and Florence in the late 1580s and early 1590s, and provides a further early example of the translation of the Ferrarese model for the grand-ducal court around the time that the high-profile plays of Tasso and Guarini were gaining attention. *Clorilli* also enriches our understanding of pastoral drama produced by and for women in the period, and the 'vanished performances' which are coming to light, such as Laura Guidiccioni and Emilio de' Cavalieri's pastoral ballets.[181] Bernardi's play thus provides an alternative perspective on elite culture to the more extensively documented activities in the grand-ducal court and male academies in Florence and Ferrara. As such, *Clorilli* contributes to the ongoing review of the historiography of culture in this period, by stimulating enquiry into the gendering of spheres of production and reception, and female-centred contexts which could enable other voices and forms of generic experimentation.

Notes

1 For the hypothesized title *Clorilli*, based on the main female protagonist's name and on eighteenth-century references to her (lost) play as *Clorillo* or *Clorindo*, see Moreali, 'Memorie', 356v; L*St*, V:169, and Section 1.3. For the dating of *Clorilli*'s composition, see Section 2.1.2.

2 Javitch, 'Emergence', 139–40, 148–62; Weinberg, 'History', I:349–423; S*Pa*, 12–60. Aristotle's *Poetics* was translated into Latin by Alessandro Pazzi de' Medici in 1536; the first printed commentary was by Francesco Robortello in 1548.

3 On pastoral dramaturgy and Ferrara, see for example PSc, 151–80 (and *passim* for broader geography of the genre); Bruscagli, '*L'Aminta*'; SPa, 12–31; Selmi, '*Classici e Moderni*'; for the historiography of pastoral drama, see also Riccò, '*Ben mille*'.

4 Ingegneri, *Della poesia* [1598], 4, 25 ('ben mille pastorali').

5 The pastoral plays of Torelli, Campiglia and Andreini are all available in bilingual critical editions in the 'Other Voice in Early Modern Europe' series, as is the later one of Valeria Miani (see Bibliography). For women writers of pastoral drama, see CPr, 92–118; SPa, 98–128; Coller, *Women*, 133–45. For an earlier female-authored play, see Moderata Fonte's *Le feste* (1581; published 1582), CPr, 88–91.

6 Rossi, *Battista Guarini*, 181–228; Sampson, 'The Mantuan Performance'; Fenlon, *Music*, I:146–52, 159–61; Coluzzi, *Guarini's 'Pastor fido'*, ch. 2; and Selmi, 'Guarini, Battista'.

7 CPr, 27; on literary 'conversion', see also xvi, xviii–xx, 19–50, 92–106. Both Torelli's *Partenia* and Campiglia's *Flori* circulated widely; Bernardi may have learnt of *Flori* through her poetic correspondent Angelo Grillo, who engaged poetically with Campiglia. See Campiglia, *Flori*, III.6.148 and paratextual verse; Cox and Sampson, 'Introduction' to Campiglia, *Flori*, 4, 11, 32, 33. On Grillo, see Sections 1.2.2, 1.2.4–7 and 3.1.2–3.

8 Denores, *Discorso* [1586], 200. On the *Pastor fido* debate, see Weinberg, *History*, II:1074 –105; also Selmi, '*Classici e Moderni*', 11–74; SPa, 137–41.

9 [Guarini], *Il Verrato*, 818; for *Verato secondo*, see n. 18 below.

10 [Guarini], *Il Verrato*, 765–80.

11 Compare Ottavio Rinuccini's augury for Bernardi's happy release from suffering by the Virgin in his verse response to her *canzone*; see Section 3.1.4 (ii) stanzas 4–5. See also Giovanni Battista Leoni's popular spiritual tragicomedy *La conversione del peccatore a dio* (1591), dedicated to Christine of Lorraine.

12 By contrast, Torelli, Campiglia and Andreini subtitled their plays *favola boschereccia* or *pastorale*. For contemporary references to Bernardi's play as 'favola pastorale', see Pocaterra, *Dui dialoghi* [1607], 16; and Moreali, 'Memorie', 356v ('Clorillo [*sic*], favola pastorale'). The possibility remains of a retrospective addition of a title when the manuscript was drafted (1603?); for dating, see Section 2.2.2.

13 [Guarini], *Il Verato secondo* [1593, col. 1592].

14 Ingegneri, *Della poesia*, 6–7, also 4 ('le Mirtille' presumably references Andreini's *Mirtilla*, by then in its sixth edition) and 25 (Torelli's *Partenia*). See Riccò, '*Ben mille*'.

15 'admettendo le vergini in palco e le donne oneste, quello che alle commedie non lice, danno luoco a nobili affetti, non disdicevoli alle tragedie istesse', Ingegneri, *Della poesia*, 7.

16 On Ingegneri's subtle self-promotion, Riccò, '*Ben mille*', 252; and Sampson, 'Performing'; on female performances, Sampson, '"Drammatica secreta"'; Gerbino, *Music*, 202–39; Treadwell, '"Simil combattimenti"'.

17 'Costei coll'ingegno, & colla voce gli studi delle Muse onorando aggiunse nuova dolcezza co'l suo canto a i suoi versi. Ardì anch'ella felicemente di tesser Favola Pastorale, in cui vendica il proprio sesso di que' Poeti, che ne' biasimi feminili una ingiusta Gloria vanno cercando', Pocaterra, *Dui dialoghi*, 16. This introductory section on Pocaterra, including his collected verse, is separately numbered (1–46) and follows the dedicatory letter to Cardinal Alessandro d'Este in the edition in the Bodleian Library, Oxford, Vet. F1.f.227. This section does not appear in the first 1592 edition, dedicated by the author to Duke Alfonso II. On Bernardi's poetic and musical skills, see Sections 1.2.1 and 1.2.2.

18 Durante and Martellotti, *Le due 'scelte'*, 1:66. For Tasso's membership of the Accademia Ferrarese (1570–post 1587), though incarcerated in Sant'Anna from 1579, see the *Italian Academies Database* (*IAD*). Guarini may have belonged to the same academy; see *Verato secondo*, attributed to Guarini, by an unidentified 'Attizzato Accademico Ferrarese'. Like Alessandro Guarini, Guidobaldo Bonarelli della Rovere was an Intrepidi academician and is cited in Pocaterra's *Due dialoghi* (1607). For the Accademia di Lettere, Armi e Musica, see Solerti, 'Statuto'.

19 Cox, 'Members, Muses', 148–51, 156; on the *virtuosa*, Cardamone, 'Lifting', I:110–5.

20 For details on the 25, 26 or 32 academies that operated in sixteenth-century Ferrara, see respectively Quondam, 'L'Accademia', 53, 288; Maylender, *Storia*; Prandi, Il 'Cortegiano', 50–5.

21 Selmi, 'Maggi, Vincenzo'.

22 Pocaterra, *Dui dialoghi*, 8.

23 Though for Guarini's problematic relations with the Ferrarese court from 1583 until his departure in 1593, Rossi, *Battista Guarini*, 52–4, 76; for Guarini's lyric output in this period, Vassalli, 'Appunti'.

24 Cited in Carter, 'Renaissance', 10.

25 Newcomb, 'Alfonso Fontanelli'; Tomlinson, 'Madrigal, Monody'.

26 *CPr*, 93; and Section 2.2.1.

27 Cremonini, *Ritorno di Damone*, Prefatory letter, 2v; see also Schmitt, 'Cremonini, Cesare'.

28 Ingegneri, *Della poesia*, 4, 34 n. 8; Pelagalli and Scarpa, 'Fontanelli, Alfonso'. None of the pastoral pays noted in the Pocaterra preface are termed *tragicommedia*; Luigi Putti (founder of the Accademia Ferrarese) apparently composed some 'Pastorali egloghette' (Pocaterra, *Dui dialoghi*, 12). Other pastorals with Estensi connections include: Gabriele Zinano, *Il Caride* (1583), Paolo Brusantini, *L'Alcida* (lost) and *Filaura* (manuscript, Modena, BEM It. 166 = alfa.K.3.10) Muzio Manfredi, *La Semiramis* (1593) and *Il contrasto amoroso* (1602).

29 Bonarelli, *Phyllis of Scyros*; *SPa*, 203–4.

30 See n. 69 and n. 87.

31 *La Cavaletta* in Tasso, *Gioie*, 4r–39r.

32 *CPr*, 55, 56, 295 n. 7.

33 Cavaletti's 'Ninfa del Mincio a caso in un bel choro' appears in G. B. Licino's anthology of *Rime di diversi celebri poeti* (1587). See also Ceserani, 'Bertolai, Orsola'; *CLy*, 172, 357, 393; Cox, 'Members, Muses', 153–4. For the *concerto*'s evolution, Newcomb, *Madrigal*; Durante and Martellotti, *Cronistoria* (224–5 for Licino's anthology); Stras, *Women and Music*, esp. 241–88.

34 Vassalli, 'Appunti', 4, 12; Rossi, 'Battista Guarini', 52–4.

35 Chater, '"Un pasticcio"', 139.

36 Solerti, 'Statuto', esp. 64–5.

37 Cox, 'Members, Muses', 151–5; 146–8 (for Campiglia and Torelli). See also Torelli, *Partenia*, 17–20, 22–3; Campiglia, *Flori*, 6–7, 13–4, 31. Cf. Isabella Andreini's membership of the Accademia degli Intenti of Pavia (1601) long after her *Mirtilla* (1588); Sampson, 'Amateurs', 199–201.

38 Durante and Martellotti, *Cronistoria*, 183; Cox, 'Members, Muses', 134, 149, 158; Sampson, 'Reforming Theatre', 66, 68.

39 Cox, 'Members, Muses', 140–1.

40 'di materia amorosa toscanamente questionare, o discorrere, e ciò alla presenza de' Prencipi, e Prencipesse, e della nobiltà cosi di Dame, come di Cavaglieri solennemente invitati', Pocaterra, *Dui dialoghi*, 8.

41 Serassi, *Vita di Tasso*, 144–5: 'L'Uomo in sua natura ama più intensamente e stabilmente che la donna.'

42 Cox, 'Members, Muses', 153–4; *SPa*, 206.

43 For a comparison of *Clorilli* with six other contemporary female-authored pastoral plays, see *CPr*, 107–8, 92–118; Coller, *Women*, 133–51.

44 *Met* V, 55–166.

45 I.2.67; ([Clorilli] 'Forsen[n]ata gridai la notte e'l giorno / per le foreste', I.2.60–1; Cf. *OF*, XXIII.124–5 and 134–6); also Tasso *Aminta*, I.1.221–31 (Tirsi's madness for love). All references to plays give act, scene and line number where relevant. On women recovering their liberty in all-female groups, see Fonte's *The Worth of Women*, 48–50, 53–4, 56, 113–4, 230, 237–8; for the self-sufficiency of Diana's nymphs in pastoral, Campiglia, *Flori*, 22–3.

46 I.5.27–8 and 67–8. Cf. *Am* II.3.1050–1, where an appeal is similarly made to the lover's virility; Aminta is advised indirectly to assault his beloved, whether his desire is reciprocated or not (I.3. 1081–5, 1119–24).

47 Cf. Tasso's more sensual account of Aminta's revival by Silvia, *Am*, V.1.102–5. Also 'Ninfa gentil' (85) in the Marciana codex; see Section 2.2.4.

48 Fillinio refers to Aminta's example in III.4.142–5. For textual echoes of *Aminta*, see notes to the translation *passim*, especially V.5.

49 *CPr*, 98.

50 *SPa*, 199–202.

51 Richard Andrews, 'The Dilemma of Chastity and Sex in Pastoral Drama', unpublished paper for Symposium at University College London, 1997; see also *PSc*, 156.

52 For an unusual representation of a nymph who has consummated her love, see Valeria Miani, *Amorosa speranza* (1604), I.3, fol. [12]v.

53 Cf. Torelli, *Partenia*, II.6.393–418; and 'Introduction', 36–37, 40. For rare examples of female characters who resist marriage in pastoral drama to observe chastity (and avoid incest), see Alberto Lollio's *Aretusa* (1567) and Livio Pagello's *Cinthia* (ms. c. 1579). Campiglia's protagonist in *Flori* desires a chaste union to pursue intellectual goals.

54 Cf. Ingegneri's *Danza di Venere*, where Amarilli (first played by an aristocratic girl) appears in nine of 24 scenes across all four acts (see Section 2.1.1). In numerical terms, the character who appears in most scenes of Bernardi's *Clorilli* is the tragicomic Coribante (11, in Acts 1–3, and 5); Dalinda appears in four scenes (Acts 4–5).

55 1.2.158–64, Cf. *Aminta*, III.1.1312–34 (Chorus), and Shakespeare, *As You Like It*, IV.1.1876–87.

56 *CPr*, 114.

57 *CPr*, 115. For Orsina Cavaletti's madrigal 'Sdegno la fiamma estinse' (1587), voiced by the male lover, which was very popular with musicians, see *CLy*, 172.

58 Nicholson, '"She speaks poniards"', 4, also 9–14; see also Andreini, *Lovers' Debates*, and Franco, *Terze rime* (1575), for example, *capitoli* 14, 16, 17. On Sienese games, Bargagli, *I trattenimenti*, e.g. II, 393–401 ('Giuoco della disfida'); McClure, *Parlour Games*, esp. ch. 3 'The Games of Girolamo and Scipione Bargagli'.

59 Bracciolini's *L'amoroso sdegno* was printed 1597, but apparently written six or seven years earlier in 1590/91. In IV.2–4 Clori is 'tamed' by her lover Acrisio's display of anger; for Acrisio's imagined attack, 40r.

60 Torelli, *Partenia*, 'Introduction', 45.

61 Vazzoler, 'Le pastorali', especially 281–5.

62 [Fillinio] 'io pur *ritorno* a *rivedervi*, e'n voi / ben *riconosco* . . .' (II.1.2–3, italics mine); lines 8 and 11 begin: 'Riconoscete'.

63 Aristotle, *Poetics*, 6.4 (pp. 18–9); 8.2 (pp. 26–7); Guarini, *Verrato*, 801–2. Brother–sister recognition, though typical of comedy, is relatively unusual in pastoral, but see Giovanni Pona, *Tirrheno* (1589), III.2, based on Euripides's *Iphigenia in Tauris*; and with the threat of incest: Giraldi Cinthio's unfinished *Favola pastorale*, Lollio's *Aretusa*, Ingegneri's *Danza di Venere*, Torelli's *Partenia*.

64 Groto, *Pentimento* (1576), III.7; Chiabrera, *Gelopea* (1614), III.2; Guarini, *Pastor fido*, III.8. For this device used off-stage, see Shakespeare, *Much Ado About Nothing*, III.3.144–64, IV.1.88–114.

65 Benson, *Invention*, 94–101; on *Orlando furioso*'s reception in Florence, see Plaisance, 'I dibattiti'; for its performance, see for example, Henke, *Performance*, 89–91; Treadwell, '"Simil combattimento"'; Nicholson, 'Romance'; Stras, *Women and Music*, esp. chs 3–4.

66 For accusations, III.6; IV.3; and explanation, V.1.112–9.

67 The term *spettacolo* is used to describe Dalinda's apparent death at the fountain (II.1.25); the satyr's attack (III.3.1); the sight of Clorilli's apparent betrayal of Filemone (III.5.4) and of Clorilli's suicide attempt (IV.3.216); and Filemone's imagined suicide (III.7.11).

68 Maravall, *Culture*, 263. On the paradigm shift in Baroque theatre to emphasize spectacle, see Snyder, 'Introduction' to Andreini, *Love in the Mirror* [1622], 4–5.

69 I.1.95–7. Cf. the two elderly fathers' differing interpretations of a recent storm, in Bonarelli's *Filli di Sciro (Phyllis of Scyros)*, I.1. For ambiguous prophetic dreams, see also Torelli, *Partenia*, I.4; IV.4.

70 IV.4.91–103; Coribante suggests this was the body of Alcasto, IV.4.120–26.

71 II.4, n. 124; and see Section 1.2.1.

72 I.2. 83–7. Cf. themes of female naivety and experience in Fonte's *Worth of Women*, 55, 171, 181, and *passim*. For Bernardi's own apparently unhappy marriage, see Sections 1.2.1, 1.2.2 and 1.2.4.

73 Torelli, *Partenia*, II.3, II.6, 'Introduction', 36–7; cf. the protagonist's claim of freedom in choice of partner and type of union in Campiglia's *Flori* (V.1–2). On the Catholic Church's challenges to abuses in arranged marriages, see Ferraro, *Marriage Wars*, 147.

74 I.1.145–6.

75 *CPr*, 108.

76 *CPr*, 109; for a possible male response to this polemic in the anonymous verse following the manuscript play, see Section 2.2.4.

77 II.5.26–9.

78 Compare the visual allegory of fair-faced Fraud holding out a honeycomb and disguising

a sting in her tail in Agnolo Bronzino's *Venus, Cupid and Time* (*Allegory of Lust*) (1540–5), gifted by Cosimo I de' Medici to Francis I of France.

79 II.5.69–71.

80 In Solerti, *Albori*, II:59–63; Boggini records the manuscript in BNCF Palatino 249, 'Per un'edizione', 28.

81 Ugolini, *The Court*, esp. 3–12, 84–144. Cf. Tasso's polemical anti-courtly speech by Mopso, *Am*, I.2.555–607.

82 Castiglione, *Cortegiano*, III.50, 54; *OF*, X.5–9; Torelli, *Partenia*, I.3.339–74, and 'Introduction', 33; Campiglia, *Flori*, II. 5, also II. 2; Coller, *Women*, 217, 144–45; Weaver, *Convent Theatre*, 101.

83 Fonte, *Worth of Women* (*Il merito delle donne*), 45 n. 4, 46–8, 119–20, 189–92, 258–9 and *passim*.

84 For Fonte's Ferrarese connections, C*Pr*, 307 n. 160; C*Ly*, 173.

85 C*Pr*, 109; and Section 1.2.3.

86 For Marfisa d'Este and the *balletto delle donne*, see Treadwell, '"Simil combattimento"'; Gerbino, *Music*, 230–5; also Sections 1.2.2–3.

87 For the *Discorsi*, see Perella's Introduction to Bonarelli, *Phyllis of Scyros*, xx–xxiv; S*Pa*, 206. On Angelo Grillo's literary pseudonym Livio Celiano in his love poetry, see Section 1.2.2. On the popular *Lettere amorose di Madonna Celia gentildonna Romana* (1562) as possible 'female impersonations' by a male writer, see Ray, *Writing gender*, 13, 232 n. 47; though see C*Wo*, 317 n. 5.

88 For Ormindo as a possible reference to the poet Giulio Cesare Croce, see Section 1.2.5.

89 C*Pr*, 127; S*Pa*, 77. Scarpati, 'Il nucleo', 92.

90 I.2.32; Clorilli had responded that if Filemone married another, she would 'love him as much as he loved me' ('riamarlo / quanto ei m'amava', I.2.88–9).

91 I.4.55–6, 58. Cf. The priest Nicandro charging Amarilli for (falsely imputed) adultery ('noi soli a noi stessi / fabbri siam pur de le miserie nostre'), in *Pastor fido* IV.5.81–2.

92 Campiglia, *Flori*, 'Introduction', 21–8. Compare the refuge convents provided for elite secular women from abusive families or in times of personal stress; Cusick, *Francesca Caccini*, 55–7 (Florence); Stras, *Women and Music*, 25 (Ferrara).

93 Following the model of pastoral comedies such as Shakespeare's *A Midsummer Night's Dream* and *As You Like It*, the 2018 performance of *Clorilli* at NYU Florence directed by Eric Nicholson ended with a choral dance on a separate elevated 'green' stage (see '*Clorilli* video recording', at 1'36"). See Section 2.4.5.

94 *Clorilli* V.5 and notes to translation; cf. Tasso, *Aminta*, Chorus V, and Prologue, I.1, II.2, V.1.

95 Paradoxically, Dalinda's praise of the chaste Lidia (V.3.69–71) references Petrarch's spiritual verse for Laura (*C* lxi 'Benedetto sia 'l giorno').

96 For *à clef* names, see notes to *Clorilli*.

97 For occasional manuscript verse for Cosimo II's christening by Rinuccini, see BNCF Palat. 249, 59r–62r; and by G. B. Strozzi Jr (unattributed), Chater, 'Poetry', 349. On Cosimo II, see *Clorilli*, n. 13, 16, 39, 51.

98 Moreali, 'Memorie', 356v; see Section 1.3. Torelli's manuscript *Partenia*, explicitly set at a Farnese villa in Collecchio, similarly does not record a performance, though documents show it was rehearsed if not staged at the court of Guastalla; see Sampson and Burgess-Van Aken, 'Introduction' to Torelli, *Partenia*, 42–5.

99 Fantoni, 'Simbolismo', and 'Courts', 261, 271–2; Bizzocchi, 'Tra Ferrara e Firenze'.

100 Cox-Rearick, *Dynasty*; Fantoni, 'Simbolismo', 21.

101 IV.4.113; for the reference to the astrological sign of Taurus, I.2.141–3, and translation n. 51. For Cosimo's commemoration, see Vincenzio Panciatichi, *Orazione funerale* (1598).

102 Prologue, line 7; see also Prologue, 29, 36, 95; IV.2.14; IV.3.37; V.1.133; V.4.3. On Medici villas, see Saslow, *Medici Wedding*, 134–7.

103 *Clorilli*, II.6.79–80. Butters, 'Christine', 129, 134; on Villa La Petraia, Saslow, *Medici Wedding*, 135.

104 Butters, 'Christine', 134–5; *Clorilli*, II.6, n. 18 and 106. On Cavalieri's 'camerata' with Guidiccioni at Villa Careggi near Fiesole, see Kirkendale, *Emilio de' Cavalieri*, 188–9.

105 Wright, 'Some Medici Gardens', 49–59; for Marfisa d'Este's visit to Pratolino, see Section 1.2.3 and *Clorilli*, n. 82; Goode, 'Pratolino'.

106 Spalding, 'Allori, Alessandro'; Daddi Giovanozzi, 'Di alcune incisioni', 88–91; Kirkendale,

Emilio de' Cavalieri, 92, 98, 200–1; on the pastoral stage set, see Cavicchi, 'Imagini', esp. 50; for the (lost) wall fountain of the Mugnone with a reclining figure of Fiesole at the Medici Boboli Garden, see Wiles, *The Fountains*, 34.

107 'prima al proprio fonte / tornerà l'onda del Mugnon . . . / che . . . mai più si dica: – / Clorilli a Filemone s'è fatta amica', I.2.188–92.

108 Coller, *Women*, 137; P*Sc*, 214–9.

109 Godard, 'Première Représentation', 226–51; S*Pa*, 63–4; Clubb, 'Pastoral Play', 69; Quarta, 'Spazio scenico', esp. 308, 313.

110 P*Sc*; see *Clorilli* IV.2.11, II.5.276.

111 C*Pr*, 114.

112 II.7.46, 54–5.

113 For Ferdinando de Medici's interests in gambling and women when Cardinal, see Fragnito, *Storia*, 72, 90–3, 151, 153–5.

114 Cf. *Am*, II.1.572–648; C*Pr*, 319–20 n. 106; S*Pa*, 80. See for the marginalia marking out occasional episodes, *Clorilli*, II.5.71 and 264; also II.6.28 and 169.

115 Graziani, '*Translatio Arcadiae*'; on the Turin performance, S*Pa*, 141–8.

116 Plaisance, 'I dibattiti'; Weinberg, *History*, II:954–1073.

117 P*Sc*, 172.

118 On Florentine theatre see, for example, Mamone, *Il teatro* and *Dei*. Early Florentine tragedies include Giovanni Rucellai's *Rosmunda* and *Oreste* (1515–20).

119 Machiavelli (attrib.), *Discorso o Dialogo intorno alla nostra lingua* (*c.* 1515–6), §69.

120 For Florentine pastoral *intermedi*, see for example those for Machiavelli's comedies (*Mandragola*, *c*.1518 and *Clizia*, 1525), and several official Medici-sponsored comedy performances, from Antonio Landi's *Commodo* (1539) to Girolamo Bargagli's *La pellegrina*, sixth *intermedio* (1589). See Gerbino, *Music*, 197.

121 See, for example, Tylus, 'The Work'.

122 Gualterotti, *La Virginia* (1584), dedication to Duke of Savoy, Florence, 15 November 1582, 3–4.

123 Plaisance, 'I dibattiti', 385. Though for Florentine musicians and the Ferrarese *musica secreta* in 1583 and 1584, Durante and Martelotti, *Cronistoria*, 152–5, 162–6.

124 For a semi-official account, see de' Rossi, *Descrizione del magnificicentiss* (1585). For political-religious reasons why Bardi's comedy was not printed, see Plaisance, 'I dibattiti', 368, also 373, 388.

125 Rossi, *Battista Guarini*, 71 n. 1; for two of Guarini's three choruses ('Le contadine' and 'Le Maghe trionfanti d'amore'), see Guarini, *Opere*, II:108–9.

126 Pasquazi, 'Le Annotazioni', see 191–2 and *passim*. For Guarini's contacts within the Crusca academy, including Giovanni de' Bardi, see Rossi, *Battista Guarini*, 87; letter from Salviati to Guarini, 26 April 1586, in Guarini, *Lettere*, 347–9.

127 Borghini, *Diana pietosa* (1586), dedicatory letter to Baldassar Suares, fol. *3r.

128 Plaisance, 'I dibattiti', 370; Palisca, 'The Alterati'.

129 'fu udita da parecchi gentilhuomini dell'Accademia degli Alterati, scienziate e di bel giudizio'; 'ne sian rimasti confusi, non che ammirati', Salviati, Letter to Guarini, 8 October 1586, in Pasquazi, 'Le Annotazioni', 210.

130 Rossi, *Battista Guarini*, 88; for Guarini's letter of thanks for admission to the Accademia Fiorentina, 11 November 1587, Salvini, *Fasti consolari*, 285–6.

131 Carter, *Jacopo Peri*, I:17; Rossi, *Battista Guarini*, 93–4.

132 Rossi, *Battista Guarini*, 123–6, 129–30. Guarini was elected Arciconsolo of the Accademia della Crusca, and contributed a dialogue between Juno and Minerva to the marriage festivities of Maria de' Medici and Henry IV in 1600.

133 Lupi, *I sospetti*, 134, and dedicatory letter to Girolamo Papponi, Florence, 30 October 1588. Two editions were produced by the Florentine publisher Bartolomeo Sermartelli, one in Lucca 'ad istanza di Matteo Galassi e Compagni, librari'. On Cristoforo Castelletti's pastoral *I torti amorosi* (1581) and other theatre performances in Ferdinando's elite-clerical circles in Rome, see Fragnito, *Storia*, 64–7, 74–5; for further Roman pastorals, P*Sc*, 173.

134 Contarini's *La fida ninfa* was published in two editions in 1598, and at least four more in 1599; it appeared revised with the subtitle *Darinello* in 1620.

135 Fenlon, 'Golden Age', 199, 207.

136 Fenlon, 'Golden Age', 218; Kirkendale, 'L'opera', 372–3 and *Emilio de' Cavalieri*, 185–212; Palisca, 'Musical Asides', 342–3, 345.

137 Rinuccini, *L'Euridice* and *Dafne* (1600); only six fragments of Peri and Corsi's setting of *Dafne* survive. For the probable dating of *Dafne* performances, see Carter, *Jacopo Peri*, 29–39; also Palisca, 'Musical Asides', 349–55; Magini, 'Cronache', 54–6. On competing claims for precedence in the new type of song, see Carter and Goldthwaite, *Orpheus*, 256–7.

138 Smith, 'Leonora Orsini'; Murphy, *Murder*.

139 Gough, 'Marie de Medici', 140; Chiarelli, 'Before and After'.

140 Fenlon, 'Golden Age', 214–6; Gough, 'Marie de Medici', 140.

141 Carter, 'Music and Patronage', esp. 70 n. 68; Kirkendale, *Emilio de' Cavalieri*, 189–90.

142 On *Disperazione*, see Kirkendale, *Emilio de' Cavalieri*, 192; on *Euridice*, see Carter and Goldthwaite, *Orpheus*, 113.

143 Fenlon, 'Preparations'; Gough, 'Marie de Medici', 139–40; Cusick, *Francesca Caccini*, 3. For a later Florentine *concerto*, including Caccini's second wife and two daughters, see Carter, *Jacopo Peri*, 22, 24 and n. 71; Newcomb, *The Madrigal*, ii:200.

144 'la Signora Principessa Maria [de' Medici], et la Signora Lionora sorella del Signor Virginio [Orsini] havevano incominciato a metter su una musica di donne nelle loro stanze', ASM, Ambasciatori, Firenze, b. 28, Ercole Cortile, Florence, 2 January 1588 to Duke Alfonso II, Ferrara, in Fenlon, 'Preparations', 216 n. 29.

145 Gerbino, *Music*, 214; compare Muzio Manfredi's *Il contrasto amoroso* (1602), and Angelo Ingegneri's *Danza di Venere* (1584), composed specifically for young aristocratic ladies, see Sampson, 'Performing', 115.

146 Cusick, *Francesca Caccini*, esp. xix; Cusick refers particularly to theatre during Christine of Lorraine's regency (1606–36). See also for Ferrara, Stras, *Women and Music*.

147 Aristotle *Poetics*, 4.4, 50b (pp. 12–3); 9.1 (pp. 31–2); 12.1–2 (pp. 46–7); S*Pa*, 171.

148 On choruses, Aristotle, *Poetics*, esp. 8.9, pp. 30–1; and in pastoral drama, Selmi, 'Classici e Moderni', 179–99; S*Pa*, 99–100, 130.

149 'contenendo la Pastorale attion privata, non è capace del choro', Manfredi, *Lettere brevissime* [1606], 11 January 1591, Nancy, 11; and Torelli, *Partenia*, ed. Sampson and Burgess-Van Aken, 48.

150 See Sections 1.2.4 and 3.1.5 (vi).

151 Tasso's 'Amore Fuggitivo' (stanzas 2–3), first published with Tasso's *Aminta* in his *Rime* (1581) but often not considered an authentic part of the play; see Tasso, *Opere*, I; S*Pa*, 80–1; and *Clorilli* (translation), n. 2.

152 On *Aminta*, see Kirkendale, *Emilio de' Cavalieri*, 190–1. For Luigi Groto's request for 'musiche, o spettacoli muti' as *intermedi* for his pastorals, Groto, *Lettere famigliari* (1601), letter to Giovanni Fratta, 15 March 1582, 124r.

153 For the probably identification of 'L. B.' as Bernardi, see Section 3.1.4. The five madrigals appear in BNCF, Palat. 249, 35r–36r, immediately preceding Rinuccini's response to Bernardi's *canzone*, 36r–37v. The first four of the five poems appear in the same order (with slight variants) in a mid-seventeenth-century manuscript miscellany held in the Corsiniana library of Rome containing poetry associated with musical performance, *Canzoniere*, 45.G.9 (Cors. 960), 51v–52v. Rinuccini visited Ferrara with Giovanni de' Bardi and Jacopo Corsi in early 1590, Boggini, 'Per un'edizione', 27.

154 'A me che tanto v'amo' ('To me who so loves you'), BNCF, Palatino 249, 36r. This madrigal is found in a slightly later companion miscellany of Rinuccini's verse too (BNCF, Palat. 250, 69v); in another also containing Bernardi's verse, Siena BCI I. XI. 11, 38v (Chiarelli, 'Per un censimento', 143; and Section 3.1.1); and in the 1622 Giuntina of Rinuccini's verse, edited by his son Pierfrancesco (80). It was set to music by Pietro Maria Marsolo, *maestro di cappella* at Ferrara cathedral and music teacher within the Intrepidi academy of Ferrara, in *Secondo libro de' Madrigali a quattro voci* (Venice: G. Vincenti, 1614).

155 'Amor è fatto insidioso arciero' ('Love has become a treacherous archer') and 'Con bellissima man leggiadra arciera' ('With her beautiful hand the lovely archer'), BNCF, Palatino 249, 35r–v (nos. 2 and 3; also in the companion MS Palatino 250, 63v, 67r). For this theme also in Bernardi's madrigal 'Vago Cielo ov'Amore', set to music by Philippe de Monte, see Section 3.1.4.

156 ('vorrei sentire / i vostri dolci accenti e poi morire'), BNCF, MS Palatino 249, 36r (no. 5, 'Delle sirene al suono'). For a similar erotic conceit, see Rinuccini's *stanze* for Bernardi, stanza 5, in Section 3.1.4 (ii).

157 Characters which could potentially be doubled are: Linfadusa, Alfesibeo and Alcone, Satiro, Aurindo, Licandro, Licasta. It seems unlikely to have been the case for Dalinda. For doubling in the *Clorilli* production, see Section 2.4.3 and Appendix.

158 Gerbino, *Music*, 202–15; Sampson, 'Performing', '*Drammatica secreta*', and S*Pa*, 175–8.

159 'le scene pastorali si fanno tosto e vi va poca spesa, e la cosa è bella, e onorata', letter of Muzio Manfredi to Ferrante Gonzaga, 18 March 1587, in Torelli, *Partenia*, 'Introduction', 42.

160 On *commedia* actresses, see, for example, Henke, *Performance and Literature*, ch. 6; MacNeil, *Music and Women*; Kerr, *Rise of the Diva*; also Gerbino, *Music*, 194–201; and Brown, Campbell and Nicholson's 'Introduction' to Andreini, *Lovers' Debates*.

161 Solerti, *Albori*, I:54 n. 1. On Andreini's performances, see Vazzoler, 'Pastorali', 284–5.

162 In BNCF, Magl. VII, 15, referenced in MacNeil, *Music and Women*, 64–66, 300–5, also 49.

163 III.2–3. *Commedia* elements were vividly brought out by Elia Nichols (Satyr) in the 2018 *Clorilli* production; see video at 53'53"–55'28"; and Section 2.4.3.

164 'FILL. Tu non la lasciarai? Tosto 'l vedremo. / SAT. Ecco io la lascio. Ah perfida Clorilli[!]', III.3.7–8.

165 Coller, *Women*, 133–73, esp. 138–45; C*Pr*, 101, 112–4. On *theatergrams*, see Clubb, *Italian Drama*, 6–26.

166 Kirkendale, 'L'opera', 373 n. 36.

167 Chater, '"Un pasticcio"', 150; Innamorati, 'Il riuso', Henke, *Performance*, 45–9.

168 The NYU performance of *Clorilli* captured the essentially lyric pathos of Filemone by having him appear strumming a guitar, accompanying his first words (See video at 22'02").

169 Perella, *Critical Fortune*, 26–32; for erotic verse following *Clorilli* in the Marciana manuscript, see Section 2.2.3; for Bernardi's lyric verse, see Section 3.

170 Rosand, *Opera*, 361–2 (quotation), 361–86; Refini, 'Parole tronche'. See also Coller, 'Ladies'.

171 My thanks to Wendy Heller for her comments on this point. Wilbourne, *Seventeenth-Century Opera*, 61, and for *commedia dell'arte*'s influence on the operatic lament, 51–91. Compare the famous laments of the eponymous heroines in Rinuccini/Peri's *Euridice* (27 lines), and Rinuccini/Monteverdi's *Arianna* (146 lines); see Carter, 'Lamenting Ariadne?', 404 n. 24. For solo singing connected from the mid-sixteenth century especially with theatre and *commedia dell'arte*, see Newcomb, *Madrigal*, 15–9; and Nosow, 'The Debate'.

172 Rosand, *Opera*, 363.

173 Cusick, 'Not One Lady', 25, 30–35; Refini, 'Parole tronche', esp. 142–4; Wilbourne, *Seventeenth-Century Opera*, 52–4, 58–9.

174 On Archilei singing (and dancing) in a trio of female performers in the sixth of the 1589 *intermedi* (which Emilio Cavalieri and Laura Guidiccioni played a key part in creating), see Saslow, *Medici Wedding*, 157; Magini, 'Cronache', 57–8. For *Disperazione*, Palisca, 'Musical Asides', 345; Kirkendale, *Emilio de' Cavalieri*, 192. On the typically limited roles in operas for female singers before *Arianna*, see Carter, 'Lamenting Ariadne?', 401.

175 Carter, 'Lamenting Ariadne?'; on the recitative style, Tomlinson, 'Madrigal, monody', 86–95.

176 See above Sections 2.1.4 and 1.3.

177 Butters, 'Christine', 116, and 119, 137 n. 29, 141 n. 158, 160–3. For Grand Duke Ferdinando's interest in the garden design, see Luchinat and Galletti, *La villa*, 12–31.

178 Butters, 'Christine', 123, 126.

179 Cusick, *Francesca Caccini*, 39–60.

180 Bernardi's 'Voi l'oro delle stelle' highlights the name 'Flavia'; see Section 3.1.5 (iii). On Flavia Peretti, see Murphy, *Murder*, 348; Morucci, 'Poets and musicians', esp. 54–6 (Campiglia); Boerio, 'Peretti Damasceni, Flavia'; and C*Wo*, 143. See *Clorilli*, n. 101–2.

181 Fenlon, 'Golden Age'.

2.2 The Marciana manuscript of *Clorilli*

Lisa Sampson

The known works attributed to Leonora Bernardi of Lucca – a full-length pastoral play and 11 poems in different genres – collectively present an active and highly regarded cultural protagonist operating at the intersection of print, scribal and oral cultures from the 1580s until her death in 1616. This oeuvre appears shaped by dialogues across various connected cultural communities in Lucca, Ferrara and Florence in which Bernardi played a more or less visible role, as well as by social transmission further afield. However, the works also raise numerous methodological complexities in terms of determining authorship, textual agency and reception. Such issues will be explored in this section, with particular reference to the *Tragicomedia pastorale* (here entitled *Clorilli*) attributed to Bernardi on the basis of an encoded attribution in the manuscript and other strong circumstantial evidence. This long neglected play exists in a single, enigmatic codex in the Marciana Library of Venice (MS It. IX, 239 (=6999)), where it is followed by a collection of extremely heterogeneous verse by various, mostly unattributed authors, ranging from the satirical and obscene to the sacred. Her own verse and its reception also in music is discussed in more detail in Section 3. Bernardi's case is seen in this chapter as problematizing how 'women's historical identities were constructed, dramatized, and transmitted for the reader's assessment' – and also concealed.[1]

2.2.1 Authorship, anonymity and agency

Bernardi's works were evidently produced for highly exclusive audiences and settings such as courts, academies and lay religious groups, for reasons connected with her social class, her problematic status as a widow with a scandalous past, and possibly also for political reasons, as discussed in Section 1. It is therefore no surprise that only five of her poems are known to survive in print under her own name, all in anonymous or male-authored collections, though some appear unattributed in printed music part books (see Section 3). The rest of her corpus gathered in this volume, including her play – probably a small proportion of her overall output – has been found in manuscript anthologies or loose sheets, dispersed across archives and libraries from Venice and Florence to Siena. The manuscripts all appear to be scribal copies, rather than autograph manuscripts, and their compilation is complex to trace. A significant factor here is the inconsistent presentation of Bernardi's first and married names (Eleonora/Leonora/Dianora and Belatti/Bellatti/

Bellati/Bellata/Bel[l]atta), and the reversal at times of her patronymic and married name. This difficulty is compounded by the use of code for her naming in *Clorilli*, which from the outset suggests a guarded attitude to authorship by the author herself and by those who transmitted her works. On the other hand, a Sienese codex (BCIS, I.XI.11) supplies Bernardi's name for four poems which were left anonymous in printed music anthologies, following common practice (see Sections 3.1.1 and 3.2). This collection indicates the value given to Bernardi's works in some settings – and also that further works of hers could be similarly identified in the future, including perhaps her lost religious poem *Eustachio*, which may possibly be connected with the anonymous play of this title held in the Biblioteca Estense of Modena.[2] However, this mixed picture alerts us to the troubled category of 'authorship' in Bernardi's case, and to how it affects our understanding of her surviving works.

Bernardi's few attributed printed works carefully fashion an acceptable social identity mostly on the basis of her spiritual and Marian verse, authorized by male interlocutors, most notably by the renowned cleric and poet Angelo Grillo (*c.* 1557–1629).[3] By contrast, her verse transmitted anonymously in musical settings and in manuscript – including *Clorilli* – presents secular themes and sometimes witty conceits and even polemical ideas, especially on women, and it seems connected more with occasional use for musical or dramatic performance. The extent of Bernardi's agency in determining where or how her works were transmitted is, however, open to question. In her reluctance to have her work printed, Bernardi differed from many Italian women writers of her time, but she mirrors some earlier prominent aristocrats such as Vittoria Colonna and Veronica Gambara. They had eschewed this public and commercial medium for their poetry to preserve their modesty and protect them from the slur of vanity and ambition, as required by contemporary gender and class decorum.[4] Barbara Torelli's *Partenia*, the earliest documented female-authored pastoral play, prepared for a court performance in *c.* 1586, was never printed for probably the same reasons, though this was perhaps also to avoid a public critical backlash linked to contemporary neo-Aristotelian literary debates on drama.[5]

To date, *Clorilli* appears uniquely, to our knowledge, in an anonymous manuscript miscellany MS It. IX, 239 (=6999) among the Italian manuscripts of the Biblioteca Marciana, Venice.[6] The title page of this codex (M) reads from the top *16[0]3* | *Libro di diverse rime* (*Book of various verse*), with a second title beneath of *Tragicomedia Pastorale della* | *Sig.ra Xqᶜbefm Hqxmllm* | *Gentildonna luchesse* (Fig. 5). The author of the untitled 'Pastoral Tragicomedy' is thus revealed only as a 'gentlewoman from Lucca', indicating the author's gender, class and 'nation'. The nineteenth-century paper catalogue of the Italian Manuscripts Classe IX 'Poeti' tentatively ascribes the play to '(Lisabetta Coriglia?)' or Isabella Coreglia, the best-known seventeenth-century female poet of Lucca and the author of two printed pastoral plays, *Dori* (1634) and *Erindo il fido* (1650).[7] This doubtful attribution may explain why the codex had barely been consulted before I first ordered it up in 2008. Virginia Cox's deciphering of the encoded name as 'Leonora Belatta' in 2011, supported by compelling correspondences between the play and documentation on the historical woman, has since enabled important new bio-bibliographical and literary investigation on Bernardi. Further documentary finds presented in this volume on her literary career and locations (especially in Section 1) now provide firm evidence for her authorship.[8] This chapter aims to probe the question further by considering the play in light of the complex codex in which it appears. It will explore the apparently intentional secrecy surrounding its authorship in relation to the cultural system and shared conventions that underpinned the play's transcription and early reception.[9] The encoded name and the play on anonymity generally within the codex are linked to its suggested destination for a restricted and privileged 'in-group' of readers, so as to evade the scrutiny of outsiders. Anonymous works were, after all, considered suspect and banned from publication in the Pauline Index of 1559. It is argued that rhetorical and performative practices of secrecy, and themes of literary masking, simulation and dissimulation evident in the play pervade the entire codex.[10]

2.2.2 The production of the Marciana manuscript

It will be helpful to start with a description of the physical attributes of the codex in which Bernardi's play appears, and an outline of its contents, which are detailed more fully in the Appendix (2.2.5). Her *Tragicomedia Pastorale* (fols 1r–66r) presents the first and most substantial work in this complex codex of 206 leaves. This is followed directly (on the verso of the final leaf) by a miscellany of 137 unattributed poems (*diverse rime*), of which the authors hitherto identifiable are all male; they include some leading contemporaries such as Tasso, Guarini and Marino. The distinctively different final quire of the codex (fols 200–11; numbered in ink 201–212) contains a collection of 16 sonnets, eight each by the Capuchin friar Lodovico da Monte Falco (Montefalco) and Giovanni Morotti di Lucca. One further madrigal is added to the pasted back cover sheet with some corrections, making a total of 154 poems. The codex is of presentation standard for Bernardi's play and the last quire, and much of the rest of the verse. However, from fol. 144 there are inconsistencies in the original ink page numbering, and later there are various blank leaves; some leaves have also been cut out, leaving stubs.[11] (References will therefore follow the regular pencilled numbers added from fol. 157 at a later date, as explained in the Appendix.) The ruled margins of some of the blank leaves indicate that more verse was expected to fill them, since otherwise blank spaces or pages are not deliberately left in the codex (except in the last quire), apart from an empty half page after Marino's unattributed 'Canzone on a widow' ('Canzone sopra una vedova', 113, 172r). This and other internal and external factors discussed below suggest the codex was compiled as a fair copy of selected works for private use, over a period of time, perhaps from *Clorilli*'s surmised performance in the early 1590s to around the 1620s, but was abandoned still incomplete. It lacks any paratexts and an index.

The quarto codex is in good condition, though there is a little evidence of wear on the title page and on the page edges. The parchment cover seems to be original and has been secured at the top and bottom with a blue and yellow cord; the bottom cord has been torn, leaving a small hole on the cover. Some restoration to the inside spine has been undertaken more recently. The codex has a glued-on front cover sheet; the leaves are mostly in octave gatherings, though the final quire is of 12 leaves and appears to have been inserted at a later stage before the last leaf, which is glued to the back cover. Some unidentifiable traces of writing on the top right of the verso of the final leaf of this quire (211v) indicate that a different sheet from the existing back cover had originally followed it, perhaps a coversheet or letter accompanying the verse. A supplementary loose sheet folded as a bi-folio summarizing the contents was evidently inserted at a later date inside the back (or front) cover. This list is in the hand of Marco Forcellini, and matches the description of M in his 1748–9 catalogue of the manuscripts of the Venetian book collector Apostolo Zeno (1668–1750).[12]

The paper and hands indicate that the final quire of the codex was prepared in a separate context, though the leaves were bound together at the same time. The paper used for fols numbered 1–199 (the tragicomedy and a collection of *rime* following) is yellowy and a little worn round the edges, and measures 207 × 156mm. The quality is reasonable, but not exceptional, suggesting private use. Occasionally, there is a slight bleeding through of ink from the other side, though this does not affect legibility. The watermark presents a cross in outline in an ovoid, which was common in northern Italy around the turn of the seventeenth century, and is similar to examples from Lucca 1612 and Turin 1650. It appears regularly across the centre binding, as consistent with the quarto format.[13] The paper used for the final quire (fols numbered 200–11), however, appears slightly lighter in colour and has a watermark which, in addition to the cross, gives also the initials 'A' and 'E' below. This watermark bears strong similarities with ones recorded in Lucca 1618–28, which coincides with the internal indications of this quire's composition.[14] This last section – the only one which names authors and patrons who are connected to Lucca, as detailed below – includes a blank folio coversheet and the two connected sonnet collections, each set of verse being separated by a folio title page (unlike the verse in the rest of the codex).

At least two different and unidentified transcribing hands (A and B) are evident within the codex itself (excluding the loose bi-folio). Neither appears consistent with the sample of Bernardi's hand in the single known autograph letter (Fig. 4). Hand A, which transcribes the majority (if not all) of the codex (fols 1r–199v), including the play, *rime* and sheet pasted on the back cover, has a differently angled slant from Bernardi's, and in the lower parts the 'g' and 'p' are also differently formed, as is the capital 'D'. This non-match is predictable, since hand A was apparently still transcribing verse in the codex in or after 1612 (a *canzone* commemorates Battista Guarini's death that year), by which time Bernardi had largely retreated from public life and may also have lost her sight.[15] Given the explicit eroticism (heterosexual and homosexual), the violent satire and sacrilegious content of some of the verse that directly follows the play, as discussed below, it seems more plausible that this hand was that of an educated male.

Hand A transcribes the play in a practised and relatively elegant humanistic cursive, with swash capitals and small pen flourishes at the endings of some scenes and acts (see Figs 6–9). This transcription indicates the scribe's Tuscan and possibly Lucchese origins through its linguistic features; it is neatly presented and is generally precise. The few corrections that have been made mainly consist of minor transcription errors emended by the inscribing hand, such as letters or words added discreetly in small letters above an insert mark in the text, occasional erasures or strikethroughs, as indicated in the notes to the critical edition (Section 2.3). In the poetry that follows there is more variability in hand A in terms of size and formation, especially as the layout can be uneven and sometimes cramped. This is in part necessitated by having to accommodate many different genres of verse (from longer *capitoli* and octave stanzas to brief madrigals), but the hand also occasionally

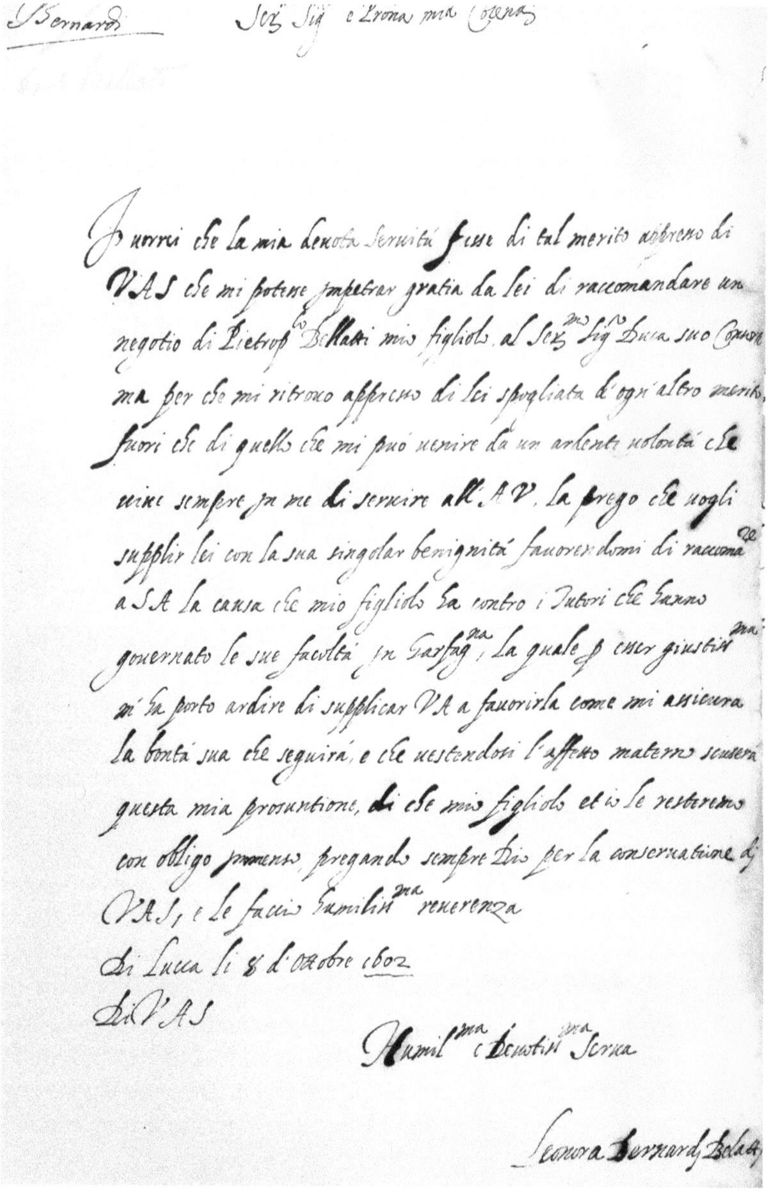

Bernardi

Ser.ma Sig.ra e Prona mia Col.ma

Io vorrei che la mia devota servitù fusse di tal merito appresso di V.A.S. che mi potesse impetrar gratia da lei di raccomandare un negotio di Pietro Paolo Bellati mio figliolo al Ser.mo Sig.r Duca suo Consorte ma per che mi ritrovo appresso di lei spogliata d'ogni altro merito, fuori che di quello che mi può venire da un ardente volontà che vive sempre in me di servire all'A.V. la prego che vogli supplir lei con la sua singolar benignità favorendomi di raccomandare a S.A. la causa che mio figliolo ha contro i Tutori che hanno governato le sue facoltà in Garfag.na, la quale per esser giustissima mi ha porto ardire di supplicar V.A. a favorirla come mi assicura la bontà sua che seguirà, e che vestendosi l'affetto materno scuserà questa mia prosuntione, di che mio figliolo et io le resteremo con obligo perenne, pregando sempre Dio per la conservatione di V.A.S., e le faccio humilissima reverenza

Di Lucca li 8 d'ottobre 1602

Di V.A.S.

Humil.ma e devotiss.ma Serva

Leonora Bernardi Bellati

Figure 4 Archivio Estense, Cancelleria, Carteggi e documenti di particolari 107 (Bellati) [*sic*]: autograph letter from Leonora Bernardi Belatti to Virginia de' Medici of 8 October 1602. With permission from the Ministero della Cultura – Archivio di Stato di Modena, prot. no. 2516, 27 October 2022. Reproduction prohibited.

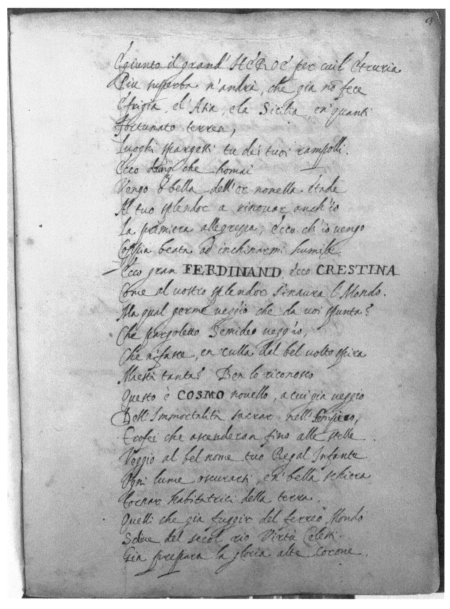

Figure 6 The prologue of [Leonora Bernardi, *Clorilli*], Venice, Biblioteca Marciana, MS It. IX, 239 (=6999), fol. 3r. With permission from the Ministero della Cultura – Biblioteca Nazionale Marciana, prot. 1501-28.10.13/3, 13 July 2021. Reproduction prohibited.

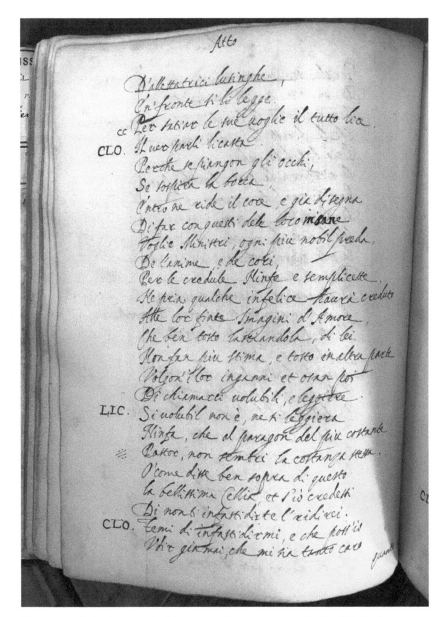

Figure 7 Distinctive marginal features in [Leonora Bernardi, *Clorilli*], Venice, Biblioteca Marciana, MS It. IX, 239 (=6999), fol. 24v. With permission from the Ministero della Cultura – Biblioteca Nazionale Marciana, prot. 1501-28.10.13/3, 13 July 2021. Reproduction prohibited.

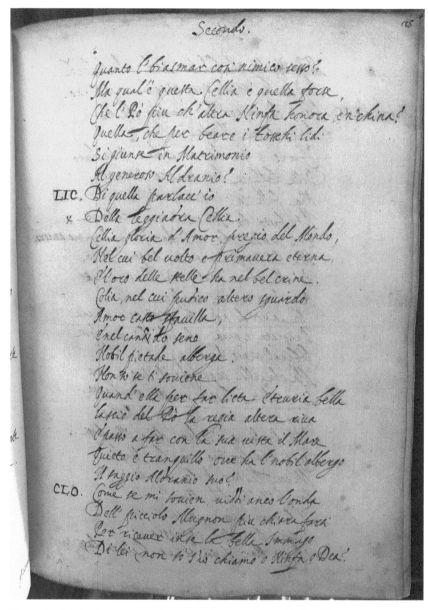

Figure 8   Distinctive marginal feature in [Leonora Bernardi, *Clorilli*], Venice, Biblioteca Marciana, MS It. IX, 239 (=6999), fol. 25r. With permission from the Ministero della Cultura – Biblioteca Nazionale Marciana, prot. 1501-28.10.13/3, 13 July 2021. Reproduction prohibited.

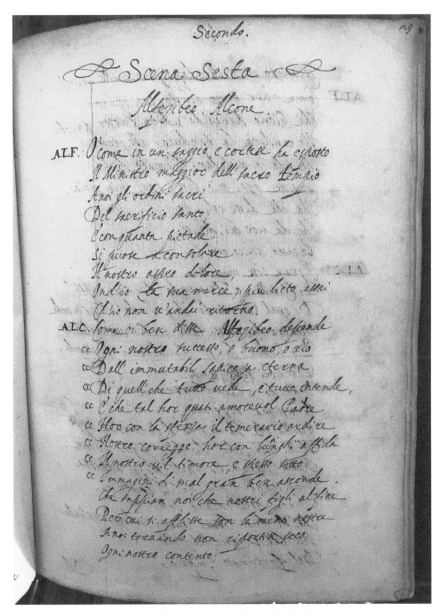

Figure 9 Distinctive marginal features and spelling of 'Alfezibeo' in [Leonora Bernardi, *Clorilli*], Venice, Biblioteca Marciana, MS It. IX, 239 (=6999), fol. 29r. With permission from the Ministero della Cultura – Biblioteca Nazionale Marciana, prot. 1501-28.10.13/3, 13 July 2021. Reproduction prohibited.

betrays signs of hurried transcription or fatigue, and may have changed over time; ink colours also vary. Differences are particularly noticeable in the sonnet commemorating a 'great' Lucchese military figure ('gran Sarti') (100), which may have been added at a later phase – or even by a different hand. The last sheet pasted onto the back cover, also by hand A, provides a correction (a missing tercet from the third poem 'Testamento di mecenate'),[16] a gloss to an occasional detail in the second *Imeneo* (84) and an additional madrigal, though intriguingly two lines at the bottom of the leaf are heavily cancelled and illegible.

For the play text, pencil-ruled margins have been used consistently (top 19 mm, left-hand *c.* 39 mm), and the format generally resembles a printed edition, though there is no indication that the manuscript was meant for this purpose. There are regular ruled lines (25 to a page), and running heads at the top of the folios with 'Atto' on the recto and the act number (e.g. 'Primo') on the facing verso. The ruled margins continue to be used also for the verse, though, as noted, the line layout is more variable. Catchwords are provided at the bottom of the verso of each folio where the following leaf contains writing. Ink numbering appears consistently at the top right of the recto for the first 143 folios (including all of the play). This continues, with a probably accidental omission of fols 144–9, through to fol. 156, which completes a gathering, and follows the sonnet commemorating Sarti (fol. 155v). Thereafter the numbering stops for four quires (157–64; 165–72; 173–80; 181–6).[17] As discussed below, these quires present some occasional verse with strong Venetian connections (nos 103–6, 108) and, strikingly, 11 poems by the polemical and highly mobile poet Giambattista Marino (1569–1625) (found in the grouping 112–23), of which most were still unprinted by 1612 and some censored beyond the 1620s.[18] Ink numbering only reappears on fol. 186v (numbered as 157) at the start of a section of religious verse, and again from fol. 199 (ink numbered as 200), just before the final quire of religious verse. This may suggest that the unnumbered folios between the ink numbers 156 and 157 (=187) were a later and more sensitive addition, and might also explain the blank pages.

Sententiae are marked in the play by using the *diple* (") in the left-hand margin at the mid-level of each line of text, observing contemporary usage (Figs 7 and 9).[19] This practice of highlighting notable sayings or references to other authoritative works was introduced in print with Aldo Manuzio's edition of Valerius Maximus's *Dictorum et factorum memorabilium* (1502), based on an earlier Greek manuscript tradition. It was widely used, for example, in Giovanni Battista Ciotti's edition of Guarini's *Pastor fido* (Venice, 1602) and outside Italy in Sir Philip

Sidney's *The Countesse of Pembrokes Arcadia* printed for W. Ponsonbie (London, 1590).[20] Occasionally, a small cross (×) also appears at the left margin, presumably as a highlight, such as for the mention of the *à clef* figure Cellia (surmised to be Marfisa d'Este) (Fig. 8). A sign resembling an upwards slanting '=' with two parallel dots above and below seems to indicate set-piece occasional speeches which may have been added, or omitted, for particular occasions (Fig. 7). Capitalization is used in the play to highlight names of key figures, especially the Medici Grand Dukes Ferdinando I and Christine of Lorraine, and Cosimo de' Medici (Fig. 6). The verse that follows the play text similarly uses capitalization and flourishes, as well as headings at various points.

The clearly identifiable second hand (B) is more professional and limited to the final quire of 12 folios. This is distinctly more elegant and formal, and the verse appears also more spaced out, with only a sonnet per page, compared to the preceding pages, where sonnets frequently appear on the page with a madrigal. This hand may be that of the unknown Scipione Massucchi, who signs his name on a separate leaf following the verse as 'the most humble servant of Signor Antonio Sarti' ('Del Sig.r Ant[oni]o Sarti humiliss[im]o S[servito]re', 211r). In any case, the scribe presumably had some connection with the religious or cultural circles of the poets of this verse, or with Sarti, the apparent dedicatee of this collection – if not with the volume itself at some stage (which would explain the above-mentioned verse commemorating 'gran Sarti', no. 100). The figures named in the final quire of M strengthen the hypothesis of a Lucchese provenance. Antonio Sarti is probably the gentleman and captain from Lucca of this name who was long in military service for Venice, serving also in Flanders and Hungary as a military architect possibly from 1592; he published treatises on the subject in 1628–30.[21] Morotti was a cleric with some history of dissent, but by 1605 he held the position of prior at S. Pietro [Pier] Somaldi in Lucca. Besides his spiritual sonnets in M, written in response to Montefalco's, he also wrote a secular poem (an *Imeneo*) published in Lucca.[22] In 1599 he was himself the dedicatee of a dialogue printed in Lucca (*Il Chiariti*) featuring the local intellectual Domenico Chiariti, who was a great admirer and publicist of Bernardi after she returned to the city that year (see Section 1.2.6). As we will see, the naming of Sarti and Morotti in the codex helps to place the production of the manuscript at least partly in Lucca, accounting for the interest in *Clorilli* and the presence of military and religious themes in the verse. The connection with Chiariti, who is described as 'an excellent musician' ('musico eccellente') – as Bernardi was herself – may also explain the significant number of poems in the codex which were popular in musical settings.[23] These include various poems set as madrigals for collective singing in parts, as commonly practised in many academies and *ridotti*, as well as texts suitable for solo singing to instrumental accompaniment in octave stanzas or *terza rima*, or lighter strophic *canzonette*.[24]

The dating of the codex remains conjectural, especially since it seems to have been compiled over a period of time. The title page gives '16[0]3'; a small hole appears towards the top of the '0', but the date is confirmed by an eighteenth-century catalogue listing the codex.[25] However, at the end of the unpaginated section of M a *canzone* (124) mourns the death of the poet and pastoral dramatist Battista Guarini ('In morte del S[ignore] Cavalier Guerini', 178r–182r), providing a *terminus post quem* of 1612. If we take 1603 as the date for the transcription of *Clorilli* – as noted, the first work in the codex – it would indicate its interest to some readers, and possibly also performers, some 11 years or more after its hypothesized preparation for performance in the early 1590s to celebrate the birth or baptism of Cosimo II de' Medici (respectively, in 1590 or 1592) as alluded to in the prologue (see Section 2.1.4). Noticeably, the play is stripped of any dedicatory or paratextual material, including gratulatory verse, which typically accompanied plays in print at least (but also Torelli's manuscript *Partenia*), and provided a sort of social and poetic shield. Such materials might potentially have been compromising for the repurposing of the text in a different political-cultural milieu such as Lucca, though, as noted, Medici rulers are visibly named (Fig. 6), notwithstanding the long history of hostility between the republic and the grand duchy.

It is not known what prompted this transcription of *Clorilli*. One possible explanation may be the compiler's desire to acquaint a new audience with Bernardi's play, or to engage with it afresh, perhaps in response to literary and musical interests, or personal and occasional circumstances. As detailed in Section 1, in 1603 Bernardi seems to have been at the height of her fame in her native Lucca, where she hosted a *ridotto* at her house attended by male poets and clerics – besides receiving visitors in her country villa, including the wife of the political exile Orazio Lucchesini. It is possible that *Clorilli* was at least read aloud or circulated in such a context, just like Guarini's *Pastor fido* was for years before being printed in 1589/90. Only later in the following year did Bernardi make her apparently dramatic decision to withdraw to a more secluded religious life (see Sections 1.2.6–7). Another possible context for transmitting Bernardi's play in 1603 was Siena. Chiariti had close connections there with Belisario Bulgarini of the Intronati academy, which reopened that year on the order of Grand Duke Ferdinando de' Medici. Bulgarini and other Sienese elites had a strong interest in pastoral, and performed Guarini's *Pastor fido* c.1592–3. Members of the Sienese Filomeli academy also published Bernardi's *canzonetta* 'Più d'altra ninfa amata' anonymously in a musical anthology in 1603, and her madrigals were evidently circulated and prized too.[26] However, the verse in M suggests that this date may be more significant for specific local political and military factors, which would explain the connection with Sarti and celebration also of other military heroes and battles. That year marked the conclusion of a second phase of wars (1601–3) between the Lucchesi and their powerful rivals, the Estensi (supported by the Medici), over bitterly disputed border territories in the Garfagnana, which were mediated by Spanish Milan.[27] Bernardi's connections with elite literary circles celebrating her in Lucca, as well as in Estense territories (where her son resided in the border town of Castelnuovo; see Fig. 1), in Florence and Massa, may hint at a more sensitive political reason why she is identified only in code and as 'Gentildonna luchesse'.[28]

2.2.3 The *diverse rime*

To fully understand *Clorilli*'s transcription and transmission we must consider its relationship with the *diverse rime* directly following it in the same hand in M. This anonymous verse lacks any obvious organizational principle besides that of *varietas*, ranging significantly in genre, content and register. Even so, the selection and placement of the verse, its themes, authors, and the more or less evident geographical and social allusions give some clues to the milieu of its reception. The poems are identified and sometimes clustered by genre (such as madrigals or sonnets), and on two occasions by language (Sicilian octaves, and Venetian sonnets and *canzoni*), and secular and religious poetry are separated. Excluding the final quire of 16 sonnets, there are: 55 sonnets (including six satirical tailed sonnets – *sonetti caudati*); 39 madrigals (including four spiritual ones and one secular one on the back coversheet); 14 *canzoni*; 9 poems in octave stanzas (two as single *strambotti*); 6 longer poems in *terza rima* (such as *capitoli* and *epistole*); and a few poems in lighter, performance-oriented forms popular by the turn of the seventeenth century, such as *ottave siciliane*, *canzonette*, *villanelle* and *balletti*. The secular verse often moves brusquely from love lyric to commemoration of death and marriage, political figures and events, religious satire and explicit eroticism; then, after a series of blank leaves there is a noticeable spiritual turn, starting with a series of madrigals for the Virgin (from fol. 186v). The more decent poetry in this eclectic selection reflects conventional themes of poetic anthologies around then and suggests its predominantly social use for a restricted audience with shared experiences and poetic tastes.[29] Such tastes evidently encompassed varied and relatively new forms such as spiritual madrigals and lighter popular ones, as well as pastoral, sensual and bizarre subjects in the emerging Baroque style, and political satire, poetic parody and censored (or self-censored) texts, which explain the interesting play on naming and anonymity in the codex.

As noted, all the verse in M is anonymous, apart from in the final quire in hand B, which complicates identification of the authorship. The Appendix (2.2.5) identifies verse where possible, though acknowledging the scope for further investigation. What has been identified of the 138 poems in hand A reveals that by 1612 (when Guarini died) only relatively few existed in named printed poetic editions or anthologies datable from around 1550 (17 per cent, or 24 poems), with 6 per cent, or 8 poems seemingly only in music part books. Textual variants, including playful reworkings (*rifacimenti*), are frequently introduced, though these are beyond the scope of this study to detail. This inclusion suggests that the compiler(s) had privileged access to texts circulating only in manuscript which could be more freely rewritten. Their manuscript status may have been connected with use for reserved performance, but in other cases seems due to its problematic content, as for the verse of Maffio Venier (1550–86) and Marino.[30] A little over half of the *rime* copied by hand A are currently of unidentified authorship (79 poems).

As in Bernardi's play, many of the references to names also remain highly elusive. The verse section opens with an 'Epistola di A. S. alla Signora F. H.' (1), possibly by Antonio Sarti, as a *rifacimento* of a manuscript poem by the Florentine Giulio Dati composed in 1593.[31] The same dedicatee seems to be implied in a later verse opening a new section after some blank leaves: 'Lettera alla S. F. H' (112), which this time re-addresses a 'Lettera amorosa' by Marino. Several poems reference female beloveds with highlighted *senhals*, following a longstanding lyric practice. The most frequent is 'Faustina', who may be identified with the Signora F. H. of these two epistles, perhaps the beloved of Sarti. A series of five poems near the start evoke variations of FAUSTINA (7, 9–12), and three more later evoke Fausta (13, 54, 94). The same woman may be the implied poetic interlocutor FA of four poems (25, 27, 29, 33), whose name is again inserted into existing madrigals by Girolamo Parabosco (27, 33) and an octave by Guarini (29), where FA (perhaps 'Fausta') replaces 'donna' (line 2). The *rime* also feature Lara (59), Viola (50) and Anna (116), potentially beloveds or courtesans.[32] This use of coded names or initials – which contrasts overtly with the encomiastic, highlighted full names of historic male or female patricians or aristocrats in other poems – suggests a teasing concealment to reinforce shared coterie connections. This practice was, for instance, cultivated in the printed familiar letters of Parabosco, who frequented Venetian *ridotti*, and later Giovanni Brusoni, a member of the libertine and all-male Accademia degli Incogniti.[33]

The verse is not arranged chronologically. The *canzone* (61) describing the elaborate festivities for the coronation in 1597 of the Venetian Dogaressa Morosina Morosini, the wife of Doge Marino Grimani (the date is added to M later in pencil), appears some pages after the sonnet marking the death of Philip II of Spain in 1598 (24). Even so, one can detect some shifts in poetic tastes and forms over the collection. The earlier part of M features various poems by mid-century poets, especially where madrigals and sonnets largely alternate (14–67); many of these were still set to music in the later century. Most prominently featured, with eight secular madrigals printed 1550–1, is the poet and musician Girolamo Parabosco (*c.* 1524–57).[34] Four of these were also discussed in his fictional dialogue *I diporti* (1551) in Day Three, which evokes the elite literary circle of Domenico Venier in Venice.[35] At least two (21, 35) are known to have been set to music well into the seventeenth century, including by leading composers such as Giaches de Wert and Philippe de (Filippo di) Monte, who had a specific interest in Bernardi's verse – Monte was also close to Medici–Orsini and imperial circles.[36] A tailed sonnet (*sonetto caudato*) in Venetian dialect references Parabosco ('Potta no mi divento una Zoeta', 76) among a series of verses by the satirical poet Maffio Venier, nephew of Domenico, both of whom at different times attended the latter's circle, which included musicians and literati. Another fairly prominent, mid-century poet is the Neapolitan Luigi Tansillo (1510?–68), who had close connections with members of the Accademia Fiorentina and whose poems were also very popular with musicians from the 1570s to well into the seventeenth century, including Wert and Monte. His verse is mostly presented in a cluster of three sonnets (95, 97–8), though, unusually, the first ('Valli nemiche, al sol superbe rupi', 95) appears also in a variant form earlier ('Valli profonde al sol nimiche rupi', 20), possibly reflecting copies made from manuscript editions or different musical settings. This verse may have been adapted by the Florentine Ottavio Rinuccini for his pastoral opera *Euridice* (1600) and was set to music in 1615 by Rinuccini's compatriot (and fellow librettist) Marco da Gagliano.[37]

Two further notable contemporary Tuscan poets figure in the *rime*. Giovanni della Casa (1503–56) – typically admired for his grave poetry – is here represented by an obscene, burlesque tailed sonnet (40) probably composed in the 1530s, and a sonnet (67), neither of which were printed in his lifetime. A famous sonnet by Francesco Beccuti 'il Coppetta' (d. 1553) ('Locar sopra li abbissi e' fondamenti') uniquely appears in two near-identical versions contiguously (134–5) in the closing section of spiritual verse (125–36). Intriguingly, this sonnet by Coppetta, which was very popular with composers in the late-sixteenth century for its 'sweet' quality, was valued less highly than della Casa's grave sonnets by Tasso's mouthpiece in his dialogue on Tuscan poetry *La Cavaletta*. This suggests an oppositional stance to Tasso in M, which, as we shall see, was noticeable also towards his verse in the *Diverse rime*.[38]

M thus indicates a taste for poetry for music from Venice, Tuscany and, to some extent, Naples and the South, areas where Bernardi's texts circulated independently among musicians (see Section 3.2). Various poetic texts suggest links also with contemporary poets and musicians active in Venice, the Florentine court or private academies, and possibly Siena (92).[39] The opening poem, 'Epistola di A. S. alla Signora F. H.' ('Epistle by A. S. to Signora F. H.'), for instance, seems to repurpose the poem 'Quintilio ad Anna' by Giulio Dati, a poet associated with Florentine literary-musical circles and pleasure companies in the 1590s, which included the poet and librettist Ottavio Rinuccini (1563–1621) and influential music patron Jacopo Corsi.[40] The poem was evidently known in various Florentine manuscripts, which suggests that M's compiler was aware of innovations and perhaps had direct private and personal channels of textual transmission.[41] Even more striking is the inclusion of several unprinted poems by the above-mentioned Venetian satirist Maffio Venier, best known now for his violent and obscene poetic exchange with the courtesan Veronica Franco in the 1570s.[42] At least eight poems of his appear in a cluster of sonnets and *canzoni* 'in Venetian' ('in lingua venetiana', 75–83) on rustic, earthy subjects, plus (likely) an obscene poem of his (108), all circulating only in manuscript. His Tuscan *canzone* on Saint Francis (131), included among the religious verse, was, however, printed from 1586.

By contrast, the Ferrarese poets Tasso and Guarini play a relatively less prominent part in M, despite their predominance in Italian lyric production from the 1580s to early 1600s and their pioneering of the lighter madrigal form (see Section 2.1.2). Only two poems by Guarini are included, both popular with musicians: his octave ('Mentr'io v'adoro', 29) has been reworked to accommodate 'FA', while the madrigal ('La bella man vi stringo', 45) was set by 14 musicians, including Monte (1593) and Giulio Caccini (1614); both also set a madrigal by Bernardi (Section 3.2.2). Interestingly, Guarini is also memorialized in association with

Venice, where he died, in a lengthy *canzone* (124) by Girolamo Priuli, apparently a Venetian senator.[43] Tasso is represented by a sole sonnet (32), despite being the leading poet of the time and his *Aminta* heavily influencing Bernardi's *Clorilli*. Notably, this sonnet was even marked specifically as being anonymous (by 'incerto') in the anthology *Scelta di rime* (1591). His *Gerusalemme liberata* also appears to be paradoxically evoked in an unidentified sonnet (16) which adapts the imagery from a key erotic scene of the epic, describing the enchantress Armida's self-adornment, to reference a nymph with skin disease.[44]

Tasso's single sonnet ('Insegna a te la tua gran Patria Roma') seems to have been chosen to match the political emphases of the *rime*.[45] It celebrates the military campaign in Paris (1589) of Alessandro Farnese, duke of Parma and governor of Flanders, who was married to Margaret of Austria, the natural daughter of Emperor Charles V. This fits with Lucca's policy of seeking support from Spain in its campaigns against Estense and Florentine aggression, and it may further explain the inclusion of verse by the Neapolitan Tansillo and Sicilian octaves. As mentioned, a sonnet honourably commemorates King Philip II of Spain's death (24). Yet one also finds a satirical and parodic 'Pater noster against the Spanish' (where the words of the prayer are limited to initial letters) – an imprecation to be rid of the foreign occupiers, described as lascivious and avaricious *maranos*.[46] In a similar vein, an unidentified sonnet (30), 'Il perder non fu mai laudabil cosa' ('Losing was never praiseworthy'), critiques the disastrous imperial campaigns and 'fortress war' in Hungary against the Turks (1595–1601) (in which Sarti may have taken part). It describes the siege of Canissa (Kanizsa, 1601) in terms of 'pricks' (*CAZZI*) alongside the 'balls' (*COGLIONI*) of the earlier defeat at Buda (1541). This sonnet wittily recasts the proemial lines of a canto from the Ferrarese Ariosto's *Orlando furioso* (XV.1.1–4), about the glory of bloodless victories, aptly recalling the poet's refusal to serve the Estense in Hungary – and perhaps his earlier governance of the Garfagnana. The closing allegorical references to genitalia for political satire evoke the Sienese academician Antonio Vignali's polemical *La cazzaria* (*The Book of the Prick*) (c. 1526), which was still covertly circulating, as well as the more generalized use of sexualized language for invective by upper-class intellectual men.[47]

Various poems in M are violently anti-clerical. Some may have been composed in circles in Lucca, where local clergy had been involved in recent clashes between the republican government and Rome; others were likely in response to the Venetian Interdict of 1606–7. For instance, the fourth poem, a prayer (*Suplica*) in *terzine* ('Scappato signor mio di pacienza', 4), apparently by Giovanni Serragli, a composer of Florentine *canti carnascialeschi* (carnival songs) found in a Roman manuscript, laments explicitly the vices and sexual frustrations of a cleric given over to 'bestial love' ('Amor alla bestiale', 79v). It parodies Petrarchan conceits, referencing desired erotic encounters, the fear of syphilis (*malfrancese*), sodomy and other abuses. In this respect, M can be linked with other manuscript codices produced at the margins of respectable society, or in private elite circles such as that of Domenico Venier, which present political satire, sensual and obscene verse relating to males as well as females, and burlesque poetry in the style of Franceso Berni or Antonio Da Molin ('Burchiella').[48] Marino's sonnet 'Fosti Città d'ogni citta fenice' (121) directly excoriates Rome and was put on the 1664 Index, together with his *Adone* (1623).[49]

Marino's sonnet appears in the unpaginated section of M, from 157r to the *canzone* commemorating Guarini's death in 1612, 178r–[182r] (poems 103–24), which was, as noted, possibly added later and comprises some more risqué verse. This section turns away from madrigals and features verse especially by the preeminent Baroque poet Marino – seven sonnets, a *canzone*, octave stanzas, a verse epistle and a *canzonetta* (a recent, popular lighter form) (112–9, 121–3) – as well as a sonnet (120) by his sometime friend Claudio Achillini (1574–1640), employed in Ferrara in 1609–21. Both poets were active in Farnese Parma in the early 1600s.[50] Much of Marino's verse in M was printed in his *La lira III* (Venice, 1614), but may have been transcribed earlier as his verse circulated widely in manuscript in academy and courtly contexts.[51] His obscene 'Amor, che meco a la noturna impresa' (known as 'Duello amoroso', 123) was suppressed from most of Ciotti's later editions from the following year.[52] As Virginia Cox has observed, Marino's verse spearheaded the 'rule-breaking' Baroque movement; this offered fresh opportunities for male elites to transgress norms of 'profeminist gallantry [that] had been the default polite gender pose for so long'.[53] It is known for challenging conventions of decorous Petrarchan poetry, with its witty conceits and 'irregularity', frank sensuality, political critique and anti-feminism, aspects all evident in his verse in the codex. Musicians would also appreciate the sonority of Marino's verse; the sonnet included by Achillini was set to music by Claudio Monteverdi.[54]

By contrast, the last part of the *Diverse rime* (fols 186v–199v), which follows four blank leaves, includes only religious and moral verse. It starts with a series of four unidentified madrigals honouring the Virgin (125–8) – the particular object of Lucchese cult from 1588 (Section 1.2.4). Given Bernardi's famed verse on this subject (Section 3.1.2), it is possible that at least some of these are hers, especially the last two, which have musical references and are somewhat shorter – though this would not indicate her authorized transmission.[55] The identified spiritual verse in M includes works by two poets with some Medici connections. Three are by the spiritual poet Marcantonio Laparelli of Cortona (d. 1591), posthumously printed in 1618 and dedicated to the grand duchess of Florence, Christine of Lorraine. These poems contemplate human wretchedness, death, the corruption of the body and faith (129, 130, 133). A *canzone* by the restless Venetian Maffio Venier (131), in service at the Medici court in 1574–5 and close to Bianca Cappello, grand duchess from 1578, describes St Francis retreating from the world to Mount Vernia (Tuscany) to follow Christ.[56] The evocation of this saint, the spiritual model for the Capuchins, sets the tone for the closing lean, virtuosic Christocentric sonnets of the codex, initiated by the friar Lorenzo da Montefalco. These are in the 'hypermannerist form' of the *sonetto continuo*, using only two or three repeated rhyme words (*vita*, *morte*, *croce*) in different alternating combinations, sometimes two in the same line.[57]

2.2.4 Reception and transmission of *Clorilli* (Florence, Lucca and Venice)

To return to our initial questions, what light does the Marciana manuscript throw on authorship and textual agency in relation to the *Tragicomedia* (*Clorilli*), and what can we deduce from the *rime* that follow? It is possible that Bernardi authorized the copying of her play for coterie scribal publication; as noted, some of the verse found in M may also have been hers – in this case, most likely the unidentified spiritual madrigals, or the more serious encomiastic and occasional verse.[58] Potentially, she could even have ventriloquized a male voice to introduce some slight sensuality, as in the case of the actress-poet Isabella Andreini. Bernardi's status and social milieu in Counter-Reformation Lucca makes this improbable, though in highly reserved settings sensual verse had very occasionally been dedicated to aristocratic female patrons, or even sung by them.[59] Given the explicitly risqué nature of some of the verse in M it seems highly implausible that Bernardi was directly involved with its preparation. More likely, her play was socially transmitted by other agents ('user publication').[60] These agents were almost certainly men, functioning within all-male contexts where the author and her work could be recognized, despite her encoded name.

Such a scenario would explain the inclusion of some verse in M which suggests an oblique response to *Clorilli*, both playful and critical.

The above-mentioned variant of the octave by Guarini (29) for FA, for instance, converts Clorilli's claim for autonomy to Armilla (III.1.25–39) to a more conventional male lover's complaint of self-loss:

> . . .   son vostro, o mio?
> Se mio son pur, perché di me non vivo,
> E vivo in voi; sì che me stesso oblio?

> . . .   *am I yours or mine?*
> *If I am my own, why do I not live for myself,*
> *and live in you; so that I forget myself?*[61]

A poem in octaves, 'Ninfa gentil' (85) (which appears in a Florentine manuscript miscellany), also seems to develop aspects of the drama that take place between Filemone and Clorilli, especially after her rejection in Act 3 has driven him to suicide offstage. The lovers in the verse in turn collapse in grief, recover and, on seeing the other apparently lifeless, drive a spear into their breast, but are cured by a passing hunter and bound in matrimony.[62] This verse is, however, followed in M by further octave stanzas 'by the same male author' ('l'istesso autore') describing the bizarre scenario of a male lover being spattered with his beloved's hymeneal blood at the peak of their passion, resulting in conceits bordering on blasphemy (86). Notably, *Clorilli*'s striking pro-feminist arguments in the *à clef* scene of Cellia (Act 2, scene 5) find a suggestive counterpart in Marino's 'A te che sola sei' ('Lettera alla S[ignora] F. H', 112). In accusing his beloved of bad faith ('nera fede', 163v), the jealous male speaker here echoes Filemone's sentiments (III.6; IV.3) and significantly reverses Cellia's warning to women (II.5) by presenting the naïve male lover tossed on an insidious sea of fickle (*volubili*) waves of female infidelity (166r, 167r). Finally, the inclusion of Marino's sensuous *canzone* ('Quest'animata notte', 113), on a darkly mysterious widow, and his obscene 'Duello amoroso' (123) deploring women's inconstancy ('sesso incostante', 177v),[63] may reflect further personalized responses by the compiler(s) of M to Bernardi and her work, perhaps reacting hostilely to her literary sociability and fame in Lucca (see Section 1.2.6) and alluding to the scandalous accusations made against her. Such a scenario was not uncommon, even for aristocratic women writers, performers or literary patrons.[64]

It has been suggested so far that the authors, themes and styles in the *diverse rime* point to the codex's use within a close-knit, reserved, male community – for social at least as much as poetic reasons. However, it remains hard to pinpoint this community, given the considerable regional and stylistic diversity of the verse, and the emphasis on anonymity and secrecy. Some clues may, however, be found in the conspicuous or semi-concealed use of names and other occasional references, especially at key parts of the codex.[65]

In this respect, Lucca and Venice form privileged poles, though a Florentine context is also suggested initially with *Clorilli* and in the religious verse. Lucca is, as noted, specifically evoked from the title page (where the *Tragicomedia*'s author is presented as a 'gentildonna Lucchesse') and at the end with Giovanni Morotti (206r). A nuptial verse (*Imeneo*, 84) references Lucca metonymically through the river Serchio, which is capitalized as a highlight, alongside playful references to the bride (possibly Giulia Nobili de' Cantarini).[66] More noticeably, Lucca is also evoked in a military context, both from a civilian perspective and through the commemoration of its war heroes. The sixth verse, a *capitolo*, describes the 'incredible spectacle' ('spettacolo stupendo', 87v) of the military gathered in the streets of Lucca, with young soldiers (including Genoese and Spaniards) dressed for battle in their fine dress and plumes, after which battle ensues, with frightening blasts. Later poems celebrate various heroes: the 'wise warrior' ('Saggio guerrier', 155v) Sarti is mourned in a sonnet (100) which mentions his invincibility and ability to overcome the strong and disarm fortresses, perhaps referencing Antonio's father Colonel Giovanni Andrea Sarti, who was in military service at least from 1570.[67] The sonnet 'O Lucchesin[i], you twice held at bay / the Estense enemy' ('Stringesti o luchesin due volte il freno / Dell'estense inimico', no. 26, 99r) likely refers to Jacopo Lucchesini, who played a heroic role during the wars in the Garfagnana territories in 1602–3, for which he was richly recognized by the republic; and perhaps also to Salvator Lucchesini, who similarly played a key role in the final phase of the Garfagnana war against Modena in 1613.[68] The 'defender of the fatherland' (line 12) is praised for brilliantly defeating the fierce opponents from the 'mountain' (presumably Montenero at the pass of Monteperpoli) through his sword and prudence (*consiglio*). It is worthy of note that another significant member of this family, Orazio Lucchesini, had been involved in the war on the other side, through espionage, and was connected with Bernardi during her time in Florence in the late 1580s. Orazio Lucchesini had been married to the Lucchese poet and singer Laura Guidiccioni, but was exiled by Lucca in 1593 as a Medici informer, and again formally in 1595 for his involvement in the failed Antelminelli conspiracy against Lucca. However, his second wife evidently had contact with Bernardi, perhaps through being related by marriage to the latter's son (Pierpaolo Belatti).[69]

The *rime* also suggest strong Venetian connections alongside the Tuscan. Besides claiming Guarini in relation to Venice (124), several other members of leading patrician families of the Republic (like the Venier, Valier and Morosini) are referenced visibly through textual highlights. The closing epigram (137), the sole verse in Latin in the codex, is addressed to Alvise Giustinian 'Morani Provisorem', recalling his role as governor (*provveditore*) in 1598–1601 of the key military fort and fishing village of Marano on the north-eastern frontier of the republic with Friuli. Giovanni da Lezze (Legge) is also praised in two sonnets (103–4), as governor (*podestà*) of Brescia in 1609–10.[70] Venice is celebrated in a sonnet by Vincentius Cardinius too (90), and an anonymous response sonnet which commends its sons 'elected to castigate unjust tyrants' (91).[71] Marino hails Venice as the ultimate 'Phoenix city' in his above-mentioned satirical sonnet ('Fosti Città d'ogni citta fenice', 121). Previously, the long *canzone* (61) celebrating the coronation of Morosina Morosini Grimani in 1597 captured the full political pageantry of the republic, describing it as a divinely favoured 'fount of Justice' (109v).[72] This sole named historical female figure in the codex is also of some interest in relation to the 'Gentildonna lucchese'. Morosini's public appearance in the familiar male ritual for the doge – as one of only two *dogaresse* crowned in the century and the last ever – had prompted some political opposition and evidently provoked male anxieties by substituting the abstract ideal of Venetia and threatening traditional gendered roles.[73]

A contrasting earthy and popular vision of Venice emerges instead from the lengthy series of 'Sonnets and canzoni in Venetian language' (75–83), which is explicitly described as being less 'polite' (*polia*) than Tuscan.[74] Indeed, a dialect 'canzon' (106) violently denounces with strong sexual imagery a 'misier Aldo' (the humanist and university professor Aldo Manuzio the younger), a 'more than perfect man of letters' ('letterao . . . plusquam perfetto', l. 16), for claiming the invalidity of his marriage (which produced offspring) to pursue his interests via the Church in Rome ('Vù fe fioli, e minchione la ghiesia?', ll. 10–1, 158v).[75] This almost incongruous clash of subjects and styles may be explained by the fact that Venetian male elites often cultivated overt political eulogy as a precautionary practice alongside their semi-clandestine indulgence in anti-feminism, eroticism and homosexuality, blasphemy, and anti-papal satire, especially in the period following the papal interdict (1606–7). Such libertine expression was later epitomized by the Incogniti Academy of Venice, and also cultivated in Medicean Florence by private circles, such as the Academy of the Borra.[76]

M, then, presents us with various possible contexts and even conflicting scenarios of reception, criticism and reappropriation of the play attributed to Bernardi, though it remains unclear how they can be linked together and why her play was included. There may have been some intention to present the codex to a casual reader looking through the start and end as a part of a conventional Petrarchan *iter*, whereby Bernardi's pastoral play would emblematize the 'earthly' stage of love, which takes a spiritual turn from no. 125 with addresses to the Virgin, the injunction to reject the 'dead' world and turn to Christ (130) and, in Morotti's closing sonnet (153), a call for a change of life through Christ ('mutar vita', 210v). This recuperative paradigm – which would parallel the author's self-imposed semi-retreat from the world (see Section 1.2.7) – is, however, broken by the various polemical secular *rime* following the play, especially in the unnumbered quires, which suggest, rather, a more irreverent and even potentially hostile context of reception. *Clorilli*'s pro-feminism (especially in II.5) is countered by anti-feminist and explicitly erotic perspectives more typical of seventeenth-century culture. Marino's sensuous verse for a veiled widow may deliberately have been included as a way of destabilizing Bernardi's ethos.

In this light and in the absence of any firm evidence, it is tempting to link the play's initial transmission and reception to male social groups within the Lucchese context who would have known Bernardi for her relatively visible role among intellectual elites in the early seventeenth century – as well as for the public scandals surrounding her personal life, and her cultivation of key religious figures such as Angelo Grillo. The subdued references in the codex to sources from Florence and especially Ferrara, key rivals of Lucca, and the strong presence of verse by dissident figures such as Maffio Venier (suspected of spying for Florence) and Marino, would fit with a grouping interested privately in exploring political and libertine ideas.[77] Orazio Lucchesini might be hypothesized as a likely candidate for the transmission to Lucca of the text of *Clorilli* between courtly circles in Florence, following the probable performance there in the early 1590s, especially given his membership of the important Oscuri academy of Lucca before his exile (1593) and his above-mentioned connection with Bernardi. A (lost) manuscript copy of the play is in fact recorded as belonging to the Lucchesini family, dedicated to the grand duchess of Tuscany, so possibly it was based on a presentation copy made for the planned performance.[78] If this was the case, it could explain *Clorilli*'s highlighted encomiastic references to the grand-ducal couple in the prologue and the description of Villa Petraia (II.6), alongside references in the verse to Jacopo Lucchesini and other Lucchese figures.

It is harder to account for the Venetian dimension to the codex. Bernardi's poetic mentor, the Benedictine monk Angelo Grillo, was present in the city in 1598 and 1612–6, but it seems hardly likely that he would have been involved in the compilation (see Sections 1.2.5 and 3.3.2) and he does not figure in the codex. Bernardi's admirer and literary networker Domenico Chiariti may, however, have facilitated contacts between Lucchese and Venetian communities, by transmitting her work and that of Morotti, since he is recorded as spending time in Venice at least in spring 1580.[79] It seems likely that other mobile, dissident males from Lucca could also have been involved in transmitting the play between groups of Lucchesi or Florentines and in Venice, and discussing it privately alongside risqué verse.

In this respect, a further tempting, if unverifiable, conjecture is that Bernardi's self-purported 'lover' Cavalier Girolamo Sbarra of Lucca was somehow involved in the compilation of the codex. As detailed in Section 1.2.3, Sbarra had in 1588 scandalously accused Bernardi publicly of an extramarital relationship with him and complicity in her husband's murder in 1585, for which Sbarra was responsible. He was thereafter banished from Lucca and the confines of Italy; Bernardi and her family also left and were temporarily exiled from Lucca. Sbarra's status as a knight of Malta in the service of Venice between the late 1560s or early 1570s until at least the mid-1580s would explain connections in the codex to military and religious figures from Lucca and Venice. Notwithstanding his formal exile in 1588, he may have continued military activity in Venetian territories further afield, perhaps in the eastern Mediterranean or in other anti-Turkish campaigns, or in more lawless and dangerous boundary regions of the republic such as Dalmatia, Marano (near Friuli) or even Brescia, which was famous for its arms production. As mentioned above, two of the men celebrated in M (Alvise Giustinian and Giovanni da Lezze) served as governors for the latter two strategic areas. It is also conceivable that Sbarra came into contact with Antonio Sarti, or his father, when or after fighting at Lepanto, given the close working relations on the battlefield between military engineers and captains, or in Hungary, Corfu, Vicenza, Flanders and other places where Sarti worked.[80] This might further explain the inclusion of burlesque sonnets in M satirizing the Turks (44) – and also on Lepanto (46) and the disastrous Hungarian campaigns of Canissa and Buda (30), as well as the response to Tasso's sonnet in praise of Alessandro Farnese (34), possibly by Walter Scott of Buccleuch, a Scot active in Flanders in the late-sixteenth century.[81] Sbarra's status as a marginal military figure would explain the irregular and libertine nature of the verse in M. His violent and erotic past history with Bernardi could also account for the prominent place given to her work, and the apparently personalized response to it in M through anti-feminism and satire.

Until further evidence emerges, however, it is impossible to establish firmer hypotheses for how the codex was compiled – and when or why it was left unfinished. Sarti was still professionally active in 1630 when he added a postscript to a work on military architecture by his son, so M could still have been in preparation after that time.[82] The next certain information of M's whereabouts is not until 1748–9, when M had been acquired by and catalogued for the bibliophile Apostolo Zeno, whose name appears on the note stuck to the inside front cover (Fig. 5).[83] How this codex arrived in Zeno's collection is unclear: it may have come from one of the suppressed religious houses in Venice or have been a private bequest. From this collection it passed to the library of the Dominicans of Santa Maria del Rosario (Gesuati) and in 1811 to the Biblioteca Marciana.[84] At all events, the codex points to how Bernardi's play text was transmitted far beyond the social and geographical setting of the elite Ferrarese circles and Florentine court in which it was originally composed or performed. It suggests how *Clorilli* – in contrast to Bernardi's poetry, discussed in Section 3 – potentially attracted prurient interest, criticism and intentional obscuration.

Notes

1 Smith, 'Fictions', 48; C*Wo*, esp. xxv–xxvii.
2 Rizzi and Griffiths, 'Renaissance of Anonymity', 205–7; on 'lost' plays and possibilities for serendipitous discoveries, see McInnis and Steggle, 'Introduction'; and Williams, 'What's a lost play?'. See also [Anon.], 'Il S. Eustachio', BEM, MS It. 12 = a.P.9.12; for Bernardi's *Eustachio*, C*Pr*, 256, and Section 1.2.7.
3 C*Pr*, 66–8, 255–6, *LP*, 244–8, 279–80, and Sections 1.2.2, 1.2.4, 1.2.6–7; 3.1.2–3.
4 C*Wo*, 64–75, 80–91; Richardson, *Manuscript Culture*, 16–8, 23; Torelli, *Partenia*, 11–5; Sampson, '"Non lasciar"'.
5 Torelli, *Partenia*, 13–14, 25–6, 48–9, and Section 2.1.1.
6 This codex is not catalogued in *Iter italicum* or in *Inventari dei manoscritti*; nor is it in the Italian national manuscripts database *Manus online*. Accessed 11 March 2023. https://manus .iccu.sbn.it/.
7 Coller, *Women*, 174–245, and Section 1.3.
8 C*Pr*, 93, see also 66–8, 97–9, 107–9, 255–6; and C*Ly*, 244–8, 279–80.
9 Rizzi and Griffiths, 'Renaissance of Anonymity'.
10 McCall and Roberts, 'Introduction', 7–9; Snyder, *Dissimulation*, xiii–xx; for anonymity as a deliberate category, Feldman, 'Authors', esp. 166, 185–6. See also Section 2.1.3.
11 See Appendix 2.2.5.
12 BMV, Manoscritti Zeniani, Cod. It., XI, 285 [=7165], 503–4.
13 Piccard, *Wasserzeichen Kreuz*, 14, II. no. 653; see 144 nos 1005 (Turin) and 1006 (Lucca). Thanks to Dott.ssa Elisabetta Sciarra and Dott.ssa Elisabetta Lugato of the Biblioteca Marciana, Venice, for their generous assistance with analyzing the manuscript.
14 Piccard, *Wasserzeichen Kreuz*, 14, II. nos 1012–13, 1015–16; all from Lucca, except 1012 (Turin).

15 M, 178r[–182], see Section 1.2.7.

16 An adaptation of Cesare Caporali's bernesque heroic poem *Vita di Mecenate* (1604), Book X. All references to verse follow numbering in Appendix 2.2.5. On Caporali's intermittent relations with Ferdinando I de' Medici, see Mutini, 'Caporali, Cesare'.

17 The quires are all octaves in the codex except: fols 181–6; 195–9 + 212 (glued to back cover).

18 See censored poems 121, 123; Russo, *Marino*; and Section 2.2.3.

19 Hunter, 'The Marking'.

20 Castellani, 'Sulla formazione', I:79–81, 'Le virgolette', I:82–4; Parkes, *Pause and Effect*, 57–8, 303; for the English context, see Hunter, 'The Marking', 171–88.

21 Breman, *Books*, 301–3; Sarti, *I crepuscoli*. Antonio Sarti may also have authored a lost *Aurora delle opere di fortificazione e di guerra* (Venice, 1626), see LSt, VI:139–40. For military themes, see Sections 2.2.2 (Hungary) and 2.2.4.

22 Morotti, *Himeneo* (1589). See also Ragagli, 'La Repubblica', 177, 249; ASL, Notari, Rog. Stefano dei Rocchi, 7 October 1605.

23 Rubric for a verse by Maria de Ferrari ('Cantava il pastor Chiaro in dolci accenti'), in *Scelta di rime*, 'Tavola', 161, and 38. See Section 1.2.6 and Appendix 2.2.5.

24 Canguilhem, 'Singing Poetry'; for overlaps between verse anthologies and madrigal corpuses, see Feldman, 'Authors', esp. 166.

25 Manoscritti Zeniani, Cod. It., XI, 285 [=7165], fol. 504, CIV.1. The designation CIV.1 appears in pencil on the frontispiece of M; see Fig. 5.

26 Pecci and Tantucci, *Canzonette*. For Bernardi's poems in the Sienese codex (S1) compiled 1600–30, see Sections 3.1.1, 3.1.5 and 3.2.3; and Coluzzi, *Guarini's 'Pastor fido'*, ch. 2 and n. 121.

27 Tommasi, *Sommario*, Books 3–4:478–91; Ragagli, 'La Repubblica', 16, 263 and 137 (conflicts 1583–4); on the Garfagnana, see Sections 1.1.1, and 1.2.1 (Bernardi's move to Castelnuovo).

28 For the suggestion that Bernardi might have been associated with political information-gathering for Lucca after her return there in 1599, see Section 1.2.6.

29 CPr, 52–3.

30 Richardson, *Manuscript Culture*, 130–1.

31 (1) refers to the verse numbering of M, see Appendix 2.2.5.

32 The uncapitalized Bianca (63), a madrigal of unambiguous praise may allude to Bianca Cappello (second wife of Grand Duke Francesco de' Medici, godfather of Bernardi).

33 Muir, 'Why Venice'; Favaro, 'La retorica', 22–5; Parabosco, *Il primo libro*.

34 M nos 21, 23, 27, 33 and 56 appear in Parabosco, *Il primo libro* (1551); nos 35 and 41 in the miscellany *Libro terzo delle rime* (1550); no. 57 only in Parabosco's dialogue *I Diporti* (1551).

35 Poems 21, 23, 41, 57. On this work, see Quaintance, *Textual masculinity*, 58–61, 69–73.

36 Lindell and Mann, 'Monte, Philippe de [Filippo di]'. See Section 3.2.1.

37 Bujic, 'Figura poetica', 39–40. See Toscano, 'Tansillo'.

38 *La Cavaletta overo della poesia Toscana*, in Tasso, *Gioie di rime* (1587); see Section 2.1.2. For Tasso's *Aminta*, see Section 2.1.

39 For Siena, D'Accone, *The Civic Muse*, 706. For a madrigal by the Venetian composer Bartolomeo Barbarino, who set a text by Bernardi, see Appendix 2.2.5, 17; Miller, 'The Composers of San Marco', 143; also see Section 3.3.2.

40 Fantappiè, 'Rinuccini, Ottavio' and 'Strozzi, Piero Vincenzo'. Dati, *Disfida*, 121–9.

41 Cf. 'Se dal grave dolor sotto il cui pondo' in BNCF, Palat. 249, 68vff, which includes Rinuccini's poetic responses to Bernardi's famous *canzone* 'Se pur fin su negli stella(n)ti chiostri', as well as possibly other verse prepared for Bernardi's *Clorilli*, and a *canzone* for the birth of Cosimo II. See Gentile, *I codici palatini*, 1:375 and Section 3.1.4. For another Florentine witness presumed by Rinuccini (Biblioteca Riccardiana e Moreniana, Florence, Codici Moreniani 216), see Chiarelli, 'Per un censimento', 159.

42 Rosenthal, *The Honest Courtesan*, 17–19, 42–57.

43 *Varie poesie* (1618), 1–7. For authorship, see Spada, *Giardino*, 379; Melzi, *Dizionario*, vol. 1, s.v. 'Academico Veneto Sconosciuto'.

44 'Non si legiadro spiega in bella mostra / glorioso Pavon l'occhiute piume' M 96v, cf. *GL*, 16.24.

45 Tasso *R*, 1684.

46 M poem 60; cited in Novati, 'Una poesia politica', 150–2.

47 Moulton, 'Introduction' to Vignali, *La cazzaria*, 1–8, 21–35, 45–56; for printed editions, see Richardson, *Manuscript Culture*, 131.

48 On Venier, see Rosenthal, *Honest Courtesan*; CPr, 177–95, and Ferrari, 'Il *Lamento*', 8–13 and *passim*; Quaintance, *Textual Masculinity*; Richardson, *Manuscript Culture*, 114–3, 169–70.

49 *Index Librorum Prohibitorum* (Rome, 1664), 333. For Lucchese anti-clericalism, see Ragagli, 'La Repubblica', 138–9.

50 Russo, *Marino*, 25, 28–9.

51 On *Lira III*, Russo, *Marino*, 128–38; Sacchini, 'Da Francesco Petrarca', 250–2.

52 Russo, *Marino*, 131–3.

53 CPr, 178.

54 Asor Rosa, 'Achillini, Claudio'. See Appendix 2.2.5, poem 120.

55 127: 'Hor che di Dio la Madre' ('Now that the mother of God'); 128: 'Mira nel Ciel qual splende' (Behold how [the brightest crown] shines in Heaven').

56 Favaro, 'Venier, Maffio'; Rosenthal, *The Honest Courtesan*, 45, 49.

57 CPr, 55.

58 CPr, 53–5. For an early spiritual madrigal by a Ferrarese contemporary of Bernardi, Sidonia Zerbinati (1580s–early 1590s), see Pocaterra, *Due dialoghi*, 13, Section 2.1.2.

59 For occasional lascivious songs probably prepared for Duchess Renée D'Este of Ferrara and perhaps her daughter(s) in the 1540s, and for Isabella d'Este singing a lewd song privately in male company, see Stras, *Women and Music*, 79–80, 99.

60 Richardson, *Manuscript Culture*, 34–44.

61 'Mentr'io v'adoro, voi m'havete, a scivo', M 99v, ll. 2–4 (*Rime*, 1598); cf. Dalla Casa, *Il Secondo Libro*, 1590.

62 Cf. *Clorilli*, IV.3, V.1.

63 On 'Duello amoroso', suppressed in Ciotti's 1615 edition, see Russo, *Marino*, 131–3.

64 CWo, 195–227; Sampson, 'Performing', 111.

65 Cf. for this issue regarding 'social poetry' in print, see Cox, 'The Social World'.

66 The names capitalized are 'Nello', 'Nobil', 'Medico' and 'Giulia' 'Cantarini'. The significance of the emblem is mentioned on the back page of the codex. Possibly, there is an allusion to Daniello de' Nobili, who belonged to the Accademia degli Oscuri of Lucca and prepared an account of it in 1619 (Bertacchi, *Storia*, 4–8).

67 Breman, *Books*, 302.

68 Tommasi, *Sommario*, 468–9, 478–91, 519, 525; Ragagli, 'La repubblica', 262.

69 See Sections 1.1 and 1.2.5–6; Magini, 'Cronache', 45–46, 56, 60–1.

70 Goy, *Chioggia*, 286. It is unclear whether the Alvise Giustinian who co-founded the San Moisè theatre in 1620 is a homonym (Mangini, *I teatri*, 43). For da Legge, M, 157r; Gullino, 'Da Lezze, Giovanni'.

71 'eletti a castigar tirani ingiusti', M 153r.

72 Wilson, '"Il bel sesso"', esp. 74–6, 84.

73 Wilson, '"Il bel sesso"', 76–8, 83–4, 93, 107.

74 M 122v (70); see Quaintance, *Textual Masculinity*, 87–90, 96–113, 128–33.

75 'Ah' misier Aldo a che Ziuogo Zioghemo?'; see for similar version in an undisclosed Marciana manuscript, Pilot, 'Il divorzio', 69. The verse title recalls Venier's satire of Franco, 'An fia cuomodo? A che muodo zioghemo?', Rosenthal, *The Honest Courtesan*, 51, 55–6.

76 Muir, 'Why Venice?', 331–3, 338–9, 341–3; De Miranda, 'Lamberti'.

77 For Venier's suspected espionage given his close relations with Bianca Cappello, see Rosenthal, *The Honest Courtesan*, 49.

78 Moreali, 'Memorie', 356v; L*St*, 9: 5, 169, and 52 (Oscuri Academy).

79 Goselini, *Lettere*, 105–8. See above for his connections with Morotti, and Section 1.2.6.

80 For Sbarra at Lepanto, see Ruscelli, *Imprese illustri*, 42–3; for the knights of Malta's sway over Counter-Reformation Lucchese clergy, see Ragagli, 'La Repubblica', 139–40; for Sarti, see Breman, *Books*, 302; Hale, *Renaissance War Studies*, 104, 125. Maffio Venier was Bishop of Corfu from 1583 until his death in 1586.

81 Petrina, 'Walter Scott', 688–9; Nelson Novoa, 'Double Alterity'. For a reference to the war in Savoy around the turn of the seventeenth century, see M, no. 110.

82 'Scrittura del Precettor dell'Autore', in Sarti, *La simmetria*, 81–95.

83 See note 12.

84 BMV, Archivio dei possessori, s.v. 'Zeno, Apostolo'. Accessed 22 April 2023. https://archivio possessori.it/archivio/549-zeno-apostolo.

2.2.5 Appendix:
The Codex Biblioteca Marciana, Venice MS It. IX, 239 (=6999)

The lists below set out the contents of the heterogeneous codex in which Leonora Bernardi's pastoral drama ([*Clorilli*], *Tragicomedia Pastorale*) appears with a collection of mostly anonymous verse (*diverse rime*), as discussed in detail in Section 2.2. The information is intended as a guide to the manuscript and invites further, more detailed examination beyond the scope of this volume, especially regarding variants and musical settings.

The five columns of the table present: 1) the folio numbers, which appear on the top right of the recto, mostly in inked numbering; where the original numbering is missing or appears incorrectly, they are given in italics and follow the later pencil numbering; 2) numbering of verse for the *diverse rime* section, though this is not given in the manuscript; numbers underlined indicate their anonymity or unclear authorship; 3) title if given, and first line (in inverted commas, following original punctuation and spelling); 4) metre or form (see below for abbreviations); and 5) notes on sources or other relevant features of the verse. Musical settings of the verse up to Bernardi's death (1616) are here indicated in abbreviated form unless there are biographical or literary reasons for expansion. Fuller details are available from the databases listed in the Appendix bibliography.

B	*Balletto / Ballata*
C	*Canzone*
Ctt	*Canzonetta*
Ep	Epigram
E.r.	*Endecasillabo rime baciate* (hendecasyllables in couplets)
E.s.	*Endecasillabo sciolto* (unrhymed hendecasyllables)
e+s	*Endecasillabo* (hendecasyllable) and *settenario* lines used without fixed pattern
M	Madrigal
O	Octaves
O.s.	*Ottave siciliane*
S	Sonnet
S.c.	*Sonetto caudato* (tailed sonnet)
T	*Terzine* (tercets)
V	*Villanella*

Physical description

Condition: relatively good, though binding of front cover is loose. Paper is yellowy and of mediocre quality, though the last quire (numbered 200–11) is lighter in colour. Brown ink is used for the first part of the codex, but especially for fols 158r–182r a darker ink is used, with lighter brown again for fols 186v–199v. The hand (A) which probably transcribes all except the last quire is unidentified and legible, though of varying neatness. The last quire is in a different, more elegant hand (B).

Binding: original in vellum; all the quires were originally bound together. The blue and yellow cord is visible and shows some damage at the bottom.

Measurements: 207mm × 157mm.

Watermark: for fols 1–198 a cross outline in an ovoid is visible at bi-folio folds (for example, fols 21–2) consistent with the octave format. The watermark is found in late-sixteenth/early seventeenth-century northern Italy, and can be linked to examples from Lucca 1612 and Turin 1650 (Piccard, *Wasserzeichen Kreuz*, 14, II. no. 653; see 144 nos 1005 (Turin) and 1006 (Lucca)). The last quire, (see fols 206–7), has capital initials A and E below the oval, recalling a type found especially in Lucca 1618–28 (cf. Piccard, nos 1012–1013, 1015–6; all from Lucca except 1012 (Turin)).

Composition: frontispiece + 206 leaves, consisting of 26 quires: 17 octaves 1–137 ($1–8^8$, $9–16^8$, etc. to $129–136^8$); [18] 137–42 (+ stubs, see below), [19] $143–56^8$ [*sic*; see below on omitted page numbers]; [20] $157–64^8$, [21] $165–72^8$, [22] $173–80^8$; [23] $181–6^6$; [24] $187–194^8$; [25] 195–9 + 212 (back cover sheet)^8; [26] $200–11^{12}$ (separate inserted quire). Verse is sometimes transcribed across quires.

Blank leaves: 160v, 182v–186r, 198r, 200r–v (cover sheet for last quire), 211v (last quire cover sheet).

Stubs: between fols numbered 136–7 (1), 140–1 (1), 194–5 (3?).

Pagination: 1–143 (original hand, ink numbering, recto top right), [144–9, page numbers omitted], 150–56 (original ink numbering); 157–86 (pencil numbering added later); 187 (pencil numbering; ink original numbering 157); 188–98 (pencil numbering); 199–211 (pencil numbering; ink numbering restarts from 199, but given as 200); 212 (not numbered and glued to back cover).

Catchwords: on verso of each leaf where the following one contains writing.

Tragicomedia pastorale

1r		16[0]3 / Libro di diverse / Rime / Tragicomedia Pastorale della / Signora Xq^cbefm Hqxmllm / Gentildonna lucchesse		Titlepage
1v		Madrigale: *Venere alla Autora* 'Il dolce e caro figlio'	M	
2r–4v		Prologo: *Linfadusa fata* 'Di molte una son io'	e+s	
5r		Interlocutori		Cast list
5v–66r		[Tragicomedia pastorale]	e+s	Acts 1–5

Diverse rime

66v–71v	*1*	Epistola di A.S. alla Signora F. H.: 'Se dal grave dolor sotto il cuo pondo'	T	Cf. 'Quintilio ad Anna' in Dati, *Disfida* [1593], 121–9
71v–73r	*2*	Canzone in lode della rosa: 'Casta consorte Clori'	C	
73v–79r	*3*	Testamento di mecenate: 'Non restò barba consumata, o bianca'	T	cf. Caporali, *Vita di Mecenate* [1603], X.184–489
79v–84r	*4*	Suplica: 'Scappato signor mio di pacienza'	T	Giovanni Serragli (Rome, BCR, Cors. 43 A f. 34r; 44 C 22, f. 282r (Carboni, I: 550)
84r–87v	*5*	Himeneo: 'O' somaro del fonte d'Aganippe'	e+s	Highlight 'CIATTO'
87v–91r	*6*	Capitolo: 'Hor ch'io solo mi sto signor mio caro'	T	
91r–92r	*7*	Canzone: 'Amor m'invita / Dolce mia vita'	C	Highlight 'F.A.U.S.T.I.N.A.'
92r–92v	*8*	Canzone: 'Vedrò la Neve ardente'	C	
93r–94r	*9*	Canzone: 'Ecco Maggio, è seco ha flora'	C	Highlight 'FAUSTINA'
94r–95r	*10*	Baletto: 'Vorei fuggire / senza martire'	B	Highlight 'FAUSTINA'
95r	*11*	Vilanella: 'Le lagrime, ch'io sparsi un tempo Ahi lasso'	V	Highlight 'FAUSTINA'. Anon. (Gio. Giacomo Algardi?), *Poesie varie*, collection for Agostino Caraccio pittore, Bologna, Biblioteca Universitaria, in Ms.It. 1686 (3797), I–M, 25 (1916), 46.

95v	*12*	Sogno: Am[ant]te: 'Per che piangi hò Amore?'	e+s	Dialogic verse; highlight 'FAUSTINA'
95v	*13*	Madrigale: 'Haime, che hai? Piango, perche?'	M	Refers to 'FAUSTA'
96r	*14*	Per un svenimento: 'Chiuse i bei lumi, e impallidissi il volto'	S	
96r	*15*	Madrigale: 'Tu neve io foco son e nel tuo gelo'	M	
96v	*16*	Si lodano le pitigine: 'Non si legiadro spiega in bella mostra'	S	Cf. Tasso, *GL*, 16.24
96v	*17*	Madrigale: 'L'alma un sospir mi tolse'	M	Set to music by Amadio Freddi (Venice, 1605) and Bartolomeo Barbarino for solo and three voices (Venice, 1610, 1617) and ms. Bibl. Herzog August (Miller, 'The Composers of San Marco', 145, 148)
97r	*18*	S'ama et non s'arde: 'Vissi beato all'hor, che il vostro foco'	S	
97r	19	Madrigale: 'Pomo acerbetto sei'	M	Filippo Alberti, in Caporali, *Le piacevoli rime*, 190; Alberti, *Rime* (1602); [Il Confuso Accademico Ordito], *Il gareggiamento* (1611), I: Bellezze, 5v (only first stanza). Musical setting by Basilio Cossa, *Madrigaletti a tre voci* (Venice, 1617)
97v	20	Sonetto: 'Valli profonnde al sol nimiche Rupi'	S	Cf. Tansillo, *Canzoniere*, Sonnet XI, 'Valli nemiche al Sol, superbe rupi' (see below no. 95). Set to music in Fidelis, *Il primo libro* (1570), no. 3; da Gagliano, *Musiche* (1615), no. 20 (a 1)

97v	*21*	Madrigale: 'Donna s'io resto vivo'	M	Parabosco: in *Libro terzo*; Parabosco, *Il primo libro*; *I diporti*, Day 3, 292–3; Musical settings: Nasco, *Primo libro* (1554) [editions 1555, 1561, 1584], 13; Merulo, *Primo libro* (1566), 29; Monte, *Libro quinto* (1574), 13; Piccioni, *Primo libro* (1577), 7; Anerio, *Madrigali* (1585), 11; Pallavicino, *Terzo libro* (1585), 3 [1606, 1607]; Della Rota, *Primo libro* (1600), 24; Facio, *Primo libro* (1601), 14 (see RePIM, NV)
98r	*22*	Sonetto: 'Gioisca il Ciel hor mai l'aria, e la terra'	S	
98r	*23*	Madrigale: 'Poi ch'io vivo lontano'	M	Parabosco, *Il primo libro*, 3v; *I Diporti*, Day 3, 306
98v	*24*	Sonetto: 'Sia tomba al Gran [F]ilippo l'ampia mole'	S	For death of Philip II of Spain (1598)
98v	*25*	Madrigale: 'Petto dove'l mio cor? Nol sai? No' io'	M	Highlight 'FA'
99r	*26*	Sonetto: 'Stringesti o luchesin due volte il freno'	S	
99r	*27*	Madrigale: 'Se comprendeste si la doglia mia'	M	Parabosco, *Il primo libro*, 3r. Variants include highlighted 'FA'
99v	*28*	Sonetto: 'Mi tira sì l'acerba et dura pena'	S	
99v	*29*	Madrigale: 'Mentr'io v'adoro, voi m'havete, a scivo'	M	Guarini, 'Ottave amorose', 1, in *Rime* (1598), 135v. Variants include splitting line 2 and replacing 'Donna' with 'FA'. Musical setting: Cf. Dalla Casa, *Il secondo libro* (1590), 11–14; Liberti, *Secondo libro* (1609)
100r	*30*	Sonetto: 'Il perder non fu mai laudabil cosa'	S	Highlights CAZZI and COGLIONI, with reference to Canissa and Buda campaigns. Cf. Ariosto, *OF*, 15.1.1–4
100r	*31*	Madrigale: 'S'io v'amo, et s'io v'ho amato, un dì vedrete'	M	

100v	32	Proposta: 'Insegna a te la tua gran Patria Roma'	S	Tasso, *R* 1493 'Al duca Alessandro Farnese'; in *Scelta di rime*, I, 116 (attrib. to 'Incerto'), 160 (Tavola: 'Al Duca di Parma, per lo soccorso dato a Pariggi')
100v	33	Madrigale: 'S'io non piango, e sospiro'	M	Parabosco, *Il primo libro*, 4v. Variants include highlighted 'FA'
101r	_34_	Risposta: 'Insegna a me l'ardir non Spagna, o Roma'	S	Response sonnet to Tasso's no. 32. In BMV MS, IX, 175, coll. 6283 (CIV.8), fol. 116r (paired with Tasso's 'Insegna a te'), possibly by or known to Walter Scott of Buccleuch in Flanders 1590s–*c.*1609. Appears with variants in the manuscripts of William Fowler (Edinburgh 1560– London 1612), National Library of Scotland, MS Hawthornden 2065, 138r, see Petrina, 'Walter Scott', 688–9
101r	35	Madrigale: 'Voi volete ch'io moia'	M	Parabosco, in *Libro terzo* (1550), 159v. Set to music by 15 composers 1554–1619, including Philippe de Monte (1562); Orlando de Lasso (1577) and Giaches de Wert (1581) (RePIM)
101v	36	Proposta: 'O voi ch'apresso menate tal'otta'	S.c.	Bernesque sonnet, attributed to Antonio Caetani against Giulio Cesare Gonzaga, prince of Bozzolo, in Tassoni, *La secchia rapita*, 302 (*Rime*). Variants in M
101v	_37_	Madrigale: 'Mira che bella cosa'	M	
102r	38	Risposta: 'Io non son Duca, ne somiglio il Potta'	S.c.	Tassoni, *La secchia rapita*, 302–3 (*Rime*). Response to no. 36, impersonating ('in nome di') G. C. Gonzaga
102r	_39_	Madrigale: 'Madonna se volete / ch'un dono in nome vostro io porti altrui'	M	(Sensual)

102v	40	Sonetto: 'S'en vece di midolle piene l'ossa'	S.c.	Giovanni Della Casa for Antonio Bernardi, a philosopher from Mirandola (c. 1542), 15 manuscript versions with variants; printed 1728–9. Variants in M include 'Ser Jacopuzzo' for 'Ser Antoniuzzo'. Burlesque, obscene verse, using satirical topos of riddle-sonnet, see Zaccarello, 'Alcune "Rime piacevoli"', 290–306
102v	41	Madrigale: 'Donna ben sapreb'io'	M	Parabosco, 'Donna ben sapre' io', in *Libro terzo*; *I diporti*, Day 3, 308–9. Musical setting by Anerio, *Madrigali* (1585), 10
103r	_42_	Sonetto: 'Fu ton padre a dui figli Azzo e Giorone'	S.c.	'Proposta d'un dubbio legale. Del Semplice. "Fu Ton padre a duoi figli: Azzo e Girone"', for which a reply follows by '[il] Modesto', MS Bologna, Biblioteca Universitaria 805 (1211), *Poesie varie* (I–M, 19 (1912), 171)
103r	_43_	Madrigale: 'Bacimi vita mia, ne ti sia grave'	M	To music by Bartolini, *Il primo libro* (1606), no. 5
103v	_44_	Sonetto: 'Selin? Chi chiama? Io tu? Si, chi sei? L'alma'	S	[Anon.] 'Selim! – Chi chiama? – Io – Tu? – Chi sei? L'alma', BNCF, II, IX, 45, fol. 237 'Sonetto burlesco sul Turco' [c. 1560s–90s] (I–M, 11 (1901), 269)
103v	45	Madrigal: 'La bella man vi stringo'	M	Guarini, *Rime* (1598), Madrigal no. 61, 88r. Set to music by 14 composers 1590–1627, including Philippe de Monte (1593), Luca Marenzio (1599) and Giulio Caccini (1614)

104r	_46_	Sonetto: 'Que pars est o seli salamelech'	S	Anon. (attrib. 'Zambò de Val Brombana'), _Raccolta_ (1572); 40v, and Groto, _Trofeo_ (1572), 114r; musical setting by Giovan Ferretti, _Il primo libro_ (1576) [1st ed. 1573]), nos 22–23. Multilingual sonnet mocking Sultan Selim II after Lepanto found widely in print and in manuscripts in Florence, Rome (Vatican) and Portugal; see Nelson Novoa, 'Double Alterity'; Zanetti, 'Anonimo'; Fenlon, 'Lepanto', 201, 214–15
104v	_47_	Madrigale: 'Da tuoi begl'occhi Amor s'anida'	M	
104v	_48_	Sonetto: 'Che tessa il Ragno, e 'l Vermicello ordisca'	S	
104v	49	Madrigale: 'Dimmi Clori cara amata'	M	Alberto Parma, 'Filli cara e amata', in Caporali, _Rime piacevoli,_ 214 (for other variants, see RePIM); five musical settings 1586–1620, including by Monteverdi, _Primo libro a cinque voci_ (1587), no. 7
105r	_50_	Sonetto: 'VIOLA no, ma ben candido Giglio'	S	
105r	51	Madrigale: 'Dunque Damon mio caro'	M	Alberto Parma, 'Dunque Aminta mio caro', in Caporali, _Rime piacevoli_, 214. Set to music by Camillo Zanotti (1587) and Orazio Colombano (1588)
105v	_52_	Sonetto: 'Amor è un no so che, bien no so d'onde'	S	Attrib. to 'Poeta' in Vincenzo Cartari, _Imagini degli Dei degli antichi_ [Venice, rev. ed 1571], ed. Auzzas et al., [XIII], 450; for attrib. to Cartari, 594. Cf. F. Andreini, _Ragionamenti_ (1612), no. 2, p. 11
105v	_53_	Madrigale: 'Morta no; ma sepolta'	M	
106r	_54_	Sonetto: 'FAUSTA Ills. in cui spirò Natura'	S	
106r	_55_	Madrigale: 'Ogni parte risponde al vostro nome'	M	

106v	56	Madrigale: 'Non piu saette Amore'	M	Parabosco, *Il primo libro*, no. 59; set to music by Giovan Domenico Montella, *Il primo libro* (1594), 2 (lines 1–3 only)
106v	57	Madrigale: 'La dove il Nilo irriga le campagne'	M	Parabosco, *I diporti*, Day 3, p. 309 (discussed after 'Donna ben sapre' io'; see no. 41 above)
107r	<u>58</u>	Madrigale: 'Se nettar bevo fra Rubini ardenti'	M	Musical setting: Anerio, *Primo libro* (1590, 1599), 7. Dedicated to Cardinal Montalto
107r	<u>59</u>	Madrigale: 'Fida, e giusta hoggi sarà la mano'	M	Highlight 'LARA'
107v–108v	<u>60</u>	Terzetti: 'Pietà pietà ch'ogni speranza e morta'	T	[Anon.] 'Pater noster contro gli Spagnuoli'. For text and other manuscript witnesses, see Novati, 'Una poesia politica', 150–2
109r–114v	<u>61</u>	Canzone: 'Queste son ben vere letitie, queste'	C	Celebrates the coronation in Venice 1597 of Dogaress Morosina Morosini (wife of Doge Marino Grimani, r. 1595–1605). Several highlights of MOROSINA, also once PRINCIPESSA (113r) and VENEZIA. 1597 in pencil at top left of fol. 109r
115r	<u>62</u>	Sonetto: 'Discolorito, ahime, viddi il bel volto'	S	
115r	<u>63</u>	Madrigale: 'Bianca non piu di voi sul'Apenino'	M	Praise of beauty of Bianca (Cappello?)
115v	<u>64</u>	Madrigale: 'Bella si ma Crudele'	M	
115v	65	Sonetto: 'Fiume, che a l'onde tue ninfe et pastori'	S	Ongaro, *Rime*, 1600, 13; *Scelta di rime*, I, 98. Madrigal settings by Luca Marenzio (1599, 1601, 1609); Agostino Agazzari (1600); Francesco Stivori (1601) and Sigismondo d'India (1606)
116r	<u>66</u>	Madrigale: 'Tu cangi il seggio Amore'	M	
116r	67	Sonetto: 'Se ben pungendo ogni hor vipere ardenti'	S	Della Casa, in *Il Galateo . . . e le Rime* (1746), 330 (no. 72); author did not allow its publication

116v–121r	68	Ottave: 'Signor Coscrucci poi che ricercate'	O	At fol. 120v Alamanno Appiano is referenced positively, the brother-in-law of Clement VIII, nephew of Cosimo I and a knight of S. Stefano
121v–122r		Ottave siciliane:	O.s.	
	69	Proposta: 'Lu cori chi di cara sijttatu'		
	70	Risposta H: 'Lu cori chi di carasajitta tu'		
	71	'Amici mei si beni mi voleti' / (122v)		
	72	'Beati ciecchi vu che non vediti'		
	73	'Lu riscignolu adolurata cantu'		73. Possibly corresponds with the octave 'Lu Rusignulu' with guitar intabulature, in BNCF, Landau Finaly. Mss 175 ('Danze e canzonette intavolate per chitarra', early 17th century), n. 13 (Becherini, 131)
	74	'Si li campani sintirai sunari'		
122v–130v		Sonetti e canzoni in lingua venetiana:		
	75	'No ve maravigiè, sia chi se vogia'	S	75. Venier, *Canzoni*, Sonnet 25; BMV MS It. IX, 217 (=7061), 2r (proemial sonnet), MS It. IX 173 (=6282), 191v; Venier, *Canzoni*. Sonnet 25
	76	'Potta, no mi divento una Zoeta'	S.c.	76. References Parabosco l. 12
	77	'Anzoletta del Ciel senza peccà'	S	77. Venier, *Canzoni*, Sonnet 16, BMV MS It. IX, 217 (=7061), 7r; MS It. IX 173 (=6282), 218v
	78	'O Ciel come è possible che se faga'	S.c.	78. Venier, *Canzoni*, Sonnet 50 ('Ohimè! Com'è possibil che se faga'); BMV MS It. IX 173 (=6282), 'O Dio, come è possibil che se faga', 254r
	79	'Haver un pare che non creppa mai'	S.c.	79. Venier, *Canzoni*, Sonnet 61
	80	Madrigale: 'Vù m'havè vento e'l cuor'	M	80. Venier, *Poesie diverse*, 35 (printed 1613)
	81	Canzoni: 'O' man de puro latte'	C	81. Venier, *Canzoni*, Canzon piccenina (de la man), BMV MS It. IX, 217 (=7061), 14r–15v, MS It. IX 173 (=6282)

	82	'AMOR vivemo con la Gatta a i stizzi'	C	82. Venier, 'Canzon (delle strazze)/La Strazzosa', BMV MS It. IX, 217 (=7061), 79r ff; MS It. IX 173 (=6282), 27v–30r; *Poesie*, 14–19
130v–133v	83	Canzone: 'Donna pompa del Ciel unica e sola'	C	Venier, BMV MS It. IX, 173 (=6282), 24v–26v; *Poesie diverse*, 47–55 (For Barbara Contessa da Sala)
134r–136v	84	Imeneo: 'Deh sciolgi audace il canto'	C	Highlights include 'AQUILA', 'SERCHIO', 'SPOSO', 'NELLO', 'NOBIL', 'MEDICO', and 'GIULIA' 'CANTARINI'. Quite a sensual epithalamium. The symbolism of the 'Aquila' is explained on fol. 212r
137r–142r	85	Ottave: 'Ninfa gentil ma tu ninfa non sei'	O	[Anon.], MS verse miscellany of 1500–1600s, Florence, BNCF, Cl. VII, 650, fols 115–222 (I-M, 13 (1905–6), 136)
142r–152r	86	Altre ottave dell'istesso autore: 'AMOR io nel ricordo, e non fia mai'	O	
152r	87	Madrigali: 'In rimirando in alto'	M	
	88	'Nostra michante stella'	M	
152v	89	Enigoma [*sic*]: 'Di morte e terror figlia in luoghi incolti'	O	Strambotto
152v	90	Sonetto: 'S'ove nido havean sol palustri merghi'	S	Vincent[us] Cardin[us], in BCR, MS Cors. 44 B 21, 44v (Carboni, II: 585)
153r	91	Risposta: 'In questi hoggi pregiati, e ricchi alberghi'	S	
153r	92	Madrigale: 'Dolce, grave et acuto'	M	Cesare Rinaldi, in Bianciardi, *Il primo libro de madrigali* (1597)
153v	93	Sonetto funebre: 'Campion Ill.re che da sì longa guerra'	S	In top left margin header: 'Inclito heroe', but unnamed
153v–154r	94	Madrigale: 'O quanto sei simile'	M	To music in Fattorini, *La Rondinella* (1604). Highlight 'FAUSTA'

154r	95	'Valli nemiche, al sol superbe rupi / che minacciate al ciel, profonde grotte'	S	Tansillo in *Nuova scelta* (1573), 21 (cf. variant version no. 20 above); set to music by Felis, *Il primo libro* (1585), no. 20 (dedicatee Paolo Grillo); Pesenti, *Il primo libro* (1621); with final tercets 'Erme campagne', Baccusi, *Il primo libro* (1570), 20–21; Vicomanni, *Il primo libro* (1582), 7; Wert, *Il sesto libro* (1577, 1584, 1592), 15–16/ (1592) 2–3 [a 5]; Dal Pozzo, *Il quarto libro* (1612), 19–20 (NV).
154v	96	Sonetto: 'Strane rupi, aspri monti, alte tremanti'	S	Tansillo in *Nuova scelta* (1573), 21; attrib. Niccolò Amanio (*c.* 1468–pre 1528), in *Rime di diuersi* (1547), 171r. Set to music by Cipriano da Rore (1542)
154v	97	'Amor m'inpenna l'ale, e tanto in alto'	S	Tansillo, in *Libro terzo* (1550), 171r. Set as madrigals by Matteo Ruffolo (1561); Alessandro Striggio (1566; 1571); Philippe de Monte (1581); Cf. Bernardi's canzonetta 'O chi l'ale m'impenna', Section 3.1.2 (ii)
155r	98	Sonetti [*sic*]: 'Poi che spiegat'ho l'Ale al ben desio'	S	Tansillo, in *Rime di diuersi* (1553), 557, directly follows no. 97 ('Amor m'impenna')
155r–v	99	'Pastori amanti / e ninfe amate'	Ctt	5-syllable lines presented in two columns
155v	100	Sonetto: 'Fu pur nul grado hor dell'invidia è a scherno'	S	Underlines 'Sarti', 'forte' and 'il vinto'
156r	101	Canzonetta: 'Ah traditor che fai?'	Ctt	[Enrico] Radesca da Foggia, *Canzonette, madrigali* e *arie* (1606), 'Audace amante', no. 15
156v	102	Sonetto: 'Convien Signor, per le tue lodi ardire'	S	
157r	103	Sonetto: 'Corsero i tuoi gra[n]d'Avi, a briglia sciolta'	S	'LEGGE' and 'GIOVANNI' highlighted
157v	104	Sonetto: 'Sempre vivran vincendo ogni memoria'	S	'DA LEGGE' and 'GIOVANNI' highlighted
158r	105	Sonetto: 'A te nacque, a te Visse, a te Morio'	S	'VALIER' and 'PACE' highlighted

158v	*106*	Canzon: 'Ah misier Aldo a che ziuogo, zioghemo?'	C	In Venetian dialect, obscene. Ends: 'Che se' un coion vitioso in stampa d'Aldo'; cf. close variant in BMV, MS It. IX 173 (=6282), no 98, see Ferrari, 'Il lamento', transcribed Pilot, 'Il divorzio', 69 Cf. Maffio Venier's satire of Franco, 'An fia cuomodo? A che muodo zioghemo?', Rosenthal, *The Honest Courtesan*, 51, 55–6
159r	*107*	Sonetto: 'Al nuovo suon di vostre Dotte carte'	S	
159r	108	'Cagnoletto zentil che hai per uso'	E.r.	Cf. Variant in Maffio Venier, *Rime*, BMV MS It. IX, 217 (=7061), 13r; MS It. IX, 173 (=6282), 38v ('Cagnoletta mia bella / Che ti ha sì spesso in uso'); *Poesie diverse*, p. 42; Ferrari, 'Il Lamento', 24
159v	*109*	Madrigale: 'Dhe se tu credi Amore'	M	
159v–160r	*110*	'Tu sei pur giunto o Peregrin felice / alla Patria natia al bel soggiorno'	S	Marino, *Rime* (1602), 'Rime lugubri' 168, ll. 1–2: 'Hoggi a le tue contrade alme natie / Giunto se' tu felice Peregrino'
160r	*111*	'Gravida d'armi al suo dolor in preda'	S	[Anon] with rubric 'Sopra li moti di Savoia', Pesaro, Biblioteca Oliveriana, MS 578, late 1500s–1600s, miscellany especially of political-military writings (I-M, I 42 (1929), 81)
161r–169v	112	Lettera alla S. F. H: 'A te, che sola sei'	E.s.	Marino 'Lettera amorosa'. Unattributed in Remigio Romano, *Terza raccolta* (1622), 6–23; Marino, *Lettere* (1628), 266–86
170r–172r [157 ink]	113	Canzone sopra una vedova: 'Quest'animata notte'	C	Marino, *L* III, 11–15

_172v–173v_	_114_	Sopra le stelle: 'Hor l'ingegno, e le rime'	Ctt	Marino, _Hinno alle stelle_ (Palermo, 1608); also in _Nuove poesie_ (Macerata, 1614); in _Murtoleide_ (Frankfurt, 1626); and in a seventeenth-century manuscript edition; see Landi, 'Notizia', 294
_173v_	_115_	Sonetti: 'Orbe [_sic_] gravido d'aure al Ciel sospinto'	S	Marino, 'Giuoco di pallone per una donna: Globo gravido d'aure al ciel sospinto', _L_ III: 'Amori', 36
_173v–174r_	_116_	'Anna, ben tu da l'anno il nome prendi'	S	Marino, 'Alla Sig. Anna N.', _L_ III: 'Amori', 54. For manuscripts, see Landi, 'Notizie', 293
_174r_	_117_	'Negra sì, ma sei bella, o di natura'	S	Marino, 'Schiava: Nera sì, ma se' bella o di Natura', in _L_ III: 'Amori', 10. For the variant 'Negra' in a codex (Paris BNF, ital. 575) produced by 1602 for a Florentine containing verse by Rinuccini, Tasso and Isabella Andreini, see Sacchini, 'Da Francesco Petrarca', 251; for further manuscript copies in Turin (lost) and Madrid (which includes 'Anna ben tu'), and textual variants, Landi, 'Notizia' 293–4
_174v_	_118_	'Donna siam' rei di morte, errasti, errai'	S	Marino, _L_ III: 'Amori', 3 'Inferno amoroso'. Set as madrigals by Sigismondo D'India (1618), Antonio Gualtieri (1625) and Girolamo Frescobaldi (1630)
_174v–175r_	_119_	'Amor, com'esser' può, che per mia doglia'	S	Marino, _L_ III: 'Amori', 2 'Donna bella & crudele'
_175r_	_120_	'Ecco vicine, o bella tigre l'hore'	S	Claudio Achillini, _Poesie_ (1632), 193 ('Amante s'addolora per la partenza dell'Amata'). Set by Monteverdi, _Libro VII de madriga_li (1619), no. 11

175r–v	121	'Fosti Città d'ogni citta fenice'	S	Marino, 'Sonetto per una inondatione del Tebro a Roma' in *Il Padre Naso* (1626), 133; banned in *Index Librorum prohibitorum: usque ad annum 1681* (1726), 211
175v	122	'Legar [*sic*] vento leggier; fabrica, e fonda'	S	Marino, 'Donna volubile': 'Segue il vento leggier, fabrica, e fonda', *L* III: 'Amori', 19
176r–177v	123	Ottave: 'Amor, che meco a la noturna impresa'	O	Marino, *L* III: 'Duello amoroso' (omitted in the 1629 edition as banned). M omits the third of the 12 octaves
178r–182r	124	In morte del G. Cavalier Guerini: 'Questi lugubri inchiostri, e queste note'	C	Girolamo Priuli, in *Varie poesie* (1618), 1–7
186v	<u>125</u>	Madrigali: 'Gia fosti e fiore, e rosa'	M	Spiritual
186v–187r[ink 157]	<u>126</u>	'Quasi vermiglia rosa / che sul materno stelo'	M	Spiritual
187r	<u>127</u>	'Hor che di Dio la Madre / qual fiamengiante stella'	M	Spiritual
187r	<u>128</u>	'Mira nel ciel qual splende / chiarissima corona'	M	Spiritual
187v–190r	129	Della miseria humana: 'Quando tal' hora il lagrimoso ciglio'	O	Marcantonio Laparelli, *Cristiade* (1618), 248–53; 21 octaves; M gives 18
190v–192v	130	Della Morte: 'D'ossa e di vermi pien ov'han ricetto'	O	Laparelli, *Cristiade* (1618), 257–61; 18 octave stanzas; M gives 15
193r–195v	131	Canzone: 'Sacrati horrori, ove la folta chioma'	C	Maffio Venier, 'Sopra il Monte dell'Avernia ove San Francesco hebbe le stimate', first printed as *Canzone spirituale sopra il monte dell'Avernia* (1585); Tasso, *Delle rime* (1586), 171–5; BMV It. IX 271 (=6096) (see Rosenthal, *The Honest Courtesan*, 152–3); set to music in Gastoldi, *Sacre lodi* (1587), 14–22
195v–197v	<u>132</u>	Canzone: 'SPIRTI chiari e felici / da più sublimi scanni'	C	

197v	*133*	Della fede: 'Scesa dall'alto Ciel fra voi mortali'	O	Laparelli, *Cristiade*, 'Le tre virtu teologali', 247 (Fede)
198v	*134*	Sonetto: 'Lo'char [Locar] sopra gl'abbissi i fondamenti'	S	Francesco Beccuti il Coppetta (d. 1553), *Rime* (1580), 17. Much anthologized and set to music (*NV*); discussed in Tasso's dialogue *La Cavaletta*
198v–199r	*135*	'Locar sopra li abbissi e' fondamenti'	S	*135* Textual variant (corresponding to more musical settings). Many musical settings (some only part of sonnet), e.g. by Cesare Tudino (1564), 1; Gio. Battista Mosto (1578), 6; Lambert Courtois (1580), 5; Simone Balsamino, *Prime novelette* (1594)
199r [ink 200]	<u>*136*</u>	Sonetto: 'Essendo Guerra fra la terra el Cielo'	S	
199v	<u>*137*</u>	Ad Illustrissimum D[omin]um Aloysium Iustinianum M[a]rani Provisorem, Epigramma: 'Lucida se Caelum mo[n] strent, Aer terra[m] virentem'	Ep	
201r	*Title page*	Sonetti del P. F. Lodovico da Monte Falco Cappuccino (201v blank)		
202r [203 ink]	*138*	'Goder si de mentre che siamo in vita'	S	
202v	*139*	'O beati color ch'in questa vita'	S	
203r	*140*	'S'andiamo ogn'hor morendo in questa vita'	S	
203v	*141*	'Poi che morto Signor con la tua morte'	S	
204r	*142*	'Che mi giova guardarti morto in Croce'	S	
204v	*143*	Proposta: 'Se l'aspro e duro legno della Croce'	S	
205r	*144*	Risposta: 'Poi ch'hebbe acerba morte in dura Croce'	S	
205v	*145*	Dialogo: 'Chi fe l'huomo immortal venir a morte?'	S	

206r	*Title page*	Sonetti del Sig.r Giovanni Morotti di Luca [206v blank]		
207r	146	'Goder vorrei innanzi, e doppo morte'	S	
207v	147	'O beati coloro a qual in vita'	S	
208r	148	'Se cagion del mio ben è la tua morte'	S	
208v	149	'Nel verbo etterno nel condurre a vita'	S	
209r	150	'Ben mi giova guardarti morto in Croce'	S	
209v	151	Proposta: 'Se il dolce e lieve giogo de la Croce'	S	
210r	152	Risposta: 'M'adiro e piango, e chi mi puo dar vita'	S	
210v	153	Dialogo: 'Che fia dunque di me spietata morte?'	S	
211r		Del Sig.r Ant.o Sarti humiliss.o [S].re Scip. Massucchi [211v blank]		Back cover sheet
212r	154	[Glued to back cover] Terzetto che mancha al testamento . . . Del secondo Imeneo . . . Madrigale 'Da tuoi begl'occhi DONNA fui legato'	M	

Bibliography

Databases consulted

AR Archivi del Rinascimento. https://www.archivirinascimento.it.

Becherini Becherini, Bianca. *Catalogo dei manoscritti musicali della Biblioteca Nazionale di Firenze*. Kassel: Bärenreiter, 1959.

Carboni Carboni, Fabio. *Incipitario della lirica italiana dei sec XV al XX*. VIII–IX: Accademia Nazionale dei Lincei e Biblioteca Corsiniana di Roma. 2 vols. Vatican City: Biblioteca Apostolica Vaticana, 1992.

I-M *Inventari dei manoscritti delle Biblioteche d'Italia*, dir. by G. Mazzatinti (1–13), A. Sorbelli (14–75) and L. Ferrari (76–81). Florence: Leo S. Olschki, 1890–.

IUPI Santagata, Marco. *Incipitario unificato della poesia italiana*. 4 vols. Modena: Panini, [1988].

Lyra Edited by Simone Albonico, University of Lausanne, https://lyra.unil.ch.

NV Vogel, Emil, Alfred Einstein, François Lesure, Claudio Sartori, *Bibliografia della musica italiana vocale profana pubblicata dal 1500 al 1700: Nuova edizione*, 3 vols. [Pomezia]: Staderini, 1977.

RePIM Repertorio della Poesia Italiana in Musica, 1500–1700, edited by Angelo Pompilio http://repim.muspe.unibo.it/.

Primary sources

Manuscripts

Biblioteca Nazionale Marciana, Venice

Rime, canzoni, e sonetti di Maffio Veniero, BMV, MS It. IX.217 (=7061).

[Verse miscellany] BMV, MS It. IX, 173 (=6282).

Printed

Achillini, Claudio. *Poesie*. Bologna: Clemente Ferroni, 1632.

Alberti, Filippo, *Rime*. Rome: Guglielmo Facciotto, 1602.

Andreini, Francesco. *Ragionamenti fantastici*. Venice: Giacom'Antonio Somasco, 1612.

Anerio, Felice. *Primo Libro de Madrigali a sei voci*. Venice: Ricciardo Amadino, 1590; Anversa, Pietro Phalesio, 1599.

Anerio, Felice. *Madrigali . . . a cinque voci. Secondo Libro*. Rome: Alessandro Gardano, 1585.

Balsamino, Simone. *Al ser.mo Francesco Maria duca d'Urbino . . . prime Novellette*. Venice: Ricciardo Amadino, 1594.

Bartolini, Orindio (da Siena). *Il primo libro de madrigali a cinque voci*. Venice: Alessandro Raverij, 1606.

Beccuti, Francesco. *Rime di M. Francesco Coppetta de' Beccuti perugino*. Venice: Domenico, et Gio. Battista Gerra, fratelli, 1580.

Bianciardi, Francesco. *Il primo libro de madrigali a cinque voci*. Venice: Gardano, 1597.

Caporali, Cesare. *Rime piacevoli . . . del Mauro et d'altri autori* [1586]. *Accresciute . . .* Venice: Giorgio Bizzardo, 1609.

Caporali, Cesare. *Vita di Mecenate* [Venice: G. B. Ciotti, 1604], edited by Danilo Romei. [n.pl.] Lulu, 2018.

Cartari, Vincenzo. *Imagini de i dei gli antichi* [Venice, rev. ed 1571], edited by Ginetta Auzzas, Federica Martignago, Manlio Pastore Stocchi, Paola Rigo. Vicenza: Neri Pozza, 1996.

Da Gagliano, Marco. *Musiche a una dua e tre voci*. Venice: Ricciardo Amadino, 1615.

Dati, Giulio. *Disfida di Caccia tra i Piacevoli e Piattelli* [MS 1593]. Florence: Per il Magheri, 1824.

Dalla Casa, Girolamo. *Il secondo libro dei madrigali a cinque voci con i passaggi*. Venice: Ricciardo Amadino, 1590.

Della Casa, Giovanni, *Il Galateo . . . . Giuntovi il Trattato degli Uffizi comuni, l'orazione a Carlo V, l'Orazione alla Repubblica di Venezia, e le Rime*. Venice: Simone Occhi, 1746.

Fattorini, Gabriele. *La Rondinella: Secondo libro di madrigali a cinque voci*. Venice: Ricciardo Amadino, 1604.

Felis, Stefano, *Il primo libro de madrigali a cinque voci . . . risampati*. Venice: Angelo Gardano, 1585.

Ferretti, Giovan, *Il primo libro delle canzoni alla Napolitana à sei voci* [1st edn 1573]. Venice: L'herede di Girolamo Scotto, 1576.

Fidelis, Lancelot (flamengo). *Il primo libro di madrigali aerosi a quatro voci*. Venice: li figliuoli di Antonio Guardano, 1570.

Gastoldi, Giovan Giacomo. *Sacre lodi a diversi santi con una Canzone al glorioso serafico S. Francesco*. Venice: Ricciardo Amadino, 1587.

Groto, Luigi. *Trofeo della Vittoria sacra, ottenuta della Chistianiss. Lega contra Turchi nell'anno MDLXXI*. Venice: Sigismondo Bordogna & Franc. Patriani, 1572.

Guarini, Battista, *Rime*. Venice: Gio. Bat. Ciotti, 1598.

Il gareggiamento poetico del Confuso Accademico Ordito. Madrigali amorosi gravi e piacevoli. Venice: Barezzo Barezzi, 1611.

Laparelli da Cortona, Marcantonio. *La Cristiade, poema heroico . . . alla Serenissima Gran Duchessa di Toscana . . .* Rome: apud Gulielmum Facciottum, 1618.

Liberti, Vincenzo. *Secondo libro dei madrigali a cinque voci*. Venice: Ricciardo Amadino, 1609.

Libro terzo delle rime di diuersi nobilissimi et eccellentissimi autori nuouamente raccolte. Venice: appresso Bartholomeo Cesano, 1550.

Marino, Giambattista. *Della lira . . . Parte Terza* [Venice: Giambattista Ciotti, 1614]. Venice: Il Ciotti, 1629.

Marino, Giambattista. *Il Padre Naso . . . Con le sue due prigionie di Napoli, e di Torino. Con un Sonetto sopra il Tebro. . .* Paris: Eredi di Abram Pacardo, 1626.

Marino, Giambattista. *Lettere . . . Gravi, Argute, e Facete*. Venice: Giacomo Sarzina, 1628.

Marino, Giambattista. *Rime*. Venice: Giovan Battista Ciotti, 1602.

Montella, Giovan Domenico, *Il primo libro dei madrigali a cinque voci*. Naples: Nicola Antonio Stigliola a Porta Regale, 1594.

Nasco, Giovan. *Primo libro di Madrigali a quattro*. Venice: Gardano, 1555.

Nuova scelta di rime di diversi begli ingegni. Genoa: Christofforo Bellone, F.A., 1573.

Ongaro, Antonio. *Rime . . .* Farnese: Nicolò Mariani, 1600.

Parabosco, Girolamo. *I diporti.* Venice: Giovan Griffio, [1551]; London: Riccardo Bancker, 1795.

Parabosco, Girolamo. *Il primo libro delle lettere famigliari e de' suoi madrigali.* Venice: Giovan Griffio, 1551.

Pesenti, Martino. *Il primo libro de' madrigali a due tre e quattro voci.* Venice: Alessandro Vincenti, 1621.

Raccolta di vari poemi latini, greci e volgari. Fatti . . . nella felice vittoria riportata da Cristiani contra Turchi alli VII d'ottobre del MDLXXI. Venice: Sebastiano Ventura, 1572.

Radesca da Foggia, [Enrico], *Canzonette, madrigali e arie alla romana a due voci. Libro primo.* Milan: Appresso l'herede di Simon Tini, et Filippo Lomazzo, compagni, 1606.

Rime di diversi, et eccellenti autori. Raccolte da i libri da noi altre volte impressi, tra le quali se ne leggono molte non piu vedute. Venice: appresso Gabriel Giolito de' Ferrari, et fratelli, 1553.

Rime di diversi nobili huomini et eccellenti poeti nella lingua thoscana. Libro secondo. Venice: appresso Gabriel Giolito di Ferrarii, 1547.

Romano, Remigio. *Terza raccolta di bellissime canzoni alla romanesca. Per suonare e cantare nella chitara alla Spagnuola. . . Con nuova aggiunta di poesie nuove.* Vicenza: Angelo Salvadori Libraro, 1622.

Scelta di rime di diversi moderni autori, Parte prima. Genoa: Heredi di Gieronimo Bartoli, 1591.

Tansillo, Luigi. *Il canzoniere edito ed inedito, secondo una copia dell'autografo ed altri manoscritti e stampe.* Edited by Erasmo Percopo. Naples: Consorzio editoriale Fridericiana/Liguori, 1996. Accessed 31 May 2022. http://www.Bibliotecaitaliana.it.

Tasso, Torquato. *Delle rime . . .: Parte quarta, e quinta.* Genoa: Ad instanza di Antonio Orero, 1586.

Tassoni, Alessandro. *La secchia rapita. L'oceano e le rime.* Edited by Giorgio Rossi. Bari: Laterza, 1930.

Varie poesie di molti eccellenti autori in morte del . . . Cavalier Battista Guarini. Milan: Gio. Battista Bidelli, 1618.

Venier, Maffio. *Canzoni e sonetti.* Edited by Attilio Carminati, Manlio Cortelazzo, Tiziana Agostini Nordio. Venice: Corbo e Fiore, 1993; Rome: Biblioteca Italiana, 2004. Accessed 11 March 2023. http://www.bibliotecaitaliana.it/.

Venier, Maffio. *Poesie di Maffeo Veniero arcivescovo di Corfù.* Edited by Bartolommeo Gamba. Venice: Al negozio di libri all'Apollo, dalla tipografia di Alvisopoli, 1817.

Venier, Maffio. *Poesie diverse.* Edited by Attilio Carminati, preface by Manlio Cortelazzo. Venice: Corbo e Fiore, 2001.

Secondary sources

Fenlon, Iain. 'Lepanto: The arts of celebration in Renaissance Venice', *Proceedings of the British Academy*, 73 (1987): 201–36.

Ferrari, Mattia. 'Il *Lamento dei pescatori veneziani* e il ms. Marc. It. IX 173 (=6282), Tesi di Laurea, relatore Prof. Lorenzo Tomasin, University of Ca' Foscari Venice, 2011–12.

Landi, Marco. 'Notizia di alcuni manoscritti di rime mariniane', *Studi secenteschi*, 62 (2021): 282–95.

Miller, Roark Thurston. 'The Composers of San Marco and Santo Stefano and the Development of Venetian Monody (to 1630)', PhD diss. University of Michigan (1993).

Nelson Novoa, James W. 'Double Alterity in a Celebratory Sonnet on the Battle of Lepanto', *eHumanista*, 21 (2012): 421–36.

Novati, F. 'Una poesia politica del Cinquecento: Il Pater noster dei Lombardi', *Giornale di Filologia Romanza*, 5 (1879): 122–52.

Petrina, Alessandra. 'Walter Scott of Buccleuch, Italian poet?', *Renaissance Studies*, 24.5 (2010): 671–93.

Pilot, Antonio. 'Il divorzio di Aldo Manuzio il giovane', *Ateneo Veneto*, 27 (1904): 62–74.

Rosenthal, Margaret F., *The Honest Courtesan: Veronica Franco, citizen and writer in sixteenth-century Venice.* Chicago: University of Chicago, 1992.

Zaccarello, Michelangelo. 'Alcune "Rime piacevoli" di Giovanni Della Casa e la tradizione burlesca', in *Giovanni della Casa Ecclesiastico e Scrittore. Atti del Convegno di Firenze-Borgo S. Lorenzo, 20–22 novembre 2003*, edited by Stefano Carrai, 281–306. Rome: Edizioni di storia e letteratura, 2007. Accessed 12 June 2022. https://iris.univr.it/retrieve/handle/11562/318239/2181/CAP7_Zaccarello_DellaCasa.pdf.

Zanetti, Umberto. 'Anonimo della battaglia Lepanto', [2006], 196–200. Accessed 7 October 2022. https://www.pieralbertoverlato.it/_files/ugd/344e7d_fc7599a6b4a644b2b107110f5b79d9bd.pdf.

Clorilli, A Pastoral Tragicomedy: A bilingual annotated edition

By Leonora Bernardi, Gentlewoman of Lucca

Italian text edited by Lisa Sampson, translation by Anna Wainwright, and notes by Lisa Sampson and Anna Wainwright

Transcription criteria

Lisa Sampson

The transcription of the *Tragicomedia pastorale* in the Marciana manuscript MS It IX, 239 (=6999), here presented in print for the very first time, aims to balance fidelity to the original, on the one hand, and the needs of the modern reader, on the other. The clarity of the copying hand and the generally good state of preservation of the manuscript makes it possible to reproduce the text and formatting without significant editorial interventions (see Section 2.2). However, this is not a diplomatic transcription. Relevant physical aspects and presumed errors are noted, and the following modifications to the text have been made for the sake of accessibility:

- The few abbreviations found in the text, which are not used consistently, have been silently written out in full (e.g. *no'* > *non*; *-q*[flourish] > *-que* (e.g. *dunq.* > *dunque*); *Sig.^{ra}* > *Signora*; *feliciss.^o* > *felicissimo*; *illus.^r* > *illustre*; *q.a* > *questa*).
- The use of *ij* has been standardized to *ii* (e.g. *templij* > *templii*; *odij* > *odii*, *injurij* > *injurii*).
- The use of *h* has been modernized (e.g. *havesser* > *avesser*; *heroi* > *eroi*; *hor* > *or*; *anticho* > *antico*; *vagha* > *vaga*, *dhe* > *deh*).
- *-(t)ti* has been standardized to *-z* (e.g. *gratia* > *grazia*; *precipitio* > *precipizio*; *condittion* > *condizion*).
- Apostrophes are added or normalized according to modern usage (e.g. *el reggi* > *e'l reggi*; *l'asciò* > *lasciò*).
- Further editorial interventions have been indicated by square brackets and explanations are given in the footnotes.

Questions of orthography (including the use of apostrophes), adjustment of word boundaries, accentuation and punctuation have occasionally required a more flexible approach, given their very fluid usage within the manuscript, as is typical for the period before the establishment of firm and universally used linguistic and grammatical norms. Orthography is inconsistent even for proper names (e.g. oscillation of *Fillinio/Filinio*; *Crestina/Cristina*). In Dalinda's long lament at the end of Act 4 (scene 5), *rivela* and *rivella* are used interchangeably in the refrain 'Tu fonte testimone *rivela/rivella* altrui' and even within the same line one can find variants: 'spera *ancor* Filemon *anchor* confida' (I.5.107 [17v]). In cases where a standard form exists, this is given throughout; any oscillations and editorial changes are indicated in square brackets, or in a footnote (unless subject to the modifications listed above). Where the variants used are commonly found (e.g. *luoco*, *loco*, *luogo*; *longo* (for *lungo*); *dui*, *duo* (for *due*)) these are preserved in the transcription. M contains various Tuscan forms, some of which are common, such as *li* (for third person dative pronoun of both genders, *gli* and *le*); others are referenced in notes.[1]

Word boundaries have on occasions been adapted silently to follow modern usage in order to facilitate comprehension. This may involve separating words (e.g. *intestessa* > *in te stessa*; *avostri* > *a vostri*; *agara* > *a gara*) and joining words (*in vece* > *invece*; *per fin* > *perfin*; *dall'hor* > *d'allor*). However, words have only been joined or split where this does not involve *raddoppiamento sintattico* (e.g. *per che* > *perché*, *poi che* > *poiché*; but not *già mai* > *giammai*, or *a la* > *alla*).

The use of accents and diacritics is also rather haphazard in the manuscript and has been adapted where necessary to follow modern usage in order to aid comprehension. For example, redundant elements have been removed (e.g. accent on *tù*, apostrophe in *A' così*); accents have been added to distinguish words (e.g. *di* (of) / *dì* (say, day) or *voi* (you) / *vòi* (*vuoi*, you want)) or occasionally to indicate stress in unusual verbal formations; and apostrophes have been added to indicate that omitted letters follow normal usage (e.g. *l' sole* > *'l sole*).

Capitalization in the manuscript has been slightly adapted to follow standard modern usage, so capitals have, for instance, been removed for unmarked proper nouns (e.g. 'Ninfe' and 'Pastori'; 'per far preda d'Augei le reti han tese'). It is retained where it highlights content or proper names and allegorizations. Whereas the original manuscript capitalizes each line at the start, as typical also in early printed editions, the present volume observes internal punctuation rules, with the aim of facilitating the sense of the verse and making the sentence structure clearer to the modern reader.

The original punctuation in the manuscript is generally reasonably easy for the modern reader to follow, though it is somewhat on the light side and is unevenly used in places. For this reason, the present edition adheres where possible to the original usage, though some punctuation has been strengthened (e.g. commas replaced with colons or full stops), or adjusted to aid comprehension. Occasional stray dots and dashes visible on the manuscript have made some interpretation necessary at times in light of the content. The most significant intervention has been the addition of long dashes to mark reported speech, again for the aid of the modern reader. The undifferentiated use in the original manuscript of a question mark (see Fig. 8) to indicate both questions and exclamations has occasionally resulted in a necessary distinction being made to clarify the sense.[2] The edition reproduces M's use of the *diple* (") in the left-hand margin at the mid-level of each line of a segment of text to indicate notable sayings (*sententiae*) or references to other authoritative works (see Figs 7 and 9).[3] Other forms of marginal pointing are indicated and explained in the notes.

As was common in pastoral plays following Tasso's *Aminta*, *Clorilli* is in verse of mixed hendecasyllable (*endecasillabo*) and heptasyllable (*settenario*) lines. In M all lines start at the left margin, including some occasional lines divided between two speakers (*antilabe*), a rhetorical device adopted from Greek tragedy which increases the drama and pace.[4] Where *antilabe* is inferred it is indicated according to normal editorial practice, by indenting the second half-line, and numbering only whole lines. Where line breaks in M appear to have been introduced erroneously (e.g. leaving lines of three syllables) or have apparently been omitted (e.g. leaving a line of at least 14 syllables, IV.4.108–9), these are adjusted and noted. Also noted are the few cases where lines appear in an inconsistent metre.

Notes

1 Rohlfs, *Grammatica storica*, II: §457.
2 While question marks had a long tradition pre-print, exclamation marks were still rarely used in print at the turn of the seventeenth century in vernacular texts, and had only recently been codified in Orazio Lombardelli's *L'arte del puntar* (1585); see Castellani, 'Sulla formazione', I:75–8.
3 On the *diple*, see 2.2.2.
4 Rutherford, *Greek Tragic Style*, 42.

Note on the translation

Anna Wainwright

This is both the first time that Leonora Bernardi's pastoral tragicomedy *Clorilli* has appeared in print and the first time it has been translated from Italian into English – or into any language, for that matter. It has been thus both a daunting and liberating task, as I was neither burdened by earlier translations nor able to be helped by them. The English text is based on the only known copy of the play, which is located in a manuscript housed in the Biblioteca Nazionale Marciana in Venice and which Lisa Sampson describes in detail in Section 2.2.

Throughout the lengthy process, I was fortunate to be able to hear – and see – an abridged version of my translation performed live in English: once at NYU's La Pietra campus in Florence in Spring 2018, and then again at the University of New Hampshire in Spring 2019, both in Eric Nicholson's marvellous and agile adaptation. These performances, as well as a semester's worth of rehearsals with students for the production in New Hampshire, allowed me to further refine particular phrasings after hearing them repeatedly spoken aloud. I am indebted to Dr Nicholson for his lively collaboration and the many elegant and lyrical touches he lent to parts of the text in his stage adaptation, many of which have been retained in the present edition. I am also thankful to Anna Newman and Amy Boylan at the University of New Hampshire for collaborating with me on the 2019 production.

I have chosen to translate the play into prose, while remaining as faithful as possible to the author's use of alliteration, assonance and other stylistic flourishes. My twin concerns as I translated the text were providing clarity of meaning for the anglophone reader, and maintaining the particular tone and style of the early modern Italian original. To this end, I have sought as much as possible to be faithful to Bernardi's original intent, except in cases when to do so would make the English irretrievably awkward. I have also regularly used somewhat archaic turns of phrase in English without leaning too heavily into ostentatiously stylized parlance, and have avoided overly familiar or casual contemporary expressions.

Bernardi's characters often speak in the present tense in order to recount events that took place in the past with more life, as is common in Renaissance drama, and I have maintained the present tense in some of these instances. The frequent *sententiae* or adages sprinkled throughout the play have been put into italics. I have added very few stage directions, doing so only when it seemed absolutely necessary in order to explain to readers or actors a sudden change in tone or situation.

As is standard in translations of early modern Italian, I have broken up many of the longer sentences into two or more shorter ones, and have occasionally replaced pronouns with characters' names for clarity. This is most important in scenes which concern the two male protagonists, who are wittily, if inconveniently, named Filemone and Fillinio. Names of prominent mythical figures have been anglicized (e.g. Jove, Cupid, Venus), but more obscure or entirely invented names have been left in the original (e.g. Sicano, Italo, Gloridaura). Because the Grand Duchess is generally styled as 'Christine' in anglophone scholarship, I have followed suit; governed by the same logic, her husband, the grand duke of Florence, is referred to as Ferdinando.

In addition to the important contributions from Dr Nicholson, as well as welcome and helpful input from Eugenio Refini, I am profoundly grateful to the volume's editors, Virginia Cox and Lisa Sampson. It has been a privilege to explore and discover Leonora Bernardi's life and works in collaboration with them, and they have offered their expertise and support throughout the translation of this challenging and delightful text, adding many an invaluable turn of phrase to the English version.

Clorilli, A Pastoral Tragicomedy

Tragicomedia Pastorale della
Signora Xq^cbefm Hqxmllm
Gentildonna lucchesse / [1ᵛ]

Madrigale

Venere alla Autora

Il dolce e caro figlio   1
afflitta madre i' cerco: e che ridete
gentil signora? Voi forse l'avete?
Ahi mi date sospetto
che rinchiuso non stia nel vostro petto: 5
rendetel prego, che di furto tale
n'avereste voi ancor pena immortale. / [2^r]

Prologo

Linfadusa fata

Di molte una son io   1
del gran D[e]mogorgon² dev[o]te³ ancelle
che con potere et con sapere immenso
il fato altrui come a noi piace andiamo
spesso cangiando; onde da voi mortali   5
fate siam dette. Io Linfadusa sono,
abitatrice di questi alti colli
perfin d'allor che 'l generoso Atlante
li coronò di grandi eccelse torri.
Io quella fui che prima   10
Dardano il gran rampollo
che in te già germogliò patria felice
in più feconda terra trasportai.
Però che da poter maggior del mio
a me fu l'alta sua cura commessa,   15

---

¹ For full title page, see 2.2.5 Appendix.
² *Dimogorgon*. Unless otherwise stated, all notes reference M.
³ *devete*.

Pastoral Tragicomedy by
Signora Xqᶜbefm Hqxmllm
Gentlewoman of Lucca / [1ᵛ]

Madrigal

Venus to the Author

I, a suffering mother, am searching
for my dear, sweet son.[2] And why do you laugh,
gentle lady? Do you perhaps have him yourself?
Alas, you make me fear
he may be hidden within your breast:
Give him back, pray, for such a theft
would earn you eternal punishment. / [2^r]

Prologue

The fairy Linfadusa[3]

I am one of many devoted handmaidens of the great Demogorgon.[4] With our great power and wisdom, we often change the fates of men as it pleases us. Thus we are called fairies by you mortals. I am Linfadusa, a dweller in these glorious hills ever since generous Atlas crowned them with great, lofty towers.[5]

It was I who first brought to more fertile soil the great shoot Dardanus, who first germinated in you, happy fatherland.[6] A power greater than I entrusted me with the illustrious care of Dardanus, just as

com'ebbe Eraclitea la cura anch'ella,
di Sica[n]o[4] il fratel, e Gloridaura
d'Italo il glorioso da cui serba
la bellissima Italia anch'oggi il nome.
Dardano fu mia cura et mio diletto,   20
gradito e caro, et da cui già discese
di gloriosi eroi sì lunga serie: / [2ᵛ]
eroi felici, per cui già la vita
mi fu diletta. Et quando, ahi rimembranza,
viddi cadente il fortunato Impero   25
felicissimo un tempo, et da me cadde
per lunghissimo spazio ogni speranza
né più potei soffrir d'andar intorno
per quei monti rimirando, ahi lassa,
raccorre il mietitor le spighe e l'erba   30
dove al Ciel s'inalzar palagi e templii:
racchiusa entro l'orror d'un antro scuro
l'immortalità mia gran tempo piansi;
e se col mio saper non vedea lungi,
che ancora a più sovrani invitti eroi   35
saresti ancor Fiesole bella serva,
prevedendo d'Egeria il tristo caso
in lacrime conversa già sarei.
Ma fortunata speme
che pur al fin dopo sì lungo tempo   40
che 'l seme tuo nell'alma mia spargesti
maturisi.[5] Pur oggi si rinnova
il bel secol dell'oro
che felice fiorì, mentre fioriva
del gran Dardano mio la nobil prole.   45
Ecco che pure al fortunato Impero / [3ʳ]
è giunto il grand'EROE per cui l'Etruria
più superba n'andrà, che già non fece
e Frigia, e l'Asia, e la Sicilia, e 'n quanti
fortunato terren,   50
luoghi spargesti tu dei tuoi rampolli.
Ecco dunque che omai
vengo, o bella dell'or novella etade,

[4] *Sicamo*.
[5] *maturisi: si maturi*.

Eraclitea cared for his brother Sicano, and Gloridaura for glorious Italo, from whom most beautiful Italy takes her name.[7]

Dardanus was my charge and my delight, beloved and dear, and such a long line of glorious heroes descended from him: / [2ᵛ] fortunate heroes, who made my life so dear. And when – alas, what a memory! – I saw that fortunate, once-happy empire crumbling, every hope of mine collapsed for a very long time as well. Nor could I bear to wander these mountains any longer, alas, and see the reaper harvest corn and hay where palaces and temples once stretched to Heaven. Confined to the gloom of a shadowy cave, I lamented my immortality for a long while. And if I had not long foreseen that you, lovely Fiesole,[8] would one day serve yet loftier, more triumphant heroes, I would have melted into tears, presaging the sad story of Egeria.[9]

But fortunate hope! For now, at last, so long after you planted the seed in my soul – now may it ripen! This very day the great Golden Age, which flourished when the noble offspring of my great Dardanus flourished, is born again.

Behold, the great HERO has returned to this fortunate empire, / [3ʳ] so that Etruria will lord it over Phrygia and Asia and Sicily, and, fortunate land, in every place where you once planted your shoots.[10] Behold, thus! For now, at last, I have come as well, O wondrous new Age of Gold,

al tuo splendor a rinovar anch'io
la primiera allegrezza; ecco ch'io vengo,   55
coppia beata, ad inchinarmi umile.
—   Ecco gran FERDINAND, ecco CR[I]STINA[6]
come al vostro splendor s'inaura l'mondo.
Ma qual germe vegg'io che da voi spunta?
Che pargoletto semideo vegg'io,   60
che 'n fasce, e 'n culla dal bel volto spira
maestà tanta? Ben lo riconosco,
questo è COSMO novello, a cui già veggio
dell'immortalità sacrar nel[7] Tempio,[8]
trofei che ascenderan fino alle stelle.   65
Veggio al bel nome tuo Regal Infante
ogni lume oscurarsi e 'n bella schiera
tornar abitatrici della terra
quell[e][9] che già fuggir del ferreo mondo
schive del secol rio Virtù Celesti.   70
Già prepara la gloria alte corone / [3ᵛ]
di palme e lauri, onde il tuo capo cinga,
già molli di sudor Sterope e Bronte
della più fina adamantina tempra
nobil' arme preparano, et già s'ode   75
di incudi risonar l'atra fucina.
O qual ti serba il fato alte vittorie.
O quante domerà provincie, e regni,
la valorosa destra?
Che qual fulmin di foco   80
atterrerà le più superbe cime.
Già veggio, o veder parmi
i più gelati Sciti
le mani al petto, e le gran teste inchine
piegar devoti al tuo regal aspetto.   85
Cresci felice Augusto, e cresca teco

---

[6] CRESTINA; capitalization in original (see Fig. 6). Christine of Lorraine signed her name as 'Chrestina'; more commonly she was known as Cristina (see below, l. 110), though other variants were also used ('Cristiana' or 'Cristierna'), Butters, 'Christine', 139 n.118. A dash appears in the left margin.

[7] nell'.

[8] Tempio: alterations and slight blot in this word, apparently to cancel an 'r' between the 'i' and 'o' (possibly originally '[I]mpero').

[9] quelli.

to renew that first happiness with your splendour: here I come to kneel before this blessed couple.[11]

Behold, great FERDINANDO, behold, CHRISTINE, how your splendour gilds the world![12] But what new shoot do I see, which has sprung up from the two of you? What sweet demigod of a child do I see, who even in his swaddling clothes and cradle exudes such majesty from his beautiful face? Ah! I recognize him! This is the new COSIMO; already I can see the trophies consecrated to him in the Temple of Immortality, ascending to the heavens.[13] I can see that the great name of your royal infant will outshine all lights, and the Heavenly Virtues, who fled the Iron World horrified by that wicked age, will return in a fair flock to inhabit the earth once more.[14] Glory is already preparing sublime crowns / [3ᵛ] of palm and laurel to adorn your head; Steropes and Bronte are already damp with sweat as they prepare your noble arms from the finest tempered adamant; already one can hear the dark forge echo with the sound of anvils.[15] Oh, what great victories Fate holds in store for you! Oh, how many provinces and kingdoms your valorous right hand will conquer, as, like a lightning bolt, it razes the proudest peaks! Already I see, or it seems to me I see, the Scythians in their icy wastes, hands to chest, and their great heads bowed, kneeling in devotion before your royal countenance.[16]

Grow, happy Augustus, and may my hope grow alongside you, and,

la speme mia, cresca et crescendo avanza
i Lorenzi, i Giovanni
i Cosmi, e 'l gran Francesco.
Cedino al tuo valor   90
gli Eustacchii, Balduini, e i Gottofredi
e quanti altri fiorir guerrieri illustri
dall'una, e l'altra gloriosa stirpe.
Ma tu solleva omai l'altera fronte
Fiesole bella, e se già fosti   95
dal tuo gran fondatore / [4ʳ]
coronata di torri alte, e superbe
oggi pur t'ergerai felice al Cielo
coronata di gloria

"10 che per lunga stagion non cade o crolla.   100
Felice madre già, ma più felice
oggi serva di grandi invitti eroi.
Limpidissimo fonte
che del gran Ferdinando irrighi i campi
al tuo, soave e grato mormorio,   105
lasciando il be[l] Permesso, et Ippocre[n]e,[11]
liete verranno ad abitar le Muse,
e canteran con voci alte e canore
de' tuoi gran Semidei le vere lodi.
Canteran di voi saggia CRISTINA   110
la pietate, il valor, la cortesia,
che qual sol fiammeg[g]iante
splender vi fan di chiari raggi adorna.
Ma quai preveggio tristi avvenimenti
che in così lieti, e sì felici giorni,   115
oggi pur avveranno in questi colli
tra questi pastorali abitatori?
E se l'età dell'or pur oggi splende,
come a lor non risplende? or m[e] n'aveggio[12]
Amor n'è la cagion. Empio tiranno   120

" che l'alme altrui, come a lui piace invole / [4ᵛ]
" di tormento e di noia.

---

[10] *diple* (") in left-hand margin indicates a *sententia*, following a commonly used typographical practice in Italy from 1502, and earlier in manuscripts; see Transcription criteria; 2.2.2 and Fig. 9.
[11] *bell'*; *Hippocreme*.
[12] *m' n'aveggio*.

in growing, outstrip the Lorenzos, and the Giovannis, the Cosimos and the great Francesco.[17] May the Eustaces, the Baldwins and the Godfreys cede to your valour, and all the other valiant warriors from both branches of your glorious family tree.[18] But you, beautiful Fiesole, at long last raise up your lofty brow! And though you have already been crowned by your great founder / [4ʳ] with tall, proud towers, today you will ascend to Heaven, crowned with a glory *that will not crumble or collapse for many an age*. I am already a happy mother, but even happier today as the servant to such great, invincible heroes.

Clearest fountain, you who bring life to the fields of the great Ferdinando! The Muses will leave behind beautiful Permessus and Hippocrene, and happily come here to live by your soft, graceful murmuring,[19] and sing the true praises of you great demigods with noble and resounding voices. They will sing of you, wise Christine, of your piety, valour, courtesy, all of which, like a flaming sun, adorn you with spectacular rays.

But what are these unhappy events I foresee? In such happy and joyous days, will they really occur in these hills, among the shepherds who make their home here? And if the Golden Age does shine today, why, then, does it not also shine on them?

Now I see! Love is the reason. A cruel tyrant who *steals away the souls of others* / [4ᵛ] *with torment and sorrow as he so pleases.*

“   Amor cieco fanciullo,
“   che 'l fren della ragion togliendo altrui
       scorge sovente i miserelli amanti   125
       a precipizio e morte.
       E ben oggi il vedrete,
       né già senza pietade,
       nel più gentil pastor di queste selve.
       Udirete oggi risonar i colli,   130
       di focosi sospir d'amaro pianto,
       nuovi rivi vedrete irrigar l'erbe.
       Ma ben v'annunzio ancora,
       che lieto fin avranno i lor martiri,
       ché non voglio io che turbi,   135
       ancor picciola nube,
       il bel seren della chiare speranze.
       Dunque col mio potere,
       tornerò lieti i tristi avversi casi,
       e sgombrato il dolor dai cori afflitti   140
       di pianto invece, e di sospir dogliosi,
       farò sonar i colli e le campagne,
       di liete voci, et di sua[v]i accenti.

Fine del prologo / [5ʳ]

Love is a blind little boy who, taking the bridle of reason from others, all too often sees poor wretched lovers to ruin and death.[20] And today you will, not without pity, see him reign over the noblest shepherd of these woods. Today you will hear the hills resound with the fiery sighs of bitter lament,[21] and you will see new streams of tears drench the grass.

But I also announce to you that their miseries will have a happy ending,[22] for I do not want even with the smallest cloud to obscure the great light of shining hope. So, with my power, I will transform the nymphs' and shepherds' sad, unfortunate stories into happy ones, and lift the pain from afflicted hearts. Instead of woeful sighs and laments, I will make the hills and the countryside resound with happy voices, and ring out with the sweetest and loveliest of sounds.

End of prologue / [5ʳ]

Interlocutori

Alfesibeo	)	
Alcone	)	Vecchi
Armilla	)	
Clorilli	)	Ninfe
Dalinda	)	
Licasta	)	
Filemone	)	
Coribante	)	Pastori
Fillinio	)	
Ruscone		Satiro
Aurindo	)	Nunzio
[Licandro[13]		Nunzio] / [5ᵛ]

---

[13] M omits the second messenger, who first appears in Act 5 scene 1.

Players

Alfesibeo	)	
Alcone	)	Old men
Armilla	)	
Clorilli	)	Nymphs
Dalinda	)	
Licasta	)	
Filemone	)	
Coribante	)	Shepherds
Fillinio	)	
Ruscone		Satyr
Aurindo	)	Herald(s)
[Licandro[23]	)]	/ [5ᵛ]

ATTO PRIMO

Scena prima

Alfesibeo,[14] *Alcone*

ALF.	O come bella in oriente appare	1
	con la fronte di rose e co[n] crin[15] d'oro	
	più dell'usato l'Alba.	
	O come lieti e vaghi	
	al suo nuovo apparir ridono i colli	5
	e con dolci concenti	
	salutano gli augeletti il nuovo giorno.	
	Ond'io più del[l]' usato assai per tempo	
	sorgo a dar lode al creator dell'Alba,	
	pien di nuova speranza,	10
	che in questo dì giocondo	
	termin' avran le mie[16] sì lunghe pene.	
	Fa' tu Giove immortal che così sia.	
	Ma non veggio da lungi	
	venir Alcone il mio caro compagno?	15
	È esso certo, se già non m'inganna	
	la debol' vista per sì lunga etade.	
ALC.	Né più felice, né più caro incontro	
	non poteva venirmi del mio amato	
	e caro Alfe[s]ibeo, e s'è presaga	20
	di un lieto giorno una lieta mattina / [6r]	
	fortunato sarà questo, e felice.	
ALF.	Ove così per tempo, et così solo	
	eri inviato Alcone? Al tempio forse?	
ALC.	Al tempio tu l'hai detto.	25
	E veniva rivolgendo nella mente	
	un sogno che poche ore innanzi 'l giorno	
	m'empié di tema, e di letizia[17] il petto.	

---

[14] *Alfezibeo* (see Fig. 9). The cast list gives 'Alfesibeo', the standard Italian pastoral form which is used in this edition, though the play text adopts a form with 'z'. See *Clorilli* translation, n. 26.

[15] Between 'co' and 'crin' an 's' has been erased.

[16] *miei.*

[17] *empie . . . lettizia.*

ACT ONE

Scene One

Alfesibeo, Alcone

Alfesibeo

Oh, how the Dawn appears in the east today, even more beautiful than usual, with her rosy brow and golden hair.[24] Oh, how the hills laugh, beautiful and happy at this latest appearance, and how the little fowls salute this new day with their sweet harmonies. Whereby, earlier than usual, I rise to give praise to the dawn's creator, full of fresh hope that this cheerful day will end my long sufferings. O immortal Jove, let it be so!

But wait! Is that not my dear friend Alcone I see, approaching from afar?[25] Yes, it is him, if my eyes, weakened by old age, do not deceive me.

Alcone

Neither a happier nor a sweeter meeting could occur than one with my beloved, dear friend Alfesibeo.[26] And if a happy morning foreshadows a happy day, / [6ʳ] this one will certainly be fortunate and pleasant.

Alfesibeo

Where are you going this early all by yourself, Alcone? To the temple,[27] perhaps?

Alcone

I was on my way to the temple, just as you say. And as I made my way there, I was thinking about a dream I had just a few hours before daybreak. It filled my breast with both happiness and foreboding.

ALF.	Anch'io nella medesima ora appunto	
	viddi sogno simil, ma come vani	30
	li[18] ho sempre reputati, io non li credo.	
ALC.	Se ben talor fa[l]laci	
	riescono, è pur ver che anche talvolta	
	il ver predisse altrui verace sogno.	
ALF.	Sì ma tra mille e mille	35
	bugiardi e vani un ver ne trovi appena.	
	Pur dimmi Alcone amato il tuo, che poi	
	anch'io diro[t]ti[19] il mio.	
ALC.	E' mi parea	
	che una leggiadra mia gentil colomba,	
	che nodrito m'avea molti e molt'anni	40
	con gran diletto e cura,	
	fuor del mio sen con improviso volo	
	uscisse per seguire il più gentile	
	colombo che formasse unqua natura;	
	ond'io rimasi sbigot[t]ito e 'n vano / [6ᵛ]	45
	tentai di ritrovarla,	
	e mi parea che al fine	
	si calasse alla fonte de' cipressi,	
	ove trovò che in terra	
	gi[a]cea[20] l'amato suo colombo estinto.	50
	Sussur[r]ò flebilmente,	
	e con l'ugna e col rostro,	
	cruda a sé stessa lacerossi il petto,	
	si divelse la piuma, e del suo sangue	
	fe' pioggia miserabile e funesta.	55
	E già parea vicina all'ora estrema	
	quando da questi boschi	
	ecco spiegar il volo	
	a gemella compagna, e non sì tosto	
	la vidde in tal stato, che veloce	60
	bec[c]ò di tal virtude o fronda od[21] erba	
	che in un momento risanolla, e poscia	
	seco si rinselvò, né più la viddi,	

---

[18] gli.
[19] diroti, i.e. ti dirò. Cf. line 70.
[20] gicea.
[21] ad.

Alfesibeo

I had a similar dream myself, at the very same hour! But since I have always considered dreams to be of little importance, I give them no credence.

Alcone

Though they often turn out to be false, it also happens that a good dream has occasionally predicted the truth.[28]

Alfesibeo

Yes, but among thousands and thousands of false and vain dreams, you will scarcely ever find a single true one. But tell me yours, beloved Alcone, and then I will tell you mine.

Alcone

In my dream, I had a beautiful and noble dove, whom I had raised for many years with great pleasure and care. She flew away from me unexpectedly to follow the most noble male dove ever to live; I was left dismayed, and tried in vain / [6ᵛ] to find her again. At last, I seemed to see her swoop down into the cypress fountain. There she found her beloved mate, lying dead on the ground. She murmured faintly, and, turning cruelly on herself, tore at her breast with her claws and beak, ripping away her plumage. Her blood rained down in a piteous, dire stream.[29] It seemed that she was already nearing her final hour when suddenly, from these very woods, she flew off to a sister dove. Once her friend saw her in this terrible state, she began to peck at grass and herbs of such virtue that they cured my dove at once. Then she went back into the forest with her companion. I did not see my dove for a long time, until

se non dopò gran tempo che solinga
tornossi a questa fonte.   65
ove trovò l'amato suo compagno
oltre ogni creder vivo,
onde più che mai bella, a me più cara
lieta ritornò seco al nido antico.
Questo è 'l mio ALFESIBEO[22], dirotti / [7ʳ]   70
quel[23] che io temo, e quel ch'io spero. E prima
tu ti dèi ricordar che quando al Cielo
si ritornò la mia[24] diletta Nisa,
che mi lasciò Dalinda
mia cara amata figlia,   75
la qual mentre con g[i]oia io preparava
di darla per sposa a Filemone,
ché d'accordo eravamo Ergasto et io,
partissi,[25] non so come, ascosamente
una notte da me; notte infelice,   80
ché le tenebre tue poscia durate
son sempre in questo cor, né già mai nuova
n'ebbi meschin[o][26]; or dicea meco
forse l'amico sogno in cotal guisa
della mia dolce figlia   85
il bramato ritorno a me predice.
O se ciò fosse ver, felice vecchio,
pur rivederesti ancora
la tua cara Dalinda.
Ma quando mi sovvien che esangue e smorta   90
giacer vidd'io la colombella estinta
tutto mi raccapriccio,[27] et bramo allora
che sian bugiardi [i] sogni, et da me lungi
così sinistri infortunati auguri.
Così tra dubbio e speme, / [7ᵛ]   95
tra contento e dolore
mi vivo Alfe[s]ibeo.

---

[22] *ALFEZIBEO.*
[23] *Quell'.*
[24] *mia*: insertion above.
[25] *partissi*: in standard Italian *si partì.*
[26] *meschin*: addition surmised, as existing line has no more than 10 syllables.
[27] *raccapricciò*: the accent may be a transcription error perhaps influenced by past tense 'vidd'io' (line 91); *raccapriccio* in the present tense better fits the sense.

she returned alone to the fountain, where she discovered her beloved, who, contrary to all expectation, was still alive. She then came back to her old nest, happier, dearer and more beautiful to me than ever.

This was my dream, dear Alfesibeo. Now I will tell you / [7^r] what I hope, and what I fear. First, you must remember that when my beloved Nisa departed this life to ascend to Heaven, she left behind Dalinda, my dear beloved daughter.[30] I had been planning Dalinda's marriage to Filemone with great joy, after an agreement made with Filemone's father Ergasto.[31] Then, one night, she ran away from me in secret, I know not how. Unhappy night, your long shadows have stayed in my heart! I have had no news of her since, much to my woe.

Just now, I was thinking that perhaps this kind dream is a prediction of my sweet daughter's longed-for return home. Oh, if it were true, you would see your sweet Dalinda again, you fortunate old man![32] But when I remember how I saw the little dove lying drained of blood, all life extinguished, I am horrified once more, and long to believe that dreams are no more than lies, and that these unfortunate and sinister portents have no meaning for me. And this is how I live, Alfesibeo: between doubt and hope, / [7^v] between happiness and sadness.

ALF.
Gran cose invero
mi narri, ma se tanta legge[28]
di perfetta amicizia   100
v[u]ol che l'amico al caro amico scopra
ogni pensier occulto,
ben ardisco pregarti,
per quella che tra noi fin da['] prim'anni
vera amicizia è stata,   105
che tu mi faccia noto
la cagion della fuga di Dalinda
di che non mai t'ho domandato prima
per non rinovellar col tuo dolore
il mio dolor insieme;   110
però che il mio Fillinio
rim[em]branza[29] crudel, in quella stessa
fece egli ancor da me partita
per più non ritornar. Fillinio mio,
amato figlio e caro,   115
or sarà mai ch'io ti riveda et oda?

ALC.
Se ben io so che le parole mie
son mantice al dolor che 'l cor m'affligge,
io pur dirò per compiacerti quanto / [8ʳ]
brami saper da me, se ben di questo   120
certo io non son, ma sol n'ho qualche indizio.
Se ti dicea pur d'i[n]anzi,
che già conchiuso con Ergasto av[e]a
d'unirla in matrimonio al figlio, or sappi
che sempre che di ciò seco parlai   125
mostrossi al desir mio ritrosa e schiva,
dicendo pur che seguitar Diana
volea, non Imeneo. Né mai ragione
che per farle cangiar pensiero o voglia
io le recasse incontro   130
fece alcun frutto, ma salda e costante
stette nel primo dir. Io che credea
vergogna verginal, non ostinata
durezza questa sua, conchiusi il tutto,
sperando che 'l gentile   135

---

[28] Lines 98–99: unusually these are respectively of 5 or 6, and 9 syllables.

[29] *Rimbranza*: presumably a copy error for *rimembranza*, which would give the line the standard 11 syllables.

Alfesibeo

You recount truly amazing things to me. But in keeping with the law of perfect friendship, which requires that every hidden thought be revealed to one's bosom friend, dare I ask, because we have been friends so long: can you explain why Dalinda ran away? I have never asked you before, because I did not want to renew my own pain along with yours; I felt grief for my own Fillinio, O bitter memory, who at that very same time left me too never to return again.[33] My own Fillinio! My dear beloved son, will I ever see you again, ever hear your voice?

Alcone

Although I am well aware that my words can only serve to stoke the sadness that afflicts my heart, I can certainly tell you what / [8ʳ] you wish to know from me, even if I am not fully certain of it myself, but have only some signs. Now, you must know that despite my agreement with Ergasto, Dalinda was always wary of and resistant to my desire to see her married and declared that she would rather be a follower of Diana than of Hymen.[34] Nor did any argument that I put forward to try to make her change her thoughts or wishes ever bear fruit; instead, she remained resolute and faithful to her original decision. Since I believed this stemmed from virginal bashfulness, rather than firm determination, I carried on with the arrangements. I hoped that the noble appearance of the

aspetto del pastor, con le sue vaghe
et accorte maniere, avesse al fine
a levarle dal cor questa sciocchezza.
Così li diedi la nuova[30]
delle future nozze.   140
A così fiero annunzio ella rimase
pallida, muta, fredda, e quasi priva
di sentimento, et dopo un gran silenzio / [8ᵛ]
in cotai voci irata al fin proruppe:
— Sazia, Padre crudel con la mia morte   145
la voglia tua che io t'obedisco e cedo —[31]
mi disse, e tacque, e dui fonti di pianto
da gl'occhi scatur[ir][32]. Si tolse poscia
da me furiosa, et dall' albergo fuori
uscì soletta, e poi che alquanto spazio   150
fu dimorata, ritornò più lieta,
in vista più tranquilla e tutta umile.
Ma quando apparve in ciel l'alba novella,
del giorno ch'io sperai più fortunato
d'ogni altro, più tranquillo (o come spesso   155
"   nostro folle sperar riman deluso),
più non veggio Dalinda, e quella casa
che esser casa dovea di gioia e festa
fu ripiena di pianto e di sospiri.
Partì da me Dalinda, né so dirti   160
s'Amor le fosse scorta o pur Diana.
A me fia sempre amara,
e l'una e l'altra. Allor d'ogni mio bene,
e d'ogni speme mia rimasi privo.
ALF.   "   Se ben biasmar le cose a cui rimedio   165
"   alcun non è forse follia rassembra,
io pur dirollo. Alcone errasti allora / [9ʳ]
che contro la sua voglia
di legarla pensasti
a quel sì forte laccio   170
"   che scioglier non si può se non per morte.
"   Ché se in ogni altra cosa al padre i figli

---

[30] Line of 8 syllables.
[31] Long dashes added to mark reported speech.
[32] *scaturì*. Standard Italian *scaturirono* (intransitive verb *scaturire*).

shepherd Filemone,[35] with his pleasing and refined manners, would banish my daughter's foolish thoughts, and so I told her the news of her future marriage.

In response to this bitter announcement, she turned pale, mute and cold; indeed, she seemed to have lost all feeling. After a long silence, / [8ᵛ] she cried out in an angry voice: 'Cruel father, may your wish be fulfilled by my death, for I shall yield and obey you!' She said this to me, and then she went quiet. Two fountains of grief sprang from her eyes. She left me in a fury, and fled the house by herself.[36] Then, after some time had passed, she returned, and seemed happier, calmer and most humble. But when the next day's dawn appeared in the sky, on that day I had hoped would be more fortunate and tranquil than any other – oh, *how often our crazy hopes are dashed!* – Dalinda was gone, and our house, which should have been bursting with joy and celebration, was instead filled with sadness and sighs![37]

Dalinda left me. I do not know whether to tell you Love was her escort, or Diana. Whether it be one, or the other, does not matter; either would be a bitter truth. And ever since, I have remained deprived of every good, of every hope.

Alfesibeo
Even if it seems like folly to lament things that cannot be mended, I will say this: Alcone, you made a mistake back then / [9ʳ], when you tried to tie her against her wishes in a knot so strong *it could only be loosened by death. For even if in every other matter children are subject to their father,*

"	soggetti sono, in questo libertade
"	ha lor concesso la Natura e Dio;
"	d'unirsi come a lor diletta e piace.

       soggetti sono, in questo libertade
       ha lor concesso la Natura e Dio;
       d'unirsi come a lor diletta e piace.   175
       Or se contravenisti in farle forza
       alle legge[33] degli uomini, e del Cielo
       soffri pazientemente
       l'amaro frutto che di ciò raccogli.
       Ma ti consola ancor, e spera e credi,   180
       che stabil non fu mai cosa terrena,
       ché dopo l'oscura atra tempesta
       più vago un bel seren mostrarsi suole,
       Spera, il mio caro Alcone,
       però che al fin di freddo orrido inverno   185
       Primavera rimena i fiori e l'erbe.

ALC.   Ancor ch'io la ragion ridire non sappia
       pur incognita speme
       mi serpe dolcemente al core intorno.
       Ma tu, d[eh],[34] narra caro Alfe[s]ibeo   190
       qual il tuo sogno fu.

ALF.   Mentre che andiamo / [9ᵛ]
       al tempio per via il tutto narrerotti.
       Vedi che 'l sol nascente
       indorando le cime a' monti, a noi
       vieta il più far dimora in questo luoco?   195
       Dunque pria che più s'erga andianne al tempio
       ché i prieghi matutini al sommo Giove
       son più de gli altri accetti, et chi per tempo
       prega, per tempo ottien ciò che dimanda.

Scena seconda

Armilla, Clorilli

ARM.   Così Clorilli il tuo bel Filemone   1
       per te s'andrà qual neve al sol struggendo?
       E tu più cruda d'una tigre ircana
       prenderai sempre in gioco i suoi tormenti?
       Ah, sono in tutto spente le faville   5

---

[33] Tuscan, non-Bembist form (for *leggi*). Cf. I.4.4 *leggi*, rhyming with *reggi* in line above.
[34] *dhe* in original throughout.

in this one thing Nature and God have conceded them their liberty: to unite among each other as they please and see fit.[38] If you transgressed the laws of men and of Heaven by forcing her to marry, you must patiently suffer the bitter fruit you now harvest.

But console yourself now, and hope and believe: *for no earthly thing ever stayed fixed, and after a dark and gloomy storm, a more beautiful and serene sky often appears.* Hope, my dear Alcone, *for at the end of the cold, horrid winter, spring returns with blooms and green grasses.*[39]

Alcone
Although I do not know how to explain why, an indescribable hope still snakes sweetly around my heart. But come, dear Alfesibeo, tell me about your dream.

Alfesibeo
I will tell you everything / [9ᵛ] as we make our way to the temple. You see, the fledgling sun now turns the mountains' peaks gold, so we cannot stay here any longer. Let us go to the temple then, before the sun rises higher, *for morning prayers are more pleasing to the supreme Jove, and those who pray betimes are sooner granted their wishes.*

Scene Two

Armilla, Clorilli[40]

Armilla[41]
And so, Clorilli, will your beautiful Filemone melt away on your account, like snow in the sun? And will you, crueller than a Hyrcanian tigress, continue to ridicule his torments?[42] Alas, have all the sparks from that

di quella fiamma che già t'arse il petto
per Filemone tuo, per Filemone
un tempo del tuo cuor anima e vita?
Ma qual fu la cagione
che sopita d'amor sì nobil fiamma   10
destò nel tuo be[l]³⁵ sen fiamma di sdegno?
Dimmi, e quando commisse
il tuo fidel amante
cosa che meritasse odio o disprezzo? / [10ʳ]
Se di sposar Dalinda   15
promisse al vecchio padre,
sai che fu tuo consiglio, e tuo commando.
Non ti disse egli al fonte de gli allori
(io medesima, l'udii) — Clorilli amata,
empio voler de' miei crudi parenti   20
cerca di tormi a te per farmi sposo
d'un'altra ninfa, anzi la vita mia
vogl[i]on tor[r]e a me stesso; or che far debbo?
Che mi consigli cara ninfa mia? —
Allor tu fera — Dunque Filemone —   25
gli rispondesti — contradir vor[r]ai
al padre tuo, che già carco d'etade
da te spera veder novella prole?
Segui pur la sua voglia,
sèguila pur Filemon, certo e sicuro   30
che ancor io t'amerò quanto tu m'ami —.
Questo finto parlar fu la cagione
che al giogo marital, piegando il collo
fe' contento il voler del vecchio padre.
Ma con quanta sua doglia,   35
ben sallo chi lo vidde andar errando,
chiamando il nome di Clorilli, e Morte,
che desse fine alle sue pene amare.
Ma pia[c]que al Ciel di così grave affanno / [10ᵛ]
ben tosto trarlo, che partì Dalinda   40
da queste selve ascosamente, prima
che egli avesse da lui la bianca mano
di cerchio d'oro adorna.
Ma che pro? S'egli pur di pena in pena

³⁵ *bell.*

flame which once burned in your breast for Filemone been extinguished? He, who was once the life and soul of your heart?

But why was the amorous flame of such a noble lover smothered, and a disdainful one awakened in its place? Tell me, when was it that your faithful lover committed so terrible an offence to merit your hatred and contempt? / [10ʳ] If he promised Dalinda's old father that he would marry her, you know it was because of your advice, and your command. Did he not say to you at the fountain by the laurels? (I heard it myself):

'My beloved Clorilli, it is the wicked desire of my cruel relatives to wrench me from you and marry me to another nymph, which is the same as ripping my life from me. What should I do? What do you suggest I do, my dear nymph?' And then you, cruel one, responded:

'So, Filemone, you would go against your father, already burdened with age, who hopes to see you with children? Obey his wish, obey it Filemone, certain and sure that I will love you as well as you have shown yourself to love me.'[43]

These false words were the reason he obeyed his elderly father's wish and bent his neck to the marital yoke. But he did it with much sorrow, for you know very well that he was often seen wandering, crying out the name 'Clorilli' and begging Death to rescue him from his bitter grief. But it pleased Heaven to free him of such terrible grief most quickly / [10ᵛ], for Dalinda secretly left these woods, disappearing before he had the chance to decorate her white hand with a circle of gold.[44] But what good has it done, if he is just moving from one pain to another?

	va trapassando, e di così lungo pianto	45
	non raccoglie che pianto. Ah' fera ninfa	
	come ti soffre il core	
	di vederlo vicino a morte corso,	
	e non darli soccorso?	
CLO.	Quando, Armilla, mi tolsi dal[36] drappello	50
	dell'altre ninfe io già non mi credea	
	che di costui parlar tu mi dovessi,	
	di costui che odio tanto, e tanto abborro,	
	che più non odia il gregge nostro il lupo.	
	Tempo fu che io l'amai	55
	più di questi occhi assai, più de la vita,	
	e quando ei diè la fè di matrimonio	
	a la bella Dalinda	
	credei morir di doglia.	
	Forsen[n]ata gridai la notte e 'l giorno	60
	per le foreste. Allor quanti Pastori	
	disser — Clorilli è fuor del senno uscita? —	
	Quante volte vicina a darmi morte / [11ʳ]	
	fui, lassa? E ben può farne aperta fede	
	Silvia mia fidelissima compagna,	65
	con l'aiuto di cui con lungo affanno	
	pur ricovrai la libertà primiera.	
ARM.	Dannoso acquisto, poiché in van si perde	
	il più bello, il più saggio, il più gentile	
	pastor, che unqua vedesse il tosco clima.	70
CLO.	Il più fidel dovevi aggiunger anco.	
	Ma per toglierti Armilla	
	ogni ragion che a ragionar tu m'abbia	
	mai più di Filemone,	
	sappi che una non pur, ma mille volte	75
	d'esser mio sposo m'affermò giurando.	
	Or mentre io lieta attendea	
	delle promesse nozze il giorno e l'ora,	
	et ei mi vien a dir che 'l padre vuole	
	che ei tolga un' altra ninfa, e mi domanda	80
	di ciò consiglio, e vuol ch'io li[37] commandi	
	quel che far deggia in così dubbio caso.	

---

[36] *dall'*.
[37] Tuscan form for *gli*, used e.g. line 110; see Rohlfs, *Grammatica storica*, II: §457.

And he reaps nothing from such endless lamentation but further lamentation! Oh, cruel nymph, does it not hurt your heart to see him so close to death, and not help him?

Clorilli
Armilla, when I took leave of our band of nymphs, I did not think it was so you would speak to me of this man, whom I hate and abhor so greatly that our flock does not loathe the wolf more! There was a time when I loved him, yes, far more than these eyes, more than life itself. And when he pledged his troth to the beautiful Dalinda, I thought I would die of sadness. Out of my mind with grief, I passed day and night wailing in the forest. How many shepherds asked 'Has Clorilli gone out of her mind?'[45] Alas, how many times did I come close / [11ʳ] to killing myself? Certainly Silvia, my most faithful companion, can attest to this.[46] With her help, and after long suffering, I was able to recover my original liberty.

Armilla
A perilous liberty, since by gaining it, you lost the most beautiful, the wisest, the kindest shepherd Tuscany has ever seen.

Clorilli
You'd have done well to add 'the most faithful' to that description.

But Armilla, to strip you of all your arguments and reasonings on behalf of Filemone, know that he swore to me not once but a thousand times that he would become my husband. Now while I was happily waiting to learn the day and the hour of the promised nuptials, he comes along to say that his father wants him to marry another nymph![47] He asks me what I advise, and wants me to tell him what to do in this uncertain case.

Io che così vecchia, né di lui signora
era, che a consigliare, che a comandar
fussi atta, altro risponder non potei   85
se non che egli seguisse
la voglia di suo padre,
promettendoli ancor di riamarlo / [11ᵛ]
quanto ei m'amava. Or se d'amor fu segno
romper la data fede e disprezzarmi   90
lascerò giudicarlo a te medesma.
E s'io lo sprezzo e fuggo, al[l]' amor suo
altra mercè non si convien che questa.
Mi dolse, e sallo il Ciel, ch'egli restasse
sì tosto privo di Dalinda sua;   95
ma già non mancheranno a Filemone
altre ninfe, e di me più belle assai,
a Filemon figlio d'Ergasto, a cui
pastor ugual³⁸ non han le nostre selve
per nobiltà di sangue, e per ricchezza,   100
a Filemon che tutto quel possiede
che a nobile Pastor più si conviene.
Non perda dunque inutilmente il tempo
in seguir chi lui fugge, e chi lo sprezza,
ma segua chi lui segue, e chi lo stima.   105

ARM.   Non puote altri seguir che te, sua vita,
che così stabilmente
le sue stelle ordinaro.
E vedi ben che non potendo d'altra
esser che tuo, così tosto li tolse   110
il Ciel Dalinda, e non fia d'altra mai
il miser Filemon che di Clorilli.

CLO.   E se d'altra esser non può per esser mio, / [12ʳ]
anch'io per esser mia
non posso esser d'altrui.   115

ARM.   Graziosa Clorilli
come puote esser mai
che, in un soggetto ove Natura pose
quanto di bello e buono oggi è tra noi,
regni sì brutto vizio   120
di ingratitudine e di dimenticanza.

³⁸ uugual.

I, neither wizened with age, nor mistress over him, was not fit to advise or command him; I could only respond by telling him to follow the wishes of his father, promising him that I would continue to love him / [11ᵛ] as much as he loved me. Now whether *that* was a sign of love – to break his sworn faith and disrespect me – I will let you judge for yourself. And so if I scorn him and run from him, it is a fitting reward for his love. Heaven knows I was sorry he should have been so soon deprived of his Dalinda. But Filemone will not lack the attention of other nymphs now, women much more beautiful than me. Filemone, son of Ergasto, has no equal among the shepherds in our woods, neither in noble blood nor in wealth. Filemone possesses all that is most fitting for a noble shepherd. Let him not waste his time uselessly, in pursuit of the one who runs from him and despises him, but instead may he pursue those who pursue him, and who admire him.[48]

Armilla
He cannot pursue anyone but you, you are his life, for so the stars ordained it![49] It is clear he cannot be anyone's but yours; this is why Heaven robbed him of Dalinda so quickly. The wretched Filemone will never belong to any woman but Clorilli.

Clorilli
And just as he cannot belong to another, because he is mine, / [12ʳ] I too, because I am mine, cannot belong to another.[50]

Armilla
Charming Clorilli, how is it possible that someone to whom Nature has granted all the beauty and goodness of this age can be ruled by the ugly vices of ingratitude and neglect?

CLO.	Io non fui ingrata in alcun tempo mai,
	amata Armilla, che per finto amore
	perfettissimo resi e vero amore,
	come resi disprezzo per disprezzo.[39] 125
	E troppo del passato mi ricordo,
	e mi dolgo, e mi pento
	con sì candida fe' d'aver amato
	uom [in]fedele [e] ingrato.[40]
ARM.	Di ciò sola cagion fossi tu stessa. 130
	Ah che poteva egli altro,
	che obedir al tuo impero
	a cui lo fe' soggetto Amore e 'l Cielo?
	Or se la colpa è tua debbe egli solo
	dunque patir sì lunga e fiera pena? 135
	Ma poniam che egli errasse, ah non ti basta,
	non ti basta crudele
	perfino a questo giorno
	d'averlo tormentato? / [12ᵛ]
	Già la seconda volta 140
	è ritornato il sole
	nell'animal che fa bel segno in Cielo
	per Europa gentil, dacché tu 'l privi
	del chiaro sol de' tuoi bei lumi ardenti,
	et insieme lo privi 145
	d'ogni contento e gioia
	onde al fin ne morirà, misero amante.
	Allor, allor fia sazia
	l'ostinata tua voglia
	che ei darà fin morendo alla sua doglia. 150
	Ma con che core potrai soffrir, o fiera,
	di dar morte a colui che di te vive?
	D[eh] cangia bella Ninfa, cangia omai
	sì cruda voglia e fiera
	acciò che non arrechi 155
	morte al meschin, a te vergogna e biasmo.
CLO.	Non dubitar Armilla,
	ché non corre uom sì tosto a darsi morte.

---

[39] *disprezzo?*: the punctuation mark in M seems inconsistent.

[40] *uom fedele et ingrato*: 'fedele' in M appears inconsistent with the overall sense of the passage and the pairing with 'ingrato', referring to Filemone. To maintain the line's heptasyllable (*settenario*) metre, 'et' is altered to 'e' to allow synalepha.

Clorilli

I was never ungrateful, adored Armilla, for I returned false love with most perfect and true love, just as I returned scorn for scorn. I remember too much from the past, and I regret it and rue that I loved such an inconstant and ungrateful man with such blind faith.

Armilla

You alone were the cause of this. What could Filemone do other than obey your rule, to which Love and Heaven made him subject? Now if the fault is yours, must he alone suffer such long harsh pain? But let's say that he did make a mistake, oh, is this not enough for you, is it not enough, even for someone as cruel as you, to have tormented him for so long? / [12ᵛ] The sun has now revolved twice around the Bull, who appears boldly in the Heavens for noble Europa, since you robbed him of the clear sun of your beautiful ardent eyes, and thus of all happiness and joy.[51] Your wretched lover will die of this loss! Then, and only then, will your stubborn desire be satisfied, when he puts an end to his pain with death. But, O cruel one, with what heart will you be able to suffer being the cause of death of one who lives for you? Change, beautiful nymph, change your cruel and proud desires at once, so that you do not bring death to that wretch, and grief and blame to yourself.[52]

Clorilli

Do not fear, Armilla, men are never in a hurry to kill themselves.

	Anch'io ci fui vicina	
	ma sia lodato il Ciel, io vivo e parlo.	160
	Ma quando anco sì fuor del[41] senno uscito	
	fosse pur Filemone	
	che si desse la morte	
	a me non so veder che biasmo arrechi.	
ARM.	O che sublime[42] onor, che chiare lodi, / [13ʳ]	165
	che pregi fiano i tuoi d'aver ucciso	
	un che t'amava più degl' occhi suoi?	
	Superba ingrata ninfa, in che pur fidi	
	tanta alterezza, in quella chioma d'oro?	
	In quelle fresche rose?	170
	Tosto l'aurato crin verrà d'argento.	
	Tosto l'or[r]ido inverno	
	coprirà d'alte brine il volto e 'l seno,	
	e le purpuree rose	
	viole diverran languide, e smorte.	175
	Allor dirai pentita,	
	se ben non gioverà — quanto mi disse	
	Armilla il vero. Ah, fossi io pur stata,	
	più saggia, e men crudele — .	
	Or va', sèguita pur l'empio costume	180
	ninfa, ostinata,	
	ché io più di Filemone non ti parlo.	
CLO.	Et io voglio vedere	
	pria che il dì giunga a sera	
	se questo dardo mio	185
	atterrar può qualche selvaggia fiera.	
	Io ti conchiudo Armilla	
	che prima al proprio fonte	
	tornerà l'onda del Mugnon, e prima	
	vedrai d'Atlante il monte andar errando / [13ᵛ]	190
	che tra ninfe e pastori mai più si dica: —	
	Clorilli a Filemone s'è fatta amica —	
	Or io mi parto. A Dio, rimànti in pace.	
ARM.	Segui, segui le fere,	
	fera di lor più cruda, e fuggi pure	195
	ove vestigio uman l'arena stampi.	

[41] *dell'*.
[42] *subblime*.

I too was close to killing myself but, Heaven be praised, I am still alive and speaking. But even if Filemone were so out of his mind that he surrendered to death, I don't see how you could blame me.

Armilla

Oh, what sublime honour, what brilliant praise, / [13ʳ] what esteem will be yours, to have killed one who loved you more than his own eyes!

You proud, ungrateful nymph, do you place such pride and happiness in your golden locks, in those fresh roses? Before long, your golden brow will turn silver. Soon, hideous winter will cover your face and breast in so much hoarfrost, and those crimson roses will become lifeless and wan violets.[53] Then, even though it will no longer be of any use, you will say, repentant: 'How true Armilla's words were! Oh, if only I had been wiser, and less cruel.' Now go on, obstinate nymph, chase after your wicked desires. I won't speak to you of Filemone anymore.

Clorilli

And before day turns to evening, I will see if this arrow of mine can fell some wild beast. I conclude, Armilla, by saying that you will sooner see the waves of the Mugnone return to their source,[54] and sooner see the Atlas mountains go wandering,[55] / [13ᵛ] than you will hear it said amongst nymphs and shepherds, 'Clorilli is Filemone's lover once more.' Now I take my leave. Farewell, and peace be with you.

Armilla

Follow the beasts, for you are a crueller beast than they. Go, and flee every vestige of humanity that marks the sand![56]

Scena terza

Armilla

ARM.   A[vr]ebbeno[43] i mie[i] prieghi   1
        tante volte inte[nerito], e[44] le minaccie
        amollito la dura alpestre cima
        di questo orrido monte,
        e pur chi 'l crederia, non han potuto   5
        render men duro il cor d'una fanciulla?
        Misero Filemone,
        s'altra speme non hai che nel mio aiuto,
        poco più da sperar omai t'avanza.
        Pur mi giova seguir la bella impresa,   10
    "   che se picciola stilla
    "   consumò talor marmi, e pietre salde,
    "   a ponderoso rivo
    "   di lacrime, sospir, prieghi, e minaccie
    "   qual resister potrà forza o durezza?   15

Scena quarta

Filemone / [14ʳ]

FIL.   Amor ben con ragion sei detto Dio,   1
        e Dio di tutti gli altri il più possente,
        poiché non sol governi il mondo, e 'l reggi
        con le tue sante leggi
        e sol muovi le stelle, e gl' elementi   5
        con discordie concordia unisci e tempri;
        ma fin la giù, ove non giunge il sole
        è noto il tuo potere, e ben provòllo
        per Proserpina bella
        il crudo Re, che alle nude ombre impera.   10
        Ma come è? Che se 'l ciel, l'inferno, e 'l mondo
        teme il tuo gran potere,[45] che sol Clorilli

---

[43] *Averebbeno*: form of 'avere', used frequently but not throughout in M; here, as elsewhere, the shortened form is surmised to fit the metre (*settenario*).

[44] *Interati,e*: the sense of the original is unclear. The writing appears compressed as if written at a later stage to fill a gap. The hypothesized 'intenerito' is problematic, however, as it creates a hypermetric line.

[45] *potere*: possibly *poter*, since this line currently has at least 12 syllables.

Scene Three

Armilla

My entreaties would have moved, and my threats softened, the craggy peak of this bleak mountain many times over. Who would believe they could not soften a maiden's heart? Wretched Filemone, if my help is your only hope, you have little more to hope for now! Yet I shall pursue this noble endeavour, *for if a small drop of water has occasionally worn down marble and hard rock, what kind of strength or hardness will be able to resist a thundering river of tears, sighs, prayers and threats?*

Scene Four

Filemone / [14ʳ]

Love, it is for good reason you are called a god, and the most powerful of all the gods. For not only do you govern the world, and rule it with your holy laws, and alone move the stars, and unite and temper the elements that are in discord;[57] but even deep below the reach of the sun, your power is known, and that cruel King who rules the naked shades below felt it with beautiful Proserpina.[58] But how is it that Heaven, Hell and Earth all fear your great power, and Clorilli alone scorns you and flees from you?

[e][46] ti sprezzi e ti fugga? O Dio possente,
come soffri tu mai, come consenti
che in cor di donna tanto orgoglio alberghi?   15
E tu ninfa crudel, se 'l mio languire
è tal che può nelle più crude fiere
destar pietà, perché nel tuo bel seno
non si desta ella omai? Perché non sorge
più che mai chiaro il sol degl'occhi tuoi   20
a quest'occhi infelici? O cara e bella
dolce cagion un tempo / [14ᵛ]
del lieto viver mio, mentre non solo
t'era caro il mio amore, ma mi giuravi
che senza quel né cara né gradita   25
ti sarebbe la vita,
come s'è dileguato[47] in un baleno
quel mio fortunatissimo sereno?
Avessi almen d'un bel cristallo il petto
e 'n lui volgessi tu l'altiero sguardo,   30
che vedresti il mio duol acerbo e fero,
come pian pian va consumando il core.
Ma poiché questo non consente il Cielo;
D[eh] perché non comprendi,
da questo mesto e pal[l]ido sembiante,   35
da' miei sospiri ardenti,
da quest'occhi conversi in tristi fonti
quanto è grave il dolor che mi tormenta?
Allor o fera, o cruda,
crederai il mio martire   40
che te lo farà noto il mio morire[48].
Allor forse pentita
della tua ferità piangerai morto
quel misero pastor che tu di vita
crudelmente privasti, o se ciò fosse   45
fortunata, e dolcissima mia morte. / [15ʳ]
Ma che bramar degg'io
cosa che turbi al mio bel sol i rai?
Mori pur Filemone e lieta vivi
Clorilli, e del tuo mal cura non prenda,   50

---

[46] *ei.*
[47] *diliguato.*
[48] *Mortire*: presumed copying error due to assonance with *martire* in line above.

O powerful God, how can you possibly bear it? How can you allow such pride to dwell in a lady's heart? And you, cruel nymph: if my pining can provoke pity in the most savage beasts, how can it not awaken pity in your beautiful breast? Why does the sun of your eyes not rise brighter than ever before, to greet these unhappy eyes? O dear and beautiful one, you were once the sweet reason for a time / [14ᵛ] of great joy in my life, when not only was my love dear to you, but you swore to me that without it, life would be impossible to enjoy. How can that most fortunate and tranquil time have disappeared in an instant? If only my breast were made of the finest crystal, I could direct your haughty gaze inside it, so you could see my bitter and wild grief, which is slowly consuming my heart.[59] But since Heaven does not permit this – ah! Why do you not understand from my sad and wan appearance, from my ardent sighs, from these eyes transformed into sad fountains, just how grave the pain is that torments me? O fierce one, O cruel one, you will only believe in my martyrdom once you have made me die. Then, perhaps regretful of the wound you caused, you will weep for the miserable shepherd you so cruelly robbed of life. Oh, if that were so, how fortunate, how very sweet my death would be! / [15ʳ]

But why must I continue to wish for a thing that would obscure the rays of my beautiful sun? Just die, Filemone, and let Clorilli live happily, untouched by your suffering.

ché non merti pietà, poiché pietade
a te medesmo usar tu non sapesti.
Non altri che tu stesso
ti privò di Clorilli.
Tu crudel fab[b]ro fosti   55
delle miserie tue.
Che poteva il voler del vecchio padre,
se 'l tuo cieco volere
non consentiva all'altrui voglia? Ormai
muori pastor sventurato, poi   60
ché tra tanto dolore
speme non hai che ti mantenghi in vita.

Scena quinta

Coribante, Filemone

COR.	Pur al fin ti trovai	1
	Filemone gentil. D[eh] vie[n]e meco	
	a piè del colle, ove Aronte e Tirsi	
	per far preda d'augei le reti han tese.	
FIL.	Vanne pur Coribante, ch'io qui solo / [15ᵛ]	5
	mi rimar[r]ò piangendo.	
COR.	Non è tempo di pianto,	
	or che la vaga Primavera	
	rallegra i colli, gli uomini, e le fere,	
	e s'odon d'ogni intorno	10
	di ninfe, e di pastor canti soavi.	
FIL:	Cantai mentre il mio foco ardea il core	
	della mia bella ninfa.	
	Cantai mentre dal puro e vago cielo	
	d'una serena fronte	15
	piover viddi dolcezza.	
	Cantai mentre ver me benigne e liete	
	le mie spendenti stelle	
	rotaro i raggi lor lucenti e belli.	
	Or che per sorte mia spent'è quel foco,	20
	e 'nvece di dolcezza	
	piove dal mio bel Ciel ira et asprezza;	
	or che le vaghe stelle	
	son fatte a' miei desir empie e rubelle	

For you do not deserve pity, since you did not know how to grant pity to yourself. No one else robbed you of Clorilli. You were the cruel forger of your own misery. How could your father's will have prevailed, if your blind will had not surrendered to him? Die now, you wretched shepherd, since you have no hope of staying alive in so much pain!

Scene Five

Coribante, Filemone

Coribante
So I found you at last, gentle Filemone! Now come with me to the foot of the hill, where Aronte and Tirsi have stretched their nets to trap birds.[60]

Filemone
You go on ahead, Coribante, / [15ᵛ] for I will stay here alone to weep.

Coribante
Now is not the time for lament, now that glorious Spring reanimates the hills, men and beasts, and the sweet songs of nymphs and shepherds are heard from every corner of the forest.

Filemone
I sang as my ardour enflamed the heart of my lovely nymph. I sang as I saw sweetness rain down from the serene countenance of a bright and cloudless sky. I sang as my twinkling stars turned their beautiful and bright rays toward me, joyous and benevolent.[61] It is now my fate to have that fire extinguished, and instead of sweetness, anger and bitterness pour down from my beautiful Heaven; now that the lovely stars have been made wicked and resistant to my desires, I will cry until the day

		piangerò finché fòre	25
		esca con 'l pianto un dì lo spirto e 'l core.	
COR.	"	Inutil pianto ad uom viril non lice	
	"	sempre versar, o Filemone amato.	
FIL.		S'io sperassi piangendo / [16ʳ]	
		intenerir quel duro alpestre core	30
		ben fora il pianto inutilmente e vano,	
		ma in sì tranquillo stato	
		non mi ritrovo, Coribante mio,	
		che del mio lagrimar mercede attenda.	
		Piango e piangendo spero	35
		non soccorso o pietade,	
		ma che sì dura vita	
		ormai finisca, e si risolva in pianto.	
COR.	"	Spesso parol' e prieghi	
	"	ponno più che le lagrime e sospiri.	40
		Cessa dunque dal pianto, e parla, e priega.	
FIL.		Come vòi tu ch'io prieghi?	
		Come vòi tu ch'io parli	
		a chi sol per fuggirmi	
		il guardo [h]a pronto, e l'piede?	45
		Posto che d'ascoltarmi ancor le piac[c]ia;	
		che potrebbero in lei	
		le mie rozze parole e rozzi prieghi	
		interrotti da pianti e da sospiri?	
		se Armilla, Armilla stessa, a cui son note	50
		tutte le vie perché gelato seno	
		senta foco d'Amor, non ha potuto	
		una favilla sola / [16ᵛ]	
		dopo lungo pregar destarle il core.	
COR.		D'ostinato voler, d'alma indurata	55
		avrai tu veri segni, e veri effetti.	
		Ma spera Filemon, forse anco Armilla	
		non ha del suo valor fatto ogni prova.	
		E quando pur al fin tanto ostinata	
		fosse costei, che mai sempre d'odiarti	60
		fosse disposta, tu con un disprezzo	
		nobile e generoso	
		spezza quelle catene onde t'avvinse	
		alla sua servitù tiran[n]o Amore.	
		E se aver non può luogo quella legge	65

when my spirit and heart expire from grief.

Coribante
A virile man should not pass his time shedding vain tears, beloved
Filemone.[62]

Filemone
If I hoped that crying / [16ʳ] would soften that hard, craggy heart, then
my tears would certainly be vain, but I do not find myself in so tranquil a
state that I expect any mercy in return for my weeping, dear Coribante.
I cry, and in crying I wish not for help, nor for pity, but that this hard life
will be over soon, and finish up in lament.

Coribante
Often words and prayers do more than tears and sighs. Stop your crying,
then, and speak, and beg!

Filemone
How do you expect me to beg? How do you expect me to speak to one
whose gaze and feet are always set to flee me? Let's suppose that it still
pleased her to listen to me, what effect could I hope to achieve from my
rough words and prayers, broken up by tears and sighs? If even Armilla
– Armilla herself, who knows all the ways to stoke Love's fire in a frozen
breast – could not rouse one single spark / [16ᵛ] from her heart after such
a lengthy appeal?

Coribante
You see there the true signs and true effects of a stubborn will and a
hardened soul. But keep hoping, Filemone: Armilla may not have tried
everything in her power yet. And if in the end, your nymph is so obstinate
that she is prepared to hate you forever, then with proud and noble scorn
break those chains that have bound you as a slave to that tyrant Love!

"   che ogni amato riami, abbila quella
"   che l'odiato riodii, e tu qual prima
      torna virile e forte.
      Torna in te stesso Filemone, e mira
      come disprezzi il fior de' tuoi begl'anni   70
"   che in un punto, trapassa in pianto e 'n doglia.
      Vedi come il tuo gregge,
      debole e fiacco, a pena
      portar può il peso delle smorte membra.
      Non vedi, ancor non vedi   75
      che più non sembri Filemon, che un tempo
      fu letizia e splendor di questi colli,
      così caro alle ninfe, et a['] pastori?/ [17ʳ]
      Ma sembri un uom selvaggio, un uom di più
      d'una ninfa crudel soggetto, e schiavo,   80
      che ti fugge, e ti sprezza, anzi t'abborre!
      Torna omai Filemon, torna in te stesso,
      ricovra omai la libertà primiera,
      e nell'antico seggio
"   ragion ritorni, onde la trasse Amore.   85
FIL. Se come ben conosco e vere e sagge
      le tue ragioni, in mio poter fosse anco
      il poterle seguir, le seguirei.
      Ma che posso io s'Amore
      ogni poter, ogni voler mi tolse?   90
      Non sono io mio, nò Coribante gentile.
      A lei donai me stesso da quel giorno
      che, troppo ardito, osai
      fisso mirar de' suoi begl'occhi il lume.
      Or s'è voler di lei ch'io mora amando   95
      morrommi, e fia il morir soave e dolce.
      Superar sol vorrei questa mercede,
      che avanti al morir mio
      — Mori — dicesse — Filemone addio —.
      E tu pastor gentile   100
      se mai l'altrui dolor ti punse il core,
      fa che di tanto dono al punto estremo
      la bella ninfa mia mi sia cortese.
COR. O de' meschini amanti / [17ᵛ]
      misera condizion, quanto sei grave   105
      quanto sei degna di pietà; ma spera

And if that law whereby *all who are loved, love in return* cannot apply,[63] then let this other law apply, *that all who are scorned, scorn in return*. And become virile and strong as you were before. Become yourself again, Filemone, and see how you waste the bloom of your best years, *which in an instant are lost to lament and misery*.

See how your flock, weak and feeble, can barely support the weight of their own weakened limbs! Don't you see, do you still not see that you no longer resemble the Filemone who was once the pride and joy of these hills, so dear to all the nymphs and shepherds? / [17ʳ] You seem instead like a wild man, subject and slave of a cruel nymph, who runs from you, and scorns you, even abhors you! Come back now, Filemone, become yourself again, recover your original liberty. And in the ancient seat, *let Reason return, from where Love drew it out*.[64]

Filemone

Because I certainly recognize your arguments as true and sage, I would follow them were it in my power. But how can I, since Love has stripped me of all power and will? No, I am not myself, kind Coribante. I gave myself to her the day that I dared to gaze, too fixedly and ardently, into the light of her beautiful eyes. Now if it is her will that I die from love, I will die, and my death will be sweet and gentle.[65] I would only like to receive this one mercy: that before my death, she might say 'Die, Filemone, farewell.' And you, kind shepherd, if ever grief for another pierced your heart, try to ensure that my beautiful nymph lends me this courtesy in my final moments.

Coribante

O wretched lovers! / [17ᵛ] O miserable condition, how grave you are, how worthy you are of pity.

	spera ancor Filemon, ancor confida	
	nell'aiuto d'Armilla, e nel mio insieme.	
	Quel cor che poco avanti	
	fu d'amante nemico,	110
	volto in amore lo sdegno,	
	amante di nemico ancor vedrai.	
	Spera ancor dunque, e 'ntanto	
	andiamo a ritrovar Tirsi et Aronte.	
FIL.	Andianne ove tu vòi, ma non mi lice	115
	sperar sorte felice.	

ATTO SECONDO

Scena prima

Fillinio

[FILL.]⁴⁹	Selve beate e care	1
	io pur ritorno a riverdervi, e 'n voi	
	ben riconosco i lochi	
	de' fortunati miei dolci diletti.	
	Tra voi sacrati eroi,⁵⁰	5
	tra voi dolce gustai	
	quel ch'io non spero di gustar più mai.	
	Riconoscete voi quel misero pastore	
	che un tempo risonar sì dolcemente	
	fe' in quei monti il nome di Dalinda? / [18ʳ]	10
	Riconoscete voi quell'infelice	
	Fillinio, che da voi fece partita	
	per seguir la sua vita?	
	Io quello sono, io quello	
	che fatto albergo d'infinita doglia	15
	in voi vengo a riporre	
	questa infelice spoglia.	
	O Dalinda, mia vita, o mio bel sole,	
	ove ascondi a' tuoi raggi? È forse vero	

⁴⁹ All references to Fillinio are abbreviated to FILL. (following M), as distinct from FIL. (for Filemone).
⁵⁰ *Herroi.*

But hope, Filemone, continue to hope. Keep trusting in Armilla's help, and in mine as well. You will yet see that heart, a little while ago an enemy to its lover, trade scorn for love, and go from enemy to lover. So keep hoping! In the meantime, let us go find Tirsi and Aronte.

Filemone
We shall go where you want, but I cannot hope for a happy fate.

Act Two

Scene One

Fillinio

Woods blessed and dear, I return to see you again, and well do I recognize in you the sites of my sweet, fortunate pleasures. Among you, hallowed heroes, among you I tasted a sweetness I cannot hope to taste again. Do you recognize this miserable shepherd, who once made the name Dalinda resonate so sweetly across these mountains? / [18^r] Do you recognize that unhappy Fillinio, who left you to follow his life's path? I am he, I am he, now become an abode of infinite pain. I come back to you to lay this unlucky mortal husk to rest.

O Dalinda, my life, O my beautiful sun, where do you hide your rays?

che sei passata a far più bello il Cielo?   20
O pur, e vivi e spiri ancor, e m'ami?
Ancor Fillinio sventurato, ancora
tenti dar loco a mal nudrita speme?
Ancor fuggi di morir? Non ti rimembra
lo spettacol crudele,   25
che a questa fonte già vedesti il dardo
e 'l vel che pur ancor di lei riserbì,
di ciò non ti fan fede?
Non vedi questa fonte
come ella ancor ritiene   30
del bel sangue di lei vermigl[i]e l'onde?
Non vedi impresse nella terra ancora
l'orme della spietata e cruda belva?
Voi pur luci meschine
vedeste atre vestigie   35
della morte di lei che a voi die luce
né vi chiudeste a sempiterna notte. / [18ᵛ]
Tu man che poco dianzi
avevi ricevuto
da quella bianca man la fede impegno   40
ben fosti pronta a torre
il bel dardo di lei,
ma fosti pigra ad infiammarmi il core.
E tu cor dispietato
ben ricevesti in te l'imagin viva   45
della mia bella Diva,
or ella estinta giace, e tu pur vivi?
Ancor vivi e spiri;
O pastor infedel, non ti ricorda
che tu le promet[t]esti   50
d'esserle appresso ogn'or fedel compagno?
Così dunque l'osservi
la data fede? E così gir la lasci
sola, a incogniti lochi?
Non vedi che qui intorno   55
invisibile ancor rimira il loco
delle miserie tue, della sua morte?
Ah non senti, non senti
che rimprovera a te la data fede?
E ti chiama, e t'aspetta, o che più tardi?   60

Is it perhaps true that you have passed on, to make Heaven more beautiful? Or rather do you still live and breathe, and love me?

Unlucky Fillinio, will you still harbour a hope so poorly nursed? Do you still run from death? Do you not remember the cruel spectacle? For it was here at this fountain that you saw the arrow, and the veil, which you still preserve; do they not bear witness to what you saw?[66]

Do you not see this fountain, how its waters are still tinged vermilion with her blood? Do you not see the tracks of that pitiless and cruel beast still impressed upon the earth? Wretched eyes of mine, you saw the dark traces of the death of that nymph who once gave you light, and yet you still have not closed to face eternal night. / [18ᵛ] You, hand, who received a promise of faith from that white hand shortly before, you were certainly ready to take up her noble arrow, and yet you were slow to set my heart aflame. And you, pitiless heart, you welcomed within you the living image of my beautiful goddess. Now she lies dead, and yet you still live? Still you live, and breathe!

O faithless shepherd, do you not remember that you promised her you would always stay near her, her faithful companion? So this is how you observe the promise you gave? And so you let her go alone, to unknown places? Do you not see that she is here, invisible, still gazing at the site of your misery, of her death? Oh, do you not feel, do you not feel her reproaching you for the promise you gave? And she calls you, and waits for you, oh, why tarry further?

Non riconosci il suono
della angelica voce? Io vengo, io vengo
ecco pronto io ti seguo.
Ma o cruda mia sorte / [19ʳ]
anco il morir mi vieti   65
col venir di costui?
Asconderom[m]i in questa grotta. E poi
che egli sarà partito
ove morì il mio ben morommi anch'io.

Scena seconda

Filemone

FIL.   Mi disse Coribante   1
ch'io l'aspettassi in questo luoco, ove
detto m'avrebbe[51] quanto
fatto avesse per me con la mia ninfa,
ma nol veggio apparire.   5
Dio voglia pur che questa sua tardanza
non sia nunzia del mal che mi sovrasta,
e che quella speranza
che egli tentò di porre
in questo disperato petto mio   10
di morte più crudel cagion non sia.
Ma pur lo veggio da lontano, e parmi
in vista molto lieto.
D[eh] per pietade Amore
fa che egli apporti il fine   15
del mio fiero dolore.

Scena terza / [19ᵛ]

Coribante, Filemone

COR.   Bu[o]ne nuove t'arreco   1
Filemone gentil; pon fine al pianto.
FIL.   Che? Si contenta forse
la cara ninfa mia dirmi ch'io mora?

---

[51] *averebbe*: adjusted to fit seven-syllable line.

Do you not recognize the sound of her angelic voice? I am coming, here I am, coming, ready to follow you.

But O cruel fate of mine, / [19r] will you continue to delay my death by sending this man?[67] I will hide myself in this cave. And then when he has left, in that place where my beloved died, I will die as well.

Scene Two

Filemone

Coribante told me to wait for him here, and in this spot he would tell me how he interceded for me with my nymph. But I do not see him appear. I hope to God that his tardiness is not a sign of the evil hanging over me. And may that hope, which he attempted to stir in this desperate breast of mine, not cause an even crueller death!

But look, I see him from afar, and he seems to wear a most happy expression. Oh, for pity's sake, Love, let him bring an end to my fierce pain!

Scene Three / [19ᵛ]

Coribante, Filemone

Coribante
I bring you good news, gentle Filemone. Put an end to your grieving!

Filemone
What? Does it please my dear nymph, perhaps, to tell me to die?

COR.		Che parli di morir? Tempo è di vita,	5
		e di vita lietissima e felice.	
FIL.		O me beato, ha forse il freddo core	
		di nuovo acceso con sua face Amore?	
COR.		Questo non so, so ben che Armilla ha detto	
		di far ogni suo sforzo, e si confida	10
		piegarla ad ascoltar le tue parole	
		prima che 'l sol nell'ocean s'asconda.	
FIL.		Fugacissima speme	
		come tosto ti involi	
		dagli infelici amanti?	15
		E questa è Coribante	
		quella felice nuova	
		per cui mandar doveva in bando il pianto?	
		Or non t'ho detto che ben mille volte	
		che ella m'ascolti, ha invan tentato Armilla?	20
COR.		E che sai tu che al fin non le riesca?	
	"	Annosa e dura querci[a]	
	"	non atterra un sol colpo,	
	"	ma, se da forte mano / [20r]	
	"	son raddoppiate le percosse, al fine	25
	"	cede, e precipitosa in giù rovina.	
FIL.		Ah che più facil fora	
		raccorre in rete le lieve aure e 'l mare	
		chiuder dentro in confin di picciol urna,	
		che di rigida ninfa	30
		l'ostinato voler cangiar pregando.	
COR.	"	Ogni cosa col tempo al fin si piega.	
		Né già creder vogl'io	
		che sì fedel servire,	
		non debba riportar qualche mercede.	35
FIL.		Privo d'ogni mercede	
		mi rende la mia fera aspra ventura.	
COR.	"	Cangiasi ogn'or la sorte	
	"	di trista in lieta, ancor mercede avrai.	
FIL.		E che sperar poss'io?	40
	"	L'Amor premio è d'Amore, amar mi nega	
		la mia cruda Clorilli.	
COR.	"	Et Amor anco avrai, che è dove regna	
	"	bellezza, e cortesia.	
	"	Et se avvien che talor nube di sdegno	45

Coribante

Why do you speak of death? It is time for life, and for the most joyous and happy kind of life at that!

Filemone

Oh, how blessed I am! Has Love's torch perchance set her cold heart ablaze once more?

Coribante

That I do not know; but I do know that Armilla said she would make every effort, and she is certain she can persuade Clorilli to listen to your words before the sun hides itself in the ocean.

Filemone

Most fleeting hope, why do you steal away from unhappy lovers so quickly? And Coribante, is this that happy news for which I should have banished my tears? Have I not told you that Armilla has tried in vain to get her to listen to me at least a thousand times?

Coribante

And how do you know she will not succeed in the end?

A single blow does not fell the aged and sturdy oak. But if the strokes are redoubled by a strong hand, / [20ʳ] *in the end the oak yields, and crashes to the ground below.*[68]

Filemone

Ah, it would be easier to gather soft breezes in a net, and to enclose the sea within the confines of a little urn, than to change the obstinate will of a merciless nymph through entreaties!

Coribante

Everything yields in the end, with time.

Nor can I believe that such faithful service will bring no reward.

Filemone

My cruel, harsh destiny deprives me of all mercy.

Coribante

Fate is everchanging, turning sadness into happiness. You will have mercy yet.

Filemone

And how can I hope?

Love's prize is Love, yet my cruel Clorilli denies me.

Coribante

And you will again have Love, which can be found where beauty and courtesy reign. And if it should happen that from time to time a cloud of

	"	l'asconda agli occhi altrui	
	"	pur la discopre al fine	
	"	col ventilar dell'ali[52] ardente Amore.	
FIL.		Non osa amor d'approssimar le piume / [20ᵛ]	
		al bel guardo di lei,	50
		che quasi ardente sole	
		ogni cosa creata arde e consuma.	
COR.	"	E pur il sole ancora	
	"	oltre il suo proprio ardore	
	"	sente il foco d'Amore.	55
FIL.		Sai perché Coribante?	
	"	Perché a guisa di secco arido legno	
	"	al calor d'altro foco	
	"	arde più facilmente a nuovo foco.	
	"	Ma che gelata neve	60
	"	si scaldi, occhio mortal non vide unquanco.[53]	
COR.	"	Non sai se Mongibello	
	"	estolle al Ciel la cima	
	"	c[a]rca di neve, e dentro ha fiamme eterne?	
FIL.		Ma non sai s'in Clorilli	65
		è fiamma ciò che appare,	
		e giel ciò che s'asconde?	
COR.	"	Si dilegua anco il gielo	
	"	a pos[s]ente calore.	
FIL.	"	S'ammorza ogni gran fiamma	70
	"	con freddo algente g[h]iaccio.	
COR.		Oggi sarà quel giorno	
		dunque, che Filemone	
		sarà privo d'Amore, / [21ʳ]	
		o ver Clorilli amante.	75
FIL.		E perché Coribante?	
COR.		O che 'l suo g[h]iaccio ammorzerà il tuo foco,	
		o che al tuo foco il g[h]iaccio	
		di lei dileguarsi.	
FIL.		Non fia né l'uno, né l'altro.[54]	80
		Che non consente Amore	

---

[52] *ventillar del'ali.*

[53] *unquancho*: in modern Italian *giammai.*

[54] Line 80 has at least eight syllables. Filemone's initial 'Non' may have been intended as an addition to the end of the previous line, to create here a seven-syllable line (with synalepha on *lei*).

scorn should hide this ardour from another's eyes, burning Love will uncover it in the end, with the beating of his wings.

Filemone
Love does not dare allow his wings / [20ᵛ] to approach her beautiful gaze, which burns and consumes everything in sight, much like the brilliant sun.[69]

Coribante
And yet even the sun feels the fire of Love as well as its own heat.[70]

Filemone
Do you know why, Coribante?
　　Because just as is the wont of dry, arid wood, Love burns more easily in the heat of a new fire than in any other fire. But for frozen snow to be warmed is something no mortal eye has ever seen.

Coribante
Don't you know that though Mongibello's snow-covered peak reaches to Heaven, it contains an eternal flame at its core?[71]

Filemone
But don't you know that in Clorilli's case, it is the flame that is visible, and the frost that remains hidden?

Coribante
Frost also melts away in the face of mighty heat.

Filemone
Every great flame is extinguished in cold, freezing ice.

Coribante
Then today will be the day when either Filemone will be robbed of Love, / [21ʳ] or Clorilli will become a lover.

Filemone
And why, Coribante?

Coribante
Either her frost will dampen your fire, or your fire will melt her frost.

Filemone
It shall be neither one, nor the other! For Love does not allow me to

		che avanti il mio bel sole	
		serbi un medesmo stato,	
		ma tutto g[h]iaccio fammi, o tutto foco.	
COR.	"	All'ardor de' tuoi lumi	85
	"	dileguerassi il g[h]iaccio.	
	"	Al g[h]iaccio del suo core	
	"	s'ammorzerà l'ardore.	
FIL.		E perché ciò non segua,	
		ella si starà longi;	90
		né potran punto i preghi	
		d'Armilla a far ch'al suo voler si pieghi	
		ad ascoltarmi mai.	
COR.		Ben farà sì. Ma non veggio da lungi	
		venir Armilla? E par tutta ridente,	95
		spera d'aver per te buone novelle.	
FIL.	"	Non ardisce sperar misero amante	
	"	che tante volte ha già sperato indarno.	

Scena quarta / [21ᵛ]

Armilla, Coribante, Filemone

ARM.	Non così gran fatica,	1
	sotto il pondo del ciel sostenne Atlante,	
	quant'in piegar la voglia	
	d'una ninfa ostinata ho soffert'io.	
	O che ho detto, o che ho fatto; e se non fosse	5
	la pietà che mi stringe	
	degli infelici amanti,	
	so dir io che più volte	
	avrei[55] lasciata questa impresa a mezzo.	
	Ma ecco Filemone, e Coribante.	10
	Ben trovati pastor, o come appunto	
	fa che mi incontrai in voi, felice sorte.	
COR.	Che apporti di nuovo	
	cortessissima Armilla?	
ARM.	Pur al fin mi promesse d'ascoltarti	15
	la tua bella Clorilli.	

---

[55] *Averei*: adjusted to fit hendecasyllable metre (cf. I.3.1).

remain steady in the presence of my lovely sun. He makes me all ice, or all fire.

Coribante
The ardour in your eyes will melt her frost. The frost in her heart will dampen your heat.

Filemone
She will keep her distance to ensure that does not happen. Nor will Armilla's pleas ever suffice to persuade her to give me ear.

Coribante
She certainly will. But do I not see Armilla approaching from afar? And she seems to be all smiles, and hopes to have good news for you.

Filemone
A wretched lover does not dare hope, for he has already hoped many times in vain.

Scene Four / [21ᵛ]

Armilla, Coribante, Filemone

Armilla
Atlas himself did not suffer such labour supporting the weight of Heaven as I have suffered to bend the will of such an obstinate nymph! Oh, what I have not said, oh, what I have not done! And if I were not gripped with pity for these unhappy lovers, I can say that I would have abandoned this enterprise halfway through more than once. But here are Filemone and Coribante. Well met, shepherds! It seems a happy chance brought about this meeting.

Coribante
What news do you bring, most courteous Armilla?

Armilla
Your beautiful Clorilli has finally promised me that she will listen to you.

FIL.		O che sent'io[56]
		Et è pos[s]ibil ciò? D[eh] cara ninfa
		dimmi di grazia il vero?
ARM.		Di poca fede, ah credi
		ch'io ti burlassi in questo, è certo, è vero.	20
FIL.	"	In disperata rocca
	"	è così avvezza a star l'alma infelice, / [22ʳ]
	"	ove non giunse già mai
	"	che fer[e] dogl[i]e[57], e guai,
	"	che 'l timor fida scorta	25
	"	di lei non l'assicura
	"	di metter dentro alle guardate mura
	"	gente inimica e forte,
	"	ond'egli ne riceva esilio e morte.
	"	Però che non sì tosto	30
	"	s'appresentano al core[58]
	"	per entrarvi la speme con la gioia
	"	che sorgendo il timore
	"	esclude l'una, e fa che l'altra moia.
		Onde s'io non do fede	35
		a' tuoi veraci detti,
		Armilla, a ciò mi muove un pensier solo:
		che potrebb'esser che ella fastidita
		da' tuoi prieghi importuni
		ti concedesse allora	40
		quanto le domandavi,
		ma che non abbia in cor già d'osservarlo.
ARM.		Non temer che Clorilli
		delle promesse sue mancasse mai.
FIL.		D[eh] voglia, Armilla, il Ciel, che così sia,	45
		ma del contrario temo.
COR.		A quel ch'io veggio
		è morta ogni speranza nel tuo petto. / [22ᵛ]
	"	Ma di che nutri Amore
	"	se l'è di lui nutrice, e da lei prende
	"	qual vezzoso bambin continuo lat[t]e[59]?	50

---

[56] M does not indent broken lines where split between speakers (*antilabe*).
[57] *fero dogle*.
[58] Lines 30–1 appear in M as a single 14-syllable line.
[59] *l'ate*.

Filemone

Oh, what new emotion is this? And is this possible? O dear nymph, pray, do you tell me the truth?

Armilla

Ah! Are you of such little faith that you believe I would tell you this in jest? It is certain, it is true.

Filemone

The unhappy soul is used to dwelling in a desolate fortress, where nothing ever visits but savage sorrows and woes, / [22^r] *for Fear, its faithful companion, does not permit the soul to bring any fierce enemies within its guarded walls which might banish or slay it. So, no sooner might Joy, together with Hope, begin to approach the heart to beg entry, than Fear, rising up, drives one away, and slays the other.*[72]

So if I do not give faith to your true words, Armilla, it is because only one thought moves me: perhaps, pestered by your importunate prayers, she relented to your demands in the moment, but in her heart she does not intend to follow through.

Armilla

Do not fear, for Clorilli never goes back on her promises.

Filemone

O Armilla, may Heaven make it so; but I fear she will.

Coribante

From what I see, all hope in your breast has died. / [22^v] *But how can Love be nourished, if Hope is his wet nurse, and he can only thrive by avidly suckling at her breast, like a bonny babe?*

FIL.		Si nutre di dolore,	
		d'amare rimembranze.	
ARM.	"	Se di venen si nutre	
	"	tosto dovrà morire.	
COR.		M'allegro Filemone	55
		che tosto sarai fuor[60] di questo affanno.	
FIL.		Di vita sì che io sarò tosto fuori.	
		Ma quando parlerògli[61] Armilla, quando?	
ARM.		Sian restate d'accordo	
		di venir fra mezz'ora in questo luoco,	60
		ove potrai parlargli.	
		Ma sai che ti ricordo Filemone;	
		pon da canto le lacrime e sospiri,	
		e tanti tuoi lamenti, che ora è tempo	
		d'esser ardito, e valoroso amante.	65
FIL.		Sei stata amante in alcun tempo Armilla?	
ARM.		Fui sempre e sono, e sarò finché io viva.	
FIL.		Et amasti da vero[62]?	
ARM.		Come s'amai da vero?	
		Amai più che me stessa il mio Licone	70
		mentre visse tra noi;	
		e poi che morte acerba / [23r]	
		tolse dal suo bel velo	
		l'anima bella e colocolla in Cielo,	
		quasi nume divin l'amo e l'onoro.	75
FIL.	"	Dunque debbi saper[63] che vero Amore	
	"	è privo d'ogni ardire.	
ARM.		Se Amor è Dio sì valoroso e forte	
		come s'egli pur regna nel tuo core	
		che dia loco al timore	80
		dimmi chi n'è cagione?	
FIL.		Quella che amare e riverir m'insegna.	
ARM.		S'egli ti insegna ad amare[64]	
		debbe insegnarti ancor d'esser ardito,	
	"	che 'n generoso core	85
	"	ardito si dimostra e forte Amore.	

[60] *fuor*: inserted in superscript.
[61] *parlerogli*: Tuscan form (standard Italian: *le parlerò*).
[62] *da dovero*. Surmised version fits the seven-syllable line, and produces an echo in the following line.
[63] *sapere*. Apocope surmised to fit hendecasyllable.
[64] Line 83 has at least eight syllables.

Filemone
Love feeds on pain, on bitter memories.

Armilla
If Love nourishes itself with poison, it will soon die.

Coribante
I am happy, Filemone, for soon you will be past this heartache.

Filemone
Yes, for soon I will be past life itself! But when will I speak with her, Armilla, when?

Armilla
We agreed to come in half an hour to this place, where you will be able to speak to her. But I must remind you, Filemone, to put aside your tears, and sighs, and all these endless laments, for now is the time to be a daring and valorous lover![73]

Filemone
Have you ever been in love, Armilla?

Armilla
I always was, and I am, and I will be as long as I live.

Filemone
Were you ever truly in love?

Armilla
What do you mean, was I ever truly in love? I loved my Licone more than I loved myself while he lived amongst us![74] And since bitter Death / [23ʳ] wrenched his beautiful soul from its beautiful earthly veil and set it in Heaven, I have loved him and honoured him almost as a divine spirit.

Filemone
Then you must know that true Love lacks all daring.

Armilla
If Love is such a strong and valorous god, and reigns in your heart, why does he allow Fear a place there as well? Tell me, who is the cause of this?

Filemone
She whom he teaches me to love, and to worship.[75]

Armilla
If he teaches you to love, he should also teach you to be bold, *for Cupid shows himself, bold and strong, in the noble heart.*

	Ma tempo è ormai ch'io vada	
	a ritrovar Clorilli.	
	A te lascio la cura	
	di condur Filemone	90
	all'ora destinata.	
COR.	Va pur che io condurollo	
	ma prima voglio andar alla capanna.	
FIL.	Venir voglio anch'io teco, andianne.	
COR.	Andiamo.	

Scena quinta

Licasta, Clorilli / [23ᵛ]

LIC.	Punto più che tardavi a comparire	1
	non mi trovavi, ove sei stata tanto?	
CLO.	Mi sopragiunse Armilla in quello stante	
	che io raggiunsi la damma, e ch'io l'uccisi,	
	e come sempre suol con le sue ciancie	5
	oltre al dover mi tenne a bada, et io	
	da lei non mi toglieva	
	col prometterli quanto ella bramava	
	v'era che far tutto oggi, avanti ch'io	
	potessi a te venir, Licasta mia.	10
LIC.	Ancor sèguita Armilla	
	di importunarti⁶⁵ per quel Filemone?	
CLO.	Segue ostinata, e pare	
	che pur ora incominci, ond'io per tormi	
	questa noia d'intorno	15
	alla fin gl'ho promesso	
	d'ascoltar Filemone; ma ti prometto⁶⁶	
	che seguirà con sì poca sua gioia	
	che forse pentirassi	
	d'averlo procurato.	20
LIC.	O son pur importuni	
	gli uomini amanti, o che fingon d'amare	
	per meglio dir, però che a dirti il vero	
	Clorilli mia, poco do fede o nulla	

---

⁶⁵ *impurtunarti*.
⁶⁶ Line 17 has 12 syllables.

But now it is time for me to go find Clorilli. [*To Coribante*] I leave to you the task of bringing Filemone back at the appointed hour.

Coribante
Go on. I will bring him, but first I will go to the cottage.

Filemone
I will come, too. Let's be going!

Coribante
Let's go.

Scene Five

Licasta, Clorilli / [23ᵛ]

Licasta
You nearly arrived too late to find me here. Where were you for so long?[76]

Clorilli
Armilla caught up with me just when I had overtaken the doe and killed it. And as always, she kept me with her idle chatter much longer than necessary. And I would have been there all day if I had not managed to pry myself away by promising her all that she desired so I could come to you, my dear Licasta.

Licasta.
Is Armilla still badgering you on behalf of that Filemone?

Clorilli
She continues most obstinately, and it seems as if this is only the start of it! To save myself this annoyance, in the end I promised her I would listen to Filemone; but I promise you it will bring him so little joy, he will perhaps regret having procured my ear.

Licasta
Oh, they are true importunates, men who love – or rather, men who pretend to love! But to tell you the truth, my dear Clorilli, I give little

alle querele lor, a' lor lamenti; / [24ʳ]   25
perché son mastri rari
di mentite parole, e così bene
san travestir la fraude, in amor parlo,
che la diresti la verità stessa.
Pria di pal[l]ido velo   30
le ricopron la sozza or[r]ida faccia,
poscia candido manto
di lagrime contesto
gli omeri le ricopre.
La gola cinge intorno   35
prezioso monile,
di giuramenti in vento convertiti,
che in prima vista ti sembrian diamanti,
ma se t'accosti, poi tu li ritrovi
fragilissimo vetro.   40
Vaga ghirlanda il crin di varii fiori
l'adorna, e cinge di sospir mentiti.
Poi dall'instabil mar delle lor voglie
da finta conca han tratto
di fallaci promesse   45
due vanissime perle
che pendon dall'orecch[i]e,
a cui posto han nome d'Amore, e fede.
S'adornan poi le mani
di varie gemme, con tersi smanigli,   50
che gli hanno dato il nome / [24ᵛ]
d'allettatrici lusinghe,[67]
e'n fronte si li legge:[68]

"   per saziar le sue voglie il tutto lice.

CLO.   Il ver parli Licasta,   55
perché se piangon gli occhi,
se sospira la bocca,
entro ne ride il core, e già disegna
di far con questi del[l]e loro insane
voglie ministri ogni più nobil preda   60

---

[67] Line 52 has eight syllables.
[68] Presumed *gli si legge*. The Tuscan (non-Bemban) form *li si legge* is known (Rohlfs, *Grammatica storica*, §475). The inversion (*si gli* for *gli si*) is also not unusual in today's Tuscan, especially in the western area, including Pisa and Lucca (personal communication from Eugenio Refini, 11/12/2021).

or no faith to their moans and their laments. / [24^r] For they are rare masters of lying words, and they know how to disguise Fraud so well in matters of Love, I mean, so effectively, that you would say it was the very truth.

First, they cover Fraud's horrid filthy face with a pale veil, and then they cover her shoulders with a pure mantle of tears.[77] A precious necklace wraps around her throat, made of promises that blow away on the wind. For at first glance, you would think them diamonds, but if you get close, you will discover that they are made from the most fragile glass. They adorn her hair with a beautiful garland of various flowers, circling it with lying sighs. Next, out of the inconstant sea of their desires, they have extracted false promises from a false conch: these two hollow pearls hang from her ears, which have been given the names Love and Faith. Then, they adorn her hands with various gems and polished bracelets, all of which have been given names / [24^v] of enticing flattery. And on Fraud's forehead read the words: '*to satisfy one's desires, all is permitted*'.[78]

Clorilli
You speak the truth, Licasta, for while their eyes weep and the mouth sighs, inside, the heart laughs. And now it plots with the ministers of their mad desires to capture that noblest of prey:

de l'anime e de' cori
per le credule ninfe e semplicette.
Né pria qualche infelice avrà creduto
alle lor finte imagini d'Amore
che, ben tosto lasciandola, di lei   65
non fan più stima, e tosto in altra parte
volgon' i lor inganni, et osan poi
di chiamarci volubili e leggiere.

LIC.   Sì volubil non è, né sì leggiera,
ninfa che al paragon del più costante   70
=   pastor non sembri la costanza stessa.[69]
O come disse ben sopra di questo
la bellissima Cellia, et s'io credessi
di non ti infastidir te 'l ridirei.

CLO.   Temi di infastidirmi, e che poss'io   75
udir già mai che mi sia tanto caro / [25ʳ]
quanto 'l biasmar così nemico sesso?
Ma qual'è questa Cellia, è quella forse
che 'l Pò più ch'altra ninfa onora e 'nchina?
Quella, che per beare i toschi[70] lidi   80
si giunse in matrimonio
al generoso Aldranio?

LIC.   Di quella parlav'io
x   della leggiadra Cellia,[71]
Cellia gloria d'Amor, pregio del mondo,   85
nel cui bel volto è primavera eterna,
e l'oro delle stelle ha nel bel crine.
Cel[l]ia, nel cui pudico altero sguardo
Amor casto sfavilla,
e nel candido seno   90
nobil pietade alberga.
Non so se ti soviene
quand'ella per far lieta Etruria bella
lasciò del Pò la regia altera riva,
e passò a far con la sua vista il mare   95

---

[69] Line 71: mark in left-hand margin of two parallel lines (=) sloping upwards to the right, with two horizontal dots in parallel with the lines, above and below (Fig. 7). This is repeated below line 264, marking out a polemical *à clef* passage (lines 72–263) perhaps used for a particular performance or added from a separate manuscript source. Cf. II.6.28 and 169.

[70] *Tosschi.*

[71] Line 84: a small cross mark appears in the left margin, presumably as a highlight for the encomiastic *à clef* section following (Fig. 8).

the souls and hearts of these simple, trusting nymphs. No sooner will some unfortunate nymph be taken in by their false images of Love than they will quickly leave her, for they will no longer respect her, and they will soon direct their deceits in another direction. And they dare to call *us* inconstant and fickle!

Licasta
The most unfaithful and fickle nymph would seem like Constancy itself compared to even the most steadfast of shepherds. Oh, how well the lovely Cellia spoke on this subject![79] And if I thought I would not bore you, I would tell you the story.

Clorilli
You worry that you will bore me! But what can I possibly hear that might be as dear to me / [25ʳ] as criticism of this sex that is so much our enemy?

But who is this Cellia? Can she be the one the Po River honours and reveres above all other nymphs? She who, to bless the Tuscan shores, joined herself in matrimony with the noble Aldranio?[80]

Licasta
I was speaking of her, indeed, of the charming Cellia. Cellia, glory of Love, prize of the world, in whose beautiful visage lies eternal spring, and who holds the gold of the stars in her hair. Cellia, in whose proud and honest gaze chaste love sparkles forth, and in whose pure breast noble piety resides. I don't know if you remember when she left the proud, royal banks of the Po to bring happiness to lovely Etruria? When she

	quieto e tranquillo ove ha 'l nobil albergo	
	il saggio Aldranio suo?	
CLO.	Come se mi sovien, viddi anco l'onda	
	del[72] picciolo Mugnon più chiara farsi	
	per ricever in sè la bella immago	100
	di lei (non so s'io chiamo o ninfa o dea)[73] / [25ᵛ]	
	mentr' ella col bel piè calcando l'erbe	
	lungo le rive sue n'andava al Arno.	
LIC.	Tu ti dèi ricordar ancor che tutte	
	le paesane ninfe	105
	corsero a prova a render il tributo	
	delle bellezze lor, manco possenti	
	alla bellezza imperiosa sua.	
	Il tributo fu amor puro e costante.	
	Tra molte che v'andar, v'andammo ancora	110
	Ilia la saggia mia compagna, et io.	
	Et ella come suol, con le sue grate	
	accoglienze, così ne fece sue,	
	che a noi di noi non restò cosa alcuna	
	pregiata e cara che di lei non fosse	115
	liberalissimo[74] dono.	
	Ma che ella seguendo il suo viaggio	
	sconsolate lasciò queste compagne,	
	e maggiormente noi, ci risolvemmo	
	d'andarla a riveder dove ella fosse.	120
	Così ci trasferimmo ove la Magra	
	mesce le sue dolci acque	
	con le salse del mare	
	e la trovammo assisa	
	sopra l'incolta spiaggia,	125
	che in mar fissa tenea l'altere luci / [26ʳ]	
	in guisa tal che di noi non s'accorse	
	al primo comparir; ma quando poi	
	ne vidde, tutta lieta ella n'accolse.	
	La cagion li chiesi io perché sì intenta	130
	affissava nel mar le luci, et ella	
	cortese, mi rispose:	

---

[72] dell'.

[73] ?: surmised transcription error for end parenthesis (see Fig. 8).

[74] Line 116 is an eight-syllable line. Possibly syncope envisaged (*libralissimo*) to maintain *settenario*, as common in Lucchese (Castellani, *Grammatica storica*, 311).

went to dwell by that sea where Aldranio has his noble lodging, stilling its waves with her fair sight?[81]

Clorilli

What do you mean, do I remember? I too saw the waters of the little Mugnone made brighter when the beautiful image was reflected in them of this . . . I know not whether to call her nymph or goddess, / [25ᵛ] when she trod the grass along its banks with her lovely foot as she made her way to the Arno.[82]

Licasta

You must also remember, then, that all the nymphs of the surrounding countryside rushed to compete in rendering tribute to her superior beauty with their own lesser beauty. Their tribute was pure and constant Love. Among the many were my mannerly companion Ilia and I.[83] And Cellia, as she is wont, greeted us most warmly, winning us to her so entirely that nothing remained to us in ourselves, nothing that was precious or valuable, that was not her most bountiful gift.

But as she carried on with her journey, leaving her companions inconsolable, especially the two of us, we resolved to go and see her again in her new home. So we travelled to where the Magra mixes its sweet waters with the salt of the sea.[84] There we found her seated above the untamed beach, with her lofty gaze so fixed upon the sea / [26ʳ] that she was not aware of us when we first appeared, though when she saw us, she welcomed us most gladly. I asked her why she stared so intently upon the sea and she answered me graciously:

— Stava pur or mirando
di questo nostro mar l'instabil campo,
e ne venia facendo un paragone   135
all'incostanza, a la volubil fede
de gli uomini; e dicea tra me medesma:
O come quieto appare
in vista l'ocean, come tranquillo!
Come son piane l'onde, e qual promette   140
bonaccia a' naviganti! Ma se poi
dalle cave spelonche[75] Eolo disserra
ancor picciolo vento
vedi farsi quel pian montagne d'onde,
vedi in cruda tempesta   145
cangiar quel primo sì tranquillo aspetto,
e guerra minacciando, aperta[76] guerra
al misero nocchiero.
Tali gli uomini son, de[h][77] mentre ascosi
tengono i lor volubili pensieri   150
nell'or[r]ide caverne
del lor[78] perfido core; / [26^v]
mansueti li scorgi, e 'n vista umili,

    x   e par spirar da placidi sembianti.[79]
Ma non sì tosto mal accorta ninfa   155
spiega le vele de su[o]i bei desiri
per questo mar, che sembra amico e piano,
che in un momento essi allentando il freno
all'infinita schiera
delle volubil voglie   160
la travolgon in guisa
che di toccar le stelle ora le sembra,
or del profondo abisso[80]
la più profonda parte
premer col piede; alfine   165
in quell'empie voraggini assorbita
resta miseramente.

---

[75] speloncche.
[76] apperta.
[77] de.
[78] Dell'or.
[79] x: small cross indicated in left margin of line 154, presumably highlighting allusion to Tasso's *Rime* mclxxxix; see *Clorilli* translation, n. 87.
[80] abbisso.

'I was looking out just now at the shifting expanses of this sea of ours, and I was fashioning a parallel with the inconstancy and the fickle faith of men. I said to myself:

"How calm does the ocean appear to us, how tranquil? How low and even are the waves, promising fair weather to sailors? Yet if Aeolus releases even his meekest wind from the hollow caves, then you will see that low plane transform into mountains of waves.[85] You will see that formerly tranquil surface transform into a cruel tempest, and threatening war, open war on the miserable helmsman.

Just so, mark, are men! While they keep their fickle thoughts hidden deep in the horrid caverns of their perfidious hearts, / [26ᵛ] they will look gentle and mild to you nymphs, breathing only peaceful semblances.[86] But no sooner does a guileless nymph unfurl the sails of her fine desires upon this sea that seems so very benign and calm, than, in an instant – unleashing the reins of the infinite horde of their voluble volitions – they throw her into such turmoil that she seems now to rise to meet the stars; now to tread the lowest point of the abyss, until finally she is miserably devoured by the unholy depths.

E se tranquillo appare
allo spuntar del sole, a mezzogiorno
lo scorgi fatto orribile e tremendo.   170
Dimmi qual è quel uomo
che in un pensiero stesso
lo ritrovin già mai la luna e 'l sole?
Anzi dicev'io mal che in un pensiero
lo ritrovan non pur la luna e 'l sole,   175
ma le stagioni e gl'anni.
Stanno a guisa di scogli
ripercossi dall'onde / [27^r]
di fe' pura e costante a lor nimica,
fermi e costanti solo   180
nell'incostanza loro.
Dentro al verace sen gemme e tesori
assorbe il mar; sì col desir ingordo
ogni[81] ricchezza avidamente accoglie
dell'uom la avara mente;   185
vaga più che d'onor, d'argento, et d'oro.
Mostri nudrisce il mar, nutre ancor l'uomo
quasi Proteo novello
di bruttissime foche[82] immenso stuolo.
Desir lascivi, e 'mpuri,[83]   190
molli pensier, e vili
oziosi diletti,
e mille altri infiniti
or[r]endi mostri e sozzi
ch'io non ti narro, omai vedendo il sole   195
spegner nell'ocean gli accesi raggi.—
Così pose ella fin al suo parlare,
e me condusse seco
al[84] fortunato albergo.

CLO.   Fu degno paragone   200
             di così saggia ninfa.

LIC.   Mi scordavo di dirti
             che mentre che ella incominciò a parlare
             a caso soprag[g]iunse Ormindo il forte,

[81] *Ongi.*
[82] *focche.*
[83] *empuri.*
[84] *All'.*

And if the sea seems tranquil at the break of day, by noon you will see it become horrid and fearsome.

Tell me, is there a man in whose mind the moon and the sun may be found at the same time? Nay, I was speaking falsely, for men can hold not only the moon and the sun in their minds, but also the seasons, and the years. They are like rocks in the sea, battered by waves / [27ʳ] of pure faith and constancy, which are enemy to them, for they are steadfast and constant only in their inconstancy.[87] Within its true breast, the sea contains gems and treasures; and, in the same way, the miserly mind of man avidly hoards wealth, desiring silver and gold above honour. The sea nourishes monsters, while man, like a new Proteus, breeds an immense flock of the foulest sea-calves:[88] lascivious, impure desires, sensual and vile thoughts, idle pleasures, and a thousand other horrendous and vile monstrous things that I will not describe to you, now that I see the sun's fiery rays extinguished in the ocean."'

Thus she ended her speech, and brought me with her to her happy abode.

Clorilli
The wise nymph made a worthy comparison.

Licasta
I forgot to tell you that just as she began to speak, the strong Ormindo

il qual con tai parole 205
affermò ciò che disse. / [27ᵛ]
— Ninfe è ver, lo confesso
che con giusta ragione
armate le veraci lingue vostre
ai nostri veri biasmi. 210
Noi troppo temerarii
fummo biasmando voi,
ma come errante nube
per poco spazio asconde agli occhi altrui
la chiarezza del sole, 215
così non han potuto
le nostre lingue impure
torvi quello splendor che 'l Ciel vi infuse.
A voi fu madre la Natura, a noi
fierissima matrigna. 220
Sì ché ne muove a invidia,
e però con menzogne
quel ben che pose in voi coprir tentammo:
perché vie più celati
s'ascondessero in noi tanti difetti. 225
Ma voi qual fiammeggiante
piropo, che più splende ov'è più scuro,
risplendete più chiare e più lucenti
tra le false calu[n]nie e finti biasmi.
Noi di inganni e di fraude 230
ci armammo, io lo confesso,
per apportarvi guerra, / [28ʳ]
ma resospinte l'armi
dal fortissimo scudo
della vostra innocenza 235
in noi fecer le piaghe,
a noi portar la guerra
con le nostre armi. Voi
contro di noi nobil vittoria aveste;
appendendole poi come trofei 240
al tempio de la vostra invitta fede.
Donne che per beare
scendesti a noi dalli stellati chiostri
quasi numi del ciel v'onori il mondo,
e se tanto dir lice anco v'adori. — 245

arrived,[89] and affirmed what she said with his own words: / [27ᵛ]

'Nymphs, it is true, I confess that you are right to arm your truthful tongues against our true faults. We were too rash in blaming you, but just as an errant cloud can only hide the sun's brightness from others' eyes for a moment, so were our tongues unable to rob you of the splendour with which Heaven has endowed you. Nature was mother to you, to us a most ferocious stepmother. She thus moved us to envy, but we tried to cover the good in you with lies to hide our own defects more fully;[90] but just as a flaming, shining pyrope shines more brightly in the dark,[91] so do you also shine forth with even more light among false accusations, and fake blame. I confess that we armed ourselves with fraud and deceptions to make war on you. / [28ʳ] But our weapons, repelled by the great shield of your innocence, wounded us instead, and we made war on ourselves with our own arms. You won a noble victory over us, hanging our weapons as trophies in the temple to your unshakeable faith. You, ladies who descended from the starry cloisters to bless us – everyone honours you, almost as though you are deities from Heaven, and if I may say so, they also worship you.'[92]

CLO.		Pur tra tanti bugiardi uomini infidi	
		un se ne ritrovò fido e verace;	
		ma tra quanti infedeli	
		mai furno e mai saranno	
		il più infidel, non credo,	250
		che si possa trovar di Filemone.	
LIC.	"	E' son tutti macchiati d'una pece,	
		sorella mia, e quanto a me disposta	
		son di fuggirli come ho fatto sempre	
		per seguir la mia Delia.	255
		Quell'è gioir, quella è felice vita	
		che si vive di lei seguendo l'orme. / [28ᵛ]	
		A voi nuocer non ponno	
		le lor perfide voglie e lor inganni.	
CLO.		Quanto mi duol Licasta,	260
		che io ciò non viddi e non conobbi prima.	
LIC.		Assai per tempo t[e]'n'accorgi, e puoi	
		seguir sì dolce vita.	
CLO.	=⁸⁵	Seguir vò'l tuo consiglio, e quanto prima	
		vò levarmi da torno Filemone.	265
LIC.		D[eh] riposianci un poco a questa fonte,	
		che a confes[s]arti il ver son quasi stanca.	
CLO.		Non ci fermian già qui, Licasta mia,	
		che questo è 'l luogo appunto	
		ove io debbo parlar con Filemone,	270
		e non vorrei che a sorte egli venendo	
		pensasse che bramosa di parlargli	
		avessi prevenuto il suo venire,	
		e che per ciò sperasse	
		che l'odio mio fosse del tutto estinto.	275
LIC.		Et ove andremo?	
CLO.		Alla fonte sotterra	
		quivi poco lontana,	
		ivi dissi ad Armilla	
		che mi ritroverebbe.	
LIC.		Andiamo adunque. / [29ʳ]	

---

⁸⁵ Marginal mark, as in line 71, possibly to demarcate a passage added or removed for an edition or performance.

Clorilli

Well, at least one was found who was true and faithful, even among so many liars and unfaithful men! But among so many faithless men, I do not believe there ever was or ever will be anyone more faithless than Filemone.

Licasta

They are all tarred with the same brush, sister of mine. For my part, I am disposed to flee from them as I always have, to follow my Delia.[93] This is joy; this is the happy life, to live following her path. / [28ᵛ] Then they cannot hurt you with their perfidious desires and their deceits.

Clorilli

How it saddens me, Licasta, that I did not see and understand this earlier.

Licasta

You have realized it quite soon enough, and can follow this sweet life.

Clorilli

I will follow your advice and free myself from Filemone as soon as I can.

Licasta

Come, let's rest a while at this fountain, for to tell you the truth, I am a little tired.

Clorilli

Let's not stop here, dear Licasta, for this is the very place where I must speak with Filemone. And I would not want him to come across me by chance, and think I had come eager to speak with him before he arrived, for he might hope that my hatred for him has been extinguished.

Licasta

And where shall we go?

Clorilli

To the fountain underground, that place not far from where I told Armilla she would find me.

Licasta

Let's go then. / [29ʳ]

Alfe[s]ibeo Alcone

ALF.	O come in un' saggio e cortese ha esposto	1
	il ministro maggior del[86] sacro tempio	
	a noi gli ordini sacri	
	del sacrificio santo;	
	e con quanta pietade	5
	si puose a consolare	
	il nostro aspro dolore,	
	ond'io la sua mercè più lieto assai	
	ch'io non v'andai ritorno.	
ALC.	Come ei ben disse, Alfe[s]ibeo, depende	10
"	ogni nostro successo, o buono o rio,	
"	dall'immutabil sapienza eterna	
"	di quel[87] che tutto vede e tutto intende,	
"	e che talor quasi amorevol Padre	
"	or con la sferza il temerario ardire	15
"	nostro corregge, or con lusinghe[88] affida	
"	il nostro vil timore, e spesso sotto	
"	immagini di mal gran ben asconde.	
	Che sappian noi che nostri figli al fine,	
	per cui sì afflitte son le menti nostre,	20
	a noi tornando non riportin seco	
	ogni nostro contento; / [29ᵛ]	
	cresciuto in mille doppii, in mille guise?	
ALF.	Come è ver tutto questo, così spero	
	che Giove avendo udito i nostri preghi	25
	ne renderà la perduta allegrezza.	
	Che solo in riveder l'amato figlio	
=	consiste ogni mio ben, ogni mia gioia.[89]	
	Ma che disse egli poi	
	che da voi mi divise	30
	Ergasto, amico mio?	

---

[86] *dell'*.
[87] *quell'*.
[88] *si* of *lu[si]nghi* is written above as insertion.
[89] Line 28: left marginal mark as for II.5.71, 264. This pointing is used also below in line 168, which suggests that lines 29–168 are marked off, possibly due to their occasional and enco-miastic function for a performance linked to the Medici consorts, Ferdinando I and Christine.

Scene Six

Alfesibeo, Alcone

Alfesibeo

Oh, how wisely and courteously did the high priest of the holy temple show us the sacred orders of the holy sacrifice; and how kindly he set himself to consoling our bitter grief. Thanks to him, I come back much happier than I went.

Alcone

As he said very well, Alfesibeo, *each one of our successes, whether bad or good, depends on that immutable eternal knowledge of Him, who sees all, and understands all. Much like a loving father, from time to time He now corrects our foolish daring with the whip, now bolsters our abject fears with encouraging words. And often beneath what seems to be bad there hides great good.*[94]

How do we know, in the end, that our children, who so trouble our minds, will not bring back all our happiness, / [29ᵛ] grown a thousand times and in a thousand ways, by returning to us?

Alfesibeo

How true all of this is! So I hope Jove, having heard our prayers, will restore to us our lost happiness. For my every good, my every joy, depends entirely on seeing my beloved son again. But what else did he say, after my friend Ergasto took me from you?

ALC.   O gran cose mi disse
      di Cristilla e Dinando, amanti e sposi!
      Di quel Dinando il grande, a cui si vede
      quanto da questi colli occhio mortale   35
      può veder lungi biondeggiar le spiche
      per i bei colti campi.
      Dinando, a cui l'Etruria
      lietissima soggiace;
      quello che ha riposto il fortunato seggio[90] 40
      nella città che da fior piglia il nome,
      nella città nella qual oggi a prova[91]
      fioriscono i più nobili costumi,
      mercè del[92] chiaro sole
      che di duoi lumi unito a doppio splende 45
      nel bel seren del Cielo
      del fortunato Impero. / [30r]
      Del[93] gran Dinando e di Cristilla bella,
      grazia d'aura cortese
      che dal bel petto spira   50
      della saggia Cristilla.
      Né mai sì altero rese Arno gentile
      il suo tributo al mare,
      quanto dopoi, che da' più ricchi onori
      lieto spogliò la Mosa,   55
      Mosa che già per la saggia Cristilla
      se n' gìa superba al paro
      dell'imme[n]so oceano.[94]
ALF.   O fortunata etade
      a cui lice veder   60
      non so s'io debba dir Giove o Dinando,
      non so s'io debba dire
      Giunone o pur Cristilla,
      congiunti in maestà sedersi insieme,
      che ben Giove n'assembra il gran Dinando 65
      al valor, all'impero,

---

[90] Line 40 has at least 12 syllables.
[91] *approva*.
[92] *dell'*.
[93] *dell'*.
[94] *orceano*.

Alcone

Oh, he told me great things about Cristilla and Dinando, lovers and consorts![95] That great Dinando, thanks to whom the corn gleams yellow across the beautiful, cultivated fields as far as the human eye can see. Dinando, to whom most happy Etruria is subject, he who has placed his fortunate seat in the city that takes its name from the flower – the city wherein today the most noble customs can be clearly seen to bloom, thanks to the bright sun that emanates from two lights united in double splendour in the beautiful calm of Heaven above this fortunate Empire.[96] / [30ʳ]

He told me of the great Dinando, and of beautiful Cristilla; wise Cristilla, who exudes courtly air from her fair breast. Never before did the noble Arno render its tribute to the sea so proudly as after he happily stripped the Meuse of its richest honours – the Meuse, which once thought itself the equal of the immense ocean thanks to the sage Cristilla.[97]

Alfesibeo

Oh, what a fortunate age, when it is possible to witness . . . I do not know if I should call him Jove or Dinando, I do not know whether to call her Juno, or rather Cristilla, joined in majesty to reign together. For great Dinando certainly resembles Jove, in valour, in empire.

che ben Giunon simiglia
Cristilla, all'alto senno, al bel sembiante.

ALC. Mi dicea Corebo, il buon ministro,
che appunto or quanto più ardeva il sole   70
sì ri[parò]⁹⁵ da' fervidi calori
nella sublime⁹⁶ lor capanna altera,
che dalle pietre già si prese il nome, / [30ᵛ]
onde Petraia è detta;
pietra che assai più che diamante splende,   75
mercè de la virtù che a lei comparte
il chiaro sol di dui be' lumi ardenti.
Ivi dice egli che Cristilla bella,
anzi nuova Diana,
cinta di ninfe intorno   80
scacciavano dall'alma ogni tristezza.

ALF. E quali eran le ninfe,
a cui benigna sorte
tanta grazia concesse?

ALC. V'era la leggiadrissima Amarilli,   85
Amarilli gentile,
che sembra agli occhi altrui celeste Aurora,
qual'or più vaga suole
sorger dal[l'] Ocean, figlia del sole;
Aurora, che mill'alme e mille cori,   90
se ben giovane spunta
dall'orizonte⁹⁷ appena, arde et infiamma.
Or che farà, quando l'aurato crine
Febo l'illustrerà col suo splendore?
V'era la casta Onoria,   95
Onoria onor di queste nostre selve,
Onoria che con dotta man può dare
quasi la voce e 'l moto
a figura che pinga in carte o 'n tela. / [31ʳ]
Coppia ben degna, che di lor ragioni   100
ogni più doppia, ogni più saggia lingua,
ambe unite di sangue al gran Dinando
ambe care a Cristilla.

---

⁹⁵ *si ripprarò.*
⁹⁶ *subblime.*
⁹⁷ *orizzonte.*

For Cristilla certainly resembles Juno, in her great wisdom, and in her noble appearance.[98]

Alcone

The good priest Corebo was telling me that just when the sun was at its hottest,[99] he took refuge from the raging heat in their sublime and lofty dwelling, which takes its name from the stones, / [30ᵛ] and so is called Petraia. It is a stone that sparkles even more brightly than a diamond, thanks to the excellence that shines on it from the bright sun, composed of two such beautiful ardent lights.[100] There, he says, the beautiful Cristilla was like a new Diana who, with her circle of nymphs, chased all sadness from their souls.

Alfesibeo

And who were the nymphs upon whom kind fate bestowed such grace?

Alcone

Fairest Amarilli was there – noble Amarilli, who looks to those who gaze on her like heavenly Aurora, daughter of the sun, when, at her most beautiful, she rises from the Ocean.[101] An Aurora, who inflames a thousand souls and a thousand hearts, even though, young as she is, she has only just appeared on the horizon. Now what will she do when Phoebus casts his brilliance on her golden hair?

Chaste Onoria was there – Onoria, the honour of these woods of ours. Onoria, who with her wise hand can almost grant voice and motion to a figure she paints on paper or in tapestry.[102] / [31ʳ] A pair most worthy of celebration by every wise and eloquent tongue, both united by blood with the great Dinando, both dear to Cristilla.

ALF.	Ove è questa Petraia	
	che già non mi sovviene	105
	d'averla mai veduta?	
ALC.	Vella[98] qui dirimpetto,	
	vedi come alto estolle	
	la superba capanna al ciel la cima.	
	Vedi l'altere mura.	110
	Entro a lor si raccoglie	
	quanto più di pregiato altrove abbonda.	
ALF.	O gran macchina, o quella, o s'io potessi	
	veder quell' che di bello in sè n'asconde,	
	felice me. Ma tu che già l'hai vista	115
	di tante meraviglie	
	nàrrane alcune, cortese Alcone.[99]	
ALC.	Per molto che io dicessi	
	sarebbe appena una minima stilla	
	d'un infinito mare	120
	di cose elette e rare	
	che lì dentro si scorgon. Ivi sempre	
	primavera verdeggia / [31ᵛ]	
	col suo fiorito nembo.	
	Fioriscono ivi eterni	125
	odorati giardin d'aranci e cedri.	
	Sm[e]raldi[100] han l'erbe l'ingemmati prati	
	che non sentir' già mai tempesta o verno.	
	Ivi tra lauri e mirti	
	lieti scherzan a gara	130
	gl'augei, e cantando	
	tempron suave note i lusignoli.	
	O se vedessi i liquidi cristalli,	
	in quante guise, in quanti varii modi	
	apportan vaga vista;	135
	qual par che vogli andar superbo al Cielo,	
	qual[101] con più larga vena	
	versa precipitoso.	
	Altri insieme raccolti	

---

[98] *Vella*: in modern Italian *vedila*.
[99] *nàrrane alcune,* | *cortese Alcone*. Line break removed to fit metre.
[100] *Smiraldi*.
[101] *e qual*: it is presumed that 'e' is a transcription error, as it would make the line eight syllables.

Alfesibeo

Where is this Petraia? For I do not believe I have ever laid eyes on it.

Alcone

Here you see it opposite! See how tall the proud dwelling rises up into the heavens. See the lofty walls. Within them, more precious things are collected than can be found anywhere else.

Alfesibeo

Oh, what a great edifice! Oh, if I could see the beauty hiding within, oh, how happy I would be! But you, courteous Alcone, who have already seen all its many marvels – tell me about some of them!

Alcone

However much I could recount would be but a tiny drop in the infinite sea of rare, choice things to be found inside. Spring blooms continually there, / [31ᵛ] with a shower of flowers. Sweet smelling gardens of orange and lemon trees flower evermore. The grasses of the budding sparkling lawns are emerald, and have never felt storms or winter. There, the happy birds challenge each other playfully among the laurel and myrtle, and the singing nightingales temper their sweet notes.[103]

Oh, if you could see the liquid crystals,[104] and how they manifest glorious visions in so many ways, in so many different forms! One fountain seems to shoot up proudly towards Heaven; another pours forth water from its largest artery. Yet more unite to form a tranquil pool so

forman tranquillo stagno, 140
sì trasparente e chiaro
che annoverar potresti
ogni minuta arena
che forma a lui l'inargentato fondo,
ove i pesci vedresti 145
in bella schiera andar lascivi errando.
Ma che dirò de' marmi
scolpiti in varie forme?
Qua ti sembra veder latrar un cane, / [32r]
là fuggirsi un cignal cui con gran forza 150
rozzo villan lanciando un dardo atterra.
In altra parte vedi Ercole invitto
far varie prove. Ma che vò contando
quel che a pena capir pensiero umano
puote? Non ché ridir 155
rustica lingua incolta?
E ben conosco che troppo alto ascesi,
troppo ardisco io rozzo pastor e vile.
Ma voi coppia beata,
voi nostri semidei, voi nostri Duci, 160
perdonate benigni,
condonate all'affetto
onde ha vestit[o]¹⁰² l'alma
il temerario ardire.

ALF.   "   Alma che a Giove d'agguagliarsi intende 165
       "   d'un umil cor gradisce il puro affetto,
       "   né di lingua devota a sdegno prende
       "   lode che al suo valor non s'alzi uguale.
       =   Ma tempo è omai che andiamo¹⁰³
           alle nostre capanne, 170
           ove in dolce riposo
           caccieremo il digiuno.

ALC.   Andian, che gli anni miei
           più braman di riposo,
           che d'andar¹⁰⁴ tutto il dì vagando intorno. / [32v] 175

---

¹⁰² *vestita*.
¹⁰³ Line 169: mark in left margin, as above in line 28.
¹⁰⁴ *d'landar*.

transparent and clear that you could count every minute grain of sand that makes up the silvery deep, where you might see wanton fish go wandering together in pleasing schools.[105]

But what can I say about the many marbles sculpted into different forms? Here, you might think you see a dog barking, / [32^r] and there, a wild boar tries to flee, just before he is felled by a coarse peasant forcefully launching a spear. Just over there, you can see invincible Hercules performing his many feats of strength.[106]

But why do I continue to recount what the human mind can barely understand, let alone recount it with an unpolished, rustic tongue? And I certainly know that I climbed too high. I, a rough and base shepherd, dare too much.[107]

But you, blessed couple, you are our demigods, you are our leaders. Graciously pardon my harmless words, accept my affection, which has clothed my soul in reckless daring.

Alfesibeo
The soul who seeks to reach the heights of Jove pleases through the pure affection of a humble heart; nor does Jove scorn praise from a devoted tongue which does not rise equal to his merit.[108]

But now it is time for us to return to our dwellings, where, in sweet repose, we will break our fast.

Alcone
Let's go, for my many years are more avid for repose than for wandering around all day. / [32^v]

[*They leave.*]

Scena settima

Satiro

" Cacciato dalla fame   1
" esce dal bosco[105] il fiero lupo e corre
" rapido là ove saziar più crede
" l'avidissime brame.
Non altrimenti or me fame amorosa   5
sospinto ha fu[o]r delle spelonche[106] sacre,
ove mia Deità sovente alberga,
e vengo in questa selva, ove tal volta
suol per diporto suo venir Clorilli,
Clorilli perfidissima, che abborre   10
sì questa forma mia, sì questo aspetto
venerabile e forte, e qual conviensi
appunto a un semideo.[107]
Clorilli ingrata, chi sprezzi e fuggi?
Un'orso? un tigre? un fiero basilisco?   15
ch[e][108] col guardo t'uccida? Io che son Dio
in queste selve, che con la mia forza
far acquisto potrei dell'amor tuo,
mi compiaccio pregarti,
et a' preghi aggiungo[109]   20
doni preziosimi e graditi,
e tu mi sprezzi et or recusi? O folle
mal consigliata ninfa. / [33ʳ]
Dui cerviotti[110] l'altro ier vezzosi e molli
tolsi a la madre, e la vaga Curilla   25
tentat' ha per avergli ogni sua arte,
promettendo di darmi in ricompensa
vaso non tocco ancor da labbia umana,
ove da dotta man si vede scolto
del semicapro Dio l'antico amore   30
con la triforme Dea,

---

[105] *bosccho.*
[106] *delle speloncche*: *delle* inserted in superscript.
[107] Lines 13–14: *appunto a un semideo Clorilli ingrata | chi sprezzi e fuggi?* Line break adjusted to fit *hendecasyllable/settenario* metre (avoiding a line of maximum six syllables).
[108] *Ch'*: added just to left of the text.
[109] Lines 19–20 written as a single line in M of not less than 12 syllables; split to preserve metre.
[110] *cervviotti.*

Scene Seven

Satyr

Driven by hunger, the fierce wolf emerges from the forest and hastens to where he thinks he is most likely to satisfy his most ravenous desires. No differently has amorous hunger now driven me out from the sacred caves, where my goddess often dwells.[109] And I come to this wood, where Clorilli often comes alone to amuse herself. Most perfidious Clorilli, who so detests my form, so detests my venerable and strong countenance, which befits a demigod![110]

Ungrateful Clorilli, whom do you scorn and evade? A bear? A tiger? A fierce basilisk, who can kill you with one glance?[111] I, who am a god in these woods, and could conquer your love by force, choose instead to court you, and add precious and welcome gifts to my entreaties – and yet still you scorn me, and now you refuse me? O vain, ill-advised nymph! / [33^r]

The other day, I took two soft and wanton young deer away from their mother, and the lovely Curilla used all her wiles to try to obtain them. She promised to reward me with a vessel untouched by human lips, upon which, sculpted by a gifted hand, one can see the ancient love of the half-goat God for his triform goddess.

di te più bella assai; né le dispiacque
il [s]uo[111] feroce e grazioso aspetto,
e mi soggiunse che se quel non era
condegno guiderdon[e]   35
di quanto ella bramava[112]
m'avrebbe[113] fatto don del amor suo.
Et io per seguir te sprezzo i suoi doni
e non curo il suo amor, e tu non curi
perfida ninfa un Dio così fedele?   40
Ma perché folle vo seguendo i preghi
s'io mi posso valer di quel che in dono
mi concesse Natura? E se la forza
ebbi a che non l'adopro, e te rapisco
quel che da lei non posso avere in dono?   45
O disconviene a un Dio l'esser rapace?
A sua posta sconvenga, anco pur Giove
per rapir[e] l'amato Ganimede
in aquila cangiossi, e 'n pioggia d'oro
per ingannar la semplicetta Danai / [33ᵛ]   50
or in cigno, or in toro, or in Diana,
in fiamma, in serpe, in mille strane forme
cangiossi per rapir d'amor i frutti.
E chi vorrà biasmarmi s'ancor io
seguo del[114] maggior Dio l'essempio? Or questa   55
non è virtu da grande? Se 'l gran Giove
l'ha posta in uso? Or dunque
varrommi della forza, e mal tuo grado
verrai Clorilli in mio potere, e pure
ch'io sazii la mia voglia a me che importa   60
che sia tuo danno o mia rapina? Io voglio
nascondermi colà tra quei virgulti;
ivi starò aspettando
rapace cacciator la preda al varco.

---

[111] *tuo*: Satiro must be referring to Pan here (though 'te' in line 31 refers to Clorilli).
[112] Lines 35–6: written as a single line in M of not less than 13 syllables.
[113] *m'averebbe*.
[114] *dell'*.

Diana is much more beautiful than you, but she was not put off by *his* fierce, graceful appearance.[112] And Curilla added that she would give me the gift of her love if her offer was not adequate compensation for what she requested. And to follow you, I spurn her gifts and care nothing for her love and yet, still, perfidious nymph, you care not for such a faithful god?

But why do I foolishly obey your wishes, if I can make use of what Nature gave me? And if I was granted strength, why do I not use it, and rob you of what I cannot have as a gift? Or is it not fitting for a god to be rapacious? Was it also unseemly, then, when Jove changed into an eagle to rape his beloved Ganimede, and into a shower of gold to deceive innocent Danae? / [33ᵛ] He changed first into a swan, then into a bull, then into Diana; he changed into a flame, into a serpent, and into a thousand other different forms to seize the fruits of love.[113]

And who will blame me if I too follow the example of that most powerful god? Is this not the way of great men, if Jove himself has already done the same? Now, then, I will use force, and in spite of yourself, Clorilli, you will see yourself under my power. What does it matter to me whether you are damaged, or prey of mine, as long as I satisfy my own desire?

I will hide myself in those shrubs. There I will be waiting for my prey at the pass, a ravenous hunter.

ATTO TERZO

Scena prima

Armilla, Clorilli

ARM.		Disponti o mia carissima Clorilli	1
		d'udir benignamente Filemone,	
		e lascia omai tant'odio e tanto sdegno,	
		che se troppo più dura	
		al fin torrà la vita a quel meschino.	5
		E potrai più, crudel, rimirar morto / [34ʳ]	
		chi pur un tempo amasti?	
		D[eh] sovvèngati omai	
	"	che maggior gloria acquista	
	"	cortese vincitor, che doni al vinto	10
	"	e vita e libertade,	
	"	che quel che fiero e crudo	
	"	d'aspre catene al vinto alfin l'uccide.	
		A te vinto si rende	
		l'amante tuo, né libertà ti chiede,	15
		ma sol vita domanda,	
		per viver sempre tuo fedel e servo.	
CLO.		Per compiacerti Armilla	
		promesso ho d'ascoltarlo, e ascolterollo	
		cortesemente, or non ti basta questo?	20
ARM.		Non che non basta, voglio	
		che tu l'ascolti amante, e non nimico.	
CLO.		Nemica non son io, né manco amante.	
ARM.	"	Se nimica non sei, sei dunque amante.	
CLO.	"	Amante di me stessa, e non di lui.	25
ARM.	"	Et ei vive in te stessa adunque l'ami.	
CLO.		Vive in me stessa, et in qual parte Armilla?	
		Dal cor lo discacciai,	
		la memoria il perdette,	
		e 'l pensier mio quanto più può lo fugge. / [34ᵛ]	30
ARM.		Ei vive, tuo malgrado,	
		delle stelle, e del Cielo.	
		Dimmi quest'occhi belli,	
		queste dorate chiome,	

ACT THREE

Scene One

Armilla, Clorilli

Armilla

Prepare yourself, O my dearest Clorilli, to listen to Filemone kindly. It is time to abandon all your hatred and contempt. For if this lasts too much longer, the poor wretch's life will be over! And, cruel one, will you be able to gaze again upon that man when he is dead, / [34ʳ] he whom you once loved? Just remember now: *The generous victor achieves greater glory by granting life and liberty to the conquered, than one who, cruel and fierce, [puts] his captive in rough chains, and kills him in the end.*114 Your conquered lover has surrendered to you. And he does not ask you for liberty, but only for life, so he may live forever as your faithful servant.

Clorilli

To please you, Armilla, I have promised to listen to him, and I will listen to him courteously. Now is that not enough for you?

Armilla

The point is not whether it is enough; I want you to listen to him as a lover, not an enemy.

Clorilli

I am not an enemy, but neither am I a lover.

Armilla

If you are not an enemy, then you are a lover.

Clorilli

A lover of myself, and not of him.

Armilla

And he lives within you, thus you love him.

Clorilli

So he lives within me – in which part, then, Armilla? I chased him from my heart, my memory erased him, and my thoughts evade him as much as they can. / [34ᵛ]

Armilla

He lives there in spite of you, in spite of the stars and in spite of the heavens. Tell me, these beautiful eyes of yours, these golden locks, this

		questo candido sen, e questo volto	35
		son parte di Clorilli, o pur d'altrui?	
CLO.		Mie son, se in me le tocchi.	
ARM.		Se sol da queste Filemone ha vita	
		or non vive egli in te?	
CLO.		Non m'hai tu detto	
		ben mille volte che questi occhi miei	40
		gli hanno ferito il core?	
ARM.		L'ho detto, e più che mai di nuovo il dico.	
CLO.	"	O chi ferisce uccide, e non dà vita.	
ARM.	"	Dallo scorpion' ancora	
	"	vien la morte, e la vita.	45
CLO.		Et in che modo Armilla?	
ARM.	"	Le piaghe che in altrui vivendo impresse,	
	"	che mortali sarian morto risana.	
CLOR.		E mi vorresti morta Armilla dunque	
		per apportar salute a Filemone?	50
		E perché tanto m'odii?	
ARM.		Che io t'odii, o mia Clorilli? Anima mia,	
		che io t'odii? Questo no, perché t'amo assai / [35ʳ]	
		di me medesma, ma col dir intendo	
		che se da' tuoi begli occhi	55
		avventi a Filemon acuti strali,	
		da' medesimi ancora	
		piove tanta dolcezza	
		che le piaghe risana aspre e mortali.	
CLO.		Se dunque è sano a che cercar aita?	60
		Meglio è ch'io non li parli, e via men' vada,	
		acciò che non talvolta	
		quest'occhi, poi che l'avesser ferito,	
		non piovesser invece di dolcezza	
		ira di sdegno, et egli	65
		si rimanesse senza alcun soccorso.	
ARM.		O quanto ninfa al danno altrui sei scaltra.	
	"	Or non sai tu che piaga	
	"	d'avvelenato strale	
	"	si molce sì, ma non si sana mai?	70

snowy breast, and this face, do they belong to Clorilli, or to another?

Clorilli
They are mine, if it is in me that you mark them.

Armilla
And if Filemone lives only for these things, does he not then live in you?

Clorilli
Have you not already told me a thousand times that these eyes of mine wounded his heart?

Armilla
I did say this, and I say it again now, more than ever.

Clorilli
Oh, he who wounds, kills, and does not give life.

Armilla
The Scorpion gives both death and life.[115]

Clorilli
And in what way, Armilla?

Armilla
Through its death it heals the wounds it made when living, which would otherwise be fatal.

Clorilli
And so you would want me dead, Armilla, to make Filemone well? Oh, why do you hate me so much?

Armilla
O my Clorilli, you think I hate you? How could I hate you, my dear soul! This is not so, for I love you more / [35ʳ] than I love myself. But I mean to say that even if you send sharp arrows at him from your beautiful eyes, from those same eyes pours forth a great sweetness that can heal those cruel and fatal wounds.

Clorilli
If he is healed, then why seek help? It is better for me not to speak to him, and take my leave, lest after wounding him, these eyes rain down anger and scorn rather than sweetness, leaving him helpless.

Armilla
O nymph, how sly you are in hurting others!
Now don't you know that the wound from a poisoned arrow can be soothed, but never heals?[116]

CLO.	E che nel guardo mio	
	mortifero venen sta fors[e][115] ascoso?	
ARM.	Ben sai che vi s'asconde.	
CLO.	Dunque di basilisco[116],	
	o d'altro or[r]ibil serpe	75
	son nata Armilla? Ah tu mi ingiurii troppo.	
ARM.	Non già dal ventre della vaga Alcippe	
	tel' portasti Clorilli, ma dopoi	
	Mastro eccellente in disusata foggia / [35ᵛ]	
	temprollo, e te n'asperse.	80
CLO.	Di grazia dimmi il Mastro, e di che tempre	
	sia quel venen che dentro agl'occhi ascondo.	
ARM.	Il gran Mastro fu Amor che prima tolse	
	dal[117] bel manto dell'Alba	
	le più candide part[i][118],	85
	e poscia della Notte	
	tolse il suo più negro oscuro Cielo,	
	alle stelle rapì quella scintilla	
	di celeste rugiada.	
	Il tutto insieme infuse, e raffinollo	90
	al suo più ardente foco,	
	e di poi lo ripose	
	negl'occhi di Clorilli.	
CLO.	Alle favole pur[']	
ARM.	Favole dunque[119]	
	stimi tu queste mie? Né ti rammenta	95
	che 'l tuo leggiadro sguardo	
	fu quel che fece pria mortal ferita	
	nel cor di Filemone;	
	et egli è quel che lo sostien in vita,	
	se ben in vita languida et inferma.	100
CLO.	E credi Armilla che tanto potere	
	abbia uno sguardo?	
ARM.	Come s'io 'l credo? / [36ʳ]	
	Or non sai tu ciò che quel gran pastore,	

[115] *forsi*: Tuscan (non-Bemban) form.
[116] *basilisccho*.
[117] *dall'*.
[118] *parte*.
[119] *Favole dunque*: five syllable line; presumed *antilabe* with line above, though 'pure' has been adjusted to fit hendecasyllable metre.

Clorilli
So is deadly poison perhaps hidden in my gaze?

Armilla
You know full well it is hidden in you.

Clorilli
Was I born of a basilisk, then, or another horrible snake, Armilla? Oh, you wound me greatly![117]

Armilla
You did not carry this poison when you emerged from beautiful Alcippe's womb, Clorilli, but only after the excellent Master, in uncommon garb, / [35ᵛ] tempered it and sprinkled it over you.[118]

Clorilli
Tell me, by grace, who this Master was, and how he tempered the venom I hide in my eyes.

Armilla
This great Master was Love, who first took the whitest parts from the lovely mantle of the Dawn, and then the blackest part of the sky from the Night. He robbed the stars of their sparkling celestial dew. He mixed all these things together, distilled the brew over his brightest burning fire and then set it in Clorilli's eyes.[119]

Clorilli
Ah, so we are on to fairy tales now!

Armilla
You think these words of mine a fairy tale, do you? Do you not remember that it was your beautiful gaze that first mortally wounded Filemone's heart? And it is this gaze that keeps him alive, even if it is a weak and sickly life.

Clorilli
And do you believe, Armilla, that a gaze can have such power?

Armilla
What do you mean, 'do you believe'? / [36ʳ] Don't you know what that

	che in riva nacque al bel Sebeto, e poi	
	vicino al Po cantò si dolcemente,	105
	scrivesse già di dui luci serene?	
CLO.	Che ne scrisse Armilla?	
ARM.	Così diss'egli — Ah luci belle —, e disse	
	— Ah voi non v'accorgete	
	che a vostri rai rinovellar vi lice	110
	un cor quasi fenice,[120]	
	e le piaghe saldar che aperte avete. —	
CLO.	Favole di poeti, sogni, et ombre.	
ARM.	Quando Amore sdegnato	
	per punir in un dì ben mille offese,	115
	ti manderà nel core	
	quel venen dolce che piacendo ancide	
CLO.	Non farà, s'io non voglio.	
ARM.	Non farà se non vòi? Credilo pure,	
	ma farà che tu voglia.	120
	Resta, ch'io voglio andar per Filemone,	
	che così li promissi,[121]	
	e ti ricordo intanto	
	che ammollito lo sdegno	
	lieta ti mostri, e mansueta in volto.	125
CLO.	Va pur, ch'io farò quanto mi comandi.	

Scena seconda / [36ᵛ]

Clorilli, Satiro

CLO.	Costei folle si crede	1
	con queste sue sì ben ordite ciance	
	di levarmi dal cor questo odio immenso,	
	ch'io porto a Filemone,	
	ma presto s'avvedrà quanto s'inganna.	5
SAT.	Di qua non vien nissun, né di là manco.	
CLO.	Prima con le mie man mi darei morte	

[120] *fenice*: written over an erasure. Lines 109–13 quote from a *canzone* of Tasso, *R* ccclxix, ll. 76–80; see translation of *Clorilli*, n. 121.
[121] *promisi* in modern Italian.

great Shepherd born on the shores of the clear Sebeto, who later sang so sweetly by the Po, wrote once about two bright eyes?[120]

Clorilli
What did he write about them, Armilla?

Armilla
Here is what he said:
'Ah, beautiful lights,' he said,
'Ah, don't you realize that your rays
are able to renew a heart almost like a phoenix,
and to heal the wounds that you have opened?'[121]

Clorilli
The fables of poets. Dreams and shadows!

Armilla
When angry Love punishes you one day for a thousand offences, by sending to your heart that sweet poison which kills by pleasing . . .

Clorilli
He will not if I don't want it.

Armilla
He will not if you do not want it? Believe that if you like, but he will make you want it. Stay, and I will fetch Filemone, as I promised him. And meanwhile, I remind you to soften your anger, and to show yourself happy and gentle in your expression!

Clorilli
Go on, I will do what you command of me.

Scene Two / [36ᵛ]

Clorilli, Satyr

Clorilli
[*To herself*] This crazy woman believes that she will lift the immense hatred I bear for Filemone from my heart with her well-contrived chatter. But we will soon see how she deceives herself!

Satyr
[*Aside*] No one is coming, from over here or over there! From this direction or from that!

Clorilli
[*Aside*] I would sooner kill myself with my own hands . . .

SAT.	Ogni cosa è sicura.	
CLO.	che mai tornar amante.	
SAT.	Sù sù non più dimora.	10
	O ninfa bella, e cara, io t'ho pur giunta![122]	
CLO.	Ohimè, lassa, che veggio? Oimè son presa!	
	Armilla, Armilla torna,	
	torna cara compagna! Oimè meschina.	
SAT.	Non ti varrà gridar ninfa spietata.	15
CLO.	Pastor' oimè, correte, aita, aita!	
SAT.	Vienne pur là in quell'antro,	
	se non vòi ch'io ti stra[s]cini malvagia.	
CLO.	Pastor' correte! Aita, ohimè[123] son morta.	

Scena terza

Fillinio, Satiro, Clorilli

FILL.	O spettacol['][124] crudele. / [37r]	1
	O satiro malvagio	
	lascia cotesta ninfa,	
	se tu non vòi provar la forza mia.	
SAT.	Ch'io la lasci? Non no, simil pazzia	5
	già non farà Ruscone.	
FILL.	Tu non la lasciarai? Tosto 'l vedremo.[125]	
SAT.	Ecco io la lascio. Ah perfida Clorilli[!]	
FILL.	Pàrtiti qui d'intorno,	
	e rinsèlvati omai bestia villana.	10

[122] Here and below the end-of-line question marks in the original have been surmised as exclamation marks according to the sense.
[123] *hoime*: insertion above text.
[124] *spettacolo*. Surmised to fit *settenario* metre, as line 1 has eight syllables.
[125] *vederemo*. Adjusted to fit *settenario* metre.

Satyr
[*Aside*] All is secure.

Clorilli
[*Aside*] . . . than become a lover again.

Satyr
[*Aside*] Come on now! The time has come! [*To Clorilli*] O beautiful and dear nymph, I have surely caught you!

Clorilli
Aye me, alas, what do I see? Alas, am I taken? Armilla, Armilla, come back, come back, my dear companion! Alas, wretched me!

Satyr
There is no use screaming, pitiless nymph.

Clorilli
Shepherds, alas, come quickly! Help! Help!

Satyr
Come with me into this cave if you don't want me to drag you, you wicked nymph!

Clorilli
Shepherds, come running! Help me, aye me, I am dead!

Scene Three

Fillinio, Satyr, Clorilli

Fillinio
Oh, cruel spectacle! / [37ʳ] O contemptible satyr, leave this nymph alone, unless you want to feel the strength of my blows.

Satyr
Why would I release her? No no, Ruscone will never do such a crazy thing![122]

Fillinio
You won't let her go? We'll soon see about that![123]

Satyr
Here, I'll let her be. O deceitful Clorilli!

Fillinio
Be gone from here! Retreat back into the forest, you boorish beast.

Scena quarta

Clorilli, Fillinio

CLO.	Pastor io ti ringrazio	1
	del[126] cortese soccorso,	
	ché certo se non eri, o che veggio?	
	Non è questo Fillinio,	
	il mio caro fratello?	5
	O fratello dolcissimo, ti veggio	
	o pur mi sembra di vederti? Dormo,	
	o pur son desta? È l'aura, od ombra?	
	O pure è l'imagin vera di Fillinio[127]	
	questa ch'io miro? D[eh] se gli è pur vero,	10
	che tu sia il mio fratello	
	parla, e giungi la destra a la mia destra. / [37ᵛ]	
FILL.	Fillinio io son Clorilli,	
	carissima sorella, il ver rimiri	
	che dopo un longo esilio	15
	ritorno a riveder l'antico albergo.	
CLO.	Dolcissimo Fillinio io pur t'abbraccio,	
	e ti veggio, e ti tocco e 'l credo appena;	
	qual sì duro destin Fil[l]inio mio	
	da noi ti tolse? E perché al vecchio padre,	20
	a la sorella tua	
	celasti la cagion del tuo partire?	
FILL.	Amor empio tiran[n]o,	
	come ti narrerò, da voi mi tolse.	
	Ma che è del padre nostro,	25
	vive egli? E come porta	
	la grave soma di sì lunga etade?	
CLO.	Vive il nostro buon padre,	
	fatto da grave età debole, e stanco.	
	Tempo ben fu che io mi credea ch'al Cielo	30
	si ritornasse, abbandonando il mondo:	
	tanto dolor recògli il tuo partire.	
	O qual è per sentir dolcezza al core	
	dell'improviso tuo dolce ritorno,	
	bramato tanto, e sospirato tanto.	35

---

126 *Dell'*.
127 This line has at least 12 syllables.

Scene Four

Clorilli, Fillinio

Clorilli
Shepherd, I thank you for your courteous rescue, for certainly if you had
not been here . . . *[recognizes her brother]* Oh, what do I see? Is this not
Fillinio, my dear brother? O sweetest brother, am I really seeing you, or
do I just think I am? Am I sleeping, or am I awake? Is this just the breeze,
or a shadow? Or am I really seeing the true image of Fillinio? Oh, if it
really is true that you are my brother, speak, and take my right hand in
yours! / [37ᵛ]

Fillinio
I am Fillinio, Clorilli, my dearest sister. What you see once again is true.
After a long exile, I have returned to see my former abode once more.

Clorilli
Sweetest Fillinio! So I really am embracing you, I see you, and I touch
you, and I can hardly believe it. What cruel fate took you away from us,
my Fillinio? And why did you hide the cause of your departure from your
old father, from your sister?

Fillinio
That wicked tyrant Love took me from you, as I will tell you. But what
of our father, is he still living? How does he carry the great burden of his
advanced age?

Clorilli
Our good father lives, although his old age has made him weak and
tired. There was a time when I thought he would ascend to Heaven,
abandoning the world, your departure brought him so much pain. Oh,
what joy he will feel in his heart at your unexpected, sweet return, so
long wished for, and sighed for!

	Ma perché tardo più, perché non corro	
	al[128] vecchio padre mio, / [38ʳ]	
	nunzia di felicissime novelle?	
FILL.	Non far Clorilli, acciò che non tal volta	
	quel che in lui non puotè l'aspro dolore	40
	d'improv[v]isa partita	
	non cagionasse soverchia allegrezza	
	d'improv[v]isa tornata.	

                 " Che 'l soverchio[129] gioir tal volta uccide.

CLO.   Tarderò dunque ancor, ma narra intanto   45
              quel ch'io ti domandava!

FILL.   Poiché tu mi comandi
              ch'io rinuovi parlando il mio dolore,
              odi del fratell'[130] tuo, cara sorella
              l'istoria miserabile e dolente.   50

              Io non passava di dui anni ancora
              il terzo lustro, che fero destino
              guidommi in parte ove tra molte ninfe
              quasi splendente sol tra chiare stelle
              stava la leggiadrissima Dalinda,   55
              al cui possente lume
              qual semplice farfalla
              corsi invaghito, e non sì tosto a lei
              i' m'appressai, che d'invisibil fiamma
              arso mi sentii il core.   60
              Conobbe ella il mio incendio, e conobb'io, / [38ᵛ]
              che qual fiamma per me li corse al core
              quasi in quel punto, e mi stimai felice.
              Crebbe l'amor, crebbe l'ardir in noi
              in guisa tal ch'io mi credea ch'a pena   65
              lo potesse ammorzar di Morte il gielo.
              Con lei passava i giorni, e lei con meco
              dolcemente godea
              or[a] d'un fresco rivo[131]
              il lento mormorare,   70
              ora di vaghi augelli

---

[128] *all'*.
[129] *sovercchio*.
[130] *fratell'*: M has cancelled final '-o' and added apostrophe, to fit the hendecasyllable metre.
[131] Line 69 unusually has only six syllables. *Ora* surmised, as for line 71, matching the balanced pairings throughout lines 61–76.

But why do I still delay, why do I not run to my old father, / [38ʳ] a herald for this happiest of news?

Fillinio
Don't do it, Clorilli, lest what caused such bitter pain with my sudden departure cause excessive happiness at my sudden return. *Too much happiness sometimes kills.* [124]

Clorilli
I will delay then, but meanwhile, answer my question!

Fillinio
Since you ask me to renew my pain in speaking to you, dear sister, you shall hear your brother's miserable and sorrowful story. I had not yet turned seventeen when cruel destiny guided me to a place where among many nymphs lived the most beautiful Dalinda, like a shining sun amid a field of bright stars. [125] I rushed toward her bright light like a moth, [126] and as soon as I drew near her, I felt an invisible flame overwhelm my heart. She recognized my fire. I knew / [38ᵛ] that the same flame flared in her heart in that instant, and I was happy. Our love grew, and courage grew in us alongside it, so I believed that even Death's icy grip could not extinguish it. I passed my days with her, and with me she sweetly relished now the slow murmuring of a cool stream, now the sweetest harmony of lovely birds.

dolcissimi concenti,
né mai levos[s]i il sole,
né mai tuffò nell'onda i bei crin d'oro,
che non lasciasse, o rivedesse insieme   75
Dalinda bella il suo fedel Fillinio.
Ma cangiò ria fortuna
ben tosto in fosche notti i dì sereni;
però che in pensier venne
al padre di Dalinda   80
di darla per sposa a Filemone.
Che non diss'ella, e che non fece[132] solo
per schivar[e][133] le mal gradite nozze?
Ma non potè, che l'ostinato vecchio
contra voglia di lei pur le conchiuse.   85
A così strano caso ambi dui giunti / [39ʳ]
non sapevam che farsi; al fin arditi
ci risolviam'[134] d'abbandonar fuggendo
i patrii letti, e più felice stanza
andar cercando a' nostri amori amica.   90
Così restammo di trovarci insieme
a questa fonte la seguente notte.
O come lento mi parea che 'l sole
cacciasse i suoi destrier, o come pigre
erano al trapassar l'ore notturne,   95
pur giunse al fine l'ora bramata. Or quando
io mi credea partire
impro[v]viso dolor t'assalt' in guisa,
che buona pezza ti tenghian per morta;
pur rivenisti al fine, et io partimmi   100
del mio disegno al men più tardi un'ora,
e veloce m' n'venni, ov'io credea
che già stesse spettando
la dolce vita mia.
Ohimè, che invece sua   105
trovai segni di morte atri, e funesti.
Giunto alla fonte altro non sento, o veggio,
che un tacito silenzio, e pien d'orr[or]e
rimiro d'ogn' intorno, e scorgo al fine

[132] *fece?*: question mark has been moved to end of phrase.
[133] *schivar*. The line has only 10 syllables.
[134] *risolviam'*: correction apparently of *risolvemo*; 'a' inserted above.

The sun never rose, nor did it plunge its beautiful golden tresses into the waves, without seeing the beautiful Dalinda in company with her faithful Fillinio.

But cruel Fortune changed those serene days into dark nights, for the thought entered her father's mind to marry her to Filemone. What did she not say, what did she not do, just to avoid the dreaded wedding! But she could not escape it, for the obstinate old man concluded the arrangements even so.

Finding ourselves in such a difficult situation, / [39ʳ] we did not know what to do. In the end we resolved with daring to flee and abandon our fathers' homes, and go in search of a place happier and friendlier to our love. So we agreed to meet at this fountain the next night. Oh, how slowly it seemed to me that the sun drove its steeds, how lazily the night seemed to pass, before the awaited hour finally arrived![127] But at the moment I planned to depart, you were overcome by a sudden pain, so that for a good while we believed you were dead.[128] You recovered in the end, and I left at least an hour later than I had planned, and went quickly to the place where I believed my sweet life was already waiting for me.

But alas! Instead, I found dark and gloomy signs of her death.[129] Reaching the fountain, I hear nothing but a terrible silence and see only a heavy darkness. I peer all around, and finally discover the tracks of

di mostruosa belva 110
l'orme nel suolo impresse. / [39ᵛ]
Veggio del chiaro fonte
l'onda fatta sanguigna,
e mentre sbigottito io pur rimiro
ecco agl'occhi mi s'offre in terra un dardo, 115
che fregiato avea la parte estrema,
né molto indi lontano un bianco velo
tutt'asperto di sangue.
Io li prendo ambe dui, li miro intorno
e tu luna crudel prestasti il lume 120
a così fiera vista? E veggio impresso
nel dardo di Dalinda, ahi vista amara,
l'amato nome, indi conobbi il velo.

CLO.   O fiero caso, o degno di pietade.

FILL.   Così della mia vita io viddi i segni 125
che estinta si giacea,
stata, ohimè, troppo prezioso pasto
di famelica belva;
volsi gridar, ma 'l varco
al suon chiuse il dolore. 130
Uccider' io mi volsi,
ma mi ritenne in vita
solo il desio di raccor le reliquie
delle sue belle membra
per finir poi dopo il pietoso offizio, 135
e la vita e 'l dolore. / [40ʳ]
Così cercando andai
tre volte intorno, e dentro in ogni loco
tutta questa foresta,
né altro vi trovai ch'orror solinghi. 140
Allor mi venne al cor molti pensieri,
rimembrandomi pur, ch'Aminta anch'egli
ingannato da un dardo,
e da un candido velo,
Silvia morta credè, che era pur viva, 145
che esser forse potrebbe che Dalinda,
dall'orror de la morte impaurita,
e dall'aspetto dell'or[r]ibil fiera,
lasciando il dardo, e 'l vel, fuggisse errando.
Allor di nuovo la ricerco, e chiamo, 150

a monstrous beast imprinted in the ground. / [39ᵛ] I see the waters of the clear fountain made bloody, and as I look around me, dismayed, there before my eyes on the ground is an arrow with a decorated tip, and not very far from it a white veil, all spattered with blood. I pick up both and look around. Ah cruel moon, how could you lend light to such a terrible sight? I see stamped into Dalinda's arrow – oh, bitter sight! – my beloved's name, and then I recognized the veil.¹³⁰

Clorilli
O cruel Fortune! Oh, how pitiable!

Fillinio
And thus I saw the signs that my life itself was lying dead, the most precious prey of the ravenous beast. I wanted to scream, but pain strangled my voice. I wanted to kill myself. Only the desire to collect the relics of her beautiful limbs kept me alive, and, once this pious duty was done, to end my life and with it my pain.¹³¹ / [40ʳ]

And so I went looking around three times, and in every corner of this forest. But I found nothing but lonely darkness.¹³² Many thoughts flooded into my heart, and I remembered that Aminta too was deceived by an arrow and a white veil, and thus believed that Silvia was dead, when she was really alive.¹³³ So it could be that in the same way, Dalinda left behind the arrow and veil and ran away, frightened by the horrible beast's countenance, and the horror of death.

And so I search for her again, and call out,

ma solo al mio chiamar Eco[135] risponde.
Credetti, perché sovragiunto il giorno,
temendo ella tornar al vecchio padre,
né volendo aspettar in questo loco
ove per la frequenza de' pastori   155
sarebbe stata ritrovata, e vista,
sì fosse tolta via d'Etruria, ond'io
pronto mi messi a seguitarla dove
più che ragion mi conducea il fato.
Perduta finalmente quella speme / [40ᵛ]   160
ch'io seppi a' miei desir ir fabricando,
mi risolvei tornare
all'infelice patria.
Così viddi Clorilli
spenti del mio bel sol gl'accesi rai,   165
così giunt' all'occaso ogni mia gioia.

CLO.   O dolenti successi
possenti a trar da queste pietre il pianto
quanto del tuo dolor m'incresce e duole.
O come volentier con la mia vita,   170
e col mio sangue stesso,
ricomprerei la vita di Dalinda.

Scena quinta

Clorilli, Filemone, Fillino

CLO.   Ohimè, che questo pianto   1
a me trafigge il core,
d[eh] lascia ch'io 'l raccogli in questo velo.
FIL.   O spettacol dolente, ah,[136] che veggio?
CLO.   Ma sarà forse[137] meglio   5
ridursi dentro alla paterna casa[138]
FIL.   O disleal Clorilli.

---

[135] *Ecco.*
[136] *ha.*
[137] *forsi.*
[138] The start of this line has a sign of erasure in the left margin where 'CLO.' was written erroneously.

but only Echo responds to my cry.[134] I believed that because her wedding day had arrived, she was afraid to return to her old father, and didn't want to stay in this place where she would surely be discovered and seen, since it is so frequented by shepherds, and so she left Etruria. I decided immediately to follow her, led less by reason than by fate. When I finally lost that hope, / [40ᵛ] which I knew I was constructing with my desires, I resolved to turn back to my unhappy homeland. And thus I saw the burning rays of my beautiful sun extinguished, Clorilli, and with it all my joy ended.

Clorilli
Oh, what sorrowful events, fit to draw laments from these stones themselves! How your pain saddens and grieves me. Oh, how willingly I would trade my life, and my blood itself, to give Dalinda life again!

Scene Five

Clorilli, Filemone, Fillinio

Clorilli
Alas, your weeping pierces my heart! Oh, let me wipe your tears with this veil.

Filemone
[*Arriving, aside*] Oh, sorrowful sight, ah, what do I see?[135]

Clorilli
But perhaps it would be better to return to our father's house . . .

Filemone
[*Aside*] O disloyal Clorilli.

CLO.	ove meglio potrai
	ristorar col riposo la stanchezza[139] / [41ʳ]
	di sì longo viaggio. 10
FILL.	Non mi par ben ch'io venga,
	per la cagion che poco dianzi ho detta.
FIL.	E lo veggio? E lo soffro?
FILL.	Intanto potrai dir al vecchio padre
	che hai nuova ch'io son vivo, in breve speri 15
	ch'io sia per ritornar in queste parti.
CLO.	E quando poi vorrai ch'egli ti veggia?
FILL.	Al più longo domani, in questo mentre,
	cara sorella mia, tiemmi celato.
CLO.	Farò quanto domandi. O mio Fillino 20
	io non posso saziarmi d'abbrac[c]iarti.
FIL.	O miser'[140] Filemone.
FILL.	Ecco di qua un pastore, Clorilli a Dio.

Scena sesta

Clorilli, Filemone

CLO.	È questo Filemone? Certo egli è desso.[141] 1
	Per compiacer Armilla
	bisogna a mio mal grado ch'io l'aspetti.
FIL.	O perfida, e crudel, o impura, indegna
	di me, tu quella sei ch'ardisci 5
	di chiamar[142] infedele
	il più fido pastor che viva al mondo? / [41ᵛ]

[139] *stancchezza.*
[140] *misero.* Line has eight syllables; adjustment surmised to fit *settenario* metre.
[141] Line 1 has at least 12 syllables.
[142] *chiamar*: '-mi' struck through at end of word.

Clorilli

... where you will be able to rest more easily, and recover from your fatigue / [41ʳ] after such a long journey.

Fillinio

I don't think I should come, for the reason I told you earlier.

Filemone

[*Aside*] Am I really seeing this? How can I bear it?

Fillinio

In the meantime, you can tell our old father you have news I am alive, and that you hope I am to return to these parts shortly.

Clorilli

And when will you let him see you?

Fillinio

Tomorrow at the latest. In the meantime, keep me hidden, my dear sister.

Clorilli

I will do what you ask. O my Fillinio, I cannot stop myself from embracing you.

Filemone

[*Aside*] O miserable Filemone!

Fillinio

A shepherd comes this way. Clorilli, farewell.

Scene Six

Clorilli, Filemone

Clorilli

[*Aside*] Is this Filemone? Surely it is he! To please Armilla, I must wait for him against my wishes.

Filemone

O, you treacherous and cruel, O you impure nymph, you do not deserve me! Are you the one who dares to call the most faithful shepherd in the world unfaithful? / [41ᵛ]

	Tu sei quell'impudica	
	che per seguir Diana ogn' uom' disprezzi?	
	Pur l'impudiche[143] voglie	10
	che sotto manto d'onestà coprivi	
	saran mal grado tuo palesi, e conte.	
	Ecco perché mi fuggi!	
	Per seguir altrui, e pensi	
	ricoprir sì gran fallo, e sì gran torto	15
	sott'ombra di disdegno? Et a me rivolti[144]	
	dell'accuse, e de' biasmi il ferro acuto?	
	Io disleal? Io traditor son detto	
	senza amor, senza fè?[145] O sommo Giove	
	a che riserbi le saette ardenti?	20
	Vendica tant'inganno, e tanta fraude.	
CLO.	O bel principio, o che gentile amante,	
	non m'aspettava già simil parole.	
FIL.	Io non credeva anch'io	
	d'averti a ragionar in cotal guisa,	25
	perfida, e pur conviemmi a mio dispetto.	
CLO.	Vaneggi Filemone? E che parlare	
	è questo tuo? Fa ch'io l'intenda anch'io.	
FIL.	Di non intender fingi,	
	quel che tu sai certissimo? Quest'occhi	30
	pur or non t'han veduto / [42^r]	
	stringerti[146] al seno il tuo novello amante?	
CLO.	E questo a te ch'importa? O importar deve?	
FIL.	Che importar deve a me?	
	Veder ch'altri possegga[147]	35
	la mia cara mercede,	
	veder in poter d'altri	
	quel ch'ogni ragion vuol che pur sia mio,	
	veder, che a me spietata,	
	a me dài morte, ad altri vita.	40
	Domandi anche che importa?	

---

[143] *impudicche*.
[144] Line 16 has at least 12 syllables.
[145] Question mark moved from line 18 following *detto* to fit the sense.
[146] *stringesti*. The catchword on fol. 41v reads *stringerti*, which fits the sense.
[147] Lines 34–5 are written in M as a single line of at least 13 syllables. The line break reinforces the anaphora (*veder*) in lines 37 and 39 below.

Are you that unchaste nymph who, to follow Diana, scorns all men? Yet the immoral desires that you were hiding beneath that cloak of honesty shall be revealed and broadcast despite your attempts. Is this why you flee from me? In order to pursue others? And you think you can hide such a great error, such a great injury, beneath a mask of disdain? And you throw accusations and blame back at me like a sharp sword? Am *I* disloyal? Am *I* called a traitor, without love, without faith? O highest Jove, why do you hold back your burning arrows? Avenge this great deception, and this great fraud!

Clorilli
Oh, fine proem![136] Oh, what a gentle lover! I was not expecting such words.

Filemone
Nor did I think I should need to speak to you in such a manner, perfidious nymph; and yet I must, against my will.

Clorilli
Are you mad, Filemone? What manner of speaking is this? Speak in a way I may also understand.

Filemone
Do you pretend not to understand that which you most certainly do? Did my own eyes not just now see you / [42ʳ] clasp your new lover to your breast?

Clorilli
What does that matter to you? Or why should it matter?

Filemone
Why should it matter to me? To see another possess my sweet recompense?[137] To see in the hands of another what by right should be mine? To see that she who is pitiless towards me, giving me only death, gives life to others! You ask why this matters?

CLO.	Io ne domando sì, di qual mercede
	favelli tu, che vedi in poter d'altri,
	che pur sia tua? Che vita, e di che morte
	vai tu gracchiando?
FIL.	Tu sei la mercede, 45
	ch'al mio lungo servir si convenia.
	Tu per legge[148] d'Amore
	è già gran tempo che sei fatta mia,
	e tu m'uccidi allora,
	che togliendoti a me ti doni altrui. 50
CLO.	S'io cercassi, o gradissi il tuo servire,
	ragion avresti a domandar mercede,
	ma lo fuggo, e lo sprezzo. Altra pur servi
	che ti gradisca, e quanto a morte o vita, / [42ᵛ]
	non so quel che dir vogli; 55
	so ben che 'l tuo morir non cerco o bramo,
	né de la vita tua punto mi cale.
FIL.	Troppo lo so, se ben in altro tempo
	mostrasti pur ch'ella ti fusse grata.
CLO.	S'in alcun tempo mai, 60
	ch'io non voglio negar, caro mi fusti,
	ben mi porgesti ancor giusta cagione
	ond'io l'amor in odio convertissi.
FIL.	E qual cagion crudel addur potrai,
	se non che a nuovo amor rivolt' hai 'l core? 65
	E ti vergogni a palesarlo altrui,
	per non far nota insieme
	della tradita fè l'indegna colpa.
CLO.	Lo sai ben ch'io t'odio, e sai ben anco
	s'allor t'amai, che d'amor fusti degno. 70
	Scortese Filemon non men che infido.
	Per contentar Armilla
	ab[b]astanza ho sofferto. A Dio, mi parto.
FIL.	Clorilli ohimè non ti partir, perdona,
	perdona a questa lingua, 75
	ch'Amor e sdegno spinse
	fu[o]r di camino a dir quell' ch'io non volsi.
	Ascolta ancor ti prego / [43ʳ]
	queste del[149] viver mio parole estreme.

148 *leggie.*
149 *dell'.*

Clorilli

Yes, I do ask. What recompense are you speaking of, that you see in others' possession and that should be yours? What life, and what death, are you raving about?

Filemone

You are the recompense that befits my long service. *You*, by the law of Love, have already been mine for a long time. And you slay me when, robbing me, you give yourself to others.

Clorilli

Had I sought, or gratefully acknowledged, your devotion, you would be right to ask for this recompense, but I flee from it and despise it. Serve another nymph, any who pleases you. As for death or life, / [42ᵛ] I do not know what you mean by all this. I know that I do not desire or wish for your death; nor do I care a fig for your life!

Filemone

I know that all too well, even if there was once a time when it seemed to mean something to you.

Clorilli

If there was once a time (and I shall not deny it) when you were dear to me, it is also true that you gave me good reason to convert my love into hatred.

Filemone

Oh, and what reason can you adduce other than that you turned your heart to a new love, cruel one? You are ashamed to reveal it, as it would also make known the ugly fault of your infidelity.

Clorilli

You know very well that I hate you, and you also know very well that if I loved you once, it is because you deserved it then. You are no less discourteous than you are unfaithful, Filemone. I have suffered quite long enough at Armilla's behest. Farewell, I take my leave.

Filemone

Clorilli, alas, do not leave. Pardon, pardon this tongue, which Love and Anger led astray,[138] making me say what I did not mean. Give ear a little longer, I beg of you, / [43ʳ] to these, the last words of my life.

CLO.	Ecco mi fermo, or via spedisci presto.	80
FIL.	Alza leggiadra ninfa i tuoi bei lumi,	
	rimira in questo volto esangue e smorto	
	con tutti i suoi martir dipinto 'l core;	
	ivi intender potrai	
	parte del mio dolore,	85
	parte diranne ancor la flebil voce,	
	se tra l'agonia[150] e 'l duol non verrà meno.	
	Già la seconda volta	
	la primavera a noi fatt'ha ritorno,	
	rendendo a' colli, a le campagne, a' boschi	90
	or pregiati onori,	
	da che tu privi quest'alma meschina	
	di quel ben che cortese donatrice	
	un tempo le donasti,	
	cibo un tempo vital, cibo soave.	95
	Da indi in qua, qual il mio stato sia,	
	qual questa vita misera, e infelice,	
	qual il dolor di cui l'alma si nutre	
	io non lo dico, che ben poco fora	
	s'io il potessi ridire;	100
	ma da questo il comprendi,	
	che fatto è nuovo Inferno il petto mio, / [43ᵛ]	
	in cui s'accoglie ogni più grave pena.	
	Qui la picciola colpa ch'io commisi[151]	
	seguendo il tuo volere,	105
	e quel del padre mio,	
	fatto nuovo av[v]oltoio	
	divora il mesto core.	
	Indi nuovo I[s]sione l' stabil ruota	
	volgo da la cangiata mia fortuna	110
	nel mio pensiero, e de['] miei gravi mali	
	la gravissima pietra ogn'or sostengo.	
	Stassi ardente desio nelle chiar' onde,	
	e famelico ogn'or di la[u]te mense	
	vede apparecchio grande,	115
	ma quando estinguer pensa	
	la sete per saziar l'avide brame	

[150] *angonia.*
[151] *commissi.*

Clorilli

Here I am, then. Get on with it!

Filemone

Charming nymph, lift the beauteous beams of your eyes and behold once more in this drained and deathly visage my heart, portrayed in all its torments. There you will read at least a part of my suffering.[139] Another part my faint voice will tell, if it does not fade to silence amid my agony and grief.

Spring has now returned a second time – restoring its prized glories to the hills, the fields, the woods – since you deprived this wretched soul of that good that you once bestowed on it as a gracious gift: sustenance that once kept me alive, and tasted sweet as well! I shall not tell you what my state has been since you left me, how wretched and unhappy my life, how my soul feeds on pain, for if I could describe it in words it would be a far smaller thing.

But this you will understand: my breast has become a new Inferno, / [43ᵛ] home to the greatest of torments. Here the small fault that I committed, in following your desire, and that of my father, has become a new vulture devouring my miserable heart.[140] A new Ixion, I turn the steady wheel of my altered fortune in my thoughts and bear up the massive stone of my crushing ills. I share his burning desire for fresh water; famished, he always sees an abundant table of choice food arrayed before him; but just as he thinks he is finally about to quench his thirst, to satisfy his avid hunger,

si fuggon l'acque e le vivande, ond'egli
stassi sempre famelico e digiuno.
Qui da verace fiamma,   120
sfavilla ampia fornace,
e qui d'orrido gielo
provo l'algente sido,
e tant'altri tormenti
ch'a raccontargli solo   125
non ch'a soffrirli inso[p]portabil pena.[152] / [44r]
Ivi tra tanti guai siede regina
qual Proserpina bella
la bella immagin['] tua.

CLO.   Nell'Inferno mi tieni?   130
Trammene Filemone, che non m'aggrada
sì tenebrosa stanza.

FIL.   Trartene non poss'io, ben tu potresti
farla con gl'occhi tuoi, serena e chiara.

CLO.   Non son di quel poter che forse pensi.   135

FIL.   Ah non so io per prova
se son quei dui begl'occhi, anzi dui soli,
possenti a rischiarar abbissi e notti?
E ben lo sai tu ancor, ma serbi altrove
a scoprir la virtù de['] raggi loro.   140

CLO.   Quando pur gl'occhi miei
avesser tal valor, non creder ch'io
volessi rischiarar le notti tue;
anzi s'avver[r]à mai ch'io pur t'incontri
chiusi terrolli, o volgerolli altrove.   145

FIL.   Se quelle vaghe luci
che le tenebre mie rischiarar ponno,
vai pur tormi Clorilli,
perché in etterno orror misero viva,
per levarti ogni tema, ogni sospetto / [44v]   150
ch'io te miri gia[m]mai,
per mai più non gli[153] aprir, vo' chiuder gl'occhi.
Ma d[eh] per quell'Amore,
che mi portasti un tempo,
per quell'ore sì dolci,   155

---

[152] Line 126: this clause seems to depend on the main verb 'provo' (line 123).
[153] *li* in standard Italian.

both food and drink vanish before his eyes, so that he remains forever ravenous and starved. An enormous furnace burns with real flame here, and here I feel the searing cold of bitter frost, and so many other torments that even to speak of them, let alone to suffer them, brings unbearable pain. / [44ʳ] There, amid all these woes, your beautiful image reigns as queen, like beautiful Proserpina.

Clorilli
You would place me in Hell? Take me out of there, Filemone. Such a shadowy chamber is not to my liking.

Filemone
I cannot take you out of there, but with your eyes, you could make that same chamber tranquil and bright.

Clorilli
They are not as powerful as you might think.

Filemone
Ah, don't I know well from my own experience that those two beautiful eyes – two suns, rather – are powerful enough to illuminate the night, and great caves? You know this very well yourself, but you prefer to direct the power of their rays elsewhere.

Clorilli
Even if my eyes did have such powers, do not think that I would want to brighten your nights! Quite the opposite: should I ever happen to meet you, I will either keep them closed, or turn them in a different direction.

Filemone
Clorilli, if you intend to deprive me of those glorious rays that could illuminate my dark nights, so that I shall live miserably in eternal darkness, then to spare you from the fear and danger / [44v] that my own eyes will ever cast sight on you again, I will close them, never to open them again. But, pray, for the sake of that love you once bore me, for those hours so sweet, and those happy, serene days that we passed

	ch'a dì lieti e sereni	
	traemmo insieme allor concordi amanti,	
	tempra lo sdegno tuo con la mia morte.	
	Spegna l'antiche offese il sangue mio.	
CLO.	Non pensar Filemone	160
	ch'io cangi al tuo parlar pensiero, o voglia.	
	Rimanti in pace, io parto.	
FIL.	Così mi lasci in pace,	
	così crudel mi lasci al punto estremo?	

Scena settima

Filemone

[FIL.]	Ah tu potevi pur bella Clorilli	1
	d'una parola sola	
	mostrarti al mio morir cortese almeno,	
	tu potevi pur dir, — Filemone, mori —.[154]	
	Ma non ti basta cruda,	5
	ch'io sparga il sangue e mora,	
	se questa miser' alma / [45^{r}]	
	non passa disperata ad altra vita?	
	Perché tacita almeno	
	non ti fermasti spettatrice allegra	10
	allo spettacol fiero	
	che della morte t'apparecchiava?	
	So pur che lieta vista	
	questo trafitto core	
	averebbe a gli occhi tuoi spietata offerto.	15
	Ma via corresti forse	
	nunzia del mio morir, de' tuoi trofei,	
	a rallegrarti col tuo nuovo amante,	
	e mio fiero nimico;	
	cagion non pur ch'io mora, e mora a torto	20
	ma quell' che è via peggior che morte assai	
	mi toglie il mio morir la mia Clorilli,	
	né soffre che morendo	
	i languidi occhi in lei rivolger possa,	
	e questi andrà delle mie spoglie altero?	25

[154] Line 4: 12-syllable line.

together as lovers in harmony, let my death temper your anger, and let my blood extinguish my past offences.

Clorilli
Filemone, do not think your speeches will change my mind or desire. Peace be with you. I am leaving.

Filemone
Is this how you leave me in peace? Do you leave me thus, cruel one, at the moment of my death?

Scene Seven

Filemone

O beautiful Clorilli, with but a single word you could have shown yourself to be merciful, at least at my death. You could even have said: 'Die, Filemone!' But is it not enough for you, cruel one, that I shed blood, and die, unless my wretched soul / [45ʳ] passes into the next life in misery? Why did you not at least stop at being a happy, silent spectator at the cruel spectacle Death was staging for you? I certainly know, pitiless one, that this tormented heart would have offered a happy sight to your eyes. But perhaps you ran away to spread the news of my death – of your triumph – and to celebrate with your new lover, my cruel enemy. Thus, not only do I die, and die wronged, but – far worse than death itself – my Clorilli deprives me of my own death and will not suffer that I turn my languid eyes towards her in my dying moments. And my rival will triumph over my remains?

Io n'andrò misero amante a morte,
ei rimarrà godendo ogni mio bene?
Morirò sì, ma prima
farò che mora anch'egli;
[n]é[155] s'n'andrà superbo / [45ᵛ]   30
un mal nato rivale
di riportar la spoglia
della mia trista vita.
E tu fiera Clorilli,
che della morte mia tanto bramosa   35
ti dimostrasti, a pien non goderai.
Tempera l'al[l]egrezza
della mia cruda morte
il duol che proverai
per la morte del tuo gradito, e vago.   40
Io pur con queste mani
gli aprirò il petto e 'l core
con questo dardo mio.
Vendicherò l'offese,
e goderò che in un istesso tempo   45
verserete ambo il sangue,
egli dalla ferita, e tu da gl'occhi.
Ma che vaneggi Filemon['], che pensi?[156]
Se mentre fosti in vita
con ogni tuo poter cercasti sempre   50
di compiacerli[157] ogn'ora
vorrai del viver tuo nell'ore estreme
dispiacerle e turbarla?
Se per piacere a lei te stesso uccidi
vorrai contaminar così bell'opra   55
col recargli dolor dell'altrui morte? / [46ʳ]
Viva pur lieto il fortunato amante,
mora pur Filemon senza vendetta.
Così, così mi giova
irne tra l'ombre inferne.   60
A dio selve, a dio colli,
a morir, a morire.

---

[155] *He.*
[156] Line 48: 'Filemone' has been apocopated to avoid a 12-syllable line.
[157] *compiacerli*: Tuscan form of indirect pronoun (*-gli*) for both genders; cf. line 53 (*-le*).

I will go to my death a wretched lover, and he will remain to enjoy my every good? Yes, I will die, but first I will make him die as well; a lowly rival shall not proudly / [45ᵛ] reap the spoils of my sad life.

And you, proud Clorilli, who have so desired my death, you will not enjoy it in full. Your delight at my cruel death will be tempered by the pain you will feel at the death of your beloved and handsome lover. I will open up his breast with these very hands and pierce his heart with my arrow! I will avenge his offences and I will revel in the fact that you will both spill blood at the same time: he from his wound, and you from your eyes.[141]

But what are you ranting about, Filemone, what are you thinking? If in living, you tried with all your power to please her, do you want to make her unhappy, to grieve her, in the final hours of your life? If you kill yourself to make her happy, do you wish to ruin such a beautiful deed by bringing her pain through another's death? / [46ʳ]

Let the fortunate lover live happily, and let Filemone die without *vendetta*. And so it pleases me to go among the infernal shadows. Farewell woods, farewell hills, I go to die, to die!

Armilla

[ARM.]	Filemon, Filemone	1
	non ti partir, aspetta[!]	
	Egli[158] va sì veloce	
	come s'avesse l'ali;	
	fia pur meglio ch'il segua,	5
	che sì turbato parmi	
	che di qualche gran mal dubito forte.	
	O Clorilli, o Clorilli	
	quanto ancor piangerai tant'alterezza.	

ATTO QUARTO

Scena prima

Coribante, Armilla

COR.	E credi certo Armilla,	1
	che 'l superbo disprezzo di Clorilli	
	sarà stato cagione / [46ᵛ]	
	che 'l miser[159] Filemon sia giunto a morte?	
ARM.	Assai per certo il tengo,	5
	perché com'io t'ho detto	
	ar[r]ivai in questo loco	
	in quell'istante appunto	
	che egli partissi furioso, in volto	
	tutto cambiato e di color di morte.	10
COR.	Perché non 'l seguitasti?	
ARM.	Ben fui pronta a seguirlo,	
	ma sì ratto n'andava, e sì veloce,	
	che in poco spazio lo perdei di vista.	
COR.	D[eh] perché allor non fusti almen presente	15
	che parlava a Clorilli?	
	Fors' impedito avresti	

---

[158] *E'lgli.*
[159] *miser*: letter 'o' following is cancelled to preserve the hendecasyllable metre.

Scene Eight

Armilla

Filemon, Filemone, don't leave, wait! He moves so quickly, as though he had wings![142] I had better follow him, for he seems to me so distraught that I suspect something terrible. O Clorilli, O Clorilli, how much more you will weep because of your pride!

ACT FOUR

Scene One

Coribante, Armilla

Coribante
And do you really believe, Armilla, that Clorilli's haughty scorn has driven / [46ᵛ] wretched Filemone to his death?

Armilla
I certainly do! For as I told you, I arrived in this place at the very instant he was leaving. He was in a wild state, his face entirely transformed, and deathly pale.[143]

Coribante
Why did you not follow him?

Armilla
I was most ready to follow him, but he was moving so swiftly, and at such a speed, that I soon lost sight of him.

Coribante
Ah, then why were you not at least present when he spoke to Clorilli? You

		raffrenando di lei l'orgoglio e l'ira	
		così strano accidente.	
ARM.		Io venni con Clorilli in questo loco	20
		per questo effetto, et parendomi poi	
		che Filemone oltre il dover tardasse	
		a comparir, mi partii per condurlo,	
		temendo che il suo solito timore	
		lo ritenesse, ma non l' ritrovai,	25
		onde mi volsi per tornar. Intanto	
		io rincontrai per via	
		Nicilla, che di un certo infortunio / [47ʳ]	
		cominciò meco a ragionar, e 'n questo	
		passommi il tempo, ch'io non m'n'ac[c]orsi.	30
		Ma tu che notte e giorno	
		sempre esser suoli al caro amico appresso,	
		perch'al maggior bisogno	
		l'abbandonasti, e lo lasciasti ir solo?	
COR.		Perché così vols'egli,	35
		io che pensato avria[160] caso sì strano	
		come volse restai.	
ARM.		O pastor infelice	
		ben eri tu presago	
		della sua trista sorte.	40
		O quanto bisognò pregar, e dire	
		per far ch'egli poi gisse	
		a ritrovar la morte,	
		ah foss'io stata muta.	
COR.	"	Ecco che premio porta	45
	"	al fin chi fa signore	
	"	della mente e del cor tiran[n]o Amore.	
ARM.	"	Amor quanto diverso	
	"	da te medesmo in questa età rassembri.	
	"	Già non solevi tu funesto arciero	50
	"	spinger dell'arco tuo strali mortali,	
	"	ma saette vitali,	
	"	al cui dolce ferir non elmo, o scudo, / [47ᵛ]	
	"	ma 'l petto inerme, e ignudo,	
	"	offerian' lieti i pastorelli amanti.	55

---

[160] *haveria.*

might have stopped this terrible event by soothing her pride and anger.

Armilla
I accompanied Clorilli here for this very reason, and since it seemed to me Filemone was strangely late in arriving, I was afraid his typical fears were holding him back, and left to bring him here. But I did not find him. As I turned to come back, I happened to meet Nicilla on the road, who began to recount / [47ʳ] a certain misfortune of hers to me.[144] And the time flew by, without my realizing it.

But you, who hover around your dear friend night and day – why did you abandon him in his hour of greatest need, and allow him to go alone?

Coribante
Because that is what he wanted! Although I had feared such a strange occurrence, I stayed away as he wanted.

Armilla
O unhappy shepherd, you were certainly an augur of his sad fate! Oh, how many prayers and words did I employ, only to cause him to go and meet his death. Ah, if only I had stayed quiet!

Coribante
This is the prize that comes to the man who makes Love master of his mind, and tyrant of his heart.

Armilla
Love, how different from your usual self you seem in this age. You, deadly archer, used to shoot not lethal arrows from your bow, but rather life-giving darts, to whose sweet wounds innocent shepherd-lovers presented no helmet nor shield, / [47ᵛ] *but simply their naked, unarmed breast.*

		Nel[161] tuo bel foco l'alme	
	"	rinovellar solea[n] vita più lieta,	
	"	or qual funesto rogo	
	"	pal[l]ido splende di tua face il lampo,	
	"	e saette di morte	60
	"	sembran di tua faretra Amor gli strali.	
	"	Tu che senz'alma un cor serbavi in vita	
	"	morir or lasci i tuoi più fidi amanti?	
	"	Tu che l'altrui desir, l'altrui speranze,	
	"	dolce nutrivi, or d'ogni speme in bando	65
	"	disperati abbandoni al duolo in preda	
	"	i tuoi più cari[?] Han fors[e][162] l'armi tue	
	"	quell'antica virtù, Signor, perduto	
	"	che recava ne' cor diletto e gioia?	
	"	Fors[e] ministro sol d'affanno e pena	70
	"	ferir ben può, ma risanar non vale	
	"	l'arco, ch'un tempo medico e guerriero	
	"	portar soleva in un piaga e salute.	
	"	O pur di Signor placido[163] e cortese	
	"	tiranno disleal, sei fatto crudo,	75
	"	vago di sangue, sol vago di morte?	
COR.	"	Non è da sé diverso / [48r]	
	"	come tu credi Amore,	
	"	qualor di doglia e di dolor ministro	
	"	l'alme tormenta e cori;	80
	"	ben è da sé diverso	
	"	se mai dolcezza a suoi seguaci apporta.	
		Misero Filemone,	
		con[164] troppo duro essempio oggi l'insegni,	
		se non è vano, il timor nostro e 'l dubbio.	85
ARM.	"	Ahi fia pur troppo ver. Di rado avviene	
	"	che 'l mal trovi ritegno.	
		Ma vien di qua la fera;	
		ecco l'ingrata ninfa,	
		come superba viene	90
		da così illustre impresa.	

---

[161] *Nell*.
[162] *forsi*. As in line 70 below.
[163] 'Placido' is capitalized in M.
[164] *Con*: two erroneously written letters (apparently 'he') are cancelled after 'C'.

Souls once renewed themselves in your beautiful fire and found a happier life. But now your torch flickers like a funeral pyre with a ghastly gleam; the darts from your quiver, Love, now seem more like Death's arrows. You, who once kept hearts alive without souls, do you now leave your most faithful lovers to die? You, who nourished the desires and sweet wishes of others, do you now abandon those dearest to you, who are desperate, without hope and prey to grief? Have your weapons perhaps lost that ancient power, Lord, that brought so much happiness and joy to hearts? Perhaps your bow – which was once both warrior and healer, providing both the wound and its salve – has now become nothing but a minister of pain and suffering. It can still wound well enough, but it can no longer heal. Or, rather, are you now transformed from a kind and courteous Lord into a cruel and treacherous tyrant?[145]

Coribante
Love is not so changed / [48ʳ] *as you think when he acts as a minister of pain and suffering, tormenting hearts and souls. He is not his true self when he brings sweetness to his followers.* Wretched Filemone, you show this with all too cruel an example today unless our fears and worries are mistaken.

Armilla
Ah, sadly it may be too true. Rarely are such tragedies checked. But here comes the fierce nymph herself now, here is that ungrateful one.[146] How proudly she comes, after such an illustrious enterprise!

Scena seconda

Clorilli, Armilla, Coribante

CLO.	Per tutta questa selva	1
	t'ho ricercata Armilla,	
	pur al fin ti trovo.[165] Dimmi ti prego	
	veduto avresti a sorte Filemone	
	doppo ch'io gli parlai?[166]	5
ARM.	E che cura ti muove	
	a ricever di lui? / [48ᵛ]	
CLO.	Temo di qualche male,	
	perché poi ch'io mi tolsi	
	sdegnosa di parlargli,	10
	volendo andar all'antro di Tesbina	
	trovai questo suo dardo[167] per la via.	
	E mi diss'ella, che l'avea veduto	
	scender verso Mugnon tanto veloce	
	che parea forsennato,[168]	15
	né saputo altro ha dirmi.	
COR.	Or godi empia Clorilli,	
	che questi indizi fian purtroppo veri.	
ARM.	Or ecco, ingrata ninfa,	
	della tua crudeltà miseri frutti.	20
	Ecco che al fin per te rimast' estinto	
	un pastor sì gentile e sì leggiadro.	
	Or più non sentirai	
	ricordar quell'odioso infedel nome.	
	Vivi or ninfa crudel, vivi a te stessa,	25
	va pur con l'altre fere	
	a incrudelir ne' boschi, e nelle selve;	
	pastor più non avrai che di te pensi.	
	O sfortunato amante,	
	per chi sei corso a morte?	30
	Per una dispietata, / [49ʳ]	
	che d'una lagrimetta, o d'un sospiro,	
	non t'è cortese almeno?	

---

[165] *trovoi.*
[166] *parlai*: 'r' inserted above.
[167] *dordo.*
[168] *forzennato*: the 's' resembles a 'z', as for the 's' in 'Alfesibeo' above.

Scene Two

Clorilli, Armilla, Coribante

Clorilli
I looked all over the forest for you, Armilla. At last I have found you! Tell me, pray, did you happen to see Filemone after I spoke with him?

Armilla
And what makes you ask for news of him now? / [48ᵛ]

Clorilli
I fear something terrible. For after I left him, angry from our conversation, and headed to Tesbina's cave, I found this arrow of his along the path.[147] And Tesbina told me that she had seen him heading down to the Mugnone so quickly he seemed out of his mind. She could tell me nothing more.

Coribante
Take pleasure in this, wicked Clorilli, for sadly these signs may well be true!

Armilla
Now see, ungrateful nymph, here are the miserable fruits of your cruelty! Here, at long last, this noble and gallant shepherd dies because of you. Now you will never hear his odious and faithless name spoken again! Go on and live, cruel nymph, live for yourself alone, go join the other wild ones to make the woods and forests cruel! You will no longer be burdened by a shepherd who thinks only of you. O unfortunate lover, is this the woman for whom you leapt to your death? For one who is without pity, / [49ʳ] who is not even gracious enough to honour you with one small tear, or a sigh?[148]

CLO.	Non sarà fors[e] morto,
	Armilla non temere. 35
ARM.	Che deggio più temer se 'l mal è certo?
CLO.	E che certezza n'hai?
	Ho pur udito dire
"	ch'ogn uom' a suo poter fugge la morte.
ARM.	O quante volte, o quante 40
	egli ci fu vicino,
	ma sempre fino a qui l'abbian salvato
	or Coribante, or io,
	or ben ci sarà corso,
	poi che da noi fiero destin partillo. 45
COR.	Rimànti Armilla, io voglio
	veder s'io lo ritrovo, o vivo o morto,
	e non passerà molto
	che recarvi potrò nuove più certe.

Scena terza

Clorilli, Armilla, Aurindo

CLO.	Misera vita mia se pur è vero, 1
	Armilla, che sia morto Filemone.
ARM.	Anzi sarai lietissima e felice / [49ᵛ]
	che più non avrai
	chi con prieghi noiosi ti importuni. 5
CLO.	D[eh] non voler crudele
	con le parole tue
	trafigger più quel core,
	che purtroppo l' trafigge aspro dolore.
AUR.	O secolo inumano, 10
	che in te nutrisci sì spietata ninfa!
ARM.	Odo una voce, e par tutta dogliosa.
AUR.	O miser Filemone,
	tu pur ti giaci estinto
	nell'età tua più verde, e più fiorita? 15

Clorilli
He may not be dead, Armilla, do not fear.

Armilla
What have I to fear anymore, if the worst is certain?

Clorilli
And what certainty do you have of his death? I have heard it said *that every man escapes death if he can.*[149]

Armilla
Oh, how many times, oh, how many times he came close to death! But until now we have always saved him, either Coribante or I. Now he may well have rushed to his death, after cruel fate kept him from us.

Coribante
Stay, Armilla! I will see if I can find him, whether living or dead. It will not be long before I can bring you back more certain news.

Scene Three

Clorilli, Armilla, Aurindo[150]

Clorilli
My life will be wretched, Armilla, if Filemone is truly dead.

Armilla
To the contrary, you will be most joyous and happy, / [49ᵛ] for he will no longer bother you with his tiresome entreaties.

Clorilli
Ah, do not say such cruel things! You further torment my heart, which is already tormented with bitter pain.

Aurindo
[*Aside*] Oh, what a cruel age, to have nurtured such a pitiless nymph!

Armilla
I hear a voice, and it seems most sorrowful.

Aurindo
[*Aside*] O wretched Filemone, do you really lie dead in the prime of your life?

CLO.	Ohimè, che questo è Aurindo	
	che parla della morte	
	di Filemone. Ahi lassa.[169]	
ARM.	Pastor di dove vieni, e di che morte	
	parlavi fra te stesso?	20
AUR.	Meco venia piangendo	
	la morte del più fido, e più[170] gentile	
	pastor di queste selve;	
	di Filemone io parlo.	
CLO.	A così fiero annunzio	25
	io non esco di vita?	
ARM.	Narra pietoso Aurindo / [50ʳ]	
	questa dolente istoria.	
AUR.	Se dal dolor concesso	
	mi sarà tanto spirto	30
	ch'io la possa narrare	
	volentier narrerolla,	
	tanto più ch'io ci veggio	
	chi della morte sua stat'è cagione.	
CLO.	Ohimè, che mille morti	35
	ben aspett'io dalle parole tue.	
AUR.	Lungo il Mugnon io m'n'andava solo,	
	sciolto d'ogni pensier quando repente	
	viddi venir correndo Filemone,	
	attraversando il fiume.	40
	Io che ben mille volte	
	preso m'avea un pietoso diletto	
	d'udirlo di nascosto lamentare,	
	dell'empia crudeltà della sua ninfa,	
	credessi certo allora	45
	che in quei solinghi luochi	
	dell'amorose cure	
	sgravar volesse lamentando[171] il core,	
	onde da lungi lo seguii. Ma quando	
	fu di quel[l'] erto monte al[172] mez[z]o asceso,	50

---

[169] Lines 17–8: in M the two lines are differently divided (after 'Filemone'), forming a 12-syllable line, and unusually a three syllable line ('Ahi lassa'). The line break has been adjusted to form two regular heptasyllable lines. Cf. 4.4.108–9.
[170] *piu*: inserted above *e gentile*.
[171] *lamentanto*.
[172] *all'*.

Clorilli

Aye me, here comes Aurindo, who speaks of Filemone's death. Alas!

Armilla

Shepherd, where are you coming from, and whose death were you lamenting?

Aurindo

As I made my way here, I was weeping over the death of the most faithful and kind shepherd in these woods. I speak of Filemone.

Clorilli

[*Aside*] Can I remain alive after hearing such dreadful news?

Armilla

Tell us this woeful story, kind Aurindo. / [50ʳ]

Aurindo

If grief allows me the strength to tell the story, then I will willingly recount it, the more so because I see here before me the nymph who was the cause of his death.

Clorilli

[*Aside*] Alas, your words will bring me a thousand deaths!

Aurindo

I was walking along the Mugnone by myself, free from all care, when suddenly there was Filemone running towards me, crossing the river. I, who a thousand times before had taken a hidden, piteous pleasure in listening to him lament the wicked cruelty of his nymph, was certain that he wanted to unburden his heart by lamenting his lovelorn state in that solitary place.[151] So I followed him at a distance. But when he had climbed halfway up the steep mountain which bears the name of the son

	che del figlio d'Amor riserba il nome / [50ᵛ]	
	fermossi, et io da lui lontano alquanto	
	mi ascosi entro un cespuglio,	
	ove senz'esser visto	
	le sue parole udía.	55
CLO.	O mia fera sventura!	
AUR.	Ivi fermos[s]i tacito, et immoto,	
	in giù guardando buona pezza stette[173]	
	fisso mirando il precipizio orrendo.	
	Al fin levando gl'occhi	60
	parve ch'un cotal poco	
	rasserenasse la turbata faccia.	
	Poi dall'alma un sospiro	
	così profondo trasse,	
	che ben certo credei	65
	che seco uscisse anch'ella,	
	e con queste parole accompagnollo.	
CLO.	Ohimè, ohimè!	
ARM.	O caso dispietato.	
AUR.	— Poscia che dall'altezza	
	della tua grazia, o Clorilli crudele,	70
	miseramente caddi	
	in questo abisso[174] di miseria estrema	
	della disgrazia tua,	
	è ben ragion ancora	
	che 'l mio corpo meschino / [51ʳ]	75
	da questa altezza omai	
	precipitando vada	
	a ritrovar la più profonda parte	
	di questa orrida balza. —	
	Tacque per breve spazio e 'n questo mez[z]o	80
	da gl'occhi scaturì con larga vena	
	d'amarissime lagrime un torrente.	
	Poscia del sen si trasse	
	candido velo, e 'n lui fissò lo sguardo.	
	Indi soggiunse: — O vel quanta mutanza	85
	vist'ho, poi ch'io ti viddi.	
	Ah non promise[175] a me la ninfa nostra,	

---

[173] M shows in left margin traces of an erasure of the speaker's name ('AUR').
[174] *abbisso.*
[175] *promisse.*

of Love, / [50ᵛ] he stopped.[152] I concealed myself in a bush some way off, where I could hear his words without being seen.

Clorilli
[*Aside*] Oh, my cruel misfortune!

Aurindo
He rested there where he had stopped, quiet and still, looking down for a long while, gazing down the horrible precipice. Finally, raising his eyes, his troubled countenance seemed to have cleared a little. Then he drew from his soul so deep a sigh that I fully believed his very soul would escape with it.

Clorilli
[*Aside*] Alas, alas!

Armilla
[*Aside*] Oh, what a terrible tale!

Aurindo
[*Quoting Filemone*] 'O cruel Clorilli, just as I fell miserably from the heights of your favour into the abyss of extreme misery that is your disfavour, it is only right that my wretched body / [51ʳ] should plummet down from this peak and land at the very foot of this fearsome crag!'

He fell silent briefly in the middle of his speech, and a torrent of the bitterest tears sprang from his eyes. Next, he pulled the white veil from his breast, and, fixing his gaze upon it, he added: 'O veil, how much change have I witnessed since I first saw you! Ah, did our nymph not promise,

quando fusti di lei cortese dono,
che qual è 'l tuo candor
sarebbe stato quel della [s]ua[176] fede;   90
e che com' un alpestre orrido scoglio
si sta saldo al soffiare
de' più rabbiosi venti
così sarebbe stat'ella in amarmi.
Ah' come al vento sparte,   95
furon quelle promesse!
Che pur l'ha macchiat'ella
la bianca[177] fede, e 'n altra parte ha posto
il tesor prezioso / [51ᵛ]
del suo bramato Amore.   100
Altri dunque si gode
la mia Clorilli, et io
pur a morir m'n' vado!
E tu malfido testimon di fede
prègoti resti ancor — ; e in questo dire   105
squarciò come vedete questo velo,
e da sé rigittollo.
Poi come fuor del senno uscito fosse
squarciossi i panni intorno
con folgorante sguardo acceso in volto.   110
Tornò poscia di marmo,
e con volto di morte
disse queste parole.

CLO.   Di marmo ho ben il core
se non si stilla in pianto.   115

AUR.   — Osi ancor temerario
d'accusar la tua ninfa
d'infedeltà? Non sai
Che tu fusti il primiero
a torre a lei la fede   120
per darla ad altri? Tu fusti l'infido,
tu quel che grave oltraggio a lei facesti,
et ancor vivi, e 'nvendicata resta
la bella ninfa tua? / [52ʳ]
Ah' perché chiami tua   125

---

[176] *tua*: presumed transcription error, since 'tuo' in line 89 refers to the apostrophized veil, which is compared with Clorilli's 'fede'.
[177] *bianccha*.

when she gave you to me as a gracious gift, that your pure whiteness would be matched by the purity of her faith? Just as a bleak alpine peak stands firm against the most furious winds, so would she be steadfast in her love for me.[153] Alas, how these promises have blown away in the wind! For she sullied her faith and placed the precious treasure / [51^v] of her love – which I so desired! – elsewhere. My Clorilli enjoys the company of another, and so I go to my death. And you, fickle witness of her promise, pray remain.' And with these words, he tore up the veil, as you can see, and threw it far away. Then, as if he were out of his mind, he tore at his clothes, a deranged expression on his face. Then he became as still as marble, and with a deathly expression, said these words . . .

Clorilli
[*Aside*] My own heart must be made of marble, if it does not drip with tears!

Aurindo
'Do you still have the temerity to accuse your nymph of infidelity? Do you not know that you were the first to rob her of your promise, and give it to another? *You* were the faithless one, *you* the one who committed that grave offence. And yet you still live, and your beautiful nymph remains unavenged? / [52^r] Ah, why do you call her yours if you once rejected

	se già la ricusasti?	
	E se ella or ti recusa	
	giustissimo rifiuto è questo suo.	
	Ella non m'ama dunque,	
	et io non moro? Ah mori	130
	mori meschino, e teco	
	morirà la fe' tua morta.[178]	
	O Clorilli, o Clorilli,	
	ecco che Filemone	
	vendica l'ingiurie tue,	135
	ecco Clorilli io moro.— E così detto	
	precipitos[s]i in un momento al basso.	
ARM.	O pastor infelice,	
	come per ben amare	
	hai ricevuto in guiderdon la morte.	140
CLO.	Dispietato dolor tu non m'uccidi?	
	Forse pietà ti sembra	
	tener un mostro di miseria in vita?	
	O vòi che la mia man con questo dardo	
	in me faccia vendetta	145
	del suo dolce signore?	
	Son pronta ad obbedirti,[179]	
	io son pronta a seguirti	
	o Filemon amato, / [52ᵛ]	
	in morte e in vita odiato,	150
	ma fors[e] questo ferro	
	contro altro ferro non avrà[180] possanza,	
	che di ferine tempre	
	ben è questo mio petto,	
	poiché sì lungo pianto	155
	non lo potè ammollire.	
	Tu caro Filemone	
	hai finito il tuo corso	
	uscendo di miserie,	
	et io per la tua morte	160
	trafitta ohimè da doppia e cruda morte	

---

[178] Line 132 has at least eight syllables. Either 'tua' or 'morta' could be omitted for a seven-syllable line.

[179] *Io son pronta ad obbedirti*: 'Io' surmised as a copyist's insert (mirroring line 148), since line 147 has at least eight syllables.

[180] *havera*. Adjusted to avoid a line of at least 12 syllables.

her? For if she rejects you now, hers is a most just refusal. She does not love me, and yet I still live? Ah, die! Die, you wretch, and your dead promise will die with you. O Clorilli, O Clorilli, behold, Filemone avenges the injustices you've suffered. Behold, Clorilli, now I die.' And with these words, he threw himself in an instant to the ground below.

Armilla

O unhappy shepherd! Why was death your reward for loving truly?

Clorilli

Pitiless grief, why do you not kill me? Perhaps it seems like pity to you to keep a monster of misery alive? Or do you wish that this arrow would avenge its sweet lord with my own hand? I am ready to obey you, I am ready to follow you, O Filemone, beloved / [52ᵛ] in death, though despised while he was alive! But perhaps this bit of iron will hold no power against my ferrous heart. For this breast of mine is certainly of a feral nature, since he was unable to soften it with his long lament.

Dear Filemone, you have completed the course of your life, leaving behind all miseries. I, alas, am wounded twice over by your death. Cruel

ancor rimango in vita?
In te mio Filemone
mort'è l'anima mia,
e se pur questa spoglia   165
ancor ha voce e moto,
questo è misero effetto
che adopra[181] in me vendicatrice doglia
per uccidermi ogn'or ben mille volte;
perché solo una morte   170
di questa vita vile
non è degna vendetta
della perdita fatta
della tua vita nobile e gentile. / [53ʳ]
E tu mia cara Armilla, a che più tardi   175
a vendicar di Filemon la morte?
Io fui quell'empia fera
che il suo morir bramai,
io lo condussi al precipizio in cima,
io scellerata ninfa   180
giù lo precipitai.
Tu che l'amasti in vita
vèndicalo ora in morte.
Ecco il dardo di lui,
che solo a questo effetto   185
il suo signor lasciollo
aprimi il petto omai,
e del[182] mio fero core
fa ferocissimo scempio.[183]
Ecco io te l'appresento   190
senza difesa ignudo.
Perché, perché non l' fiedi?
ARM.   Miserissima ninfa
troppo tardi pietosa,
e troppo tardi accorta,   195
vivi infelice, vivi,
soffri questi martir[i][184]
in premio del tuo grave empio fallire. / [53ᵛ]

[181] *addopra*.
[182] *dell'*.
[183] Line 189 is at least eight syllables.
[184] *martire*: in M this creates a rhyming couplet with 'fallire' in the line below.

death, how is it that I am still alive? My soul died with you, my Filemone, and if this mortal husk of mine still has voice and movement, this is the grievous effect that despair has on me, to avenge my actions and kill me a thousand times over – for one death alone is not enough to avenge the loss of your noble and gentle life.[154] / [53ʳ]

And you, my dear Armilla, why do you delay in avenging Filemone's death? I was that cruel beast who longed for his death; I led him to the precipice on the mountain's peak; I was the treacherous nymph who threw him to the ground below. You, who loved him in life, avenge him now in death.

Here is the arrow left behind by its master for this sole purpose. Open my chest, and destroy my heart as cruelly as you can. Here, I offer it to you, defenceless and naked. Why, why do you not pierce my breast?

Armilla

Most miserable nymph, you have become merciful too late. You have realized it all too late! Live, unhappy wretch, live and suffer these torments as reward for your truly wicked error.[155] / [53ᵛ]

CLO.	Crudel mi nieghi dunque
	quel che ogni ragion vòl che a me si dia? 200
	Io rea dell'altrui morte
	troverò del[185] morir chiuse le porte?
	Ma che? Troppo pietosa
	è la tua mano Armilla
	per così crudo effetto. 205
	Questa mia che crudele
	negò di dar la fede
	al mio fido pastore,
	passerà questo seno.
	O Filemone amato 210
	rimira questo colpo,
	godi della vendetta
	di sì fera nimica
	e ricevi quest' alma.
ARM.	O Clorilli, o Clorilli, e che far pensi? 215
AUR.	O spettacol dolente!
ARM.	O Clorilli infelice!
	Se più tardavo a ritenerli il braccio
	certo si avrebbe[186] uccisa.
	Lasciami questo dardo. 220
CLO.	Non mi vietar Armilla
	che questa mano, ob[b]ediente ancella / [54ʳ]
	al mio giusto volere,
	segua quell' che tu cruda
	non volesti eseguire. 225
ARM.	Lasciami questo dardo!
	O pastor dammi aiuto
	ch'io gliel'[187] tolga di mano.
AUR.	Lascial' misera ninfa,
	e non voler di nuovo 230
	con la tua morte uccider Filemone;
	ma in te riserba viva
	la memoria di lui.
	Vivi certa e sicura
	ch'ei t'ama ancor, come mostrò morendo. 235

[185] dell'.
[186] haverebbe: in standard Italian sarebbe.
[187] gnel. Compare similar Tuscan, more popular form 'gnene' ('gliele'); Rohlfs, Grammatica storica, II: §467.

Clorilli

You cruelly deny me, then, what is due to me for so many reasons? I, who am responsible for the death of another, now find death's doors closed to me? But why? Your hand is too compassionate for such cruelty, Armilla. This hand of mine, which refused to trust my faithful shepherd, will plunge the arrow into my breast. O beloved Filemone, witness this blow, relish the revenge on such a cruel enemy and accept this soul.

Armilla

O Clorilli, O Clorilli, what do you think you're doing?[156]

Aurindo

Oh, what is this sorrowful spectacle?

Armilla

O unhappy Clorilli! If I had waited any longer to take her arm, she would surely have killed herself. [*To Clorilli*] Give me this arrow!

Clorilli

Do not stop me, Armilla, for this hand is an obedient servant / [54ʳ] to my just desire, let it carry out what you, cruel one, refused to do.

Armilla

Give me the arrow! O shepherd, help me, so that I may wrench it from her hand!

Aurindo

Hand it over, wretched nymph. Do not try to kill Filemone anew with your death, but keep his memory alive within you. Live certain and secure in the knowledge that he still loves you, as he demonstrated by dying.

CLO.	Dunque se ancor ei m'ama	
	è ben ragion ch'io il segua.	
	Ma concedimi Aurindo	
	quel velo; miser avanzo	
	del suo giusto furore,	240
	acciò che meco resti	
	per questo breve spazio	
	di vita che mi avanza.[188]	
AUR.	Eccotel' ninfa, ma depon' ti prego	
	quel pensier ch'al morir folle ti mena. / [54ᵛ]	245
CLO.	E tu crudel Armilla	
	rendemi questo dardo.	
ARM.	Non ti pensar mai più di riaverlo,	
	né meno di seguire	
	così fiero inuman proponimento.	250
CLO.	Io te lo lascio, e vado	
	a ritrovar il corpo	
	del[189] miser' Filemone.	
	Ivi darò pur fine	
	al mio giusto desire,	255
"	Che ben può nulla chi non può morire.	
ARM.	Pastor seguir la voglio	
	per impedirle l'opra.[190]	
AUR.	Et io voglio ire a ritrovar Ergasto,	
	da ché mia sorte vòl che sia avviso[191]	260
	di sì rie novelle.[192]	

Scena quarta

Coribante, Dalinda

COR.	Lodato il Ciel, che se togliè di vita	1
	pur oggi Filemone,	
	ancor ci ricompensa, e ne consola	
	con renderci Dalinda, e viva e sana.	

---

[188] *avvanza.*
[189] *dell'.*
[190] *per impedirle l'opra*: original version of line 258 of M. This has been partly cancelled and added to, to read 'per impedirle~~a~~ ~~l'opra~~, a Dio'.
[191] Lines 260–1: *vòl che sia avviso.*
[192] *da ché mia sorte / vòl che sia avviso di sì rie novelle*: line break adjusted to fit metre.

Clorilli

So if he still loves me, there is good reason for me to follow him. But grant me that veil, Aurindo, that miserable vestige of his just rage. Let it stay with me for the short stretch of life that I have left.

Aurindo

Here it is, nymph. But I beseech you to abandon that previous intention, which will lead you to a mad death. / [54ᵛ]

Clorilli

And you, cruel Armilla, give me back this arrow.

Armilla

Do not think you will ever get it back, certainly not to see through such an inhuman, savage idea.

Clorilli

I leave it to you then and will go to find wretched Filemone's body.[157] And there I will satisfy my just desire, because *she can do nothing, who cannot die.*[158]

Armilla

Shepherd, I must follow her and stop this desire of hers.

Aurindo

And I must go find Ergasto; Destiny dictates that I alert him to this horrible news.

Scene Four

Coribante, Dalinda[159]

Coribante

May Heaven be praised! For even if it wrenched Filemone from life today, still it rewards and consoles us by giving us Dalinda back alive and well.

DAL.		Ch'io viva Coribante[193] / [55ʳ]	5
		effetto è sol d'empio destino ingiusto	
		che per maggior mio mal mi tiene in vita!	
COR.		Ma qual cagion, dimmi Dalinda amata,	
		ti sospinse a lasciar la propria casa,	
		e 'l vecchio genitor? E perché lungi	10
		da noi stata ti sei sì lungo tempo?	
DAL.		Se ben il mio dolore	
		a cui fiera, e cruda rimembranza	
		non altrimenti che rivo per pioggia	
		andrà crescendo, il tutto narrerotti.	15
		Tu ti dèi ricordar che quando Alcone	
		conchiuder volle l'infelice nozze	
		di me con Filemone['],[194] che quasi fuori	
		per soverchio[195] dolor del senno uscii.	
COR.		Del tutto mi ricordo, né potei	20
		saper da te qual fosse la cagione	
		che a sprezzar[196] ti inducea pastor sì degno?	
DAL.		Perdonami cortese Coribante,	
		s'a te celato io tenni	
		la fiamma che nel cor m'accese Amore,	25
		così volse egli, e così volli anch'io.	
COR.	"	Chiusa fiamma è più ardente e più tormenta;	
	"	mal saggio è chi l'asconde, e non la scopre. / [55ᵛ]	
DAL.		Ma sì chiaro era il foco che mi ardea	
		che per somma ventura	30
		ebbi di incenerir nelle sue fiamme.	
		Io so che tu conosci il mio Fillinio,	
		Fillinio onor di queste selve, e gloria	
		del fiesolano monte; a quest', ahi[197] lassa,	
		vivo io così congiunta	35
		d'Amor quanto di fede	
		et egli nel mio foco ardeva il core.	
COR.		Se ugual[198] era la fiamma	
		la cagion era uguale.	

---

[193] *Coribante?*: the question mark has been replaced with an exclamation mark at the end of the sentence to fit the sense.
[194] *Filemone*: apocope surmised to avoid a 12-syllable line.
[195] *sovercchio.*
[196] *sprezzor.*
[197] *hai.*
[198] *uugual.*

Dalinda

That I live, Coribante, / [55ʳ] is only due to most terrible and unjust destiny, for it keeps me alive to create the worst misery.

Coribante

But tell me, beloved Dalinda, what forced you to abandon your home, and your old father? And why did you stay so far from us for such a long time?

Dalinda

Although my pain will grow greater by reliving this horrible and cruel memory, just as a stream expands after rain, I will tell you everything.[160] You must remember that when Alcone decided to join me in an ill-fated marriage with Filemone, I nearly went out of my mind from extreme pain.

Coribante

I remember it all – but I could never learn from you why you were moved to scorn such a worthy shepherd.

Dalinda

Please forgive me, kind Coribante, if I kept the flame that Love had lit in my heart hidden from you. So he wished it, and so I wished it as well.

Coribante

A hidden flame burns more brightly,[161] *and flickers more violently – only a fool would try to cover it, rather than reveal it.*[162] / [55ᵛ]

Dalinda

But the fire that burned inside me was so brilliant, I deemed it the greatest fortune to burn to ashes in its flames. I know that you are acquainted with my Fillinio; Fillinio, the pride of these woods, and the glory of the Fiesolan mountain. Alas, to this man I am bound, by Love as by sworn faith – and his heart, similarly, burned in my fire.

Coribante

If the flame was the same, the cause was the same.

DAL.	Così beati un tempo	40
	vivemmo, finché 'l Cielo	
	volse cangiar il mio felice stato	
	nel più infelice che già mai scorgesse	
	nel suo torto viaggio intorno il sole;	
	perché al mio vecchio padre	45
	venne quel rio pensiero,	
	cagion ch'andasse ogni mia gioia in bando.	
	Perché non avend'io già mai voluto	
	consentir'[199] alle nozze, ch'ei bramava,	
	che né la[200] fede data al mio Fil[l]inio	50
	d'essergli sposa, né l'amor immenso	
	ch'io le[201] portava a me lo consentiva, / [56ʳ]	
	contro mia voglia al fin conchiuse[202] il tutto.	
	Et io, misera me, forzata fui	
	d'ordinar con Fillinio	55
	d'abbandonar la patria, e 'l padre, e queste	
	amatissime selve.	
	Ahi mia fera ventura[!]	
	Ben dissi l'ordinai, che molto lungi	
	al concorde voler seguì l'effetto.	60
COR.	Di furioso Amor folle consiglio	
	fu questo tuo, Dalinda.	
DAL.	Così l'ordine demmo	
	di ritrovarci di notte a questa fonte.[203]	
	Io prima di lui giunsi,	65
	e mentre sola in sì deserto loco	
	stava aspettando il suo venir, et ecco	
	un ferocissimo orso che veloce	
	verso di me con famelica rabbia	
	furioso venia; io dal timore	70
	di subito[204] assalita,	
	non avendo altro schermo a mia difesa	
	alla fuga mi volsi, e così bene	
	mi riuscì, che salva	
	al fin uscii da' suoi feroci artigli,	75

[199] An erroneous letter in *consenti[?]r* is blotted out.
[200] *ne[l]la*: the first 'l' appears blotted out.
[201] *le*: *gli* in standard Italian.
[202] *concchiuse*.
[203] Line 64 has at least 12 syllables.
[204] *subbito*.

Dalinda

And so we lived blessedly for a time, until Heaven decided to turn my happy state into the most unhappy one that the sun ever witnessed in its troubled voyage around earth.[163] For that wicked idea came to my father, an idea that caused all of my joy to vanish.[164] I had never agreed to the marriage he so desired; the promise given to my Fillinio that I would become his bride, and the immense love I felt for him, would not allow me to. / [56ʳ] In the end, my father determined everything against my wishes. And I, poor wretch that I am, was forced to plan with Fillinio to abandon my home, and my father, and these beloved woods. Alas, how cruel my luck is! I said I planned it, but events turned out very differently from our mutual desires.

Coribante

Dalinda, your counsellor on this matter was Love gone mad.[165]

Dalinda

We made a plan to meet at night by this fountain. I arrived before him, and while I was alone in this deserted place waiting for him to arrive, suddenly a most ferocious bear was hurtling towards me in a blind ravening fury.[166] Fear immediately assailed me, and, having no other means to defend myself, I fled. I managed to escape from his ferocious

e mi nascosi entro una grotta, dove / [56ᵛ]
stetti fin quasi all'apparir del giorno
tutta tremante e tim[i]da.[205] Ma poi,
più che mai forte risorgendo Amore,
posto in fuga il timore,   80
e desiosa di trovar Fillinio,
mi ricondussi in questo luogo. Ahi[206] lassa,
che ben lo ritrovai,
ma non già in quella guisa ch'io bramava;
trovailo (ohimè, che a rimembrarlo io moro)   85
lacero il volto, e 'l petto,
nel proprio sangue involto
giacer (misera me) nel suolo estinto.

COR.   O miserando caso
          degno d'eterno duol, d'eterno pianto.   90

DAL.   Lo trovai (lassa) estinto,
          et ancor negom[m]i il fero destino[207]
          di poter contemplar l'amato volto,
          perché ivi l'empia belva
          via più che in altra parte   95
          sfogato avea la rabbia,
          né apparia di lui
          altro che parte de' suoi biondi crini;
          e se non era il vestir bianco, e un cinto
          azzurro di zenzado, ch'io gli diedi,   100
          che agli omeri a traverso avea legato, / [57ʳ]
          in dubbio sarei stata
          che quel fosse[208] Fillinio.
          O dubbio avventuroso
          se pur durava. O sconoscenza amara!   105

COL.   Di biondo pel, di vestir bianco,[209] un cinto
          azzurro di zenzado,
          quanto tempo è Dalinda,
          che seguì questo caso?[210]

---

[205] *timeda*.
[206] *hai*.
[207] *il mio fero destino*: 'mio' is surmised as a copyist's addition, making line 92 at least 12
syllables.
[208] *fosse*: heavily cancelled letter after the 'o'.
[209] *bianccho*: the second 'c' is blotted out.
[210] Lines 108–9 split a single line in M of at least 14 syllables.

talons, and I hid myself in a cave, where / [56ᵛ] I stayed until near daybreak, fearful and trembling all over. But then Love came surging up once more, stronger than ever, and I set aside my fear. Wanting to find Fillinio, I came back here. Oh, alas! For I did find him, but not in the state I was hoping to. (Aye me, I die remembering it now!) His face and breast were ripped apart; he was lying covered in his own blood, O wretched me![167] On the earth, dead.

Coribante
Oh, pitiful case, worthy of eternal sorrow, of eternal lament!

Dalinda
I found him – alas! – dead, and cruel destiny again denied me the chance to contemplate his lovely face. For the horrible beast had unleashed his rage there far more than other places, and nothing was left of him but a few of his blond locks. If it were not for the white clothes, and the blue band of sendal I had given him, and which he had tied across him, / [57ʳ] I would not have known if it was Fillinio.[168] Oh, this would have been fortunate doubt, if only it had lasted. Oh, bitter ignorance!

Coribante
Blond hair, white clothes, a band of blue sendal . . . how long is it since you witnessed this?

DAL.	Dui anni sono, in quella notte appunto	110
	che sogliono i pastori il dì seguente	
	onorar con solenni giochi, e feste	
	dell'estinto Cosmino il gran sepolcro.[211]	
COR.	Avea altri segnali	
	quel misero pastor, che per Fillinio	115
	conoscer lo potessi?	
DAL.	Non altri.	
COR.	Or ti consola,	
	che forse ancor sarà vano il sospetto	
	che della morte avesti di Fillinio.	
	Perché il pastor che tu vedesti morto	120
	forse fu 'l forte Alcasto,	
	il qual io viddi in quella istessa notte	
	affrontarsi col orso, e 'l viddi uc[c]iso,	
	et i medesmi panni avea appunto	
	che tu mi narri, e quella cinta dono / [57ᵛ]	125
	era della sua ninfa.	
DAL.	Ahi ben lo riconobbe il cor dolente,	
	che sentito per altri non avrebbe[212]	
	e per Fillinio mio tanto dolore.	
COR.	Certo che il tuo dolor sarà ancor vano,	130
	credilo a me Dalinda.	
	Anzi ti voglio dir, che spero[213]	
	che Fillinio sia vivo, e 'n queste selve.	
DAL.	Crudel pietade è questa tua, se cerchi	
	con falsa speme ritenermi in vita.	135
COR.	Se non è falso quel che poco avanti	
	Ruscon mi disse, dolendosi meco	
	d'un pastor che l'avea battuto, il quale	
	disse che al volto gli sembrò Fillinio,	
	non sarà falsa ancor questa speranza.	140
	Ma di grazia trattieni un poco ancora,	
	finché 'l ver meglio intenda, in questo loco,	
	che or or ritorno, e saprò dirti il tutto.	
DAL.	Troppo son chiara omai, troppo son certa	
	della sventura mia,	145
	ma pur per compiacerti Coribante	

[211] *sepolcchro.*
[212] *haverebbe.*
[213] Line 132 has nine syllables.

Dalinda

It has been two years, since the very eve of the day when shepherds commemorate the departed Cosmino, passing the time in solemn games and festivals at his majestic tomb.[169]

Coribante

Did the wretched shepherd bear any other signs that helped you to recognize him as Fillinio?

Dalinda

No others.

Coribante

Now console yourself, for the suspicion you had about the death of Fillinio may still be proven wrong. The shepherd you saw lying dead may have been the strong Alcasto, whom I saw battling the bear that very night. I saw the bear kill him, and he had on the very same clothes that you describe to me, and that band was a gift / [57ᵛ] from *his* nymph.[170]

Dalinda

Ah, but my woeful heart recognized him, for it would not have felt such grief for anyone but Fillinio.

Coribante

Believe me, Dalinda, for I am certain your grief will yet be proven vain. I will tell you, what is more, that I suspect that Fillinio is alive and in these woods.

Dalinda

This pity of yours is cruel, if you seek to keep me alive with false hope.

Coribante

If what Ruscone just told me is not false, when he bemoaned a shepherd who had trounced him and whose face he said resembled Fillinio's, then your hope will not be false either.[171] But pray, stay here a little longer, until I better understand what is true and can return to tell you the whole story.

Dalinda

I am now most certain. I am most sure of my misfortune. But to please

COR.   son contenta aspet[t]arti.
            Or vanne, ma di grazia torna presto!
            Io vo, tu non partire. / [58ʳ]

                        Scena quinta

                        Dalinda

[DAL.]   Non t'annidare in questo afflitto seno   1
            o mal sicura speme;
            pàrtiti, che non hai tu qui pur loco,
            ch' io pur a questo fonte
            viddi spento di vita il mio Fillinio,   5
            qual empia orrenda belva
            lacerò le sue membra.
            Qui di tiepido sangue
            viddi farsi un ruscello,
            et ancor veggio, ahi lassa,   10
            che riserbano i fiori
            il purpureo color delle lor fogl[i]e.
            Tu fonte testimon rivela²¹⁴ altrui
            del mio fero dolor l'acerba istoria.

            Io che sì pronta fui   15
            a lasciar del mio padre
            lo sconsolato albergo
            per seguir te dolcissimo Fillinio,
            così tarda or ti seguo?
            Ma perdona cor mio questa tardanza,   20
            che ben contro mia voglia ancor son viva. / [58ᵛ]
            Tu fonte testimon rivela altrui
            del mio fero dolor l'acerba istoria.

            Io che animosa, e forte,
            spezzai d'ogni periglio   25
            la più terribil forma,

---

²¹⁴ *rivella*. This spelling is found once more in the refrains (line 42). The line spaces following the refrain are an editorial addition.

you, Coribante, I am happy to wait for you. Now go on. But by grace, come back quickly!

Coribante
I will go now. Don't leave! / [58^r]

Scene Five

Dalinda

O tenuous hope, do not make yourself a nest in this troubled breast of mine. Leave, you are not welcome here! For I saw Fillinio here at this very fountain, his life extinguished, after a wicked, hideous beast ripped his body apart. I saw his blood stream out when it was not yet cold, and I can see that the flowers still preserve a scarlet hue on their petals now.

You, fountain and witness, reveal my fierce pain's bitter history to others.[172]

I, who was so ready to abandon my father's unhappy house to follow you, sweetest Fillinio, how can I be so slow in following you now? But pardon this delay, heart of mine, for it is against my will that I am still living. / [58^v]

You, fountain and witness, reveal my fierce pain's bitter history to others.

I, who was spirited, and strong, and scorned the worst form of every

così poscia temei
d'un orso il fiero aspetto
perché più fiero aspetto a me porgessi?
Tu fonte testimon rivela altrui   30
del mio fero dolor l'acerba istoria.

Io sì cruda allor fui,
che io viddi a eterno occaso
giunti que' chiari soli
che le tenebre mie rendean sì chiare   35
né fuori uscii di vita?
Ah' ben volssi morire;
tu me l' vietassi, o Lidia, empia cagione
delle mie lunghe pene.
Tu riserbasti a più duri tormenti   40
quest'alma afflitta, et a più cruda morte.
Tu fonte testimon rive[l]a altrui
del mio fero dolor l'acerba istoria.

Et anco oggi di nuovo
son ritenuta in vita   45
da fal[l]ace speranza? / [59ʳ]
Ma fia lo spazio breve
di questo viver mio,
che se già questo dardo,
tu mio sommo diletto,   50
mentre con questo braccio
godeva d'atte[r]rar selvaggia fera,
per lui fia tratto a fine
la disperata doglia,
fiera crudel, che entro il mio cor s'annida.   55
Tu fonte testimon rivela altrui
del corto viver mio l'acerba istoria.

Sol tanto spazio voglio
di vita che mi resti
che Coribante torni;   60
non già perch'io mi creda
che la venuta sua
mi debba consolare,
ma perché d'aspettarlo li promissi;

danger – how, then, could I have feared the fierce sight of a bear, so that you could offer me an even more horrible sight?

You, fountain and witness, reveal my fierce pain's bitter history to others.

Was I so cruel then? For I saw those bright sun-like eyes, which turned all my shadows to light, closed in eternal dusk. And yet I still did not die? Oh, I certainly wanted to die; O Lidia, you denied me this, you were the wicked cause of my long suffering.[173] You kept this suffering soul alive for harsher torments, and for a crueller death.

You, fountain and witness, reveal my fierce pain's bitter history to others.

And am I still kept alive by fraudulent hope today? / [59ʳ] But let this life of mine be over soon! For just as you, arrow, were once my greatest delight, when I relished the killing of savage beasts by my own hand, so let this same arrow put an end to my desperate pain, which inhabits my heart like a cruel beast.

You, fountain and witness, reveal my brief life's bitter history to others.

I only want my life to last long enough for Coribante's return, not because I believe that his arrival will comfort me, but because I promised I would wait for him.

poi seguirò dolente 65
lo spirto di Fillinio
che forse anco qui intorno
desioso m'aspetta.
Intanto, fin ch'ei giunga
Asconderom[m]i dentro a quella grotta. / [59ᵛ] 70
Tu fonte testimon asconde altrui
del corto viver mio l'acerba istoria.

ATTO QUINTO

Scena prima

Licandro, Coribante

LIC.	O giorno fortunato, o giorno lieto,	1
	giorno felice e chiaro,	
	ben degno ch'io ti scriva in saldi marmi[!]	
	Dalinda è viva, Fil[l]inio è trovato,	
	Filemon non è morto, e di Clorilli	5
	l'odio tutto in amor è convertito.	
	Felic[i] avvenimenti, o qual mi ingombra,	
	Coribante gentil, letizia il core.	
	Ma Dalinda ove è, che pur dicea	
	che t'aspettava appunto in questo loco?	10
COR.	Non puote esser lontana,	
	né tarderà a venir. Intanto dimmi	
	di grazia, il mio Licandro, in che maniera	
	salvasti Filemon dal[l]' alta rupe,	
	di dove disse Aurindo	15
	che cader l'avea visto?	
LIC.	Il ver disse Aurindo, / [60ʳ]	
	che di morir disposto	
	precipitossi, ma benigno fato	
	al disperato suo voler s'oppose	20
	com'io ti narrerò.	
COR.	Dì ch'io t'ascolto.	
LIC.	Lungo il Mugnon sul[l]'erba verde e fresca	
	io mi giacea dolce, allettando il sonno	
	per ristorar l'affaticate membra,	
	quando alto grido, e spaventevol molto,	25

Then I will dolefully follow Fillinio's spirit, which perhaps still waits longingly for me in these parts.[174] Until he arrives, meanwhile, I will hide myself inside that cave. / [59ᵛ]

You, fountain and witness, hide my brief life's bitter history from others.

ACT FIVE

Scene One

Licandro,[175] Coribante

Licandro
O fortunate day, O happy day, bright and happy day! So worthy that I shall inscribe you into strong and enduring marble. Dalinda is alive, Fillinio is found, Filemone is not dead and Clorilli's hatred has been wholly converted into love. Happy events, O gentle Coribante, how happiness overwhelms my heart! But Dalinda, where is she? For surely she said she would wait for you in precisely this place?

Coribante
She cannot be far, nor will she be long to arrive. In the meantime, pray tell me, my dear Licandro, how did you manage to save Filemone, when Aurindo said he saw him fall from that high cliff?

Licandro
Aurindo spoke the truth. / [60ʳ] Filemone hurled himself down, intent on death. But kind fate denied his desperate will, as I will recount to you.

Coribante
Tell me, I am all ears!

Licandro
I was lying on the fresh and green grass alongside the Mugnone, flirting with sweet slumber to restore my weary limbs, when a loud and most

di cima al colle mi ferì l'orecchia
e scacciò il sonno: ond'io, levando gli occhi
ove io sentii lo spaventevol suono,
viddi cotal ruina, e tal tempesta
venir precipitando un uom dal sommo,   30
che a ripensarvi solo agg[h]iaccio e tremo.[215]
Subito[216] salto in piedi, e corro dove
penso trovar quel miser uom in pezzi.
"   Ma come volle il Ciel, santa innocenza,
"   quando a te mancò mai schermo, e difesa?   35
Terminò del cader l'alta ruina
appunto dove a piè dell'alto monte
accresciuto per pioggia il picciol fiume
lasciò d'acqua ripien['][217] concavo seno, / [60ᵛ]
che quasi sembra un piccioletto stagno.   40
Ivi cadd'egli appunto; io con un salto
ratto mi getto a nuoto[218] entro a quel[l'] onda,
in breve spazio lo sospingo a riva.
Ivi intanto eran giunti Silvio e Tirsi,
tratti dal caso, o pur dal grido stesso   45
ch'a me interruppe il sonno, et uniti insieme
risvegliandolo, di peso sopra l'erba[219]
lo ponemmo a giacere; e fatti accorti
del lieve respirar che non in tutto
abbandonat' avea l'anima e sensi,   50
chi gli rallenta il sen, chi gli riasciuga
la chioma, e 'l volto, e chi con altri uffizii
ravvivar cerca gli smar[r]iti spirti.
Mentre siam' tutti a la bel[l'] opra intenti
sentian di pianto feminile[220] intorno   55
doloroso concento. Ecco infuriata
d'Alfe[s]ibeo la figlia che veloce
ver noi venia, battendo palma a palma,
pur Filemon gridando ad alta voce.
Allor fisso mirando il corpo esangue   60

---

[215] *triemo.*
[216] *Subbito.*
[217] *Repieno*: line 39 has 12 syllables in M; apocope is surmised.
[218] *nutoto.*
[219] Lines 46–7 have at least 12 syllables.
[220] *feminille.*

frightful cry pierced my ear and chased sleep away. At this, raising my eyes in the direction whence I heard the terrible sound, I saw such a fall, and heard such a commotion: a man tumbling down from the top of the cliff! Even to think back to it I tremble and go cold. Quickly I jump to my feet and run to the spot I think I will find that poor man in pieces.[176]

But, as Heaven wished it (holy Innocence, when did you ever lack for shield or protection!),[177] his long fall was interrupted at the foot of the great cliff, just where a little stream, swollen with rain, had filled a hollow, / [60ᵛ] making what looked almost like a little pond. He fell right into it. With a hasty jump, I dive straight into the water, and quickly push him to the bank.

In the meantime, Silvio and Tirsi had arrived, drawn either by chance or by the same cry which had interrupted my slumber,[178] and we joined together to revive him. We heaved his body onto the grass, and from his light breathing discerned that his soul and senses had not yet fully abandoned him. One of us works to loosen the breast of his garment; another dries off his locks and face; and another tries to recover his lost senses through other means.

While we are all intent on this weighty task, we hear the mournful tones of female lament nearby. Then we saw Alfesibeo's daughter coming towards us quickly in a fury, beating palm against palm, crying out loudly for Filemone.[179] Then looking intently at the pale body,

riconosciam che Filemone è quello
che nelle braccia de' suoi cari amici
era vicino a terminar la vita.
Qual dolor ci trafisse il cor nel petto / [61ʳ]
chi spirto ha di pietà per sé lo stimi.   65
Giunse intanto Clorilli, e giunt'appena
fermò gl'occhi in quel volto esangue²²¹ e smorto,
ch'allargando le braccia abbandonossi
tutta sul petto a Filemon, e svenne.
O che pietosa vista a gl'occhi nostri[!]   70
Al pianto che da gl'occhi di Clorilli
gli cadea sul volto a Filemone
rinvenne, e gl'occhi aprendo gravi e stanchi,²²²
nelle luci di lei, che in sé tornata
fisso lui rimirava, anch'ei s'affisse;   75
così si rimirar taciti immoti
per breve spazio. Indi in un punto stesso
duo tai sospir dall'una all'altra bocca
uscendo si incontrar, ch'io mi credei
che l'una e l'altra anima bella insieme   80
lasciando il mondo se ne gisse al Cielo.
Di nuovo ella cadendo in abbandono
ricongiunse il bel viso al suo bel viso.
Ambi parlar volean, ma s'udia solo
tra lagrimosi baci e tra sospiri   85
un roco mormorio, che di pietade
facea lagrimar que' colli intorno.
Pur Filemon che dall'alta ruina / [61ᵛ]
altro danno non ebbe che 'l timore,
come poscia si vidde; alzando gli occhi   90
diede di vita a noi certa speranza,
e le braccia movendo al sen si strinse
la sua Clorilli, ch'ormai fatta certa
della sua vita, baldanzosa e lieta
a seder sollevollo in su l'erbetta;   95
quivi con quanta gioia, e quanta festa,
con quai segni d'amor, con quai parole
soavi e care, l'uno amante all'altro

²²¹ *essangue.*
²²² *stancchi.*

we recognize that it is Filemone who is so close to death in his dear friends' arms![180] Such grief pierced our hearts then, / [61ʳ] as anyone who feels pity can understand. Clorilli reached us then, and just as she did, she fixed her eyes on Filemone's pale and lifeless face. Opening her arms wide, she threw herself on Filemone's breast and fainted.

Oh, what a piteous sight before our eyes! Tears fell from Clorilli's eyes onto Filemone's face and he awoke. Opening his heavy, weary eyes, he looked into hers; having come back to her senses, her gaze was also fixed on him. And so they gazed at each other for a brief moment, wordless and still. Then, at the same instant, two sighs escaped from each of their mouths to meet together; so great were these sighs that I was certain their beautiful souls were leaving the world to ascend to Heaven together.[181] Her beautiful countenance joined with his, as she swooned yet again with abandon. They both tried to speak, but amidst their tearful kisses and sighs all that was audible was a wordless murmuring that made the surrounding hills weep with pity.[182]

Filemone confirmed our hopes as he raised his eyes: as we now saw, he had suffered no injury from his great fall, / [61ᵛ] only fear, and, opening his arms, he clasped his Clorilli tightly to his chest. Now that she was reassured that he was alive, she, happy and bold, raised him up to sit on the grass. With what joy and cheer, what signs of love, and what soft and tender words, one lover revealed to the other the ardent fire in their

	scopriva del suo cor l'ardente foco,	
	questo mi taccio, che stimar non puote	100
	uman pensier, nonché ridirlo altrui.	
COR.	O fortunati amanti	
	il Ciel conservi eternamente in voi	
	pura fé, casto amor, vita felice[!]	
	Ma raddoppia il contento,	105
	che mi rendi nel cor, Licandro mio,	
	con darmi nuova di Fillinio ancora,	
	che oggi come pur sii s'è ritrovato?	
LIC.	Mentre tra lor gl'[a]v[v]enturosi amanti	
	rammemorando già de' loro amori	110
	i diversi successi, or lieti or tristi,	
	chiese a Clorilli Filemon chi fosse / [62ʳ]	
	quel pastor che da lei sì caramente	
	raccolto fu cagion del gran periglio.	
	Che era Fillinio il suo fratello amato	115
	gli rispos'ella, che di lungo esilio	
	ove lo tenne Amor gran tempo absente	
	ritornava a veder le patrie mura,	
	il vecchio padre²²³ e' suoi diletti amici.	
COR.	Caro Fillinio mio, tu sei pur vivo?	120
"	O Fortuna regina	
"	di quanto copre il Ciel, come ben sai	
"	tornar felice e lieto	
"	qualor t'aggrada ogni infelice stato.	
"	Oggi pur, tua mercè,	125
"	quanto turbonne Amor si fa sereno.	
	Ma dove potrei io trovar Fillinio,	
	che pur vorrei questo felice giorno	
	per doppie nozze ancor veder più lieto?	
LIC.	Questo non ti saprei dir per l'appunto,	130
	ma dal grido comun là tratt' anch'egli	
	sarà da' nuovi sposi dove a gara²²⁴	
	del fiesolano monte	
	è concorso ogni ninfa, ogni pastore.	
	Ma poiché non si vede / [62ᵛ]	135
	da nessun luoco comparir Dalinda,	

---

²²³ *Padre*: inserted above.
²²⁴ *aggara*.

hearts – of this I will be silent, for human thought cannot embrace it, still less convey it to others.

Coribante

O fortunate lovers! May Heaven forever preserve pure faith, chaste love and a happy life in you! But my Licandro, might you redouble this joy you bring to my heart by giving me whatever news you have of Fillinio, who has also returned today?

Licandro

As those lucky lovers were recalling the vicissitudes of their love, some happy, some sad, Filemone asked Clorilli about the shepherd / [62ʳ] she had lovingly embraced, who had been the reason for his brush with death. She answered that it was her beloved brother Fillinio, who had returned from a lengthy exile whereby Love had long kept him absent to revisit the walls of his homeland again, his old father and his dear friends.

Coribante

My dear Fillinio, are you really alive?

O Fortune, queen of all that Heaven surveys, how deftly you can turn any unhappy state to a happy and blithe one, whenever you choose![183] *Today, by your mercy, you now make serene what Love had unsettled.*

But where might I find Fillinio? For I would like to see this happy day made even happier through a double wedding.[184]

Licandro

I would not know exactly where to tell you, but from the common cry yonder my guess is that he is with the bride and groom at the Fiesolan mountain, where all the nymphs and shepherds have rushed to foregather. But since / [62ᵛ] Dalinda does not appear from any direction,

non voglio più tardar
a dar questa felice e lieta nuova
a' padri di Clorilli e Filemone,
che sol per questo effetto io mi partii.   140
Ma temo, tanto mi son qui fermato,
che da' figlioli stessi avran la nuova,
pur non vo' rimaner d'andarvi anch'io,
tornerò poscia anch'a veder Dalinda.

COR.   Va pur, e se per sorte   145
t'incontrassi in Fillinio, fa che sappia
come Dalinda et io l'andiam cercando.

LIC.   Farò quanto comandi
tanto più volentieri ch'io vedo ancora
ch'ei lei vada cercando,   150
perché la voce è sparsa omai tra tutti
del suo ritorno et forz' è ch'a quest'ora
sia giunt'anch'all'orecchia di Fillinio.

COR.   Anch'io lo credo; or vanne dunque, a Dio.

Scena seconda

Coribante

COR.   Ma dove sarà gita,   1
ch'io non la veggio in alcun luoco?
Forse per tema di non esser vista / [63ʳ]
si sarà ascosa, o vero
temendo che la speme ch'io li diedi   5
della vista del suo caro Fillinio
fallac[e] sia se ne sarà di nuovo
fuggita in qualche parte.
O pur d'amaro assenzio
oggi non turbi il Cielo   10
questa nostra dolcezza.

I will not delay any longer in giving this happy and joyful news to Clorilli and Filemone's fathers. It was only for this that I left the celebration. But I fear I have stayed here so long they will hear the news from their own children! Even so, I shall not refrain from going there myself. I will return afterwards to find Dalinda.

Coribante
Go on ahead. And if by chance you happen upon Fillinio, let him know Dalinda and I are looking for him.

Licandro
I will do what you ask more than willingly now that I see that he is still searching for her. For by now, word of her return has spread amongst everyone, and by this hour it must have reached Fillinio's ears.

Coribante
I believe so as well; now go on then, farewell!

Scene Two

Coribante

But where could she have gone, why do I not see her anywhere? Perhaps she has hidden herself / [63^r] for fear of being seen. Or else, fearing the hope I gave her of seeing her dear Fillinio was false, she has fled again.

Oh, may Heaven not make bitter wormwood of our sweet happiness today!

Dalinda, Coribante

DAL.	Coribante non torna, et io meschina	1
	quasi a raggio di sol falda di neve	
	mi vo pur consumando.	
COR.	Ove volgerò il passo	
	per ritrovarla? O Dalinda, o Dalinda	5
	ove sei tu nascosa?	
DAL.	Eccolo appunto.	
COR.	O sia lodato il Ciel che a' miei desiri	
	cortese aspira, o Dalinda, o Dalinda,	
	il tuo Fillinio è vivo, e sano e lieto.	
DAL.	Il mio Fillinio è vivo?	10
COR.	È vivo il tuo Fillinio, et oggi pure[225]	
	di te cercando a questa fonte è stato, / [63ᵛ]	
	così Clorilli sua sorella afferma.	
DAL.	E mi cerca Fillinio?	
COR.	E ti cerca Fillinio, et di desio	15
	di rivederti si consuma e strugge.	
DAL.	Felicissimo giorno,	
	giorno felice et lieto,	
	prescritto al piacer mio,	
	giorno che l'alma acqueti	20
	del suo caro desio.	
	Sempre festoso e caro	
	a me ritornerai.	
	Così 'l tuo bel sereno	
	nubilosa tempesta	25
	non ricopra già mai,	
	ma sempre a prova i fiori	
	fiorischin per le piaggie,	
	e pargoletti Amori	
	danzando lieti a questa fonte intorno	30
	rendin solenne il memorabil giorno.	
	Si rinselvin le fiere	
	più feroci et più forti,	
	et solo a liet[e][226] schiere	

---

[225] Line 11: written in M as two lines, split after 'Fillinio'.
[226] *lieti*.

Scene Three

Coribante, Dalinda

Dalinda

[*Aside*] Coribante is not coming back, and I am wretched, wasting away almost like a snowflake melted by a ray of sun![185]

Coribante

[*Aside*] Which way should I go to find her? O Dalinda, O Dalinda, where have you hidden yourself?

Dalinda

[*Aside*] Here he comes now!

Coribante

Oh, may Heaven be praised, for it kindly grants my wishes. O Dalinda, O Dalinda, your Fillinio is alive, and healthy, and happy!

Dalinda

My Fillinio is alive?

Coribante

Your Fillinio is alive, and he has been searching for you today by this very fountain. / [63ᵛ] So says his sister Clorilli.

Dalinda

And Fillinio is looking for me?

Coribante

And Fillinio is looking for you! And he is consumed by desire – melting with desire! – to see you again.

Dalinda

O happiest day – happy and cheerful day, decreed for my delight.[186] Day that quiets the soul of its dear desire, you will always be joyous and dear in my memory. May your beautiful calm skies never be eclipsed by storm clouds, but always see flowers flowering by the shores, and may little Cupids dancing happy around this fountain solemnize this memorable day. May the strongest and most ferocious beasts return to the forest, and only happy nymphs and shepherds join our merry band, and may the

venghin ninfe e pastori,   35
e da' monti vicini / [64ʳ]
calin' le boscareccie e sacre dive,
e con lieti sembianti
celebrino il gioire
di noi felici amanti.   40
E voi chiare e fresch'acque,
non vi turbi già mai
la vostra onda tranquilla
stuol d'assetato armento,
ma sol Diana con le vaghe ninfe,   45
al più cocente ardore,
bagni le membra in queste pure linfe.
Chi mi dà un nuovo core
ov'io possa albergare
quest'allegrez[z]a mia?   50
Che sì avvezzo al dolore
è questo mio, che tutta
non la potria capire.
O Fillinio, mia vita,
è pur ver che tu viva?   55
Oggi quest'occhi miei
pur saranno beati
della tua dolce vista.
O Dalinda felice,
fortunati martiri,   60
dolcissime mie pene / [64ᵛ]
s'a così lieto fine
guidar voi mi dovevi.
O Lidia mia, da te pur riconosco
questo presente bene.   65
Tu contro al mio volere
ne' tuoi sacrati orrori,
viva m'hai riserbata a tanta gioia.
Sia benedetto 'l giorno
ch'in te m'avvenni, et benedette l'ore   70
ch'io son vissuta teco.
O pur mill'anni e mille
a te si giri il Ciel cortese et pio:
a' tuoi casti pensier sempre secondi,
Lidia gentil, per cui felice or vivo.   75

sylvan and sacred goddesses descend from the nearby mountains / [64ʳ] and smilingly celebrate the joy of us happy lovers.

And you, clear and fresh waters,[187] may your tranquil waves never be troubled by thirsty herds of cattle, but may only Diana and her winsome nymphs bathe their limbs in these pure springs in the most searing heat of the day.

Who will give me a new heart, where I can house my happiness? For mine is so used to woe that it could not offer shelter to so much joy.

O Fillinio, my own life, is it really true that you are alive? Today these eyes of mine will be blessed by the sweet sight of you.

O happy Dalinda, my sweet sufferings are fortunate torments, / [64v] if they were leading me to my happy ending with you.[188]

O my Lidia, it is you I must thank for my present happiness. You kept me alive against my wishes in your sacred shadows and sustained me for this joy. Blessed be the day that you found me and blessed are the hours that I lived with you![189] Oh, may kindly and holy Heaven revolve around you and reward your holy thoughts for many an age, noble Lidia, for you are the reason why I am alive and happy today.

COR.	Dunque con Lidia sempre,
	de la gran Dea ministra,
	stata ti sei ne la spelonca sacra
	da ché noi ti perdemmo?
DAL.	Sempre d[i]poi nel suo solingo albergo	80
	stata son'io, che morto
	falsamente credetti il mio Fillinio:
	ella m'accolse allor che disperata
	per uccidermi avea già pronto il dardo,
	e mi condusse a la solinga stanza.	85
	Ivi con saggi detti, e dolci preghi, / [65ʳ]
	m'ha conservata a sì felice vita.
COR.	Sempre felice e lieta
	sia tu Lidia gentil, né lasci il Cielo
	senza degna mercede opra sì bella.	90
	Ma qual pastor vegg'io
	che verso noi vien sì festoso e lieto?
	Egli è 'l gentil Aurindo.

Scena quarta

Aurindo, Coribante, Dalinda

AUR.	O leggiadra Dalinda, egl'è pur vero	1
	che del tuo bello aspetto
	sei ritornata a far Fiesol più bello?
DAL.	Il Ciel cortese Aurindo
	come tu vedi al fin m'ha ricondotto	5
	a queste selve, a questi colli amati.
	Ma di Fillinio mio che dir mi sai?
AUR.	Di casa Ergasto or vengo, ov' egli insieme
	con Filemon e con Clorilli è giunto
	con infinita schiera	10
	di pastori et di ninfe,
	lieto, che la sorella è fatta sposa
	di Filemon. Ma vi è più lieto assai
	del tuo ritorno, e si consuma e strugge, / [65ᵛ]
	egli non pur ma tutta quella gente,	15
	di rivederti. Or che più tardi? Vanne
	a raddoppiar le feste e l'allegrezze
	pria che per trovar te di là si parti.

Coribante

Then you were with Lidia, priestess of the great goddess, in her sacred cave from the moment we lost you?[190]

Dalinda

I was in her solitary abode the whole time, since when I first falsely believed my Fillinio to be dead. She took me in when I was desperate, ready to kill myself with my arrow, and she led me to the solitary chamber. There she restored me to happy life / [65ʳ] with wise words and sweet prayers.

Coribante

May you always be happy and cheerful, noble Lidia, and may Heaven not neglect to grant you worthy recompense for such a gracious deed! But what shepherd is this I see coming towards us, so joyous and gay? It is the noble Aurindo!

Scene Four

Aurindo, Coribante, Dalinda

Aurindo

O charming Dalinda, is it really true that you have returned with your fair countenance to make Fiesole more beautiful?

Dalinda

As you can see, gentle Aurindo, the Heavens have brought me back to these woods, to these beloved hills. But what news can you tell me of my Fillinio?

Aurindo

I come now from Ergasto's house, where Fillinio arrived together with Filemone and Clorilli, and an endless number of shepherds and nymphs, happy because his sister has been made Filemone's bride. But he is even happier about your return, and is most impatient / [65v] to see you – not just he but everyone is. Now, why delay any longer? Go and double the celebration and merriment before they leave in search of you!

DAL.	E tu non vòi venire?	
AUR.	Verrò poi ancor io,	20
	com' abbia dato[227] una rivista al gregge.	
COR.	Andia[n] Dalinda, andian, che non partisse.[228]	
DAL.	Prestami l'ali Amore,	
	ch'io voli ov'è 'l mio ben, ov'è l'mio core.	
COR.	Aurindo, se Licandro	25
	vedessi a sorte dilli[229] ove noi siamo.	
AUR.	Dirogliel' s'io l'incontro.	

Scena quinta

Aurindo

[AUR.]	Chi creduto averebbe	1
	che Filemon precipitando fosse	
	d'ogni sua contentezza al sommo asceso,	
	e che Fillinio errando	
	doppò sì longo et periglioso esilio	5
	trovato avesse anch'ei riposo et pace?	
"	O quanto ascose sono / [66r]	
"	ad uom mortal le vie	
"	onde ne sorgi alle tue gioie Amore.	
"	Te mai non biasmi o 'ncolpi	10
"	perché tra scogli e scirti	
"	d'amorosa tempesta	
"	talor ondeggi travagliato amante;	
"	dopo il soffrir crudele	
"	di repulse e di sdegni	15
"	venti contrarii all'amorose voglie	

---

[227] *doto*. The initial *Com'* is an emendation in M of *Come*.
[228] *Andiamo*: apocope (and repeated verb form 'andian') surmised, as line 22 has at least 12 syllables.
[229] Tuscan (non-Beman) form of *digli*.

Dalinda

And won't you come as well?

Aurindo

I will return, after I have checked on my flock.

Coribante

Let's go, Dalinda, let's go, lest he leave before we arrive.

Dalinda

Love, lend me your wings, so that I might fly to where my happiness is, where my heart is!

Coribante

Aurindo, if by chance you see Licandro, tell him where we are.

Aurindo

I will tell him if I chance upon him.

Scene Five

Aurindo

Who would have believed that by falling, Filemone would have reached the summit of his every happiness?[191] And that by wandering after such a long and hard exile, Fillinio would also have found rest and peace?

O Love, how hidden are / [66ʳ] the ways by which mortals ascend to your joys![192] May no one blame or condemn you if a beleaguered lover sometimes struggles amidst the rocks and gales of an amorous tempest, for after the cruel torment of scorn and rejection,[193] which are winds unfavourable to his amorous desires,[194] the calm harbour of Love is even more sweet.

“   vie più dolci d'Amor la calma e 'l porto.
Ma d[eh] non voglia mai la ninfa mia
far del mio amor sì perigliosa prova.
Creda quest'occhi ch'io   20
fermo talor sì desiosi in lei
senza risch[i]o mortale,
al mio verace amor acquistan fede
pianti, sospir, e domandar mercede.

Il fine

But, ah, may my nymph never test my love in such a perilous way![195] May she trust in these eyes that I fix so longingly on her, without the need for mortal risk, and may her faith in my true love be won through tears, sighs and begging for mercy.[196]

The End

Notes

1 On the coded name 'Leonora Belatta', see *CPr*, 93 and Section 2.2; for full title page, see Section 2.2.5.

2 Venus's errant son, Cupid, prefigures the key theme of erotic love typical of pastoral plays. Compare the very different representation of Venus's search for Cupid in Tasso's 'Amore Fuggitivo' (stanzas 2–3), possibly meant as a postlude to *Aminta* (printed in Tasso, *Rime* (Ferrara, 1581)), see Section 2.1.5 and 111 n. 151. For madrigals by Bernardi and their musical settings, see Section 3.

3 For Linfadusa, an immortal enchantress (*fata*) who appears only in the prologue, see Section 2.1.3 and 2.1.5. The name appears invented, perhaps as portmanteau of *linfa* (sap, vital lymph) suggesting springtime, regrowth and pure springs (associated with Diana and her nymphs as at V.3.47) and Medusa, one of the mythological Gorgons (thanks to Jane Tylus for this suggestion). The term *fata* is linked with the idea of fate or destiny (Italian *fato*, antiquated pl. *le fata*); in classical mythology, three ancient goddesses or *parcae* spun the threads of human destinies.

4 Demogorgon was the progenitor of the pantheon of pagan gods and associated also with Orphic singing, according to a mythographic tradition started chiefly by Boccaccio's *Genealogie deorum gentilium libri* (*Genealogy of the Pagan Gods*) and popular especially in Florence (Coleman, 'Boccaccio's Demogorgon', 1–6). A 1583 Medici performance of Giovanni Fedini's comedy *Le due Persilie* featured Demogorgon in the first inter-act spectacle (*intermedio*) set to music by Jacopo Peri.

5 Atlas was an ancestor of Noah and the founder of Fiesole, according to mythologizing accounts of Florence's legendary Etruscan past such as that found in Sansovino, *Le antichità*. See Bizzocchi, 'Tra Ferrara e Firenze', esp. 10–1. For Fiesole (Phaesyle) as the daughter of Atlas, see Wright, 'Some Medici Gardens', 56 n. 69. In classical mythology, the titan Atlas is condemned by Jove to hold up the heavens eternally, and later transformed into the Atlas mountain range (*Met* IV.639–61).

6 Dardanus was a legendary hero of divine birth, who was variously considered the founder of Dardania, the kingdom of Troy, or Corythus in Etruria (Tuscany). Pierfrancesco Giambullari (Florence, 1495–1555) presented Dardanus as the son of Atlas, who fled to Candia and then Phrygia to found the kingdom of Troy. For Dardanus as the Etruscan progenitor of the Trojan Aeneas, see *Aen* III.167, 170; VII.209; IX.10. On Virgil's partiality for the Etruscans, see Horsfall, 'Corythus', 76–9. On the importance of the myth of Florence's Etruscan foundations for the Medicean principate to legitimate Cosimo I de' Medici's political status and territorial expansion as a counternarrative to the Roman line, see Fantoni, 'Il simbolismo', 17–26; Fantoni, 'The Courts', 271–2; Bizzocchi, 'Tra Ferrara e Firenze', 7–9, 14–5; Cipriani, *Il mito etrusco*, 85–6, esp. 173–215.

7 Eraclitea and Gloridaura are invented names like Linfadusa. According to a legend cultivated during the Medicean principate, Sicano and Italo were two of a long succession of ancient Etruscan kings (Cipriani, *Il mito etrusco*, 195). The Florentine chronicler Giovanni Villani (1280–1348) identifies them as the brothers of Dardanus; Sicano founded Sicily, Dardanus later founded Troy; Italo stayed at home to rule Fiesole (Villani, *Nuova cronica*, I.8–9).

8　Fiesole (Roman *Faesulae*) was a key city in the ancient Etruscan confederacy (c. ninth–eighth century BCE) strategically positioned on a hill above Florence. Taken by the Romans in 283 BCE, it reached its cultural height under Augustus. Under the Medici principate it was celebrated as part of the Tuscan empire (Etruria) famous for its piety and learning. It was, for instance, represented allegorically in the ephemeral structures for the 1589 dynastic wedding; see Cipriani, *Il mito etrusco*, 85n55, 180–3; Bocci Pacini, 'Faesulae'.

9　The nymph Egeria was wife to Numa, the peaceful ancient ruler of Latium. On Numa's death, Egeria fled inconsolable from the city to the forest. Diana took pity on her, and transformed her into a spring, traditionally identified with the one nearby Porta Capena in Rome (*Met* XV.478–561).

10　Medicean Tuscany is presented as the 'reborn' Golden Age ancient Etruscan empire and compared to glorious ancient powers across the world.

11　The classical myth of the Golden Age, often evoked in pastoral plays, was characterized by innocence, peace, justice and plenitude, in order to satirize the corrupt present (the Age of Iron, see n. 14 below) or, as here, for eulogy. See *Met* I, Hesiod, *Theogony*; *Ecl* IV and *Aen* VI.792–4, and esp. *Am* Chorus 1, II.1; *SPa*, 76–9; Costa, *La leggenda*; Levin, *The Myth*. For the cultivation of the Golden Age myth by the Medici in the arts since the time of Cosimo the Elder, see Houghton, 'Renaissance'; Cox-Rearick, *Dynasty*.

12　Ferdinando de' Medici became Grand Duke of Tuscany (1587–1609) after renouncing the cardinalature, and on 20 February 1589 he married by proxy in Blois Christine of Lorraine (1565–1637), a daughter of Charles III of Lorraine and Claude of Valois, and granddaughter of Catherine de' Medici (d. 5 January 1589) and Henry II of France; see Section 2.1.4–5.

13　Cosimo II's birth (12 May 1590), as the first male heir, was widely celebrated as ensuring Medici continuity, fulfilling a succession of triumphantly returning Medicean Cosimos. Cf. *Ecl* IV, thought to commemorate the birth of the 'saviour child' from the union of Anthony and Octavian's sister, Octavia, ushering in a new Golden Age.

14　Honour, truth, loyalty, piety and Justice (Astraea) fled in the Age of Iron, the wickedest of the four ages of mankind (*Met* I.128–50); for Astraea's return with the 'saviour child', see *Ecl* IV.6.

15　Steropes and Brontes were two of the Cyclops who, along with their brother Arges, forged Zeus's thunderbolts in Tartarus. According to Hesiod, they resembled gods except for their single eye in the middle of their forehead (*Theogony*, 139–46).

16　A eulogistic comparison to Jove casting lightning bolts, cf. *Clorilli* III.6.19–20. Ferdinando de' Medici is compared to Jove at II.6.65. The Scythians were a fearsome ancient warrior tribe whose influence extended across Central Asia, from China to the northern Black Sea bordering Europe. The reference suggests the extent of the infant's future empire and military might. Ironically, Cosimo II (r. 1609–21) would be a sickly and unheroic ruler.

17　The names evoke several key Medici family members and the dynasty's strategic concern with continuity. The former Grand Duke Francesco (1541–87) was Ferdinando's older brother and Bernardi's godfather; see Section 1.2.1. On Cosimo I's adoption of the image of Emperor Augustus (like Charles V), and Ferdinando's cultivation later of the formulae of empire in the arts, see Fantoni, 'The Courts', 261, 271, and 'Il simbolismo'; Houghton, 'Renaissance', 426–7.

18　Christine's dynasty is traced back via her father, Charles III Duke of Lorraine (1543–1608), to the hero of the First Crusade, Godfrey of Bouillon, who conquered Jerusalem in 1099 with his brothers Eustace (Eustazio) and Baldwin (Baldovino), as immortalized in Tasso's *Gerusalemme liberata* (1581). On Godfrey's exploits and their depiction in the courtyard of La Petraia, see Butters, 'Christine', 123, 174–5.

19　The Tuscan fountain is described as outdoing the waters on the classical Mount Helicon, the stream Permessus and the spring Hippocrene, considered the source of poetic inspiration. Both were sacred as the bathing place for the muses (Hesiod, *Theogony*, 5–6). On the fountain's centrality in the play, see Sections 2.1.4 and 2.4.2.

20　Lines 120–4: cf. *Inf* V.39 ('la ragion sommettono al talento'), V.100–7 (anaphora 'Amor'). The god Love or Cupid is traditionally depicted as a winged boy with a bow and arrow; lovers are generally defenceless against him. See above n. 2, and for a play on this convention, with Love disguised as a shepherd, *Am* Prologue, 1–19.

21　Lines 130–1: cf. *Am* Prologue, 76–77: 'Queste selve oggi ragionar d' Amore / s'udranno in nuova guisa.'

22 A meta-theatrical reference to the play's happy ending. Linfadusa thus acts as a liminal figure, commenting on and determining the action in opposition to Love in order to second divine dynastic prophecy.

23 Name omitted in manuscript at fol. 5r; see 2.3.2.

24 The classical goddess Dawn (Êôs or Aurora) was traditionally depicted as beautiful and rosy-fingered, driving away the night in her chariot drawn by winged horses. Bernardi's pastoral observes the neo-classical unity of time, so the play's action takes place within a single day.

25 The name Alcone (Alcon) appears only once in Virgil's *Eclogues* (V.9) and not in earlier pastoral. Though less commonly used in pastoral drama, it is found in Giovanni Battista Pona, *Tirrheno* (1589), Act V, and in Muzio Manfredi, *Il contrasto amoroso* (1602), V.6, fols 132–3.

26 Alfesibeo (Alphesiboeus) is a traditional name for a shepherd, following *Ecl* VIII (interlocutor), V.73. The name is found in various pastoral verse, probably referencing real figures, for example in Dante's *Eclogue* IV, Sannazaro's *Arcadia*, *Prosa* and *Eclogue* X and *Am* V.1.1928. For the oscillation of spelling (Alfezibeo) in the manuscript play (M), see *Clorilli*, note to 1.1 and Fig. 9.

27 Temples commonly form part of the pastoral landscape (following Sannazaro's *Arcadia*, esp. *Prosa* III) and the pastoral stage, though notably not in Tasso's *Aminta*. They could sometimes take elaborate forms, as for a production of Agostino Beccari's *Sacrificio* (1587). See the engravings to the Ciotti edition of Guarini's *Pastor fido* (1602), esp. Act IV; Ivaldi, *Le Nozze Pio-Farnese*, 9–10; and Cavicchi, 'Immagini e forme'.

28 Allegorical dreams and visions of problematic truth-status are commonly recounted in tragedies, pastoral plays and epic poetry. According to classical tradition, dreams may pass through the gates of horn or ivory; the first are prophecies of real events, the second are false and deceptive. The difficulty lies in distinguishing between them, and in interpretation. See Penelope's dream in Homer, *Odyssey* XIX, which similarly uses bird metaphors.

29 The dove is an animal loaded with Christological symbolism, representing peace, God's promise to man (Genesis 8:6–11) and the Holy Spirit. Here the dove represents Alcone's daughter, Dalinda; the 'dead dove' is her lover Fillinio, who is correctly shown to be still alive.

30 The name Nisa (Nysa) is referred to in *Ecl* VIII.18, and thereafter found in Renaissance pastorals such as Alberto Lollio's *Aretusa* (1564), Gabriello Chiabrera's *Alcippo* (1614) and Giovanni Capponi's *Orsilla* (1615). Pastoral drama (and Renaissance theatre generally) mostly avoids representing mothers; though for maternal figures in *Clorilli*, see Section 2.1.5.

31 Ergasto is a traditional pastoral name probably derived from the Greek ἐργαστήρ (labourer) and used, for example, for characters in Sannazaro's *Arcadia*, Tasso's *Aminta* and Guarini's *Pastor fido*.

32 Alcone's daughter Dalinda, with her beloved Fillinio, forms one of the two pairs of protagonists in the play, though she does not appear on-stage until Act 4, scene 4. The name Dalinda recalls a character from *OF* V; see Section 2.1.3.

33 The name Fillinio appears uncommon in pastoral drama; it is perhaps an adapted or portmanteau name (*philos* meaning friend or beloved), recalling the traditional female pastoral name 'Filli' (Phyllis). Characters named Fil(l)ino appear in Paolo Bozzi's, *Fillino* (1597); Dionisio Rondinelli's *Il pastor vedovo* (1599); and Guidubaldo Bonarelli's *Filli di Sciro* (1607) for a comic shepherd boy.

34 Diana is the Roman goddess of the hunt (Artemis in Greek mythology), who swore off marriage to dedicate herself to the single life and is traditionally surrounded by her devotee nymphs. Hymen is the god of matrimony, generally identified as the son of either Apollo and one of the Muses, or Dionysus and Aphrodite.

35 The name Filemone (from the Greek *philema*) means 'kiss' or some sort of affection, and it may in Christian culture imply also showing brotherly forgiveness (see St Paul's letter to Philemon). It also (perhaps ironically) recalls the Greek myth of the devoted couple, Philemon and Baucis, who were rewarded for their hospitality to the disguised gods Zeus and Hermes by being saved from death, and who were granted the wish to die at the same moment (*Met* VIII).

36 The diminutive *soletta* adds an emotional nuance difficult to capture in English, appending great vulnerability to her departure in solitude.

37 Italics are used to indicate *sententiae*, which in the manuscript are highlighted with two

c-shaped dashes in the left margin (*diple*). These were likely designed for readers rather than for performance. See Section 2.2.2, and Fig. 9.

38 Marriage was reaffirmed as a sacrament during the Council of Trent (1545–63), as was the importance of spouses freely choosing their own partner to avoid the abuses of forced marriages. See Section 2.1.3 and Act 3 scene 4; for Bernardi's own, seemingly unhappy marriage, see Section 1.2.4.

39 The motif of the return of spring points to the happy outcome of the tragicomedy and motifs of rebirth and renewal associated with the Medici (see Cox-Rearick, *Dynasty*). It may also refer to the actual time of year of the performance, possibly for the birth of Cosimo II de' Medici (12 May 1590) or his baptism in late April 1592. Cf. Linfadusa's Prologue, lines 133–7.

40 The name Clorilli is uncommon in pastoral drama but suggests a portmanteau of two traditional classical pastoral names, Clori (Chloris, or Flora the goddess of flowers; see Section 2.4.1) and Amarilli (Amaryllis), as well as perhaps recalling Tasso's virago heroine of *Gerusalemme liberata*, Clorinda. The opening scene follows Tasso's *Aminta* I.1 and many other pastorals in presenting an older confidante persuading her charge to love; see Clubb, *Italian Drama*, 15–8.

41 The name Armilla is uncommon in pastoral drama, though see Serono, *La fida Armilla* (1610) and Aleardi, *L'Origine di Vicenza* (1612) (offstage character). See also the tragedies of Maffio Venier (d. 1586) (*Hidalba*, 1596) and Valeria Miani (*Celinda*, 1611); Miani's features an Armilla similarly as a confidante favouring sensual love (Coller, *Women, Rhetoric*, 94–5). For Maffio Venier's verse in the Marciana manuscript containing *Clorilli*, see Section 2.2.4, and Appendix 2.2.5.

42 The tigers of Hyrcania (in modern-day Iran) were believed to be the fiercest on earth, and often in literary comparisons signify emotional cruelty and hardheartedness. See *Aen* IV.459; *Am* I.2.365.

43 Clorilli's speech is deliberately ambiguous. Filemone tragically fails to understand the condition she sets for her love.

44 Wedding rings were an important part of the betrothal process and marriage pact in early modern Italy, and a first promise of a lifelong commitment. Bernardino da Siena (1380–1444) insisted that once a ring had been exchanged and the wedding consummated, the marriage was permanent. The *fede* was often designed as two hands clasped together in a clear reference to a contractual agreement, a style going back to the Romans. See Lombardi, 'Marriage', esp. 98–100.

45 For the trope of the shepherd-lover roaming the forest mad with grief, see esp. *OF* XXIII.124–5, 134–6; cf. *Am* I.1.312–22 and Armilla's description of Filemone above. Clorilli's 'forsennata gridai' (line 59) recalls the abandoned Armida ('forsennata gridava') in *GL* XVI.40.1, and see stanzas 39–51. For a famous setting of Armida's stanza by Giaches de Wert as a madrigal (in *Ottavo libro*, 1586) for the Ferrarese *concerto delle dame*, see Maniates, *Mannerism*, 81–2; Stras, *Women and Music*, 261. On Clorilli's rejection of lament, see Sections 2.1.3 and 2.1.5.

46 Silvia self-consciously suggests the protagonist nymph of Tasso's *Aminta*, a virgin huntress resistant to love who was conquered by pity for her beloved.

47 Much of this section is written in the present tense, often used to lend vividness or *enargeia* to narrated accounts of events and to give greater emphasis to feelings.

48 A topos used by scornful beloveds to reject their lovers. Cf. Silvia in *Am* I.1.192–6.

49 The idea of astral determinism, where human fates are predestined by the stars (planets) was commonplace from antiquity, for example in Neoplatonic thought. Attitudes to astrology varied greatly among Christian thinkers, since it conflicted with the central doctrine of free will.

50 Cf. The declaration of independence by Ariosto's famous warrior woman Marfisa: 'Io sua non son, né d'altri son che mia' ('I am not his, nor am I anyone's but my own'), *OF* XXVI.79.7.

51 The 'Bull' is an astrological reference to Taurus, and to Zeus's abduction of the nymph Europa in the form of a bull. 'Twice around the Bull' suggests that it has been two years since Clorilli and Filemone were lovers, and that it is the season of Taurus, or springtime. The 'bel segno' ('great sign') made in the sky likely refers to Florentine hopes for a new Golden Age beginning with the reign of Ferdinando and Christine, and the birth of Cosimo II, also under the sign of Taurus. See Wainwright, 'The Fair Warrior'.

52 Cf. the repeated call by Dafne for Silvia to 'change' and follow love, *Am* I.1.97–8, 129, 256.

53 The poetic trope of *carpe florem*, exploiting the 'spring' of youthful love before the 'winter' of old age and death, dates to classical times; see Ausonius, 'De rosis nascentibus' ('On budding roses'), also Robert Herrick, 'To the Virgins, to Make Much of Time' (1648), in *Poetical Works*, 84. See also *Am* I.1.264–72; *GL* XVI.15.5–8.

54 The Mugnone river flows from Fiesole and joins the Arno in Florence. The use of adjacent rivers to signify towns and cities was common in Renaissance poetry and typical of pastoral, as in Sannazaro's *Arcadia*. The figure of *adynaton* (*impossibilia*) is commonly used in pastoral poetry.

55 On Atlas, see Prologue, n. 5.

56 *C* xxxv, l. 4.

57 Cf. *Par* XXXIII.145 ('l'amor che move il sole e l'altre stelle'). For the idea of Love's inscrutable laws and providential rule, *Am* V.1.1839–47. *Concordia discors* is the classical concept of the four discordant elements creating a perfect harmony together, theorized by Empedocles and Pythagoras and given its Latin name by Horace.

58 Proserpina (Greek: Persephone) was the daughter of the earth goddess Demeter. She was abducted by Pluto (Hades), the god of the underworld, and reigned over that realm during winter, returning to earth during the spring.

59 The crystal heart, its transparency allowing internal feelings to be seen by others, was a common Renaissance literary topos, especially in Pietro Bembo's *Asolani* (1505). See Bolzoni, *Il cuore di cristallo*.

60 Coribante's name suggests the ancient Greek Corybants (Korybantes), armed divine young males who performed ecstatic dances, though the character here is associated with reasoned male friendship; see Section 2.4.4. Coribante was also the name of one of the mythic Etruscan kings along with Dardanus, Sicano and Italo referenced by Linfadusa in the Prologue (Cipriani, *Il mito etrusco*, 195). Coribante's mention of Aronte and Tirsi (or Thyrsis, an archetypal pastoral name associated with Tasso himself in *Aminta*) evokes a wider community of shepherds engaged in traditional rustic pursuits, and accentuates Filemone's solitude.

61 The effect of anaphora by repeating 'I sang' ('cantai') at the start of three closely spaced lines, is one of the many lyric features found in Filemone's laments, see Section 2.1.5.

62 Cf. Tirsi's injunction to Aminta to be a 'bold man' ('uom ardito'), *Am* II.3.1051; see Section 2.1.3.

63 An allusion to the damned courtly lover Francesca's famous dictum, *Inf* V.103 ('Amor, ch'a nullo amato amar perdona'), here parodied in Coribante's inversion.

64 An appeal to conventional Aristotelian binary thought on the sexes, whereby the male was associated with reason and the mind, the female with the passions (including love) and the body, which justified the latter's subordinate status.

65 Lines 95–6: it is impossible to capture fully in translation the distinctive lyricism and aural effects of Filemone's speeches; see Section 2.1.5.

66 The fountain serves as the central point for the play's action; see n. 19 above. Fillinio's horrified description of the bloody spectacle he saw there when arriving to meet his lover Dalinda alludes to the classic tale of Pyramus and Thisbe (*Met* V.55–166). For a more detailed description of this *antefatto* and the misleading tokens pointing to Dalinda's death, see *Clorilli* III.4; and for Dalinda's version of events, IV.4.

67 The text implies that Fillinio prepares to attempt suicide on-stage out of despair, but retreats to keep his return secret. Bernardi hereby follows Guarini's recommendations for pastoral tragicomedy to temper tragic (as well as comic) emotions, by removing the terror, and representing only the danger of death, [Guarini], *Il Verrato*, 1051.

68 Lines 22–6: this *sententia* recalls Virgil's image of Aeneas as a storm-tossed oak ('velut annoso validam cum robore quercum') remaining resilient to Dido's pleas to return her love (*Aen* IV.441–9), adding a striking gender reversal.

69 Filemone evokes the myth of Icarus, the son of Daedalus, who perished when he flew too close to the sun, melting the wax in the wings his father had made for him (*Met* VIII.183–235). See also Petrarch's topos of the poet-lover being like a moth drawn, despite the danger, to the powerful flame of his love; *C* xix.

70 The god of Love (Cupid) characteristically bears a flaming torch with the power to kindle fire in, or melt the ice of, a cold beloved's heart. See *C* cxxv, ll. 11–3. Apollo (Phoebus), the Greco-Roman sun god, was himself conquered by Love various times, most famously for the nymph Daphne (*Met* I).

71 Mongibello is the Italian name of Mount Etna, the Sicilian volcano.

72 Petrarch similarly describes the soul as a besieged fortress, victim to warring emotions; *C* cclxxiv.

73 Cf. Armilla's instruction in I.5; and Tirsi's to Aminta, *Am* II.3.1051.

74 Licone is the name of the speaker lamenting his beloved's cruel indifference in Jacopo Sannazaro's *Eclogae piscatoriae* (*Piscatory Eclogues*) II, 'Galatea' (*c.* 1523). Armilla's fidelity to her dead lover highlights her virtuous observance of chastity as a widow (*univir*), as codified by St Paul and St Jerome, and modelled in the Renaissance most famously by Vittoria Colonna. Bernardi herself never remarried after her husband was murdered when she was 26; see Section 1.2.3.

75 Cf. *C* v, l. 9 ('cosí laudare et reverire insegna'); for love as producing fear as well as daring, *C* clxxxii.

76 Licasta appears only in this single scene of the play. For the suggestion that she may be a figure for the author, see Section 1.2.3. The name is unusual in pastoral drama, but is used for a tragic figure who laments the death of her lover (Agelao) in Bernardo Tasso's *Amadigi* LVIII.5–7. In Giambattista Marino's notorious *Adone* (1623), XIV, Licasta is the cross-dressed alter ego of the eponymous anti-hero. For Marino's verse in the manuscript, see 2.2.3 and 2.2.5 (Appendix).

77 In this extended, original, and highly mannerist Fraud metaphor, Licasta turns on its head the traditional misogynistic trope of the fickle and deceptive female beloved (as famously decried by the Satyr in Guarini's *Pastor fido*, I.5.29–80). Men are described as the real frauds in their relations with women. See Section 2.1.3.

78 Line 54 evokes the provocatively licentious dictum of Tasso's Golden Age chorus, *Am* I.681: 's'ei piace ei lice' ('if it pleases it is allowed').

79 This section on Cellia is highlighted in the manuscript by marginal markings (lines 71 and 264), possibly indicating its occasional function. The name Cellia evokes both the idea of a jest or hoax (*celia*) and concealment (*celare*). Bernardi's friend and correspondent, the aristocratic Benedictine monk Angelo Grillo, used a similar double pun in fashioning the pseudonym Livio Celiano, under which he circulated secular love poetry (McHugh, *Petrarch*, ch. 5). A Celia features also as the second protagonist nymph of Bonarelli's *Filli di Sciro* (1607), stimulating an academic debate concerning her 'double love'. See Section 2.1.2. On Bernardi's relationship with Grillo, see Section 1, esp. 1.2.1, 1.2.4, 1.2.6–7, Section 2.1, 106 n. 7, and Section 3.1.3.

80 The Po runs through the north of Italy, including Ferrara. The further reference to Cellia's marriage to a Tuscan 'Aldranio' strongly suggests that the nymph represents in pastoral disguise the Ferrarese princess and flamboyant cultural patron Marfisa d'Este (c.1554–1608), who in 1580 married Alderano II Cybo-Malaspina (1552–1606), marquis of Massa and Carrara, on the Tuscan coast near the border with Liguria. See Section 1.2.2.

81 The reference to 'Aldranio's noble lodging' is to the palace of the Cybo-Malaspina at Massa, which Duke Alberico I, Marfisa's father-in-law, began to build in 1563 for his new state.

82 The passage describes a journey by Marfisa d'Este and her retinue to Florence (metonymically evoked by the river Arno), passing through Fiesole (evoked by the river Mugnone). It suggests a visit Marfisa took with her husband, involving a brief stay with Grand Duke Francesco de' Medici and his consort Bianca Cappello at their villa Pratolino in August 1587. See Section 1.2.3, and Masetti Zannini, *Marfisa d'Este*, 142 n. 6. For Pratolino as a possible setting for the play, see Section 2.1.4.

83 Ilia appears to be an *à clef* character but her identity is obscure. She may represent a lady from the Florentine court or Tuscan aristocracy.

84 The mouth of the Magra River is around 12 miles north of Massa.

85 Aeolus is the god of the winds, which he kept enclosed in a large cave on the island of Aeolia. When unleashed, the winds could wreck ships in sea storms, as in the case of the fleet of Aeneas (*Aen* I, 52–4), and King Ceyx (*Met* XI). See also Homer, *Odyssey*, X.1. Virgil's episode forms the backstory to Sperone Speroni's controversial tragedy *Canace* (1542), in which Eolo (Aeolus) murders the infant son born from his own twin's incestuous love.

86 Cf. *R* mclxxxix 'Mal non prendea co' placidi sembianti' ('Per le nozze della Sig. . . . Malpiglia'). Tasso's poem may be directed to Lucrezia Malpiglia, daughter of his Lucchese friend Vincenzo Malpigli, who married in August 1591 around the time of *Clorilli*'s possible performance. Tasso praises the new bride for having always been armed against Love's weapons and

'l'arte di leggiadri amanti' ('the art of fair lovers'). Ironically, Lucrezia scandalously had her husband, Lelio Buonvisi, killed in 1593 by her lover. Grand Duke Ferdinando I intervened in the investigation and Lucrezia retreated as a nun to the Lucchese convent of Santa Chiara before being imprisoned in 1609–18 (Bongi, *Storia*). The image of the woman as the boat on a sea of lovers inverts the conventional Petrarchan image of the lover as a boat on a storm-tossed sea, which represents his state of amorous turmoil (e.g. *C* cxxxii); for a possible verse response in the Marciana manuscript, see Section 2.2.4.

87 This paradoxical image inverts the usual metaphorical significance attached to rocks in the sea, of firmness of purpose; here it is the rock of men's inconstancy that is battered in vain by the waves of women's constancy and good faith.

88 Proteus was a sea god, famous for changing into many forms (*Met* VIII). The translation 'sea-calves' for *foche* derives from John Florio's *Queen Anna's World of Worlds* (1611), consulted online at http://www.pbm.com/~lindahl/florio/search/205r.html, 30 January 2023.

89 The pro-feminist Ormindo suggests another *à clef* character, impossible to identify. A candidate might be the Bolognese poet Giulio Cesare Croce (1550–1609), who wrote a poem in praise of women and against misogyny, dedicated to Marfisa d'Este; see Section 1.2.5 and 63 n. 128. In Bonarelli's *Filli di Sciro*, the elderly shepherd Ormino is the father of Celia.

90 For the argument that men denigrate women because they are envious of them, see Moderata Fonte's near-contemporary dialogue, *Il merito delle donne* (written by 1592; published posthumously in 1600). See *The Worth of Women*, transl. Cox, 61.

91 A pyrope is a fiery red gem. Giulio Cesare Croce used this same positive term of comparison in his defence of women dedicated to Marfisa d'Este; see Croce, *La gloria delle* donne, A3r.

92 Lines 242–3 recall the opening line of Bernardi's famous *canzone* to the Virgin, 'Se pur fin su negli stella(n)ti chiostri', probably written in 1588, shortly before *Clorilli* (see Sections 1.2.4 and 3.1.2), as well as the danced finale of Emilio Cavalieri's oratorio *Rappresentazione di anima e corpo* (1600), with libretto by Padre Agostino Manni ('chiostri altissimi e stellati'); see Kirkendale, *Emilio de' Cavalieri*, 246.

93 Delia is an alternative name for Diana; see n. 34.

94 Alcone's sententious words explicitly refer to the chief Roman god Jove or Jupiter (Zeus in Greek mythology), but they are infused with the Christian idea of divine omniscience and providence underpinning human actions, as was characteristic of Counter-Reformation pastoral drama. See Sampson, '"Deggio ferma"'; Clubb, *Italian Drama*, 110–3, 178–80.

95 This playful encomium to Grand Duke Ferdinando (Dinando) and Grand Duchess Christine (Cristilla) was possibly inserted for a particular performance (or edition) of the play for which they were intended as the primary audience (see marginal marks at lines 28 and 169). The grand-ducal couple are praised in conventional terms – he is a new Jove, she a new Juno – indicating hopes that their union would solidify Florence as a new global power. See Wainwright, 'The Fair Warrior'.

96 The city is, of course, Florence ('Florentia'), which was historically associated with the lily or iris (*giglio fiorentino*); see Bergstein, 'Marian Politics', and *Par* XVI.148–54. The lily has associations with Marian purity and recalls the heraldic symbol of the French monarchy (fleur-de-lis) used by Florence from 1266. The Medici adopted the French royal insignia in their family blason from 1465 and used it to mediate Franco-Florentine relations; see Sturm-Maddox, 'Catherine de Medici'. The flower also points symbolically to rebirth, the arrival of spring and celebrations for Flora, the goddess of flowers (Ludi Florales, 28 April–3 May), as well as to the florin, the Florentine coin and symbol of prosperity. The 'double splendour' signals the equal power of the Medici–Lorraine consorts.

97 The Meuse flows from France (through the Duchy of Lorraine), north to Belgium and the Netherlands, emptying into the North Sea.

98 Juno (Hera in Greek mythology) was the chief Roman goddess, and the wife of Jove. She was associated with all areas of women's lives, and especially marriage and childbirth.

99 Corebo (from the Greek 'Κόροιβος' (Κόροιβος), meaning 'credulous') recalls Coroebus, a heroic young Trojan in *Aen* II who dies trying to save the priestess Cassandra. This pastoral figure may allude to the then archbishop of Florence, Alessandro Ottaviano de' Medici (1574–1605, later Leo XI), who had a Reformist agenda and a rather conflictual relationship with Ferdinando de' Medici, especially in the 1580s, though he played a key political role in securing Maria de' Medici's marriage to Henry IV of France; see Sanfilippo, 'Leone XI'.

100 Villa La Petraia came into Medici possession in 1544, and was gifted by Grand Duke Cosimo to his son Ferdinando while he was still a cardinal. It underwent extensive renovations beginning in 1588 and throughout the 1590s, after it was gifted to the grand duchess upon her marriage to Ferdinando in August 1589. It became her personal domain, which she enjoyed with her children and her ladies-in-waiting. See Section 2.1.4.

101 The name Amarilli must allude to a prominent court lady. Given the positioning of this name first in the list and aural similarities, it may evoke the young princess Maria de' Medici (1575–1642), the daughter of Grand Duke Francesco de' Medici and Joanna of Austria (and niece of Ferdinando I), who in 1600 married King Henry IV of France. The beautiful goddess of dawn, Aurora, in some accounts, rose from the sea in her winged chariot. Hesiod's *Theogony* presents her as the sister, rather than the daughter, of the sun god (Phoebus Apollo), but here the reference suggests that she is a virgin destined for a great marriage. The reference to her golden hair ('l'aurato crine') recalls also Bernardi's madrigal in praise of 'Flavia' (Section 3.1.5 iii, lines 1–2), possibly the cultural patron and protagonist Flavia Peretti Damasceni (1574–1606), grand-niece of Pope Sixtus V. In 1589 she married Virginio Orsini, following the machinations of his uncle, Grand Duke Ferdinando de' Medici, and was active in the latter's court. See Fragnito, *Storia*, 139, 141, 144–55, 164–7; Section 2.1.5.

102 The *à clef* reference to Onoria may suggest Leonora (Nora) Orsini, the daughter of Ferdinando's sister, the murdered Isabella de' Medici. Leonora was culturally active at the Florentine court in her youth, together with her cousin Maria de' Medici. Leonora's skills in painting or weaving (*tela*) are not documented, but, like her mother, she was a skilled musician and may have had an education in the visual arts. Maria de' Medici is, however, known to have created artworks (a woodcut and sketch) in the late 1580s and became an important art patron in France (Johnson, 'Imagining Images', 128). The reference may otherwise be to her sister-in-law, Flavia Peretti Damasceni Orsini (see note above), to whom her 'guardaroba' Andrea Arbustini dedicated a manuscript on making tapestries (*Libro per fabricar tele . . .* 1606), Boerio, 'Peretti Damasceni, Flavia'. For Leonora, see Smith, 'Leonora Orsini', 123–4; Murphy, *Murder*, 227–9, 348; for Leonora's abusive marriage in 1592, Cusick, *Francesca Caccini*, 50. For Leonora and Flavia, see Section 2.1.5.

103 Like the many other Medici villas developed during the reign of Ferdinando I, La Petraia had an elaborately designed and terraced garden, as figured in the lunette of Giusto d'Utens (1599–1602). Christine of Lorraine, a keen garden designer like her consort, designed a new garden for her villa which included specimens from various places, including Crete; see Butters, 'Christine', 134. The description alludes to the Golden Age topos of the garden in the state of eternal spring, though without any reference to erotic pleasure (cf. *Am* Chorus 1, and especially Armida's enchanted garden in *GL* XVI).

104 *C* ccxix, l. 3; see also Giovanni Gastoldi's madrigal set to a text of Pietro Malombra, 'Al mormorar dei liquidi cristalli', in *Il Trionfo di Dori* (1592), no. 27. For the aqueduct which filled La Petraia's great fishing pool (*vivaio*) and produced 13 water jets (mainly for irrigation) and for its single important fountain, see Luchinat and Galletti, *La villa*, 31–2. For the use in Medici villas of freestanding fountains displaying elaborate and ingenious sculpture, among other types of fountains, see Wiles, *The Fountains*, 19–31; and Goode, 'Pratolino'.

105 Christine loved recreational fishing in addition to hunting, and La Petraia had a reflecting pool well stocked with fish on the terrace below La Petraia's garden façade; Butters, 'Christine', 134.

106 The description of marble sculptures of pastoral and mythological subjects fits a tradition of *ekphrasis* in pastoral, and sophisticated play on nature and art, e.g. *Ecl* III; Sannazaro, *Arcadia*, III. In reality, La Petraia was richly decorated by leading court artists, with a frescoed courtyard by Ludovico Cardi da Cigoli (1559–1613); Saslow, *Medici Wedding*, 135.

107 Pastoral was traditionally associated with the lowest style and rustic matters, and so unsuitable in rhetorical terms for epic subjects (such as the Jove-like Ferdinando I). Here the self-conscious stylistic slippage playfully recalls *Ecl* VI and *Am* II.2.1024–35, which similarly introduce encomia.

108 Lines 166–9 (highlighted) closely echo the last tercet of Laura Battiferri's 1560 encomiastic sonnet for Eleonora di Toledo, Ferdinando I de' Medici's mother 'Felicissima donna, a cui s'inchina': 'Non le sdegnate prego, che'l gran Giove, / che fece e muove il sol, non prende a sdegno / l'umili offerte d'un divoto core' ('Do not disdain them, pray, for the great Jove, who made the sun and moves it, does not scorn the humble offerings of a devout heart'); *CLy*, 289.

109　The satyr may be referring to Diana, the powerful goddess who dwelt in wooded groves and was fiercely opposed to love, or the woodland goddess Pomona.

110　The semi-divine satyr – half-human, half-goat – was a characteristic, if marginalized, figure in pastoral drama. Normally male, this figure commonly formed a negative foil for the courtly shepherd-lover, being characterized by 'uncivilized' behaviour, including violence, sexual and behavioural excesses. By the late Renaissance there was a long tradition dating back to the ancient Greek satyr play of representing satyrs, visually, in literature and on-stage, including in contemporary court spectacles; see Nicholson, 'Crossing borders', and Section 2.1.5.

111　On the basilisk, see n. 117.

112　The 'half-goat God' is Pan and the 'triform goddess' is Diana, associated with Selene (or Luna) and Hecate. While the goddess is devoted to chastity (except in the case of the youth Endymion), the sculpted image may represent the mythological subject of Pan offering gifts to the goddess, as in Annibale Carracci's popular *Pan and Diana* fresco (Palazzo Farnese, Rome, 1597–1602). Similar precious artefacts as gifts or prizes are described in *Ecl* esp. III, V; Sannazaro, *Arcadia*, II, prosa, §8; Beccari, *Sacrificio*, III.2; and Lollio, *Aretusa*, III.4. For the contrast of love won by gifts with freely given love, typical of the Golden Age, see *Am* Chorus 1.

113　The Satyr (Ruscone) here references Jove's many transformations to justify an amorous assault on Clorilli; nearly all are included in Arachne's woven depiction of the abuse by the gods in *Met* VI. Jove transformed into an eagle to rape Asterie and Ganymede (*Met* VI.106 and X.155–62); a shower of gold which descended on Danae (IV.609–11, VI.105); a swan, in the rape of Leda (VI.112); a bull, to kidnap Europa (II.844–75); the goddess Diana, to seduce the nymph Callisto (II.405–531); a flame with Aegina (VI.118); and a serpent with Persephone (VI.114). Jove also transformed into a satyr to rape Antiope (VI.108–9).

114　In ancient Rome vanquished enemies were led in chains alongside the spoils of battle in ritual processions or triumphs. Armilla appeals to Clorilli, as victor in the 'battle' of love (the *domina* or 'donna'), to show the classical virtue of clemency towards her lover Filemone. Clorilli is presented here as a powerful and cruel dominatrix-beloved, following a topos from medieval lyric poetry.

115　The scorpion is the first of a series of symbols used here to reference love (and the beloved) as both deadly and life-bringing. Diana sent a scorpion to kill Orion after he threatened that he would kill every beast on earth; Jove made both into constellations following their battle. The scorpion thus gifted to Orion both death and immortality. The scorpion became linked also to deception and hypocrisy in love, and in the Renaissance the scorpion (and the scorpion type) became associated with the venereal disease syphilis. For the ambivalent iconology of the scorpion type, see Cohen, *Animals*, 263–90.

116　Armilla references the pains of unrequited love inflicted by the beloved, who can wound, kill and return to life (see *Am* II.2.836–8). Cupid was believed to shoot arrows tipped with gold and lead, which respectively fill their victims with uncontrollable desire and aversion (see *Met* I). It was a literary topos developed from *stil novo* models (see *C* clii) and combined with Christian misogyny to consider love as a sweet poison, and the female beloved as poisoner or serpent. On this topos in artistic and learned Florentine circles, see Gaston, 'Love's Sweet Poison', 249–88, esp. 274–81.

117　The basilisk is a hybrid mythological creature able to kill with both poison and its deadly gaze (Pliny the Elder, *Natural History*, Book 8, ch. 33). It is often referenced in Renaissance literature in discussions of the power of one's eyes – the portals to the soul, through which love enters, according to love phenomenology immortalized in *stil novo* poetry.

118　Alcippe was the daughter of Ares (Greek god of war). She was raped by Halirrhothius, son of Poseidon, who was caught in the act and killed by Ares. In Tasso's *Aminta* (I.1.177), the confidante (Dafne) similarly recalls her young charge's divine mother (Cidippe).

119　The idea of Love distilling elements of cosmic beauty in Clorilli alludes to Neoplatonic ideas and alchemical processes of interest to various members of the Medici family (notably Grand Duke Francesco), besides the topos of Zeuxis's painting of Helen of Troy by selectively imitating the most beautiful models (Cicero, *De Inventione*, II). Cf. Tasso's witty discussion of 'l'uccider piacendo' inspired by ''l gran maestro' – in this case, Nature and the female confidente (*Am* II.2.836, 840–4; also Chorus 2).

120　A reference to the most famous poet of the day, Torquato Tasso (1544–95), whose major works, and especially the pastoral drama *Aminta*, are alluded to consistently throughout the play. The Sebeto river empties into the Bay of Naples, where Tasso's birthplace Sorrento lies. The Po flows among other places through Ferrara, where Tasso served the ruling Este dynasty for much of his adult life.

121 Cf. 'O con le Grazie eletta e con gli Amori,' *R* ccclxix, ll. 76–80. Tasso's *canzone* is addressed to 'La Bruna', maidservant to the countess of Scandiano, Leonora Sanvitale. Sanvitale was a celebrated singer in the *concerto delle dame* at the Este court, arriving in Ferrara shortly after her marriage to Giulio Tiene, count of Scandiano, in 1575. She died in 1582, before we know Bernardi to have been at the Ferrara court. Cf. Tasso's self-quotation on the beloved's deceptive gaze in *Am* I.1.320–2. Tasso's poem references the phoenix, a mythic unique bird, who continually burns to ash and is then reborn.

122 The name Ruscone is unfamiliar in pastoral, but perhaps derives from the Latin 'ruscus' for a spiky (wild) plant. With the Italian augmentative suffix (*-one*) it approximately translates as 'great oaf'. Satyrs on the occasions when they are named in pastoral drama tend to observe classical names derived from Virgil, *Eclogue* IV (e.g. Cromi in Torelli's *Partenia*). A satyr called Rustico appears, though, in a Ferrarese play by Bernardi's contemporary Cesare Cremonini (*Le pompe funebri*, 1590).

123 The text here implies a fight between Fillinio and Ruscone, with the latter losing. Struggles involving satyrs on- and off-stage were common in pastoral drama, usually involving shepherds defending nymphs. Occasionally, nymphs themselves fight off the satyr's advances, as in the pastorals of Beccari, Andreini and Guarini, which provide possibilities for physical comedy (*lazzi*). See Section 2.1.5.

124 The *sententia* may recall the athlete Diagoras of Rhodes, who died from happiness after witnessing his sons' triumph at the Olympic Games of 448 BCE, as well as contemporary medical theories on the emotions. Annibale Pocaterra, a physician and poet contemporary with Bernardi in Ferrara, claimed in his *Dialogues on Shame* (1592) that joy 'causes the heart to swell up', leading to an outpouring of vital spirits 'comparable to a serious wound'. Gundersheimer, 'Renaissance concepts of shame', 50. On Pocaterra, see Section 2.1.2.

125 Fillinio's description of being not two years past his third 'lustro' (from Latin 'lustrum', a period of five years) has been simplified in the translation.

126 For the topos of the lover being like a moth attracted dangerously to the flame (his beloved), see *C* cxli.

127 Helios, the personification of the sun, is often depicted as driving a chariot pulled by horses across the sky.

128 The present tense ('tenghian') is again used in the Italian to add a sense of urgency.

129 This entire section is written in the present tense in the original Italian. Fillinio emphasizes the archetypal tragic emotions of horror or fear and pity.

130 Fillinio's story follows the much-imitated tragic tale of the star-crossed young lovers Pyramus and Thisbe, who had been prevented by their parents from marrying. In Ovid's version, Thisbe arrived first at the lovers' secret tryst but ran away from an encounter with a lioness, leaving behind her veil, which was falsely seen as a sign of her death by Pyramus, who killed himself, prompting Thisbe's suicide thereafter (*Met* IV, 55–166). The story underpins Tasso's *Aminta*, where Silvia's spear and blood stained veil are similarly found, this time with seven wolves nearby (*Am* III.2; and see *Am* IV.1), though the failure of her lover's suicide attempt allows a happy ending.

131 Cf. *Am* IV.2.1792–8. Clorilli wants to do the same in IV.3.251–3.

132 Cf. *C* clxxvi.

133 A playful allusion to the eponymous hero of *Aminta*, who wrongly interpreted his beloved Silvia's bloody veil as a sign of her death; cf. *Am* III.2.1401–6.

134 Echo was cursed by Juno to speak only the last words spoken to her as a punishment for her previous garrulousness; as a result, Echo was unable to tell Narcissus of her great love for him, and after his death she wasted away, leaving behind only her voice (*Met* III.339–401). Echo devices were often staged in pastoral plays following classical and humanistic models for pleasing poetic and musical effect, as well as to provide revelatory or prophetic responses, e.g. most famously Guarini's *Pastor fido* (IV.8), but also previously in Barbara Torelli, *Partenia* (III.3), Maddalena Campiglia, *Flori* (III.6), Leone De' Sommi, *Irifile* (III.2), Muzio Manfredi, *Semiramis boschereccia* (III.4, for comic effect) and Ingegneri, *Danza di Venere* (V.1, for ambiguous information). See generally, Imbriani, 'L'Eco responsiva', 279–314; in relation

to English literature and theatre, Loewenstein, *Responsive Readings*; and in Ferrarese music, Stras, *Women and Music*, 256.

135 This staged episode where Fillinio thinks he sees Clorilli embracing a new lover recalls especially *OF* V.46–54, where Ariodante believes he is seeing his beloved Ginevra betraying him with a rival suitor. This scenario, which draws on earlier sources, is used also in contemporary pastorals e.g. by Luigi Groto (*Pentimento amoroso*, III.7) and Guarini (*Pastor fido*, III.8); and is central to Shakespeare's *Much Ado About Nothing*. See Section 2.1.3.

136 A *principium* or proem was the beginning of a speech in classical rhetoric, usually intended to win the benevolence of the audience (*captatio benvolentia*). As Clorilli's ironic praise underlines here, Filemone's *principio* has precisely the opposite effect.

137 *Mercede*, meaning reward or recompense, and also mercy, kindness and compassion, was a key term in medieval and Renaissance love lyric, designating the benign response (or favours) lovers hoped to win from their beloved through their devoted love. On translating this term in contemporary performance, see Section 2.4.3.

138 Erotically induced anger (*amoroso sdegno*) was a fashionable subject in courtly lyric verse of this period; see, for example, the madrigals by Orsina Cavaletti and Isabella Andreini in *Cly* 172, 175. Within pastoral drama, the theme is especially associated with Francesco Bracciolini's play *Amoroso sdegno* (1611); see Section 2.1.3.

139 The notion of the face as the image of the heart within recalls Filemone's wish to have 'a heart of crystal' (1.4.29) so that Clorilli could read his feelings clearly.

140 Filemone's psychological hell resembles the classical vision of Tartarus, as described most famously in *Aen* VI. The torments alluded to are those of Tityos, whose liver is torn by a vulture; Ixion, broken on an eternally spinning wheel; and Tantalus, doomed to extreme hunger and thirst while tortured with visions of running water and banquets. The gravity of these classical figures' crimes (respectively, attempted rape (Tityos); murder and adultery (Ixion); the murder and serving up as food of a son (Tantalus)) underline the lightness of Filemone's 'small fault'.

141 Cf. Guarini, *Pastor fido*, III.8: the protagonist shepherd Mirtillo's desire for vendetta on his supposed love rival after witnessing an apparent betrayal.

142 Cf. *Am* III.2.1465: this scene similarly features the shepherd-lover rushing to commit suicide.

143 Shepherds and nymphs often go mad from unrequited love in pastoral drama and the pastoral mode generally, since the green setting allowed it 'more plausibly to represent certain [heightened] areas of emotional and psychological experience than comedy and tragedy' (*SPa*, 4). Madness allowed interesting stage performances (e.g. Ingegneri, *Danza di Venere*; Campiglia, *Flori*). The specific reference to Filemone in IV.2 as 'furioso' and 'forsennato' (out of his mind) recalls the madness of Ariosto's knight Orlando from unrequited love for Angelica (*OF* XIV.4.2). See also Clorilli's former love-madness ('forsen[n]ata', I.2.59 and n. 45 above.

144 The casual allusion to the nymph Nicilla may refer to an unidentified figure known by Bernardi's audience.

145 Armilla contrasts the destructive passions caused by Love and the god's cruelty towards his subjects (i.e. Filemone) with the pleasures of reciprocated love traditionally enjoyed in the Golden Age (cf. *Am* Chorus 1, esp. lines 682–94).

146 The play on the words 'fiera' or 'fera' (proud or cruel, or beast) points to Clorilli's delight in hunting wild beasts and her beast-like cruelty; see for the same pun, e.g. I.2; I.3.399–400. As suggested in Act 1 scene 2, Armilla references the common anti-feminist topos of branding female beloveds who do not reciprocate love as 'ingrates' (*ingrate*) and presenting them with future hellish torments if they do not repent (e.g. Boccaccio's *Decameron*, V.8; *OF* XXXIV.6–44; and *Am* I.1.282–96).

147 Tesbina's cave is mentioned only on this occasion in the play. This unidentified offstage location suggests a feminine space linked with Diana's nymphs.

148 Compare the more forgiving attitude of Tasso's confidante (Dafne) towards her charge in the corresponding scene in *Am* IV.1. Armilla's sentiment is, however, echoed by Tasso's Tirsi in *Am* III.1 and the chorus (*Am* IV.1.1628–9).

149 This common-sense maxim may recall *Am* III.1.1312–14. Suicide was deemed a mortal sin by the Church and against natural law and charity, as formulated for example by St Augustine (*City of God*, I.17–27) and St Aquinas (*Summa Theologiae*, II:2, 64, 5).

150 As in Tasso's *Aminta*, Bernardi features two messengers to recount false deaths, though both

her messengers are male. The messenger's narration offered the scope for virtuosic rhetorical performance, following classical tragedy. Aurindo appears a more tragicomic figure in the closing scene of the play.

151 Aurindo points self-consciously to the aesthetic pleasure derived from listening to love laments, a sub-genre then popular in oral poetry, song and theatre, derived from the Petrarchan and lyric tradition; see Sections 2.1.5.

152 It is unclear if a real mountain is alluded to here; one possible candidate is Monte Morello, the highest peak in the Florentine valley north-west of the city. Bernardi may be following Tasso's *Aminta* in evoking a place not identified with the Medici court in Act 4; see Quarta, 'Spazio scenico'; SPa, 74.

153 This draws on Petrarchan tropes of the steadfast, rock-hard nature of true love. Bernardi here conflates elements from two scenes of Tasso's *Aminta*: III.2, where Aminta mistakenly takes Silvia's bloody veil as a sign of her death; and IV.2, his reported speech before jumping to his death from a cliff from grief at Silvia's supposed death. They are adapted to fit with Filemone's misplaced belief in Clorilli's infidelity.

154 Referring to the Neoplatonic idea of the duality of the soul and the body, Clorilli suggests that her soul has migrated to her now-dead beloved, while her body lives on as an empty husk, and will continually suffer the pain of this loss.

155 The Italian 'empio fallire' brings a note of moral, even religious, censure. Deaths (including suicides) were normally avoided on stage out of decorum. Cf. the wicked nymph Corisca's acknowledgement of her sin (*peccato*) and formal pardon in Guarini's *Pastor fido*, V.9.

156 Clorilli has snatched up Filemone's arrow to kill herself onstage out of penitence, but she is prevented by Armilla. Cf. Aminta's suicide attempt offstage, *Am* IV.2.

157 Cf. *Am* IV.2.1792–3, where Silvia asks Dafne to help her find her lover's body. This is Clorilli's final exit from the stage.

158 *C* clii, l. 14: 'ben può nulla chi morir non pote'; cf. *GL* XX.131.

159 This is the first appearance of the more tragic female lover of the play, anticipated from the first scene of the play. Her account completes the narration of the 'frame' story (*antefatto*) by Fillinio in Act 2 scene 1.

160 Dalinda's style tends to be hyperbolic and poetic, in contrast to the clear, straightforward speech of Clorilli, which is more in keeping with comedy. See Section 2.1.3.

161 *C* ccvii, l. 66.

162 See also *GL*, VI.60.5–6. It was commonly believed that recounting unrequited (or lost) love lessened the pain. See Torelli, *Partenia*, I.1.37–43; though for a counter-example, see I.4.55–8.

163 Cf. *C* cclxxxvii, l. 6.

164 Cf. Alfesibeo's disapproval of this marriage arrangement by Dalinda's father (Alcone), I.1.172–84.

165 Dalinda's romance-style elopement to preserve her faithful love is explicitly condemned for contravening social norms, yet implicitly condoned given the play's happy outcome, see CPr, 108.

166 For earlier partial accounts of events, see II.1 and III.4. Cf. Silvia's encounter with a wolf in *Am* IV.1.1490–1527. On animals in pastoral drama, including the bear in Shakespeare's *A Winter's Tale*, see Clubb, 'The Tragicomic Bear'; Clubb, *Italian Theatre*, especially 140–6; and Nicholson, 'Crossing Borders', 343–4, 353–5.

167 Historic present is again used ('lacero').

168 Sendal ('zenzado', or *zendalo, zendado*) is a type of thin silken material. This band served as a token for Dalinda's (false) recognition of Fillinio's death, following Aristotelian principles for tragedy (*Poetics*, XVI). Cf. *Am* IV. 2.1738–42, Ergasto's account of his unsuccessful attempt to save Aminta from jumping off a cliff by grabbing the band of *zendado* around the shepherd-lover's waist.

169 A reference to the death of the first grand duke of Florence, Cosimo I de' Medici (1519–74). This continued to be commemorated thereafter in Florence on 21 April, as Cosimo remained an important presence in Florentine life and imagery. Funeral rituals and games modelled on those in classical epic (*Aen* V; Homer, *Iliad*, Book XXIII) have a long association with pastoral: see *Ecl* V, Sannazaro, *Arcadia*, *Prosa* V and Eclogue V; *Prose* X–XI, and, more contemporary to Bernardi, Campiglia, *Flori* (1588), III.4–5; Cremonini, *Le pompe funebri* (1590).

170 The gory description of Alcasto, a shepherd unrecognizably disfigured from being mauled to

death by a bear, is unusual in *Clorilli* and suggestive of a mannerist interest in death. It avoids, however, the morbid eroticism suggested in Bracciolini's *Amoroso sdegno* (V.2, fol. 54r) and in Erminia's desire for her seemingly dead beloved, Tancredi, in *GL* XIX.107; see *SPa*, 211. The name Alcasto recalls the fierce and proud crusader in Godfrey of Bouillon's army, who is ignominiously defeated by the enchanted forest in *GL* XIII.24–30. It may also suggest to the reader the brutal spectacle of Bernardi's husband's murder; see Section 1.2.3.

171 See Act 3, scene 3.

172 Dalinda's solo lament in which she expresses her conflicted state between grief and hope is punctuated by a two-line *ritornello*, separating out the stanzas. The first three refrains are identical; the final two have the same variant in the last line. Laments became very popular in the period, especially with the rise of virtuoso actresses and singers, and often formed the emotional high point of opera; see Rosand, *Opera*, 361–86, Refini, 'Parole tronche'; and Section 2.1.5.

173 Lidia, who cured and helped Dalinda, was pre-empted in Alcone's dream as the 'gemella compagna' ('twin companion') to his 'beautiful dove' (Dalinda) (I.1.59). The name Lidia may recall the early Christian convert of St Paul, who opened her house to him (Acts 16:11–15; 40). Though it is used also for an 'ingrate' in *OF* XXXIV, especially stanzas 11–43. In this context it more likely references a pious noblewoman (see also Act 5 scene 3). A possible candidate is the cultivated Leonora Cybo Vitelli (1523–1594), herself a poet and sister of Alberico I Prince of Massa, who retreated as a widow in 1575 to the convent of Le Murate in Florence; see Cruciata, 'An enigmatic portrait', 49–55.

174 Dalinda imagines Fillinio's soul may still be in the vicinity, waiting to reunite with hers once she is dead, suggesting the Neoplatonic notion of the separation of the soul from the earthly body, a recurrent theme throughout the play. On Neoplatonism in pastoral plays (including those of Maddalena Campiglia and Barbara Torelli), though the genre was more commonly associated with erotic love, see *SPa*, 39–42, 102, 104, 116–8, 121, 183.

175 Licandro appears only once in this play, as the second messenger; the manuscript omits his name from the cast list, probably a scribal error. His opening words bring an abrupt tonal shift after Dalinda's lament. Cf. Elpino in *Am* V.1. The pastoral name Licandro was used later, e.g. in Girolamo Manna's *Licandro* (1634) and in Mary Wroth's *Urania* (1621).

176 Cf. Ongaro, *Alceo* (1582), V.2 (Alceo similarly falls in water and is hauled out by fishermen); in *Am* V.1.1904–23, Aminta is saved by vegetation breaking his fall.

177 Cf. *GL* VIII.41.7–8.

178 Silvio and Tirsi are common pastoral names, used, for example, for the 'second shepherds' respectively of Guarini's *Pastor fido* and Tasso's *Aminta*. Their evocation reminds the audience of the broader pastoral community, in the absence of an onstage chorus.

179 Alfesibeo's daughter is Clorilli. Cf. *Am* V.1928: the physician Alfesibeo is called to save Aminta. Cf. *Am* III.1.1228, 'Dafne veggiam, che battea palma a palma'.

180 Licandro alternates between the past and present tense throughout his recounting of Filemone and Clorilli's dramatic reunion.

181 This Neoplatonic idea of soul-swapping between lovers as they finally kiss is often coupled with a more physical dimension in pastoral plays, e.g. in Ongaro, *Alceo*, V.2, fol. 52r.

182 Cf. *C* cclxxix, l. 3: 'roco mormorar di lucide onde'.

183 Lady Fortune or Fortuna is considered the goddess of fate, as well as of happy love, and is generally depicted as a blindfolded woman turning a wheel; see *Inf* VII.67–97. See also Albrecht Dürer's famous engravings of the unstable goddess: 'Small Fortune', 1495–96, and 'Nemesis (The Great Fortune)', 1501–2.

184 Marriages are traditional endings for comedy, as well as the tragicomic pastoral, and often multiple marriages are staged or announced to resolve interweaving plotlines. Here both couples are married offstage.

185 Cf. *C* ccxxxii, l. 19: 'consumando mi vo di piaggia in piaggia', as well as the broader Petrarchan topos of the snow being melted by the sun.

186 Dalinda's exclamation picks up on Licandro's opening words of the final act and is a last insistence on the motif of time and return which appears throughout the play (as in Petrarch's *Canzoniere* with its 15 anniversary poems commemorating the poet's first sight of his beloved Laura and her death). Dalinda's speech is highly patterned, similar to her *ritornello* at the end of Act IV – preponderantly in *settenari* and with quite a few rhymes, including at least one in juxtaposition ('intorno / giorno').

187 Cf, *C* cxxvi, 'Chiare, fresche et dolce acque'. Dalinda suggests the peaceful image of Diana and her nymphs bathing secluded in the waters of the fountain (just as Petrarch's Laura did in the Sorgue river). The insistence on renewal, and on water, may also suggest a reference to the Medici baptism presumably commemorated with the performance of the play.

188 Dalinda brings back the 'lieto fine' or 'happy ending' we are promised by Linfadusa in the Prologue (line 134). On the *tragedia di lieto fine* and the 'happy ending' in pastoral, linked with providential design and appealing to audience tastes, see *SPa*, 20–1, 24–5, esp. 48–50.

189 This line recalls *C* lxi, 'Benedetto sia 'l giorno, et 'l mese, e l'anno', in which Petrarch praises all the different forms of time (day, month, year, age, hour, moment) in which he first set sight on Laura.

190 Dalinda's seclusion in the 'sacred cave' of Diana is suggestive of a convent; it carefully guarantees the nymph's chastity during the years she lived apart from her family and her beloved. See also IV.5.38–41.

191 Cf. *Am* V.1.1848–9. Aurindo's closing speech is replete with allusions to Tasso's *Aminta*.

192 Cf. *Am* V.1.1843–6.

193 Cf. *Am* Chorus V.1993–4: 'soavi disdegni / e soavi repulse'.

194 Cf. *C* cxxviii, l. 105, 'venti contrari a la vita serena'.

195 The desire to avoid suffering in love recalls the more cynical, comedic stance of Tirsi in *Aminta* II.2.948–9 ('coglile e gusta / le dolcezze d'amore senza l'amaro'), and the final chorus. Cf. the desire for reciprocated love in the Golden Age chorus, *Am* I.

196 *Am* I.1.161, 'pianti, sospiri, e dimandar mercede'.

2.4 Green acts in green shades: Adapting and staging *Clorilli* at Villa La Pietra, Florence, spring 2018

Eric Nicholson

> [I]f the pastoral drama is performed in summer, as seems to be most fitting, in an outdoor place and during the daytime, it suffices that the stage is prominent and green, and that it brings spectators pleasure at first sight. And this can be done with ease, representing the most joyous seasons with fronds and flowers and fruit-bearing trees.

> [S]e la favola pastorale si avrà da rappresentare di estate, come par che più si convenga, in loco aperto, et di giorno, bastarà che la sua scena sia eminente et verdeggiante, et che, nello scoprirsi, porga vaghezza a' veditori. Et questo si fa agevolmente, rappresentando con le frondi e coi fiori, et con gl'arbori fruttuosi, le staggioni più alegre.
>
> <div align="right">(Leone De' Sommi, <i>Quattro dialoghi in materia di rappresentazioni sceniche</i>, c. 1570)[1]</div>

> Annihilating all that's made
> To a green thought in a green shade.
> (Andrew Marvell, 'The Garden', c. 1665)[2]

2.4.1 Green worlds

The choice of colours is a fundamental decision for any theatrical production. For an early modern pastoral play intended for outdoor performance, the use of green as a leading colour is an almost inevitable one, as affirmed by Leone De' Sommi, commentator, poet, playwright, impresario and high-profile member of late-sixteenth-century Mantua's Jewish community. From its inception in classical times, pastoral literature has had the green world of nature as both its setting and prime identity marker. In the case of Leonora Bernardi's *Clorilli*, this greenness is integral as well as multifaceted. The very name of the play's female protagonist incorporates the Greek word *chloris*, meaning green, especially the light green of the fresh moist grass and tender leaves of early spring, and it evokes the presiding goddess Chloris, a nymph associated in mythology with female sexuality.[3] Moreover, as Andrew Marvell's well-known couplet stresses, this kind of newly arrived (and returned) springtime 'green' can metaphorically evoke youthful ingenuousness and the phenomenon of 'the first (green) time'.

Appropriately, then, the outdoor production of *Clorilli, a pastoral drama by Leonora Bernardi of Lucca (1559–1616)* that I produced and directed with NYU Florence's La Pietra Players for a springtime public performance on 11 May 2018 was a green one, in multiple senses.[4] While the season was not yet the summer that De' Sommi recommends, the days of April and early May during which we rehearsed were getting longer and warmer, and were indeed filled with lush greenery, since our chosen performance venue was the extensive series of terraced garden spaces behind the imposing, three-storey main Villa La Pietra building, which dates from the fifteenth to the eighteenth centuries and now serves as the NYU Florence study abroad administrative base. Having little or no actual theatrical experience, many of the students of the cast and crew were themselves 'green'.[5] Perhaps the most significant and paradoxical aspect of the production's greenness was the fact that it was the English premiere – and the first ever revival of any kind – of a play written around the early 1590s, and possibly performed only once then. A theatrical bud had been waiting on a stem for over 400 years, and it was finally blossoming. Our goal, therefore, was to work through and past the potential limitations of this 'first time' condition and apply them to fruitful artistic outcomes. This process also relied on the work of our production coordinator Virginia Cox, together with scenic designer Cameron Anderson, with advice on the music by Emily Wilbourne.

The green worlds of our staging of *Clorilli* themselves necessitated an experimental coordination of time and space, in the modes of site-specific theatre, and of Performance As Research (PAR). Although resistant to definition, PAR is a methodological approach that favours process over result, heterogeneity and interdisciplinary practice over any single-perspective, unitary theory; it emphasizes physical, sensual and kinetic criteria in experimental, potentially transformative expressions of embodied knowledge. When used in a university-supported theatrical production such as ours, PAR is also a way to include and validate artistic activity in a research context, to coordinate creative play with academic study – in short, to practise 'investigating by doing'. As Annette Arlander puts it, 'PAR foregrounds performance or doing as a method in producing research material or data, or as a method in sharing research results, or any combination of these'.[6] Moreover, by an uncanny coincidence, NYU's campus in Florence is located across the valley from the neighbouring hilltop town of Fiesole: the slopes and streams of this area figure prominently in the script of the play (see Section 2.1.4). In this way, our performance venue, with its green leaves, fronds and flowers, was not only pre-designed for staging all kinds of early modern pastoral drama, but also happened to be situated in the very terrain envisioned by Leonora Bernardi as the setting for *Clorilli*. These topographical and historical circumstances made our production a truly site-specific one, in which the outdoor playing space became a sort of character, and an integral thematic as well as narrative element, especially because we used not one but four different locations, dispersed through the Villa La Pietra gardens (see Fig. 10).

We thus were able to pursue the organic coordination of 'performance, place, and public' that theorist/practitioners such as Cliff McLucas and Mike Pearson have favoured and achieved.[7] Concomitantly, there was a homogeneous 'time machine' effect: since the La Pietra site and palazzo had been owned by the aristocratic Capponi family, allies of the ruling Medici dynasty of Tuscany, it could suitably 're-host' and 're-enact' the circumstances that pertained to probably the first and only previous performance of the play, likely in the presence of Grand Duke Ferdinando I and his consort Christine of Lorraine, at the Medici villa La Petraia or in Fiesole itself, in honour of their first-born son Cosimo (see Section 2.1.4). In our specific case, then, these factors informed two crucial interpretive moves, one of them textual, the other physical. First, we adapted the Prologue of the play, spoken in the original script by a *fata* ('fairy') named Linfadusa, who introduces the setting as the Tuscan hills and then directly addresses Ferdinando and Christine.[8] The performer of the part – the impressively versatile professional actress Elia Nichols – dressed in an elegant, late-Renaissance style crimson dress and holding a folio-sized, leather-bound 'book of the play', first identified herself as Linfadusa, but then revealed that she was Bernardi. This 'transformation' led to one of the most notable departures in our performance text from the original Italian script:

> Oh, clearest fountains, you who bring life to the fields of Tuscany, of the great Granduca Ferdinando – the Muses will gladly come here, to this Villa, and to these Gardens, to live by your soft, graceful murmuring . . . They will sing of the wise Granduchessa Christine – of her piety, her valour, her courtesy, all of which, like a blazing sun, adorn her with spectacular rays. And . . . they will see and hear this play that I have written, called *Clorilli*.[9]

Second, as Linfadusa/Bernardi concluded her Prologue, with its coy usage of the time-travelling 'Golden Age' trope often found in pastoral

Figure 10 Plan of Villa La Pietra showing the itinerary through the
performance spaces of the NYU Florence production of *Clorilli* on 11 May 2018:
(A) Opening Song and Prologue; (B) Act I, Scene 1; (C) Act I, Scene 2 to the end
of Act V; (D) Final Dance. Reproduced with the permission of NYU Florence.
Additional artwork by Paul Greene.

plays to celebrate patrons, she shifted into the role of usher: she invited the more than 100 audience members, who had been standing for over five minutes in an open space immediately behind the villa itself (position 'A' in Fig. 10), to walk via pathways lined by Baroque sculptures and topiary hedges towards the performance area of the play's first scene.

This 'promenade' *mise en scène* sought to impart the lived, mobile sensation of travelling from the grey-yellow stone and stucco world of Italian civilization and its built environments to the green-leafed world of nature.[10] This movement itself performed a key element of pastoral's traditional agenda, namely the voyage out from the corrupt city and vice-threatened court into prelapsarian Arcadia. At the same time, the audience's displacement was itself an act of de-familiarization, of gaining kinetic and embodied knowledge that prompted them to become active participants and learners, rather than merely passive observers. Granted, the redemptive world of nature in our production was only a simulation, demarcated and distilled as a *hortus conclusus* rather than being an authentic, uncultivated 'Golden Age' wilderness. Nonetheless, the site itself shaped and transformed our work in progress, and thus crucially involved physical, 'situated knowledge', of the kind delineated by Lynette Hunter: 'situated knowledge becomes a situated textuality, knowledge always in the making, focused on the process'.[11]

To nurture this process, we made a strong invitation – it might also be termed gentle pressure – to the audience to alter their habitual behaviours and consciousness, through a mildly Dionysiac initiation itinerary, first past the 'First Basin' (*Prima Vasca*, see Fig. 10), then beneath low-hanging branches and down a series of ramps and steps into a vast garden-amphitheatre, about 25 metres in diameter. Here the audience beheld the centrepiece of a large circular stone basin (*Seconda Vasca*, facing position 'B' in Fig. 10), with a Grecian-style colonnade/pergola as its backdrop, in turn framed by the hills of Fiesole on the horizon (see Fig. 11). As sunset approached, this was no longer the literal space of the La Pietra gardens, but an imaginary and even oneiric one. The basin was filled with floating miniature origami paper boats, illuminated by candles. The elderly shepherds Alcone and Alfesibeo entered, to perform the first scene of the play. Then Leonora Bernardi reappeared, now leading a group of classically robed technical assistants (Ali Del Vecchio, Clara Hillis and Maia Reeb), who held up a gauzy white curtain to enlarge the shadow of a papier-mâché dove-puppet with flapping wings, manipulated by Nichols/Bernardi herself (Fig. 12). This evoked the traditional symbol for love, innocence and purity, but it was no ordinary dove, as its 'feathers' were actually strips of paper with reproductions

Figure 11   View of the Villa La Pietra Gardens with Fiesole in the distance. Image courtesy of NYU Florence.

Figure 12   Performance of *Clorilli* at Villa La Pietra, NYU Florence, 11 May 2018, directed by Eric Nicholson. Leonora Bernardi and the 'Dove' from Alcone's Dream in *Clorilli* (Act I, Scene 1). Elia Nichols as Bernardi, with Ali Del Vecchio, Clara Hillis and Maia Reeb. Image courtesy of NYU Florence.

of the original handwritten lines of the script. They visually rendered the words being uttered by the elderly shepherd Alcone, recounting the prophetic dream he had dreamed of a beautiful, cherished dove he had raised, lost and re-discovered. Cameron Anderson had ingeniously prepared and – with the help of her assistant, Andrew Child – constructed the dove-puppet, whose fragility and elusive textuality reflected the folded paper sheets bobbing up and down in the ornate fountain below. With this physical device, we sought to accentuate the script's own liquid qualities, while foreshadowing the central presence of another actual 'fountain' in the scenes to come.

2.4.2 Water

Clorilli is suffused with water, in word and action, in figurative and literal ways. From the elegy of the 'limpidissimo fonte' ('clearest fountains') made by Linfadusa in the Prologue (line 103) to the nymph Dalinda's lengthy apostrophe/blessing of the 'clear and fresh waters' (V.3.42) at the end of the play, water permeates the script.[12] In a notable flashback recounted in Act 2, the nymph Licasta narrates at length her encounter with the lady 'Cellia, glory of Love, prize of the world' (a coded reference to Bernardi's friend, the real-life princess of Ferrara, Marfisa d'Este) above a beach 'beside the sea that bathes the shore of the Cinque Terre', and quotes the same Cellia's comparison of the volatile sea to 'the inconstancy and the fickle faith of men', for 'if the sea seems tranquil at the break of day, by noon you will see it become horrid and fearsome. The sea nourishes monsters, while man, like a new Proteus, breeds an immense flock of the foulest sea-calves.'[13] This speech evokes water at the macrocosmic level, but other lines emphasize it in the microcosmic form of human tears: Dalinda's father Alcone weeps for the loss of his daughter; the young shepherd Filemone weeps for his rejection by Clorilli; and later Clorilli herself weeps for the apparent death of Filemone. Fortunately, her tears fall on Filemone's face, and they help to revive her suicidal lover after his own fortunate fall into a natural pool of water.

This turning-point event, enabling the change of the play's ending from tragic to happy, occurs off-stage, but Bernardi's script calls for the continual on-stage presence of a fountain. This central scenographic component connects the play's enacted scenes with both its 'backstory' and its climactic (off-stage) event of a lover's leap into water. Two years before the time of the play's performed action, at 'this fountain' Dalinda had dropped her veil as she fled a menacing bear, who then attacked another shepherd (named Alcasto); Dalinda's beloved Fillinio then had found the bloodstained veil, mistakenly concluding that Dalinda was the bear's victim, and in Act 2 scene 1 he arrives at the fountain, whose waters 'are still vermilion with her blood'.[14] Two acts later, sharing the same mistaken belief that the bear had killed her lover, Dalinda herself returns to the fountain, and speaks/chants an incantatory apostrophe-refrain: 'You, fountain, reveal my fierce pain's bitter history to all.'[15] When, however, in the next and concluding act Dalinda receives the unexpected, joyous news that Fillinio is alive and looking for her, she predicts that an eternally verdant, flowering springtime will grace the surrounding hills, and 'young little Cupids' will happily dance 'around this fountain'.[16]

Inevitably, then, water became a key dramaturgical trope and material presence in our production in both the playing areas used for the play itself following the Prologue (see Fig. 10, 'B' and 'C'). As mentioned, the first open amphitheatre area ('B') had a large stone basin; in the second main playing space/audience seating area used from Act 1 scene 2 through to Act 5, we built a small circular pool as a visual-physical counterpoint. This quadrangular performance zone is located just beyond and slightly below the amphitheatre (labelled 'C' in Fig. 10). In fact, it is an extension, reached by a flight of wide stairs, of the La Pietra gardens' principal *teatro di verzura* (literally, 'greenery theatre'; labelled 'Teatrino' at position 'D' in Fig. 10), which has a raised and raked stage, parallel topiary hedges forming eighteenth-century-style 'flats', and low trimmed shrubs backing the footlights.[17] The main performance space used for *Clorilli* similarly has a grassy lawn-floor, as well as a backdrop formed by dark green, trimmed laurel trees, seven metres wide and five metres high. At the exact centre of this playing area we placed our fountain, composed of a circular hard plastic tub, disguised by a ring of short, thin, beige-coloured slabs, bedecked with actual moss, sprigs and a green cloth garland, and filled with reflecting water on which floated a few more of the small origami paper boats crafted by Anderson and her assistants. The upper, horizontal ring of the structure was likewise composed of small stone slabs, purposefully left unpolished and loose-fitting to give the impression of Cyclopean masonry, of the kind found at primordial sacred sites such as Stonehenge. To extend the 'fountain effect', and to add local historical atmosphere as well as symmetry to the arrangement, we flanked the circular pool with two large, metre-high *orci*, the traditional terracotta urns used in Tuscany to store oil or wine.

Given the intricacy and sophistication of the script's poetic language, we sought to offset the natural green, 'environmental' set elements with overtly artificial ones: this mixture of, and contrast between, Nature and Art is indeed one of the principal aesthetic-philosophical concerns of the pastoral mode, from ancient to modern times. A pertinent example of this tradition is Sebastian Serlio's 1545 design for the 'Satyric scene', which combines human-crafted stone huts with wild shrubs and leafy trees.[18] Thus, when Fillinio mentioned still-visible 'vermilion' blood, he pulled a long swath of crimson-coloured cloth out of one of the urns. Likewise, Anderson and her team created beautiful, oversized, bright orange, white and yellow papier-mâché flowers which could be seen rising, or 'blossoming', above the actual, carefully trimmed low hedge running along the perimeter of the playing area. Their improbable size and shapes, combined with their evident artificiality, prompted associations with Lewis Carroll's Alice books, sustaining the dream-like implications of the play in performance. These human-made flowers contrasted with the real daisies in the headbands of the shepherdesses Coribante and Aurinda,[19] as surely as the crimson cloth did with the real water in the central pool, which the athletic nymphs Clorilli and Licasta often used to rinse their arms and hands.

Even more artificially and symbolically, a pair of broad, light blue lengths of fabric were hung from a metal rod arching over the walkway leading into the amphitheatre area, as a transformative pseudo-waterfall/portal into the make-believe Arcadian world of the pastoral tragicomedy. Once through the portal, audience members proceeded past two wide terracotta troughs filled with water, placed adjacent to the permanent narrow irrigation channel of the gardens themselves. Finally, the blending of the natural green set and its watery elements with artificial embellishments reached its most conspicuous and contemporary technological expression through the full-colour, partially animated digital images inventively designed by Anderson and periodically projected on the leafy screen looming behind the main playing area. These projections punctuated and accompanied crucial moments in the script. Among these was the above-cited flashback story of Cellia in Act 2. Here the reproduction of a sixteenth-century portrait of Marfisa d'Este suddenly appeared on the screen, giving way to a sequence of rolling waves and storm-at-sea effects, with an origami boat morphing into an early modern vessel harried by a fabulous marine monster with giant curved horns. Appropriately, this last-named transformative digital image was based on a woodcut of a 'marine satyr' published in 1560 (in Zurich, by Christoph Froschover).

2.4.3 Rejections, separations and confrontations

With its tragicomic focus on the pangs of disprized love, *Clorilli* thus aptly deploys water to configure its physical as well as emotional landscape – the 'wind and the rain' of sorrowful lovers' sighs and tears. This dominant motif marks the ambiguous fluidity and changeability that emerge in the play's tragicomic portrayal of the dangers and vicissitudes of love. Our task as interpreters of the play's dramatic, literal and symbolic agenda meant exploring and rehearsing its various episodes of rejection, separation and consequent confrontation during the first four acts, which tend towards self-inflicted death and tragedy. In this process, crucial questions of translation, editing, logistics and pedagogy also were a key priority, particularly since our audience was a general anglophone one, and not a specialized group of scholars well-versed in Italian Renaissance literature. Time constraints and other practical considerations made it impossible to attempt a staging of the full play text with costly 'period' costumes and props. It likewise would have been misguided and potentially confusing to emulate the play's prevalently verse lines – unrhymed, hendecasyllabic *versi sciolti*, for the most part – and proto-Baroque rhetorical syntax in our English script. My task in cutting lengthy speeches for the performance script was facilitated by Anna Wainwright's excellent full translation for the present edition, which wisely opted for prose and a modernized English, well-suited for twenty-first-century readers and audiences.[20]

A key example of the choices made in interpreting the play's symbolic agenda is found in Act 3 scene 6. This could be called the dramatic core of the play, since it features the much-awaited and long-deferred interview between the ex-lovers Clorilli and Filemone, wherein the nymph definitively rejects the shepherd, partially in response to his having broken off their planned engagement under ungentle pressure from his father to marry another woman (Dalinda). Filemone's impassioned 40-line plea to Clorilli in the Italian text (lines 87–127) derives credible dramatic motivation from his state of near desperation. Yet the intricate poetic lines of the speech present practical difficulties for a young, inexperienced actor to memorize and make compelling for contemporary ears. There was the risk of unnecessary dilation in maintaining the somewhat hyperbolic and repetitive rhetorical flourishes of the original text. Thus, elaborate passages were sometimes scaled down into concise, less eloquent but more playable versions, as these quotations demonstrate:

Già la seconda volta
la primavera a noi fatt'ha ritorno,
rendendo a' colli, a le campagne, a' boschi
or pregiati onori,
da che tu privi quest'alma meschina (III.6.87–91)

Spring has now returned a second time – restoring its prized glories
to the hills, the fields, the woods – since you deprived this wretched
soul (Wainwright)

More than a year ago, you deprived this wretched soul (Wainwright
and Nicholson, 38)

A few lines later, Filemone uses the familiar 'living hell' metaphor to
express his emotional distress, and expands on it through detailed
citation of the Tantalus myth: 'both food and drink vanish ... so
that he remains forever ravenous and starved'.[21] This vivid reference
communicated Filemone's anguish as well as poetic consciousness to
educated late-Renaissance Europeans, but today it would impede the
theatrical pace, especially for actors and listeners who are less familiar
with classical allusions. Therefore, it sufficed to retain the character's
opening declaration, 'my breast has become a new Inferno, home to the
greatest of torments', and to skip 17 lines ahead to his conclusion: 'Here
a great furnace sparks with real flames, and here I feel the searing cold of
bitter frost.'[22] This translation and editing choice had the added value of
preserving both the Italianate locution 'Inferno' and the emblematic 'icy
fire' oxymoron of Petrarchan love lyric.

Jeremy Crocker, the young student actor playing Filemone, fully
understood and persuasively rendered these literary contextual associa-
tions. Still more importantly for a live performance, he applied his study
of the poetry of Dante and Petrarch in the classroom to his embodiment
of the character at this precise moment of the script: the hyperbolic,
Dantesque 'Inferno' image motivated him to stand up from a kneeling
position in front of Clorilli, and to 'act out', in the central downstage
area and with sincere vehemence, the extremity of his suffering. This
sequence was a revealing example of the 'ludic knowledge' encouraged
by the PAR model, since Crocker only arrived at this interpretive
discovery through the trial and error of multiple rehearsals, particularly
the final ones in our actual 'found space' in the La Pietra gardens. His
convincing energy and movements aptly pushed toward sentimental
excess, giving all the more impetus for Miranda Schumacher, playing

Clorilli, to counter Filemone's self-pitying, accusatory remonstrations with sceptical irony. We therefore kept the final mythological citation in his speech, namely his claim that in the 'inferno' of his breast 'sits your [Clorilli's] lovely image as queen, lovely as Persephone on her frozen throne'.[23] These lines were physically translated by Filemone returning to his kneeling pose in front of Clorilli, who was seated not on a grand regal throne but rather on an actual wooden stump, covered by a patch of green cloth. In this position, dressed not in queenly robes but in her athletic outfit of loose-fitting, muslin warm-up trousers and plain white tank-top shirt, Schumacher could ironically smile and aptly convey her character's amused but also bemused reactions. Having previously clapped her hands in mock approbation of his earlier tirade against her, she now replied with the curt, prosaic English 'You would place me in Hell?', followed by her sarcastically disdainful quip 'Take me out of there, Filemone. Such a dark, shadowy chamber is not to my liking.'[24]

While Schumacher's Clorilli clearly enjoyed exerting her wit, she also connected her mocking deflation of Filemone's grandiloquent Petrarchan lover's tropes to the convincing expression of genuine emotional pain on her part. Again, PAR made this possible through our use of theatre rehearsal games that allowed for the ludic testing out of verbal options and inflections, in tandem with physical and psychological ones. Schumacher and Ellie New, our versatile assistant director, also brought depth, nuance and complexity to the proto-feminist qualities of Bernardi's script through the *performed* transformation of their critical insights, drawing on relevant scholarship.[25] Performance thus becomes a dynamic bridge between a late-sixteenth-century text and twenty-first-century awareness and sensibilities. For example, an early modern ideological assumption of masculine privilege is inherent in the Petrarchan lover Filemone's expectation of *mercede* (recompense or reward) from the lady he loves and 'serves'; for him it is part of the natural order of interpersonal things, rather than a masculinist social construct. Filemone had previously accused Clorilli of both betrayal and lack of chastity, since he had seen her embracing her brother Fillinio, whom Filemone mistakenly thinks is her new lover. Spiteful jealousy comes through in his claim that only he should 'possess' his 'sweet reward' (Clorilli herself), and in the self-dramatization of his emotional state as one of life and death. Clorilli responds by interrogating her ex-lover's language and deconstructing its sexist presumptions.

Here again the rehearsal process provided instruction and guided us to artistic decisions that analysis alone could not accomplish. With the aim of imparting a 'Shakespearean' resonance to the English lines, I first opted for 'recompense' over 'reward' as the translation of 'mercede'. This was revealed to be a mistake, because the second word resonates much more clearly and urgently in our contemporary social world; any 'Shakespearean' gain needed to yield to the much more significant gain of accessibility for today's audience. This final choice was validated by the strong, widely shared and even audibly engaged response to Schumacher's sarcastic, stage whisper-echo of Crocker's abject plea for his supposed 'reward':

> FIL: You feign not to understand what you know most certainly. Did my own eyes not just now see you clasp your new lover to your breast?
> CLO: What does that matter to you? Or what should it matter?
> FIL: What should it matter to me? To see another man possess my sweet reward? To see in the hands of another what by right should be mine? To see that she who is pitiless towards me, giving me only death, gives life to others. You ask why this matters?
> CLO: Yes, I do ask. What reward are you speaking of, that you see in others' possession and that 'should' be yours? What life, and what death, are you jabbering on about?
> FIL: *You* are the reward that befits my long service. *You* by the law of Love have already been mine for a long time. And you slay me when, robbing me, you give yourself to others.
> CLO: If I had looked for, or gratefully acknowledged, your devotion, you would be right to ask for this 'reward', but I flee from it and despise it.[26]

Without pre-designing the effect, then, but by trying out viable and not-so-viable options, we managed to make Bernardi's critique of male rhetorical deception and abusive inconstancy towards women palpable for our live 2018 audience. Filemone's lamenting protestations to Clorilli, laden as they are with insinuating, potentially disingenuous poetic conventions and masculinist claims of ownership, also imply a kind of sexual aggression and violence: as Anna Wainwright argues, this effect shows how Bernardi modulates the typical pastoral figuration of the lustful satyr, by suggesting that supposedly virtuous, respectable men such as Filemone can do nymphs just as much harm as can their social inferiors.[27]

As noted, *Clorilli* deploys the familiar pastoral technique of contrasting and debating various opinions on the merits and defects of

Figure 13 Armilla quotes Torquato Tasso 'about two bright eyes' in *Clorilli* (Act III, Scene 1). Luzmyrna Crespo as Armilla, Miranda Schumacher as Clorilli, performed at Villa La Pietra, NYU Florence, 2018. Image courtesy of NYU Florence.

amorous desires, and on the challenge to either accept or reject them, made popular by plays such as Tasso's *Aminta* (1573) and Isabella Andreini's *Mirtilla* (1588). Thus, Clorilli's friend Armilla urges her to acknowledge Love's power, and to allow for the possibility of reconciliation with Filemone (Fig. 13), while her other friend, Licasta, advises her to shun the company of men and take delight in the freedom of life with huntress nymphs amidst the hills, woods and fountains. In effect, Clorilli is caught between these two energies of attraction and rejection. To accentuate this duality, the highly gifted student actress Luzmyrna Crespo was cast as both Armilla and Licasta. With subtle shifts in the use of her vocal resonators, slight alterations to her hair – letting it down for Armilla, tying it back more athletically for Licasta – and the use of a light blue shawl, she was able to convey distinct aural and visual contrasts between the two characters, while keeping them on a continuum of widely differing attitudes.

Our other conspicuous use of 'doubling' aimed to convey even more marked contrasts and counterpoints. Elia Nichols, who had opened the show in aristocratic period costume as Leonora Bernardi/Linfadusa/Prologue, returned to play Ruscone the Satyr in Act 3, decked out in boots, imitation buckskin leggings, shaggy black 'furry' jacket, long fake beard and a pair of large curving horns (Fig. 14).[28] Through her vocal and kinetic development of this physical impersonation of 'hyper-masculinity' in our rehearsal process, Nichols deftly accomplished a satire on juvenile

Figure 14   The satyr Ruscone approaches Clorilli in *Clorilli* (Act III, Scene 2). Elia Nichols as Ruscone, Miranda Schumacher as Clorilli, performed at Villa La Pietra, NYU Florence, 2018. Image courtesy of NYU Florence.

aggressiveness and ludicrous 'macho' boasting – Ruscone claims he is a 'semi-god' and compares himself to Jove – that had as its foundation the viewpoint of a female author. She/'he' thus became a comical, masquerading mirror to Filemone, who for his part is 'feminized' by the 'weakening' effects of love, as expressed through his abject laments.[29] Like his shepherd counterpart, Ruscone complains of Clorilli's past, off-stage rejection of his gifts and attempted genteel courtship. He then utterly fails to capture her by force on-stage. In the original text, Clorilli's call for help is heard by her brother Fillinio, who performs the classic rescuer of the damsel-in-distress, quickly and decisively chasing away her 'boorish beast' assailant. Still, Clorilli's clipped, somewhat laconic cries, combined with Ruscone's final re-labelling of her as 'deceitful', prompted us to pursue a modern interpretive choice, achieved through a minimal modification of the script: Schumacher's nymph showed her skill at strongly and astutely defending herself against the presumptuous assault of Nichols' blustering, clumsily posturing satyr.[30]

This mainly risible confrontation thus offered a tonal contrast to the pathos and seriousness of the ensuing scenes, the first one featuring Clorilli's joyous reunion with Fillinio, and the second her acerbic verbal rebukes and ultimately poignant leave-taking of Filemone. Here, as elsewhere, we employed a few anachronistic and popular cultural devices to amplify the discordant and provocative strains already sounded by Bernardi's script. Nichols' Ruscone mustered up some courage with the help of long swigs of cheap lager from an oversized, bright green can, while Clorilli's and Licasta's long, imitation bronze, diamond-headed spears and multiple leather armbands referenced the outfits of the Amazonian warriors in the recently released film *Wonder Woman* (2017). After all, Bernardi repeatedly connected her own Italian present with the imaginary past of the Golden Age pastoral green world. Just as Tasso had done in *Aminta* with its topical glances at the Este court of Ferrara and transparent code-names for real-life contemporaries such as himself, Sperone Speroni and Giovan Battista Pigna, Bernardi references Ferdinando de' Medici as Dinando and Christine of Lorraine as Cristilla.[31]

In connecting the Arcadian past with her own present, Bernardi also reinforces her critique of outdated and oppressive patriarchal customs, most specifically the practice of marriages contracted by fathers against their daughters' will. This theme is developed especially in the first scene, where the audience learns through exchanges between the aged shepherds Alcone and his friend Alfesibeo that it was Alcone's determination to have his daughter Dalinda marry Filemone, the shepherd Ergasto's son, that precipitated the entire potentially tragic plot of the play. Defying her father's command, Dalinda eloped with Fillinio, and the lovers have been missing for nearly two years. Meanwhile, Filemone obeyed his father's pact with Alcone, and broke off his engagement with Clorilli. Although we found it necessary to cut many lines from the long-winded speeches of Alcone (played by the director, Eric Nicholson) and his friend Alfesibeo (played by the first-year student actor Maurice Bensmihen), we did retain the latter's pointed chiding of the former:

> For even if in every other matter children are subject to their father, in this one thing Nature and God have conceded them their liberty: to unite among each other as they please and see fit.[32]

Although it chimed well with Counter-Reformation ideals about marriage, such decisive advocacy of direct, mutual and exclusive consent between intimate partners might have sounded boldly unconventional in its original performance context, but it commands nearly universal approval over 400 years later.[33] 'What love has brought together let no manipulative fathers put asunder' might serve as an encapsulating gloss on Bernardi's play, which, in keeping with a major innovative trend in Cinquecento comedy, endorses the agency of determined young women in love.[34] If the insensitive cruelty of oppressive fathers and the reckless egoism of male lovers push *Clorilli* towards tragedy through separations, rejections and attempted suicide, then the wise counsel, patient devotion and steadfast friendship shown by the female characters enable a dramatic swing toward a comedic resolution.

2.4.4 Projections and reunions

Our *mise en scène* sought to recognize and elucidate this gender-inflected pattern through several specific textual and musical choices, together with special scenic effects and embellishments. We therefore preserved in our translation the female Prologue's promise, now spoken by Bernardi herself: 'with my power, I will change the nymphs' and shepherds' sad, unfortunate stories to happy ones, and lift the sadness from afflicted hearts. Instead of sorrowful sighs and laments, I will make the hills and the countryside sing with happy voices.'[35] Even before Bernardi's entrance on the Villa La Pietra terrace, a woman's voice was heard, as Schumacher sang (to live violin accompaniment by Isabel Schmieta) the *canzonetta* 'Più d'altra ninfa amata' by Mariano Tantucci (1603), with text by Bernardi herself,[36] while the stage assistants Rachael Ryu and Nela Kreglicka stood on the villa's first floor balcony, scattering natural flower petals which glimmered in the late afternoon light. As a kind of foreshadow, several origami boats bobbed up and down in a nearby stone basin, anticipating their metamorphosis into images in the first of four extended digital projections on the leafy screen. As explained above, this projection transmitted the portrait of Marfisa d'Este, to illustrate her advice (in the guise of 'Cellia') that women beware the deceptive, untrustworthy love-suits of men, using the metaphor of storm-tossed boats.[37] Women's counsel, education and solidarity are thus highlighted here, as they are in our performance script's Act 3 scene 1, when Armilla continues to persuade Clorilli to give Filemone a hearing. Armilla extols the 'great master' Love as the force that gave Clorilli her beauty and charisma (Fig. 13). As a visual supplement to this paean of love's powers, our next digital projection featured a full-colour, embellished and animated enlargement of Caravaggio's 'Amor vincit omnia', depicting the winged, frontally naked, early adolescent Cupid. Thus, even and indeed especially during the play's phase of separations and confrontations, women's supportive energies gained expression in our production, through both voice and vision.

In a related, interpretive sense, we projected this *leitmotiv* of women's solidarity onto a significant change to the play's configuration of its characters. The 'sage counsellor shepherd' is another standard feature of the pastoral repertoire: Theocritus' Corydon, Sannazaro's

Carino, Tasso's Tirsi and Guarini's Linco are notable examples, and Bernardi appoints this role to Coribante, often described as 'kind' and 'gentle' in the script. Coribante is a somewhat startling onomastic choice for a calm, mature and kindly male shepherd, since *coribanti* were known as the youthful, often militaristic, dancing and drum-beating celebrants of the goddess Cybele. Since Bernardi evidently took some liberty in altering this character's usual associations, we made a similar move and changed his gender to female, casting the student actress Ruolan Chen for the part. Although somewhat comically ineffectual in advising disdainful manliness and preventing the younger, intensely passionate characters such as Filemone from rushing toward violent extremes, our Coribante was a voice of encouragement, proverb-speaking moderation and cool-headed wisdom. To Dalinda's grief-stricken account of Fillinio's apparent killing by the bear, the older character responds with fact-seeking questions about the evidence.[38] Coribante affirms that she had seen the bear kill *Alcasto*, not Fillinio, and counters Dalinda's reliance on emotive intuition ('my aching heart recognized my lover, and it would not have felt such pain and grief for anyone but Fillinio') with an exhortation to 'know the truth'.[39] Coribante cites to Dalinda her news of Fillinio's presence in Etruria, learnt from Ruscone off-stage (who had encountered Fillinio, as the audience has witnessed).[40] Thus we applied the PAR approach once more to the scripted material, using our embodied modifications, to enact the play's turn towards reunion, even as dramatic tensions linger between life-sustaining intellect and self-destructive passion.

Indeed, these tensions reach a climax in the following scene (IV.5). Here Dalinda remains alone, seemingly determined to resist Coribante's advice and to regress towards a replay of the classic Pyramus and Thisbe double suicide plot, based on the wilful misinterpretation of circumstantial evidence. Reunion and reconciliation can only be attained through struggle, and our staging aimed to body forth this idea through Curtin's full commitment to crawling on the grass, after being left temporarily alone by Coribante, and inaccurately declaring:

> I saw Fillinio's life extinguished at this very fountain. That wicked, horrendous wild beast ripped his body apart. Here I saw tepid blood form a stream, and alas, I see that the flowers still hold a scarlet hue on their petals.[41]

At this point Curtin gracefully began her slow, precise and dance-like approach to the fountain itself, and with a lowering of her vocal resonator

Figure 15 Dalinda chants the line 'You, fountain, reveal my fierce pain's bitter history to all', in *Clorilli* (Act IV, Scene 5). Rory Curtin as Dalinda, performed at Villa La Pietra, NYU Florence, 2018. Image courtesy of NYU Florence.

and a chant-like rhythm, she intoned the first of four repetitions of the refrain, 'You, fountain, reveal my fierce pain's bitter history to all' (Fig. 15). As our musical adviser Emily Wilbourne recommended, we strove for a heightened, early opera type of rendition of this repeated line and the monologue that it punctuated, evoking arias for abandoned, forsaken or maddened ('forsennata') female heroines such as Armida and Ariadne. Several of these surviving pieces remain part of the Baroque musical repertoire, such as Monteverdi's 'Lamento di Arianna' and 'Lamento della ninfa'.[42] This latter nymph's lament, with its mournful and insistently repeated 'non mi tormenti', served as a fitting reference point for our interpretation of Dalinda's near-delusional state at this climactic moment of the play.

Yet, thanks to the crucial, life-sustaining interventions of Coribante and Dalinda's off-stage friend Lidia, Bernardi's script rejects the tragic Pyramus and Thisbe/Romeo and Juliet archetype, and instead converts its own imminent tragedy into a comedy of reconciliation and nuptial festivity. To sustain this trope of conversion in our production, Licasta – who had earlier voiced the anti-male, anti-marital argument – was included in the final comedic resolution. In the original script, the male shepherd Licandro recounts in the first scene of Act 5 Filemone's miraculous survival of his leap from the cliff into the deep, pool-like waters of the stream below. However, in our version it was Licasta who told this tale, and who exulted over his reunion with Clorilli, as well as the returns of Fillinio and Dalinda, and the consequent general happiness of the pastoral community. Again, our PAR-guided experimentation enabled us to reinforce these effects, through the doubling of Crespo as Armilla and Licasta. In the end, she performed a fusion of two previously polarized, mutually antagonistic energies.

2.4.5 Fusion, renewal and community celebration

Perhaps the most spectacular and most enthusiastically admired of Cameron Anderson's captivating transformative digital projections was the one which burst into view as Dalinda learnt of Fillinio's return and danced her joyful dance. On the leafy screen, the audience clearly saw – because by now the sun had fully set behind the villa – a dynamic series of multi-coloured images of a variety of flowers, some in symmetrical, kaleidoscopic patterns, blossoming amidst visions of meadows, hillsides and cascading water. There was a recall of the fantastical composite paintings of Bernardi's contemporary Arcimboldo, and an emphasis on newly flourishing love and fertility, in an effusion that was itself a fusion of early modern and post-modern artistic technologies.

The entire closing sequence, featuring a music-and-dance conclusion, was our own invention, since Bernardi's manuscript text ends with comments on love spoken by Aurindo and omits any stage directions for a possible choral performance of this kind (see Fig. 16). Live original percussion music played on a full drum kit by student musician Sherry Gao heralded the soon-to-follow group celebration, as did the immediately subsequent playing of a recorded performance

Figure 16   The full cast of *Clorilli* dances a tarantella for the finale, Villa La Pietra NYU Florence, Teatrino Verde. Image courtesy of NYU Florence.

of Monteverdi's exuberant madrigal 'Zefiro torna' ('Zephyr returns'). With its zesty and dance-supporting *chaconne* rhythms, but also sweetly melodic affirmation of the return of spring and the balmy west wind, this song was an apt choice for accompanying the play's transition towards a concluding celebratory scene. In the mythological tradition, and in the Neoplatonic philosophical milieu of Renaissance Florence, Zephyr was well known as the lover of Chloris, and therefore Monteverdi's madrigal (with lyrics by Ottavio Rinuccini) was also well-suited for the dénouement of a play about the return of Clorilli to the world of love and its promise of new life.[43] At this point, the entire cast ascended onto the *teatrino*, with Aurinda and several technical assistants guiding the audience to stand and then walk up the stairs to the area in front of the raised, grassy stage (position 'D' in Fig. 10). Our final promenade movement re-accentuated a dramaturgy of ludic transformation, as spectators once more were coaxed toward feeling themselves as participants, now in a final celebratory dance.

We may never know if some sort of musical finale took place at the play's performance before Ferdinando de' Medici and Christine of Lorraine, but the case can be made that it certainly could have been added as an appropriate festive embellishment (see Section 2.1.5). After all, songs and dances celebrating betrothals and weddings frequently cap off early modern European comedies, as in Shakespeare's *A Midsummer Night's Dream, Much Ado About Nothing,* and *As You Like It.* Thus, we ourselves were practising a renewal that aimed toward fusion, uniting special occasion-focused elements across the more than four centuries between our performance and the first premiere of *Clorilli.* In a metaphoric but also practical sense, our production – especially in its final sequence – was the present-time 'ghost' performing at the 'host' of the Medicean site: as Mike Pearson explains, such an approach deploys 'the overlay of two basic sets of architectures, those of the extant building or *host*, that which is *at* site, . . . and those of the constructed scenography or the *ghost*, that which is temporarily brought *to* site'.[44] In this regard, we decided, as much by chance as by design, to change the music at this point, shifting from the Monteverdi madrigal to another kind of Italian soundtrack, still traditional but more accessible for dancing by untrained and inexperienced performers. Our assistant director, Ellie New, also an adept choreographer, coached the cast to execute the dance steps and movements she designed for a vigorous rendition of a Pugliese *tarantella*: this was based on a recorded performance of the Briganti di Terra d'Otranto of a Dionysiac courtship 'pizzica salentina'.[45] With Sherry Gao's live percussion accompaniment, the entire cast energetically skipped, turned, jumped and zig-zagged across the lawn, holding their arms high in the air, first as a group and then in couples, Clorilli with Filemone, Dalinda with Fillinio, Armilla/Licasta with Alfesibeo, Coribante with Aurinda and Alcone with Bernardi/Ruscone (in her formal Renaissance dress, but still with satyr's horns on her head) (Fig. 16). More than could be articulated in words, then, our exultant bodies and smiling faces were expressing and affirming not only the reunion of young lovers with each other and with their fathers, but also the renewal of an entire rural society.

Once more, our production choices eclectically blended ancient and modern elements, 'popular' and 'elite' forms, 'plugged' and 'unplugged' technologies. Finally, after the early evening sunlight had given way to darkness, we employed the basic, steady lighting provided by a half-dozen Fresnel lights with pale-tinted gels in our main playing space, before making a deliberate change to both the sidelight glowing from a row of shallow round citronella candles, and the electric light shining from bulbs within blue paper 'Chinese lanterns' strung behind the green theatre stage area. The resulting pools of bright light, set against the dark green hedges and surrounding outdoor darkness, created long cast shadows and an appropriately *chiaroscuro* visual effect.

All in all, ours was an exercise in 'embodied knowledge', wherein utterance, composition and movement in space, rehearsal games and improvisations applied to memorized lines, vocal expression and musical instrumentation, trying on of various costumes for 'doubling' and other purposes, experimentation with gesture, dance and other physically interpretive options were all needed and coordinated to enact our truly fresh, English-language rendition of a 'brand new' play from the Italian past. In Baz Kershaw's terms, this approach entails a 'dislocation of knowledge by action', in the spirit of Gregory Bateson's paradox that 'an explorer can never know what he is exploring until it has been explored'.[46] We consequently trusted the process of 'un-knowing', as we explored and tried out alternative 'green' worlds in transporting an erudite, poetically sophisticated, late-Renaissance Italian text to the found spaces behind an early modern Florentine villa/early twenty-first-century global university site. In this particular theatrical context, knowing, un-knowing and re-knowing becomes a practice of *physical engagement*, to employ the terms of scientist and queer theorist Karen Barad.[47] Through the collaboration of faculty, students, staff and professional as well as non-professional theatre artists, our project strove to engage our own bodies with the specific physical context in which we were rehearsing and performing, as a rejuvenating community experience. Thus, thanks to its freshly minted theatrical ensemble, the NYU Villa La Pietra *Clorilli* production of spring 2018 aspired to transmit as well as illuminate a myriad of shared green thoughts in shared green shades.[48]

Appendix: Programme and Cast List

Clorilli

A pastoral drama by Leonora Bernardi of Lucca (1559–1616)
NYU Florence, 11 May 2018, 7.30 p.m., Gardens, Villa La Pietra

CAST (in order of appearance)

Leonora Bernardi, a poet and playwright	Elia Nichols
Alfesibeo, an elderly shepherd	Maurice Bensmihen
Alcone, an elderly shepherd	Eric Nicholson
Clorilli, a young nymph of the woods	Miranda Schumacher
Armilla, a nymph of the woods	Luzmyrna Crespo
Filemone, a young shepherd	Jeremy Crocker
Coribante, a shepherdess	Ruolan Chen
Fillinio, a young shepherd	Andrew Cohen
Licasta, a nymph of the woods	Luzmyrna Crespo
Ruscone, a satyr	Elia Nichols
Dalinda, a young nymph of the woods	Rory Curtin
Aurinda, a shepherdess and messenger	Marina Gonzalez

CREW

Director and Producer	Eric Nicholson
Assistant Director	Ellie New
Assistant Producer	Andrew Cohen
Scenography, Video and Puppet Designer	Cameron Anderson
Stage Manager	Elaine Julie
Music Direction	Andrew Cohen
Musicians	Sherry Gao, Paul Kim and Isabel Schmieta
Music Consultant	Emily Wilbourne
Dance Direction	Ellie New
Costumes and Props Coordination and Construction	Shanae Butler, Ali Del Vecchio, Clara Hillis, Lilly McClure and Lana Polito
Puppet Construction	Andrew Child and Cameron Anderson
Make-up Artist	Julia Violone
Video Recording	Domenico Cannalire

Documentary Filming	Gabriel Goh
Photographers	Michael Davidoff and
	Hasan Halai
Technical Assistance	Nela Kreglicka,
	Maia Reeb and
	Rachael Ryu

A Note on 'Clorilli': Tonight's play survives in a sole manuscript in the Biblioteca Marciana in Venice, unknown to scholarship until 2008. 'Clorilli' was written by the multi-talented and well-connected singer, musician and poet Leonora Bernardi Belatti of Lucca, famous in her day but now almost entirely forgotten. The play offers a fresh and witty take on the courtly genre of pastoral drama, made fashionable by Torquato Tasso's *Aminta* (first performed in 1573). Evidence internal to the text suggests that it was performed at one of the Medici villas in the early 1590s, for an audience including the grand dukes of Tuscany, Ferdinando de' Medici and Christine of Lorraine. Tonight's performance, in the English version, as translated by Anna Wainwright and abridged by Eric Nicholson, is the first one of 'Clorilli' in over 400 years.

THANKS and ACKNOWLEDGEMENTS:

The La Pietra Players would like to thank a number of people and resources whose invaluable support and assistance have made the production of 'Clorilli' possible: at NYU Florence, Executive Director Ellyn Toscano, Academic Director Virginia Cox, Executive Assistant for Academic and Faculty Services Stefania Bacci, Assistant Director of Accounting Elisabetta Clementi, Assistant Director for Villa La Pietra Operations Barbara Bonciani, Horticultural Associate Nick Dakin-Elliot, Visit and Event Coordinator Cristina Fantacci Cellini, Assistant Director of Academic Affairs Lisa Cesarani, Programming Coordinator Julian Lonsdale, Coordinator for Media Production Domenico Cannalire, Coordinator of Instructional Technology and Digital Initiatives Scott Palmer, Nicola Porri, Alexa Farah, Federico Nori e I Bravi Giardinieri di Villa La Pietra, Lucia Ferroni, Marija Mihajlovich, Cristina Bellini, Tanya Di Rienzo, Concetta Chirabino, Alessandra Galluzzo, Luca Ragazzo e le guardie di Villa La Pietra. At NYU New York, Dean of the Gallatin School for Individualized Study Susanne Wofford, the Italian Studies Program, the Liberal Studies Program and the Provost's Global Research Initiative.

Our special thanks, of course, to Cameron Anderson (Faculty, Brandeis University), Lisa Sampson (Faculty, University College

London), Anna Wainwright (Faculty, University of New Hampshire), Emily Wilbourne (Faculty, City University of New York), Rebecca W. Cole; and Caterina Mazzotta and Claudio Canali (AVUELLE).

We also wish to give our profuse thanks to professional actress Elia Nichols (MFA, University of Texas at Austin), for her generous and expert collaboration.

Finally, many thanks to our friends and families – grazie di tutto!

ENJOY THE SHOW! BUONO SPETTACOLO!!

Notes

1 de' Sommi, *Quattro dialoghi*, 66.
2 Marvell, *The Poems*, 152.
3 Freeman, *Searching for Sappho*, 123–4; for Chloris' rape by Zephyrus, the god of the west wind, and transformation into Flora, the Roman goddess of flowers and early spring, see Ovid, *Fasti*, 91, and Botticelli's famous painting 'Primavera' ('Spring', *c.* 1480), Uffizi Galleries, Florence.
4 See Appendix for details. I need to thank and acknowledge here the outstanding work and collaboration of the entire cast and crew of production assistants, and the administration and technical staff of NYU Florence, in particular the exceptionally skilled, patient and generous gardening and groundskeeping team of Villa La Pietra, led by Nick Dakin-Elliot and Federico Nori. For a full recording of the live performance, see *Clorilli: A Pastoral Drama by Leonora Bernardi of Lucca (1559–1616)*. Accessed 22 August 2021. https://www.youtube.com/watch?v=sCCf8al5Sw0.
5 While several cast and crew members were full-time professional theatre artists, and several of the actors and production assistants were upper division theatre majors, at least a dozen student participants were first-year undergraduates involved in their first full-scale theatrical production.
6 Arlander, 'Agential Cuts', 334.
7 Pearson, *Site-Specific Performance*, 35–7.
8 In most cases, occasional topical references to Grand Duke Ferdinand and his consort Christine were cut from the unpublished performance text: *Clorilli, a pastoral drama by Leonora Bernardi (1559–1616)*, translated by Anna Wainwright, abridged by Eric Nicholson, 2018.
9 Wainwright and Nicholson, *Clorilli*, 1.
10 Kershaw, 'Promenade performance'; and Sidiropoulou, *Authoring Performance*, 19–20.
11 Hunter, 'Situated Knowledge', 152.
12 *C* cxxvi, 'Chiare fresche et dolci acque'.
13 Wainwright and Nicholson, 21. Cf. Wainwright's translation of *Clorilli*, II.5; for Marfisa d'Este, Sections 1.2.2–3 and 2.1.5.
14 Wainwright and Nicholson, 12; also Section 2.1.4.
15 Wainwright and Nicholson, 51; Bernardi, 'Tu fonte testimon rivela altrui / del mio fero dolor l'acerba istoria', *Clorilli*, IV.5, 13–14; and Section 2.1.5.
16 Wainwright and Nicholson, 56–7.
17 Cazzato, Fagiolo and Giusti, *Teatri di verzura*.
18 Serlio, *Il Secondo libro* (1545), fol. 70v. For Serlio's assimilation of Vitruvius's satyric scene with the lavish contemporary sets of pastoral eclogues, see *SPa*, 176.
19 For mainly logistical reasons, the gender of the characters Coribante and Aurindo was changed from male to female in our production.
20 Although we preserved the same number of scenes, we cut nearly a third of the lines of the original text. For Wainwright's 'Note on the translation', see Section 2.3.
21 'si fuggon l'acque e le vivande, onde egli / stassi sempre famelico, e digiuno', III.6.127–8.
22 Wainwright and Nicholson, 38. Cf. *Clorilli*, III.6.102–3, 120–23.

23 Wainwright and Nicholson, 38. Cf. III.6, 127–9.

24 Wainwright and Nicholson, 38. Cf. III.6, 130–31.

25 The production team especially referred to C*Wo*, C*Pr*, 93–115; and S*Pa*.

26 Wainwright and Nicholson, 36. Cf. Wainwright's translation in this volume of III.6, 29–53.

27 Anna Wainwright, 'The Role of the Satyr in Bernardi's Tragicommedia pastorale [Clorilli]', unpublished conference paper, Renaissance Society of America meeting, New York City, 2014.

28 The make-up and costumes-building team was led by Julia Violone, Shanae Butler and Lana Polito. On staging satyrs, see Nicholson, 'Crossing Borders with Satyrs'.

29 Refini, '"Parole tronche".

30 See Section 2.1.5.

31 See Section 2.1.4, and notes to *Clorilli*, Prologue and II.6.

32 Wainwright and Nicholson, 5. ('se in ogni altra cosa al padre i figli / soggetti sono, in questo libertade / ha lor concesso la Natura e Dio; / d'unirsi come a lor diletta e piace'), *Clorilli*, I.1.172–5.

33 See *Clorilli*, note 38.

34 See, for example, P*Sc*; Clubb, *Italian Drama*, 65–152; Andrews, *Scripts and Scenarios*, 91–108; and Giannetti, *Lelia's Kiss*.

35 Wainwright and Nicholson, 2.

36 For the text and music, see Sections 3.1.5 (vii) and 3.2.3–4; for the madrigal prefacing *Clorilli* in the original manuscript, see Section 2.1.5.

37 Wainwright and Nicholson, 21; cf. *Clorilli*, II.5.149–67.

38 Wainright and Nicholson, 50; *Clorilli*, IV.4.106–16.

39 Wainright and Nicholson, 50–1; Cf. *Clorilli*, IV.4.127–31.

40 Wainwright and Nicholson, 51; *Clorilli*, IV.4.136–9.

41 Wainwright and Nicholson, 51; cf. *Clorilli*, IV.5.4–12.

42 Wilbourne, *Seventeenth-Century Opera*, 51–91, and Gordon, *Monteverdi's Unruly Women*. On female laments in early modern Italian literature and opera in particular, see Refini, 'Echoes of Ariadne'; also Section 2.1.5.

43 Rinuccini's madrigal text begins: 'Zefiro torna e di soavi accenti / L'aer fa grato e'l pie discoglie a l'onde / E mormorando tra le verdi fronde / Fa danzar al bel suon sul prato i fiori, / Inghirlandato il crin Fillide e Clori' ('Return O Zephyr, and with gentle gusts / Make pleasant the air and shake your foot across the waves, / And murmuring among the green branches / Make the flowers in the field dance to your fine sound; / Crowned with garlands are the locks of Phyllis and Chloris'; transl. mine). For Rinuccini and Bernardi's poetic dialogue, see Sections 3.1.4, and 2.1.5.

44 Pearson, *Site-Specific Performance*, 35–6.

45 'Tarantella Dance by Briganti di Terra d'Otranto'. Accessed 31 December 2021. https://www.youtube.com/watch?v=hjmNWAXQeFw.

46 Kershaw, 'Performance Practice as Research', 4–5.

47 Barad, *Meeting the Universe Halfway*, 342.

48 See the short documentary, filmed and edited by NYU Liberal Studies student Gabriel Goh: 'The Making of *Clorilli*'. Accessed 8 November 2021. https://www.youtube.com/watch?v=nkhnnyMlappc. Goh also assisted the principal photographer and video-maker of the project, NYU Florence Coordinator for Media Production Domenico Cannalire, to whom I extend profound thanks for his work on our production.

3
Bernardi's lyric verse and its musical settings

3.1 Leonora Bernardi, lyric poet

Virginia Cox

This edition of Leonora Bernardi's lyric verse will follow the format adopted in my 2013 anthology, *Lyric Poetry by Women of the Italian Renaissance*. The Italian text is followed by a prose translation and commentary. A difference here, however, is that significant textual variants are recorded within the manuscript and print witnesses to these poems, and full descriptions are provided for these sources (Section 3.1.1). Bernardi's poems are grouped thematically, rather than by metrical form or alphabetically by *incipit*, with one section (Section 3.1.2) devoted to her Marian verse and another (Section 3.1.5) to her love poetry. Between these, two sections (3.1.3–3.1.4) contain poems by Angelo Grillo and Ottavio Rinuccini, respectively, responding to Bernardi's most famous poem, her *canzone* 'Se pur fin su ne gli stellanti chiostri', together with two sonnets by Bernardi in response to Grillo. Transcription conventions mirror those for Bernardi's play in this volume (see Section 2.3). In Sections 3.1.3–3.1.4, the poems by Bernardi's 'respondents' are given in italic and Bernardi's poems in Roman type.

An account of the later sixteenth-century Italian lyric tradition may be found in *Lyric Poetry by Women of the Italian Renaissance*, along with descriptions of the verse forms used by Bernardi (with the exception of the *canzonetta*) and notes on the rules governing rhyme and rhythm in Italian verse.[1] The *canzonetta*, a popular form in the last decades of the sixteenth century, derived from the model of popular Neapolitan song known as a *villanella*. It had short stanzas, most typically of three or four lines, although sometimes of five or six, most commonly rhymed in couplets (e.g. ABB, AABB, ABBCC, AABBCC). Like the poetic madrigal, it freely mixed *settenari* and hendecasyllables (seven-syllable and eleven-syllable lines).[2]

3.1.1 Sources

See also Section 3.2, Table 1, for a list of printed books of music containing settings of Bernardi's verse. References to musical sources in the notes and commentaries to Bernardi's verse use the abbreviations given in that table.

Manuscripts

F

BNCF, Magl. VII, 447

?Early 17th C. Paper, 4 fols, with later numbering. Presentation-standard copy, well-spaced, in brown ink, scribal hand. Added smaller folded title page, with the heading 'Dian. Bellata Poesie Varie' ('Various Poems by Dianora [i.e. Eleonora] Bellata'). It is possible that the title relates to a printed collection of verse by Bernardi cited by the eighteenth-century erudite Giambattista Moreali under the title 'varie composizioni in versi in lode della B[eata] Vergine' ('Various Verse Compositions in Praise of the Blessed Virgin'). Moreali speaks of the work as having been published in octavo in Venice in 1610.[3]

Contains: 'Se pur fin su negli stellati chiostri', 1r–4v, headed 'Della beata Vergine. Della Sig.ra Dianora Bellatta' (1r). The text appears to be the product of collation of several versions of the poem, with some deletions and corrections (see the commentary to the poem in Section 3.1.2).

S1

BCIS, I.XI.11.

16th–early 17th C. Paper, quarto, 58 fols. *Poesie di diversi autori*. Presentation-standard copy, scribal italic hand. Collection of verse, mainly madrigals, almost all amorous in theme, apart from Bernardi's canzone, which opens the volume and two religious madrigals by Giambattista Guarini (5v) and Ottavio Rinuccini (57v). The dominant poets are Guarini and Rinuccini, with, respectively, 34 and 18 poems, followed by Bernardi with six, Giambattista Strozzi and Sinolfo Saracini with five, Livio Celiano [Angelo Grillo] with two, and Torquato Tasso, Antonio Ongaro, Tarquinia Molza, Riccardo Riccardi, Francesco Antonio de' Pazzi and Vincenzo di Buonaccorso Pitti with a single poem each. The madrigal by Tasso in the collection (11r, 'In un lucido rio') is given in an early, pre-1587 version,[4] and a note accompanies Guarini's 1581 madrigal 'Mentre vaga angioletta' (12v–13r), referring to a performance of the poem by the *concerto delle dame* in a setting by Luzzasco Luzzachi.[5] This may point to a Ferrarese source for at least parts of the collection. Some poems in the manuscript derive from musical sources: see Section 3.2.1 for further discussion.

Contains: 'Se pur fin su negli stellanti chiostri' (1r–5r, headed 'Canzone alla Vergine della Sig[nor]a Leonora Bernardi'); 'Se voi lagrime a pieno' (5r, headed 'Madrigale della medesima'); 'Se pur il ciel consente' (22v, headed 'Della S[igno]ra Leonora Bernardi'); 'Voi l'oro delle stelle' (22v, headed 'Della Medesima'); 'O meraviglia altera' (23r, headed 'Della Medesima'); 'Vago Cielo ov'Amore' (23r, headed 'Della medesima'); 'Più d'altra ninfa amata' (37r, headed 'Della S[ignor]a Leonora Bernardi').

S2
BCIS, I.XI.39.
?17th C. Paper, quarto, 430 pp. *Raccolta di poesie di vari autori*, Miscellany of vernacular verse by mainly Tuscan authors of the later 16th and 17th C (including the Lucchese Cristofano Guidiccioni), with some Venetian material, made up of separates and fascicles in different hands, preceded by an index.

Contains, as no. 23: 'Se pur fin su negli stellati chiostri, 388r–393r; headed 'Canzone alla B[eata] Vergine / De la S[ignor]a Leonora Bernardi 1588'. Index entry describes this as 'Bernardi Eleonora, Canzone.'

Printed sources of significance in establishing texts
G1
PARTE PRIMA / DELLE RIME / DEL SIG. DON ANGELO / GRILLO / NUOVAMENTE DATE IN LUCE / Con licenza de' Superiori / *In Bergamo* / CIƆIƆ XIC [1589] / *Appresso Comino Ventura*

4°. Contains: 'Se le mie preci, & humili, e devote' (113v), headed 'DELLA SIG. / LEONORA BERNARDI / A quel [sonetto], che cominicia: / *E sì chiare, e sì belle, e sì devote.* / c. 26a'; 'Questi, che porger può, care e devote' (114r, headed 'REPLICA / DELLA MEDESIMA / Al medesimo').
A note by Giulio Guastavini in the *argomenti* to the volume (unnumbered, but listed alphabetically by *incipit*) records the context of Grillo's initial *proposta*: 'Signora Leonora Bernardi ... having composed a very beautiful and graceful canzone for the Virgin Mary, this poem came into the hands of the Author, and, since it pleased him greatly, he

composed the present sonnet in its praise, replying to certain details in the said canzone' ('Haveva la Signora Leonora Bernardi ... composta una Canzone alla Vergine Maria, molto bella, & leggiadra, la quale pervenuta nelle mani dell'A. e piacendoli molto, compose il presente Sonetto in sua lode, rispondendo ad alcuni particolari di detta Canzone'). A further *argomento* referring to Bernardi is that to Grillo's reply sonnet to the Lucchese cleric Guido Tegrimi, 'Chi può vincer Vincenzo? O chi perde?', where the line 'in the song and music of your bounteous Phoenix' ('[nel] / canto e nel suon di vostra alma Fenice') is glossed as 'of the Signora Leonora Bernardi, a lady of that city [Lucca], of rare and singular beauty of body and mind, and supremely talented at singing, playing, and writing verse' ('della Sig. Leonora Bernardi, gentildonna di quella città rara, e singolare di bellezza di corpo e d'animo, & eccellentissima nel cantare, nel sonare, e nel poetare').

Sc

SCELTA DI RIME / DI DIVERSI / MODERNI AUTORI. / NON PIÙ STAMPATE. / Parte Prima. // ALLO ILL. ET MOLTO REVER. SIG. / *F. Benedetto Spinola, Cavaliere di San Giovanni.* // IN GENOVA / *Appresso gli Heredi di Girolamo Bartoli / Con licentia de' Superiori, 1591.*

8º. Contains: 'Se pur fin su ne gli stellanti chiostri' (50–3; headed 'Leonora Bellati Bernardi'). The index entry describes the poem as 'Sopra la vergine apparsa a Lucca'.

P

DUI / DIALOGI / DELLA VERGOGNA, / CON ALCUNE PROSE, / ET RIME / DEL SIG. ANNIBALE POCCATERRA / *Academico Ferrarese*, / DEDICATI /ALL'ILLUSTRI[SS.mo] ET REVERENDISS. / SIG. CARDINALE D'ESTE. // IN REGGIO, / Appresso Flauio, et Flamminio Bartholi. 1607. / *Con licenza de' Superiori.*

4º. Contains: 'Tacete (oimè) tacete' (15–6).

F1

VIAGGIO / NELLA S. CASA DI LORETO / DISTINTO IN DODECI / Giornate; / Nelle quali si contiene l'ordine / e modo, che in questo / [e] in ogni pellegrinaggio di / devotione ò di obligo si do- / verebbe tenere per ritrarne / frutto di salute. / Del P. CESARE FRANCIOTTI / della Congregatione della [Santa] Madre di Dio. In Venetia, presso Gio. Battista Combi, 1616.

24º. Contains: 'O chi l'ali m'impenna' (289–90, headed 'ALLA / SANTISSIMA / VERGINE / MARIA. Della Sign. Leonora Belatta de'

Bernardi di Lucca'); 'Se pur fin sù ne li stellanti chiostri' (291–4, headed 'ALL'ISTESSA / SANTISSIMA VERGINE. / Della medesima').

Later editions

G2

Nuova scielta delle rime morali del R. Sig. Don Angelo Grillo. In Bergamo, per Comin Ventura, 1592. 8°. Contains the same poems as G1, with no textual variants, at 197–8.

F2–F4

Viaggio alla S. Casa di Loreto distinto in dodeci giornate. In Venetia, presso Gio. Battista Combi. Three further editions: F2 (1622, 4°); F3 (1625, 24°); F4 (1627, 12°), reproducing the same two poems as F1, in the same order, without textual variants, at 41v–42r (F2); 289–94 (F3); 221–5 (F4).[6]

B

Componimenti poetici delle più illustri rimatrici d'ogni secolo, raccolti da Luisa Bergalli. Parte seconda, che contiene le rimatrici dell'Anno 1575 fino al presente. In Venezia, appresso Antonio Mora, 1726. 12°. Contains: 'Questi, che porger può, care, e devote' (35, headed 'LEONORA BELLATI / BERNARDI. / 1580') from G1, with no textual variants; also, on the same page, a sonnet misattributed to Bernardi, 'Dite, anime felici, siam pur vinte'. This is found in an anthology of 1550 under the name of Giovanni dal Bene (*Libro primo delle rime spirituali*, In Venetia, al segno della Speranza, 6v).

La

Laudi mariane ovvero rime in onore della Vergine Santissima de' più insigni poeti di tutti i secoli della letteratura italiana raccolte da Francesco Martello. Vol. IV. In Napoli, dalla Tipografia di G. Cataneo, 1853. 20 cm. Contains: 'Se fin su negli stellanti chiostri' (321–4) from Sc, with no textual variants.

Lu

Cecilia Luzzi, *Poesia e musica nei madrigali a cinque voci di Filippo di Monte (1580–1595).* Florence: Olschki, 2003. Contains: 'Se pur il ciel consente' (198) from Philippe de Monte's *Il Sestodecimo libro de madrigali a cinque voci* (1593), with a speculative attribution to Angelo Grillo. See Section 3.2.1 for discussion.

3.1.2 The Marian Muse

(i) Se pur fin su ne gli stellanti chiostri (canzone)

st 1

Se pur fin su ne gli stellanti[a] chiostri
talor penetrar osa[b]
presontuosa ancora[c] lingua mortale:
anch'io vorrei, ma con lodati inchiostri
mio core aprirti, o santa e glorïosa   5
Vergine, e gran desio m'impenna l'ale;[d]
ma a dir[e] le meraviglie altere e sole
di te mio vivo[f] Sole
gran spavento ritragge il cor mentr'io
di lui penso che 'n Pò cadde e morìo.   10

st 2

Musa, tu dunque a cui d'eterni allori
nel più vero Elicona
degna[g] corona il crin adorna[h] e cinge,
tu le tenebre mie co' tuoi splendori
rischiara, e 'l canto avviva, e tu perdona,   15
Vergin, se penna umil tue lodi pinge:
tu sostenta lo stil, tu porgi aita,
alla virtù smarrita;
mostra il sentier che[i] senza te non scerno,
battuta nave in mar senza governo.   20

st 3

Già fra[j] le meraviglie al mondo rade
scampò Vergine pia
da fama ria, portando acqua col[k] cribro,
gentil fidanza in tenebrosa etade,
e tu l'infamia d'Eva,[l] onde peria   25

---

[a] F S2 stellati.
[b] F S2 Fr1 ardisce, et osa.
[c] F S2 Fr1 entrar.
[d] S1 Sc L l'ali.
[e] F S2 Fr1 ma dir.
[f] S2 chiaro.
[g] Fr1 nobil.
[h] S1 t'adorna.
[i] S1 S2 ch'io.
[j] F Fr1 tra.
[k] S2 nel.
[l] S1 d'Eva l'infamia.

il mondo, purghi, e già non corri al Tibro
ma nel tuo seno a Dio gradito tempio.
Vergin senza essempio,
di grazie accogli il[m] fiume, e da quell'acque
vita ebbe vita, e morte estinta giacque.   30

st 4   Ecco vedova ebrea che 'n treccia, e 'n gonna,
con famosa pietate,[n]
tra schiere armate si fidò soletta,
poi riede vincitrice, altiera donna:
et tu, Vergine ebrea, tanto più grate   35
spoglie riporti, quanto più perfetta
sei tu[o] d'ogn'altra. Ecco l'empio Oloferne
giù[p] ne le parti inferne
per te legato, ecco inaudita e nova
pace a' mortali e 'n Ciel letizia a prova.   40

st 5   Veggio di regia stirpe, e d'alto core
sposa, che 'n bel sembiante
al rege avante supplice s'inchina
e 'l popol trae di grave[q] rischio fuore.
Tu dell'eccelso e sempiterno amante,   45
sposa, figliola, e madre, e 'n ciel regina,
tutte le grazie impetri, e peccatrice
turba rendi felice.
Tu ci liberi ognor da orribil morte,
o noi beati, o nostra altera sorte.   50

st 6   Or tu, che da' celesti[r] e santi giri,
Vergine eletta e pura
in valle oscura e 'n grave aspro periglio,
mi vedi omai di sì lunghi martiri,
di questa vita tenebrosa e dura,   55
deh ti mova pietà, prega il tuo figlio,
che si degni[s] col suo beato lume,

[m] F S2 un.
[n] F pitate [replacing deleted beltate]; S1 Fr1 beltate.
[o] F Fr1 sei più.
[p] Sc, L già.
[q] F grave [replacing deleted 'mortal']; S2 gran; Fr1 mortal.
[r] F superni [replacing deleted 'celesti']; S1 S2 superni.
[s] F li piacia [replacing deleted 'si degni']; S2 li piaccia.

com'è pur suo costume,
risguardar quest'afflitta anima stanca
d'ogn'altro aiuto homai povera e manca.   60

st 7   Già sai, Vergine pia, che poco è lunge
il quartodecimo anno
che 'n grave affanno io son misera involta,
e 'l core or tema, or doglia afflige e punge.
Deh volgi a me dal tuo beato scanno   65
le sante luci, e 'l umil[t] prego ascolta
di quest'indegna tua devota ancella.
Sgombra benigna stella,
sgombra tante procelle, e rasserena
la vita d'atro orror, di morte[u] piena.   70

st 8   Et se tal grazia, tua mercede, impetro,
spero più che mai lieta,
con fronte queta, il volgo e' suoi pensieri
haver a scherno: all'hor saran di vetro
suoi vani sforzi, se divino acqueta   75
favor le rie tempeste e i turbi fieri.
O mia celeste Dea, ecco l'umìle,
se ben con roco[v] stile,
fida serva a' tuoi piè. La mia salute,
opra sia di tua[w] man, di tua virtute.   80

congedo Va', poverella mia, non ti smarrire.
Se ben al gran desire
non hai manto conforme, un puro zelo[x]
fu con pietà sempre[y] raccolto 'n cielo.

[t] S1 et humil.
[u] S1 morti.
[v] Fr1 rozzo.
[w] F tue.
[x] F Fr1 Telo.
[y] F fu ~~sempre~~ con pietà sempre [deletion in original]; S2 Fr1 fu sempre con pietà.

[st 1] If even on high, within the starry cloisters, sometimes a mortal tongue dares presumptuously to venture, I too would open my heart to you with a worthy pen, holy and glorious Virgin, and a great desire feathers my wings. But from telling your rare and lofty virtues, my living

Sun, a great fear impedes my heart, as I think of him who fell into the Po and died.

[*st 2*] Muse, you whose locks are adorned and circled by a noble crown of eternal laurels in the true Helicon, dispel my shadows with your splendour and give life to my song. And you, Virgin, forgiving that a humble pen paints your praises, sustain my pen and lend support to my scattered powers. Show me the way, for I cannot discern it without you, a battered ship on the ocean with no one at the helm.

[*st 3*] Once among the rare miracles of the world, a holy virgin escaped from ill fame, carrying water in a sieve, a noble sign of faith in an age of shadows; and you purge the world of the infamy of Eve, from which it was perishing, running not to the Tiber but the beloved temple to God in your breast. Matchless Virgin, you gather up the river of grace and from those waters life has life, and death lies slain.

[*st 4*] Here is the Hebrew widow who, in skirts and braids, with famous piety entrusted herself all alone amid the armed throng, from which she returned in triumph, a great lady; and you, Hebrew Virgin, bring back finer spoils, as one more perfect than any other woman. Here is the wicked Holofernes bound by you in the regions of hell; here is a new and unwonted peace sent to mortals and joy in heaven to vie with it.

[st 5] I see a bride of regal blood and high heart, who, in lovely guise, bows a supplicant before a king and draws her people safely from mortal risk. You, bride, daughter and mother of the supreme and eternal lover, queen of heaven, ask all graces for us, rendering happy your errant horde. You free us at every hour from fearful death. How blessed we are, how lofty our fate!

[*st 6*] Now, Virgin choice and pure, you who from the celestial and holy spheres see me in a dark valley and in grave cruel danger, suffering such long torments in this hard life of shadows, let pity move you; pray your son that he deign with his sacred light, as he is wont, to shield this weary and afflicted soul, lacking and bereft of all succour.

[*st 7*] Merciful Virgin, you know it is almost the fourteenth year I have been, alas, enveloped in grave suffering. Now my heart trembles, now it is afflicted and pierced by pain. Turn your holy eyes on me from your blessed dwelling and listen to the humble prayer of your unworthy

devoted handmaiden. Banish, kind star – banish these storm clouds and bring peace to my life, full of black horror and death.

[*st 8*] And if I should attain such a grace through your mercy, I hope that, happy as never before, I shall defy the vulgar throng and its thoughts with a quiet brow, for then all its vain efforts will be as glass; and if divine favour calms the cruel storms and fierce blasts, my heavenly goddess, here is your humble faithful servant at your feet, though her style be hoarse. Let my salvation be the work of your power and your hand.

[*congedo*] Go, poor little creature, do not lose your way. Even if you do not have the garb my great desire wished for you, pure-hearted zeal was always welcome in heaven.

Sources: F, S1, S2; Sc, Fr1–Fr4, La. Rhyme scheme: AbCABCDdEE+YyZZ, without *concatenatio* and with internal rhyme in the third line. Bibliography: *CPr* 67–8; *CLy*, 244–8 (written before the reconstruction of Bernardi's biography); Cox, "'L'umil prego ascolta'".

Bernardi's most famous and circulated poem, this canzone is found in two manuscripts in Siena and one in Florence, in a printed anthology published shortly after the poem's composition, in 1591, and in a work by her acquaintance Cesare Franciotti, printed four times in Venice between 1616 and 1627. The reception of the poem suggests that the canzone was appreciated both as a literary and a devotional work.

This edition is based on the version of the text found in the first printed edition of the canzone (Sc). This is likely to reflect the version of the poem that circulated shortly after its composition in 1588 and that inspired Angelo Grillo's sonnet of praise. Sc was published in Genoa, where Grillo was stationed at the time, and it contains numerous poems by him and his circle. Two corrections have been introduced on the basis of the manuscript and print tradition: *ale* for *ali* at line 6, which is necessary for the rhyme with *mortale* in line 3 and is found in F, S2, and Fr1, and *giù* for *già* at line 38, the sole textual variant found in all printed and manuscript sources except for Sc. These may be printers' errors. Other significant variants are discussed below.

The eight-stanza canzone falls into three parts. In the first (stanzas 1–2), the *captatio benevolentiae*, the poet speaks of her inadequacy to the task she has set herself, of praising the Virgin. In the second part (stanzas 3–5), she embarks on this task, comparing the Virgin to three famous female classical and Old Testament figures: Tuccia, the Vestal

Virgin accused of unchastity, who miraculously proved her innocence by carrying water in a sieve (stanza 3); Judith, the widow of Betulia who, in the apocryphal Book of Judith, rescued her people by killing the enemy general Holofernes (stanza 4); and Esther, who, in the Book of Esther, intervened with her husband, the Persian king Ahasuerus, to save the Jewish people of his kingdom from destruction (stanza 5). The third part of the canzone (6–8), before the *congedo*, shows the poet asking the Virgin to intercede for her and rescue her from current woes, which she describes in stanza 7 as having lasted almost 14 years. As noted in Chapter 1.2.4, this takes us back to 1575, the time of Bernardi's marriage.

The three stanzas praising the Virgin by reference to famous women invite comparison with Vittoria Colonna's canzone 'Mentre la nave mia, longe dal porto', which makes similar use of *exempla* of famous women, although Colonna's are all classical.[7] Judith and Esther were frequently cited in the religious literature of the period as types of the Virgin. The Virgin, like Judith, rescued her people from destruction (in this case, spiritual destruction) through her role in the Incarnation, defeating the Devil in the process, as Judith had defeated Holofernes. She also resembles Esther in respect of her mediatory interventions with God on behalf of humankind. The mention of Tuccia, falsely accused of unchastity and vindicated by a divine miracle, gains a particular resonance when we consider Bernardi's circumstances at the time of the poem's likely composition, following her family's exile from Lucca in July 1588 (Chapter 1.2.4). The same is true of stanza 8's allusions to the hostility of the 'vulgar throng'.

An interesting feature of the poem is its dense intertextual relationship with the poetry of Petrarch and Tasso. Where Tasso is concerned, this is apparent especially in the second stanza, which very closely tracks the second stanza of Tasso's *GL* in its invocation of the heavenly Muse. The term *stellanti chiostri*, in line 1, is also frequent enough in Tasso's religious lyrics to be understood as a deliberate echo here.[8] Bernardi's allusion to the Tuccia story in the third stanza closely imitates a passage in Petrarch's *TP*, ll. 148–51. The phrase *gentil fidanza* also derives from Petrarch's *Trionfi* (*TF*, ii, l. 67: 'O fidanza gentil!'). Another echo of Petrarch is found in the last line of the first stanza, the second half of which precisely echoes line 20 of Petrarch's canzone 'Mai non vo' cantar com'io soleva' (*C* cv): the reference is to the myth of Phaeton, who borrowed the chariot of the sun from Apollo and was struck down by Jove with a thunderbolt. The last line of the second stanza (20) also contains a Petrarchan allusion (*C* cxxxii, l.11), while the description of Judith in stanza 4 echoes both *TC* iii, l. 55 and *C* cxxi, l. 4. The phrase *beato scanno* in line 65 is a rare quotation from Dante (*Inf.* II.112), while the address to the canzone in the *congedo* as *poverella mia* returns to Petrarch (*C* cxxv).

As might be expected, we also find numerous echoes in Bernardi's canzone to Petrarch's great concluding canzone to the Virgin, 'Vergine bella, che di sol vestita' (*C* xxxlxvi). See, for example, Bernardi's line 28 ('Vergine senza essempio'), and compare *C* ccclxvi, l. 53 ('Vergine sola al mondo senza exempio'), both in rhyme with 'tempio' used as a metaphor for the Virgin; Bernardi, line 46 ('sposa, figliola, e madre'), and compare *C* ccclxvi, l. 47 ('madre, figliuola et sposa'); Bernardi, line 66 ('l'umil prego ascolta') and compare *C* ccclxvi, l. 11 ('al mio prego t'inchina'). It is also possible that Bernardi's use of an internal rhyme in the third line of each stanza was inspired by Petrarch's use of such a rhyme in the thirteenth line of his.

Aside from this ornament through allusion, Bernardi's canzone shows a high degree of rhetorical ornamentation, which belies her description of her 'humble pen' in the first stanza and her 'hoarse' style in stanza 8. Especially notable for its rhetorical embellishment is stanza 1, whose rhymes include the inclusive, consonant-rich *chiostri / inchiostri*, the composite *mentr'io / morìo* and the equivocal *sole / Sole*.

An important context for Bernardi's canzone is the miracle that occurred in Lucca in March 1588, when a young soldier's arm broke spontaneously shortly after he blasphemed against the Virgin. This sparked a powerful new cult within the city, surrounding an image of the Virgin and Child near which the miracle took place (see Section 1.2.4). While Bernardi's canzone makes no obvious allusion to the image or to Lucca, there are indications that early readers made the connection; thus, the index entry for the poem in its first printed edition of 1591 (Sc) identifies its subject as 'the Virgin who appeared in Lucca'. Readers within Lucca itself would probably have noticed subtle echoes in the canzone of a sonnet by the Lucchese poet Silvia Bendinelli, 'Alta Regina, a te con umil core', published in a collection of poems by the Bendinelli family addressed to the 'Miraculous Madonna of Lucca' ('Madonna de' Miracoli di Lucca'), with a dedicatory letter dated to August 1588, a month after Bernardi's banishment from Lucca.[9] Bendinelli's sonnet offers thanks to the Virgin for rescuing the poet from a time of 'torment' in her life, figured through the image of a storm at sea, before continuing in the tercets piously to hope that Mary's continued protection will one day guide her to Heaven. Echoes of Bendinelli's sonnet are found especially in lines 68–70 of Bernardi's canzone and in the *congedo*, which borrows two of the rhyme words from Bendinelli's tercets, 'cielo' and 'zelo'. The engagement with Bendinelli's text was strategic for the exiled Bernardi, underlining her continuing emotional participation in the great collective religious experience that her native city had recently undergone.

Of the three manuscripts that transmit Bernardi's canzone, S1 has a version relatively close to that found in Sc. The other two, F and S2, contain a number of significant variants: notably 'penetrar osa / presontuosa ancora' (ll. 2–3) > 'ardisce, et osa / presuntuosa entrar'; 'ma a dir' (l. 7) > 'ma dir'; 'fu con pietà sempre' (l. 84) > 'fu sempre con pietà'. Most of these variants are also found in later printed sources (Fr1–Fr4). These could well be authorial changes introduced in response to suggestions from readers, following a frequent practice in this period, whereby authors would circulate their work to elicit critical feedback. It is not difficult to see, for example, why the more conventional and fluid 'ardisce, et osa / presuntuosa entrar' in lines 2–3 might have been preferred to the less euphonious 'penetrar osa / presuntuosa ancora', although the latter is in keeping with the strong patterns of assonance and alliteration that sometimes characterize Bernardi's style elsewhere (see her sonnet 'Se le mie preci et umili e devote' below). Notable especially is 'presontuosa ancora', which contains what Tasso would call a 'clash of vowels' (*concorso di vocali*), characteristic of epic style, in its juxtaposed 'a's.

The Florence manuscript, F, is especially interesting since it shows signs of a reader collating (at least) two versions of the poem, one close to S2, the other close to S1. The text of the poem contained in the manuscript has several deletions that restore readings close to Sc where a version close to S2 had originally been transcribed, or vice versa. In one case (l. 32), F has a variant from S1 ('beltate'), which it deletes and replaces with the version found in Sc ('pietate'). The text printed in the seventeenth century (Fr1–Fr4), which may well derive from sources close to Bernardi, is similar in many regards to F, though not identical (for example, Fr1 corresponds to Sc in preferring 'si degni' to 'li piacia' in line 57, a variant found in F and S2). Fr1 also introduces some new variants, such as 'rozzo' ('crude') for 'roco' ('hoarse') at line 78. The complexity of the textual situation suggests that the canzone circulated widely, most likely in more than the five versions attested in Sc, F, S1, S2 and Fr1. This is not unusual in situations in which authors were not concerned to oversee the printing of their work.

(ii) O chi l'ale m'impenna (canzonetta)

st 1

O chi l'ale m'impenna,
o pur m'accenna,
ov'io possa spiegar sublime 'l volo?   3
Donna de l'altro polo
a te, di cui ragiono,
Vergin'celeste, a te lo chieggio in dono.   6

st 2

Alla mia rozza cetra
chi grazia impetra
che possa risonar dolce armonia,   9
se non se' tu MARIA?
Spiega tu le parole,
tu che chiudesti entro al tuo grembo il sole: 12

st 3

Vergine, sposa, e madre,
che 'l tuo gran padre
raccogliesti nel sen casto e felice,   15
ove quasi fenice
arse in rogo d'amore
fatto in forma di servo il gran Motore.   18

st 4

Dirò forse che 'n Cielo,
con puro zelo,
all'armonia delle celesti rote,   21
quelle menti devote
con vero affetto interno
cantin' delle tue lodi il pregio eterno?   24

st 5

O dirò che le stelle,
le chiome belle,
con vago giro ti cinghino intorno,   27
o che nobile e adorno
di sol ti vesti 'l manto?
Ma troppo umile al gran soggetto è il canto.   30

[*st 1*] O, who will feather my wings, or at least give me a sign of how I can soar sublime in flight? Lady of the other Pole, to you of whom I speak, celestial Virgin – to you, I ask it as a gift.

[*st 2*] My uncouth cithara – who will plead the grace that it may resound with sweet harmony, if not you, MARY? You unfold the words, you who enclosed the Sun within your womb:

[*st 3*] Virgin, bride and mother, who received your great Father within your chaste and happy breast, where, like a phoenix, He blazed in a pyre of love, the great Motor remade in servile form.

[*st 4*] Shall I perhaps say that in Heaven, with pure zeal, in harmony with the celestial spheres, those devout minds, with true inner feeling, sing the eternal prize of your praises?

[*st 5*] Or shall I say that the stars, your beautiful tresses, wind gracefully around you, or that you adorn your mantle, so noble and fine, with the sun? But my song is too humble for this great theme.

Source: Fr1–Fr4. Rhyme scheme: aaBbcC x 5.

This *canzonetta*, first published in Cesare Franciotti's *Viaggio alla Santa Casa di Loreto*, together with Bernardi's canzone to the Virgin, shares the latter's Marian theme and its self-consciousness about the challenge of writing religious verse. In the canzone, Bernardi characterizes her pen as 'humble' (l. 16) and her style as 'hoarse' (l. 78), and she portrays herself as incapable of writing of Mary without Mary's help (ll. 17–20). Similarly, in the *canzonetta*, Bernardi characterizes her 'cithara' – her poetic instrument – as 'uncouth' and professes herself unable to attain 'sweet harmony' without the inspiration of Mary as Muse (ll. 7–10). The two poems are also linked by close verbal echoes. The rhyme 'zelo / Cielo', found at the beginning of the fourth stanza of the *canzonetta* also occurs in the *congedo* of the canzone (from whence Grillo picked it up for the B rhyme of his sonnet; see Section 3.1.3 (i) below). The phrase 'm'impenna l'ale' is found in the opening stanza of both poems, in line 1 of the *canzonetta* and line 6 of the canzone. The meaning of the phrase is complicated by the double meaning of *penna*, both 'feather' and '[quill] pen'. In both poems, Bernardi's speaker calls out to the Virgin for both spiritual salvation and the poetic inspiration to speak aptly in her praise.

The close intertexual dialogue between canzone and *canzonetta* suggests that the two poems were written as a diptych. A further, triangulating text is Psalm 54 [55] 'Give ear to my prayer, O God' (*Exaudi Deus orationem meam*), which aligns thematically with the canzone and supplies the *canzonetta*'s opening line. The predicament of Bernardi's poetic 'I' in stanzas 6–8 of the canzone resembles that of the psalmist, in that both are assailed by hostility: that of a former close friend in the psalm, that of the 'vulgar throng' in the canzone. Both speakers call out helplessly for divine help in their travails, the psalmist to God, Bernardi's poet to Mary. The first line of the *canzonetta*, 'Chi l'ale m'impenna?' echoes the famous sixth line of psalm, 'quis dabit mihi pennas sicut columbae' ('who will give me wings like a dove?'). Bernardi's phrasing also recalls the *incipits* of a famous love sonnet by Luigi Tansillo of the 1550s, 'Amor m'impenna l'ale, e tanto in alto' and a love madrigal by Tasso, 'Amor l'ale m'impenna' (*R* ccclxxv).[10] The 'conversion' of love lyric to spiritual ends was one of the great projects of later sixteenth-century literature, as was the fusion of psalmic and Petrarchan influences, influentially theorized by Gabriele Fiamma in the 1570s.[11] Bernardi's *canzonetta* exemplifies both these developments, while experimenting with the potential for religious appropriation of the fashionable post-Petrarchan metrical form of the *canzonetta*, an initiative usually associated with Grillo.

Stanza 3 of the *canzonetta* sees Bernardi engaging with two sources that were de rigueur for sixteenth-century Marian poets: Dante's prayer to the Virgin in the voice of St Bernard in *Par* xxxiii, ll. 1–21 and Petrarch's canzone ccclxvi. Line 13 of the *canzonetta*, 'Vergine, sposa, e madre' echoes Petrarch's line 47, 'madre, figliuola et sposa' (already more exactly cited in line 46 of Bernardi's canzone, which opens 'sposa, figliola, e madre'). Lines 14 and 15 of the *canzonetta*, alluding to the paradox of the Virgin as mother to God, her father, recall the *incipit* of the Dantean passage, 'Vergine madre, figlia del tuo figlio'. The final stanza of the canzonetta plays on Petrarch's portrayal of the Virgin as 'garbed in the sun' and 'crowned with stars' (*C* ccclxvi, ll. 1–2).

These familiar allusions take on interesting metapoetic resonances within the economy of Bernardi's poem, as we see them recast within the 'humble' idiom of the *canzonetta*, antithetical to the originals' high style. Bernardi's last two stanzas try out possible lyric strategies of Marian praise – speaking of the ineffable songs of the angels and the spheres (4), or of Mary adorned by the sun and stars as queen of heaven (5) – before concluding that the subject is too high for her song. The parallel openings of these two stanzas ('Shall I perhaps say . . .? Or shall I say . . .?') emphasize the poet's uncertainty, and hence, perhaps, the novelty of her enterprise. This is also, of course, an example of *praeteritio*, as Bernardi demonstrates the potential of the *canzonetta* as a vehicle for religious poetry at the same time she seems to dismiss it.

With its *rime baciate* (juxtaposed rhymes), its preponderance of short lines, and its simple language and rhymes, Bernardi's *canzonetta* epitomizes the 'unforced sweetness' that theorists saw as the defining quality of the madrigalesque poetry of the age.[12] Few lines or images require commentary. The metaphor of the stars as Mary's locks or tresses in ll. 25–6 reflects a tradition apparent in the etymology of the word 'comet' (Greek: 'long-haired') and the name of the constellation Coma Berenicis ('Berenice's Hair'). More mysterious is l. 4, which addresses the Virgin as 'lady of the other Pole'. Mary was often associated with the northern pole star, in her guise as *stella maris*, star of the sea, but an association with the South Pole is more puzzling. Bernardi may simply be emphasizing Mary's universal domain as queen of heaven.

3.1.3 In dialogue with Leonora Bernardi: Angelo Grillo

(i) *E sì chiare, e sì belle, e sì devote (sonnet)*

E sì chiare, e sì belle, e sì devote
voci, e pregar sì pio, sì caldo zelo
al ciel non tornerà? Se vien dal cielo,
e 'l detta il ciel, celesti son le note?   *4*
    Leonora sù sovra l'eccelse rote,
qua giù lasciando il suo corporeo velo,
non l'udì con la mente? Apollo in Delo
l'insegnò? Tanto sa? Cotanto puote?   *8*
    L'udì, l'apprese, e parve dir Maria:
—Figlia, ch'offristi a me lo spirto e 'l core,
vie più d'ogni altra affettuosa e pura: *11*
    divo spirto, alta tromba, e santo ardore
eccoti in vece. Ah, da mie lodi impura
lingua fia lunge, e tu mia Musa sia—.   *14*

(ii) Se le mie preci ed umili e devote (sonnet)

Se le mie preci ed umili e devote,
piene, quanto poss'io, d'acceso zelo
celeste messaggier portando al cielo,
le spiegherà con vive ardenti note,   4
    forse salir sovra l'eccelse rote
potrò, sgravata dal terrestre velo,
sprezzando il lusinghiero Apollo e Delo,
che 'n ciel solo ogni ben trovar si puote.   8
    Tu in terra, Angel divin, caro a Maria,

a cui sacrasti già devoto il core,
prega per me, che puoi, con mente pura: 11
   ch'accesa l'alma, e nel suo santo ardore
purgata e monda d'ogni macchia impura,
sua serva, e non del tutto indegna, io sia.   14

(iii) Questi, che porger può care e devote (sonnet)

Questi, che porger può care e devote
preci, con sì pietoso e santo zelo,
non è dal Ciel mandato a noi? Del Cielo
non son le sue purgate e chiare note?   4
   Questi, ch'al suon de le celesti rote
tempra 'l suo canto, avvolto in sì bel velo,
ben certo appare il biondo Dio di Delo,
ma nè tanto egli sa, nè tanto puote.   8
   Angelo dunque è certo, ed à Maria
sì caro, a cui votò già l'alma, e 'l core,
ch'in vece n'hebbe casta mente e pura: 11
   et s'ella spira in lui divino ardore,
onde si stempre ogni vil voglia impura,
sol ella oggetto a la sua penna sia.   14

(iv) *Le lodi mie, ne le tue lodi sparte (sonnet)*

Le lodi mie, ne le tue lodi sparte,
sembran vario color, mista pittura,
ch'esprima in quadro intelligenza pura
e spirto infonda a l'insensate carte.   4
   L'artificio è tuo sol, tua sola l'arte,
tu l'alto figurato, io la figura,
tu l'industre fattore, io la fattura,
tu l'Angel vero, io 'l finto in degna parte.   8
   Chi mi rimirerà, volgendo gli anni,
dirà: —Ben l'opra è di pittor famoso,
né in mare il Sol par più lucente e vago—:   11
   ma leggendo il tuo nome glorïoso,
diva ti chiamerà de gli alti scanni,
che spiri eterna vita in frale imago.   14

[i] And will such clear, fine, devout words, such pious prayer, such warm zeal not reach Heaven? If it comes from Heaven, if Heaven dictates it, if heavenly are its notes? Did Leonora not hear it in her mind on high, above the sublime spheres, leaving her corporeal veil here far below? Did Apollo teach it to her in Delos? Can she know so much? Do so much? Mary heard it, welcomed it, and seemed to say: 'Daughter, you who have offered me your spirit and heart, more impassioned and pure than any other woman, a divine spirit, lofty trumpet, and holy ardour shall be yours in exchange. Let impure tongues refrain from my praises: you shall be my Muse'.

[ii] If my humble and devout prayers, full as I can make them of burning zeal, are carried to heaven by a celestial messenger and voiced with vivid ardent notes, then perhaps I shall be able to soar above the sublime spheres, freed of my terrestrial veil, despising the flatteries of Apollo and Delos, for only in heaven may all good be found. You on earth, divine Angel, dear to Maria, to whom you long ago devoutly pledged your heart, pray for me, for you can, with a pure mind, that with my soul on fire and purged in her holy flame and freed from every stain of impurity, I may be her not wholly unworthy handmaid.

[iii] This man, who can proffer up prayers so precious and devout, with such pious and holy zeal, has he not been sent to us by Heaven? From Heaven must not such polished and brilliant notes derive? This man, who tempers his song to the sound of the celestial spheres, wrapped in so fair a veil, appears for sure like the blond god of Delos – yet Apollo does not have his wisdom and power. He must certainly be an angel, then, and so dear to Mary, to whom he has vowed his soul and heart, that she gave him in return a chaste and pure mind; and, if she inspires him with divine ardour that melts away every base or impure desire, let her alone be the object of his pen.

[iv] My praises, strewn among your praiseworthy verse, seem like various hues, a mingled painting that a pure intelligence expresses on her canvas, breathing a live spirit into the senseless pages. The artifice is yours alone, yours is the art; you are the high figured meaning, I the figure; you are the industrious maker, I the made; you the true Angel, I an angel feigned in a worthy site. Those who look back at me with the turning of the years will say: 'This work is by a famous painter; nor is the sun on the sea more lucent and lovely'. But when they read your glorious name, they will call you a goddess of the high heavens, who breathes eternal life into a frail image.

Source: G1, G2. Poem (iii) also in B. Poems (i) and (iv) also found in *Rime del molto Reverendo Padre D. Angelo Grillo* (Venice: Giovanni Battista Ciotti, 1599), 127v and 142r. Rhyme schemes: (Poems (i)–(iii)) ABBA ABBA CDE DEC, with same rhyme words in same order; (Poem (iv)) ABBA ABBA CDE DCE, with one rhyme shared with the previous sequence (-ura). Source: G1, 26r, 113v, 114r, 61r.

Sonnet exchanges were a frequent poetic practice in the Italian Cinquecento, and exchanges with prominent male poets were a key means through which female poets established their 'right of residence' in the literary sphere.[13] The exchange with Bernardi initiated by Grillo and displayed in his 1589 *Rime* is an unusually intense one, however, with Bernardi writing two *risposte* to his initial *proposta* and Grillo following up with a second sonnet of his own. Another unusual feature is that Grillo's *proposta*, rather than a general sonnet of praise, is a response to an individual poem, with a high metapoetic content. Given that the poem in question was a religious one, and that Grillo was on the verge of a historically momentous intervention in the tradition of religious verse, the exchange has considerable interest, even beyond the rare glimpse it offers of Leonora Bernardi in dialogic mode. See also Section 1.2.4 for discussion of the dramatic biographical context of this exchange.

As is recorded in a note in G1 (see the entry in Section 3.1.1), Grillo's *proposta*-sonnet (i) refers to Bernardi's Marian canzone, to whose aspiration to be heard in heaven, expressed in the first stanza and the *congedo*, it alludes in its opening lines. The quatrains of Grillo's sonnet argue that Bernardi's canzone must have been inspired by heaven itself, given its literary excellence and piety. The tercets, in an exercise in prosopopoeia, have the Virgin elect Bernardi as her chosen poet on the grounds of her devotion, giving her in return the eloquence necessary to perfect her praise. The underlying conceit is that of Mary as celestial Muse, developed by Bernardi in the second stanza of her canzone. The description of Bernardi as *affettuosa* (line 11) is significant, since *affetti* (affects, emotions) were conceived of as central within Counter-Reformation religious poetics. It was a key term, in particular, for Grillo, who, from 1596, used the term *Pietosi affetti* (*Pious Affects*) as the title for successive collections of his religious verse.

Replies to sonnets often used the same rhyme scheme as the *proposta* as a test of poetic skill. An even more challenging practice, increasingly popular in the later sixteenth century, involved using the same actual rhyme words as the *proposta*. Bernardi adopts this procedure in both her replies. Poem (ii), in particular, succeeds astonishingly well within these difficult constraints, showing very little of the strain and artificiality even skilled poets sometimes demonstrate in responses of this type. Where Grillo's sonnet had allocated part of Bernardi's poetic success to divine inspiration and part to natural talent and skill, symbolized by the classical god of poetry, Apollo (lines 7–8), Bernardi modestly disavows this, renouncing Apollo and presenting her verses merely as 'humble, devout prayers'. Bernardi's skill, is, however, much on display here. The sound patterning of her sonnet is quite intricate, with alliteration and assonance used throughout, particularly in the tercets, for harmony and variety, and some quite showy effects, such as the polyptoton *celeste / cielo* (line 3), echoing Grillo's play on the same words in line 4 of his sonnet, and the chiastic balancing of sounds in line 13 (*purgata / monda / macchia / impura*), the *monda / macchia* pairing again echoing a similar device in Grillo's sonnet, *lingua / lunge* (line 14). The pun on Grillo's religious name, Angelo (line 9) 'converts' the *senhal* device of secular Petrarchism and clarifies the reference to the 'celestial messenger' of line 3 who will amplify her humble prayers with his own 'vivid, ardent notes'.

Poem (iii) contains significant echoes of Grillo's *proposta*, in addition to using its rhyme words. Its first quatrain picks up the interrogative structure of Grillo's first quatrain, along with his motif of attributing a celestial origin to his correspondent's verse. Bernardi's attribution to him in line 2 of 'pietoso e santo zelo' echoes his characterization of her 'pregar pio' and 'caldo zelo' in the equivalent line of his sonnet. Where the tercets of Grillo's sonnet had shown Mary electing Bernardi, on the grounds of her ardent faith, to be her poet on earth, Bernardi turns this compliment around, emphasizing Grillo's own devotion to the Virgin, as expressed by his religious vows, and urging him to take up the role as Marian poet that he had attributed to her. Bernardi also echoes her own first *risposta*, placing the same pun on Grillo's religious name Angelo in the first line of the tercets, along with that of Mary, and mentioning his vows in the following line. In this second poem, she shows Mary rewarding his devotion with the gift of a 'chaste and pure mind' – appropriate adjectivization for a monk, but also for Mary herself – in a way that emphasizes the consonance between poet and divine subject matter, just as Grillo had done in her case.

An unexpected feature of the poem is the second quatrain's comparison of Grillo to Apollo, not merely for his sublime poetry, but for his physical beauty (the 'beautiful veil' that enwraps him), which gives him the appearance of the 'blond Apollo' (a characteristic epithet of the god in classical and Renaissance verse; see, for example, *TC*, I: 154).

Allusions to the beauty of a female addressee, even one the poet has never seen, are conventional in Renaissance verse, but such compliments are vanishingly rare in the case of poems by female authors to male addressees. Bernardi's compliment here helps confirm that the two poets had met in person by this time, given that Matteo Ponzone's portrait of Grillo in the Museo d'Arte Medievale e Moderna in Padua, painted in around 1611, when he was in his mid-50s,[14] shows him with relatively light hair and complexion, if with few traces of the Apollonian beauty he may have possessed in 1585, the likely time of their first meeting in Ferrara, when he was in his late 20s (Section 1.2.2).

Grillo's sonnet of response, Poem (iv), abandons the rhyme scheme and rhyme words of the three previous sonnets, while retaining a connection in the form of a single rhyme shared with the previous sequence (-ura), along with a shared rhyme word, *pura*. Grillo had used a similar device to bind together his first sonnet with the canzone of Bernardi's that inspired it, picking up the last two rhyme words from the canzone's *congedo* (*zelo*, *cielo*) and recycling them in his first quatrain. The sonnet is characteristic of late-Renaissance verse in its *concettismo*, its use of striking and ingenious conceits. In the first two lines, Grillo plays on the traditional, Horatian comparison of poetry and painting to represent Bernardi's praise poems as a brilliant, richly coloured portrait ('colours' was a standard metaphor for stylistic and rhetorical devices). Line 1 plays on the two senses of *lode / laude* in Italian (and Latin *laus, laudis*), referring to praises, but also things praiseworthy. Praises of Grillo, in the first sense, are strewn throughout Bernardi's praiseworthy verses, whose artistry is underlined by Grillo's use of the term *sparte*, which echoes *sparse* ('scattered' or 'strewn') in the same position in Petrarch's proemial sonnet. Lines 3 and 4 continue the visual arts simile, alluding first to the Neoplatonic notion of painting and sculpture as cerebral arts, translating an imaginative *concetto* into material form, and then to the Pygmalion motif of the artist's godlike ability to conjure life from dead matter (here, the 'insensate pages' on which Bernardi inscribes her words). The second quatrain describes Bernardi as expert artificer of the painted artefact Grillo, concluding paradoxically by identifying her as the true 'Angelo' and himself as a lesser, feigned version – a particularly ingenious twist on the common device in sonnet exchanges of turning a compliment back on the writer who first crafted it. The tercets evoke the figure of a future reader of the exchange, who will see Bernardi's poem-portraits as evidence of her genius, rather than of any virtue of his.

Grillo's closing poem in the exchange is remarkable in the light of contemporary gender attitudes, particularly for its casting of Bernardi in the active, godlike role of creator and himself in the passive role of 'frail image'. In Aristotelian terms, Bernardi is here associated with masculine 'form' and Grillo with feminine matter; a new Pygmalion, she 'breathes him into life'. It is difficult to think of precedents for this type of gender inversion, outside Michelangelo's madrigals for Vittoria Colonna, 'Sì come per levar, donna, si pone' and 'Non pur d'argento o d'oro', which implicitly figure Colonna as spiritual and moral 'sculptor' to Michelangelo's sculpture or cast.[15] Taken together with Bernardi's feminizing portrayal of Grillo in Poem 3 as angelically beautiful and endowed by the Virgin with a 'chaste and pure' mind, this aspect of the exchange well illustrates the gender fluidity that has been noted as a feature of Counter-Reformation religious literature generally, and particularly as a feature of Grillo's verse.[16]

3.1.4 In dialogue with Leonora Bernardi: Ottavio Rinuccini

(i) Se, come dite voi, fu sempre in cielo (madrigal)

> *Se, come dite voi, fu sempre in cielo*
> *raccolto con pietate un puro zelo,*
> *voi che del cielo un'angeletta sete*
> *perché pietosa ohimè non raccogliete*
> *questi sospiri ardenti*   5
> *nati de' miei tormenti*
> *ch'al vostro albergo intorno*
> *spargo miser'amante notte e giorno.*

If, as you say, a pure zeal was always welcomed with pity in Heaven, then why do not you, who are a little angel of Heaven, pityingly now welcome these ardent sighs, born of the torments that I, a wretched lover, bewail night and day outside your door?

Source: BNCF Palatino 249, 36v. Rhyme scheme: AABBccdD.

This madrigal, and the poem in *ottava rima* that follows, are found in a manuscript in Florence containing an ample collection of verse by Ottavio Rinuccini, seemingly prepared by a series of scribes under the poet's own supervision.[17] The madrigal is preceded by a note (at 36r) that reads 'Il seguente madrigal con le sei stanze / furon fatte sopra una canzone della Sig.ra L.B.' ('The following madrigal together with the six stanze / were written about a canzone by Signora L. B.'). Five other madrigals are found in sequence in the preceding pages, addressed to a female singer. The addressee of the poems has been hypothetically identified as the famous Ferrarese court lady Lucrezia Bendidio (1547–after 1584),[18] but the mention of a canzone in the note and the direct quotations from Bernardi's 'Se fin su ne gli stellanti chiostri' in the madrigal and canzone that follow make it clear that at least these – and perhaps the five madrigals that precede them – are addressed to Leonora Bernardi. For further discussion of Rinuccini's poems to Bernardi, see Sections 1.2.4 and 2.1.5.

Rinuccini's response to Bernardi's canzone could hardly contrast more with that of Grillo. Where Grillo, as was proper for his status as monk, addresses himself to the Marian segments of the poem (stanzas 1–5), Rinuccini's falls squarely on the autobiographical segment (stanzas 6–8), and his stance is that both of a sympathizer and a lover. The madrigal transforms the pious augury of Bernardi's closing lines that her prayer will be heard in Heaven into the amorous plea of the poet-lover that his 'angelic' mistress will attend to his woes.

(ii) S'è ver che su negli stellanti giri (stanze)

st. 1	S'è ver che su negli stellanti giri	
	nel piu vago del ciel pietà risplenda,	
	fiammeggiante di zelo, e foco spiri,	
	foco onde l'alma di pietate accenda,	
	fia ben che i pianti tuoi, che i tuoi sospiri,	5
	anima bella, il ciel pietoso intenda	
	e tuoi torbidi dì tranquilli e lieti	
	renda e del cor tante procelle acqueti. / [37ᵛ]	
st. 2	S'alle lagrime tue, s'a giusti preghi	
	sparsi in sì dolce e 'n sì soave stile	10
	vien che repugni il cielo e grazia nieghi	
	alle dimande tue, donna gentile,	
	quando più fia che lo commova e pieghi	
	di mortal cor pianto o preghiera umile.	
	Ahi, che se 'l pianger tuo non move il cielo,	15
	più non gradisce de' mortali il zelo.	
st. 3	Ma come esser può mai ch'a' preghi, a' pianti	
	d'innocente beltà neghi mercede	
	chi su nel ciel sovra le stelle erranti	

siede beato e 'l tutto scerne e vede.
Ben del pudico cor gl'onesti e santi
pensier son noti e la tua pura fede,
e, s'è giustizia in ciel, cangiarsi in gioia
già veggio ogni tormento, ogni tua noia.

st. 4   *Vivi, donna gentil, lieta e sicura,*   25
omai tranquilla, omai serena il core,
vedi che piange ognun di tua sventura
e penetr'ogni petto il tuo dolore. / [37ʳ]
Angel divin di tua salute ha cura:
ecco tornare sereni i giorni e l'ore;   30
ecco farsi al tuo mare tranquille l'onde
e spirar' l'aure a tuoi desir seconde.

st. 5   *Qual dopo tempestosa e ria procella*
più vago un bel seren mostrarsi suole
più che mai lieta ancor, più che mai bella   35
vedravvi il mondo ch'or per voi si duole.
Amor già preso ha l'arco e le quadrella
e 'n virtù de' vostri occhi aspira e vuole
quanto coverchia il ciel farsi suggetto.
Soll'io, che già trafitto ho 'l core nel petto.   40

st. 6   *Il core ho già trafitto e non men' doglio*
né curo di sanar' sì bella piaga,
grata benché mortale, e 'l suo cordoglio
quasi gioia e piacere l'anima appaga.
Soccorso al mio languire non chieggio, o voglio: 45
schiva di rinsanar', di morte vaga,
l'alma vie più che mille e mille vite
stima morir per voi, luci gradite.

[st 1] If it is true that on high within the starry spheres, in the most beautiful part of Heaven, Pity gleams, aflame with zeal, and breathing fire – fire wherewith the soul is lit with pity – then it is right that your plaints and your sighs, lovely soul, should be heard by pitying Heaven, and your dark days should be made tranquil and gay, and the many storms of your heart should be quieted.

[st 2] If your tears and your just prayers, scattered in such a sweet and pleasing style, should be refused by Heaven, and grace denied to your pleas, gentle lady, then when will ever the humble plaint or prayer of a mortal heart be granted? Alas! If your weeping does not move Heaven, then no human zeal can ever win its grace.

[st 3] But how should it ever be that He who sits blessed above the wandering stars and who sees and discerns all should ever deny mercy to the prayers and plaints of innocent beauty? The honest and holy thoughts of your chaste heart are known to Him, and your pure faith, and, if there is justice in Heaven, I see your every torment and pain soon changed to joy.

[st 4] Gentle lady, now live happy and secure, now calm and quiet your heart. You see that everyone weeps for your ill fortune and every breast is pierced by your pain. An Angel divine has care of your wellbeing, so behold the serene days and hours return. Behold, the waves of your sea become tranquil and breezes blow favourable to your will.

[st 5] Just as, after a fierce and malevolent tempest, a cloudless sky appears still more lovely, just so the world that now grieves for you will see you lovelier and gayer than ever. Love has already seized up his bow and his arrows, and he aspires and wishes to subject the whole world through the power of your eyes. I know this well, for my own heart is pierced within my breast.

[st 6] My heart is already pierced, and I do not complain, nor would I wish to cure so lovely a wound, dear to me, even if fatal, for the pain that it causes me lulls my heart as if it were joy and pleasure. I do not ask help in my languishing, caring little for healing, and longing for death. My soul would rather die for you, lovely eyes, than enjoy a thousand and a thousand more lives.

Sources: BNCF Palatino 249, 36v–38r; BNCF Fondo Baldovinetti 129.1, 40r–41r. Rhyme scheme: ABABABCC x 6 stanzas. Source: BNCF Palatino 249, 36v–37v.

Ottava rima is most familiar as the standard metre for narrative poetry in Italian, but it was also used as a lyric form, as here.[19] Rinuccini's poem takes the form of a *consolatio*, first assuring Bernardi that the prayer contained in her canzone cannot fail to be heard in Heaven (stanzas 1–3), before reminding her of the widely shared sympathy that surrounds her and predicting that, as she recovers, she will soon hold the world in sway through Love (stanzas 4–5). In the final line of stanza 5, the poet confesses himself already a victim of love for her, while, in the final stanza, he celebrates the ecstatic agonies he suffers for this love.

Like the madrigal that precedes it, Rinuccini's *stanze* poem is threaded through with linguistic echoes of the canzone to which it responds. 'Ciel[o]' occurs twice in the madrigal, and four times in the first three stanzas of the longer poem, while 'pietate' / 'pietoso' is found twice in the former and three times in the first stanza of the latter. Other repeated terms are 'zelo', found once in the madrigal (in rhyme with 'cielo'), and 'prego' / 'preghiera', found three times in *stanze* 2–3 of 'S'è ver che su negli stellanti giri', while Bernardi's plea that, with the Virgin's assistance, she will emerge from her trauma 'più che mai lieta' is echoed in stanza 5 of Rinuccini's poem (with 'lieta' already found in l. 25 and 'lieti' in l. 7). This echoing technique is suggestive of an initial audience well acquainted with Bernardi's canzone and capable of recognizing allusions to it, presumably the chorus of sympathizers referred to in the 'ognun' of l. 27 and the 'mondo' of l. 36. These early readers or listeners were doubtless also acquainted with Grillo's intervention on behalf of Bernardi, alluded to in l. 29, where an 'Angel divin' – a frequent pun on Grillo's name – is said to be watching over her.

A second copy of the poem, in a lyric miscellany in Florence (BNCF Fondo Baldovinetti 129.1) suggests a later moment of circulation of the poem when this immediate context had been lost: here, it is simply captioned, generically, '[The Poet] Consoles a Beautiful Grieving Lady' ('Consola Bella Dama dolente'). This version has a few minor variants, the most significant of which are 'sen' for 'cor' at l. 21, and ''l core e 'l petto' for ''l core nel petto' at l. 40. For a description of the contents of the manuscript (formerly Palatino 294), see Palermo, 'I manoscritti', 1. 504–6.

In addition to the evidence of the canzone's early reception presented in this section and in Section 1.2.4, Alexandra Coller has recently called attention to intriguing echoes of Bernardi's poem in a canzone by the Paduan poet Valeria Miani (*c.* 1520–after 1620), addressed to the Venetian patrician Tommaso Contarini, and published in an anthology of 1609 ('Se dal sereno Ciel divino amore').[20] Besides the consonances noted by Coller, one might also note the very similar metrical schemes of the two canzoni (without *concatenatio* and with two final rhyming couplets) and the thematic and syntactic congruences of the poems' first stanzas, both similarly meta-literary – though Miani's is secular in focus – and opening with a conditional clause.[21] Miani presumably encountered Bernardi's poem in its 1591 printed edition (Sc).

3.1.5 Songs of love

(i) Se voi lagrime a pieno (madrigal)

Se voi lagrime a pieno
non mostrate il dolore
ch'entro rinchiud'il seno,[a]
a che versate fore?[b]
Statevi dentro e soffocate[c] il core.   5

[a] Mo, Ba, Ca racchiude 'l seno; Ag che dentro asconde il seno.
[b] Mo, Ba, Ag fuore.
[c] Ag soffogate; Ba tormentate.

If you, tears, do not fully express the anguish my breast harbours within, then why do you pour out? Stay within and choke my heart.

Sources: S1; Mo, Ma, Ba, De, Ca, Ag. Rhyme scheme: ababB.

Bernardi's shortest madrigal, at five lines, was her most popular among composers, with six musical settings published between 1593 and 1617. The text given here is from S1, where the madrigal is found immediately after Bernardi's canzone. The poem is exceptionally light, with four seven-syllable lines followed by a sole hendecasyllable, and only two rhymes, both simple and vocalic (-eno, -ore). The poetic 'I' addresses her – or his – tears (we have no marks of gender), reproaching them for their inability to show forth the speaker's inner pain, presumably deriving from unreciprocated love. They must stay within and suffocate her heart. Tears and sighs often figure in sixteenth-century love poetry as the means through which lovers sought to plead their case with an obdurate love object, so the speaker's annoyance is presumably motivated by her inability to convey the depth of her love and hence to awaken a reciprocal feeling. The element of wit that readers prized in the madrigal here consists in the incongruity of the speaker venting her amorous frustration on her tears, and on the final, hyperbolic image of her tears as an inner lake capable of drowning her heart.

(ii) Se pur il ciel consente (madrigal)

Se pur il ciel consente
che fien[a] le gioie mie del tutto spente,
a che più mi riserba
in questa vita acerba?
Ahi, ben dovrei morire   5
per sottrarmi a sì grave aspro martire.

[a] Mo fian.

If heaven truly consents that all my joys are quite extinguished, then why does it keep me any longer in this soured life? Ah, I should indeed die, to escape such harsh and severe torment.

Sources: S1; Mo, Lu. Rhyme scheme: aAbbcC

Darker in tone than 'Se voi lagrime a pieno', without the leavening of wit, the six-line 'Se pur il ciel consente' is also a little denser in texture, with two hendecasyllables to four *settenari* and two consonant-rich rhymes (-ente and -erba) to one more open, vocalic rhyme (-ire). The assertiveness of the rhymes is enhanced by the rhyme scheme, composed of three successive rhymed couplets. Other consonant-heavy words are also found out of rhyme: 'tutto' (l. 2) juxtaposed with 'spente'; 'questa' (l. 4) and 'sottrarmi . . . grave aspro' (l. 6), making for a particularly heavy close. 'Acerba' in line 4 means literally 'unripe', as in fruit, but it is frequently used metaphorically, as here, to mean 'sour' or 'bitter'. The word recurs in the refrain of Dalinda's lament in *Clorilli* IV.5 ('del mio fero dolor l'acerba istoria' / 'del corto viver mio l'acerba istoria').

(iii) Voi l'oro delle stelle (madrigal)

Voi l'oro delle stelle
raccogliete nel crine
e scintillanti amorose fiammelle
nelle luci divine,
e 'l vostro vago viso,   5
FLAVIA, raccolto ha 'l bel del paradiso.
Beato chi vi mira,
e chi per voi sospira.

The gold of the stars you garner in your tresses, and sparkling flames of love in your divine gaze; and your charming visage, FLAVIA, garners within it the beauty of paradise. Blessed all those who look on you . . . and those who sigh for you.

Source: S1. Rhyme scheme: abAbcCdd.

Alone among Bernardi's madrigals, this poem is addressed to a named addressee, a 'Flavia', perhaps Flavia Damasceni Peretti (1574–1606), great niece of Pope Sixtus V, who married Ferdinando de' Medici's nephew Virginio Orsini in 1589 and became part of the circles of the Medici court (see Section 2.1.5), though the couple lived initially in Rome. If this identification is correct, this poem would provide further evidence of Bernardi's cultural interactions during her Florentine years, along with *Clorilli* and the poems by Ottavio Rinuccini collected in Section 3.1.4. The likelihood that the poem derives from a different source than the other madrigals found in S1 is increased by the fact that it is the only madrigal present there that does not appear in Philippe de Monte's *Sestodecimo libro de madrigali* (see Section 3.2.1).

'Voi l'oro delle stelle' creates a dreamily idealized vision of Flavia as the angelic lady (*donna angelicata*) of the lyric tradition, drawing on language ('divine', 'paradise', 'blessed') that led some Counter-Reformation clerics to condemn Petrarchist love lyric as blasphemous. The poem's diction is refined, using the Latinate 'crine' for hair (more usually 'capelli') and the metaphorical 'luci' (literally, 'lights') for eyes. This allusion to light, together with the references to gold, stars and sparkling flames (in fact 'flamelets', the diminutive 'fiammelle'), contribute to the visual brilliance of the first section of the poem (lines 1–6), anticipating its closing rhyme word 'paradise'. The soundscape of this passage is also densely worked, with the crisp consonant pattern of line 2 contrasting with the more liquid sounds of lines 1 and 3–4 and complemented by the assonance of the opening words ('Voi l'oro') and the alliteration in line 5 ('vostro vago viso'). While the opening image of the golden-haired lady may simply be conventional, blond hair being one of the hallmarks of the Petrarchist love object, it is worth recalling that Flavia Peretti Orsini was reputedly fair-haired herself, and that her given name, Flavia, which derives from the Latin *flava,* itself signifies 'yellow-haired', 'flaxen'. Also perhaps relevant is that Flavia Peretti was the dedicatee, along with her sister, of a 1589 print sequence illustrating extravagant braided hairstyles, Giovanni Guerra's *Varie acconciature usate da nobilissime dame in diverse città d'Italia.*[22] If she is indeed the

Flavia of the poem, it is possible that a particular 'spectacle hairstyle' may be referred to, one featuring gold ornaments or stars.[23]

After the stylistic pyrotechnics of the first six lines, the poem concludes with a rhymed couplet of utter simplicity, closing with a sly, courtly allusion to Flavia's enamoured admirers. The lines resemble the final couplet of an anonymous madrigal, probably of Ferrarese origin, set to music by Carlo Gesualdo in his *Sesto libro de' madrigali* of 1611, 'Alme d'amor rubelle' ('Beato chi v'ascolta e chi vi mira / Beato chi per voi langue e sospira').[24]

(iv) O meraviglia altera! (madrigal)

O meraviglia altera!
Ecco sceso dal Cielo
un più sereno cielo
ove continuo 'l sol[a] più vago splende,
né nube invida e fera   5
le sue bellezze al guardo altrui[b] contende.

[a] Mo il sol.
[b] Mo al guard'altrui.

O lofty wonder! Here, descended from Heaven, is a more serene heaven, where the sun shines more beautifully without cease, nor does any cruel and unwelcome cloud hide its beauties from men's gaze.

Sources: S1; Mo. Rhyme scheme: abbCaC

Close in theme and tone to 'Voi l'oro delle stelle', 'O meraviglia altera' introduces a creature – probably a woman – of miraculous beauty, figuring her as a perpetually sunny and cloudless heaven or sky. The most striking feature of the poem stylistically is the juxtaposed *rima equivoca* 'Cielo' / 'cielo', with 'Heaven' in the sense first of 'Paradise', then of 'sky'.

The motif of a Heaven-born beauty finds its philosophical roots in the Neoplatonic notion of physical beauty as reflecting the divine beauty and goodness of its Maker. The comparison of the beloved to a brilliant cloudless sky (which we also find in a speech of Filemone's in *Clorilli* I.5, lines 14-6) reflects the traditional Petrarchist comparison of the beloved to the sun, associated especially with Vittoria Colonna. The soundscape of this madrigal is particularly varied and sophisticated, with the assonance of '*mera*viglia al*tera*' of the first line, the contrasting hard and soft sounds in 'Ecco sceso' in line 2, and the vocalic patterning in the final line, with the 'e's of 'le sue bellezze' and 'contende' sandwiching the 'a's and 'u's of 'al guardo altrui'.

(v) Vago Cielo ov'Amore (madrigal)

Vago Cielo ov'Amore
nel biond'oro lucente
tempra gli aurati strali,[a]
e nella luce ardente
di due benigne e fiammeggianti stelle   5
le più spente facelle
ravviva; indi ferisce e 'nfiamma[b] il core
de' felici mortali
di nobil piaga e di celeste ardore.

[a] Mo gl'aurati strali.
[b] Mo e infiamma.

Lovely Heaven, where Cupid tempers his gilded arrows in the shining blond gold, and in the ardent light of two gracious flaming stars rekindles the most dying fires; then he injures and enflames the hearts of happy mortals with noble wounds and celestial ardour.

Sources: S1; Mo. Rhyme scheme: abcbDdAcA.

At nine lines, this is the longest of the five madrigals by Bernardi found in S1. Like 'O meraviglia altera', it uses the metaphor of a beautiful sky or heaven to convey the beauty of the love object. Here, however, the imagery is fused with that of Love, the god Eros or Cupid, who was figured in mythology as responsible for stirring erotic desire in his 'victims'. Specifically, he was armed with a bow from which he shot golden arrows to arouse desire (as well as lead ones to cause aversion), and sometimes also a torch or burning brand, with which to enflame hearts. Bernardi figures him as using the golden-blonde hair of the 'lovely Heaven' to temper his golden arrows and her brilliant eyes to rekindle his torch. To complicate the imagery further, the 'shining gold' of the celestial beauty's hair is implicitly compared to the sun, while her eyes are explicitly figured as stars.

The structure of the poem is bipartite, with lines 1–7 down to 'ravviva' a long, sinuous, flowing phrase, featuring notable use of enjambement. After 'ravviva', a strong hiatus follows, with a crisper clause narrating the actions of Love. The whole is an example of anacoluthon, where one construction succeeds another in a disjunctive manner, so the two parts do not grammatically or syntactically cohere. The last lines of the poem offer an example of *rapportatio*, where two (or more) parallel sentences or clauses are lined up in a way that juxtaposes their respective grammatical elements (subjects with subjects, verbs with verbs, etc.). Here 'injure and enflame' are the actions of the previously mentioned arrows and torch, while their effects are, respectively, the 'noble wound' and the 'celestial ardour' of line 9.

Bernardi creates a deliberate tension between the violence of Cupid's acts in l. 7 (injuring and burning) and the description of his victims in l. 8 as 'happy' (or 'fortunate'). Line 9 resolves this tension by showing the love inspired by the 'lovely Heaven' to be ennobling and 'celestial', in the Neoplatonic sense that it spiritually elevates the lover and leads him to a union with the divine. The poem thus ends where it begins, with the lady's God-given heavenly beauty. The effect is reinforced by the repetition of 'Cielo' and 'celeste' in lines 1 and 9, and by the rhyme scheme, which binds the first and last lines through the rhyme of 'Amore' / 'ardore'.

(vi) Tacete (oimè) tacete (madrigal)

Tacete (oimè) tacete,
che non si desti Amore,
che dorm'entro il mio core.
Ah, voi non v'accorgete
ch'al suon de' vostri accenti   5
egli è già desto e in me doppia i tormenti,
né par che ferir osi
voi, che turbaste i suoi dolci riposi.

Hush (alas!) hush, lest you awaken Love, who is sleeping in my heart. Ah, you do not realize that, at the sound of your tones, he has already woken and is doubling my torment – nor does it seem that he dares to wound you, who disturbed his sweet repose.

Source: P; Be. Rhyme scheme: abbacCdD.

This is the only surviving love poem of Bernardi's that is not found in S1. Metrically, it divides into two clear sections, the first all *settenari* and rhyme-patterned chiastically (abba), the second made up of two rhyming couplets with a *settenario* followed by a hendecasyllable. Cutting against this symmetrical metrical patterning, the poem divides grammatically and semantically into two sections of three and five lines. In the first, the poet warns a listener to be silent, out of fear lest they may awaken Love, who lies sleeping in the speaker's heart. In the second, it transpires that Love has already awoken and is submitting the poet to his usual erotic torments. In the second section, a further division may be marked. Lines 4–6 narrate Love's awakening, while the last two lines slyly suggest that the poem's addressee, who has awakened Love with their speaking (or singing), is themself the poet's love object – and an unresponsive object, since Love does not dare wound them in return.

The madrigal is noteworthy for its wit and ingenuity, two qualities much prized in this tradition of verse. The sleeping Cupid was a familiar motif in Renaissance painting and sculpture but placing the god in the poet-lover's heart, where she fears to feel him wake, is a novel twist. The poem explores the power of the beloved's voice in awakening desire, whether by speaking or singing. If the latter is intended, then this madrigal can be counted among the many Ferrarese lyrics that explore the erotic appeal of song and of singers. Especially close to 'Tacete (oimè) tacete', and sharing a rhyme word, 'accenti', as well as the motif of love awakened by music, is a madrigal attributed to Guarini and set by Luzzasco Luzzaschi, a composer close to the world of the Ferrarese *concerto delle dame*, 'Aura soave di segreti accenti'.[25] See also Section 2.1.5 for thematic analogies with the proemial madrigal to *Clorilli*.

'Tacete (oimè) tacete' exemplifies the extreme simplicity, even mock naivety, that characterizes this school of lyric. A good example of such calculated artlessness is the juxtaposed 'che's at the beginning of lines 2 and 3, the first used as a conjunction, the second as a relative pronoun. The rhyme 'osi' / 'riposi' in lines 7 and 8 is one of several species of embellished rhymes used in Italian verse. This is an 'inclusive' rhyme, in which one rhyme word is included in its entirety in the other.

(vii) Più d'altra ninfa amata (canzonetta)

st 1	Più d'altra ninfa amata,	
	fera Amarilli ingrata,	
	mi parto, e lasso il core.	
	Or chi non sa che senza lui si more?	4
st 2	Et o dolce mia morte,	
	se 'l ciel mi desse[a] in sorte	
	ch'avanti al morir mio	
	t'udissi dir: – caro mio Tirsi, addio –.[b]	8

st 3   E più felice ancora
            se avanti[c] a l'ultim'ora
            volgessi a me quel guardo
            ov'ancor ripensando aggiaccio et ardo.[d]   12

st 4   Ahi, ch'a me già non lice[e]
            sperar[f] sorte felice.
            Rimanti, io parto e moro,
            e partendo e morendo ancor t'adoro.   16

[a] Ta disse.
[b] Ta a dio.
[c] Ta s'avanti.
[d] S1 original reading: al qual m'incenerisco non pur ardo; T ove ancor ripensando agghiac-
cio, et ardo.
[e] Ta Ahi che sperar non lice.
[f] Ta haver.

[st 1] Beloved more than any other nymph, cruel, ungrateful Amarilli, I depart and leave you my heart. Now, who doesn't know that without it you die?

[st 2] And how sweet my death, if the heavens should grant that, before I die, I might hear you say, 'Dearest Tirsi, farewell'.

[st 3] And happier still, if before the last hour, you should turn on me that look which, only to think of it, makes me freeze and burn.

[st 4] But alas! It is not for me to hope for a happy ending. Remain here. I leave you to die – and, leaving and dying, still adore you.

Sources: S1; Ta. Rhyme scheme: aabB x 4.

The text of 'Più d'altra ninfa amata' is found in a manuscript in Siena that is our prime source for Bernardi's lyric poetry, and also, in a slightly different form, in a volume of *canzonette a tre voci* of 1603, set to music by the Sienese composer Mariano Tantucci. The edition above mainly follows the text in S1, giving the variants in Ta in footnotes. S1 has two versions of line 12, one copied into the main text, the other inserted beside it in the left margin. The line in the margin, which corresponds with a slight variant to that in Ta, has been preferred here, with S1's original line given in the notes.

'Più d'ogni ninfa amata' is reminiscent of Bernardi's *Clorilli* in its use of an implied pastoral setting, evoked by the names Tirsi and Amarilli, and in the love situation it portrays. The speaker, Tirsi, laments his fate after being abandoned by the 'ungrateful' Amarilli, just as Filemone spends much of the play lamenting his cruel treatment by Clorilli. Tirsi's emotional reversals across the four stanzas of the poem, from accusation to wistful fantasy to self-pitying despair, are also reminiscent of Filemone's affective trajectory (see, for example, Act 1 scene 4 and Act 4 scene 7, which contain similar 'parting speeches'). Aside from her Marian canzone, which emphatically connects the poetic 'I' with the author, most of Bernardi's lyrics do not identify the speaker by gender. 'Più d'altra ninfa amata' is distinctive in this regard as being male-voiced – a trait that, again, brings it closer to her dramatic writing.

Notes

1 C*Ly*, 28–34; 47–55.
2 Deford, 'The Influence', 130–1.
3 Moreali, 'Memorie', 356v.
4 Chater and Bianconi, 'Fonti poetiche', 67.
5 (12v, preceding the text) 'Del S. Guarini, fatto a posta, per che il Compositor della Musica immitando queste parole, mostra quello che può far un Musico cantando'; (13r, following the text) 'ben l'ha immitato con la sua dolcissima harmonia il S. Luzzasco, e divinamente cantato le Celesti Dame della S. ma Sa Duchessa di Ferrara'. The note is of interest, given that no extant setting of the madrigal by Luzzaschi is known; see Ossi, 'A Sample Problem', 259.
6 More detailed bibliographical descriptions of the successive editions and reprints of Franciotti's *Viaggio* (which also contains an *ottava rima* poem by Bernardi's acquaintance Nicolao Tucci, on the Virgin of Loreto), may be found in Rizzolino, 'Angelus Domini', 206–8.
7 C*Ly*, 141–5.
8 Piatti, '"E l'uom"', 67.
9 Bendinelli, *L'ode*, A4r.
10 Milburn, *Luigi Tansillo*, 54, 93–4. Tasso's madrigal circulated only in manuscript, but Bernardi may have known it from her stay in Ferrara.
11 C*Pr*, 32–4.
12 Manfredi, *Cento madrigali*, 117: 'il madrigale voglia essere dolcissimo in ogni sua parte, e nullo di sforzato havere'.
13 C*Ly*, 268–85.
14 DM*Gr*, 244.
15 Saslow (ed.), *The Poetry of Michelangelo*, 305–6 (nos. 152–3).
16 McHugh, 'Devotion'.
17 On the manuscript, and its companion manuscript, BNCF Palatino 250, see Boggini, 'Per un'edizione'.
18 Boggini, 'Per un'edizione', 27–8.
19 Calitti, *Fra lirica e narrativa*.
20 Miani, *Amorous Hope*, 35–6. For the text of the poem, see 351–2.
21 Miani's stanzas take the form ABCABCDEeDD; Bernardi's, AbCABCDdEE.
22 Boerio, 'Peretti Damasceni'.
23 For the notion of a 'spectacle hairstyle', in connection with Guerra, see Yeh, 'From Classical to Chic', 164.
24 See Durante e Martellotti, 'Carlo Gesualdo', 211-2.
25 See Durante and Martellotti, *Le due 'scelte'*, 67, n. 63, and Stras, *Women and Music*, 262–3 for the text.

3.2 The musical settings of Bernardi's poetry

Eugenio Refini

One of the ways to gauge the impact of early modern poets on the culture and society of their own time is by looking at the musical settings of their poems. As is well known to scholars of both Renaissance poetry and music, the extent to which the production of a given poet is turned into musical compositions results from a number of factors that often elude the author's purview.[1] Among these factors, dynamics of textual circulation, personal contacts and broader patterns of poetical appreciation are of particular importance. At the same time, these go hand in hand with serendipitous circumstances that are frequently hard to pin down. That said about the somewhat unpredictable ways in which poems happened to be set to music, the musical reception of poets remains a most useful tool to better understand the place they held in (and beyond) their lifetime, as well as the ways in which their work circulated. The case of the musical reception of Leonora Bernardi's poetry is, from this standpoint, a textbook one: not only do musical settings of her poems shed light on specific features of the poet's career, but they also invite us to pause on the perhaps volatile, yet productive nature of the circulation of poetry across mediums in the period (for one thing, as evidenced by the edition of Bernardi's poetry included in this volume, musical settings are important sources when it comes to establishing a critical text, for they happen to bear variant readings worthy of consideration).

Undoubtedly small when compared to musical settings of Petrarch, Ariosto, Tasso and Guarini – to name only some of the poets whose works were most frequently set to music in the Renaissance – the corpus of musical pieces based on Bernardi's lyric poetry is remarkable, particularly when one considers the ratio of settings to extant poems: out of 11 poetical pieces, six were set to music, with two poems set more than once, for a total of 12 settings (see Table 1).

The fact that several poems by Bernardi proved conducive to musical settings should not surprise us: after all, as detailed in the introduction to this study, Bernardi's artistic skills in both poetry and music were known and acknowledged in celebratory terms by her contemporaries.[2] While there is no mention in the sources of Bernardi's ability to compose music herself, her singing skills are consistent with a poetical profile fully aware of the mutually informing nature of the musical and poetical arts. With the exception of the Marian *canzone* 'Se pur fin su ne gli stellanti chiostri' and the sonnets to Angelo Grillo ('Se le mie preci ed umili e devote' and 'Questi, che porger può care e devote'), which seem to belong to a kind of poetical production meant to be read rather than performed, in her other pieces Bernardi turned to poetical forms (*madrigale* and *canzonetta*) that, in the period, were overtly marked as viable for – and almost naturally conducive to – musical intonation. As a matter of fact, the lack of documentation does not exclude the possibility – indeed a likely one – that Bernardi might have sung her own poetry. In this respect, her connection with Florentine poet Ottavio Rinuccini in the late 1580s is of particular interest: as recalled elsewhere in this volume, not only did he respond to Bernardi's *canzone*, but he also likely referred to Bernardi in a set of madrigals celebrating a female singer who accompanied herself.[3] If the prosodic variety of the pastoral *Clorilli* suggests that certain sections of the play were indeed meant to be sung, both madrigals and canzonettas belonged into genres that, during Bernardi's lifetime, were particularly successful with composers. Accordingly, all but one of Bernardi's extant madrigals ('O meraviglia altera', 'Se pur il ciel consente', 'Se voi lagrime a pieno', 'Tacete, ohimè, tacete', 'Vago cielo ov'amore') and the canzonetta 'Più d'altra ninfa amata' were set to music. (It is perhaps worth stressing that, as recalled in the annotations to the edition of the poem, even the madrigal for which no musical setting survives, 'Voi l'oro delle stelle', displays similarities with poetical pieces that did circulate through music as well.)[4] Given that Bernardi's madrigals and canzonetta were not published in print by the author, one does wonder whether the fact that they were turned into musical pieces, and first published as such, might be the main reason why they have been preserved. This hypothesis, as the following discussion will show, is not only reasonable, but also speaks to the entanglement of poetry and music-making that, between Florence and Ferrara, characterized the artistic commitment of Leonora Bernardi. In order to give a better sense of this corpus, the analysis will pursue three main axes: first, the reception of Bernardi's poetry within the tradition of the Renaissance madrigal; second, the musical afterlife of one specific poem, 'Se voi lagrime a pieno', which bridged across polyphony and the burgeoning genre of early Seicento monody; and third, the reception of the pastoral piece 'Più d'ogni altra ninfa amata' within the polyphonic tradition of the strophic canzonetta.

3.2.1 Ferrarese echoes in madrigal settings of Bernardi's poetry

As mentioned above, five of Bernardi's six extant madrigals were set to music. The nature of the settings and the specifics of the textual transmission of the lyrics suggest that they all relate to the Ferrarese context in which Bernardi's poetical and musical skills were known and celebrated. They all refer to a rather narrow chronological window (they first appeared in printed collections of polyphonic madrigals in the early 1590s, thus supporting the hypothesis that Bernardi penned the poems during her time in Ferrara in the 1580s). However, they bear witness to two different lines of circulation. Four of them ('Se pur il ciel consente', 'Se voi lagrime a pieno', 'O meraviglia altera', 'Vago cielo ov'amore') first appeared in print in 1593 as part of Philippe de Monte's *Il Sestodecimo libro de madrigali a cinque voci*.[5] The fifth item ('Tacete, ohimè, tacete') appeared instead in 1595 in Paolo Bellasio's posthumous collection *Il quinto libro dei madrigali a cinque*.[6]

The bipartite musical reception of Bernardi's five extant madrigals set to music is consistent with the two branches that witness the poetical sources. The text of the four poems set by Monte are also found in a later witness, the manuscript poetical anthology now held in Siena (S1), which attributes them to Leonora Bernardi.[7] The text of the madrigal set by Bellasio – the only poem by Bernardi not included in S1 – appeared instead a few years after Bellasio's print in Annibale Pocaterra's 1607 *Dui dialoghi della vergogna* (P), in which, as recalled in Section 2.1.2 of the volume, the piece is attributed to Bernardi within a brief account of her time in Ferrara that provides information on her poetical and musical endeavours at the Este court. Pocaterra's reference to Bernardi's involvement with the musical culture of Ferrara, particularly her familiarity with the genre of the madrigal and the fact that her poetry seemed to be conceived as 'poetry for music' in the first place, are consistent with the features of S1. The codex is a collection primarily comprised of short poems, mainly madrigals, many of which are by authors that gravitated to the Este court in the 1580s and 1590s, including Battista Guarini, Giambattista Strozzi, Angelo Grillo, Tarquinia Molza, Torquato Tasso and Leonora Bernardi herself. A peculiar feature of S1 is the fact that the vast majority of the poems were indeed set to music in the decades around 1600: of the roughly 90 items included in the manuscript, at least 60 (but the count is approximate and likely to increase upon more detailed study of the codex) are also known through musical settings in printed sources dating between 1530 and 1614 (though the main bulk of the relevant settings refers to the decades 1580–1610). Alongside useful information about the time period in which S1 was likely put together (a provisional survey of the poems suggests a date within the first three decades of the seventeenth century), the poetical materials gathered in the anthology indicate that the compiler was copying from both previous manuscript sources and musical prints. In this regard, while a detailed analysis of S1 falls beyond

Table 1 Musical settings of Leonora Bernardi's lyrics

	Mo a5	Be a5	Ta a3	Ma a5	P text	De a5	Ba a1	Le a3	Ca a1	Ag a6	S1 text
MADRIGALS											
Se pur il ciel consente	X [1]										22v
Se voi lagrime a pieno	X [13]			X [12]		X [18]	X [23]		X [13]	X [2]	5r
O meraviglia altera	X [24]										23r
Vago ciel ov'amore	X [25]										23r
Tacete bella donn'ohimè tacete		X [13]			X [p15]						
CANZONETTA											
Più d'altra ninfa amata			X [19]					X [9]			37r

Ag: Agostino Agresta, *Madrigali a sei voci di Agostino Agresta napolitano, libro primo* (Naples: Costantino Vitale, 1617).

Ba: Bartolomeo Barbarino, *Il Secondo Libro de Madrigali de diversi auttori posti in musica da Bartolomeo Barbarino, detto il Pesarino per cantare sopra il chitarrone o Tiorba, clavicembalo, o altri stromenti da una voce sola, con un dialogo di Anima e Caronte* (Venice: Ricciardo Amadino, 1607).

Be: Paolo Bellasio, *Il quinto libro de madrigali a cinque, del cavalliero Paolo Bellasio* (Verona: Francesco dale Donne, 1595).

Ca: Giulio Caccini, *Nuove Musiche e Nuoua Maniera di scriverle, con due Arie particolari per Tenore, che ricerchi le corde del Basso, di Giulio Caccini di Roma detto Giulio Romano, nelle quali si dimostra, che da tal maniera di scrivere con la pratica di essa, si possano apprendere tutte le squisitezze di quest'Arte, senza necessità del Canto dell'Autore; Adornate di Passaggi, Trilli, Gruppi, o nuovi affetti per uero esercizio di qualunque uoglia professare di Cantar solo* (Florence: Zanobi Pignoni, 1614).

De: Scipione Dentice, *Di Scipione Dentice, il quinto libro de madrigali a cinque voci* (Naples: Giovanni Battista Sottile, 1607).

Le: Nicolò Legname, *Amilla, libro secondo di canzonette a tre voci di Nicolò Legname Padovano sonatore di lauto* (Venice: Alessandro Raveri, 1608).

Ma: Ascanio Majone, *Il primo libro di madrigali a cinque voci di Ascanio Mayone napolitano organista* (Naples: Giovanni Battista Sottile, 1604).

Mo: Philippe de Monte, *Il Sestodecimo libro de madrigali a cinque voci di Filippo Di Monte maestro di cappella della sacra cesarea maestà dell'imperatore Rodolfo secondo* (Venice: Angelo Gardano, 1593).

P: Annibale Pocaterra, *Dui dialogi della vergogna* (Reggio Emilia: Flaminio Bartoli, 1607).

S1: Siena manuscript (c. 1600–20).

Ta: Mariano Tantucci and Tommaso Pecci, *Canzonette a tre voci delli Affettuoso et Invaghito Accademici Filomeli dedicate al molto illustre Sig. Filippo Santi Principe della Accademia. Libro secondo* (Venice: Giacomo Vincenti, 1603).

the scope of the present discussion, it is worth recalling that, alongside the Ferrarese component mentioned above, the manuscript witnesses poetical pieces relevant to Florence, Lucca and Siena: these include lyrics by Rinuccini (some of which appeared in Giulio Caccini's *Nuove musiche*) and a few attributed to the Sienese Sinolfo Saracini, likely copied from the *Secondo libro de' madrigali a cinque voci* (1590) of the Lucchese, but Florence-based, Cristofano Malvezzi.[8] The fact that most of the attributions spelled out in S1 do not appear in the musical sources from which they might have been taken is also indicative of the compiler's familiarity with the texts and their authors, a familiarity that – as far as Bernardi's case is concerned – is easier to imagine when one considers the web of relationships, direct and indirect, that informed her poetical career and personal acquaintances between Lucca, Florence, Ferrara and Siena.

If the transmission of Bernardi's madrigals in both manuscript and print raises conjectures more than allowing for evidence-based statements about their circulation, even less solid are the assumptions one can make about the musical settings. Yet they deserve to be looked at as important pieces of the multifaceted process that enabled the transmission of the poems themselves. In this respect, Bernardi's madrigals included in Philippe de Monte's *Il Sestodecimo libro de madrigali a cinque voci* (1593) are of particular interest, for their number (four) cannot be simply explained as the result of occasional and/or fortuitous settings. Quite the contrary, when examined within the broader scope and structure of Monte's book, they hint at the composer's direct involvement with the Ferrarese context (hence the possibility of intersections with the same circles that Bernardi was acquainted with).

The Flemish composer (1521–1603), who had spent several years in Italy, and whose training was much indebted to concurrent developments in Italian polyphony, was, since 1568, kapellmeister at the Hapsburg court.[9] Primarily based in Prague, he continued to travel across Europe. Monte was a prolific composer in many musical genres. His 34 books of secular madrigals (published between 1554 and 1603) encompass the several stylistic changes and experimentations that the genre went through during the second half of the sixteenth century. Comprising more than 1,000 madrigals composed over 50 years, Monte's production is representative of the broad array of poetical choices that informed the genre. Such a large number of compositions suggests that he likely relied on the most easily accessible poetical sources, namely, those available in print. However, the *Sestodecimo libro* (*Sixteenth Book*), in which the four Bernardi madrigals appear, does mark a turning point in the composer's handling of his sources.

While in his previous books Monte drew on poetry that was mostly accessible through printed editions (an outstanding example of such practice is the *Fifteenth Book*, which derives its material almost entirely from the 1587 *Rime di diversi celebri poeti dell'età nostra*, one of the most successful poetical anthologies of the time), the composer turns here to poems that, not yet printed, were circulating in manuscript.[10] The fact that most poems included in the *Sixteenth Book* are by authors who had close relationships with Ferrara makes the collection fairly consistent; after all, the Ferrarese dimension of Monte's poetical choices had been developing steadily since the *Eleventh Book* of 1586. Indeed, as indicated by Cecilia Luzzi's study of Monte's madrigals, through the late 1580s and the 1590s the composer gave clear preference to the *madrigale libero*, privileging the works of poets such as Battista Guarini, Torquato Tasso and Annibale Pocaterra. These markedly 'Ferrarese' poems are shorter than those used in earlier collections, and particularly suitable for musical setting.[11]

Within Monte's poetical choices of these years, a key place is held by Angelo Grillo and his alter ego, Livio Celiano. The importance of Grillo as a poetical source for Monte has been highlighted by Luzzi, whose remarks prove unintentionally very useful to the discussion of the musical reception of Bernardi's verse.[12] Unfamiliar with the Lucchese noblewoman, the scholar does notice that her madrigals (which, as is the case with all the poems, are anonymous in Monte's print) bear stylistic similarities with those by Grillo set by the Flemish composer as part of the same collection. While Luzzi's suggestion that those poems might be attributed to Grillo himself does not hold in light of recent scholarship on Bernardi, the hypothesis has the merit of stressing the connection between Grillo and Bernardi, which, as detailed in Sections 1.2 and 3.1.3, is key to Bernardi's poetical progress and artistic fame. In that respect, it is worth recalling that a Genoese acquaintance of Grillo, the composer Giovanni Battista Dalla Gostena (*c.* 1530–98) was a disciple of Monte, who included some of Dalla Gostena's madrigals in his own *Terzo libro de madrigali a quattro voci* of 1585.[13] While there is no direct evidence of a triangular relationship, the possibility that Grillo-related materials (including, maybe, poems by authors who were in touch with him) reached Monte via intermediaries such as Dalla Gostena is all but far-fetched. Ultimately, the Ferrarese flair of Monte's poetical choices, and, more specifically, his interest in the works of poets such as Grillo provide us with a reasonable set of intersections that may explain the presence of Bernardi's madrigals in the collection. Further insights into the place her poetry holds within it come from a closer look at the settings.

Bernardi's madrigal 'Se pur il ciel consente' is the first piece in Monte's *Sestodecimo libro*, thus bearing a proemial function that makes it stand out among the other madrigals.[14] While it was common for composers to pay special attention to the items that would appear in threshold positions (such as the first and the last compositions in a given collection), it is nonetheless difficult to make assumptions about the specific meaning that those poems might have had in the eyes of the composers themselves. This is particularly true in cases such as Monte's, whose books of madrigals are not only numerous, but also conspicuous in terms of the items included in each book (incidentally, the *Sixteenth Book* is comprised of 29 madrigals). Given Monte's fast compositional pace, it is unlikely that much thought was put into his poetical choices and the arrangement of the pieces within each collection, which most probably depended on the availability of poetical materials. However, as the very case of the *Sixteenth Book* indicates, the fact that the composer did not rely solely on printed poetry suggests that he had indeed access to patterns of poetical circulation that entailed personal exchanges with other individuals and some sort of proactive research of materials that would be significant to his project. For this very reason, it is fair to assume that, even if the collection as a whole does not reach the architectural consistency of madrigal books such as those of Claudio Monteverdi and Luca Marenzio, the opening piece ends up holding special value.

For one thing, 'Se pur il ciel consente' opens the *Sixteenth Book* under the aegis of *gravitas*. As indicated by Luzzi, Monte's collection seems to uphold the rhetorical category of *gravitas* in terms that recall the discussion of poetry and music laid out by Tasso in the dialogue *La Cavaletta* (yet another crucial source when it comes to the musical and poetical cultures of late-Cinquecento Ferrara).[15] As such, the interest in the achievement of *gravitas* in both style and subject matter brings Monte close to developments in the madrigal that were also pursued in those years by composers such as Giaches de Wert and Monteverdi. This particular feature of the *Sixteenth Book* is also the one that speaks more evidently to the composer's penchant for Grillo's poetry. With seven madrigals based on poems by Grillo's alter ego, Livio Celiano, which Monte likely selected from the same 1587 *Rime di diversi* he had been using for the *Fifteenth Book*, Grillo is indeed the most represented poet in the collection.[16] Given the prominent role of Grillo's poetry within the book, the presence of Bernardi's four madrigals proves all the more noteworthy, for, with four pieces, she surpasses even Guarini, whose presence in the book is limited to three items.[17] After all, poetical affinity is particularly evident, as observed by Luzzi, when it comes to comparing the proemial madrigal 'Se pur il ciel consente' with Grillo's 'Se non ti sazia Amore' and 'Così cari e begl'occhi', respectively items 9 and 17 in the collection, for they all share the same prosodic structure and rhyme scheme (aAbbcC).[18]

As far as the relationship between the lyrics and the setting is concerned, Monte is not particularly involved with word painting or other tools that tie text to music. Rather, his setting of 'Se pur il ciel consente' aims to identify a sort of stylistic register – *gravitas* is, in fact, the most effective way to describe it – which is then developed consistently throughout the book. One would hardly find overt madrigalisms in Monte's setting, in which the poem is used more as the marker of an emotional status than as a text to be described through music. What the composer does is to highlight the syntactic structure of the madrigal: the question introduced by the if-clause (lines 1–4) and the final statement about the poet's desire to die in order to avoid suffering (lines 5–6) are clearly identified as the two main sections of the piece, suggesting that Monte was more concerned with structural balance than with a word-for-word musical rendering of the text. As regards compositional technique, the setting displays Monte's refined skills in harmony and counterpoint, perhaps more derivative than properly original, yet experienced and able to convey a consistent stylistic idea throughout the piece.[19]

In similar fashion, Monte's other settings of Bernardi's verse clearly build on the stylistic *gravitas* that informs the poems themselves, even when they are not concerned with pain and suffering. 'O meraviglia altera' and 'Vago cielo ov'Amore' (items 24 and 25 in the collection), which, incidentally, follow three poems by Grillo, pause on the multivalent image of the heavens, which allows for a multi-layered discourse involving both Love and God. As such, they constitute a sort of triptych with the following piece in the series, the anonymous 'Chi vuol veder il cielo', yet another variation on tropes of visibility such as the sky and the veiling effect of clouds. If these settings – undoubtedly refined, yet rather vague when it comes to word painting – do not display any feature worthy of note in terms of the ways in which Bernardi's lyrics are interpreted, the fourth madrigal, 'Se voi lagrime a pieno', is possibly the most interesting one. The piece begins by evoking a sombre atmosphere, likely a musical reflection on the poetical image of the tears. While, once again, no madrigalism stands out, the composition unfolds by gradually filling the melodic and harmonic space, reaching the peak of its dramatic progress towards the end. As is the case with 'Se pur il ciel consente', the internal organization and subdivision of the piece follow the syntactic structure of the poem. The last line (yet another statement following a question, as in the proemial madrigal) coincides with the poet's recommendation that tears, as they are unable to express the poet's internal anguish, stay inside and choke the poet's heart.

While no significant textual variant exists between the lyrics witnessed by Monte's print and S1, the situation is different when one turns to the other materials. The poetical text of the madrigal set by Paolo Bellasio ('Tacete, bella donn'ohimè, tacete') and published in his 1595 posthumous fifth book of madrigals reads differently from the version witnessed by Pocaterra's *Dialoghi* of 1607, the most notable divergence being the lack of a gendered address in the latter version.[20] While the poet's addressee in Bellasio is explicitly female ('bella donna') – likely a change introduced by the composer in order to clarify the situation evoked by the poem – Pocaterra's version is gender-neutral. By addressing the interlocutor without specifying their gender, the poem as it reads in Pocaterra's print allows for a situation in which the most common gender dynamic (male lover vs. female beloved) might be reversed, hence fitting Bernardi's own position. Another variant, probably due to euphonic preferences, is found in line 6, where the madrigal reads 'egl'è *homai* desto e *doppia 'n me* i tormenti' ('he has already woken and is doubling my torment') against the phrasing found in Pocaterra, 'egli è *già* desto e *in me doppia* i tormenti' (my italics).

Beyond these differences, which are consistent with the textual mobility that characterized poetry for music, often altered by composers in order to fit their needs, Bellasio's setting is of great interest for two other reasons. First, the composer's choice to set this specific madrigal within his collection is noteworthy in that it illustrates yet another channel of circulation for Bernardi's poetry, one not necessarily involved with the Ferrarese context. A native of Verona, Bellasio (1554–94) spent much of his professional career in and around Rome, while maintaining ties with his hometown, particularly with the Accademia Filarmonica.[21] With no immediate connections with the circles attended by Bernardi, Bellasio might have got hold of her poetry in many ways. An interesting clue comes from the same collection in which Bernardi's madrigal was published, specifically from the presence of two sonnets by one of the most famous Lucchese poets of the Cinquecento, Giovanni Guidiccioni (1480–1541). Widely available in several anthologies since the 1540s, poems by Guidiccioni were set to music quite often throughout the second half of the sixteenth century. The two items set by Bellasio, however, were not set by other composers, and his choice to include them in the same volume as Bernardi's madrigal might point towards some sort of regional connection.[22]

Second – and differently from Monte's approach – Bellasio does engage the poetical text, thus offering a veritable 'reading' of the poem. The imperative 'Tacete' that frames both the address ('bella donna') and the exclamation ('ohimè') is highlighted by a pause following the first iteration, as if the poetical voice were conveying the idea of silence entailed by the line. The device is all the more striking when compared to the homophonic and homorhythmic rendering of the explanatory clause ('che non si dest'Amore') (see Section 3.2.4: 5, bar 4), followed by another instance of hesitation, signalled by a reduction of the vocal mass, possibly suggesting the stillness and quietness that characterize Love's sleep within the poet's heart ('che dorm'entro 'l mio core'). The second section opens with another exclamation, 'Ah', reiterated through the various voices at various heights and always followed by a descending interval that mimics the vocal fluctuation of a lament or sigh. A sense of excitement and confusion is then conveyed by the repetition of the words 'voi non v'accorgete', where the same musical figure made of quavers diffracts across the various voices, which only reunite in the acknowledgement that Love has now been irremediably awoken. As far as harmony is concerned, the most striking part of the madrigal is the following one. In conjunction with the reference to the fact that, by awakening, Love is doubling the poet's torment ('e doppia 'n me i tormenti'), Bellasio turns to particularly harsh harmonies: first, a diminished fourth (B natural and E flat), then a chromatic transition (C sharp, D, E flat) (see Section 3.2.4: 5, bars 15–19). The sense of harmonic difficulty conveyed by this passage contrasts with the final section of the madrigal, where the poet acknowledges that while Love is indeed making them suffer, he is also sparing the one (namely, the beloved) who awakened him. The melismatic treatment of the verb 'turbaste' – a clear example of word painting – then makes room for the madrigal's conclusion, which reinstates the sense of sweet harmony evoked by the poem's last two words, 'dolci riposi'.

Within this largely conjectural study of the musical reception of Leonora Bernardi's poetry, the madrigal on the 'sleeping Cupid' holds special value for it invites yet another serendipitous comparison. Curiously enough, the first line of the version witnessed by Pocaterra's print ('Tacete, ohimè, tacete') is the same as the initial line of a madrigal on the same theme by Francesco de Lemene (1634–1704), set as a duet around 1710 by none other than George Frideric Handel.[23] If the other similarities found in the two texts (beyond the perfect correspondence of their *incipits*) might well be explained through the widespread circulation of poetical tropes, the affinity between the two pieces is worth highlighting, for it reminds us that – when it comes to the study of the intersections of poetry and music – dynamics of transmission, imitation and intertextual allusion are less predictable than more traditional patterns of circulation might suggest.

3.2.2 Bernardi's 'tears' across polyphony and monody

Less conjectural than the afterlife of 'Tacete (ohimè) tacete', yet open to several hypotheses, is the reception of the madrigal 'Se voi lagrime a pieno' beyond the Monte setting of 1593. The only madrigal by Bernardi to be set on multiple occasions, 'Se voi lagrime a pieno' is also the only one that made it beyond the geographical areas in which the poet's life unfolded (its prominence within the musical reception of Bernardi's poetry might be the reason why the compiler of S1 put it at the beginning of the manuscript anthology, right after another hit of Bernardi's, the Marian canzone). With three further polyphonic settings and two monodic renderings, Bernardi's poetical address to her own tears fits the *poetica degli affetti* that was at the core of concurrent developments in both secular polyphony and accompanied monody at the turn of the century – a kind of poetics that was also one of the primary concerns of poets and authors in the decades around 1600.[24] Tears, suffering and the tension between inward emotions and their outward expression proved particularly fruitful at a time when, on the one hand, composers of madrigals renewed the genre by looking for striking emotional conflicts and, on the other, the inventors of the 'new music' (to borrow Caccini's infamous phrasing) were focusing on the rhetorically effective display of passions and affects that the human voice is – on its own – able to convey. While, as recalled above, the specific reasons for the reuse of a given poetical source across several settings may be hard to detect, it is undeniable that Bernardi's 'Se voi lagrime a pieno' provided composers with a most effective emotional palette conducive to likewise effective musical settings in both polyphony and monody.

The reception of the madrigal following Monte's setting of 1593 discussed above speaks both to regional consistency in terms of stylistic experimentation and to the tightness that informs patterns of poetical circulation, particularly when – as is likely the case with 'Se voi lagrime a pieno' – a given poem's transmission started with the musical print in which it first appeared. The three further settings of the madrigal indicate that its reception was a mainly Neapolitan fact: Ascanio Majone set it in *Il primo libro di madrigali a cinque voci* (1604), where the poem is the twelfth item in a collection of 21 pieces;[25] it was then reprised by Scipione Dentice in *Il quinto libro de madrigali a cinque voci* (1607), where the madrigal is given considerable prominence by being placed at the end of the book;[26] and finally it reappeared in Agostino Agresta's first book of *Madrigali a sei voci* (1617), where the poem holds the second position, right after the proemial piece.[27] Given the geographical proximity of the three composers, it is all too natural to imagine that the first collection in the series – Majone's – may be the one that brought the poem to Naples. At least for Agresta, who shares with Majone a peculiar reading of line 3 ('che dentro asconde il seno') against the rest of the textual tradition ('ch'entro rinchiud'il seno'), this might well be the case. The most plausible hypothesis is that Majone, a renowned organist and harp player, and particularly famous for his instrumental compositions (often based on previous vocal music), drew on Monte's 1593 *Sestodecimo libro*.[28] He is possibly the individual who introduced the variant reading in line 3 so as to make it more euphonic and apt for the setting. Given that Majone's *Primo libro* is a markedly Marinist collection (six poems appear in it by Marino, alongside authors such as Pomponio Torelli, Guido Casoni and Torquato Tasso), it is difficult to argue for more direct ties with the Ferrarese context within which Bernardi's poems were originally conceived. At the same time, the presence of the variant reading does not cut out the possibility of an alternative version of Bernardi's madrigal circulating through other channels. After all, the cases of Torquato Tasso and Carlo Gesualdo, among others, remind us that important forms of poetical and musical interaction existed between centres such as Ferrara and Naples throughout the second half of the sixteenth century.[29]

Differently from Agresta, who follows the variant found in Majone (hence the reasonable hypothesis that he knew his fellow Neapolitan composer's setting), Scipione Dentice shares Monte's reading. The detail calls for some caution when it comes to assuming that Dentice's decision to set the poem was inspired by Majone. In fact, nothing excludes the possibility that Dentice – the youngest member of a famous family of musicians, with ties beyond Naples, particularly in Rome – turned to Monte directly.[30] The hypothesis is consistent with Dentice's other poetical choices in his 1607 *Quinto libro*, which, with seven poems by Guarini, and only one by Marino, is oriented towards the Ferrarese tradition of the *madrigale libero* more than to the newish trend inaugurated by Marino himself, whose success among musicians had been quickly increasing in the aftermath of the appearance of the 1602 *Rime*.[31]

In spite of significant differences (especially evident when one compares the high quality of Majone and Dentice's settings with Agresta's rather flat rendering of the poem), the three Neapolitan madrigals share a concern with the expression of emotions through harmonic choices that, consistently with local developments in vocal music, were undoubtedly more peculiar than those found in Monte. Majone begins by introducing the listener to a lugubrious soundscape filled gradually by the voices. Entering one after the other, they create an opposition between the higher and the lower registers, before reuniting on the homophonic enunciation of line 3, which is repeated twice, highlighting the image of the tears harboured within the breast (see Section 3.2.4: 7, bars 5–8). The actual question 'a che versate fuore?' ('why do you pour out?') is rendered through a series of fast-moving statements chasing one another. The preposition 'a', followed by pauses, plays with the semantic multiva-lence entailed by its acoustic ambiguity ('a' as a preposition within the sentence's syntax vs. 'a' as a sign for sighs, exclamations and lamenta-tions). An unusual dissonance is produced in conjunction with the recom-mendation that tears stay inside (see Section 3.2.4: 7, bar 12). After a strong cadenza on the last word of the poem ('core'), both the question and the command are repeated, thus stressing the bipartite structure of the poem. In a similar vein, Dentice – whose setting, despite the different reading of line 3, seems to be aware of Majone's – begins in a very sombre tone, with a harsh dissonance on the word 'dolore' (B flat) (see Section 3.2.4: 9, bar 6), and a homophonic statement on line 3 that highlights the inward movement at the core of the text (in a way, it is 'inside', and not 'outside', that the various voices – as well as the tears – come together). As in Majone, the second part, introduced by the question ('A che versate fore'), develops through a series of quicker figures that gradually fill the acoustic space. While both Majone and Dentice respond critically to the text by staging the *concetto* conveyed by the lyrics, Agresta's six-voice setting is undoubtedly remarkable in terms of structure and harmony, but less so where the interpretation of the lyrics is concerned.

In a conjectural geography of the musical afterlife of Bernardi's 'Se voi lagrime a pieno', it would be tempting to hypothesize that the circulation of the poem through collections of madrigals lay behind its reuse within the newly invented monodic style of singing that, during Bernardi's own lifetime, was about to become the most prominent one in vocal music, particularly in genres as diverse as song, opera and the cantata – and possibly one that Bernardi herself had a chance to try out.[32] The two monodic settings of 'Se voi lagrime a pieno' – Bartolomeo Barbarino's and Giulio Caccini's – bring us back north of Rome and elicit numerous questions. Whereas most of them are destined to remain unanswered, an overview of these compositions may deepen our understanding of the multiple channels through which the work of poets intersected that of musicians.

Less famous than Giulio Caccini, Barbarino (c. 1568–c. 1617) is one of the founding fathers of the new monodic style whose origins are normally associated with composers who gravitated between Florence and Rome (alongside Caccini himself, these included Jacopo Peri and Emilio de' Cavalieri, among others).[33] Barbarino, who was originally from Le Marche, was both a composer and a performer, widely known as organ player and singer. An acclaimed 'falsettista', he had remarkable vocal skills, which are witnessed by the virtuosic nature of many of his compositions. His published works, secular and sacred, appeared in Venice at the beginning of the seventeenth century, but – as declared by the composer himself in the preface to his 1610 book of *mottetti sacri* – dated back to the 1590s, when he was in the service of the Della Rovere family.[34] We know that he was one of the singers at the Casa di Loreto in 1593 and 1594; between 1594 and 1602 he worked for Monsignor Giuliano della Rovere in Urbino, where he was likely involved with entertainments for the duke's court as well; he was the principal organist of Pesaro cathedral 1602–5, and then for a short period of time, he worked in the service of the bishop of Padua. Between 1608 and 1624, he pursued a freelance career (mainly as a virtuoso singer) in Venice. He is last documented in 1640.

Most of the poems set in his two books of solo-voice songs are by poets who had ties with the court of Urbino, but Barbarino set lyrics by other authors as well, including Guarini and Ottavio Rinuccini.[35] Of great interest when it comes to assessing the possible reasons behind his selection of 'Se voi lagrime a pieno' is the fact that Barbarino had six settings published in Angelo Grillo's *Canoro Pianto di Maria Vergine sopra la faccia di Christo estinto* (*Sung Lament of the Virgin Mary over the Face of the Dead Christ*, 1613), a collection of monodies edited by composer Angelico Patto and dedicated to a close acquaintance of Grillo's, the Venetian erudite Giacomo Barozzi.[36] As a prominent contributor to this publication, Barbarino, who was based in Venice at the time, was likely in touch with Grillo himself, who had relocated to Venice in 1612 (where he stayed until 1616).[37] Whereas the degrees of separation between Barbarino and Bernardi are not negligible, the connection they both had with Grillo is undoubtedly one that needs to be recalled when trying to establish possible channels through which her poetry circulated and might have reached the musician.

In Barbarino's 1607 *Secondo Libro de Madrigali*, 'Se voi lagrime a pieno' is the closing piece of the collection.[38] The fact that the same position was held by the poem in Dentice's *Quinto libro*, published in Naples earlier that year, makes one speculate whether there might be a relationship between the two works. While it is unlikely that Dentice's setting had any influence on Barbarino's as far as the score is concerned (in fact, the two pieces do not bear any particular similarity), we cannot exclude the possibility that Dentice's book of madrigals might have contributed to Barbarino's decision to close his own collection with 'Se voi lagrime a pieno'. However, the text set by Barbarino introduces a variant reading of the last line, where 'soffocate il core' ('choke my heart') is replaced by 'tormentate il core' ('torment my heart'), yet another example of the slipperiness of the textual circulation of this kind of poetry. The variant 'tormentate' might be the result of the composer's own intervention on the text, possibly due to the expressive potential of the verb, which, in fact, allows for effective word painting (though it should be stressed that the variant 'soffocate' would also call for rhetorically powerful madrigalism, perhaps even more appealing to a composer, given its explicitly acoustic implication).

Aside from this specific matter, Barbarino's is certainly the most interesting among the musical compositions based on Bernardi's poetry. It is one of the composer's most virtuosic pieces, extremely demanding in terms of vocal range and melismatic singing. Interestingly enough, the song is scored for bass: alongside the re-gendering effect of this choice (while higher vocal registers were not necessarily an index of femininity in the period, lower voices were typically marked as male), the scoring of the piece is consistent with the vocal skills Barbarino himself was famous for (as a falsettista, he was able to move swiftly through the pitches), suggesting that the setting might be a trace of the musician's performative endeavours. Notable features include the rhythmical characterization of tears through a figuration of dotted quavers that imitate the movement of sighs – a treatment of the vocal line that returns in the rendering of the verb 'tormentate' (see Section 3.2.4: 8, bar 13). Also, when lexical references to pain are explicit, as in conjunction with the iterations of the word 'dolore' and twice on 'tormentate', Barbarino makes use of ascending chromaticism, thus creating effects of harmonic tension that evoke the physical strain caused by tears (see Section 3.2.4: 8, bars 5–6 and 14). Particularly remarkable in Barbarino – and a sign of his concerns as a virtuoso – is the use of melismas such as those on 'versate' and 'core', which are both long and, especially towards the peak of the dramatic climax at the end of the piece, rather high in pitch.

In a similar vein, if stylistically more in line with the Florentine approach to monody, is Giulio Caccini's setting of 'Se voi lagrime a pieno', which was included in the second collection of the composer's by then famed 'new songs', the *Nuove musiche* of 1614 (as is well known, the first instalment of *Nuove musiche* dated back to 1602).[39] Given the peculiar nature of Barbarino's setting, especially the composer's preoccupation with virtuosic vocal technique, it is fair to assume that, in this case, Caccini 'followed' in Barbarino's footsteps. Indeed, the two settings show several similarities, though Caccini rebranded the poem according to his own way of handling the human voice, most notably through the use of melismas that had been characterizing Florentine monody since the 1589 intermezzi.[40] One difficulty with the hypothesis that Caccini knew the poem through Barbarino's setting is that his reading does not share the variant 'tormentate', coinciding instead with the one ('soffocate') witnessed by all the other sources. Yet both Caccini and Barbarino read 'racchiude' instead of 'rinchiud(e)' in line 3 (they share, in this respect, the reading found in Monte). Needless to say, the agreement on 'racchiude' is less noteworthy than the divergent reading 'soffocate' vs. 'tormentate'; furthermore, it should be recalled that Caccini was based in Florence and that he was familiar with the same artistic and musical contexts in which Bernardi had been well known. (It is worth recalling, for instance, her connection to Rinuccini, a poet whose work Caccini knew well.) On the one hand, the possibility that Caccini knew her poetry independently from Barbarino remains open; on the other hand, as suggested by the similarities found in the settings, one should be reminded that the two scenarios were not mutually exclusive.

Caccini's rendering of Bernardi's madrigal highlights the emotional situation evoked by the lyrics. In order to do so, the composer tries to make the voice express the lover's physiological response to the pain suffered. The somewhat hesitant pace of the opening, with the conditional allocution 'Se voi' first interrupted and then repeated at a higher pitch, aims to stress the pathetic dimension of the piece. Similarly, the gradual expansion of melismas in the reiterations of the poetical lines allows for a display of highly virtuosic vocal technique that, not foreign to the skills of singers such as Bernardi herself, moved the focus from the verbal text to the sonic and purely acoustic matter of the voice, thus enhancing its affective power. To this end, madrigals such as Bernardi's proved particularly effective: short and revolving around one or two poetical tropes (love's tears, in this case), they allowed for the translation of the poetical statement into the vocal representation of an emotional condition.

As far as similarities between Caccini and Barbarino's compositions are concerned, while none of them provide us with absolutely certain proof that Caccini's is indebted to Barbarino's, they do call for some attention. Alongside a similar treatment of melismatic passages, which are, incidentally, a constant feature in the works for solo voice of both composers, three details stand out. First, both introduce a melismatic vocalization on the word 'pieno': given the fact that this particular device is not solicited by the meaning of the lexical item per se (in other words, a melisma on 'pieno' is not a self-evident form of word painting), it is fair to wonder whether one composer might have taken the idea from the other. Second, the transition from the question ('A che versate fuore?) to the final statement ('Statevi dentro') is, in both pieces, marked by a long melisma (specifically, on the word 'versate'), followed by a pattern which bears similarities in both the rhythm and the melodic line (see Section 3.2.4: 8, bars 10–12; 11, bars 10–12). Third, in both settings, the final iteration of the question coincides with an upward leap (of an octave in Barbarino, of a fourth in Caccini) that enhances the sigh-like nature of the preposition 'a' (within the phrasing 'A che versate fore?'), making it sound as if it were an exclamation. Less surprisingly, the two pieces end on flamboyant melismatic passages.

3.2.3 Sienese connections and textual variants: The nymph's canzonetta

A different facet of Bernardi's poetical and musical profile is the one that looks at the pastoral tradition, which, in the decades around 1600, often intersected with the field of lyric poetry. If *Clorilli*, as discussed in detail in Section 2 of this volume, bears witness to the author's ability to move swiftly across the prosodic variety of pastoral plays (which includes lyric forms such as the madrigal), the canzonetta 'Più d'altra ninfa amata' lets us have a glimpse into another form that, in the period, was becoming more and more popular among composers. Normally set for two or three voices, canzonettas were light-hearted compositions, primarily meant for entertainment.[41] Differently from madrigals, canzonettas were strophic in nature and were normally set as such. Bernardi's pastoral canzonetta, whose lyrics are also included in S1, has come to us in two musical versions, one by the Sienese Mariano Tantucci and one by the Paduan Nicolò Legname.

Particularly interesting to the present discussion is the setting by Mariano Tantucci, known as the 'Affettuoso' in the Sienese Accademia dei Filomeli, for it may shed light on further channels of transmission for Bernardi's poetry during her lifetime. 'Più d'altra ninfa amata' is included in the collection of *Canzonette a tre voci* that Tantucci published in 1603 together with his fellow Tommaso Pecci, known as 'Invaghito' in the academy.[42] Given the Sienese context of the volume, the connection between Bernardi's poem and the composer is probably to be found in Bernardi's Sienese acquaintances, specifically those witnessed by the correspondence between Domenico Chiariti and Belisario Bulgarini discussed in Section 1.2.6. Unfortunately, not much is known about the Accademia dei Filomeli under the aegis of which the volume of *Canzonette* was printed (the book was dedicated to one Filippo Santi, by then head of the academy).[43] Yet the reference to the academic context is of interest for two main reasons. First, in light of the numerous academic gatherings that characterized the cultural and social life of late-Renaissance Siena, of which Belisario Bulgarini himself was a prominent figure, the possibility that lyric poems such as those by Bernardi circulated in town is undoubtedly plausible. Second, the Sienese presence of the canzonetta bears witness to a context in which composers such as Tantucci and Pecci, who were members of literary academies, were likely involved with the discussion and appreciation of poetical sources ahead of setting them to music.[44] Evidence of this kind of process seems to come from the very textual tradition of Bernardi's canzonetta: Tantucci's 1603 print witnesses a conspicuous variant for line 12 ('ove ancor ripensando agghiaccio, et ardo') that, interestingly enough, coincides almost verbatim with a variant added on the margin of S1 ('ov'ancor ripensando aggiaccio et ardo'), an alternative to the reading of the main text ('al qual m'incenerisco non pur ardo'). The presence of both readings in S1 suggests that the compiler of the manuscript anthology had access to multiple versions of the poem, possibly both manuscript copies and Tantucci's musical print. If this detail further supports the idea that whoever copied S1 was very familiar with musical materials, it should also be highlighted that Tantucci's version of the poem includes other minor variant readings (specifically in lines 13 and 14) that are not found in the manuscript and that prevent us from any conclusive statement about the relationships between the sources.

A few years later, Bernardi's poem reappeared in another collection of canzonettas, Nicolò Legname's 1608 *Amilla: Libro secondo di canzonette a tre voci*.[45] Given the importance that the Pecci–Tantucci anthologies had in the spread of the genre, it is likely that Legname got hold of the poem through their print. A direct relation between the two is suggested by the fact that Legname has not only the same reading for line 12 as in Tantucci, but he also shares all the other smaller variant readings found in his predecessor's version. The only remarkable difference is a significant authorial change for line 2, where the address 'Fera Amarilli ingrata' becomes 'Fera mia Milla ingrata' so as to make the poem fit the thematic frame of Legname's volume, which is entirely devoted to the celebration of a woman called 'Amilla'.

Both Tantucci and Legname treat Bernardi's 'Più d'ogni ninfa amata' according to the compositional style that was typical of the early Seicento canzonetta repertoire. Tantucci opts for a minor key that highlights the melancholic side of the poem, while preserving its overall light nature. Entirely set in binary metre, the canzonetta flows straightforwardly from beginning to end, privileging the simplicity evoked by the pastoral context. Slightly more articulate is Legname's setting, which introduces a triple metre section for the last line of each stanza, thus varying the rhythmic pattern and enhancing the dance-like nature of the canzonetta.

Far from both the harmonic experimentations of the polyphonic madrigals and the virtuosic vocal lines of monodic songs, the settings of the canzonetta return us to yet another piece of the heterogeneous musical life (and afterlife) of Bernardi's poetry. While it is reasonable to assume that the poet was not directly involved with any of the case studies discussed in this chapter, these examples contribute to shedding light on the soundscape that Bernardi herself was familiar with. If it is impossible to recover her voice as a performer, the extant documentation about the musical reception of her verse may help us – modern readers of Bernardi's long forgotten poetry – get closer to the poetical and musical world that enabled it.

3.2.4 Transcriptions of the musical settings

Davide Daolmi and Eugenio Refini

This section includes the musical settings of Bernardi's poetry that have been discussed in detail in Sections 3.2.1–3. They are presented in chronological order based on their first publication dates:

1. 'Se pur il ciel consente', five-part madrigal (Monte, 1593, 1);
2. 'Se voi lagrime a pieno', five-part madrigal (Monte, 1593, 13);
3. 'O meraviglia altera', five-part madrigal (Monte, 1593, 24);
4. 'Vago cielo ov'Amore', five-part madrigal (Monte, 1593, 25);
5. 'Tacete, bella donna, oimè, tacete', five-part madrigal (Bellasio, 1595, 13);
6. 'Più d'altra ninfa amata', three-part canzonetta (Tantucci, 1603, 19);
7. 'Se voi lagrime a pieno', five-part madrigal (Majone, 1604, 12, 14);
8. 'Se voi lagrime a pieno', solo voice (bass) and continuo (Barbarino, 1607, 23, 35–6);

9. 'Se voi lagrime a pieno', five-part madrigal (Dentice, 1607, 18, 22);
10. 'Più d'altra ninfa amata', three-part canzonetta (Legname, 1608, 9);
11. 'Se voi lagrime a pieno', solo voice (soprano) and continuo (Caccini, 1614, 13, 19–20);
12. 'Se voi lagrime a pieno', six-part madrigal (Agresta, 1617, 2, 4).

Only two settings have been edited in modern times: Monte's 'Se pur il ciel consente' (Luzzi, *Poesia e musica*, 265–8) and Caccini's 'Se voi lagrime amare' (Caccini, *Nuove musiche*, ed. Hitchcock, 42–5).

Transcription criteria

The present edition follows conservative parameters, with minimal interventions: clefs and bar divisions have been modernized; idiosyncratic spellings in the lyrics have been preserved; accidentals in brackets are added by the editors, including courtesy ones; fermatas have been added to breves at the end of each piece.

Editorial interventions

1. Monte, 'Se pur il ciel consente', Canto, bar 6: A] B in print
2. Monte, 'Se voi lagrime a pieno', bars 10–11: tempo variation signalled by numbers in square brackets
4. Monte, 'Vago cielo ov'Amore', Basso, bar 3: second E] F in print
6. Tantucci, 'Più d'altra ninfa amata': Canto I is missing in the extant sources; the present edition includes a hypothetical reconstruction of the part, given here in smaller font
10. Legname, 'Più d'altra ninfa amata', Canto, bar 14: whole note, pause] dotted whole note in print. This intervention avoids the E F Clash, the last part of the bar being considered a different chord.

Notes

1 Haar, *Italian Poetry and Music*; Tomlinson, *Monteverdi*; Pirrotta, *Scelte poetiche*; Wilson, *Singing to the Lyre*.
2 See Sections 1.2.1 and 1.2.2 of this volume.
3 See Sections 1.2.4 and 3.1.4 for Rinuccini's reply to the canzone, and Section 2.1.5 for the madrigals.
4 See Section 3.1.5.
5 Monte, *Il Sestodecimo libro*, 1, 13, 24, 25 (these numbers identify both pages and the position held by the pieces within the volume).
6 Bellasio, *Il quinto libro*, p. 13.
7 Siena, BCI, MS. I.XI.11 (S1); see Section 3.1.1 of this volume. The manuscript includes the madrigal 'Voi l'oro delle stelle', for which no musical setting seems to be extant.
8 The presence of four poems attributed to Saracini ('Quella, che per candore', 'Quando la bella mano', 'Pura neve baciando', 'Hor lasso, e con qual arte', 23v–25r), which are also witnessed

by Cristofano Malvezzi's second book of madrigals of 1590, is one of the instances suggesting that the compiler was, at least in some cases, copying from musical printed sources.

9   For an overview of Monte's biography and career, see Lindell and Mann, 'Monte, Philippe de'; more specifically on the madrigal collections that interest the present discussion, see Luzzi, *Poesia e musica*.

10 *Rime di diversi celebri poeti*; Luzzi, *Poesia e musica*, 106.

11 Luzzi, *Poesia e musica*, 172.

12 Luzzi, *Poesia e musica*, 109.

13 On Grillo's acquaintance with Dalla Gostena, see Grillo, *Parte prima*, 12v ('Queste sì note son, questi concenti') and related index entry; DM*Gr*, 67, 70. On Dalla Gostena's acquaintance with de Monte, see Prefumo, 'Dalla Gostena'.

14 Monte, *Il Sestodecimo libro*, 1.

15 Luzzi, *Poesia e musica*, 172–3; on the musical implications of Tasso's dialogue, see Carapezza, 'Tasso e la seconda prattica'.

16 Monte, *Il Sestodecimo libro*, 4 ('Ahi le mie fiamme ardenti'), 9 ('Se non ti sazia amore'), 17 ('Così cari begl'occhi'), 19 ('Porta gl'occhi d'amor nel vago viso'), 21 ('Occhi se voi sapeste'), 22 ('Cara stagion novella'), 23 ('Vaghi fiori odorati').

17 Monte, *Il Sestodecimo libro*, 12 ('Non son Tirsi non sono'), 14 ('Non fu senza vendetta'), 20 ('La bella man vi stringo').

18 Luzzi, *Poesia e musica*, 109.

19 For a more detailed analysis and modern edition of the madrigal, see Luzzi, *Poesia e musica*, 174–5, 265–8.

20 Bellasio, *Il quinto libro*, 13; Pocaterra, *Dui dialoghi*, 15–6; see Section 3.1.5.

21 Meloncelli, 'Bellasio'; Myers, 'Bellasio [Belasio]'.

22 Bellasio, *Il quinto libro*, 'Alla bell'ombra della nobil pianta' and 'E con lei poi che dritta s'erge al cielo'.

23 George Frideric Handel, 'Tacete, ohimè, tacete', HWV 196, duet for soprano, bass and continuo; for the lyrics, see de Lemene, *Poesie diverse*, 368, 'Amor dorme': 'Tacete, ohimè, tacete; | entro fiorita cuna | dorme Amor, nol vedete? | Tacete, ohimè, tacete. | Non sia voce importuna, | che gli turbi il riposo, ov'hora giace: | sol quando Amore ha posa, il Mondo ha pace.'

24 Wilson, Buelow, and Hoyt, 'Rhetoric and music'; McClary, *Desire and Pleasure*.

25 Majone, *Il primo libro*, 14.

26 Dentice, *Il quinto libro*, 22.

27 Agresta, *Madrigali a sei voci*, 4.

28 Fabris, 'Majone'; Jackson, 'Mayone'.

29 Perotti, *I madrigali autografi*.

30 Larson, 'Dentice family'.

31 Marino, *Rime*.

32 Carter and Fortune, 'Monody'.

33 Hockley, 'Bartolomeo Barbarino'; Miller and Roche, 'Barbarino, Bartolomeo'; Miller, 'Bartolomeo Barbarino'; Assenza, 'L'itinerario artistico'.

34 Hockley, 'Bartolomeo Barbarino', 84.

35 Barbarino, *Madrigali*; Barbarino, *Il Secondo Libro*.

36 *Canoro pianto di Maria Vergine*.

37 Matt, 'Grillo'.

38 Barbarino, *Il Secondo libro*, 35–6.

39 Caccini, *Nuove musiche* (1614), 19–20; for a modern edition of the collection, see Caccini, *Nuove musiche* (1978), xiv, 43–5.

40 Treadwell, *Music and Wonder*.

41 Assenza, *La canzonetta*.

42 Pecci and Tantucci, *Canzonette*, 19. On Tommaso Pecci, whose profile and activity have been studied in some detail, see Moppi, 'Pecci'; on his activity as a madrigal composer, see Mazzeo and Rigacci, eds, *Tommaso Pecci*.

43 See the entry on the Accademia dei Filomeli in the British Library's *Italian Academies Database*, https://www.bl.uk/catalogues/ItalianAcademies/Default.aspx, accessed 1 February 2023.

44 Assenza, *La canzonetta*, 195–202.

45 Legname, *Amilla*, 9; on Legname as a composer of canzonettas, see Assenza, *La canzonetta*, 202–4.

1.
Se pur il ciel consente
[Monte 1593, 1]

2.

Se voi lagrime a pieno
[Monte 1593, 13]

3.
O meraviglia altera
[Monte 1593, 24]

4.
Vago cielo ov'amore
[Monte 1593, 25]

5.
Tacete, bella donna, oimè, tacete
[Bellasio 1595, 13]

Più d'altra ninfa amata

[Tantucci 1603, 19]

7.
Se voi lagrime a pieno
[Majone 1604, 12]

8.
Se voi lagrime a pieno
[Barbarino 1607, 23]

9.
Se voi lagrime a pieno
[Dentice, 1607, 18]

10.
Più d'altra ninfa amata
[Legname 1608, 9]

11.
Se voi lagrime a pieno
[Caccini 1614, 13]

12.
Se voi lagrime a pieno
[Agresta 1617, 4]

Bibliography

See also Sections 2.2, 3.1.1 and 3.2 for manuscript and print sources containing Leonora Bernardi's works, and Section 2.2.5 for sources relevant to the Marciana manuscript of her pastoral tragicomedy.

Archives

Florence (Archivio di Stato)

ASF, Archivio Mediceo del Principato, filza 2902.
ASF, Miscellanea Medicea, 129.

Lucca (Archivio di Stato)

ASL, Archivio dei Notari. Accessed 17 July 2021. http://www.easlu. beniculturali.it.
ASL, Consiglio generale, Riformagioni pubbliche 82.
ASL, Inv. 26. Trenta, Tommaso. 'Carte di Tommaso Trenta'.
ASL, Principale, Diplomatico, Sbarra 1551–1600. Accessed 4 April 2022. http://www.easlu.beniculturali.it.
ASL, Principale, Sentenze e bandi, 480.
ASL, Principale, Sentenze e bandi, 676.

Modena (Archivio di Stato)

ASM, Archivio Estense, Cancelleria, Carteggi e documenti di particolari, 18 (Aldobrandini).
ASM, Archivio Estense, Cancelleria, Carteggi e documenti di particolari, 107 (Bernardi and Belatti).

Manuscripts

Florence (Biblioteca Nazionale Centrale)

'Poesie di vari autori'. BNCF, Fondo Baldovinetti 129.1 (formerly Palat. 294).

Rinuccini, Ottavio. 'Poesie varie'. BNCF, Palat. 249.
Rinuccini, Ottavio. 'Poesie varie'. BNCF, Palat. 250.

Lucca (Biblioteca Statale)

Baroni, Giuseppe Vincenzo. 'Notizie genealogiche delle famiglie lucchesi'. BSL, mss. 1101–39.

Modena (Biblioteca Estense)

Guarini, Marcantonio. 'Diario di tutte le cose accadute nella nobilissima città di Ferrara', 2 vols. BEM, a.H.2.16.

'Il S. Eustachio'. BEM, ms It.12 = a.P.9.12

Moreali, Giovanni Battista. 'Memorie della Sig.a Eleonora Belatti'. BEM, It. 846 (a.0.8.18, formerly I. H. 8), cc. 354*r*–357*v*.

Rome (Biblioteca dell'Accademia dei Lincei e Corsiniana)

Canzoniere, BCR, 45.G.9 (Cors. 960).

Siena (Biblioteca Comunale degli Intronati)

Bulgarini, Belisario and Domenico Chiariti. 'Lettere'. BCIS, C. II. 25.

Venice (Biblioteca Marciana)

[Bernardi, Leonora.] '16[0]3 Libro di diverse rime, Tragicomedia Pastorale della Sig.ra Xq^cbefm Hqxmllm [Leonora Belatta] Gentildonna luchesse'. BMV, MS It. IX, 239 (= 6999)

'Manoscritti Zeniani'. BMV, Cod. It., XI, 285 [=7165].

Sbarra, Cavalier Girolamo. Letter to Sforza Pallavicino, 29 June 1572, from Zara [Zadar]). BMV MS It. X, 40 (= 6415), 77*r*–81*v*.

Vicenza (Biblioteca Bertoliana)

Pagello, Livio. *Cinthia, comedia boscareccia* (c. 1579). BBV, ms Gonzati, no. 169.

Printed primary texts

Agresta, Agostino. *Madrigali a sei voci . . . libro primo*. Naples: Costantino Vitale, 1617.

Aleardi, Lodovico. *L'Origine di Vicenza, favola boschereccia*. Vicenza: Francesco Grossi, 1612.

Alighieri, Dante. 'Le egloghe di Dante'. *Biblioteca dell 'Archivum Romanicum'*, vol. 103. Edited by Giovanni Reggio. Florence: Olschki, 1969.

Andreini, Isabella. *Lovers' Debates for the Stage*, edited and translated by Pamela Allen Brown, Julie D. Campbell and Eric Nicholson. New York and Toronto: ITER, 2022.

Andreini, Isabella. *Mirtilla, A Pastoral: A Bilingual Edition*, edited by Valeria Finucci, translated by Julia Kisacky. Toronto: Iter Press / Tempe: Arizona Center for Medieval and Renaissance Studies, 2018.

Aquinas, Thomas. *Summa Theologiae*, translated by Fathers of the English Dominican Province, 3 vols. New York: Benziger, 1948.

Ariosto, Ludovico. *Orlando furioso*, edited by Edoardo Sanguineti and Marcello Turchi, 2 vols. Milan: Garzanti, 1964. Accessed 17 March 2023. www.letteraturaitaliana.net.

Aristotle, *Poetics*, translated by Malcolm Heath. Harmondsworth: Penguin, 1996.

Augustine. *The City of God against the Pagans*, edited by R. W. Dyson. Cambridge: University of Cambridge Press, 1998.

Baldini, Bernardino. *Bernardini Baldini lusus ad M. Antonium Baldinum fratris filium*. Milan: Pacifico da Ponte, 1586.

Barbarino, Bartolomeo. *Madrigali di diversi autori*. Venice: Ricciardo Amadino, 1606.

Barbarino, Bartolomeo. *Il secondo libro de madrigali de diversi auttori posti in musica da Bartolomeo Barbarino, detto il Pesarino per cantare sopra il chitarrone o tiorba, clavicembalo, o altri stromenti da una voce sola, con un dialogo di Anima e Caronte*. Venice: Ricciardo Amadino, 1607.

Bargagli, Scipione. *I trattenimenti*, edited by Laura Riccò. Rome: Salerno Editrice, 1989.

Beccari, Agostino. *Il sacrificio, favola pastorale*. Ferrara: Francesco di Rossi da Valenza, 1555.

Bellasio, Paolo. *Il quinto libro de madrigali a cinque*. Verona: Francesco dalle Donne, 1595.

Bembo, Pietro. *Gli Asolani*. In *Prose della volgar lingua, Gli Asolani, Rime*, edited by Carlo Dionisotti. Turin: UTET, 1966.

Bendinelli, Scipione. *L'ode di M. Scipione Bendinelli alla Madonna de' Miracoli di Lucca*, translated by Massinissa Bendinelli. Lucca: Vincenzo Busdraghi, 1588.

Biralli, Simon [Scipione Bargagli]. *Delle imprese scelte . . . volume secondo*. Venice: Giovanni Alberti, 1610.

Boccaccio, Giovanni. *Decameron*, edited by Vittore Branca. Turin: UTET, 1956.

Boccaccio, Giovanni. *La Theseide . . . d'ottava rima nuovamente ridotta in prosa per Nicolao Granucci di Lucca, aggiuntovi un breve dialogo nel principio e fine dell'opera dilettevole e vario*. Lucca: Vincenzo Busdraghi, ad istantia di Giulio Guidoboni, 1579.

Bonarelli, Guidubaldo. *Discorsi . . . in difesa del doppio amore della sua Celia*. Ancona: Marco Salvioni, 1612.

Bonarelli, Guidubaldo. *Phyllis of Scyros* [*Filli di Sciro*, 1607], edited and translated by Nicolas J. Perella. New York: Italica Press, 2007.

Borghesi, Diomede. *La prima [-seconda] parte delle lettere*. Padua: Lorenzo Pasquati, 1584.

Borghini, Raffaello. *Diana pietosa, comedia pastorale*. Florence: Giorgio Marescotti, 1586.

Bozzi, Paolo. *Fillino, favola pastorale*. Venice: Giovanni Battista and Giovanni Bernardo Sessa, 1597.

Bracciolini, Francesco. *L'amoroso sdegno, favola pastorale*. Milan: Agostino Tradate, 1597.

Bulgarini, Belisario. *Riprove delle particelle poetiche sopra Dante disputate da Ieronimo Zoppio Bolognese . . . scritte nell'idioma toscano di Siena*. Siena: Luca Bonetti, 1602.

Bulgarini, Belisario. *Annotazioni, ovvero chiose marginali . . . sopra la prima parte della difesa, fatta da M. Iacopo Mazzoni, per la Commedia di Dante Alighieri*. Siena: Luca Bonetti, 1608.

Caccini, Giulio. *Nuove musiche e nuova maniera di scriverle*. Florence: Zanobi Pignoni, 1614.

Caccini, Giulio. *Nuove musiche e nuova maniera di scriverle* (1614), edited by H. Wiley Hitchcock. Madison: A-R Editions, 1978.

Camilli, Camillo. *Imprese illustri di diversi, co' discorsi di Camillo Camilli . . . Parte prima [terza]*. Venice: Francecso Ziletti, 1586.

Campiglia, Maddalena. *Flori: A Pastoral Drama*, edited with introduction and notes by Virginia Cox and Lisa Sampson; translated by Virginia Cox. Chicago: University of Chicago Press, 2004.

Canoro pianto di Maria Vergine sopra la faccia di Christo estinto: a una voce da cantar nel chitarone o altri instromenti simili . . . poesia del reverendissimo Padre Abbate Grillo; raccolta per Don Angelico Patto Academico Giustiniano; et posto in musica da diversi auttori con un dialogo, et madregale; tramutati da l'istesso. Venice: Bartolomeo Magni, 1613.

Caporali, Cesare. *Le piacevoli rime . . . Con un'aggiunta di molte altre rime, fatte da diversi eccellentissimi ingegni.* Venice: Giorgio Angelieri, 1589.

Caporali, Cesare. *Vita di Mecenate.* Venice: Giovanni Battista Ciotti, 1604.

Capponi, Giovanni. *Orsilla, favola boschereccia.* Venice: Violati, 1615.

Casentini, Gasparo. *Il vero suggetto della miracolosissima Madonna scoperta in Lucca alli 30 di marzo 1588. Con alcune bellissime laudi sopra la città di Lucca, nuovamente poste in luce per Gasparo di Bartolomeo Casentini, textore di domaschi in Lucca.* N. p. [Florence], n. d.

Chiabrera, Gabriello. *Alcippo, favola boschereccia.* Genoa: Giuseppe Pavoni, 1614.

Chiabrera, Gabriello. *Gelopea, favola boschereccia.* Mondovì: Henrietto de Rossi, 1604.

Cittadini, Celso. *Tre orationi.* Siena: Salvestro Marchetti, 1603.

Contarini, Francesco. *La fida ninfa.* Vicenza: ad istanza di Francesco Bolzetta, 1598.

Cremonini, Cesare. *Le pompe funebri, overo Aminta, e Clori, favola silvestre.* Ferrara: Vittorio Baldini, 1590.

Cremonini, Cesare. *Ritorno di Damone.* Venice: Giovanni Battista Ciotti, 1622.

Crescimbeni, Giovan Mario. *Della bellezza della volgar poesia.* Rome: Antonio de' Rossi, 1712.

Crescimbeni, Giovan Mario. *Rime di Alfesibeo Cario, custode d'Arcadia.* Rome: Giovanni Battista Molo, 1695.

Croce, Giulio Cesare. *La gloria delle donne.* Bologna: Alessandro Benacci, 1590.

de Lemene, Francesco. *Poesie diverse.* Milan and Parma: Pazzoni and Monti, 1699.

Dati, Giulio. *Disfida di caccia tra i Piacevoli e Piattelli . . . nè mai fin qui comparsa in luce,* edited by Domenico Moreni. Florence: Magheri, 1824.

Denores, Giason. *Discorso . . . intorno a quei principj, cause et accrescimenti che la Commedia, la Tragedia, ed il Poema Eroico ricevono dalla*

Filosofia Morale e Civile . . . (1586), in Battista Guarini, *Opere*, 5 vols, II (1738): 153–206. Verona: Tumermani, 1737–8.

Dentice, Scipione. *Il quinto libro de madrigali a cinque voci*. Naples: Giovanni Battista Sottile, 1607.

de' Ricci, Giuliano. *Cronaca (1532–1606)*, edited by Giuliana Sapori. Milan and Naples: Ricciardi, 1872.

de' Rossi, Bastiano. *Descrizione del magnificentiss. apparato e de' maravigliosi intermedi fatti per la commedia rappresentata in Firenze nelle felicissime nozze degl'illustrissimi, ed. eccellentissimi signori il signor don Cesare d'Este e la signora donna Virginia Medici*. Florence: Giorgio Marescotti 1585.

de' Sommi, Leone. *Irifile* [1555/6?], edited by Giuseppe Dalla Palma. In 'L'Irifile e la cultura letteraria di Leone de' Sommi (con un'edizione critica del testo)', *Schifanoia* 9 (1990): 139–225.

de' Sommi, Leone. *Quattro dialoghi in materia di rappresentazioni sceniche*, edited by Ferruccio Marotti. Milan: Il Polifilo, 1968.

Feronio, Silvio. *Il Chiariti, dialogo del molto illustre Conte Silvio Feronio*. Lucca: Vincenzo Busdraghi, 1599.

Fonte, Moderata. *Il merito delle donne, scritto da Moderata Fonte in due giornate. Oue chiaramente si scuopre quanto siano elle degne, e più perfette de gli huomini* [1600], edited by Adriana Chemello. Venice: Eidos, 1988.

Fonte, Moderata. *The Worth of Women Wherein Is Clearly Revealed Their Nobility and Their Superiority to Men* [1600], edited and translated by Virginia Cox. Chicago: Chicago University Press, 1997.

Forcìroli, Francesco. *Vite dei modenesi illustri*. Modena: Aedes Muratoriana, 2007.

Fortuna, Simone. *Le nozze di Eleonora de' Medici con Vincenzio Gonzaga descritte da Simone Fortuna*, edited by Guglielmo Enrico Saltini and Carlo Gargioli. Florence: Heirs to Le Monnier, 1868.

Franciotti, Cesare. *Pratiche spirituali intorno a tre maniere di morte, che nella sacra scrittura si trovano*. Venice: Giovanni Battista Combi, 1622.

Franco, Veronica. *Terze rime*. Venice: n.p., 1575. In *Poems and Selected Letters*, edited and translated by Ann Rosalind Jones and Margaret F. Rosenthal. Chicago: University of Chicago Press, 1998.

Gamurrini, Eugenio. *Istoria genealogica delle famiglie nobili toscane, et umbre*, 5 vols. Florence: Francesco Onofri et al., 1668–85.

Garzoni, Cesare. *Historia della gloriosa immagine della Madonna de' Miracoli, trasportata in S. Piero Maggiore di Lucca*. Florence, s. n., 1588.

Giraldi [Cinthio], Giambattista. *Egle, Lettera sovra il comporre le Satire atte alla scena, Favola pastorale*, edited by Carla Molinari. Bologna: Commissione per i Testi di Lingua, 1985.

Goselini, Giuliano. *Lettere*. Venice: Paolo Meietti, 1592.

Goselini, Giuliano. *Rime del S. Giuliano Goselini, riformate e ristampate per la quarta volta*. Venice: heirs of Pietro Deuchino, 1581.

Grillo, Angelo. *Delle lettere . . . volume primo [-terzo]*, 3 vols. Venice: Giovanni Battista Ciotti, 1616.

Grillo, Angelo. *Parte prima [-seconda] delle rime del sig. don Angelo Grillo, nuovamente date in luce*. Bergamo: Comino Ventura, 1589.

Grillo, Angelo. *Pietosi affetti*, edited by Myriam Chiarla. Lecce: Argo, 2013.

Groto, Luigi. *Lettere famigliari*. Venice: Giovachino Brugnolo, 1601.

Groto, Luigi. *Pentimento amoroso*. Venice: Bolognino Zaltiero, 1576.

Gualterotti, Raffaello. *La Virginia, rappresentazione amorosa*. Florence: Bartolomeo Sermartelli, 1584.

[Guarini, Battista]. *Il Verrato, ovvero difesa di quanto ha scritto M. Giason Denores contra le tragicomedie, et le pastorali . . .* [1588]. In *Opere di Battista Guarini*, edited by Marziano Guglielminetti, 731–821. Turin: UTET, 1971.

[Guarini, Battista]. *Il Verato secondo, ovvero Replica dell'Attizzato Accademico Ferrarese in difesa del Pastor fido*. Florence: Per Filippo Giunti, 1593 [col. 1592].

Guarini, Battista. *Lettere*. Venice: Giovanni Battista Ciotti, 1615.

Guarini, Battista. *Opere*, 5 vols. Verona: Tumermani, 1737–8.

Guarini, Battista. *Il pastor fido*. In *Il teatro italiano*, vol. 2: *La tragedia del Cinquecento*, edited by Marco Ariani. Turin: Einaudi, 1977. Accessed 17 March 2023. www.letteraturaitaliana.net.

Guarini, Battista. *Il Pastor fido, tragicommedia pastorale . . . di curiose, & dotte annotationi arricchito, & di bellissime figure in rame ornato*. Venice: Gio. Battista Ciotti, 1602.

Guarini, Battista. *Rime*. Venice: Giovanni Battista Ciotti, 1598.

Guasco, Annibale. *Lettere*. Venice: Giovanni Battista Bertoni, 1603.

Gussoni, Andrea. 'Relazione dello stato di Firenze'. In *Relazioni degli ambasciatori veneti al Senato*, edited by Eugenio Alberi, series 2, vol. 2: 353–97. Florence: Tipografia e Calcografia all'insegna di Clio, 1841.

Herrick, Robert. *The Poetical Works of Robert Herrick*, edited by Frederick William Moorman. Oxford: Oxford University Press, 1921.

Hesiod. *Theogony*. In *Theogony, Works and Days, Shields*, translated with an introduction and notes by Apostolos N. Athanassakis. Baltimore, MD: Johns Hopkins University Press, 2004.

Homer. *The Iliad of Homer*, translated by Richmond Lattimore. Chicago: University of Chicago Press, 2011.

Homer. *The Odyssey*, translated by Emily Wilson. New York: W. W. Norton & Company, 2018.

Ingegneri, Angelo. *Danza di Venere*. Vicenza: Nella Stamperia Nova, 1584.

Ingegneri, Angelo. *Della poesia rappresentativa e del modo di rappresentare le favole sceniche* [Ferrara, 1598], edited by Maria Luisa Doglio. Modena: Panini, 1989.

Laparelli, Marcantonio. *Cristiade, poema heroico*. Rome: Gulielmum Facciottum, 1618.

Legname, Nicolò. *Amilla: Libro secondo di canzonette a tre voci*. Venice: Alessandro Raveri, 1608.

Libro terzo delle rime di diuersi nobilissimi et eccellentissimi autori nuouamente raccolte. Venice: Bartholomeo Cesano, 1550.

Leoni, Giovanni Battista. *La conversione del peccatore a dio, tragicomedia spirituale*. Venice: Francesco De Franceschi Senese, 1591.

Lollio, Alberto. *Aretusa, comedia pastorale*. Ferrara: Valente Panizza Mantoano, 1564. In Agostino Beccari, Alberto Lollio and Agostino Argenti, *Favole*, edited by Fulvio Pevere, 131–99. Turin: RES, 1999.

Lombardelli, Orazio. *L'arte del puntar gli scritti*. Siena: Luca Bonetti, 1585.

Lupi, Pietro. *I sospetti, favola boschereccia*. Florence: Bartolomeo Sermartelli, 1589.

Machiavelli, Guido di Niccolò. *Tizia*, edited by Paolo Caserta. Rome: Bulzoni, 1996.

Machiavelli, Niccolò. *Discorso o dialogo intorno alla nostra lingua*. In *Tutte le opere*, edited by Mario Martelli. Florence: Sansoni, [1971]. Accessed 17 March 2023. www.bibliotecaitaliana.it.

Majone, Ascanio. *Il primo libro di madrigali a cinque voci*. Naples: Giovanni Battista Sottile, 1604.

Malombra, Pietro. *Il trionfo di Dori*. Venice: Angelo Gardano, 1592.

Manfredi, Muzio. *Cento madrigali*. Mantua: Francesco Osanna, 1587.

Manfredi, Muzio, *Il contrasto amoroso, pastorale*. Venice: Giacomo Antonio Somascho, 1602.

Manfredi, Muzio. *Lettere brevissime*. Venice: Giovanni Battista Pulciani, 1606.

Manfredi, Muzio. *La Semiramis, boscareccia*. Bergamo: Comino Ventura, 1593.

Manna, Girolamo. *Licandro, tragicomedia pastorale*. Rome: per il Mascardi, appresso Pompilio Totti, 1634.

Marino, Giambattista. *Adone*, edited by Giovanni Pozzi. Milan: Adelphi, 1988.

Marino, Giambattista. *Della lira . . . Parte Terza* [Venice: Giambattista Ciotti, 1614]. Venice: Il Ciotti, 1629.

Marino, Giambattista. *Rime*. Venice: Giovan Battista Ciotti, 1602.

Marracci, Ippolito. *Bibliotheca Marianae . . . . pars secunda*. Rome: Francesco Cavalli, 1648.

Marvell, Andrew. *The Poems of Andrew Marvell*, edited by Nigel Smith. London: Longman, 2006.

Massa, Giovanni Maria di. *Memorie di Ferrara, 1582–1585*, edited by Matteo Provasi. Ferrara: Deputazione Provinciale Ferrarese di Storia Patria, 2004.

Matraini, Chiara. *Lettere e rime*, edited by Cristina Acucella. Florence: Firenze University Press, 2018.

Matraini, Chiara. *Le opere in prosa e altre poesie*, edited by Anna Mario. Perugia: Aguaplano, 2017.

Matraini, Chiara. *Rime e lettere*, edited by Giovanna Rabitti. Bologna: Commissione per i Testi di Lingua, 1989.

Matraini, Chiara. *Selected Poetry and Prose*, translated by Eleanor McLachlan, with an introduction by Giovanna Rabitti. Chicago: University of Chicago Press, 2007.

Miani, Valeria. *Amorosa speranza, favola pastorale*. Venice: Francesco Bolzetta, 1604. In *Amorous Hope, A Pastoral Play: A bilingual edition*, edited and translated by Alexandra Coller. Chicago: Chicago University Press / Iter, 2021.

Miani, Valeria. *Celinda, A Tragedy: A bilingual edition*, edited by Valeria Finucci and translated by Julia Kisacky. Toronto: Iter Press, 2010.

Minutoli, Antonio di Bonaventura. *Memorie di un medico lucchese (1555–1606)*, edited by Riccardo Ambrosini and Albarosa Belegni. Lucca: Accademia Lucchese di Scienze, Lettere ed Arti, 1993.

Monte, Philippe de [Filippo di]. *Il Sestodecimo libro de madrigali a cinque voci di Filippo Di Monte maestro di cappella della sacra cesarea maestà dell'imperatore Rodolfo secondo*. Venice: Angelo Gardano, 1593.

Morganti, Belisario. *Deiparae Virginis Lucae miracula edentis encomium*. Lucca: Vincenzo Busdraghi, 1588.

Morotti, Giovanni. *Himeneo nelle felici nozze di Flaminio Gigli e della signora Sara Buonvisi*. Lucca: Busdraghi, 1589.

Narratione della partenza del Sereniss. S. D. Cesare da Este . . . con le feste et trionfi fatte nell'entrata dell'Illustriss. et Reverendiss. Cardinale Aldobrandino legato. Pavia: Andrea Viani, 1598.

Nigrisoli, Andrea. *Delle canzonette a quattro voci di Andrea Nigrisoli da Ferrara. Libro primo. La sola parte dell'alto*. Ferrara: Vittorio Baldini, 1585.

Ongaro, Antonio. *Alceo, favola pescatoria*. Venice: Francesco Ziletti, 1582.

Ovid. *Fasti*, translated by Anne and Peter Wiseman. Oxford: Oxford University Press, 2011.

Ovid. *Metamorphoses*, translated by Rolfe Humphries. Bloomington: Indiana University Press, 1960.

Palma, Girolamo. *Liber primus allegationum per eum conscriptarum in causis gravissimis*. Lucca: Salvatore Marescandoli and Brother, 1680.

Panciatichi, Vincenzo. *Orazione funerale del caualiere Vincenzio Panciatichi. Da lui recitata il dì 21. d'aprile l'anno 1598 nell'annuale essequie del gran duca Cosimo, nella chiesa della religion di Santo Stefano in Pisa*. Florence: per Filippo Giunti, 1598.

Parabosco, Girolamo. *Il primo libro delle lettere famigliari . . . Et il primo libro de' suoi madrigali nuouamente posti in luce*. Venice: Giovan Griffio, 1551.

Parabosco, Girolamo, *I diporti . . . Divisi in III giornate* [1st edn *c.* 1550]. Venice: Gio. Battista Ugolino, 1586.

Pecci, Tommaso and Mariano Tantucci, *Canzonette a tre voci delli Affettuoso, et Invaghito Accademici Filomeli . . . libro secondo*. Venice: Giacomo Vincenti, 1603.

Petrarca, Francesco. *Canzoniere*, edited by Gianfranco Contini. Turin: Einaudi, 1964. Accessed 17 March 2023. www.letteraturaitaliana .net.

Petrarca, Francesco. *Trionfi*, edited by Guido Bezzola and Raffaello Ramat. Milan: Rizzoli, 1957. Accessed 17 March 2023. www.letter aturaitaliana.net.

Pocaterra, Annibale. *Dui dialoghi della vergogna, con alcune prose, et rime*. Reggio: Flavio and Flaminio Bartoli, 1607.

Pona, Giovanni Battista. *Tirrheno pastorale*. Verona: Girolamo Discepolo, 1589.

Renieri, Antonio. *Il vero soggetto d'Amore*. Lucca: Vincenzo Busdraghi, 1566.

Rime di diversi celebri poeti dell'età nostra: nuovamente raccolte, e poste in luce. Bergamo: Comino Ventura and Associates, 1587.

Riminaldi, Ippolito. *Consiliorum seu reponsorum in causis gravissimis redditorum, et in septem libros tributorum*, 7 vols. Frankfurt: Johann Nikolaus Ruland and Peter Ruland, 1609.

Rinuccini, Ottavio. *La Dafne . . . Alla Sereniss. Gran Duchessa di Toscana*.

Rappresentata . . . dal Signor Iacopo Corsi. Florence: Giorgio Marescotti, 1600.

Rinuccini, Ottavio. *L'Euridice d'Ottavio Rinuccini rappresentata nello sponsalitio della christianiss. Regina di Francia, e di Navarra*. Florence: Cosimo Giunti, 1600.

Rondinelli, Dionisio [Dionigi]. *Il pastor vedovo, favola boscareccia*. Vicenza: Giorgio Greco, 1599.

Ruscelli, Girolamo, and Vincenzo Ruscelli. *Le imprese illustri del S[ign] or Hieronimo Ruscelli, aggiuntovi nuovamente il quarto libro, da Vincenzo Ruscelli da Viterbo*. Venice: Francesco De Franceschi Sanese, 1584.

Sannazaro, Jacopo. *Opere volgari*, edited by Alfredo Mauro. Bari: Laterza, 1961.

Sansovino, Francesco. *Le antichità di Beroso Caldeo sacerdote, et d'altri scrittori*. Venice: Altobello Salicato, 1583.

Sarti, Antonio. *I crepuscoli del torneo. Delle militari avvertenze. Del Capitan Antonio Sarti. Gentilhuomo Luchese . . . in XII. Libri*. Venice: Evangelista Deuchino, 1628.

Sarti, Paolo. *La simmetria dell'ottima fortificatione regolare*. Venice: Evangelista Deuchino, 1630.

Saslow, James M., ed. *The Poetry of Michelangelo—An Annotated Translation*. New Haven: Yale University Press, 1991.

Scelta di rime di diversi moderni autori, Parte prima. Genoa: Heredi di Gieronimo Bartoli, 1591.

Segni, Piero. *Orazione di Pier Segni cognominato nell'Accademia della Crusca l'Agghiacciato, recitata da lui nella detta Accademia, per la morte di m. Iacopo Mazzoni*. Florence: Giorgio Marescotti, 1599.

Sergiusti, Filippo. *De Virginis imagine novis Lucae miraculis coruscante carmen*. Siena: Luca Bonetti, 1588.

Serlio, Sebastiano. *Il Secondo libro di perspetti[v]a di Sebastiano Serlio Bolognese*. Paris: Jean Barbé, 1545.

Serono, Horatio [Orazio]. *La fida Armilla, favola pastorale*. Venice: Evangelista Deuchino and Gio. Battista Pulciani, 1610.

Shakespeare, William. *Arden Shakespeare Complete Works*, edited by G. R. Proudfoot, Ann Thompson and David Scott Kastan. London: Bloomsbury Publishing, 2014.

Spada, Giovanni Battista (O. P.). *Giardino de gli epiteti, traslati, et aggiunti poetici*. Bologna: Heir of Vittorio Benacci, 1665.

Speroni, Sperone. *Canace e Scritti in sua difesa*, edited by Christina Roaf. Bologna: Commissione per i Testi di Lingua, 1982.

Tasso, Torquato, *Aminta*, edited by Bruno Maier. Milan: Rizzoli, 1963. Accessed 17 March 2023. www.letteraturaitaliana.net.

Tasso, Torquato. *Delle opere di Torquato Tasso, con le controversie sopra la Gerusalemme liberata*, 12 vols. Venice: Stefano Monti and N.N., 1735–42.

Tasso, Torquato. *Delle rime del Signor Torquato Tasso, parte seconda. Di novo date in luce, con gli Argomenti & Espositioni dello stesso Autore.* Brescia: Pietro Maria Marchetti, 1593.

Tasso, Torquato. *Delle rime et prose del Sig. Torquato Tasso, parte quarta.* Venice: Giulio Vasalini, 1586.

Tasso, Torquato. *Gerusalemme liberata*, edited by Lanfranco Caretti. Milan: Mondadori, 1957. Accessed 17 March 2023. www.letteratura italiana.net.

Tasso, Torquato. *Gioie di rime, e prose*. Venice: appresso Giulio Vasalini, 1587.

Tasso, Torquato. *Le rime*, edited by Bruno Basile. Rome: Salerno, 1994. Accessed 17 March 2023. www.letteraturaitaliana.net.

Tasso, Torquato. *Opere*, I. *Aminta, Amor fuggitivo, Intermedi, Rime*. II. *Rime, Rinaldo, Il re Torrismondo*, edited by Bruno Maier. Milan: Rizzoli, 1964.

Torelli Benedetti, Barbara. *Partenia, a Pastoral Play*, edited and translated by Lisa Sampson and Barbara Burgess-Van Aken. Toronto: Iter Inc./Centre for Reformation and Renaissance Studies, 2013.

Varie poesie di molti eccellenti autori in morte del . . . Cavalier Battista Guarini. Milan: Gio, Battista Bidelli, 1618.

Venier, Maffio. *Hidalba [Idalba]*. Venice: Andrea Muschio, 1596.

Villani, Giovanni. *Nuova cronica*, edited by Giuseppe Porta. Parma: Fondazione Pietro Bembo/Guanda, 1991.

Virgil. *The Aeneid*, translated by Sarah Ruden. New Haven: Yale University Press, 2008.

Virgil, *Eclogues*. In *Eclogues; Georgics; Aeneid I–VI*, edited by G. P. Goold, translated by H. Rushton Fairclough. Cambridge, MA: Harvard University Press, 1999.

Wroth, Mary. *The Countess of Montgomery's Urania Parts 1 and 2*, edited by Josephine Roberts. Binghamton, NY: Medieval and Renaissance Texts and Studies, 1995 and 1999.

Zinano, Gabriele, *Il Caride, fauola pastorale*. Ferrara: Vittorio Baldini, 1583.

Secondary texts

Adorni Braccesi, Simonetta. *'Una città infetta': Lucca nella crisi religiosa del Cinquecento*. Florence: Olschki, 1994.

Adorni Braccesi, Simonetta. 'Il dissenso religioso nel contesto urbano lucchese del Cinquecento'. In *Città italiane del '500 tra Riforma e Controriforma*, 225–39. Lucca: Maria Pacini Fazzi, 1988.

Adorni Braccesi, Simonetta. 'Gigli, Matteo', *DBI* 54 (2000).

Adorni Braccesi, Simonetta. 'Giuliano da Dezza, cacaiuolo: nuove prospettive sull'eresia nella Lucca del XVI secolo', *Actum luce* 1 (1980): 89–138.

Adorni Braccesi, Simonetta, and Simone Ragagli. 'Guidiccioni, Alessandro', *DBI* 61 (2004).

Andrews, Richard. *Scripts and Scenarios: The performance of comedy in Renaissance Italy*. Cambridge: Cambridge University Press, 1993.

Arlander, Annette. 'Agential Cuts and Performance as Research'. In *Performance as Research: Knowledge, methods, impact*, edited by Annette Arlander, Bruce Barton, Melanie Dreyer-Lude and Ben Spatz, 133–51. London and New York: Routledge, 2018.

Asor Rosa, Alberto. 'Achillini, Claudio', *DBI* 1 (1960).

Assenza, Concetta. *La canzonetta dal 1570 al 1615*. Lucca: LIM, 1997.

Assenza, Concetta. 'L'itinerario artistico di un cantore virtuoso dalle Marche al Veneto'. In Bartolomeo Barbarino, *Canzonette e sonetti a una e due voci (Venezia, 1616)*, edited by Concetta Assenza, v–xxx. Bologna: Ut Orpheus, 2003.

Bandini Buti, Maria. *Poetesse e scrittrici*, 2 vols. Milan: Tosi, 1941–2.

Barad, Karen. *Meeting the Universe Halfway: Quantum physics and the entanglement of matter and meaning*. Durham, NC: Duke University Press, 2007.

Benson, Pamela J. *The Invention of the Renaissance Woman: The challenge of female independence in the literature and thought of Italy and England*. University Park, PA: Pennsylvania State University Press, 1992.

Berengo, Marino. *Nobili e mercanti nella Lucca del Cinquecento*. 2nd edition. Turin: Einaudi, 1999.

Bergstein, Mary. 'Marian Politics in Quattrocento Florence: The Renewed Dedication of Santa Maria del Fiore in 1412', *Renaissance Quarterly* 44.4 (1991): 673–719.

Bertacchi, Angelo. *Storia dell'Accademia Lucchese. Tomo I*. Lucca: Tipografia Giusti, 1881.

Bertelli, Sergio. *Trittico: Lucca, Ragusa, Boston: Tre città mercantili tra Cinquecento e Seicento*. Boston, MA: Donzelli, 2004.

Bertoni, Luisa. 'Antelminelli, Bernardino', *DBI* 3 (1961).

Biagi-Ravenni, Gabriella. 'I Dorati, musicisti lucchesi, alla luce di nuovi documenti d'archivio: Premessa bibliografica', *Rivista italiana di musicologia* 7.1 (1972): 39–81.

Bizzocchi, Roberto. 'Tra Ferrara e Firenze: Culture genealogico-nobiliari a confronto'. In *L'arme e gli amori: Ariosto, Tasso and Guarini in Late Renaissance Florence*, 2 vols, edited by Massimiliano Rossi and Fiorella Gioffredi Superbi, 1: 3–15. Florence: Olschki, 2004.

Bocci Pacini, P. 'Faesulae'. In *The Princeton Encyclopedia of Classical Sites*, edited by Richard Stillwell et al. Princeton, NJ: Princeton University Press, 1976. Accessed 11 August 2021. http://www.perseus.tufts.edu/hopper/text?doc=Perseus:text:1999.04.0006:entry=faesulae.

Boero, Stefano. 'Peretti Damasceni, Flavia', *DBI* 82 (2015).

Boggini, Daniele. 'Per un'edizione critica delle *Poesie* di Ottavio Rinuccini', *Rivista di letteratura italiana* 19/2–3 (2001): 11–60.

Bolzoni, Lina. *Il cuore di cristallo: Ragionamenti d'amore, poesia, e ritratto nel Rinascimento*. Turin: Einaudi, 2010.

Bonazzi, Francesco. *Elenco dei cavalieri del S. M. Ordine di San Giovanni di Gerusalemme*. Naples: Libreria Detken & Rocholi, 1897.

Bongi, Salvatore, ed. *Inventario del R[eale] Archivio di Stato di Lucca*, vol. 1. *Archivio diplomatico, carte del Comune di Lucca, parte prima*. Lucca: Tipografia Giusti, 1872.

Bongi, Salvatore. *Storia di Lucrezia Buonvisi lucchese raccontata sui documenti*. Lucca: Bartolomeo Canovetti, 1861.

Borsellino, Nino. 'Bargagli, Scipione', *DBI* 6 (1964).

Brady, Aoife. 'Lavinia Fontana: Trailblazer, Rule Breaker'. In Aoife Brady, Maria Canavan and Letizia Marcattili, *The Crowning Glory: Lavinia Fontana's Queen of Sheba and King Solomon*, 16–33. Dublin: National Gallery of Ireland, 2021.

Bratchel, M. E. 'Chronicles of Fifteenth-Century Lucca: Contributions to an Understanding of the Restored Republic', *Bibliothèque d'Humanisme et Renaissance* 60 (1998): 7–23.

Breman, Paul. *Books on Military Architecture Printed in Venice: An Annotated Catalogue*. Boston: Brill, 2002.

Bruscagli, Riccardo. 'L'*Aminta* del Tasso e le pastorali ferraresi del '500'. In *Studi di filologia e critica offerti dagli allievi a Lanfranco Caretti*, 2 vols, 1: 279–318. Rome: Salerno, 1985.

Bujic, Bojan. '"Figura poetica molto vaga": Structure and Meaning in Rinuccini's *Euridice*', *Early Music History* 10 (1991): 29–64.

Butters, Suzanne S. 'Christine of Lorraine and Cultural Exchanges in the Countryside: International Customs in Local Settings'. In *Medici Women as Cultural Mediators (1533–1743) / Le donne di casa Medici e il loro ruolo di mediatrici culturali fra le corti d'Europa*, edited by Christina Strunck, 111–47. Milan: Silvana, 2011.

Caiazza, Ida. 'Alvise Pasqualigo e il suo romanzo epistolare: le *Lettere amorose* dalla "relazione" alla "corrispondenza"'. *Italianistica* 43.1 (2014): 77–106.

Caiazza, Ida. 'Pasqualigo, Alvise', *DBI* 81 (2014).

Calitti, Floriana. *Fra lirica e narrativa: Storia dell'ottava rima nel Rinascimento*. Florence: Le Cáriti, 2004.

Campbell, Julie. 'Marie de Beaulieu and Isabella Andreini: Cross-Cultural Patronage at the French Court', *Sixteenth-Century Journal* 45.4 (2014): 851–74.

Canguilhem, Philippe. 'Singing Poetry *in compagnia* in Sixteenth-Century Italy'. In *Voices and Texts in Early Modern Italian Society*, edited by Stefano Dall'Aglio, Brian Richardson and Massimo Rospocher, 113–23. London: Routledge, 2016.

Caponetto, Salvatore. *Aonio Paleario (1503–70) e la Riforma protestante in Toscana*. Turin: Claudiana, 1979.

Capucci, Martino. 'Coreglia, Isabetta', *DBI* 29 (1983).

Carapezza, Paolo Emilio. 'Tasso e la seconda prattica'. In *Tasso, la musica, i musicisti*, edited by Maria Antonella Balsano and Thomas Walker, 1–15. Florence: Olschki, 1988.

Carbonaro, Davide. 'L'altro Cesare: Il Venerabile Cesare Franciotti (1557–1627) dei Chierici Regolari della Madre di Dio, insigne predicatore e maestro di spiritualità eucharistica', *Annales oratorii* 6 (2007): 187–210.

Cardamone, Donna G. 'Lifting the Protective Veil of Anonymity: ca. 1300–1566'. In *Women Composers: Music through the ages*, edited by Martha Furman Schleifer and Sylvia Glickman, 8 vols, I: 110–15. New York: G. K. Hall, 1996.

Carter, Tim. *Jacopo Peri, 1561–1633: His life and works*, 2 vols. New York; London: Garland, 1989.

Carter, Tim. 'Lamenting Ariadne?', *Early Music* 27.3 (1999): 395–405.

Carter, Tim. 'Music and Patronage in Late Sixteenth-Century Florence: The Case of Jacopo Corsi (1561–1602)', *I Tatti Studies in the Italian Renaissance* 1 (1985): 57–104.

Carter, Tim. 'Renaissance, Mannerism, Baroque'. In *The Cambridge History of Seventeenth-Century Music*, edited by Tim Carter and John Butt, 1–26. Cambridge University Press, 2005.

Carter, Tim and Nigel Fortune. 'Monody', *Grove Music Online* (2001). https://doi.org/10.1093/gmo/9781561592630.article.18977.

Carter, Tim and Richard A. Goldthwaite. *Orpheus in the Marketplace: Jacopo Peri and the economy of late Renaissance Florence*. Cambridge MA: Harvard University Press, 2013.

Castellani, Arrigo. *Grammatica storica della lingua italiana*. Bologna: Il Mulino, 2000.

Castellani, Arrigo. 'Le virgolette di Aldo Manuzio', *Studi linguistici italiani* 22 (1996): 106–9.

Castellani, Arrigo. 'Sulla formazione del sistema paragrafematico moderno', *Studi linguistici italiani* 21 (1995): 3–47.

Catelli, Nicola. 'Molza, Tarquinia', *DBI* 75 (2011).

Cavicchi, Adriano. 'Imagini e forme dello spazio scenico nella pastorale ferrarese'. In *Sviluppi della drammaturgia pastorale nell'Europa del Cinque-Seicento*, edited by Maria Chiabò and Federico Doglio, 45–86. Viterbo: Union Printing, [1992].

Cazzato, Vincenzo, Marcello Fagiolo and Maria Adriana Giusti. *Teatri di verzura: La scena del giardino dall'antico al Novecento*. Florence: Edifiri, 1993.

Ceruti, Antonio. *Appunti di bibliografia storica veneta contenuta nei mss dell'Ambrosiana*. Venice: Marco Visentini, 1877.

Ceserani, Remo. 'Bertolai, Orsola', *DBI* 9 (1967).

Chater, James. '"Un pasticcio di Madrigaletti?" The early musical fortune of *Il pastor fido*'. In *Guarini, la musica, i musicisti*, edited by Angelo Pompilio, 139–55. Lucca: Libreria Musicale Italiana, 1997.

Chater, James. 'Poetry in the Service of Music: The Case of Giovambattista Strozzi the Younger (1551–1634)', *The Journal of Musicology* 29.4 (Fall 2012): 328–84.

Chater, James, and Lorenzo Bianconi. 'Fonti poetiche per i madrigali di Luca Marenzio', *Rivista italiana di musicologia*, 13.1 (1978): 60–103.

Chiarelli, Francesca. 'Before and After: Ottavio Rinuccini's *Mascherate* and Their Relationship to the Operatic Libretto', *Journal of Seventeenth-Century Music* 9.1 (2003). Accessed 14 December 2021. https://www.sscm-jscm.org/jscm/v9/no1/chiarelli.html.

Chiarelli, Francesca. 'Per un censimento delle rime di Ottavio Rinuccini', *Studi italiani* 4 (1990): 133–63.

Cipriani, Giovanni. *Il mito etrusco nel Rinascimento fiorentino*. Florence: Olschki, 1980.

Clubb, Louise George. *Italian Drama in Shakespeare's Time*. New Haven; London: Yale University Press, 1989.

Clubb, Louise George. 'The Pastoral Play: Conflations of Country, Court and City'. In *Il teatro italiano del Rinascimento*, edited by Maristella de Panizza Lorch, 65–73. Milan: Edizione di Comunità, 1980.

Clubb, Louise George. 'The Tragicomic Bear', *Comparative Literature Studies*, 9.1 (1972): 17–30.

Cohen, Simona. *Animals as Disguised Symbols in Renaissance Art*. Leiden: Brill, 2008.

Coleman, James K. 'Boccaccio's Demogorgon and Renaissance Platonism', *Italian Studies* 74.1 (2019): 1–9.

Coli, Massimiliano. *La cronaca del monastero domenicano di S. Giorgio di Lucca*. Pisa: ETS, 2009.

Coller, Alexandra. 'Ladies and Courtesans in Late Sixteenth-Century *Commedia Grave*: Vernacular Antecedents of Early Opera's *Prime Donne*', *Italian Studies* 62.1 (2007): 27–44.

Coller, Alexandra. *Women, Rhetoric, and Drama in Early Modern Italy*. London: Routledge, 2017.

Collina, Beatrice. 'La gloria delle donne "in rozzi accenti"'. In *La festa del mondo rovesciato: Giulio Cesare Croce e il carnevalesco*, edited by Elide Casali and Bruno Capaci, 157–75. Bologna: Il Mulino, 2002.

Coluzzi, Seth. *Guarini's 'Il pastor fido' and the Madrigal: Voicing the Pastoral in Late Renaissance Italy*. Abingdon: Routledge, 2023.

Costa, Gustavo. *La leggenda dei secoli d'oro*. Bari: Laterza, 1972.

Cox, Virginia. '"Consenti, o pia, ch'in lagrimosi canti": St. Birgitta in the Poetry, Thought, and Art Patronage of Angelo Grillo'. In *The Legacy of Birgitta of Sweden: Women, politics, and reform in Renaissance Italy*, edited by Unn Falkeid and Anna Wainwright. Leiden: Brill, forthcoming, 2023.

Cox, Virginia. 'The Female Voice in Italian Renaissance Dialogue', *MLN* 128.1 (2013): 53–78.

Cox, Virginia. *Lyric Poetry by Women of the Italian Renaissance*. Baltimore, MD: Johns Hopkins University Press, 2013.

Cox, Virginia. 'Tasso's *Malpiglio overo de la corte*: The Courtier Revisited', *Modern Language Review*, 90.4 (1995): 897–918.

Cox, Virginia. 'Members, Muses, Mascots: Women and Italian Academies'. In *The Italian Academies, 1525–1700: Networks of Culture, Innovation, and Dissent*, edited by Jane E. Everson, Dennis V. Reidy and Lisa Sampson, 132–67. Cambridge: MHRA/Routledge, 2016.

Cox, Virginia. 'Note: Italian Dialogues Incorporating Female Speakers', *MLN* 128.1 (2013): 79–83.

Cox, Virginia. *The Prodigious Muse: Women's writing in counter-reformation Italy*. Baltimore, MD: Johns Hopkins University Press, 2011.

Cox, Virginia. 'Re-thinking Counter-Reformation Literature'. In *Innovation in the Italian Counter-Reformation*, edited by Shannon McHugh and Anna Wainwright, 15–55. Newark: University of Delaware Press, 2020.

Cox, Virginia. 'The Social World of Italian Lyric'. In *Petrarchism, paratexts, pictures: Petrarca e la costruzione di comunità culturali nel Rinascimento*, edited by Bernhard Huss and Federica Pich, 195–212. Florence: Franco Cesati, 2022.

Cox, Virginia. '"L'umil prego ascolta": A votive canzone to the Miraculous Madonna of Lucca (1588)'. In *Rivelazioni, letture, preghiera: Donne nell'Italia della prima età moderna*, edited by Erminia Ardissino and Elisabetta Selmi. Rome: Edizioni di Storia e Letteratura, forthcoming, 2023.

Cox, Virginia. *Women's Writing in Italy, 1400–1650*. Baltimore, MD: Johns Hopkins University Press, 2008.

Cox-Rearick, Janet. *Dynasty and Destiny in Medici Art: Pontormo, Leo X, and the two Cosimos*. Princeton, NJ: Princeton University Press, 1984.

Cruciata, Roberta. 'An Enigmatic Portrait of Leonora Cybo at Palazzo Falson', *Treasures of Malta* 57 (Summer 2013): 49–55.

Cusick, Suzanne G. *Francesca Caccini at the Medici Court: Music and the circulation of power*. Chicago: University of Chicago Press, 2009.

Cusick, Suzanne G. '"There Was Not One Lady Who Failed to Shed a Tear": Arianna's Lament and the Construction of Modern Womanhood', *Early Music* 22.1 (1994): 21–41.

D'Accone, Frank A. *The Civic Muse: Music and musicians in Siena*. Chicago: University of Chicago, 1997.

Daddi Giovanozzi, Vera. 'Di alcune incisioni dell'apparato per le nozze di Ferdinando de' Medici e Cristina di Lorena', *Rivista d'Arte* 22.1 (1940): 85–100.

Danesi, Daniele. *Cento anni di libri: La biblioteca di Belisario Bulgarini e della sua famiglia, circa 1550–1660*. Ospedaletto-Pisa: Pacini, 2014.

Deford, Ruth I. 'The Influence of the Madrigal on Canzonetta Texts of the Late Sixteenth Century', *Acta musicologica* 59.2 (1987): 127–51.

Del Gallo, Elena. 'Franciotti, Cesare', *DBI* 50 (1998).

De Miranda, Girolamo. 'Lamberti, Marco', *DBI* 63 (2004).

Durante, Elio, and Anna Martellotti. *'Amorosa fenice': La vita, le rime, e* la fortuna di Girolamo Casone da Oderzo (c. 1528–1592). Florence: Olschki, 2015.

Durante, Elio, and Anna Martellotti. 'Carlo Gesualdo e i poeti di Ferrara: fedeltà infedele al testo poetico'. In *La musica del Principe. Studi e prospettive per Carlo Gesualdo*, edited by Luisa Curinga, 187–218. Lucca: Libreria Musicale Italiana, 2008.

Durante, Elio, and Anna Martellotti. *Cronistoria del Concerto Delle Dame Principalissime di Margherita Gonzaga d'Este*. Florence: SPES, 1979.

Durante, Elio, and Anna Martellotti. *Don Angelo Grillo O. S. B. alias Livio Celiano, poeta per musica del secolo decimosesto*. Florence: SPES, 1989.

Durante, Elio, and Anna Martellotti. *Le due 'scelte' napoletane di Luzzasco Luzzaschi*, 2 vols. Florence: SPES, 1998.

D'Urso, Francesco. '"Ed egli puote risposta dare e mai non fece inganno" (T. Tasso): La raccolta di *consilia* di Ippolito Riminaldi'. *Historia et ius* 4 (2013), paper 5 (1–22). Accessed 21 June 2021. http://www.historiaetius.eu/num-4.html.

Eisenbichler, Konrad. *The Sword and the Pen: Women, poetry and politics in Siena*. Notre Dame, IN: University Press of Notre Dame Press, 2012.

Everson, Jane, Dennis V. Reidy and Lisa Sampson, eds. *The Italian Academies, 1525–1700: Networks of culture, innovation, and dissent*. Cambridge and Abingdon: MHRA and Routledge, 2016.

Eycken, Sarah. 'Tuccia and her Sieve: The *Nachleben* of the Vestal in Art'. MA thesis, KU Leuven, 2017–18.

Fabris, Dinko. 'Majone, Ascanio', *DBI* 67 (2006).

Fantappiè, Francesca. 'Rinuccini, Ottavio', *DBI* 87 (2016).

Fantappiè, Francesca. 'Strozzi, Piero Vincenzo', *DBI* 94 (2019).

Fantoni, Marcello. 'The Courts of the Medici 1532–1737'. In *The Princely Courts of Europe: Ritual, politics and culture under the Ancien Régime 1500–1750*, edited by John Adamson, 255–73, 334–5. London: Weidenfeld and Nicolson, 1999.

Fantoni, Marcello. 'Il simbolismo mediceo del potere fra cinque e seicento'. In *L'arme e gli amori: Ariosto, Tasso and Guarini in Late Renaissance Florence*, 2 vols, edited by Massimiliano Rossi and Fiorella Gioffredi Superbi, I: 17–26. Florence: Olschki, 2004.

Favaro, Francesca. 'Venier, Maffio', *DBI* 98 (2020).

Favaro, Maiko. 'La retorica della schiettezza: Sulle *lettere amorose* (1642) di Girolamo Brusoni', *The Italianist* 37:1 (2017): 20–35.

Feldman, Martha. 'Authors and Anonyms: Recovering the Anonymous Subject in Cinquecento Vernacular Objects'. In *Music and the*

Cultures of Print, edited by Kate Van Orden, 163–99. New York: Garland, 2000.

Fenlon, Iain. 'A Golden Age Restored: Pastoral Pastimes at the Pitti Palace'. In *L'arme e gli amori: Ariosto, Tasso and Guarini in Late Renaissance Florence*, 2 vols, edited by Massimiliano Rossi and Fiorella Gioffredi Superbi, I: 199–229. Florence: Olschki, 2004.

Fenlon, Iain. 'Preparations for a Princess'. In Iain Fenlon, *Music and Culture in Late Renaissance Italy*, 205–28. Oxford: Oxford University Press, 2002.

Ferrari, Mattia. 'Il *Lamento dei pescatori veneziani* e il ms. Marc. It. IX 173 (=6282)', Tesi di Laurea, relatore Prof. Lorenzo Tomasin, University of Ca' Foscari Venice, 2011–12.

Ferraro, Joanne. *The Marriage Wars in Late Renaissance Venice*. Oxford: Oxford University Press, 2001.

Ferretti, Francesco. 'L'ecfrasi mistica negli *Pietosi affetti* di Angelo Grillo'. In *Tra norma e trasgressione: Letteratura e immagini sacre in Italia nell'epoca della Controriforma*, edited by Andrea Campana, Fabio Giunta and Edoardo Ripari, 112–22. Città di Castello: I libri di Emil, 2019.

Foa, Anna. 'Castrucci, Giovanni Battista', *DBI* 22 (1979).

Fragnito, Gigiola. *Storia di Clelia Farnese: Amori, potere, violenza nella Roma della Controriforma*. Bologna: Il Mulino, 2013.

Freeman, Philip. *Searching for Sappho: The lost songs and world of the first woman poet*. New York: Norton, 2016.

Gaston, Robert W. 'Love's Sweet Poison: A New Reading of Bronzino's London "Allegory"', *I Tatti Studies in the Italian Renaissance* 4 (1991): 249–88.

Gentile, Luigi. *I codici palatini*, 2 vols. Rome: I Principali Librai, 1889.

Gerbino, Giuseppe. *Music and the Myth of Arcadia in Renaissance Italy*. Cambridge: Cambridge University Press, 2009.

Giannetti, Laura. *Lelia's Kiss: Imagining gender, sex, and marriage in Italian renaissance comedy*. Toronto: University of Toronto Press, 2009.

Giuli, Matteo. 'Dietro la quiete del vicino. Fazioni, congiure, e "discolati" a Lucca (1522–1600)'. In *Pistoia violenta: Faide e conflitti sociali in una città italiana dall'età comunale allo Stato moderno*, edited by Giampaolo Francesconi and Luca Mannori, 143–73. Pistoia: Società Pistoiese di Storia Patria, 2017.

Giuli, Matteo. 'Al servizio della Repubblica: un approccio prosopografico alla politica estera lucchese'. In *Sulla diplomazia in età moderna:*

Politica, economia, religione, edited by Renzo Sabbatini and Paola Volpini, 125–48. Milan: Franco Angeli, 2011.

Godard. Alain. 'La Première Représentation de l'*Aminta*: La Court de Ferrare et son double'. In *Ville et Campagne Dans la Littérature Italienne de la Renaissance*, 2 vols, II: *Le Courtisan Travesti*, edited by André Rochon and Anna Fontes-Baratto, 187–301. Paris: Université de la Sorbonne Nouvelle / Centre di Recherche sur la Renaissance Italienne, 1977.

Goode, Patrick. 'Pratolino'. *Grove Art Online*, 2003. https://doi-org.libproxy.ucl.ac.uk/10.1093/gao/9781884446054.article.T069260

Gordon, Andrew. 'Material Fictions: Counterfeit Correspondence and the Culture of Copying in Early Modern England'. In *Cultures of Correspondence in Early Modern Britain*, edited by James Daybell and Andrew Gordon, 85–109. Philadelphia: University of Pennsylvania Press, 2016.

Gordon, Bonnie. *Monteverdi's Unruly Women: The power of song in early modern Italy*. Cambridge: Cambridge University Press, 2004.

Gough, Melinda J. 'Marie de Medici's 1605 *ballet de la reine* and the Virtuosic Female Voice', *Early Modern Women: An Interdisciplinary Journal* 7 (2012): 127–56.

Goy, Richard J. *Chioggia and the Villages of the Venetian Lagoon: Studies in urban history*. Cambridge: Cambridge University Press, 1985.

Graziani, Françoise. '*Translatio Arcadiae*, de la *tragicommedia pastorale* à la *favola in musica*'. In *L'arme e gli amori: Ariosto, Tasso and Guarini in Late Renaissance Florence*, 2 vols, edited by Massimiliano Rossi and Fiorella Gioffredi Superbi, I: 135–58. Florence: Olschki, 2004.

Grell, Ole Peter. *Brethren in Christ: A Calvinist network in reformation Europe*. Cambridge: Cambridge University Press, 2011.

Guccini, Gerardo. 'Intorno alla prima "Pazzia d'Isabella". Fonti – Intersezioni –Tecniche', *Culture teatrali* 7.8 (2002–3): 167–207.

Guerzoni, Guido. *Le corti estensi e la devoluzione di Ferrara del 1598*. Modena: Archivio Storico, 2000.

Guidotti, Fabrizio. 'Vecoli, Bernardino', *DBI* 98 (2020).

Gullino, Giuseppe. 'Da Lezze, Giovanni', *DBI* 31 (1985).

Gundersheimer, Werner L. 'Renaissance Concepts of Shame and Pocaterra's *Dialoghi Della Vergogna*', *Renaissance Quarterly* 47.1 (1994): 34–56.

Haar, James. *Italian Poetry and Music in the Renaissance, 1350–1600*. Berkeley: University of California Press, 1986.

Hale, John R. *Renaissance War Studies*. London: Hambledon Press, 1983.

Henke, Robert. *Performance and Literature in the Commedia dell'Arte*. Cambridge: Cambridge University Press, 2002.

Hewlett, Mary. 'Fortune's Fool: The Influence of Humanism on Francesco Burlamacchi'. In *The Renaissance in the Streets, Schools, and Studies: Essays in honor of Paul F. Grendler*, edited by Konrad Eisenbichler and Nicholas Terpstra, 125–56. Toronto: Centre for Renaissance and Reformation Studies, 2008.

Hewlett, Mary. 'A Republic in Jeopardy: Cosimo I de' Medici and the Republic of Lucca'. In *The Cultural Politics of Cosimo I de' Medici*, edited by Konrad Eisenbichler, 9–22. Aldershot: Ashgate, 2001.

Hockley, Nancy. 'Bartolomeo Barbarino e i primordi della monodia', *Rivista Italiana di Musicologia* 7.1 (1972): 82–102.

Horsfall, Nicholas. 'Corythus: The Return of Aeneas in Virgil and His Sources', *The Journal of Roman Studies* 63 (1973): 68–79.

Houghton, L. B. T., 'Renaissance and Golden Age Revisited: Virgil's Fourth Eclogue in Medici Florence', *Bibliothèque d'Humanisme et Renaissance* 76.3 (2014): 413–32.

Hunter, G. K., 'The Marking of Sententiae in Elizabethan Printed Plays, Poems, and Romances', *The Library* 5–6: 3–4 (1951): 171–88.

Hunter, Lynette. 'Situated Knowledge'. In *Mapping Landscapes for Performance as Research*, edited by Lynette Hunter and Shannon Rose Riley, 151–4. Basingstoke: Palgrave Macmillan, 2009.

Imbriani, Vittorio. 'L'Eco responsiva nelle pastorali italiane', *Giornale napoletano di filosofia e lettere* 2.11 (1872): 279–314.

Innamorati, Isabella. 'Il riuso della parola: Ipotesi sul rapporto tra generici e centoni'. In *Origini della commedia improvvisa o dell'arte*, edited by Maria Chiabò and Federico Doglio, 163–85. Rome: Torre d'Orfeo, 1996.

Inventari dei manoscritti delle Biblioteche d'Italia, edited by G. Mazzatinti et al. Florence: Olschki; Forlì: Bordandini, 1890–.

Ivaldi, Armando Fabio. *Le Nozze Pio-Farnese e gli apparati teatrali di Sassuolo del 1587: Studio su una rappresentazione del primo dramma pastorale italiano, con intermezzi di G. B. Guarini*. Genoa: ERGA, 1974.

Jackson, Roland. 'Mayone, Ascanio', *Grove Music Online* (2001). https://doi.org/10.1093/gmo/9781561592630.article.18177.

Javitch, Daniel. 'The Emergence of Poetic Genre Theory in the Sixteenth Century', *Modern Language Quarterly* 59 (1998): 139–69.

Johnson, Géraldine A. 'Imagining Images of Powerful Women: Maria de'

Medici's Patronage of Art and Architecture'. In *Women and Art in Early Modern Europe: Patrons, collectors, and connoisseurs*, edited by Cynthia Lawrence, 126–53. University Park, PA: Pennsylvania State University Press, 1997.

Katinis, Teodoro. *Sperone Speroni and the Debate over Sophistry in the Italian Renaissance*. Leiden: Brill, 2018.

Kerr, Rosalind. *The Rise of the Diva on the Sixteenth-Century Commedia dell'Arte Stage*. Toronto: University of Toronto Press, 2015.

Kershaw, Baz. 'Performance Practice as Research: Perspectives from a Small Island'. In *Mapping Landscapes for Performance as Research*, edited by Lynette Hunter and Shannon Rose Riley, 3–13. Basingstoke: Palgrave Macmillan, 2009.

Kershaw, Baz. 'Promenade Performance'. In *The Oxford Encyclopedia of Theatre and Performance*, edited by Dennis Kennedy. Oxford: Oxford University Press, 2005.

Kirkendale, Warren. *Emilio de' Cavalieri, 'gentiluomo romano': His life and letters, his role as superintendent of all the arts at the Medici Court, and his musical compositions*. Florence: Olschki, 2001.

Kirkendale, Warren. 'L'opera in musica prima del Peri: Le pastorali perdute di Laura Guidiccioni ed Emilio de' Cavalieri'. In *Firenze e la Toscana dei Medici nell'Europa del '500*, edited by Giancarlo Garfagnini, 3 vols, II: *Musica e spettacolo: Scienze dell'uomo e della natura*, 365–95. Florence: Olschki, 1983.

Kirkham, Victoria. *Laura Battiferra and Her Literary Circle*. Chicago: University of Chicago Press, 2006.

Larson, Keith A. 'Dentice family', *Grove Music Online* (2001). https://doi.org/10.1093/gmo/9781561592630.article.07575.

Levin, Harry. *The Myth of the Golden Age in the Renaissance*. London: Faber, 1970.

Lindell, Robert, and Brian Mann. 'Monte, Philippe de', *Grove Music Online* (2001). https://doi.org/10.1093/gmo/9781561592630.article.40085.

Loewenstein, Joseph. *Responsive Readings: Versions of echo in pastoral, epic, and the Jonsonian Masque*. New Haven, CT: Yale University Press, 1984.

Lombardi, Daniela. 'Marriage in Italy'. In *Marriage in Europe: 1400–1800*, edited by Silvana Seidel Menchi, 94–121. Toronto: University of Toronto Press, 2016.

Lucchesini, Cesare. *Della storia letteraria del Ducato lucchese, libri sette*, 2 vols. Lucca: F. Bertini, 1825–31.

Luchinat, Cristina Acidini and Giorgio Galletti, with photos by Aurelio

Amendola. *La villa e il giardino della Petraia a Firenze*. Florence: EDIFIR, 1995.

Luzzati, Michele. 'Buonvisi, Bernardino', *DBI* 15 (1972).

Luzzati, Michele. 'Buonvisi, Lorenzo', *DBI* 15 (1972).

Luzzi, Cecilia. *Poesia e musica nei Madrigali a cinque voci di Filippo Di Monte (1580–1595)*. Florence: Olschki, 2003.

MacNeil, Ann. *Music and Women of the Commedia dell'arte in the Late Sixteenth Century*. Oxford: Oxford University Press, 2003.

Magini, Alessandro. 'Cronache musicali e letterarie di Lucca e Firenze nel secondo Cinquecento', *Momus* 1 (1994): 41–62.

Mamone, Sara. *Dei, Semidei, Uomini: Lo spettacolo a Firenze tra neoplatonismo e realtà borghese (XV–XVII secolo)*. Rome: Bulzoni, 2003.

Mamone, Sara. *Il teatro nella Firenze medicea*. Milan: Mursia, 1981.

Mangini, Nicola. *I teatri di Venezia*. Milan: Mursia, 1974.

Maniates, Maria Rika. *Mannerism in Italian Culture and Music*. Chapel Hill: University of North Carolina Press, 2011.

Mansi, Gerardo. *I patrizi di Lucca: Le antiche famiglie lucchesi e i loro stemmi*. Lucca: Titania, 1996.

Maravall, José Antonio. *Culture of the Baroque: Analysis of a Historical Structure* [1975], translated by Terry Cochrane. Minneapolis: University of Minnesota Press, 1986.

Marcheschi, Daniela. *Chiara Matraini: Poetessa, lucchese, e la letteratura delle donne nei nuovi fermenti letterari del '500*. Lucca: Pacini Fazzi, 2008.

Martini, Davide. 'Aggiornamento cronologico al catalogo delle edizioni impresse da Vincenzo Busdraghi'. In *Vincenzo Busdraghi (1524?–1601): Uno stampatore europeo a Lucca*, edited by Davide Martini, Tommaso Maria Rossi and Gaia Elisabetta Unfer Verre, 87–123. Lucca: Comune di Lucca, 2017.

Masetti Zannini, Gian Luigi. *Marfisa d'Este Cybo: 'Gentil fu da che nacque'*, edited by Alessandro Vincenzo Masetti Zannini. Ferrara: Este Edition, 2008.

Matt, Luigi. 'Grillo, Angelo', *DBI* 59 (2002).

Maylender, Michele. *Storia delle Accademie d'Italia*, 5 vols. Bologna: Cappelli, 1926–30; anast. repr. Bologna: Forni, 1976.

Mazzei, Rita. 'A proposito di modelli della storiografia umanistica: Un caso di circolazione culturale fra Napoli e Lucca nel primo Cinquecento', *Archivio storico italiano* 168.1 (2010): 33–88.

Mazzei, Rita. 'La Repubblica di Lucca e l'Impero nella prima età moderna: Ragioni e limiti di una scelta'. In *L'Impero e l'Italia nella prima età moderna / Das Reich und Italien in der Frühen Neuzeit*, edited by

Matthias Schnettger and Marcello Verga, 299–321. Bologna: Il Mulino; and Berlin: Duncker & Humblot, 2006.

Mazzei, Rita. *La società lucchese del Seicento*. Lucca: Maria Pacini Fazzi, 1977.

Mazzei, Rita. 'Il viaggio alle terme. Un "pellegrinaggio" d'élite fra sanità, politica, e diplomazia', *Archivio strico italiano*, 172.4 (2014): 645–90.

Mazzeo, Antonio, and Pietro Rigacci, eds., *Tommaso Pecci madrigalista senese del 1500*. Siena: Edizioni Centro Studi per la Storia della Musica Senese, 1987.

Mazzucchelli, Giovanni Maria. *Gli scrittori d'Italia*, 6 vols. Brescia: Giovanni Battista Bossini, 1753–63.

McCall, Timothy and Sean Roberts. 'Introduction: Revealing Early Modern secrecy'. In *Visual Cultures of Secrecy in Early Modern Europe*, edited by Timothy McCall, Sean Roberts and Giancarlo Fiorenza. Kirksville, MO: Truman State University Press, 2013.

McClary, Susan. *Desire and Pleasure in Seventeenth-Century Music*. Berkeley: University of California Press, 2012.

McClure, George W. *Parlour Games and the Public Life of Women in Renaissance Italy*. Toronto: University of Toronto Press, 2013.

McClure, George W. 'Women and the Politics of Play in Sixteenth-Century Italy: Torquato Tasso's Theory of Games', *Renaissance Quarterly* 61.3 (2008): 750–91.

McHugh, Shannon. 'Devotion, Desire and Masculinity in the Spiritual Verse of Angelo Grillo'. In *Innovation in the Italian Counter-Reformation*, edited by Shannon McHugh and Anna Wainwright, 145–65. Newark: University of Delaware Press, 2020.

McHugh, Shannon. *Petrarch and the Making of Gender*. Amsterdam: Amsterdam University Press, 2023.

McHugh, Shannon and Anna Wainwright, eds. *Innovation in the Italian Counter-Reformation*. Newark: University of Delaware Press, 2020.

McInnis, David and Matthew Steggle, 'Introduction: Nothing will come of nothing? Or what can we learn from plays that don't exist'. In *Lost Plays in Shakespeare's England*, edited by David McInnis and Matthew Steggle, 1–16. Hampshire: Palgrave Macmillan, 2014.

Meek, Christine. 'Il matrimonio e le nozze: Sposarsi a Lucca nel tardo medioevo'. In *I tribunali del matrimonio (secoli XV–XVIII)*, edited by Silvana Seidel Menchi and Diego Quaglioni, 359–73. Bologna: Il Mulino, 2007.

Megale, Teresa. 'Guidiccioni, Laura', *DBI* 61 (2004).

Meloncelli, Raoul. 'Bellasio, Paolo', *DBI* 7 (1970).

[Melzi, Gaetano] G. M., *Dizionario di opere anonime e pseudonime di* scrittori italiani o come che sia aventi relazione all'Italia, 3 vols. Milan: Luigi di Giacomo Pirola, 1848–59.

Miani, Gemma. 'Antelminelli, Alessandro', *DBI* 3 (1961).

Miani, Gemma. 'Arnolfini, Vincenzo', *DBI* 4 (1962).

Milburn, Erika. *Luigi Tansillo and Lyric Poetry in Sixteenth-Century Naples.* Leeds: Maney / MHRA, 2003.

Miller, Roark. 'Bartolomeo Barbarino and the Allure of Venice', *Studi musicali* 23 (1994): 263–98.

Miller, Roark Thurston. 'The Composers of San Marco and Santo Stefano and the Development of Venetian Monody (to 1630)'. PhD diss., University of Michigan, 1993.

Miller, Roark and Jerome Roche. 'Barbarino, Bartolomeo', *Grove Music Online* (2001). https://doi.org/10.1093/gmo/9781561592630. article.01983.

Mitchell, Bonner. *1598: A Year of Pageantry in Late Renaissance Ferrara.* Binghampton, NY: Center for Medieval and Early Renaissance Studies, 1990.

Miziolek, Jerzy. '"Exempla" di giustizia: Tre tavole di cassone di Alvise Donati', *Arte lombarda* 131 (2001): 72–88.

Moppi, Gregorio. 'Pecci, Tommaso', *DBI* 82 (2015).

Morucci, Valerio. 'Poets and Musicians in the Roman-Florentine Circle of Virginio Orsini, Duke of Bracciano (1572–1615)', *Early Music* 43.1 (2015): 53–61.

Moulton, Ian Frederick. 'Introduction. The Greatest Tangle of Pricks There Ever Was: Knowledge, sex, and power in Renaissance Italy'. In Antonio Vignali, *La cazzaria: The book of the prick*, edited and translated by Ian Frederick Moulton, 1–70. New York: Routledge, 2003.

Mueller, Hans-Friedrich. *Roman Religion in Valerius Maximus.* London: Taylor & Francis, 2002.

Muir, Edward. 'Why Venice? Venetian Society and the Success of Early Opera', *Journal of Interdisciplinary History* 36.3 (2006): 331–53.

Murphy, Caroline P. *Murder of a Medici Princess.* Oxford: Oxford University Press, 2008.

Mutini, C. 'Caporali, Cesare', *DBI* 18 (1975).

Myers, Patricia Ann. 'Bellasio [Belasio], Paolo', *Grove Music Online* (2001). https://doi.org/10.1093/gmo/9781561592630.article.02 582.

Nelson Novoa, James W. 'Double Alterity in a Celebratory Sonnet on the Battle of Lepanto', *eHumanista* 21 (2012): 421–36.

Nerici, Luigi. *Storia della musica in Lucca.* Lucca: Tipografia Giusti, 1880.

Newcomb, Anthony. 'Alfonso Fontanelli and the Ancestry of the Seconda Pratica Madrigal'. In *Studies in Renaissance and Baroque Music in Honor of Arthur Mendel*, edited by Robert L. Marshall, 47–68. Kassel: Bärenreiter, 1974.

Newcomb, Anthony. *The Madrigal at Ferrara, 1579–1597*. Princeton, NJ: Princeton University Press, 1980.

Nicholson, Eric. 'Crossing Borders with Satyrs, the Irrepressible Genre-Benders of Pastoral Tragicomedy', *The Italianist*, special issue: 'Genre-Bending in Early Modern Performative Culture', edited by Jessica Goethals and Eugenio Refini, 40.3 (2020): 342–61.

Nicholson, Eric. 'Romance as Role Model: Early Female Performances of *Orlando Furioso* and *Gerusalemme Liberata*'. In *Renaissance Transactions: Ariosto and Tasso*, edited by Valeria Finucci, 246–69. Durham, NC: Duke University Press, 1999.

Nicholson, Eric. '"She speaks poniards": Shakespearian Drama and the Italianate Leading Lady as Verbal Duellists', *Early Modern Literary Studies*, special issue: 'European Women in Early Modern Drama', 27 (2017): 1–16.

Nosow, Robert. 'The Debate on Song in the Accademia Fiorentina', *Early Music History* 21 (2002): 175–221.

Novati, F. 'Una poesia politica del Cinquecento: Il Pater noster dei Lombardi', *Giornale di Filologia Romanza* 5 (1879): 122–52.

Nuttall, Geoffrey. 'Filippino Lippi's Lucchese Patrons'. In *Filippino Lippi, Beauty, Invention and Intelligence*, edited by Paul Nuttall, Geoffrey Nuttall, and Michael Kwakkelstein, 84–118. Leiden: Brill, 2020.

Ossi, Massimo. 'A Sample Problem in Seventeenth-Century *Imitatio*: Claudio Monteverdi, Francesco Turini, and Battista Guarini's "Mentre vaga angioletta"'. In *Music in Renaissance Cities and Courts: Studies in Honor of Lewis Lockwood*, edited by Jessie Ann Owens and Anthony M. Cummings, 253–69. Warren, MI: Harmonie Park Press, 1997.

Palermo, Francesco. *I manoscritti palatini di Firenze, ordinati ed esposti*, 3 vols. Florence: Biblioteca Palatina (vols 1–2) and M. Cellini (vol. 3), 1853–68.

Palisca, Claude V. 'The Alterati of Florence, Pioneers in the Theory of Dramatic Music'. In *New Looks at Italian Opera: Essays in Honor of Donald J. Grout*, edited by William W. Austin, 9–38. Ithaca, NY: Cornell University Press, 1968.

Palisca, Claude V. 'Musical Asides in the Diplomatic Correspondence of Emilio de' Cavalieri', *Musical Quarterly* 49 (1963): 339–55.

Paoli, Maria Pia. 'Nell'Italia delle "Vergini belle": A proposito di Chiara

Matraini e di pietà mariana nella Lucca di fine Cinquecento'. In *Religione cultura e politica nell'Europa dell'età moderna*, edited by Carlo Ossola, Marcello Verga and Maria Antonietta Visceglia, 521–45. Florence: Olschki, 2003.

Paoli, Maria Pia. 'I Medici arbitri d'onore: Duelli, vertenze cavalleresche e "paci aggiustate" negli antichi Stati italiani (secoli XVI-XVIII)'. In *Stringere la pace: Teorie e pratiche della conciliazione nell'Europa moderna (secoli XVI-XVIII)*, edited by Paolo Broggio and Maria Pia Paoli, 129–99. Rome: Viella, 2011.

Parkes, M. B. *Pause and Effect: An introduction to the history of punctuation in the West*. Aldershot: Scolar Press, 1992.

Pasquazi, Silvio. 'Le Annotazioni al *Pastor fido* di Lionardo Salviati'. In *Poeti estensi del Rinascimento: con due appendici*, 191–233. Florence: Le Monnier, 1966.

Pearson, Mike. *Site-Specific Performance*. Basingstoke: Palgrave Macmillan, 2010.

Pelagalli, Rossella and Cristina Scarpa. 'Fontanelli, Alfonso', *DBI* 48 (1997).

Pellegrini, Amalchilde. *Spettacoli lucchesi nei secoli XVII–XIX*. Lucca: Tipografia Giusti, 1914.

Perella, Nicolas J. *The Critical Fortune of Battista Guarini's 'Il Pastor Fido'*. Florence: Olschki, 1973.

Perotti, Diego. *I madrigali autografi di Torquato Tasso a Carlo Gesualdo (Madrid, Real Biblioteca, ms. II/3281)*. Florence: Franco Cesati, 2021.

Petrina, Alessandra. 'Walter Scott of Buccleuch, Italian poet?', *Renaissance Studies* 24.5 (2010): 671–93.

Piatti, Angelo Alberto. '"E l'uom pietà da Dio, piangendo, impari": Lacrime e pianto nelle rime sacre nell'età del Tasso'. In *Rime sacre dal Cinquecento al Seicento*, edited by Carlo Delcorno and Maria Luisa Doglio, 53–106. Bologna: Il Mulino, 2007.

Piccard, Gerhard. *Wasserzeichen Kreuz*. Stuttgatt: W. Kohlhammer, 1981.

Picinelli, Roberta. *Le collezioni Gonzaga: Il carteggio tra Firenze e Mantova (1554–1626)*. Milan: Silvana, 2000.

Pidatella, Delia. 'Antonio Renieri da Colle: Lingua, accademia, trattenimento, e scuola nella Toscana del XVI secolo'. In *Colle di Val D'Elsa: Diocesi e città tra '500 e '600*, edited by Pietro Nencini, 447–65. Castelfiorentino: Società Storica della Val D'Elsa, 1994.

Piéjus, Anne. 'Musical Settings of the *Rime*'. In *A Companion to Vittoria Colonna*, edited by Abigail Brundin, Tatiana Crivelli and Maria Serena Sapegno, 314–45. Leiden: Brill, 2016.

Pieri, Marzia. *La scena boschereccia nel Rinascimento italiano*. Padua: Liviana, 1983.

Pilot, Antonio. 'Il divorzio di Aldo Manuzio il giovane', *Ateneo Veneto* 27 (1904): 62–74.

Pirrotta, Nino. *Scelte poetiche di musicisti: Teatro, poesia e musica da Willaert a Malipiero*. Venice: Marsilio, 1987.

Plaisance, Michel. 'I dibattiti intorno ai poemi dell'Ariosto e del Tasso nelle accademie fiorentine: 1582–86'. In *L'Accademia e il suo principe: Cultura e politica a Firenze al tempo di Cosimo I e di Francesco de' Medici / L'Académie et le prince: Culture et politique à Florence au temps de Côme Ier et de François de Médicis*, 375–91. Manziana (Rome): Vecchiarelli, 2004.

Prandi, Stefano. *Il 'Cortegiano' Ferrarese: I 'Discorsi' di Annibale Romei e la cultura nobiliare nel Cinquecento*. Florence: Olschki, 1990.

Prefumo, Danilo. 'Dalla Gostena, Giovanni Battista', *DBI* 31 (1985).

Quadrio, Francesco Saverio. *Della storia e ragione d'ogni poesia*, 4 [7] vols. Bologna: Francesco Pisarri, 1739–52.

Quaintance, Courtney. *Textual Masculinity and the Exchange of Women in Renaissance Venice*. Toronto: University of Toronto Press, 2018.

Quarta, Daniela. 'Spazio scenico, spazio cortigiano, spazio cortese: L'*Aminta* e il *Torrismondo* di Torquato Tasso'. In *La corte di Ferrara e il suo mecenatismo 1441–1598*, edited by Marianne Pade, Lene Waage Petersen and Daniela Quarta, 301–27. Copenhagen: Forum for Renaessancestudier / Ferrara: L'Istituto di Studi Rinascimentali, 1990.

Quondam, Amedeo. 'L'Accademia', in *Letteratura italiana*, edited by Alberto Asor Rosa, 6 vols, I: *Il letterato e le istituzioni*, 823–98. Turin: Einaudi, 1982.

Rabitti, Giovanna. 'Matraini, Chiara', *DBI* 72 (2008).

Radicchi, Patrizia. 'Alberico I Cybo Malaspina e la musica a Massa', *Studi musicali* 30.2 (2001): 321–49.

Ragagli, Simone. 'La Repubblica e il Sant'Uffizio: Il Controllo delle coscienze nella Lucca del secolo di ferro'. Tesi di perfezionamento, Scuola Normale Superiore di Pisa, 2008–9. Accessed 31 March 2022. https://ricerca.sns.it/retrieve/handle/11384/86025/376 47/Ragagli_Simone.pdf.

Ray, Meredith K. *Writing Gender in Women's Letter Collections of the Italian Renaissance*. Toronto: University of Toronto Press, 2009.

Refini, Eugenio. 'Echoes of Ariadne in the Musical Reception of Ariosto and Tasso', *Renaissance Quarterly* 73.2 (2020): 527–66.

Refini, Eugenio. '"Parole tronche et imperfette": The Lament as a "Mode" across Poetical and Musical Genres', *The Italianist*, special issue: *Genre-Bending in Early Modern Performative Culture*, edited by Jessica Goethals and Eugenio Refini, 40.3 (2020): 441–62.

Richardson, Brian. *Manuscript Culture in Renaissance Italy*. Cambridge: Cambridge University Press, 2009.

Riccò, Laura. *'Ben mille pastorali': L'itinerario dell'Ingegneri da Tasso a Guarini e oltre*. Rome: Bulzoni, 2004.

Riccò, Laura. *Gioco e teatro nelle veglie di Siena*. Rome: Bulzoni, 1993.

Rizzi, Andrea, and John Griffiths. 'The Renaissance of Anonymity', *Renaissance Quarterly* 69.1 (2016): 200–12.

Rizzolino, Salvatore. *'Angelus Domini nuntiavit Mariae': Poemetti mariani dimenticati fra* Lagrime *e* Rime spirituali *del Tasso. Appendice di testi Mariani Cappuccini tra XVI-XVII sec.*, edited by Fr. Costanzo Cargnoni. Milan: Edizioni Biblioteca Francescana, 2017.

Rizzolino, Salvatore. 'Nicolao Tucci, un amico lucchese di Angelo Grillo, e il suo poemetto lauretano nelle *Rime spirituali* di Torquato Tasso', *Lettere italiane* 74.1 (2022): 45–69.

Rohlfs, Gerhard. *Grammatica storica della lingua italiana e dei suoi dialetti*, 3 vols. Florence: Accademia della Crusca, 2021.

Rosand, Ellen. *Opera in Seventeenth-Century Venice: The creation of a genre*. Berkeley and Los Angeles: University of California Press, 1991.

Rosenthal, Margaret F. *The Honest Courtesan: Veronica Franco, Citizen and Writer in Sixteenth-Century Venice*. Chicago: University of Chicago Press, 1992.

Rossi, Vittorio. *Battista Guarini ed il 'Pastor fido': Studio biografico-critico con documenti inediti*. Turin: Loescher, 1886.

Russo, Emilio. *Marino*. Rome: Salerno, 2008.

Rutherford, R. B. *Greek Tragic Style: Form, language and interpretation*. Cambridge: Cambridge University Press, 2012.

Sabbatini, Renzo. 'Tra amministrazione pontificia, attività diplomatica per la Repubblica, e scrittura storica: la carriera variegata di Nicolao Tucci (1541–1615)', *Mélanges de l'École française de Rome – Italie et Méditeranée modernes et contemporaines* 133.1 (2021): 15–28.

Sabbatini, Renzo. 'Famiglie e potere nella Lucca moderna'. In *Famiglie e potere in Italia tra Medioevo ed età moderna*, edited by Anna Bellavitis and Isabelle Chabot, 233–61. Rome: École Française de Rome, 2009.

Sabbatini, Renzo. 'Immagini di una città-stato: Lucca nello specchio delle orazioni sacro-politiche recitate in Senato'. In *La città nel Settecento: Saperi e forme di rappresentazione*, edited by Marina Formica, Andrea Merlotti and Anna Maria Rao, 269–94. Rome: Edizioni di Storia e Letteratura, 2014.

Sabbatini, Renzo. *Le mura e l'Europa: Aspetti della politica estera della Repubblica di Lucca (1500–1799)*. Milan: Franco Angeli, 2012.

Sabbatini, Renzo. 'Paolino Velutelli: un nobile minore nella Lucca del Cinquecento', *Archivio storico italiano*, 139.4 (1981): 581–630.

Sabbatini, Renzo. *La sollevazione degli Straccioni: Lucca 1531: Politica e mercato*. Rome: Salerno, 2020.

Sabbatini, Renzo. 'Tucci, Nicolao', *DBI* 97 (2020).

Sacchini, Lorenzo. 'Da Francesco Petrarca a Giovan Battista Marino: L'Accademia degli Insensati di Perugia (1561–1608)'. In *The Italian Academies, 1525–1700: Networks of culture, innovation, and dissent*, edited by Jane E. Everson, Dennis V. Reidy and Lisa Sampson, 245–57. Cambridge: MHRA/Routledge, 2016.

Sacré, Dirk. 'Quaestiunculae palearianae', *Humanistica lovaniensia* 40 (1991): 206–43.

Saltini, Guglielmo Enrico. 'L'educazione del principe Don Francesco de' Medici', *Archivio storico italiano*, fourth series, 11.34 (1883): 157–72.

Salvini, Salvino. *Fasti consolari dell'Accademia Fiorentina*. Florence: Gio. Gaetano Tartini e Santi Franchi, 1717.

Sampson, Lisa. 'Amateurs Meet Professionals: Theatrical Activities in Late Sixteenth-Century Italian Academies'. In *The Reinvention of Theatre in Sixteenth-Century Europe: Traditions, texts and performance*, edited by T. F. Earle and Catarina Fouto, 187–203. Oxford: Legenda/MHRA, 2015.

Sampson, Lisa. '"Deggio ferma tener la santa fede": Representing the Priest in Pastoral Drama in Counter-Reformation Italy'. In *Innovation in the Italian Counter-Reformation*, edited by Shannon McHugh and Anna Wainwright, 190–215. Newark: University of Delaware Press, 2020.

Sampson, Lisa. '"*Drammatica secreta*": Barbara Torelli's *Partenia* (c. 1587) and Women in Late Sixteenth-Century Theatre'. In *Theatre, Opera, and Performance in Italy from the Fifteenth Century to the Present: Essays in honour of Richard Andrews*, edited by Simon Gilson, Catherine Keen and Brian Richardson, 99–115. Leeds: The Society for Italian Studies/Maney, 2004.

Sampson, Lisa. '"Non lasciar così facilmente publicar le cose mie": Manuscript Secular Drama in Sixteenth-Century Italy', *Italian Studies* 66.2 (2011): 161–76.

Sampson, Lisa. *Pastoral Drama in Early Modern Italy: The making of a new genre*. Oxford: Legenda, 2006.

Sampson, Lisa. 'Performing Female Cultural Sociability Between Court and Academy: Isabella Pallavicino Lupi and Angelo Ingegneri's *Danza di Venere* (1584)'. In *Chivalry, Academy, and Cultural Dialogues: The Italian contribution to European culture. Essays in honour of Jane E. Everson*, edited by Stefano Jossa and Giuliana Pieri, 107–22. Oxford: Legenda, 2017.

Sampson, Lisa. 'Reforming Theatre in Farnese Parma: The Case of the Accademia degli Innominati (1574–1608)'. In *The Italian Academies, 1525–1700: Networks of Culture, Innovation, and Dissent*, edited by Jane E. Everson, Dennis V. Reidy and Lisa Sampson, 62–76. Cambridge: MHRA/Routledge, 2016.

Sampson, Lisa. 'The Mantuan Performance of Guarini's *Pastor fido* and Representations of Courtly Identity', *Modern Language Review* 98 (2003): 65–83.

Sanfilippo, Matteo. 'Leone XI, papa', *DBI* 64 (2005).

Saslow, James M. *The Medici Wedding of 1589: Florentine Festival as Theatrum Mundi*. New Haven, CT: Yale University Press, 1996.

Scarpati, Claudio. 'Il nucleo ovidiano dell'Aminta'. In *Tasso, i classici e i moderni*, 75–104. Padua: Antenore, 1995.

Schmitt, Charles B. 'Cremonini, Cesare', *DBI* 30 (1984).

Selmi, Elisabetta. *'Classici e Moderni' nell'officina del* Pastor fido. Alessandria: Edizioni dell'Orso, 2001.

Selmi, Elisabetta. 'Guarini, Battista', *DBI* 60 (2003).

Selmi, Elisabetta. 'Maggi, Vincenzo', *DBI* 67 (2006).

Serassi, Pierantonio. *La vita di Tasso*. Rome: Stamperia Pagliarini, 1785.

Sforza, Giovanni. *F. M. Fiorentini ed i suoi contemporanei lucchesi: Saggio di storia letteraria del secolo XVII*. Florence: Menozzi, 1879.

Sidiropoulou, Avra. *Authoring Performance: The director in contemporary theatre*. Basingstoke: Palgrave Macmillan, 2011.

Smith, Candace. 'Leonora Orsini (?1560–1634)'. In *Women Composers: Music through the ages*, edited by Martha Furman Schleifer and Sylvia Glickman, 12 vols, I: *Composers Born Before 1599*, 123–26. New York: G. K. Hall, 1996.

Smith, Rosalind. 'Fictions of Production: Misattribution, prosopopoeia, and the early modern woman writer', *Journal of Medieval and Early Modern Studies* 50.1 (2020): 33–52.

Snyder, Jon R. *Dissimulation and the Culture of Secrecy in Early Modern Europe*. Berkeley and Los Angeles: University of California Press, 2009.

Snyder, Jon R. 'Introduction' to Giovan Battista Andreini, *Love in the Mirror*, edited and translated by Jon R. Snyder, 1–36. Toronto: Centre for Reformation and Renaissance Studies/Iter, 2009.

Solerti, Angelo. *Gli albori del melodramma*, 3 vols. Milan: Remo Sandron, 1904.

Solerti, Angelo. 'Laura Guidiccioni ed Emilio de' Cavalieri (i primi tentativi di melodramma)', *Rivista musicale italiana* 9 (1902): 797–829.

Solerti, Angelo. 'Statuto di una accademia ferrarese del secolo decimosesto', *Atti della Deputazione Ferrarese di Storia Patria* 4.2 (1892): 55–65.

Solerti, Angelo. *Vita di Torquato Tasso*, 3 vols. Rome: E. Loescher, 1895.

Spalding, Jack, 'Allori, Alessandro (di Cristofano di Lorenzo del Bronzino)', *Grove Art Online* (2003). https://doi.org/10.1093/oao /9781884446054.013.60000100177.

Stella, Clara. 'La parola d'autrice tra propaganda e dissenso: Alcuni appunti sulla questione politica nelle *Rime diverse d'alcune nobilissime et virtuosissime donne*'. In *Vincenzo Busdraghi (1524?–1601): Uno stampatore Europeo a Lucca*, edited by Davide Martini, Tommaso Maria Rossi and Gaia Elisabetta Unfer Verre, 42–53. Lucca: Comune di Lucca, 2017.

Stras, Laurie. 'Recording Tarquinia: Imitation, Parody, and Reportage in Ingegneri's "Hor che 'l ciel e la terra e 'l vento tace"', *Early Music* 27.3 (1999): 358–77.

Stras, Laurie. *Women and Music in Sixteenth-Century Ferrara*. Cambridge: Cambridge University Press, 2018.

Sturm-Maddox, Sara. 'Catherine de Medici and The Two Lilies', *Court Historian* 10.1 (2005): 25–36.

Tiraboschi, Girolamo. *Biblioteca modenese, o Notizie della vita e delle opera degli scrittori natii degli stati del serenissimo signor duca di Modena*, 6 vols. Modena: Società Tipografica, 1781–86.

Tomlinson, Gary. 'Madrigal, Monody, and Monteverdi's "via naturale alla imitatione"', *Journal of the American Musicological Society* 34 (1981): 86–96.

Tomlinson, Gary. *Monteverdi and the End of the Renaissance*. Berkeley: University of California Press, 1987.

Tommasi, Girolamo and Carlo Minutoli. *Sommario della storia di Lucca dall'anno MIV all'anno MDCC*. Lucca: Giovanni Pietro Vieusseux, 1847.

Toscano, Tobia R. 'Tansillo, Luigi', *DBI* 94 (2019).

Tozzi, Ileana. 'I codici miniati della Domenicana suor Eufrasia Burlamacchi al tramonto dell'età medievale', *Pecia* 14 (2011): 95–105.

Treadwell, Nina. *Music and Wonder at the Medici Court: The 1589 interludes for 'La pellegrina'*. Bloomington: Indiana University Press, 2008.

Treadwell, Nina. '"Simil combattimento fatto da Dame": The Musico-Theatrical Entertainments of Margherita Gonzaga's *balletto delle donne* and the Female Warrior in Ferrarese Cultural History'. In *Gender, Sexuality and Early Music*, edited by Todd M. Borgerding, 27–40. New York and London: Routledge: 2002.

Tylus, Jane. 'The Work of Italian Theater', *Renaissance Drama*, Special Issue: *What is Renaissance Drama?* 40 (2012): 171–84.

Ugolini, Paola. *The Court and Its Critics: Anti-court sentiments in early modern Italy*. Toronto: Toronto University Press, 2020.

Vandelli, Domenico. 'Vita di Tarquinia Molza, detta l'Unica'. In *Opuscoli inediti di Tarquinia Molza Modenese*, 3–25. Bergamo: Pietro Lancellotti, 1750.

Vandi, Loretta. 'Sister Eufrasia Burlamacchi and the Art of the Wayside', *Memorie domenicane* 46 (2015): 89–104, 295–7.

Vassalli, Antonio. 'Appunti per una storia della scrittura Guariniana: Le rime a stampa prima del 1598'. In *Guarini: La musica, i musicisti*, edited by Angelo Pompilio, 3–12. Lucca: Libreria Musicale Italiana, 1997.

Vazzoler, Franco. 'Le pastorali dei comici dell'arte: *La Mirtilla* di Isabella Andreini'. In *Sviluppi della drammaturgia pastorale nell'Europa del Cinque-Seicento*, edited by Maria Chiabò and Federico Doglio, 281–99. Viterbo: Centro Studi sul teatro medioevale e rinascimentale, 1992.

Vellutini, Mita. *Donne e società nella Lucca del '500*. Lucca: Pacini Fazzi, 2007.

Wainwright, Anna. 'The Fair Warrior in the City of Florence: Maddalena Salvetti's Poems to Christine of Lorraine'. In *Innovation in the Italian Counter-Reformation*, edited by Shannon McHugh and Anna Wainwright, 127–144. Newark: University of Delaware Press, 2020.

Wainwright, Anna. 'A Simple Virgin Speaks: Authorial Identity and

Persuasion in Isabella Cervoni's Oration to Pope Clement VIII', *The Italianist* 37.1 (2017): 1–19.

Weaver, Elissa B. *Convent Theatre in Early Modern Italy: Spiritual fun and learning for women*. Cambridge: Cambridge University Press, 2002.

Weinberg, Bernard. *A History of Literary Criticism in the Italian Renaissance*, 2 vols. Chicago: Chicago University Press, 1961.

Wilbourne, Emily. *Seventeenth-Century Opera and the Sound of the Commedia dell'Arte*. Chicago: University of Chicago Press, 2016.

Wiles, Bertha Harris. *The Fountains of the Florentine Sculptors and Their Followers, from Donatello to Bernini*. Cambridge, MA: Harvard University Press, 1933.

Williams, William Proctor. 'What's a Lost Play?: Toward a taxonomy of lost plays'. In *Lost Plays in Shakespeare's England*, edited by David McInnis and Matthew Steggle, 17–30. Hampshire: Palgrave Macmillan, 2014.

Wilson, Blake. *Singing to the Lyre in Renaissance Italy: Memory, performance, and oral poetry*. Cambridge: Cambridge University Press, 2020.

Wilson, Blake, George J. Buelow and Peter A. Hoyt. 'Rhetoric and music', *Grove Music Online* (2001). https://doi.org/10.1093/gmo/978156 1592630.article.43166.

Wilson, Bronwen. '"Il bel sesso, e l'austero Senato": The Coronation of Dogaressa Morosina Morosini Grimani', *Renaissance Quarterly* 52.1 (1999): 73–139.

Wright, D. R. 'Some Medici Gardens of the Florentine Renaissance: An Essay in Post-Aesthetic Interpretation'. In *The Italian Garden: Art, design and culture*, edited by John Dixon Hunt, 34–59. Cambridge University Press, 1996.

Yeh, Chia-Hua. 'From Classical to Chic: Reconsidering the Prints from *Varie acconciature di teste usate da nobilissime dame in diverse città d'Italia* by Giovanni Guerra, c. 1589', *Konsthistorisk tidskrift* 82.3 (2013): 157–68.

Digital/web-based resources

BMV Archivio dei possessori. Accessed 19 October 2022. https://archivio possessori.it/archivio/5-zeno-apostolo.

Clorilli: A Pastoral Drama by Leonora Bernardi of Lucca (1559–1617), directed by Eric Nicholson, NYU Florence, Villa La Pietra, May

2018. Accessed 20 August 2021. https://www.youtube.com/wat ch?v=sCCf8al5Sw0.

Italian Academies Database (British Library), Simone Testa and Lorenza Gianfrancesco, directed by Jane Everson, Denis Reidy and Lisa Sampson, assisted by Thomas Denman. Funded by the Arts and Humanities Research Council, UK, Resource Enhancement Grant, 2006–9, ref. AH/D00117X/1, and Major Research Grant, 2010–14 ref. AH/H023631/1). Accessed 2 April 2022. http:// www.bl.uk/catalogues/ItalianAcademies/Default.aspx.

Index

Note: references to tables and figures are given in *italic* type.

Bernardi, Leonora (*cont.*)
and Florence, 15, 19, 23–7, 96–8,
104–5
friendships of. *See* Chiariti,
Domenico; Grillo, Angelo; Tucci,
Nicolao
marriage of, 17–18, 29
and Massa, 24, 31
as mother, 17, 37
religious retreat of, 42–5, 50, 137
as salon hostess, 37–9, 41–2, 134
and scandal of 1588, 24–6, 31,
50–9
as singer and musician, 16, 18–19,
21, 27, 73–4, 424–6
widowhood of, 22–4, 29, 69, 113,
134, 137
See also Bernardi, Leonora, lyric
poetry by; Bernardi, Leonora,
writings by; *Clorilli* (Bernardi)
Bernardi, Leonora, lyric poetry by,
19–20, 28–9, 31, 75, 104
'O chi l'ale m'impenna' (canzonetta),
401–4
'O meraviglia altera' (madrigal),
418–9
set by Monte, 426, 431, 452–5
'Più d'altra ninfa amata'
(canzonetta), 421–3
set by Legname, 440–3, 475–6
set by Tantucci, 127, 377, 440–1,
463–4
'Questi, che porger può care e devote'
(sonnet), 405–9
'Se le mie preci ed umili e devote'
(sonnet), 404–8
'Se pur fin su ne gli stellanti chiostri'
(canzone), 28–31, 84, 104,
393–400, 424
'Se pur il ciel consente' (madrigal),
416
set by Monte, 426, 430–1, 445–8
'Se voi lagrime a pieno' (madrigal),
415
set by Agresta, 435–6, 479–83

set by Barbarino, 436–8, 439–40,
469–70
set by Caccini, 436, 438–40, 477–8
set by Dentice, 435–6, 438, 471–4
set by Majone, 434–6, 465–8
set by Monte, 426, 431–2, 449–51
'Tacete, ohimè, tacete' (madrigal),
99, 420–1
set by Bellasio, 426, 432–3,
459–62
'Vago cielo ov'amore' (madrigal),
419–20
set by Monte, 426, 431, 456–8
'Voi l'oro delle stelle' (madrigal),
112n180, 416–18, 425
Bernardi, Leonora, writings by, 31,
44–5, 73–4, 76
in manuscripts,
extant, 90–1, 113–14, 117–27,
132–3, 389–90, 397, 400
lost, 46–7, 67n229, 90, 137
naming of author in, 113–15, 127,
133, 135
in print, 31, 46–7, 113, 389–92, 397,
415, 424
reception of, 46–8, 73–4, 126–7,
133–4, 137–9
See Bernardi, Leonora, lyric poetry
by; *Clorilli* (Bernardi)
Bernardi, Settimio d'Andrea, 27, 55, 58,
68n257
Bernardi, Stefano d'Antonio, *11*, 15,
42
Bernardi, Tommaso Francesco, 47
Bernardini, Chiara, *12*, 14, 38
Bernardini, Giuseppe, 7, 14
Bernardini, Martino, 4
Bible, as source for Leonora Bernardi,
28, 398, 402–3
Boccaccio, Giovanni, 16, 347n4,
357n146
Bonarelli, Guidobaldo (Guidubaldo),
75, 78, 106n18
Filli di Sciro, 87, 92, 108n69, 349n33,
352n79

Lollio, Alberto, 108n53, 108n63, 349n30, 355n112

Lorraine, Christine of (Grand Duchess of Tuscany), 90–2, 98, 104, 172n6, 348n12, 348n18
  and *Clorilli*, 31, 72, 90–1, 104, 125, 363
    as 'Cristilla' and Juno in, 31, 90, 104, 353n95, 376
    name highlighted in, 125
  as dedicatee, 97, 101, 106n11, 133, 137, 363
  marriage of, 31, 92, 96, 101, 348n12
  as patron of performances, 97, 100, 104
  and Villa La Petraia, 91, 104, 348n18, 354n103, 354n105

love
  courtly, 73, 88, 355n110, 357n137
  female cruelty in, 88, 357n146
  fraternal, 83, 88
  male deception in, 86–8, 102
  in pastoral drama. *See* pastoral drama, love in
  Petrarchan, 73, 88, 137, 371–2, 417. *See also* Petrarch
    love object of, 128, 417–21, 432
  spiritual, 85, 109n95, 137, 403, 420
  See also debates, on love; marriage; Neoplatonism; *sdegno*

Love (god). *See* Cupid

Lucca
  conspiracies, 4, 6, 27, 40, 135
  convents, 9, 14, 353n86
  cultural life, 7–8, 28, 37–41, 44–5, 48
  economy, 2, 17–18
  education, 5, 7
  inheritance practices, 9, 42, 66n203
  music, 8
  political life, 2–4, 6–7, 14, 44
  relations with Florence, 4–6, 48, 126, 135
  religious life, 4–5, 38–9, 44, 48–50, 131–2, 141n80

  as republic, 2, 6, 8
  ridotti (social gatherings), 7, 48
    Leonora Bernardi's, 37–9, 41–2, 48, 50, 126
    male-only, 7–9, 137–8
    mixed-sex, 10, 14, 45, 60n35, 65n166
  spas (*terme*), 10, 18
  Straccioni rebellion, 4, 40
  ties with Northern Europe, 2, 4–5, 35
  ties with Spain and Empire, 5–6, 36, 127, 131, 135
  war with Modena, 6–7, 40, 62n162, 127, 135
  women's roles in, 9–14, 48–9
  See also Accademia degli Oscuri; Chierici Regolari della Madre di Dio; exiles; Garfagnana; Reform movement, in Lucca

Lucchesini family, 47, 135, 137
Lucchesini, Cesare, 47
Lucchesini, Jacopo, 135, 137
Lucchesini, Orazio, 14, 27, 39, 135
  and *Clorilli*, 137
  exiled from Lucca, 27, 39–40, 135
  as Laura Guidiccioni's husband, 14, 27, 135
Lucchesini, Salvatore, 135
Lucchesini, Scipione, 47, 90
Lupi, Pietro, 96
Luzzaschi, Luzzasco, 75, 390, 421, 423n5
Lyons, 2, 5, 7

Machiavelli, Niccolò, 94, 110n120
madrigals, 73–6, 126, 128, 389, 404, 425–42
  and *Clorilli*, 99–100, 102, 104, 168–9, 381
  exchanges of, 18, 30–1, 40, 127, 410
  Ferrarese interest in, 19, 75–8, 130, 390, 421, 425–6
  and pastoral drama, 75–6, 97, 104
  poetic features of, 73, 102, 128, 389, 404, 421

Tasso, Torquato, writings by (*cont.*)
   Amor fuggitivo, 99, 347n2
   La Cavaletta, 75, 130, 430
   Gerusalemme liberata, 20, 74, 93,
      103, 131
      character of Armida in, 131,
         350n45, 354n103, 379
      lyric verse, 45, 102, 104, 352–3n86,
         356n121, 389–90
      sonnet for Leonora Bernardi, 20–1
      verse following *Clorilli* (Bernardi),
         115, 130–1, 138
      set to music, 424, 426, 429, 435
   Il Malpiglio primo, 8
   See also debates, regarding Ariosto
      and Tasso; Grillo, and Tasso
Tegrimi, Eufrasia, 14
Tegrimi, Francesco, 40, 44–5
Tegrimi, Guido, 30, 391
Terracina, Laura, 13
Theocritus, 377
Titian (Tiziano Vecellio), 40
Tiraboschi, Girolamo, 46–7
Torelli (Benedetti), Barbara, 77
   Partenia, 71–2, 105, 106n12, 114,
      126
      arranged marriage in, 81, 85
      female roles in, 83
      love in, 85, 359n174
      performance of, 99–100, 109n98,
         114
   See also Manfredi, Muzio
Torelli, Pomponio, 435
tragicomedy, 69, 71–2, 78, 106n11,
      107n28
   Clorilli (Bernardi) as, 72, 78–9, 83,
      101, 103–4, 370
   debate on, 71–2, 74, 351n67. See
      also *Pastor fido* (Guarini)
Trenta, Cassandra di Silvestro, 68n257
Trenta, Francesco di Tomaso, 68n251
Trenta, Lorenzo, 24–5, 50–2, 68n251
Trenta, Silvestro di Curzio, *12*, 38
Trenta, Silvestro di Federico, 10, *12*
Trenta, Tommaso, 47

Trenta Bernardi, Lucrezia
   date of birth, 61n54
   as dedicatee of *Il vero soggetto
      d'amore* (Renieri), 15–16
   as Leonora Bernardi's mother, 15,
      42
   family connections of, 10–*12*, 15, 22,
      27, 42
   and scandal of 1588, 36, 54–5, 57–8
Trenta Burlamacchi, Caterina, *12*, 15
Tucci, Nicolao, 32–3, 36, 45, 48,
      66n197
   and Angelo Grillo, 29–31, 33, 40–1,
      45
   and Leonora Bernardi, 30–1, 33,
      40–1
   as writer, 40, 44–5, 49
Tuccia (Roman heroine), 28–9, 397–8
Tuscany, 2–*3*, 6, 23, 130
   as setting for pastoral, 78, 80–1,
      91–3, 363, 368
   See also Etruria; Florence; Lucca;
      Siena

Valerius Maximus, 29, 124
Vandelli, Domenico, 46–7
Vecoli, Bernardino, 42
Vellutello, Alessandro, 7
Venice
   and Angelo Grillo, 33, 138
   and Domenico Chiariti, 35, 138
   and Girolamo Sbarra, 23, 25–6, 54,
      56, 138
   Interdict, 131
   literary culture in, 127, 129–31, 136
   women's roles in, 9, 13, 136
   See also Fonte, Moderata; Lepanto,
      battle of; music, in Venice;
      Venier, see family members
Venier family, 136, 141n80
Venier, Domenico, 129, 132
Venier, Maffio, 128–30, 133, 137,
      141n75, 141n80
   dialect verse of, 130
   and Florence, 133, 137, 141n77

Venier, Maffio (*cont.*)
    Hidalba, 350n41
    See also Franco, Veronica; Venier,
        Domenico
Venus, in *Clorilli* (Bernardi), 99, 104,
    347n2
Vermigli, Pietro Martire, 4
Vignali, Antonio, 131
Virgil
    Aeneid, 26, 65n174, 351n68,
        352n85
    Eclogues, 72, 349n25, 356n122
Virgin Mary
    in Bernardi's verse, 28–9, 31,
        353n92, 389–410
    in literature, 28–9, 44–5
    in verse following *Clorilli* (Bernardi),
        127, 132–3, 137
    miracle of 1588, 28, 399
    See also Chierici Regolari della Madre
        di Dio; religious literature
visual arts
    engravings, 349n27, 359n183, 417
    garden design, 91–2, 96, 104,
        354nn103–4
    hair design, 417–18
    painting, 91, 354n106, 409, 421
        in literature, 40, 380
    portraits, 33, 91, 369, 377, 409
    sculpture, 91, 96, 421
        in literature, 354n106, 355n102,
            381
    set design, 8, 92, 94, 96, 361–2, 369.

    See also satyr drama, stage set
        for
    woodcuts, 354n102, 369
    See also Allori, Alessandro; Allori,
        Cristofano; Burlamacchi,
        Eufrasia; Fontana, Lavinia;
        Medici family, and spectacles

Wert, Giaches de [Jaches de Vuert],
    129, 147, 153, 350n45, 430
Wilbourne, Emily, 362, 379
women. *See balletto delle donne*;
        concerto delle dame; debates,
        on women; Ferrara, women's
        roles in; gender attitudes; Lucca,
        women's roles in; pastoral
        drama, performed by women;
        Siena, cultural life in (women's
        participation); women's writing;
        and under individual women's
        names
women's writing, 35, 114
    in Ferrara, 75–7
    in Florence, 13–14, 44, 97
    in Lucca, 10, 13–14, 28, 38, 46
    and misandry, 86–8
    in Siena, 13
    See also pastoral drama, written by
        women; religious literature,
        women's engagement with

Zeno, Apostolo, 116, 139
Zerbinati, Sidonia, 75

Ingram Content Group UK Ltd.
Milton Keynes UK
UKHW021531280623
424129UK00002B/17